Textbooks in Language Sciences

In this series:

1. Müller, Stefan. Grammatical theory: From transformational grammar to constraint-based approaches.
2. Schäfer, Roland. Einführung in die grammatische Beschreibung des Deutschen.

ISSN: 2364-6209

Grammatical theory

From transformational grammar to constraint-based approaches

Stefan Müller

language
science
press

Stefan Müller. 2016. *Grammatical theory: From transformational grammar to constraint-based approaches* (Textbooks in Language Sciences 1). Berlin: Language Science Press.

This title can be downloaded at:
http://langsci-press.org/catalog/book/25

ISBN:	Digital, complete work:		978-3-944675-21-3 ;
	Hardcover:	vol1:	978-3-946234-29-6; vol. 2 978-3-946234-40-1
	Softcover:	vol1:	978-3-946234-30-2; vol. 2 978-3-946234-41-8
	Softcover US:	vol1:	978-1-530465-62-0 ; vol. 2 978-1-523743-82-7

ISSN: 2364-6209

Cover and concept of design: Ulrike Harbort
Translators: Andrew Murphy, Stefan Müller
Typesetting: Stefan Müller
Proofreading: Viola Auermann, Armin Buch, Andreea Calude, Rong Chen, Matthew Czuba, Leonel de Alencar, Christian Döhler, Joseph T. Farquharson, Andreas Hölzl, Gianina Iordăchioaia, Paul Kay, Anne Kilgus, Sandra Kübler, Timm Lichte, Antonio Machicao y Priemer, Michelle Natolo, Stephanie Natolo, Sebastian Nordhoff, Parviz Parsafar, Conor Pyle, Daniela Schröder, Eva Schultze-Berndt, Alec Shaw, Benedikt Singpiel, Anelia Stefanova, Neal Whitman, Viola Wiegand
Open reviewing: Armin Buch, Leonel de Alencar, Andreas Hölzl, Gianina Iordăchioaia, Paul Kay, Dick Hudson, Paul Kay, Timm Lichte, Antonio Machicao y Priemer, Andrew McIntyre, Arne Nymos, Sebastian Nordhoff, Neal Whitman
Fonts: Linux Libertine, Arimo, DejaVu Sans Mono
Typesetting software: XeLaTeX

Language Science Press
Habelschwerdter Allee 45
14195 Berlin, Germany
langsci-press.org
Storage and cataloguing done by FU Berlin

Freie Universität Berlin

For Max

Contents

Preface xv

I Background and specific theories 1

1 Introduction and basic terms 3
1.1 Why do syntax? 3
1.2 Why do it formally? 6
1.3 Constituents 6
1.3.1 Constituency tests 7
1.3.2 Some comments on the status of constituent tests 11
1.4 Parts of speech 17
1.5 Heads 28
1.6 Arguments and adjuncts 30
1.7 Grammatical functions 35
1.7.1 Subjects 35
1.7.2 The adverbial 40
1.7.3 Predicatives 41
1.7.4 Valence classes 42
1.8 A topological model of the German clause 43
1.8.1 The position of the verb 43
1.8.2 The sentence bracket, prefield, middle field and postfield 44
1.8.3 Assigning elements to fields 44
1.8.4 Recursion 49

2 Phrase structure grammar 53
2.1 Symbols and rewrite rules 53
2.2 Expanding PSG with features 59
2.3 Semantics 60
2.4 Phrase structure rules for some aspects of German syntax 63
2.4.1 Noun phrases 63
2.4.2 Prepositional phrases 71
2.5 $\overline{\text{X}}$ theory 73

3 Transformational Grammar – Government & Binding 81
3.1 General remarks on the representational format 82
3.1.1 Transformations 82

3.1.2 The hypothesis regarding language acquisition: Principles & Parameters . . . 84
3.1.3 The T model . . . 85
3.1.4 $\overline{\text{X}}$ theory . . . 91
3.1.5 CP and IP in English . . . 94
3.1.6 The structure of the German clause . . . 97
3.2 Verb position . . . 98
3.3 Long-distance dependencies . . . 102
3.4 Passive . . . 106
3.4.1 Structural and lexical case . . . 106
3.4.2 Case assignment and the Case Filter . . . 107
3.5 Local reordering . . . 110
3.6 Summary and classification . . . 113
3.6.1 Explaining language acquisition . . . 114
3.6.2 Formalization . . . 115

4 Transformational Grammar – Minimalism 123
4.1 General remarks on the representational format . . . 123
4.1.1 Basic architecture . . . 124
4.1.2 Valence, feature checking, and agreement . . . 125
4.1.3 Phrase structure and $\overline{\text{X}}$ theory . . . 127
4.1.4 Little *v* . . . 127
4.1.5 CP, TP, *v*P, VP . . . 129
4.1.6 Adjuncts . . . 134
4.2 Verb position . . . 134
4.3 Long-distance dependencies . . . 134
4.4 Passive . . . 135
4.5 Local reordering . . . 138
4.6 New developments and theoretical variants . . . 139
4.6.1 Move, Merge, feature-driven movement and functional projections 139
4.6.2 Labeling . . . 149
4.6.3 Specifiers, complements, and the remains of $\overline{\text{X}}$ theory . . . 155
4.6.4 Minimalism, Categorial Grammar, and HPSG . . . 159
4.6.5 Selection of atomic features vs. selection of complex categories . 167
4.6.6 Summary . . . 169
4.7 Summary and classification . . . 169
4.7.1 Explaining language acquisition . . . 169
4.7.2 Formalization . . . 170

5 Generalized Phrase Structure Grammar 175
5.1 General remarks on the representational format . . . 175
5.1.1 Complex categories, the Head Feature Convention, and $\overline{\text{X}}$ rules . 176
5.1.2 Local reordering . . . 178

5.1.3 Metarules . . . 180
5.1.4 Semantics . . . 182
5.1.5 Adjuncts . . . 183
5.2 Passive as a metarule . . . 185
5.3 Verb position . . . 188
5.4 Long-distance dependencies as the result of local dependencies . . . 189
5.5 Summary and classification . . . 192
5.5.1 Valence and morphology . . . 193
5.5.2 Valence and partial verb phrase fronting . . . 194
5.5.3 Generative capacity . . . 195

6 Feature descriptions **197**
6.1 Feature descriptions . . . 197
6.2 Types . . . 200
6.3 Disjunction . . . 202
6.4 Structure sharing . . . 203
6.5 Cyclic structures . . . 205
6.6 Unification . . . 205
6.7 Phenomena, models and formal theories . . . 207

7 Lexical Functional Grammar **213**
7.1 General remarks on the representational format . . . 215
7.1.1 Functional structure . . . 215
7.1.2 Completeness . . . 218
7.1.3 Coherence . . . 218
7.1.4 Restrictions on the c-structure/f-structure relation . . . 219
7.1.5 Semantics . . . 219
7.1.6 Adjuncts . . . 222
7.2 Passive . . . 223
7.3 Verb position . . . 226
7.4 Local reordering . . . 227
7.5 Long-distance dependencies and functional uncertainty . . . 230
7.6 Summary and classification . . . 233

8 Categorial Grammar **237**
8.1 General remarks on the representational format . . . 238
8.1.1 Representation of valence information . . . 238
8.1.2 Semantics . . . 240
8.1.3 Adjuncts . . . 241
8.2 Passive . . . 242
8.3 Verb position . . . 243
8.4 Local reordering . . . 245
8.5 Long-distance dependencies . . . 246
8.5.1 Type Raising . . . 246

8.5.2 Forward and backward composition . . . 247
8.5.3 Analysis of long-distance dependencies . . . 247
8.6 Summary and classification . . . 249

9 Head-Driven Phrase Structure Grammar 255
9.1 General remarks on the representational format . . . 258
9.1.1 Representation of valence information . . . 259
9.1.2 Representation of constituent structure . . . 260
9.1.3 Linearization rules . . . 264
9.1.4 Projection of head properties . . . 265
9.1.5 Inheritance hierarchies and generalizations . . . 267
9.1.6 Semantics . . . 269
9.1.7 Adjuncts . . . 272
9.2 Passive . . . 275
9.2.1 Valence information and the Case Principle . . . 278
9.3 Verb position . . . 280
9.4 Local reordering . . . 285
9.5 Long-distance dependencies . . . 288
9.6 New developments and theoretical variants . . . 293
9.6.1 Specifier, complements and argument structure . . . 293
9.6.2 Linearization-based HPSG . . . 296
9.7 Summary and classification . . . 297

10 Construction Grammar 303
10.1 General remarks on the representational format . . . 305
10.1.1 The head-complement construction . . . 305
10.1.2 Representation of valence information . . . 306
10.1.3 Semantics . . . 307
10.1.4 Adjuncts . . . 307
10.2 Passive . . . 307
10.3 Verb position . . . 312
10.4 Local reordering . . . 314
10.5 Long-distance dependencies . . . 314
10.6 New developments and theoretical variants . . . 315
10.6.1 Berkeley Construction Grammar . . . 315
10.6.2 Sign-Based Construction Grammar . . . 318
10.6.3 Embodied Construction Grammar . . . 330
10.6.4 Fluid Construction Grammar . . . 333
10.7 Summary and classification . . . 352

11 Dependency Grammar 355
11.1 General remarks on the representational format . . . 358
11.1.1 Valence information, nucleus and satellites . . . 358
11.1.2 Adjuncts . . . 360

11.1.3 Linearization . . . 360
11.1.4 Semantics . . . 362
11.2 Passive . . . 363
11.3 Verb position . . . 364
11.4 Local reordering . . . 365
11.5 Long-distance dependencies . . . 366
11.6 New developments and theoretical variants . . . 372
11.6.1 Tesnière's part of speech classification . . . 372
11.6.2 Connection, junction, and transfer . . . 373
11.6.3 Scope . . . 379
11.7 Summary and classification . . . 379
11.7.1 Linearization . . . 380
11.7.2 Dependency Grammar vs. phrase structure grammar . . . 387

12 Tree Adjoining Grammar 403
12.1 General remarks on representational format . . . 404
12.1.1 Representation of valence information . . . 404
12.1.2 Substitution . . . 404
12.1.3 Adjunction . . . 404
12.1.4 Semantics . . . 406
12.2 Local reordering . . . 408
12.3 Verb position . . . 411
12.4 Passive . . . 411
12.5 Long-distance dependencies . . . 414
12.6 New developments and theoretical variants . . . 415
12.6.1 FTAG . . . 415
12.6.2 V-TAG . . . 417
12.6.3 The competence-performance distinction and the generative capacity of tree-local MC-LTAG . . . 419
12.7 Summary and classification . . . 425

II General discussion 429

13 The innateness of linguistic knowledge 431
13.1 Syntactic universals . . . 433
13.1.1 Head Directionality Parameter . . . 434
13.1.2 $\overline{\text{X}}$ structures . . . 435
13.1.3 Grammatical functions such as subject and object . . . 438
13.1.4 Binding principles . . . 440
13.1.5 Properties of long-distance dependencies . . . 442
13.1.6 Grammatical morphemes for tense, mood and aspect . . . 449
13.1.7 Parts of speech . . . 450

13.1.8 Recursion and infinitude . . . 451
13.1.9 Summary . . . 456
13.2 Speed of language acquisition . . . 457
13.3 Critical period for acquisition . . . 458
13.4 Lack of acquisition among non-human primates . . . 459
13.5 Creole and sign languages . . . 460
13.6 Localization in special parts of the brain . . . 461
13.7 Differences between language and general cognition . . . 462
13.7.1 Williams Syndrome . . . 462
13.7.2 KE family with FoxP2 mutation . . . 463
13.8 Poverty of the Stimulus . . . 463
13.8.1 Gold's Theorem . . . 464
13.8.2 Four case studies . . . 468
13.8.3 Unsupervised Data-Oriented Parsing (U-DOP) . . . 478
13.8.4 Negative evidence . . . 485
13.9 Summary . . . 486

14 Generative-enumerative vs. model-theoretic approaches 489
14.1 Graded acceptability . . . 491
14.2 Utterance fragments . . . 492
14.3 A problem for model-theoretic approaches? . . . 494

15 The competence/performance distinction 499
15.1 The derivational theory of complexity . . . 501
15.2 Incremental processing . . . 504

16 Language acquisition 511
16.1 Principles & Parameters . . . 511
16.2 Principles and the lexicon . . . 519
16.3 Pattern-based approaches . . . 519
16.4 Selection-based approaches . . . 526
16.5 Summary . . . 527

17 Generative capacity and grammar formalisms 529

18 Binary branching, locality, and recursion 535
18.1 Binary branching . . . 535
18.2 Locality . . . 538
18.3 Recursion . . . 547

19 Empty elements 549
19.1 Views on empty elements . . . 549
19.2 Eliminating empty elements from grammars . . . 551
19.3 Empty elements and semantic interpretation . . . 556

19.4 Evidence for empty elements 563
19.5 Transformations, lexical rules, and empty elements 563

20 Extraction, scrambling, and passive: one or several descriptive devices? 569

21 Phrasal vs. lexical analyses 579
21.1 Some putative advantages of phrasal models 580
21.1.1 Usage-based theories 580
21.1.2 Coercion 582
21.1.3 Aspect as a clause level phenomenon 584
21.1.4 Simplicity and polysemy 584
21.2 Evidence for lexical approaches 587
21.2.1 Valence and coordination 587
21.2.2 Valence and derivational morphology 591
21.3 Radical underspecification: the end of argument structure? 597
21.3.1 Neo-Davidsonianism 597
21.3.2 Little *v* and idiom asymmetries 599
21.3.3 Deverbal nominals 601
21.3.4 Idiosyncratic syntactic selections 604
21.3.5 Expletives 606
21.3.6 An exoskeletal approach 607
21.3.7 Is there an alternative to lexical valence structure? 611
21.3.8 Summary 612
21.4 Relations between constructions 612
21.4.1 Inheritance hierarchies for constructions 613
21.4.2 Mappings between different levels of representations 617
21.4.3 Is there an alternative to lexical rules? 620
21.5 Further problems for phrasal approaches 620
21.5.1 Particle verbs and commitment to phrase structure configurations 620
21.6 Arguments from language acquisition 621
21.6.1 Recognizability of constructions 621
21.6.2 Coordination and discontinuousness 623
21.7 Arguments from psycho- and neurolinguistics 628
21.7.1 Lexical rules vs. phrasal constructions 628
21.7.2 Light verbs 630
21.7.3 Arguments from neurolinguistics 631
21.8 Arguments from statistical distribution 635
21.8.1 Unsupervised Data-Oriented Parsing 635
21.8.2 Collostructions 638
21.9 Conclusion 638
21.10 Why (phrasal) constructions? 639
21.10.1 Verbless directives 639
21.10.2 Serial verbs 646
21.10.3 Relative and interrogative clauses 647
21.10.4 The N-P-N construction 649

22 Universal Grammar and comparative linguistics without UG **653**
22.1 Formal tools for capturing generalizations 653
22.2 How to develop linguistic theories that capture cross-linguistic generalizations 657

23 Conclusion **667**

24 Solutions to the exercises **671**
24.1 Introduction and basic terms 671
24.2 Phrase structure grammars 671
24.3 Transformational Grammar – Government & Binding 675
24.4 Generalized Phrase Structure Grammar 677
24.5 Feature descriptions 679
24.6 Lexical Functional Grammar 681
24.7 Categorial Grammar 682
24.8 Head-Driven Phrase Structure Grammar 683
24.9 Construction Grammar 684
24.10 Dependency Grammar 685
24.11 Tree Adjoining Grammar 686

Bibliography **689**

Index **783**
Name index 783
Language index 797
Subject index 799

Part II

General discussion

13 The innateness of linguistic knowledge

If we try and compare the theories presented in this book, we notice that there are a number of similarities.[1] In all of the frameworks, there are variants of theories that use feature-value pairs to describe linguistic objects. The syntactic structures assumed are sometimes similar. Nevertheless, there are some differences that have often led to fierce debates between members of the various schools. Theories differ with regard to whether they assume transformations, empty elements, phrasal or lexical analyses, binary branching or flat structures.

Every theory has to not only describe natural language, but also explain it. It is possible to formulate an infinite number of grammars that license structures for a given language (see Exercise 1 on page 78). These grammars are *observationally adequate*. A grammar achieves *descriptive adequacy* if it corresponds to observations and the intuitions of native speakers.[2] A linguistic theory is descriptively adequate if it can be used to formulate a descriptively adequate grammar for every natural language. However, grammars achieving descriptive adequacy do not always necessarily reach *explanatory adequacy*. Grammars that achieve explanatory adequacy are those that are compatible with acquisition data, that is, grammars that could plausibly be acquired by human speakers (Chomsky 1965: 24–25).

Chomsky (1965: 25) assumes that children already have domain-specific knowledge about what grammars could, in principle, look like and then extract information about what a given grammar actually looks like from the linguistic input. The most prominent

[1] The terms *theory* and *framework* may require clarification. A framework is a common set of assumptions and tools that is used when theories are formulated. In this book, I discussed theories of German. These theories were developed in certain frameworks (GB, GPSG, HPSG, LFG, …) and of course there are other theories of other languages that share the same fundamental assumptions. These theories differ from the theories of German presented here but are formulated in the same framework. Haspelmath (2010b) argues for framework-free grammatical theory. If grammatical theories used incompatible tools, it would be difficult to compare languages. So assuming transformations for English nonlocal dependencies and a SLASH mechanism for German would make comparison impossible. I agree with Haspelmath that the availability of formal tools may lead to biases, but in the end the facts have to be described somehow. If nothing is shared between theories, we end up with isolated theories formulated in one man frameworks. If there *is* shared vocabulary and if there are standards for doing framework-free grammatical theory, then the framework is framework-free grammatical theory. See Müller (2015a) and Chapter 22 of this book for further discussion.

[2] This term is not particularly useful as subjective factors play a role. Not everybody finds grammatical theories intuitively correct where it is assumed that every observed order in the languages of the world has to be derived from a common Specifier-Head-Complement configuration, and also only by movement to the left (see Section 4.6.1 for the discussion of such proposals).

variant of acquisition theory in Mainstream Generative Grammar (MGG) is the Principles & Parameters theory, which claims that parametrized principles restrict the grammatical structures possible and children just have to set parameters during language acquisition (see Section 3.1.2).

Over the years, the innateness hypothesis, also known as nativism, has undergone a number of modifications. In particular, assumptions about exactly what forms part of the innate linguistic knowledge, so-called Universal Grammar (UG), have often been subject to change.

Nativism is often rejected by proponents of Construction Grammar, Cognitive Grammar and by many other researchers working in other theories. Other explanations are offered for the facts normally used to argue for the innateness of grammatical categories, syntactic structures or relations between linguistic objects in syntactic structures. Another point of criticism is that the actual complexity of analyses is blurred by the fact that many of the stipulations are simply assumed to be part of UG. The following is a caricature of a certain kind of argumentation in GB/Minimalism analyses:

1. I have developed an analysis for the phenomenon P in the language S.
2. The analysis is elegant/conceptually simple/mine[3].
3. There is no possibility to learn the relevant structures or principles.
4. Therefore, the assumptions A_1 through A_n that are made in this analysis must be part of the innate knowledge of speakers.

By attributing arbitrary assumptions to UG, it is possible to keep the rest of the analysis very simple.

The following section will briefly review some of the arguments for language-specific innate knowledge. We will see that none of these arguments are uncontroversial. In the following chapters, I will discuss fundamental questions about the architecture of grammar, the distinction between competence and performance and how to model performance phenomena, the theory of language acquisition as well as other controversial questions, e.g., whether it is desirable to postulate empty elements in linguistic representations and whether language should be explained primarily based on the properties of words or rather phrasal patterns.

Before we turn to these hotly debated topics, I want to discuss the one that is most fiercely debated, namely the question of innate linguistic knowledge. In the literature, one finds the following arguments for innate knowledge:

- the existence of syntactic universals,
- the speed of acquisition,
- the fact that there is a 'critical period' for language acquisition,

[3] Also, see http://www.youtube.com/watch?v=cAYDiPizDIs. 01.12.2015.

- the fact that all children learn a language, but primates do not,
- the fact that children spontaneously regularize pidgin languages,
- the localization of language processing in particular parts of the brain,
- the alleged dissociation of language and general cognition:
  - Williams Syndrome,
  - the KE family with FoxP2 mutation and
- the Poverty of the Stimulus Argument.

Pinker (1994) offers a nice overview of these arguments. Tomasello (1995) provides a critical review of this book. The individual points will be discussed in what follows.

13.1 Syntactic universals

The existence of syntactic universals has been taken as an argument for the innateness of linguistic knowledge (e.g., Chomsky 1998: 33; Pinker 1994: 237–238). There are varying claims in the literature with regard to what is universal and language-specific. The most prominent candidates for universals are:[4]

- the Head Directionality Parameter
- $\overline{\text{X}}$ structures
- grammatical functions such as subject or object
- binding principles
- properties of long-distance dependencies
- grammatical morphemes for tense, mood and aspect
- parts of speech
- recursion or self-embedding

[4] Frans Plank has an archive of universals in Konstanz (Plank & Filimonova 2000): http://typo.uni-konstanz.de/archive/intro/. On 23.12.2015, it contained 2029 entries. The entries are annotated with regard to their quality, and it turns out that many of the universals are statistical universals, that is, they hold for the overwhelming majority of languages, but there are some exceptions. Some of the universals are marked as almost absolute, that is, very few exceptions are known. 1153 were marked as absolute or absolute with a question mark. 1021 of these are marked as absolute without a question mark. Many of the universals captured are implicational universals, that is, they have the form: if a language has the property X, then it also has the property Y. The universals listed in the archive are, in part, very specific and refer to the diachronic development of particular grammatical properties. For example, the fourth entry states that: *If the exponent of vocative is a prefix, then this prefix has arisen from 1st person possessor or a 2nd person subject.*

These supposed universals will each be discussed briefly in what follows. One should emphasize that there is by no means a consensus that these are universal and that the observed properties actually require postulating innate linguistic knowledge.

13.1.1 Head Directionality Parameter

The Head Directionality Parameter was already introduced in Section 3.1.2. The examples in (7) on page 85, repeated below as (1), show that the structures in Japanese are the mirror image of the English structures:

(1) a. be showing pictures of himself
 b. zibun -no syasin-o mise-te iru
 himself of picture showing be

In order to capture these facts, a parameter was proposed that is responsible for the position of the head relative to its arguments (e.g., Chomsky 1986b: 146; 1988: 70).

By assuming a Head Directionality Parameter, Radford (1990: 60–61; 1997: 19–22), Pinker (1994: 234, 238), Baker (2003: 350) and other authors claim, either explicitly or implicitly, that there is a correlation between the direction of government of verbs and that of adpositions, that is, languages with verb-final order have postpositions and languages with VO order have prepositions. This claim can be illustrated with the language pair English/Japanese and the examples in (1): the *no* occurs after the pronoun in the prepositional phrase, the noun *syasin-o* 'picture' follows the PP belonging to it, the main verb follows its object and the auxiliary *iru* occurs after the main verb *mise-te*. The individual phrases are the exact mirror image of the respective phrases in English.

A single counterexample is enough to disprove a universal claim and in fact, it is possible to find a language that has verb-final order but nevertheless has prepositions. Persian is such a language. An example is given in (2):

(2) man ketâb-â-ro be Sepide dâd-am.
 I book-PL-RÂ to Sepide gave-1SG
 'I gave the books to Sepide.'

In Section 3.1.4, it was shown that German cannot be easily described with this parameter: German is a verb-final language but has both prepositions and postpositions. The World Atlas of Language Structures lists 41 languages with VO order and postpositions and 14 languages with OV order and prepositions (Dryer 2013b,a).[5] An earlier study by Dryer (1992) done with a smaller sample of languages also points out that there are exceptions to what the Head Directionality Parameter would predict.

Furthermore, Gibson & Wexler (1994: 422) point out that a single parameter for the position of heads would not be enough since complementizers in both English and German/Dutch occur before their complements; however, English is a VO language, whereas German and Dutch count as OV languages.

If one wishes to determine the direction of government based on syntactic categories (Gibson & Wexler 1994: 422, Chomsky 2005: 15), then one has to assume that the syn-

[5] http://wals.info/combinations/83A_85A#2/15.0/153.0, 23.12.2015.

tactic categories in question belong to the inventory of Universal Grammar (see Section 13.1.7, for more on this). Difficulties with prepositions and postpositions also arise for this kind of assumption as these are normally assigned to the same category (P). If we were to introduce special categories for both prepositions and postpositions, then a four-way division of parts of speech like the one on page 92 would no longer be possible. One would instead require an additional binary feature and one would thereby automatically predict eight categories although only five (the four commonly assumed plus an extra one) are actually needed.

One can see that the relation between direction of government that Pinker formulated as a universal claim is in fact correct but rather as a tendency than as a strict rule, that is, there are many languages where there is a correlation between the use of prepositions or postpositions and the position the verb (Dryer 1992: 83).[6]

In many languages, adpositions have evolved from verbs. In Chinese grammar, it is commonplace to refer to a particular class of words as coverbs. These are words that can be used both as prepositions and as verbs. If we view languages historically, then we can find explanations for these tendencies that do not have to make reference to innate linguistic knowledge (see Evans & Levinson 2009a: 445).

Furthermore, it is possible to explain the correlations with reference to processing preferences: in languages with the same direction of government, the distance between the verb and the pre-/postposition is less (Figure 13.1a–b) than in languages with differing directions of government (Figure 13.1c–d). From the point of view of processing, languages with the same direction of government should be preferred since they allow the hearer to better identify the parts of the verb phrase (Newmeyer (2004a: 219–221) cites Hawkins (2004: 32) with a relevant general processing preference, see also Dryer (1992: 131)). This tendency can thus be explained as the grammaticalization of a performance preference (see Chapter 15 for the distinction between competence and performance) and recourse to innate language-specific knowledge is not necessary.

13.1.2 $\overline{\text{X}}$ structures

It is often assumed that all languages have syntactic structures that correspond to the $\overline{\text{X}}$ schema (see Section 2.5) (Pinker 1994: 238; Meisel 1995: 11, 14; Pinker & Jackendoff 2005: 216). There are, however, languages such as Dyirbal (Australia) where it does not seem to make sense to assume hierarchical structure for sentences. Thus, Bresnan (2001: 110) assumes that Tagalog, Hungarian, Malayalam, Warlpiri, Jiwarli, Wambaya, Jakaltek and other corresponding languages do not have a VP node, but rather a rule taking the form of (3):

(3) $\text{S} \rightarrow \text{C}^*$

[6] Pinker (1994: 234) uses the word *usually* in his formulation. He thereby implies that there are exceptions and that the correlation between the ordering of adpositions and the direction of government of verbs is actually a tendency rather than a universally applicable rule. However, in the pages that follow, he argues that the Head Directionality Parameter forms part of innate linguistic knowledge. Travis (1984: 55) discusses data from Mandarin Chinese that do not correspond to the correlations she assumes. She then proposes treating the Head Directionality Parameter as a kind of Default Parameter that can be overridden by other constraints in the language.

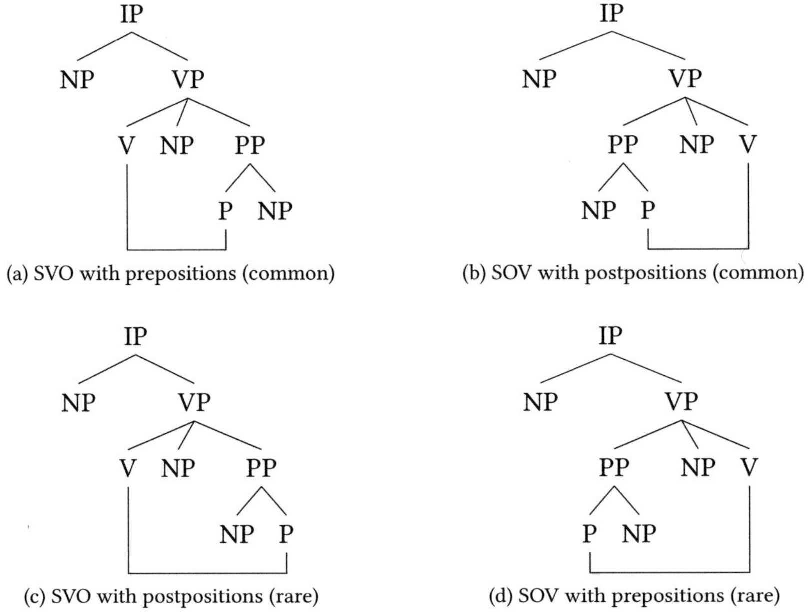

(a) SVO with prepositions (common)

(b) SOV with postpositions (common)

(c) SVO with postpositions (rare)

(d) SOV with prepositions (rare)

Figure 13.1: Distance between verb and preposition for various head orders according to Newmeyer (2004a: 221)

Here, C^* stands for an arbitrary number of constituents and there is no head in the structure. Other examples for structures without heads will be discussed in Section 21.10.

$\overline{X}$ structure was introduced to restrict the form of possible rules. The assumption was that these restrictions reduce the class of grammars one can formulate and thus – according to the assumption – make the grammars easier to acquire. But as Kornai & Pullum (1990) have shown, the assumption of $\overline{X}$ structures does not lead to a restriction with regard to the number of possible grammars if one allows for empty heads. In GB, a number of null heads were used and in the Minimalist Program, there has been a significant increase of these. For example, the rule in (3) can be reformulated as follows:

(4) $V' \rightarrow V^0\ C^*$

Here, V^0 is an empty head. Since specifiers are optional, V' can be projected to VP and we arrive at a structure corresponding to the $\overline{X}$ schema.

Apart from the problem with languages with very free constituent order, there are further problems with adjunction structures: Chomsky's analysis of adjective structure in $\overline{X}$ theory (Chomsky 1970: 210; see also Section 2.5 of this book, in particular Figure 2.8 on page 74) is not straightforwardly applicable to German since, unlike English, adjective phrases in German are head-final and degree modifiers must directly precede the adjective:

(5) a. der auf seinen Sohn sehr stolze Mann
the of his son very proud man
'the man very proud of his son'

b. * der sehr auf seinen Sohn stolze Mann
the very of his son proud man

c. * der auf seinen Sohn stolze sehr Mann
the of his son proud very man

Following the $\overline{\text{X}}$ schema, *auf seinen Sohn* has to be combined with *stolze* and only then can the resulting $\overline{\text{A}}$ projection be combined with its specifier (see Figure 2.8 on page 74 for the structure of adjective phrases in English). It is therefore only possible to derive orders such as (5b) or (5c). Neither of these is possible in German. It is only possible to rescue the $\overline{\text{X}}$ schema if one assumes that German is exactly like English and, for some reason, the complements of adjectives must be moved to the left. If we allow this kind of repair approaches, then of course any language can be described using the $\overline{\text{X}}$ schema. The result would be that one would have to postulate a vast number of movement rules for many languages and this would be extremely complex and difficult to motivate from a psycholinguistic perspective. See Chapter 15 for grammars compatible with performance.

A further problem for $\overline{\text{X}}$ theory in its strictest form as presented in Section 2.5 is posed by so-called hydra clauses (Perlmutter & Ross 1970; Link 1984; Kiss 2005):

(6) a. [[der Kater] und [die Katze]], die einander lieben
the tomcat and the cat that each.other love
'the tomcat and the (female) cat that love each other'

b. [[The boy] and [the girl]] who dated each other are friends of mine.

Since the relative clauses in (6) refer to a group of referents, they can only attach to the result of the coordination. The entire coordination is an NP, however, and adjuncts should actually be attached at the $\overline{\text{X}}$ level. The reverse case of relative clauses in German and English is posed by adjectives in Persian: Samvelian (2007) argues for an analysis where adjectives are combined with nouns directly, and only the combination of nouns and adjectives is then combined with a PP argument.

The discussion of German and English shows that the introduction of specifiers and adjuncts cannot be restricted to particular projection levels, and the preceding discussion of non-configurational languages has shown that the assumption of intermediate levels does not make sense for every language.

It should also be noted that Chomsky himself assumed in 1970 that languages can deviate from the $\overline{\text{X}}$ schema (1970: 210).

If one is willing to encode all information about combination in the lexicon, then one could get by with very abstract combinatorial rules that would hold universally. An example of this kind of combinatorial rules is the multiplication rules of Categorial Grammar (see Chapter 8) as well as Merge in the Minimalist Program (see Section 4). The rules in question simply state that two linguistic objects are combined. These kinds of combination of course exist in every language. With completely lexicalized grammars, however, it is only possible to describe languages if one allows for null heads and makes certain ad hoc assumptions. This will be discussed in Section 21.10.

13.1.3 Grammatical functions such as subject and object

Bresnan & Kaplan (1982: xxv), Pinker (1994: 236–237), Baker (2003: 349) and others assume that all languages have subjects and objects. In order to determine what exactly this claim means, we have to explore the terms themselves. For most European languages, it is easy to say what a subject and an object is (see Section 1.7); however, it has been argued that it is not possible for all languages or that it does not make sense to use these terms at all (Croft 2001: Chapter 4; Evans & Levinson 2009a: Section 4).

In theories such as LFG – the one in which Pinker worked – grammatical functions play a primary role. The fact that it is still controversial whether one should view sentences as subjects, objects or as specially defined sentential arguments (XCOMP) (Dalrymple & Lødrup 2000; Berman 2003b, 2007; Alsina, Mohanan & Mohanan 2005; Forst 2006) serves to show that there is at least some leeway for argumentation when it comes to assigning grammatical functions to arguments. It is therefore likely that one can find an assignment of grammatical functions to the arguments of a functor in all languages.

Unlike LFG, grammatical functions are irrelevant in GB (see Williams 1984; Sternefeld 1985a) and Categorial Grammar. In GB, grammatical functions can only be determined indirectly by making reference to tree positions. Thus, in the approach discussed in Chapter 3, the subject is the phrase in the specifier position of IP.

In later versions of Chomskyan linguistics, there are functional nodes that seem to correspond to grammatical functions (AgrS, AgrO, AgrIO, see page 141). However, Chomsky (1995b: Section 4.10.1) remarks that these functional categories were only assumed for theory internal reasons and should be removed from the inventory of categories that are assumed to be part of UG. See Haider (1997a) and Sternefeld (2006: 509–510) for a description of German that does without functional projections that cannot be motivated in the language in question.

The position taken by HPSG is somewhere in the middle: a special valence feature is used for subjects (in grammars of German, there is a head feature that contains a representation of the subject for non-finite verb forms). However, the value of the SUBJ feature is derived from more general theoretical considerations: in German, the least oblique element with structural case is the subject (Müller 2002a: 153; 2007b: 311).

In GB theory (Extended Projection Principle, EPP, Chomsky (1982: 10)) and also in LFG (Subject Condition), there are principles ensuring that every sentence must have a subject. It is usually assumed that these principles hold universally.[7]

As previously mentioned, there are no grammatical functions in GB, but there are structural positions that correspond to grammatical functions. The position corresponding to the subject is the specifier of IP. The EPP states that there must be an element in SpecIP. If we assume universality of this principle, then every language must have

[7] However, Chomsky (1981a: 27) allows for languages not to have a subject. He assumes that this is handled by a parameter. Bresnan (2001: 311) formulates the Subject Condition, but mentions in a footnote that it might be necessary to parameterize this condition so that it only holds for certain languages.

an element in this position. As we have already seen, there is a counterexample to this universal claim: German. German has an impersonal passive (7a) and there are also subjectless verbs (7b,c) and adjectives (7d–f).[8]

(7) a. dass noch gearbeitet wird
that still worked is
'that people are still working'

b. Ihm graut vor der Prüfung.
him.DAT dreads before the exam
'He dreads the exam.'

c. Mich friert.
me.ACC freezes
'I am freezing.'

d. weil schulfrei ist
because school.free is
'because there is no school today'

e. weil ihm schlecht ist
because him.DAT ill is
'because he is not feeling well'

f. Für dich ist immer offen.[9]
for you is always open
'We are always open for you.'

Most of the predicates that can be used without subjects can also be used with an expletive subject. An example is given in (8):

(8) dass es ihm vor der Prüfung graut
that EXPL him before the exam dreads
'He dreads the exam.'

However, there are verbs such as *liegen* 'lie' in example (9a) from Reis (1982: 185) that cannot occur with an *es* 'it'.

(9) a. Mir liegt an diesem Plan.
me.DAT lies on this plan
'This plan matters a lot to me.'

b. * Mir liegt es an diesem Plan.
me.DAT lies it on this plan

Nevertheless, the applicability of the EPP and the Subject Condition is sometimes also assumed for German. Grewendorf (1993: 1311) assumes that there is an empty expletive that fills the subject position of subjectless constructions.

[8] For further discussion of subjectless verbs in German, see Haider (1993: Sections 6.2.1, 6.5), Fanselow (2000b), Nerbonne (1986b: 912) and Müller (2007b: Section 3.2).

[9] Haider (1986a: 18).

Berman (1999: 11; 2003a: Chapter 4), working in LFG, assumes that verbal morphology can fulfill the subject role in German and therefore even in sentences where no subject is overtly present, the position for the subject is filled in the f-structure. A constraint stating that all f-structures without a PRED value must be third person singular applies to the f-structure of the unexpressed subject. The agreement information in the finite verb has to match the information in the f-structure of the unexpressed subject and hence the verbal inflection in subjectless constructions is restricted to be 3rd person singular (Berman 1999).

As we saw on page 161, some researchers working in the Minimalist Program even assume that there is an object in every sentence (Stabler quoted in Veenstra (1998: 61, 124)). Objects of monovalent verbs are assumed to be empty elements.

If we allow these kinds of tools, then it is of course easy to maintain the existence of many universals: we claim that a language X has the property Y and then assume that the structural items are invisible and have no meaning. These analyses can only be justified theory-internally with the goal of uniformity (see Culicover & Jackendoff 2005: Section 2.1.2).[10]

13.1.4 Binding principles

The principles governing the binding of pronouns are also assumed to be part of UG (Chomsky 1998: 33; Crain, Thornton & Khlentzos 2009: 146; Rizzi 2009a: 468). Binding Theory in GB theory has three principles: principle A states that reflexives such as *sich* or *himself* refer to an element (antecedent) inside of a certain local domain (binding domain). Simplyfying a bit, one could say that a reflexive has to refer to a co-argument.

(10) Klaus$_i$ sagt, dass Peter$_j$ sich$_{*i/j}$ rasiert hat.
Klaus says that Peter himself shaved has

Principle B holds for personal pronouns and states that these cannot refer to elements inside of their binding domain.

(11) Klaus$_i$ sagt, dass Peter$_j$ ihn$_{i/*j}$ rasiert hat.
Klaus says that Peter him shaved has

Principle C determines what referential expressions can refer to. According to Principle C, an expression A_1 cannot refer to another expression A_2 if A_2 c-commands A_1. c-command is defined with reference to the structure of the utterance. There are various definitions of c-command; a simple version states that A c-commands B if there is a path in the constituent structure that goes upwards from A to the next branching node and then only downwards to B.

For the example in (12a), this means that *Max* and *er* 'he' cannot refer to the same individual since *er* c-commands *Max*.

(12) a. Er sagt, dass Max Brause getrunken hat.
he says that Max soda drunk has
'He said that Max drank soda.'

[10] For arguments from language acquisition, see Chapter 16.

b. Max sagt, dass er Brause getrunken hat.
Max said that he soda drunk has
'Max said that he drank soda.'

c. Als er hereinkam, trank Max Brause.
as he came.in drank Max soda
'As he came in, Max was drinking soda.'

This is possible in (12b), however, as there is no such c-command relation. For *er* 'he', it must only be the case that it does not refer to another argument of the verb *getrunken* 'drunk' and this is indeed the case in (12b). Similarly, there is no c-command relation between *er* 'he' and *Max* in (12c) since the pronoun *er* is inside a complex structure. *er* 'he' and *Max* can therefore refer to the the same or different individuals in (12b) and (12c).

Crain, Thornton & Khlentzos (2009: 147) point out that (12b,c) and the corresponding English examples are ambiguous, whereas (12a) is not, due to Principle C. This means that one reading is not available. In order to acquire the correct binding principles, the learner would need information about which meanings expressions do not have. The authors note that children already master Principle C at age three and they conclude from this that Principle C is a plausible candidate for innate linguistic knowledge. (This is a classic kind of argumentation. For Poverty of the Stimulus arguments, see Section 13.8 and for more on negative evidence, see Section 13.8.4).

Evans & Levinson (2009b: 483) note that Principle C is a strong cross-linguistic tendency but it nevertheless has some exceptions. As an example, they mention both reciprocal expressions in Abaza, where affixes that correspond to *each other* occur in subject position rather than object position as well as Guugu Yimidhirr, where pronouns in a superordinate clause can be coreferent with full NPs in a subordinate clause.

Furthermore, Fanselow (1992b: 351) refers to the examples in (13) that show that Principle C is a poor candidate for a syntactic principle.

(13) a. Mord ist ein Verbrechen.
murder is a crime

b. Ein gutes Gespräch hilft Probleme überwinden.
a good conversation helps problems overcome
'A good conversation helps to overcome problems.'

(13a) expresses that it is a crime when somebody kills someone else, and (13b) refers to conversations with another person rather than talking to oneself. In these sentences, the nominalizations *Mord* 'murder' and *Gespräch* 'conversation' are used without any arguments of the original verbs. So there aren't any arguments that stand in a syntactic command relation to one another. Nevertheless the arguments of the nominalized verbs cannot be coreferential. Therefore it seems that there is a principle at work that says that the argument slots of a predicate must be interpreted as non-coreferential as long as the identity of the arguments is not explicitly expressed by linguistic means.

In sum, one can say that there are still a number of unsolved problems with Binding Theory. The HPSG variants of Principles A–C in English cannot even be applied to German (Müller 1999a: Chapter 20). Working in LFG, Dalrymple (1993) proposes a variant of Binding Theory where the binding properties of pronominal expressions are determined in the lexicon. In this way, the language-specific properties of pronouns can be accounted for.

13.1.5 Properties of long-distance dependencies

The long-distance dependencies discussed in the preceding chapters are subject to some kind of restrictions. For example, nothing can be extracted out of sentences that are part of a noun phrase in English. Ross (1967: 70) calls the relevant constraint the *Complex NP Constraint*. In later work, the attempt was made to group this, and other constraints such as the *Right Roof Constraint* also formulated by Ross (1967: Section 5.1.2), into a single, more general constraint, namely the Subjacency Principle (Chomsky 1973: 271; 1986a: 40; Baltin 1981, 2006). Subjacency was assumed to hold universally. The Subjacency Constraint states that movement operations can cross at most one bounding node, whereby what exactly counts as a bounding node depends on the language in question (Baltin 1981: 262; 2006; Rizzi 1982: 57; Chomsky 1986a: 38–40).[11]

Currently, there are varying opinions in the GB/Minimalism tradition with regard to the question of whether subjacency should be considered as part of innate linguistic knowledge. Hauser, Chomsky & Fitch (2002) assume that subjacency does not form part of language-specific abilities, at least not in the strictest sense, but rather is a linguistically relevant constraint in the broader sense that the constraints in question can be derived from more general cognitive ones (see p. 449). Since subjacency still plays a role as a UG principle in other contemporary works (Newmeyer 2005: 15, 74–75; 2004a: 184; Baltin 2006[12]; Baker 2009; Freidin 2009; Rizzi 2009a,b), the Subjacency Principle will be discussed here in some further detail.

It is possible to distinguish two types of movement: movement to the left (normally called extraction) and movement to the right (normally referred to as extraposition). Both movement types constitute long-distance dependencies. In the following section, I will discuss some of the restrictions on extraposition. Extraction will be discussed in Section 13.1.5.2 following it.

13.1.5.1 Extraposition

Baltin (1981) and Chomsky (1986a: 40) claim that the extraposed relative clauses in (14) have to be interpreted with reference to the embedding NP, that is, the sentences are not

[11] Newmeyer (2004b: 539–540) points out a conceptual problem following from the language-specific determination of bounding nodes: it is argued that subjacency is an innate language-specific principle since it is so abstract that it is impossible for speakers to learn it. However, if parameterization requires that a speaker chooses from a set of categories in the linguistic input, then the corresponding constraints must be derivable from the input at least to the degree that it is possible to determine the categories involved. This raises the question as to whether the original claim of the impossibility of acquisition is actually justified. See Section 13.8 on the *Poverty of the Stimulus* and Section 16.1 on parameter-based theories of language acquisition.

Note also that a parameter that has as the value a part of speech requires the respective part of speech values to be part of UG.

[12] However, see Baltin (2004: 552).

equivalent to those where the relative clause would occur in the position marked with t, but rather they correspond to examples where it would occur in the position of the t′.

(14) a. [$_{NP}$ Many books [$_{PP}$ with [stories t]] t′] were sold [that I wanted to read].
b. [$_{NP}$ Many proofs [$_{PP}$ of [the theorem t]] t′] appeared [that I wanted to think about].

Here, it is assumed that NP, PP, VP and AP are bounding nodes for rightward movement (at least in English) and the interpretation in question here is thereby ruled out by the Subjacency Principle (Baltin 1981: 262).

If we construct a German example parallel to (14a) and replace the embedding noun so that it is ruled out or dispreferred as a referent, then we arrive at (15):

(15) weil viele Schallplatten mit Geschichten verkauft wurden, die ich noch lesen wollte
because many records with stories sold were that I still read wanted
'because many records with stories were sold that I wanted to read'

This sentence can be uttered in a situation where somebody in a record store sees particular records and remembers that he had wanted to read the fairy tales on those records. Since one does not read records, adjunction to the superordinate noun is implausible and thus adjunction to *Geschichten* 'stories' is preferred. By carefully choosing the nouns, it is possible to construct examples such as (16) that show that extraposition can take place across multiple NP nodes:[13]

(16) a. Karl hat mir [ein Bild [einer Frau $\_{i}$]] gegeben, [die schon lange tot ist]$_i$.
Karl has me a picture a woman given that PRT long dead is
'Karl gave me a picture of a woman that has been dead some time.'
b. Karl hat mir [eine Fälschung [des Bildes [einer Frau $\_{i}$]]] gegeben, [die schon lange tot ist]$_i$.
Karl has me a forgery of.the picture of.a woman given that PRT long dead is
'Karl gave me a forgery of the picture of a woman that has been dead for some time.'
c. Karl hat mir [eine Kopie [einer Fälschung [des Bildes [einer Frau $\_{i}$]]]] gegeben, [die schon lange tot ist]$_i$.
Karl has me a copy of.a forgery of.the picture of.a woman given that PRT long dead is
'Karl gave me a copy of a forgery of the picture of a woman that has been dead for some time.'

[13] See Müller (1999a: 211) and Müller (2004b; 2007d: Section 3). For parallel examples from Dutch, see Koster (1978: 52).

This kind of embedding could continue further if one were to not eventually run out of nouns that allow for semantically plausible embedding. NP is viewed as a bounding node in German (Grewendorf 1988: 81; 2002: 17–18; Haider 2001: 285). These examples show that it is possible for rightward extraposed relative clauses to cross any number of bounding nodes.

Koster (1978: 52–54) discusses some possible explanations for the data in (16), where it is assumed that relative clauses move to the NP/PP border and are then moved on further from there (this movement requires so-called escape hatches or escape routes). He argues that these approaches will also work for the very sentences that should be ruled out by subjacency, that is, for examples such as (14). This means that either data such as (14) can be explained by subjacency and the sentences in (16) are counterexamples, or there are escape hatches and the examples in (14) are irrelevant, deviant sentences that cannot be explained by subjacency.

In the examples in (16), a relative clause was extraposed in each case. These relative clauses are treated as adjuncts and there are analyses that assume that extraposed adjuncts are not moved but rather base-generated in their position, and coreference/coindexation is achieved by special mechanisms (Kiss 2005). For proponents of these kinds of analyses, the examples in (16) would be irrelevant to the subjacency discussion as the Subjacency Principle only constrains movement. However, extraposition across phrase boundaries is not limited to relative clauses; sentential complements can also be extraposed:

(17) a. Ich habe [von [der Vermutung $\_{i}$]] gehört, [dass es Zahlen gibt, die die folgenden Bedingungen erfüllen]$_{i}$.
I have from the conjecture heard that EXPL numbers gives that the following requirements fulfill
'I have heard of the conjecture that there are numbers that fulfill the following requirements.'

b. Ich habe [von [einem Beweis [der Vermutung $\_{i}$]]] gehört, [dass es Zahlen gibt, die die folgenden Bedingungen erfüllen]$_{i}$.
I have from a proof of.the conjecture heard that EXPL numbers give that the following requirements fulfill
'I have heard of the proof of the conjecture that there are numbers that fulfill the following requirements.'

c. Ich habe [von [dem Versuch [eines Beweises [der Vermutung $\_{i}$]]]] gehört, [dass es Zahlen gibt, die die folgenden Bedingungen erfüllen]$_{i}$.
I have from the attempt of.a proof of.the conjecture heard that EXPL numbers gives that the following requirements fulfill
'I have heard of the attempt to prove the conjecture that there are numbers that fulfill the following requirements.'

Since there are nouns that select *zu* infinitives or prepositional phrases and since these can be extraposed like the sentences above, it must be ensured that the syntactic category of the postposed element corresponds to the category required by the noun. This means that there has to be some kind of relation between the governing noun and the extraposed element. For this reason, the examples in (17) have to be analyzed as instances of extraposition and provide counter evidence to the claims discussed above.

If one wishes to discuss the possibility of recursive embedding, then one is forced to refer to constructed examples as the likelihood of stumbling across groups of sentences such as those in (16) and (17) is very remote. It is, however, possible to find some individual cases of deep embedding: (18) gives some examples of relative clause extraposition and complement extraposition taken from the Tiger corpus[14] (Müller 2007d: 78–79; Meurers & Müller 2009: Section 2.1).

(18) a. Der 43jährige will nach eigener Darstellung damit $[_{NP}$ den Weg $[_{PP}$ für
the 43.year.old wants after own depiction there.with the way for
$[_{NP}$ eine Diskussion $[_{PP}$ über $[_{NP}$ den künftigen Kurs $[_{NP}$ der stärksten
a discussion about the future course of.the strongest
Oppositionsgruppierung]]]]]] freimachen, [die aber mit 10,4 Prozent
opposition.group free.make that however with 10.4 percent
der Stimmen bei der Wahl im Oktober weit hinter den Erwartungen
of.the votes at the election in October far behind the expectations
zurückgeblieben war]. (s27639)
stayed.back was

'In his own words, the 43-year old wanted to clear the way for a discussion about the future course of the strongest opposition group that had, however, performed well below expectations gaining only 10.4 percent of the votes at the election in October.'

b. [...] die Erfindung der Guillotine könnte $[_{NP}$ die Folge $[_{NP}$ eines
the invention of.the guillotine could the result of.a
verzweifelten Versuches des gleichnamigen Doktors] gewesen sein, [seine
desperate attempt the same.name doctor have been his
Patienten ein für allemal von Kopfschmerzen infolge schlechter Kissen
patients once for all.time of headaches because.of bad pillows
zu befreien]. (s16977)
to free

'The invention of the guillotine could have been the result of a desperate attempt of the eponymous doctor to rid his patients once and for all of headaches from bad pillows.'

It is also possible to construct sentences for English that violate the Subjacency Condition. Uszkoreit (1990: 2333) provides the following example:

(19) $[_{NP}$ Only letters $[_{PP}$ from $[_{NP}$ those people $\_{}_i$]]] remained unanswered [that had received our earlier reply]$_i$.

[14] See Brants et al. (2004) for more information on the Tiger corpus.

Jan Strunk (p. c. 2008) has found examples for extraposition of both restrictive and non-restrictive relative clauses across multiple phrase boundaries:

(20) a. For example, we understand that Ariva buses have won [$_{NP}$ a number [$_{PP}$ of [$_{NP}$ contracts [$_{PP}$ for [$_{NP}$ routes in London $\_{i}$]]]]] recently, [which will not be run by low floor accessible buses]$_i$.[15]

b. I picked up [$_{NP}$ a copy of [$_{NP}$ a book $\_{i}$]] today, by a law professor, about law, [that is not assigned or in any way required to read]$_i$.[16]

c. We drafted [$_{NP}$ a list of [$_{NP}$ basic demands $\_{i}$]] that night [that had to be unconditionally met or we would stop making and delivering pizza and go on strike]$_i$.[17]

(20a) is also published in Strunk & Snider (2013: 111). Further attested examples from German and English can be found in this paper.

The preceding discussion has shown that subjacency constraints on rightward movement do not hold for English or German and thus cannot be viewed as universal. One could simply claim that NP and PP are not bounding nodes in English or German. Then, these extraposition data would no longer be problematic for theories assuming subjacency. However, subjacency constraints are also assumed for leftward movement. This is discussed in more detail in the following section.

13.1.5.2 Extraction

Under certain conditions, leftward movement is not possible from certain constituents (Ross 1967). These constituents are referred to as islands for extraction. Ross (1967: Section 4.1) formulated the *Complex NP Constraint* (CNPC) that states that extraction is not possible from complex noun phrases. An example of extraction from a relative clause inside a noun phrase is the following:

(21) * Who$_i$ did he just read [$_{NP}$ the report [$_S$ that was about $\_{i}$]?

Although (21) would be a semantically plausible question, the sentence is still ungrammatical. This is explained by the fact that the question pronoun has been extracted across the sentence boundary of a relative clause and then across the NP boundary and has therefore crossed two bounding nodes. It is assumed that the CNPC holds for all languages. This is not the case, however, as the corresponding structures are possible in Danish (Erteschik-Shir & Lappin 1979: 55), Norwegian, Swedish, Japanese, Korean, Tamil and Akan (see Hawkins (1999: 245, 262) and references therein). Since the restrictions of the CNPC are integrated into the Subjacency Principle, it follows that the Subjacency Principle cannot be universally applicable unless one claims that NP is not a bounding node in the problematic languages. However, it seems indeed to be the case that the majority of languages do not allow extraction from complex noun phrases. Hawkins explains this on the basis of the processing difficulties associated with the structures

[15] http://www.publications.parliament.uk/pa/cm199899/cmselect/cmenvtra/32ii/32115.htm, 24.02.2007.

[16] http://greyhame.org/archives/date/2005/09/, 27.09.2008.

[17] http://portland.indymedia.org/en/2005/07/321809.shtml, 27.09.2008.

in question (Section 4.1). He explains the difference between languages that allow this kind of extraction and languages that do not with reference to the differing processing load for structures that stem from the interaction of extraction with other grammatical properties such as verb position and other conventionalized grammatical structures in the respective languages (Section 4.2).

Unlike extraction from complex noun phrases, extraction across a single sentence boundary (22) is not ruled out by the Subjacency Principle.

(22) Who$_i$ did she think that he saw $\_{i}$?

Movement across multiple sentence boundaries, as discussed in previous chapters, is explained by so-called cyclic movement in transformational theories: a question pronoun is moved to a specifier position and can then be moved further to the next highest specifier. Each of these movement steps is subject to the Subjacency Principle. The Subjacency Principle rules out long-distance movement in one fell swoop.

The Subjacency Principle cannot explain why extraction from sentences embedded under verbs that specify the kind of utterance (23a) or factive verbs (23b) is deviant (Erteschik-Shir & Lappin 1979: 68–69).

(23) a. ?? Who$_i$ did she mumble that he saw $\_{i}$?
b. ?? Who$_i$ did she realize that he saw $\_{i}$?

The structure of these sentences seems to be the same as (22). In entirely syntactic approaches, it was also attempted to explain these differences as subjacency violations or as a violation of Ross' constraints. It has therefore been assumed (Stowell 1981: 401–402) that the sentences in (23) have a structure different from those in (22). Stowell treats these sentential arguments of manner of speaking verbs as adjuncts. Since adjunct clauses are islands for extraction by assumption, this would explain why (23a) is marked. The adjunct analysis is compatible with the fact that these sentential arguments can be omitted:

(24) a. She shouted that he left.
b. She shouted.

Ambridge & Goldberg (2008: 352) have pointed out that treating such clauses as adjuncts is not justified as they are only possible with a very restricted class of verbs, namely verbs of saying and thinking. This property is a property of arguments and not of adjuncts. Adjuncts such as place modifiers are possible with a wide number of verb classes. Furthermore, the meaning changes if the sentential argument is omitted as in (24b): whereas (24a) requires that some information is communicated, this does not have to be the case with (24b). It is also possible to replace the sentential argument with an NP as in (25), which one would certainly not want to treat as an adjunct.

(25) She shouted the remark/the question/something I could not understand.

The possibility of classifying sentential arguments as adjuncts cannot be extended to factive verbs as their sentential argument is not optional (Ambridge & Goldberg 2008: 352):

(26) a. She realized that he left.
b. ?? She realized.

Kiparsky & Kiparsky (1970) suggest an analysis of factive verbs that assumes a complex noun phrase with a nominal head. An optional *fact* Deletion-Transformation removes the head noun and the determiner of the NP in sentences such as (27a) to derive sentences such as (27b) (page 159).

(27) a. She realized [$_{NP}$ the fact [$_{S}$ that he left]].
b. She realized [$_{NP}$ [$_{S}$ that he left]].

The impossibility of extraction out of such sentences can be explained by assuming that two boundary nodes were crossed, which was assumed to be impossible (on the island status of this construction, see Kiparsky & Kiparsky 1970: Section 4). This analysis predicts that extraction from complement clauses of factive verbs should be just as bad as extraction from overt NP arguments since the structure for both is the same. According to Ambridge & Goldberg (2008: 353), this is, however, not the case:

(28) a. * Who did she realize the fact that he saw $\_{i}$?
b. ?? Who did she realize that he saw $\_{i}$?

Together with Erteschik-Shir (1981), Erteschik-Shir & Lappin (1979), Takami (1988) and Van Valin (1998), Goldberg (2006: Section 7.2) assumes that the gap must be in a part of the utterance that can potentially form the focus of an utterance (see Cook (2001), De Kuthy (2002) and Fanselow (2003c) for German). This means that this part must not be presupposed.[18] If one considers what this means for the data from the subjacency discussion, then one notices that in each case extraction has taken place out of presupposed material:

(29) a. Complex NP
She didn't see the report that was about him. → The report was about him.
b. Complement of a verb of thinking or saying
She didn't whisper that he left. → He left.
c. Factive verb
She didn't realize that he left. → He left.

Goldberg assumes that constituents that belong to backgrounded information are islands (*Backgrounded constructions are islands* (BCI)). Ambridge & Goldberg (2008) have tested this semantic/pragmatic analysis experimentally and compared it to a purely syntactic approach. They were able to confirm that information structural properties play a

[18] Information is presupposed if it is true regardless of whether the utterance is negated or not. Thus, it follows from both (i.a) and (i.b) that there is a king of France.

(i) a. The King of France is bald.
b. The King of France is not bald.

significant role for the extractability of elements. Along with Erteschik-Shir (1973: Section 3.H), Ambridge & Goldberg (2008: 375) assume that languages differ with regard to how much constituents have to belong to background knowledge in order to rule out extraction. In any case we should not rule out extraction from adjuncts for all languages as there are languages such as Danish where it is possible to extract from relative clauses.[19] Erteschik-Shir (1973: 61) provides the following examples, among others:

(30) a. Det$_i$ er der mange [der kan lide $\_{i}$].
that are there many that can like
'There are many who like that.' (lit.: 'That, there are many who like.')

b. Det hus$_i$ kender jeg en mand [som har købt $\_{i}$].
that house know I a man that has bought
'I know a man that has bought that house.' (lit.: 'This house, I know a man that has bought.')

Rizzi's parameterization of the subjacency restriction has been abandoned in many works, and the relevant effects have been ascribed to differences in other areas of grammar (Adams 1984; Chung & McCloskey 1983; Grimshaw 1986; Kluender 1992).

We have seen in this subsection that there are reasons other than syntactic properties of structure as to why leftward movement might be blocked. In addition to information structural properties, processing considerations also play a role (Grosu 1973; Ellefson & Christiansen 2000; Gibson 1998; Kluender & Kutas 1993; Hawkins 1999; Sag, Hofmeister & Snider 2007). The length of constituents involved, the distance between filler and gap, definiteness, complexity of syntactic structure and interference effects between similar discourse referents in the space between the filler and gap are all important factors for the acceptability of utterances. Since languages differ with regard to their syntactic structure, varying effects of performance, such as the ones found for extraposition and extraction, are to be expected.

In sum, we can say that subjacency constraints do not hold for extraposition in either German or English and furthermore that one can better explain constraints on extraction with reference to information structure and processing phenomena than with the Subjacency Principle. Assuming subjacency as a syntactic constraint in a universal competence grammar is therefore unnecessary to explain the facts.

13.1.6 Grammatical morphemes for tense, mood and aspect

Pinker (1994: 238) is correct in claiming that there are morphemes for tense, mood, aspect, case and negation in many languages. However, there is a great deal of variation

[19] Discussing the question of whether UG-based approaches are falsifiable, Crain, Khlentzos & Thornton (2010: 2669) claim that it is not possible to extract from relative clauses and the existence of such languages would call into question the very concept of UG. ("If a child acquiring any language could learn to extract linguistic expressions from a relative clause, then this would seriously cast doubt on one of the basic tenets of UG.") They thereby contradict Evans and Levinson as well as Tomasello, who claim that UG approaches are not falsifiable. If the argumentation of Crain, Khlentzos and Thornton were correct, then (30) would falsify UG and that would be the end of the discussion.

with regard to which of these grammatical properties a language has and how they are expressed.

For examples of differences in the tense system see Dahl & Velupillai (2013b,a). Mandarin Chinese is a clear case: it has next to no morphology. The fact that the same morphemes occur in one form or another in almost every language can be attributed to the fact that certain things need to be expressed repeatedly and then things which are constantly repeated become grammaticalized.

13.1.7 Parts of speech

In Section 4.6, so-called cartographic approaches were mentioned, some of which assume over thirty functional categories (see Table 4.1 on page 142 for Cinque's functional heads) and assume that these categories form part of UG together with corresponding fixed syntactic structures. Cinque & Rizzi (2010: 55, 57) even assume over 400 functional categories that are claimed to play a role in the grammars of all languages.[20] Also, specific parts of speech such as Infl (inflection) and Comp (complementizer) are referred to when formulating principles that are assumed to be universal (Baltin 1981: 262; 2006; Rizzi 1982; Chomsky 1986a: 38; Hornstein 2013: 397).

Chomsky (1988: 68; 1991; 1995b: 131), Pinker (1994: 284, 286), Briscoe (2000: 270) and Wunderlich (2004: 621) make comparatively fewer assumptions about the innate inventory of parts of speech: Chomsky assumes that all lexical categories (verbs, nouns, adjectives and adpositions) belong to UG and languages have these at their disposal. Pinker, Briscoe and Wunderlich assume that all languages have nouns and verbs. Again critics of UG raised the question as to whether these syntactic categories can be found in other languages in the form known to us from languages such as German and English.

Braine (1987: 72) argues that parts of speech such as verb and noun should be viewed as derived from fundamental concepts like argument and predicate (see also Wunderlich (2008: 257)). This means that there is an independent explanation for the presence of these categories that is not based on innate language-specific knowledge.

Evans & Levinson (2009a: Section 2.2.4) discuss the typological literature and give examples of languages which lack adverbs and adjectives. The authors cite Straits Salish as a language in which there may be no difference between verbs and nouns (see also Evans & Levinson 2009b: 481). They remark that it does make sense to assume the additional word classes ideophone, positional, coverb, classifier for the analysis of non Indo-European languages on top of the four or five normally used.[21] This situation is not a problem for UG-based theories if one assumes that languages can choose from an inventory of possibilities (a toolkit) but do not have to exhaust it (Jackendoff 2002: 263; Newmeyer 2005: 11; Fitch, Hauser & Chomsky 2005: 204; Chomsky 2007: 6–7; Cinque & Rizzi 2010: 55, 58, 65). However, if we condone this view, then there is a certain arbitrariness. It is possible to assume any parts of speech that one requires for the analysis of at least one language, attribute them to UG and then claim that most (or maybe even all) languages do not make use of the entire set of parts of speech. This is what is suggested

[20] The question of whether these categories form part of UG is left open.

[21] For the opposite view, see Jackendoff & Pinker (2009: 465).

by Villavicencio (2002: 157), working in the framework of Categorial Grammar, for the categories S, NP, N, PP and PRT. This kind of assumption is not falsifiable (see Evans & Levinson 2009a: 436; Tomasello 2009: 471 for a discussion of similar cases and a more general discussion).

Whereas Evans and Levinson assume that one needs additional categories, Haspelmath (2009: 458) and Croft (2009: 453) go so far as to deny the existence of cross-linguistic parts of speech. I consider this to be too extreme and believe that a better research strategy is to try and find commonalities between languages.[22] One should, however, expect to find languages that do not fit into our Indo-European-biased conceptions of grammar.

13.1.8 Recursion and infinitude

In an article in *Science*, Hauser, Chomsky & Fitch (2002) put forward the hypothesis that the only domain-specific universal is recursion, "providing the capacity to generate an infinite range of expressions from a finite set of elements" (see (37b) on page 64 for an example of a recursive phrase structure rule).[23] This assumption is controversial and there have been both formal and empirical objections to it.

13.1.8.1 Formal problems

The claim that our linguistic capabilities are infinite is widespread and can already be found in Humboldt's work:[24]

> Das Verfahren der Sprache ist aber nicht bloß ein solches, wodurch eine einzelne Erscheinung zustande kommt; es muss derselben zugleich die Möglichkeit eröffnen, eine unbestimmbare Menge solcher Erscheinungen und unter allen, ihr von dem Gedanken gestellten Bedingungen hervorzubringen. Denn sie steht ganz eigentlich einem unendlichen und wahrhaft grenzenlosen Gebiete, dem Inbegriff alles Denkbaren gegenüber. Sie muss daher von endlichen Mitteln einen unendlichen Gebrauch machen, und vermag dies durch die Identität der gedanken- und spracheerzeugenden Kraft. (Humboldt 1988: 108)

[22] Compare Chomsky (1999: 2): "In the absence of compelling evidence to the contrary, assume languages to be uniform, with variety restricted to easily detectable properties of utterances."

[23] In a discussion article in *Cognition*, Fitch, Hauser & Chomsky (2005) clarify that their claim that recursion is the only language-specific and human-specific property is a hypothesis and it could be the case that are not any language-specific/species-specific properties at all. Then, a particular combination of abilities and properties would be specific to humans (p. 182–201). An alternative they consider is that innate language-specific knowledge has a complexity corresponding to what was assumed in earlier versions of Mainstream Generative Grammar (p. 182). Chomsky (2007: 7) notes that Merge could be a non language-specific operation but still attributes it to UG.

[24] The process of language is not simply one where an individual instantiation is created; at the same time it must allow for an indefinite set of such instantiations and must above all allow the expression of the conditions imposed by thought. Language faces an infinite and truly unbounded subject matter, the epitome of everything one can think of. Therefore, it must make infinite use of finite means and this is possible through the identity of the power that is responsible for the production of thought and language.

If we just look at the data, we can see that there is an upper bound for the length of utterances. This has to do with the fact that extremely long instances cannot be processed and that speakers have to sleep or will eventually die at some point. If we set a generous maximal sentence length at 100,000 morphemes and then assume a morpheme inventory of X then one can form less than $X^{100,000}$ utterances. We arrive at the number $X^{100,000}$ if we use each of the morphemes at each of the 100,000 positions. Since not all of these sequences will be well-formed, then there are actually less than $X^{100,000}$ possible utterances (see also Weydt 1972 for a similar but more elaborate argument). This number is incredibly large, but still finite. The same is true of thought: we do not have infinitely many possible thoughts (if *infinitely* is used in the mathematical sense of the word), despite claims by Humboldt and Chomsky (2008: 137) to the contrary.[25]

In the literature, one sometimes finds the claim that it is possible to produce infinitely long sentences (see for instance Nowak, Komarova & Niyogi (2001: 117) and Kim & Sells (2008: 3) and Dan Everett in O'Neill & Wood (2012) at 25:19). This is most certainly not the case. It is also not the case that the rewrite grammars we encountered in Chapter 2 allow for the creation of infinite sentences as the set of symbols of the right-hand side of the rule has to be finite by definition. While it is possible to derive an infinite number of sentences, the sentences themselves cannot be infinite, since it is always one symbol that is replaced by finitely many other symbols and hence no infinite symbol sequence may result.

Chomsky (1965: Section I.1) follows de Saussure (1916b) and draws a distinction between competence and performance: competence is the knowledge about what kind of linguistic structures are well-formed, and performance is the application of this knowl-

[25] Weydt (1972) discusses Chomsky's statements regarding the existence of infinitely many sentences and whether it is legitimate for Chomsky to refer to Humboldt. Chomsky's quote in *Current Issues in Linguistic Theory* (Chomsky 1964a: 17) leaves out the sentence *Denn sie steht ganz eigentlich einem unendlichen und wahrhaft grenzenlosen Gebiete, dem Inbegriff alles Denkbaren gegenüber.* Weydt (1972: 266) argues that Humboldt, Bühler and Martinet claimed that there are infinitely many thoughts that can be expressed. Weydt claims that it does not follow that sentences may be arbitrarily long. Instead he suggests that there is no upper bound on the length of texts. This claim is interesting, but I guess texts are just the next bigger unit and the argument that Weydt put forward against languages without an upper bound for sentence length also applies to texts. A text can be generated by the rather simplified rule in (i) that combines an utterance U with a text T resulting in a larger text T:

(i) T → T U

U can be a sentence or another phrase that can be part of a text. If one is ready to admit that there is no upper bound on the length of texts, it follows that there cannot be an upper bound on the length of sentences either, since one can construct long sentences by joining all phrases of a text with *and.* Such long sentences that are the product of conjoining short sentences are different in nature from very long sentences that are admitted under the Chomskyan view in that they do not include center-self embeddings of an arbitrary depth (see Section 15), but nevertheless the number of sentences that can be produced from arbitrarily long texts is infinite.

As for arbitrarily long texts there is an interesting problem: Let us assume that a person produces sentences and keeps adding them to an existing text. This enterprise will be interrupted when the human being dies. One could say that another person could take up the text extension until this one dies and so on. Again the question is whether one can understand the meaning and the structure of a text that is several million pages long. 42. If this is not enough of a problem, one may ask oneself whether the language of the person who keeps adding to the text in the year 2731 is still the same that the person who started the text spoke in 2015. If the answer to this question is no, then the text is not a document containing sentences from one language L but a mix from several languages and hence irrelevant for the debate.

edge (see Section 12.6.3 and Chapter 15). Our restricted brain capacity as well as other constraints are responsible for the fact that we cannot deal with an arbitrary amount of embedding and that we cannot produce utterances longer than 100,000 morphemes. The separation between competence and performance makes sense and allows us to formulate rules for the analysis of sentences such as (31):

(31) a. Richard is sleeping.
 b. Karl suspects that Richard is sleeping.
 c. Otto claims that Karl suspects that Richard is sleeping.
 d. Julius believes that Otto claims that Karl suspects that Richard is sleeping.
 e. Max knows that Julius believes that Otto claims that Karl suspects that Richard is sleeping.

The rule takes the following form: combine a noun phrase with a verb of a certain class and a clause. By applying this rule successively, it is possible to form strings of arbitrary length. Pullum & Scholz (2010) point out that one has to keep two things apart: the question of whether language is a recursive system and whether it is just the case that the best models that we can devise for a particular language happen to be recursive. For more on this point and on processing in the brain, see Luuk & Luuk (2011). When constructing strings of words using the system above, it cannot be shown that (a particular) language is infinite, even if this is often claimed to be the case (Bierwisch 1966: 105–106; Pinker 1994: 86; Hauser, Chomsky & Fitch 2002: 1571; Müller 2007b: 1; Hornstein, Nunes & Grohmann 2005: 7; Kim & Sells 2008: 3).

The "proof" of this infinitude of language is led as an indirect proof parallel to the proof that shows that there is no largest natural number (Bierwisch 1966: 105–106; Pinker 1994: 86). In the domain of natural numbers, this works as follows: assume x is the largest natural number. Then form $x + 1$ and, since this is by definition a natural number, we have now found a natural number that is greater than x. We have therefore shown that the assumption that x is the highest number leads to a contradiction and thus that there cannot be such a thing as the largest natural number.

When transferring this proof into the domain of natural language, the question arises as to whether one would still want to class a string of 1,000,000,000 words as part of the language we want to describe. If we do not want this, then this proof will not work.

If we view language as a biological construct, then one has to accept the fact that it is finite. Otherwise, one is forced to assume that it is infinite, but that an infinitely large part of the biologically real object is not biologically real (Postal 2009: 111). Luuk & Luuk (2011) refer to languages as physically uncountable but finite sets of strings. They point out that a distinction must be made between the ability to imagine extending a sentence indefinitely and the ability to take a sentence from a non-countable set of strings and really extend it. We possess the first ability but not the second.

One possibility to provide arguments for the infinitude of languages is to claim that only generative grammars, which create sets of well-formed utterances, are suited to modeling language and that we need recursive rules to capture the data, which is why mental representations have a recursive procedure that generates infinite numbers of expressions (Chomsky, 1956: 115; 2002: 86–87), which then implies that languages consist of infinitely many expressions. There are two mistakes in this argument that have been pointed out by Pullum & Scholz (2010): even if one assumes generative grammars, it can still be the case that a context-sensitive grammar can still only generate a finite set even with recursive rules. Pullum & Scholz (2010: 120–121) give an interesting example from András Kornai.

The more important mistake is that it is not necessary to assume that grammars generate sets. There are three explicitly formalized alternatives of which only the third is mentioned here, namely the model-theoretic and therefore constraint-based approaches (see Chapter 14). Johnson & Postal's Arc Pair Grammar (1980), LFG in the formalization of Kaplan (1995), GPSG in the reformalization of Rogers (1997) and HPSG with the assumptions of King (1999), Pollard (1999) and Richter (2007) are examples of model-theoretic approaches. In constraint-based theories, one would analyze an example like (31) saying that certain attitude verbs select a nominative NP and a *that* clause and that these can only occur in a certain local configuration where a particular relation holds between the elements involved. One of these relations is subject-verb agreement. In this way, one can represent expressions such as (31) and does not have to say anything about how many sentences can be embedded. This means that constraint-based theories are compatible with both answers to the question of whether there is a finite or infinite number of structures. Using competence grammars formulated in the relevant way, it is possible to develop performance models that explain why certain strings – for instance very long ones – are unacceptable (see Chapter 15).

13.1.8.2 Empirical problems

It is sometimes claimed that all natural languages are recursive and that sentences of an arbitrary length are possible in all languages (Hornstein, Nunes & Grohmann 2005: 7 for an overview, and see Pullum & Scholz (2010: Section 2) for further references). When one speaks of recursion, what is often meant are structures with self-embedding as we saw in the analysis of (31) (Fitch 2010). However, it is possible that there are languages that do not allow self-embedding. Everett (2005) claims that Pirahã is such a language (however, see Nevins, Pesetsky & Rodrigues (2009) and Everett (2009)). A further example of a language without recursion, which is sometimes cited with reference to Hale (1976), is Warlpiri. Hale's rules for the combination of a sentence with a relative clause are recursive, however (page 85). This recursion is made explicit on page 98.[26] Pullum & Scholz (2010: 131) discuss Hixkaryána, an Amazonian language from the Caribbean lan-

[26] However, he does note on page 78 that relative clauses are separated from the sentence containing the head noun by a pause. Relative clauses in Warlpiri are always peripheral, that is, they occur to the left or right of a sentence with the noun they refer to. Similar constructions can be found in German:

(i) Es war einmal ein Mann. Der hatte sieben Söhne.
there was once a man he had seven sons
'There once was a man. He had seven sons.'

It could be the case that we are dealing with linking of sentences at text level and not recursion at sentence level.

guage family that is not related to Pirahã. This language does have embedding, but the embedded material has a different form to that of the matrix clause. It could be the case that these embeddings cannot be carried out indefinitely. In Hixkaryána, there is also no possibility to coordinate phrases or clauses (Derbyshire (1979: 45) cited by Pullum & Scholz (2010: 131)), which is why this possibility of forming recursive sentence embedding does not exist in this language either. Other languages without self-embedding seem to be Akkadian, Dyirbal and Proto-Uralic.

There is of course a trivial sense in which all languages are recursive: they follow a rule that says that a particular number of symbols can be combined to form another symbol.[27]

(32) $X \rightarrow X \dots X$

In this sense, all natural languages are recursive and the combination of simple symbols to more complex ones is a basic property of language (Hockett 1960: 6). The fact that the debate about Pirahã is so fierce could go to show that this is not the kind of recursion that is meant. Also, see Fitch (2010).

It is also assumed that the combinatorial rules of Categorial Grammar hold universally. It is possible to use these rules to combine a functor with its arguments ($X/Y * Y = X$). These rules are almost as abstract as the rules in (32). The difference is that one of the elements has to be the functor. There are also corresponding constraints in the Minimalist Program such as selectional features (see Section 4.6.4) and restrictions on the assignment of semantic roles. However, whether or not a Categorial Grammar licenses recursive structures does not depend on the very general combinatorial schemata, but rather on the lexical entries. Using the lexical entries in (33), it is only possible to analyze two sentences and certainly not to build recursive structures.

(33)
a. the: np/n
b. woman: n
c. cat: n
d. sees: (s\np)/np

If we expand the lexicon to include modifiers of the category n/n or conjunctions of the category (X\X)/X, then we arrive at a recursive grammar.

Fitch, Hauser & Chomsky (2005: 203) note that the existence of languages that do not license recursive structures is not a problem for UG-based theories as not all the possibilities in UG have to be utilized by an individual language. With this view, we have actually the same situation as with parts of speech (see Section 13.1.7) that you can posit any number of properties belonging to UG and then decide on a language by language basis whether they play a role or not. An extreme variant of this approach would be that grammars of all languages become part of UG (perhaps with different symbols such as $NP_{Spanish}$, NP_{German}). This variant of a UG-based theory of the human capacity for language would be truly unfalsifiable (Evans & Levinson 2009a: 436, 443; Tomasello 2009: 471).

[27] Chomsky (2005: 11) assumes that Merge combines n objects. A special instance of this is binary Merge.

13.1.8.3 Recursion in other areas of cognition

There are also phenomena in domains outside of language that can be described with recursive rules: Hauser, Chomsky & Fitch (2002: 1571) mention navigation, family relations and counting systems.[28] One could perhaps argue that the relevant abilities are acquired late and that higher mathematics is a matter of individual accomplishments that do not have anything to do with the cognitive capacities of the majority, but even children at the age of 3 years and 9 months are already able to produce recursive structures: In 2008, there were newspaper reports about an indigenous Brazilian tribe that was photographed from a plane. I showed this picture to my son and told him that Native Americans shot at the plane with a bow and arrow. He then asked me what kind of plane it was. I told him that you cannot see that because the people who took the photograph were sitting in the plane. He then answered that you would then need another plane if you wanted to take a photo that contained both the plane and the Native Americans. He was pleased with his idea and said "And then another one. And then another one. One after the other". He was therefore very much able to imagine the consequence of embeddings.

Culicover & Jackendoff (2005: 113–114) discuss visual perception and music as recursive systems that are independent of language. Jackendoff (2011) extends the discussion of visual perception and music and adds the domains of planning (with the example of making coffee) and wordless comic strips. Chomsky (2007: 7–8) claims that examples from visual perception are irrelevant but then admits that the ability to build up recursive structures could belong to general cognitive abilities (p. 8). He still attributes this ability to UG. He views UG as a subset of the Faculty of Language, that is, as a subset of non domain-specific abilities (Faculty of Language in the Broad Sense = FLB) and the domain-specific abilities (Faculty of Language in the Narrow Sense = FLN) required for language.

13.1.9 Summary

In sum, we can say that there are no linguistic universals for which there is a consensus that one has to assume domain-specific innate knowledge to explain them. At the 2008 meeting of the *Deutsche Gesellschaft für Sprachwissenschaft*, Wolfgang Klein promised € 100 to anyone who could name a non-trivial property that all languages share (see Klein 2009). This begs the question of what is meant by 'trivial'. It seems clear that all languages share predicate-argument structures and dependency relations in some sense (Hudson 2010a; Longobardi & Roberts 2010: 2701) and, all languages have complex expressions whose meaning can be determined compositionally (Manfred Krifka was

[28] Pinker & Jackendoff (2005: 230) note, however, that navigation differs from the kind of recursive system described by Chomsky and that recursion is not part of counting systems in all cultures. They assume that those cultures that have developed infinite counting systems could do this because of their linguistic capabilities. This is also assumed by Fitch, Hauser & Chomsky (2005: 203). The latter authors claim that all forms of recursion in other domains depend on language. For more on this point, see Chomsky (2007: 7–8). Luuk & Luuk (2011) note that natural numbers are defined recursively, but the mathematical definition does not necessarily play a role for the kinds of arithmetic operations carried out by humans.

promised 20 € for coming up with compositionality). However, as has been noted at various points, universality by no means implies innateness (Bates 1984: 189; Newmeyer 2005: 205): Newmeyer gives the example that words for sun and moon probably exist in all languages. This has to do with the fact that these celestial bodies play an important role in everyone's lives and thus one needs words to refer to them. It cannot be concluded from this that the corresponding concepts have to be innate. Similarly, a word that is used to express a relation between two objects (e.g., *catch*) has to be connected to the words describing both of these objects (*I*, *elephant*) in a transparent way. However, this does not necessarily entail that this property of language is innate.

Even if we can find structural properties shared by all languages, this is still not proof of innate linguistic knowledge, as these similarities could be traced back to other factors. It is argued that all languages must be made in such a way as to be acquirable with the paucity of resource available to small children (Hurford 2002: Section 10.7.2; Behrens 2009: 433). It follows from this that, in the relevant phases of its development, our brain is a constraining factor. Languages have to fit into our brains and since our brains are similar, languages are also similar in certain respects (see Kluender 1992: 251).

13.2 Speed of language acquisition

It is often argued that children learn language extraordinarily quickly and this can only be explained by assuming that they already possess knowledge about language that does not have to be acquired (e.g., Chomsky 1976b: 144; Hornstein 2013: 395). In order for this argument to hold up to closer scrutiny, it must be demonstrated that other areas of knowledge with a comparable degree of complexity require longer to acquire (Sampson 1989: 214–218). This has not yet been shown. Language acquisition spans several years and it is not possible to simply state that language is acquired following *brief exposure*. Chomsky compares languages to physics and points out that it is considerably more difficult for us to acquire knowledge about physics. Sampson (1989: 215) notes, however, that the knowledge about physics one acquires at school or university is not a basis for comparison and one should instead consider the acquisition of everyday knowledge about the physical world around us. For example, the kind of knowledge we need when we want to pour liquids into a container, skip with a skipping rope or the knowledge we have about the ballistic properties of objects. The complexity in comparing these domains of knowledge in order to be able to make claims about language acquisition may turn out to be far from trivial. For an in-depth discussion of this aspect, see Sampson (1989: 214–218). Müller & Riemer (1998: 1) point out that children at the age of six can understand 23,700 words and use over 5000. It follows from this that, in the space of four and a half years, they learn on average 14 new words every day. This is indeed an impressive feat, but cannot be used as an argument for innate linguistic knowledge as all theories of acquisition assume that words have to be learned from data rather than being predetermined by a genetically-determined Universal Grammar. In any case the assumption of genetic encoding would be highly implausible for newly created words such as *fax*, *iPod*, *e-mail*, *Tamagotchi*.

Furthermore, the claim that first language acquisition is effortless and rapid when compared to second language acquisition is a myth as has been shown by estimations by Klein (1986: 9): if we assume that children hear linguistic utterances for five hours a day (as a conservative estimate), then in the first five years of their lives, they have 9100 hours of linguistic training. But at the age of five, they have still not acquired all complex constructions. In comparison, second-language learners, assuming the necessary motivation, can learn the grammar of a language rather well in a six-week crash course with twelve hours a day (500 hours in total).

13.3 Critical period for acquisition

Among ducks, there is a critical phase in which their behavior towards parent figures is influenced significantly. Normally, baby ducks follow their mother. If, however, a human is present rather than the mother during a particular time span, the ducks will follow the human. After the critical period, this influence on their behavior can no longer be identified (Lorenz 1970). This kind of critical period can also be identified in other animals and in other areas of cognition, for example the acquisition of visual abilities among primates. Certain abilities are acquired in a given time frame, whereby the presence of the relevant input is important for determining the start of this time frame.

Lenneberg (1964) claims that language acquisition is only possible up to the age of twelve and concludes from the fact that children can learn language much better than adults that this is also due to a critical period and that language acquisition must have similar properties to the behavior of ducks and hence, the predisposition for language acquisition must be innate (Lenneberg 1967: Chapter 4).

The assumptions about the length of the critical period for language acquisition vary considerably. It is possible to find suggestions for 5, 6, 12 and even 15 years (Hakuta et al. 2003: 31). An alternative assumption to a critical period would be to assume that the ability to acquire languages decreases continuously over time. Johnson & Newport (1989) tried to determine a critical period for second-language acquisition and they claim that a second language is learned significantly worse from the age of 15. Elman, Bates, Johnson, Karmiloff-Smith, Parisi & Plunkett (1996) have, however, pointed out that there is a different curve for Johnson and Newport's data that fits the individual data better. The alternative curve shows no abrupt change but rather a steady decrease in the ability to learn language and therefore offers no proof of an effect created by a critical period.

Hakuta, Bialystok & Wiley (2003) evaluate data from a questionnaire of 2,016,317 Spanish speakers and 324,444 speakers of Mandarin Chinese that immigrated to the United States. They investigated which correlations there were between age, the point at immigration, the general level of education of the speakers and the level of English they acquired. They could not identify a critical point in time after which language acquisition was severely restricted. Instead, there is a steady decline in the ability to learn as age increases. This can also be observed in other domains: for example, learning to drive at an older age is much harder.

Summing up, it seems to be relatively clear that a critical period cannot be proven to exist for second-language acquisition. Sometimes, it is assumed anyway that second-language acquisition is not driven by an innate UG, but is in fact a learning process that accesses knowledge already acquired during the critical period (Lenneberg 1967: 176). One would therefore have to show that there is a critical period for first-language acquisition. This is, however, not straightforward as, for ethical reasons, one cannot experimentally manipulate the point at which the input is available. We cannot, say, take 20 children and let them grow up without linguistic input to the age of 3, 4, 5, 6, ... or 15 and then compare the results. This kind of research is dependent on thankfully very rare cases of neglect. For example, Curtiss (1977) studied a girl called Genie. At the time, Genie was 13 years old and had grown up in isolation. She is a so-called feral child. As Curtiss showed, she was no longer able to learn certain linguistic rules. For an objective comparison, one would need other test subjects that had not grown up in complete isolation and in inhumane conditions. The only possibility of gaining relevant experimental data is to study deaf subjects that did not receive any input from a sign language up to a certain age. Johnson & Newport (1989: 63) carried out relevant experiments with learners of American Sign Language. It was also shown here that there is a linear decline in the ability to learn, however nothing like a sudden drop after a certain age or even a complete loss of the ability to acquire language.

13.4 Lack of acquisition among non-human primates

The fact that non-human primates cannot learn natural language is viewed as evidence for the genetic determination of our linguistic ability. All scientists agree on the fact that there are genetically-determined differences between humans and primates and that these are relevant for linguistic ability. Friederici (2009) offers an overview of the literature that claims that in chimpanzees and macaques (and small children), the connections between parts of the brain are not as developed as in adult humans. The connected regions of the brain are together responsible for the processing of lexical-semantic knowledge and could constitute an important prerequisite for the development of language (p. 179).

The question is, however, whether we differ from other primates in having special cognitive capabilities that are specific to language or whether our capability to acquire languages is due to domain-general differences in cognition. Fanselow (1992b: Section 2) speaks of a human-specific formal competence that does not necessarily have to be specific to language, however. Similarly, Chomsky (2007: 7–8) has considered whether Merge (the only structure-building operation, in his opinion), does not belong to language-specific innate abilities, but rather to general human-specific competence (see, however, Section 13.1.8, in particular footnote 28).

One can ascertain that non-human primates do not understand particular pointing gestures. Humans like to imitate things. Other primates also imitate, however, not for social reasons (Tomasello 2006b: 9–10). According to Tomasello et al. (2005: 676), only humans have the ability and motivation to carry out coordinated activities with common goals and socially-coordinated action plans. Primates do understand intentional actions, however, only humans act with a common goal in mind (*shared intentionality*). Only humans use and understand hand gestures (Tomasello et al. 2005: 685, 724, 726). Language is collaborative to a high degree: symbols are used to refer to objects and sometimes also to the speaker or hearer. In order to be able to use this kind of communication system, one has to be able to put oneself in the shoes of the interlocutor and develop common expectations and goals (Tomasello et al. 2005: 683). Non-human primates could thus lack the social and cognitive prerequisites for language, that is, the difference between humans and other primates does not have to be explained by innate linguistic knowledge (Tomasello 2003: Section 8.1.2; Tomasello et al. 2005).

13.5 Creole and sign languages

When speakers that do not share a common language wish to communicate with each other, they develop so-called pidgin languages. These are languages that use parts of the vocabularies of the languages involved but have a very rudimentary grammar. It has been noted that children of pidgin speakers regularize these languages. The next generation of speakers creates a new language with an independent grammar. These languages are referred to as *creole languages*. One hypothesis is that the form of languages that develop from creolization is restricted by an innate UG (Bickerton 1984b). It is assumed that the parameter setting of creole languages corresponds to the default values of parameters (Bickerton 1984a: 217; 1984b: 178), that is, parameters already have values at birth and these correspond to the values that creole languages have. These default values would have to be modified when learning other languages.[29] Bickerton claims that creole languages contain elements that language learners could not have acquired from the input, that is from the pidgin languages. His argumentation is a variant of the classic Poverty of the Stimulus Argument that will be discussed in more detail in Section 13.8.

Bickerton's claims have been criticized as it cannot be verified whether children had input in the individual languages of the adults (Samarin 1984: 207; Seuren 1984: 209). All that can be said considering this lack of evidence is that there are a number of demographic facts that suggest that this was the case for at least some creole languages (Arends 2008). This means that children did not only have the strings from the pidgin languages as an input but also sentences from the individual languages spoken by parents and others around them. Many creolists assume that adults contribute specific grammatical forms to the emerging language. For example, in the case of Hawaiian Creole English one can observe that there are influences from the mother tongues of the speakers involved: Japanese speakers use SOV order as well as SVO and Philippinos use VOS order as well as SVO order. In total, there is quite a lot of variation in the language that can be traced back to the various native languages of the individual speakers.

It is also possible to explain the effects observed for creolization without the assumption of innate language-specific knowledge: the fact that children regularize language can be attributed to a phenomenon independent of language. In experiments, participants were shown two light bulbs and the test subjects had to predict which of the light bulbs would be turned on next. If one of the bulbs was switched on 70% of the time,

[29] For problems that can arise from the assumption of defaults values, see Meisel (1995: 17). Bickerton (1997: 56, fn. 13) distances himself from the claim that creole languages have the default values of parameters.

the participants also picked this one 70% of the time (although they would have actually had a higher success rate if they had always chosen the bulb turned on with 70% probability). This behavior is known as *Probability Matching*. If we add another light bulb to this scenario and then turn this lamp on in 70% of cases and the other two each 15% of the time, then participants choose the more frequently lit one 80–90% of the time, that is, they regularize in the direction of the most frequent occurrence (Gardner 1957; Weir 1964).

Children regularize more than adults (Hudson & Newport 1999; Hudson Kam & Newport 2005), a fact that can be traced back to their limited brain capacity ("less is more"-hypothesis, Newport 1990; Elman 1993).

Like creolization, a similar situation can be found in certain social contexts with the acquisition of sign language: Singleton & Newport (2004) have shown that a child (Simon) that learned American Sign Language (ASL) makes considerably less mistakes than his parents. The parents first learned ASL at the age of 15 or 16 and performed particular obligatory movements only 70% of the time. Simon made these movements 90% of the time. He regularized the input from his parents, whereby the consistent use of form-meaning pairs plays an important role, that is, he does not simply use Probability Matching, but learns selectively. Singleton & Newport (2004: 401) suspect that these kinds of regularizations also play a role for the emergence of creole and sign languages. However, the relevant statistical data that one would need to confirm this hypothesis are not available.

13.6 Localization in special parts of the brain

By measuring brain activity during speech production/processing and also by investigating patients with brain damage, one can identify special parts of the brain (Broca's area and Wernicke's area) that play an important role for language production and processing (see Friederici (2009) for a current overview). Chomsky talks about there being a center of language and even calls this (metaphorically) an *organ* (Chomsky 1977: 164; Chomsky 2005: 1; Chomsky 2008: 133). This localization was seen as evidence for the innate basis for our linguistic knowledge (see also Pinker 1994: 297–314).

However, it is the case that if these parts are damaged, other areas of the brain can take over the relevant functions. If the damage occurs in early childhood, language can also be learned without these special areas of the brain (for sources, see Dąbrowska 2004: Section 4.1).

Apart from that, it can also be observed that a particular area of the brain is activated when reading. If the conclusion about the localization of processing in a particular part of the brain leading to the innateness of linguistic knowledge were valid, then the activation of certain areas of the brain during reading should also lead us to conclude that the ability to read is innate (Elman et al. 1996; Bishop 2002: 57). This is, however, not assumed (see also Fitch, Hauser & Chomsky 2005: 196).

It should also be noted that language processing affects several areas of the brain and not just Broca's and Wernicke's areas (Fisher & Marcus 2005: 11; Friederici 2009). On the other hand, Broca's and Wernicke's areas are also active during non-linguistic tasks such as imitation, motoric coordination and processing of music (Maess et al. 2001). For an overview and further sources, see Fisher & Marcus (2005).

Musso et al. (2003) investigated brain activity during second-language acquisition. They gave German native speakers data from Italian and Japanese and noticed that there was activation in Broca's area. They then compared this to artificial languages that used Italian and Japanese words but did not correspond to the principles of Universal Grammar as assumed by the authors. An example of the processes assumed in their artificial language is the formation of questions by reversing of word order as shown in (34).

(34) a. This is a statement.
b. Statement a is this?

The authors then observed that different areas of the brain were activated when learning this artificial language. This is an interesting result, but does not show that we have innate linguistic knowledge. It only shows that the areas that are active when processing our native languages are also active when we learn other languages and that playing around with words such as reversing the order of words in a sentence affects other areas of the brain.

A detailed discussion of localization of languages in particular parts of the brain can be found in Dąbrowska (2004: Chapter 4).

13.7 Differences between language and general cognition

Researchers who believe that there is no such thing as innate linguistic knowledge assume that language can be acquired with general cognitive means. If it can be shown that humans with severely impaired cognition can still acquire normal linguistic abilities or that there are people of normal intelligence whose linguistic ability is restricted, then one can show that language and general cognition are independent.

13.7.1 Williams Syndrome

There are people with a relatively low IQ, who can nevertheless produce grammatical utterances. Among these are people with Williams Syndrome (see Bellugi, Lichtenberger, Jones, Lai & George (2000) for a discussion of the abilities of people with Williams Syndrome). Yamada (1981) takes the existence of such cases as evidence for a separate module of grammar, independent of the remaining intelligence.

IQ is determined by dividing a score in an intelligence test (the mental age) by chronological age. The teenagers that were studied all had a mental age corresponding to that of a four to six year-old child. Yet children at this age already boast impressive linguistic ability that comes close to that of adults in many respects. Gosch, Städing & Pankau (1994: 295) have shown that children with Williams Syndrome do show a linguistic deficit and that their language ability corresponds to what would be expected from their mental age. For problems of sufferers of Williams Syndrome in the area of morphosyntax, see Karmiloff-Smith et al. (1997). The discussion about Williams Syndrome is summarized nicely in Karmiloff-Smith (1998).

13.7.2 KE family with FoxP2 mutation

There is a British family – the so-called KE family – that has problems with language. The members of this family who suffer from these linguistic problems have a genetic defect. Fisher et al. (1998) and Lai et al. (2001) discovered that this is due to a mutation of the FoxP2 gene (FoxP2 stands for *Forkhead-Box P2*). Gopnik & Cargo (1991) conclude from the fact that deficits in the realm of morphology are inherited with genetic defects that there must be a gene that is responsible for a particular module of grammar (morphology). Vargha-Khadem et al. (1995: 930) have demonstrated, however, that the KE family did not just have problems with morphosyntax: the affected family members have intellectual and linguistic problems together with motoric problems with facial muscles. Due to the considerably restricted motion in their facial muscles, it would make sense to assume that their linguistic difficulties also stem from motory problems (Tomasello 2003: 285). The linguistic problems in the KE family are not just limited to production problems, however, but also comprehension problems (Bishop 2002: 58). Nevertheless, one cannot associate linguistic deficiencies directly with FoxP2 as there are a number of other abilities that are affected by the FoxP2 mutation: as well as hindering pronunciation, morphology and syntax, it also has an effect on non-verbal IQ and motory problems with the facial muscles, dealing with non-linguistic tasks, too (Vargha-Khadem et al. 1995).

Furthermore, FoxP2 also occurs in other body tissues: it is also responsible for the development of the lungs, the heart, the intestine and various regions of the brain (Marcus & Fisher 2003). Marcus & Fisher (2003: 260–261) point out that FoxP2 is probably not directly responsible for the development of organs or areas of organs but rather regulates a cascade of different genes. FoxP2 can therefore not be referred to as the language gene, it is just a gene that interacts with other genes in complex ways. It is, among other things, important for our language ability, however, in the same way that it does not make sense to call FoxP2 a language gene, nobody would connect a hereditary muscle disorder with a 'walking gene' just because this myopathy prevents upright walking (Bishop 2002: 58). A similar argument can be found in Karmiloff-Smith (1998: 392): there is a genetic defect that leads some people to begin to lose their hearing from the age of ten and become completely deaf by age thirty. This genetic defect causes changes in the hairs inside the ear that one requires for hearing. In this case, one would also not want to talk about a 'hearing gene'.

Fitch, Hauser & Chomsky (2005: 190) are also of the opinion that FoxP2 cannot be responsible for linguistic knowledge. For an overview of this topic, see Bishop (2002) and Dąbrowska (2004: Section 6.4.2.2) and for genetic questions in general, see Fisher & Marcus (2005).

13.8 Poverty of the Stimulus

An important argument for the innateness of the linguistic knowledge is the so-called Poverty of the Stimulus Argument (PSA) (Chomsky 1980: 34). Different versions of it can be found in the literature and have been carefully discussed by Pullum & Scholz (2002).

After discussing these variants, they summarize the logical structure of the argument as follows (p. 18):

(35) a. Human children learn their first language either by data-driven learning or by learning supported by innate knowledge (a disjunctive premise by assumption)

b. If children learn their first language by data-driven learning, then they could not acquire anything for which they did not have the necessary evidence (the definition of data-driven learning)

c. However, children do in fact learn things that they do not seem to have decisive evidence for (empirical prerequisite)

d. Therefore, children do not learn their first language by data-driven learning. (*modus tollens* of b and c)

e. Conclusion: children learn language through a learning process supported by innate knowledge. (disjunctive syllogism of a and d)

Pullum and Scholz then discuss four phenomena that have been claimed to constitute evidence for there being innate linguistic knowledge. These are plurals as initial parts of compounds in English (Gordon 1986), sequences of auxiliaries in English (Kimball 1973), anaphoric *one* in English (Baker 1978) and the position of auxiliaries in English (Chomsky 1971: 29–33). Before I turn to these cases in Section 13.8.2, I will discuss a variant of the PSA that refers to the formal properties of phrase structure grammars.

13.8.1 Gold's Theorem

In theories of formal languages, a language is viewed as a set containing all the expressions belonging to a particular language. This kind of set can be captured using various complex rewrite grammars. A kind of rewrite grammar – so-called context-free grammars – was presented in Chapter 2. In context-free grammars, there is always exactly one symbol on the left-hand side of the rule (a so-called non-terminal symbol) and there can be more of these on the right-hand side of the rule. On the right side there can be symbols (so-called non-terminal symbols) or words/morphemes of the language in question (so-called terminal symbols). The words in a grammar are also referred to as vocabulary (V). Part of a formal grammar is a start symbol, which is usually S. In the literature, this has been criticized since not all expressions are sentences (see Deppermann 2006: 44). It is, however, not necessary to assume this. It is possible to use Utterance as the start symbol and define rules that derive S, NP, VP or whatever else one wishes to class as an utterance from Utterance.[30]

Beginning with the start symbol, one can keep applying phrase structure rules in a grammar until one arrives at sequences that only contain words (terminal symbols). The set of all sequences that one can generate are the expressions that belong to the

[30] On page 269, I discussed a description that corresponds to the S symbol in phrase structure grammars. If one omits the specification of head features in this description, then one gets a description of all complete phrases, that is, also *the man* or *now*.

language that is licensed by the grammar. This set is a subset of all sequences of words or morphemes that can be created by arbitrary combination. The set that contains all possible sequences is referred to as V^*.

Gold (1967) has shown that in an environment E, it is not possible to solve the identification problem for any language from particular languages classes, given a finite amount of linguistic input, without additional knowledge. Gold is concerned with the identification of a language from a given class of languages. A language L counts as identified if at a given point in time t_n, a learner can determine that L is the language in question and does not change this hypothesis. This point in time is not determined in advance, however, identification has to take place at some point. Gold calls this *identification in the limit*. The environments are arbitrary infinite sequences of sentences $\langle a_1, a_2, a_3, ...\rangle$, whereby each sentence in the language must occur at least once in this sequence. In order to show that the identification problem cannot be solved for even very simple language classes, Gold considers the class of languages that contain all possible sequences of words from the vocabulary V expect for one sequence: let V be the vocabulary and x_1, x_2, x_3, ... the sequences of words from this vocabulary. The set of all strings from this vocabulary is V^*. For the class of languages in (36), which consist of all possible sequences of elements in V with the exception of one sequence, it is possible to state a process of how one could learn these languages from a text.

(36) $L_1 = V^* - x_1, L_2 = V^* - x_2, L_3 = V^* - x_3, ...$

After every input, one can guess that the language is $V^* - \sigma$, where σ stands for the alphabetically first sequence with the shortest length that has not yet been seen. If the sequence in question occurs later, then this hypothesis is revised accordingly. In this way, one will eventually arrive at the correct language.

If we expand the set of languages from which we have to choose by V^*, then our learning process will no longer work since, if V^* is the target language, then the guessing will perpetually yield incorrect results. If there were a procedure capable of learning this language class, then it would have to correctly identify V^* after a certain number of inputs. Let us assume that this input is x_k. How can the learning procedure tell us at this point that the language we are looking for is not $V^* - x_j$ for $j \neq k$? If x_k causes one to guess the wrong grammar V^*, then every input that comes after that will be compatible with both the correct ($V^* - x_j$) and incorrect (V^*) result. Since we only have positive data, no input allows us to distinguish between either of the hypotheses and provide the information that we have found a superset of the language we are looking for. Gold has shown that none of the classes of grammars assumed in the theory of formal languages (for example, regular, context-free and context-sensitive languages) can be identified after a finite amount of steps given the input of a text with example utterances. This is true for all classes of languages that contain all finite languages and at least one infinite language. The situation is different if positive and negative data are used for learning instead of text.

The conclusion that has been drawn from Gold's results is that, for language acquisition, one requires knowledge that helps to avoid particular hypotheses from the start.

Pullum (2003) criticizes the use of Gold's findings as evidence for the fact that linguistic knowledge must be innate. He lists a number of assumptions that have to be made in order for Gold's results to be relevant for the acquisition of natural languages. He then shows that each of these is not uncontroversial.

1. Natural languages could belong to the class of text-learnable languages as opposed to the class of context-free grammars mentioned above.

2. Learners could have information about which sequences of words are not grammatical (see p. 453–454 of Gold's essay for a similar conjecture). As has been shown since then, children do have direct negative evidence and there is also indirect negative evidence (see Section 13.8.4).

3. It is not clear whether learners really restrict themselves to exactly one grammar. Feldman (1972) has developed a learning procedure that eliminates all incorrect grammars at some point and is infinitely many times correct but it does not have to always choose one correct grammar and stick to the corresponding hypothesis. Using this procedure, it is possible to learn all recursively enumerable languages, that is, all languages for which there is a generative grammar. Pullum notes that even Feldman's learning procedure could prove to be too restrictive. It could take an entire lifetime for a learner to reach the correct grammar and they could have incorrect yet increasingly better hypotheses along the way.

4. Learners could work in terms of improvements. If one allows for a certain degree of tolerance, then acquisition is easier and it even becomes possible to learn the class of recursively enumerable languages (Wharton 1974).

5. Language acquisition does not necessarily constitute the acquisition of knowledge about a particular set of sequences, that is, the acquisition of a generative grammar capable of creating this set. The situation is completely different if grammars are viewed as a set of constraints that partially describe linguistic structures, but not necessarily a unique set of linguistic structures (for more on this point, see Section 6.7 and Chapter 14).

Furthermore, Pullum notes that it is also possible to learn the class of context-sensitive grammars with Gold's procedure with positive input only in a finite number of steps if there is an upper bound k for the number of rules, where k is an arbitrary number. It is possible to make k so big that the cognitive abilities of the human brain would not be able to use a grammar with more rules than this. Since it is normally assumed that natural languages can be described by context-sensitive grammars, it can therefore be shown that the syntax of natural languages in Gold's sense can be learned from texts (see also Scholz & Pullum 2002: 195–196).

Johnson (2004) adds that there is another important point that has been overlooked in the discussion about language acquisition. Gold's problem of identifiability is different from the problem of language acquisition that has played an important role in the nativism debate. In order to make the difference clear, Johnson differentiates between identifiability (in the Goldian sense) and learnability in the sense of language acquisition. Identifiability for a language class C means that there must be a function f that for each environment E for each language L in C permanently converges on hypothesis L as the target language in a finite amount of time.

Johnson proposes the following as the definition of *learnability* (p. 585): *A class C of natural languages is learnable iff, given almost any normal human child and almost any normal linguistic environment for any language L in C, the child will acquire L (or something sufficiently similar to L) as a native language between the ages of one and five.* Johnson adds the caveat that this definition does not correspond to any theory of learnability in psycholinguistics, but rather it is a hint in the direction of a realistic conception of acquisition.

Johnson notes that in most interpretations of Gold's theorem, identifiability and learnability are viewed as one and the same and shows that this is not logically correct: the main difference between the two depends on the use of two quantifiers. Identifiability of *one* language L from a class C requires that the learner converges on L in *every* environment after a finite amount of time. This time can differ greatly from environment to environment. There is not even an upper bound for the time in question. It is straightforward to construct a sequence of environments E_1, E_2, … for L, so that a learner in the environment E_i will not guess L earlier than the time t_i. Unlike identifiability, learnability means that there is a point in time after which in every normal environment, *every* normal child has converged on the correct language. This means that children acquire their language after a particular time span. Johnson quotes Morgan (1989: 352) claiming that children learn their native language after they have heard approximately 4,280,000 sentences. If we assume that the concept of learnability has a finite upper-bound for available time, then very few language classes can be identified in the limit. Johnson has shown this as follows: let C be a class of languages containing L and L', where L and L' have some elements in common. It is possible to construct a text such that the first n sentences are contained both in L and in L'. If the learner has L as its working hypothesis then continue the text with sentences from L', if he has L' as his hypothesis, then continue with sentences from L. In each case, the learner has entertained a false hypothesis after n steps. This means that identifiability is not a plausible model for language acquisition.

Aside from the fact that identifiability is psychologically unrealistic, it is not compatible with learnability (Johnson 2004: 586). For identifiability, only one learner has to be found (the function f mentioned above), learnability, however, quantifies over (almost) all normal children. If one keeps all factors constant, then it is easier to show the identifiability of a language class rather than its learnability. On the one hand, identifiability quantifies universally over all environments, regardless of whether these may seem odd or of how many repetitions these may contain. Learnability, on the other hand, has (almost) universal quantification exclusively over normal environments. Therefore, learnability refers to fewer environments than identifiability, such that there are less possibilities for problematic texts that could occur as an input and render a language unlearnable. Furthermore, learnability is defined in such a way that the learner does not have to learn *L* exactly, but rather learn something sufficiently similar to *L*. With respect to this aspect, learnability is a weaker property of a language class than identifiability. Therefore, learnability does not follow from identifiability nor the reverse.

Finally, Gold is dealing with the acquisition of syntactic knowledge without taking semantic knowledge into consideration. However, children possess a vast amount of information from the context that they employ when acquiring a language (Tomasello et al. 2005). As pointed out by Klein (1986: 44), humans do not learn anything if they are placed in a room and sentences in Mandarin Chinese are played to them. Language is acquired in a social and cultural context.

In sum, one should note that the existence of innate linguistic knowledge cannot be derived from mathematical findings about the learnability of languages.

13.8.2 Four case studies

Pullum & Scholz (2002) have investigated four prominent instances of the Poverty of the Stimulus Argument in more detail. These will be discussed in what follows. Pullum and Scholz's article appeared in a discussion volume. Arguments against their article are addressed by Scholz & Pullum (2002) in the same volume. Further PoS arguments from Chomsky (1986b) and from literature in German have been disproved by Eisenberg (1992).

13.8.2.1 Plurals in noun-noun compounding

Gordon (1986) claims that compounds in English only allow irregular plurals in compounds, that is, *mice-eater* but ostensibly not * *rats-eater*. Gordon claims that compounds with irregular plurals as first element are so rare that children could not have learned the fact that such compounds are possible purely from data.

On pages 25–26, Pullum and Scholz discuss data from English that show that regular plurals can indeed occur as the first element of a compound (*chemicals-maker, forms-reader, generics-maker, securities-dealer, drinks trolley, rules committee, publications catalogue*).[31] This shows that what could have allegedly not been learned from data is in fact not linguistically adequate and one therefore does not have to explain its acquisition.

13.8.2.2 Position of auxiliaries

The second study deals with the position of modal and auxiliary verbs. Kimball (1973: 73–75) discusses the data in (37) and the rule in (38) that is similar to one of the rules suggested by Chomsky (1957: 39) and is designed to capture the following data:

(37) a. It rains.
b. It may rain.
c. It may have rained.

[31] Also, see Abney (1996: 7) for examples from the Wall Street Journal.

d. It may be raining.
e. It has rained.
f. It has been raining.
g. It is raining.
h. It may have been raining.

(38) Aux → T(M)(have+en)(be+ing)

T stands for tense, M for a modal verb and *en* stands for the participle morpheme (*-en* in *been*/*seen*/... and *-ed* in *rained*). The brackets here indicate the optionality of the expressions. Kimball notes that it is only possible to formulate this rule if (37h) is well-formed. If this were not the case, then one would have to reorganize the material in rules such that the three cases (M)(have+en), (M)(be+ing) and (have+en)(be+ing) would be covered. Kimball assumes that children master the complex rule since they know that sentences such as (37h) are well-formed and since they know the order in which modal and auxiliary verbs must occur. Kimball assumes that children do not have positive evidence for the order in (37h) and concludes from this that the knowledge about the rule in (38) must be innate.

Pullum and Scholz note two problems with this Poverty of the Stimulus Argument: first, they have found hundreds of examples, among them some from children's stories, so that the Kimball's claim that sentences such as (37h) are "vanishingly rare" should be called into question. For PSA arguments, one should at least specify how many occurrences there are allowed to be if one still wants to claim that nothing can be learned from them (Pullum & Scholz 2002: 29).

The second problem is that it does not make sense to assume that the rule in (37h) plays a role in our linguistic knowledge. Empirical findings have shown that this rule is not descriptively adequate. If the rule in (38) is not descriptively adequate, then it cannot achieve explanatory adequacy and therefore, one no longer has to explain how it can be acquired.

Instead of a rule such as (38), all theories discussed here currently assume that auxiliary or modal verbs embed a phrase, that is, one does not have an Aux node containing all auxiliary and modal verbs, but rather a structure for (37h) that looks as follows:

(39) It [may [have [been raining]]].

Here, the auxiliary or modal verb always selects the embedded phrase. The acquisition problem now looks completely different: a speaker has to learn the form of the head verb in the verbal projection selected by the auxiliary or modal verb. If this information has been learned, then it is irrelevant how complex the embedded verbal projections are: *may* can be combined with a non-finite lexical verb (37b) or a non-finite auxiliary (37c,d).

13.8.2.3 Reference of *one*

The third case study investigated by Pullum and Scholz deals with the pronoun *one* in English. Baker (1978: 413–425, 327–340) claims that children cannot learn that *one* can refer to constituents larger than a single word as in (40).

(40) a. I would like to tell you another funny story, but I've already told you the only *one* I know.
b. The old man from France was more erudite than the young *one.*

Baker (416–417) claims that *one* can never refer to single nouns inside of NPs and supports this with examples such as (41):

(41) * The student of chemistry was more thoroughly prepared than the one of physics.

According to Baker, learners would require negative data in order to acquire this knowledge about ungrammaticality. Since learners – following his argumentation – never have access to negative evidence, they cannot possibly have learned the relevant knowledge and must therefore already possess it.

Pullum & Scholz (2002: 33) point out that there are acceptable examples with the same structure as the examples in (41):

(42) a. I'd rather teach linguistics to a student of mathematics than to one of any discipline in the humanities.
b. An advocate of Linux got into a heated discussion with one of Windows NT and the rest of the evening was nerd talk.

This means that there is nothing to learn with regard to the well-formedness of the structure in (41). Furthermore, the available data for acquiring the fact that *one* can refer to larger constituents is not as hopeless as Baker (p. 416) claims: there are examples that only allow an interpretation where *one* refers to a larger string of words. Pullum and Scholz offer examples from various corpora. They also provide examples from the CHILDES corpus, a corpus that contains communication with children (MacWhinney 1995). The following example is from a daytime TV show:

(43) A: "Do you think you will ever remarry again? I don't."
B: "Maybe I will, someday. But he'd have to be somebody very special. Sensitive and supportive, giving. Hey, wait a minute, where do they make guys like this?"
A: "I don't know. I've never seen one up close."

Here, it is clear that *one* cannot refer to *guys* since A has certainly already seen *guys.* Instead, it refers to *guys like this*, that is, men who are sensitive and supportive.

Once again, the question arises here as to how many instances a learner has to hear for it to count as evidence in the eyes of proponents of the PSA.

13.8.2.4 Position of auxiliaries in polar questions

The fourth PoS argument discussed by Pullum and Scholz comes from Chomsky and pertains to the position of the auxiliary in polar interrogatives in English. As shown on page 95, it was assumed in GB theory that a polar question is derived by movement of the auxiliary from the I position to the initial position C of the sentence. In early versions of Transformational Grammar, the exact analyses were different, but the main point was that the highest auxiliary is moved to the beginning of the clause. Chomsky

(1971: 29–33) discusses the sentences in (44) and claims that children know that they have to move the highest auxiliary verb even without having positive evidence for this.[32] If, for example, they entertained the hypothesis that one simply places the first auxiliary at the beginning of the sentence, then this hypothesis would deliver the correct result (44b) for (44a), but not for (44c) since the polar question should be (44d) and not (44e).

(44) a. The dog in the corner is hungry.
b. Is the dog in the corner hungry?
c. The dog that is in the corner is hungry.
d. Is the dog that is in the corner hungry?
e. * Is the dog that in the corner is hungry?

Chomsky claims that children do not have any evidence for the fact that the hypothesis that one simply fronts the linearly first auxiliary is wrong, which is why they could pursue this hypothesis in a data-driven learning process. He even goes so far as to claim that speakers of English only rarely or even never produce examples such as (44d) (Chomsky in Piattelli-Palmarini (1980: 114–115)). With the help of corpus data and plausibly constructed examples, Pullum (1996) has shown that this claim is clearly wrong. Pullum (1996) provides examples from the Wall Street Journal and Pullum & Scholz (2002) discuss the relevant examples in more detail and add to them with examples from the CHILDES corpus showing that adult speakers cannot only produce the relevant kinds of sentences, but also that these occur in the child's input.[33] Examples from CHILDES that disprove the hypothesis that the first auxiliary has to be fronted are given in (45):[34]

(45) a. Is the ball you were speaking of in the box with the bowling pin?
b. Where's this little boy who's full of smiles?
c. While you're sleeping, shall I make the breakfast?

Pullum and Scholz point out that *wh*-questions such as (45b) are also relevant if one assumes that these are derived from polar questions (see page 95 in this book) and if one wishes to show how the child can learn the structure-dependent hypothesis. This can be explained with the examples in (46): the base form from which (46a) is derived is (46b). If we were to front the first auxiliary in (46b), we would produce (46c).

(46) a. Where's the application Mark promised to fill out?[35]
b. the application Mark [$_{AUX}$ PAST] promised to fill out [$_{AUX}$ is] there
c. * Where did the application Mark promised to fill out is?

32 Examples with auxiliary inversion are used in more recent PoS arguments too, for example in Berwick, Pietroski, Yankama & Chomsky (2011) and Chomsky (2013: 39). Work by Bod (2009b) is not discussed by the authors. For more on Bod's approach, see Section 13.8.3.

33 For more on this point, see Sampson (1989: 223). Sampson cites part of a poem by William Blake, that is studied in English schools, as well as a children's encyclopedia. These examples surely do not play a role in acquisition of auxiliary position since this order is learned at the age of 3;2, that is, it has already been learned by the time children reach school age.

34 See Lewis & Elman (2001). Researchers on language acquisition agree that the frequency of this kind of examples in communication with children is in fact very low. See Ambridge et al. (2008: 223).

35 From the transcription of a TV program in the CHILDES corpus.

Evidence for the fact that (46c) is not correct can, however, also be found in language addressed to children. Pullum and Scholz provide the examples in (47):[36]

(47) a. Where's the little blue crib that was in the house before?
b. Where's the other dolly that was in here?
c. Where's the other doll that goes in there?

These questions have the form *Where's NP?*, where NP contains a relative clause.

In (45c), there is another clause preceding the actual interrogative, an adjunct clause containing an auxiliary as well. This sentence therefore provides evidence for falsehood of the hypothesis that the linearly first auxiliary must be fronted (Sampson 1989: 223).

In total, there are a number of attested sentence types in the input of children that would allow them to choose between the two hypotheses. Once again, the question arises as to how much evidence should be viewed as sufficient.

Pullum und Scholz's article has been criticized by Lasnik & Uriagereka (2002) and Legate & Yang (2002). Lasnik and Uriagereka argue that the acquisition problem is much bigger than presented by Pullum and Scholz since a learner without any knowledge about the language he was going to acquire could not just have the hypothesis in (48) that were discussed already but also the additional hypotheses in (49):

(48) a. Place the first auxiliary at the front of the clause.
b. Place the first auxiliary in matrix-Infl at the front of the clause.

(49) a. Place any auxiliary at the front of the clause.
b. Place any finite auxiliary at the front of the clause.

Both hypotheses in (49) would be permitted by the sentences in (50):

(50) a. Is the dog in the corner hungry?
b. Is the dog that is in the corner hungry?

They would, however, also allow sentences such as (51):

(51) * Is the dog that in the corner is hungry?

The question that must now be addressed is why all hypotheses that allow (51) should be discarded since the learners do not have any information in their natural-linguistic input about the fact that (51) is not possible. They are lacking negative evidence. If (50b) is present as positive evidence, then this by no means implies that the hypothesis in (48b) has to be the correct one. Lasnik and Uriagereka present the following hypotheses that would also be compatible with (50b):

(52) a. Place the first auxiliary in initial position (that follows a change in intonation).
b. Place the first auxiliary in initial position (that follows the first complete constituent).

[36] These sentences are taken from NINA05.CHA in DATABASE/ENG/SUPPES/.

c. Place the first auxiliary in initial position (that follows the first parsed semantic unit).

These hypotheses do not hold for sentences such as (53) that contain a conjunction:

(53) Will those who are coming and those who are not coming raise their hands?

The hypotheses in (52) would also allow for sentences such as (54):

(54) * Are those who are coming and those who not coming will raise their hands?

Speakers hearing sentences such as (53) can reject the hypotheses (52) and thereby rule out (54), however, it is still possible to think of analogous implausible hypotheses that are compatible with all data previously discussed.

Legate & Yang (2002) take up the challenge of Pullum and Scholz and explicitly state how many occurrences one needs to acquire a particular phenomenon. They write the following:

> Suppose we have two independent problems of acquisition, P_1 and P_2, each of which involves a binary decision. For P_1, let F_1 be the frequency of the data that can settle P_1 one way or another, and for P_2, F_2. Suppose further that children successfully acquire P_1 and P_2 at roughly the same developmental stage. Then, under any theory that makes quantitative predictions of language development, we expect F_1 and F_2 to be roughly the same. Conversely, if F_1 and F_2 turn out significantly different, then P_1 and P_2 must represent qualitatively different learning problems.
>
> Now let P_1 be the auxiliary inversion problem. The two choices are the structure-dependent hypothesis (3b-i) and the first auxiliary hypothesis (3a-i). (Legate & Yang 2002: 155)

The position of auxiliaries in English is learned by children at the age of 3;2. According to Legate and Yang, another acquisition phenomenon that is learned at the age of 3;2 is needed for comparison. The authors focus on subject drop[37], that is learned at 36 months (two months earlier than auxiliary inversion). According to the authors, acquisition problems involve a binary decision: in the first case, one has to choose between the two hypotheses in (48). In the second case, the learner has to determine whether a language uses overt subjects. The authors assume that the use of expletives such as *there* serves as evidence for learners that the language they are learning is not one with optional subjects. They then count the sentences in the CHILDES corpus that contain *there*-subjects and estimate F_2 at 1,2 % of the sentences heard by the learner. Since, in their opinion, we are dealing with equally difficult phenomena here, sentences such as (44d) and (47) should constitute 1.2 % of the input in order for auxiliary inversion to be learnable.

[37] This phenomenon is also called *pro-drop*. For a detailed discussion of the pro-drop parameter see Section 16.1.

The authors then searched in the Nina and Adam corpora (both part of CHILDES) and note that 0,068 to 0,045 % of utterances have the form of (47) and none have the form of (44d). They conclude that this number is not sufficient as positive evidence.

Legate and Yang are right in pointing out that Pullum and Scholz's data from the Wall Street Journal are not necessarily relevant for language acquisition and also in pointing out that examples with complex subject noun phrases do not occur in the data or at least to a negligible degree. There are, however, three serious problems with their argumentation: first, there is no correlation between the occurrence of expletive subjects and the property of being a pro-drop language: Galician (Raposo & Uriagereka 1990: Section 2.5) is a pro-drop language with subject expletive pronouns, in Italian there is an existential expletive *ci*,[38] even though Italian counts as a pro-drop language, Franks (1995) lists Upper and Lower Sorbian as pro-drop languages that have expletives in subject position. Since therefore expletive pronouns have nothing to do with the pro-drop parameter, their frequency is irrelevant for the acquisition of a parameter value. If there were a correlation between the possibility of omitting subjects and the occurrence of subject expletives, then Norwegian and Danish children should learn that there has to be a subject in their languages earlier than children learning English since expletives occur a higher percentage of the time in Danish and Norwegian (Scholz & Pullum 2002: 220). In Danish, the constructions corresponding to *there*-constructions in English are twice as frequent. It is still unclear whether there are actually differences in rate of acquisition (Pullum 2009: 246).

Second, in constructing their Poverty of the Stimulus argument, Legate and Yang assume that there is innate linguistic knowledge (the pro-drop parameter). Therefore their argument is circular since it is supposed to show that the assumption of innate linguistic knowledge is indispensable (Scholz & Pullum 2002: 220).

The third problem in Legate and Yang's argumentation is that they assume that a transformational analysis is the only possibility. This becomes clear from the following citation (Legate & Yang 2002: 153):

> The correct operation for question formation is, of course, structure dependent: it involves parsing the sentence into structurally organized phrases, and fronting the auxiliary that follows the subject NP, which can be arbitrarily long:
>
> (4) a. Is [the woman who is singing] e happy?
>   b. Has [the man that is reading a book] e eaten supper?

The analysis put forward by Chomsky (see page 95) is a transformation-based one, that is, a learner has to learn exactly what Legate and Yang describe: the auxiliary must move in front of the subject noun phrase. There are, however, alternative analyses that do not require transformations or equivalent mechanisms. If our linguistic knowledge does not contain any information about transformations, then their claim about what has to be learned is wrong. For example, one can assume, as in Categorial Grammar,

[38] However, *ci* is not treated as an expletive by all authors. See Remberger (2009) for an overview.

that auxiliaries form a word class with particular distributional properties. One possible placement for them is initial positions as observed in questions, the alternative is after the subject (Villavicencio 2002: 104). There would then be the need to acquire information about whether the subject is realized to the left or to the right of its head. As an alternative to this lexicon-based analysis, one could pursue a Construction Grammar (Fillmore 1988: 44; 1999; Kay & Fillmore 1999: 18), Cognitive Grammar (Dąbrowska 2004: Chapter 9), or HPSG (Ginzburg & Sag 2000) approach. In these frameworks, there are simply two[39] schemata for the two sequences that assign different meanings according to the order of verb and subject. The acquisition problem is then that the learners have to identify the corresponding phrasal patterns in the input. They have to realize that Aux NP VP is a well-formed structure in English that has interrogative semantics. The relevant theories of acquisition in the Construction Grammar-oriented literature have been very well worked out (see Section 16.3 and 16.4). Construction-based theories of acquisition are also supported by the fact that one can see that there are frequency effects, that is, auxiliary inversion is first produced by children for just a few auxiliaries and only in later phases of development is it then extended to all auxiliaries. If speakers have learned that auxiliary constructions have the pattern Aux NP VP, then the coordination data provided by Lasnik and Uriagereka in (53) no longer pose a problem since, if we only assign the first conjunct to the NP in the pattern Aux NP VP, then the rest of the coordinate structure (*and those who are not coming*) remains unanalyzed and cannot be incorporated into the entire sentence. The hearer is thereby forced to revise his assumption that *will those who are coming* corresponds to the sequence Aux NP in Aux NP VP and instead to use the entire NP *those who are coming and those who are not coming*. For acquisition, it is therefore enough to simply learn the pattern Aux NP VP first for some and then eventually for all auxiliaries in English. This has also been shown by Lewis & Elman (2001), who trained a neural network exclusively with data that did not contain NPs with relative clauses in auxiliary constructions. Relative clauses were, however, present in other structures. The complexity of the training material was increased bit by bit just as is the case for the linguistic input that children receive (Elman 1993).[40] The neural network can predict the next symbol after a sequence of words. For sentences with interrogative word order, the predictions are correct. Even the relative pronoun in (55) is predicted despite the sequence Aux Det N Relp never occurring in the training material.

(55) Is the boy who is smoking crazy?

Furthermore, the system signals an error if the network is presented with the ungrammatical sentence (56):

(56) * Is the boy who smoking is crazy?

[39] Fillmore (1999) assumes subtypes of the Subject Auxiliary Inversion Construction since this kind of inversion does not only occur in questions.

[40] There are cultural differences. In some cultures, adults do not talk to children that have not attained full linguistic competence (Ochs 1982; Ochs & Schieffelin 1985) (also see Section 13.8.4). Children have to therefore learn the language from their environment, that is, the sentences that they hear reflect the full complexity of the language.

A gerund is not expected after the relative pronoun, but rather a finite verb. The constructed neural network is of course not yet an adequate model of what is going on in our heads during acquisition and speech production.[41] The experiment shows, however, that the input that the learner receives contains rich statistical information that can be used when acquiring language. Lewis and Elman point out that the statistical information about the distribution of words in the input is not the only information that speakers have. In addition to information about distribution, they are also exposed to information about the context and can make use of phonological similarities in words.

In connection to the ungrammatical sentences in (56), it has been claimed that the fact that such sentences can never be produced shows that children already know that grammatical operations are structure-dependent and this is why they do not entertain the hypothesis that it is simply the linearly first verb that is moved (Crain & Nakayama 1987). The claim simply cannot be verified since children do not normally form the relevant complex utterances. It is therefore only possible to experimentally illicit utterances where they could make the relevant mistakes. Crain & Nakayama (1987) have carried out such experiments. Their study has been criticized by Ambridge, Rowland & Pine (2008) since these authors could show that children do really make mistakes when fronting auxiliaries. The authors put the difference to the results of the first study by Crain and Nakayama down to unfortunate choice of auxiliary in Crain and Nakayama's study. Due to the use of the auxiliary *is*, the ungrammatical examples had pairs of words that never or only very rarely occur next to each other (*who running* in (57a)).

(57) a. The boy who is running fast can jump high. →
  * Is the boy who running fast can jump high?
 b. The boy who can run fast can jump high. →
  * Can the boy who run fast can jump high?

If one uses the auxiliary *can*, this problem disappears since *who* and *run* certainly do appear together. This then leads to the children actually making mistakes that they should not have, as the incorrect utterances actually violate a constraint that is supposed to be part of innate linguistic knowledge.

Estigarribia (2009) investigated English polar questions in particular. He shows that not even half of the polar questions in children's input have the form Aux NP VP (p. 74). Instead, parents communicated with their children in a simplified form and used sentences such as:

(58) a. That your tablet?
 b. He talking?
 c. That taste pretty good?

Estigarribia divides the various patterns into complexity classes of the following kind: FRAG (*fragmentary*), SPRED (*subject predicate*) and AUX-IN (*auxiliary inversion*). (59) shows corresponding examples:

[41] See Hurford (2002: 324) and Jackendoff (2007: Section 6.2) for problems that arise for certain kinds of neural networks and Pulvermüller (2003, 2010) for an alternative architecture that does not have these problems.

(59) a. coming tomorrow? (FRAG)
b. you coming tomorrow? (SPRED)
c. Are you coming tomorrow? (AUX-IN)

What we see is that the complexity increases from class to class. Estigarribia suggests a system of language acquisition where simpler classes are acquired before more complex ones and the latter ones develop from peripheral modifications of more simple classes (p. 76). He assumes that question forms are learned from right to left (*right to left elaboration*), that is, (59a) is learned first, then the pattern in (59b) containing a subject in addition to the material in (59a), and then in a third step, the pattern (59c) in which an additional auxiliary occurs (p. 82). In this kind of learning procedure, no auxiliary inversion is involved. This view is compatible with constraint-based analyses such as that of Ginzburg & Sag (2000). A similar approach to acquisition by Freudenthal, Pine, Aguado-Orea & Gobet (2007) will be discussed in Section 16.3.

A further interesting study has been carried out by Bod (2009b). He shows that it is possible to learn auxiliary inversion assuming trees with any kind of branching even if there is no auxiliary inversion with complex noun phrases present in the input. The procedure he uses as well as the results he gains are very interesting and will be discussed in Section 13.8.3 in more detail.

In conclusion, we can say that children do make mistakes with regard to the position of auxiliaries that they probably should not make if the relevant knowledge were innate. Information about the statistical distribution of words in the input is enough to learn the structures of complex sentences without actually having this kind of complex sentences in the input.

13.8.2.5 Summary

Pullum & Scholz (2002: 19) show what an Argument from Poverty of the Stimulus (APS) would have to look like if it were constructed correctly:

(60) APS specification schema:
a. ACQUIRENDUM CHARACTERIZATION: describe in detail what is alleged to be known.
b. LACUNA SPECIFICATION: identify a set of sentences such that if the learner had access to them, the claim of data-driven learning of the acquirendum would be supported.
c. INDISPENSABILITY ARGUMENT: give reason to think that if learning were data-driven, then the acquirendum could not be learned without access to sentences in the lacuna.
d. INACCESSIBILITY EVIDENCE: support the claim that tokens of sentences in the lacuna were not available to the learner during the acquisition process.
e. ACQUISITION EVIDENCE: give reason to believe that the acquirendum does in fact become known to learners during childhood.

As the four case studies have shown, there can be reasons for rejecting the acquirendum. If the acquirendum does not have to be acquired, than there is no longer any evidence for innate linguistic knowledge. The acquirendum must at least be descriptively adequate. This is an empirical question that can be answered by linguists. In three of the four PoS arguments discussed by Pullum and Scholz, there were parts which were not descriptively adequate. In previous sections, we already encountered other PoS arguments that involve claims regarding linguistic data that cannot be upheld empirically (for example, the Subjacency Principle). For the remaining points in (60), interdisciplinary work is required: the specification of the lacuna falls into the theory of formal language (the specification of a set of utterances), the argument of indispensability is a mathematical task from the realm of learning theory, the evidence for inaccessibility is an empirical question that can be approached by using corpora, and finally the evidence for acquisition is a question for experimental developmental psychologists (Pullum & Scholz 2002: 19–20).

Pullum & Scholz (2002: 46) point out an interesting paradox with regard to (60c): without results from mathematical theories of learning, one cannot achieve (60c). If one wishes to provide a valid Poverty of the Stimulus Argument, then this should automatically lead to improvements in theories of learning, that is, it is possible to learn more than was previously assumed.

13.8.3 Unsupervised Data-Oriented Parsing (U-DOP)

Bod (2009b) has developed a procedure that does not require any information about word classes or relations between words contained in utterances. The only assumption that one has to make is that there is some kind of structure. The procedure consists of three steps:

1. Compute all possible (binary-branching) trees (without category symbols) for a set of given sentences.
2. Divide these trees into sub-trees.
3. Compute the ideal tree for each sentence.

This process will be explained using the sentences in (61):

(61) a. Watch the dog.
     b. The dog barks.

The trees that are assigned to these utterances only use the category symbol X since the categories for the relevant phrases are not (yet) known. In order to keep the example readable, the words themselves will not be given the category X, although one can of course do this. Figure 13.2 on the following page shows the trees for (61). In the next step, the trees are divided into subtrees. The trees in Figure 13.2 have the subtrees that can be seen in Figure 13.3 on page 480. In the third step, we now have to compute the best tree for each utterance. For *The dog barks.*, there are two trees in the set of the subtrees

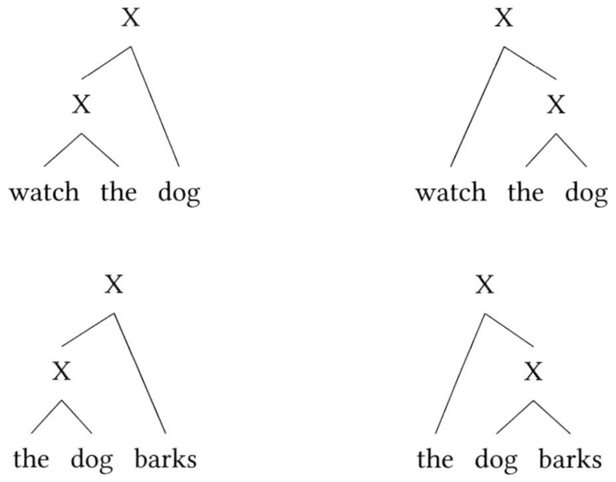

Figure 13.2: Possible binary-branching structures for *Watch the dog* and *The dog barks.*

that correspond exactly to this utterance. But it is also possible to build structures out of subtrees. There are therefore multiple derivations possible for *The dog barks.* all of which use the trees in Figure 13.3: one the one hand, trivial derivations that use the entire tree, and on the other, derivations that build trees from smaller subtrees. Figure 13.4 gives an impression of how this construction of subtrees happens. If we now want to decide which of the analyses in (62) is the best, then we have to compute the probability of each tree.

(62) a. [[the dog] barks]
b. [the [dog barks]]

The probability of a tree is the sum of the probabilities of all its analyses. There are two analyses for (62b), which can be found in Figure 13.4. The probability of the first analysis of (62b) corresponds to the probability of choosing exactly the complete tree for [the [dog barks]] from the set of all subtrees. Since there are twelve subtrees, the probability of choosing that one is 1/12. The probability of the second analysis is the product of the probabilities of the subtrees that are combined and is therefore $1/12 \times 1/12 = 1/144$. The probability of the analysis in (62b) is therefore $1/12 + (1/12 \times 1/12) = 13/144$. One can then calculate the probability of the tree in (62a) in the same way. The only difference here is that the tree for [the dog] occurs twice in the set of subtrees. Its probability is therefore 2/12. The probability of the tree [[the dog] barks] is therefore: $1/12 + (1/12 \times 2/12) = 14/144$. We have thus extracted knowledge about plausible structures from the corpus. This knowledge can also be applied whenever one hears a new utterance for which there is no complete tree. It is then possible to use already known subtrees to calculate the probabilities of possible analyses of the new utterance. Bod's model can also be combined with weights: those sentences that were heard longer ago by the speaker, will receive

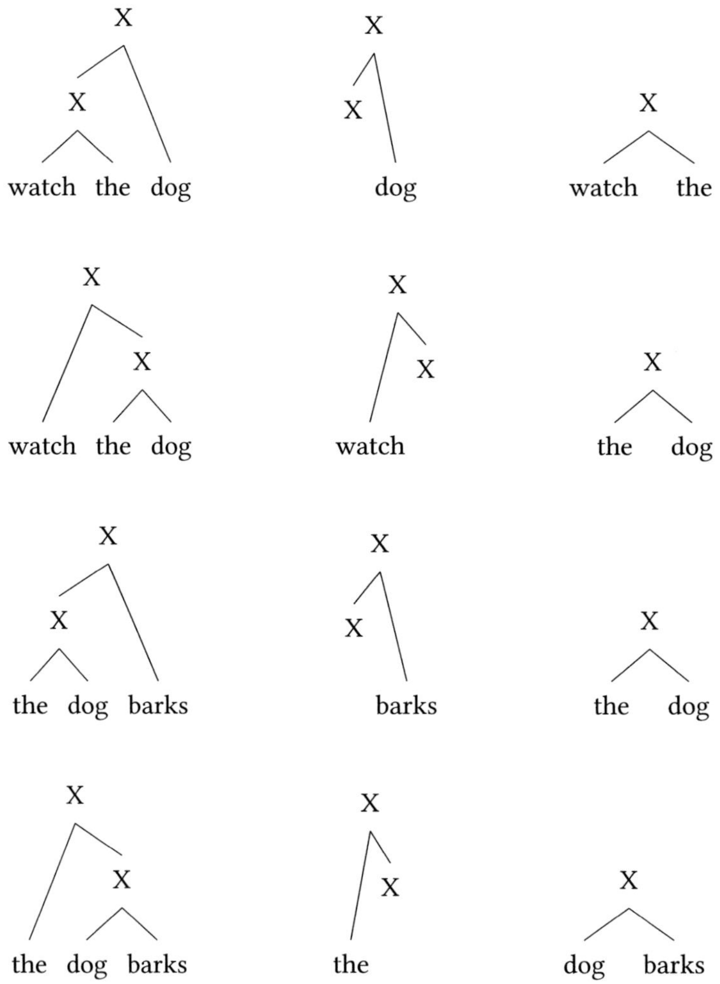

Figure 13.3: Subtrees for the trees in Figure 13.2

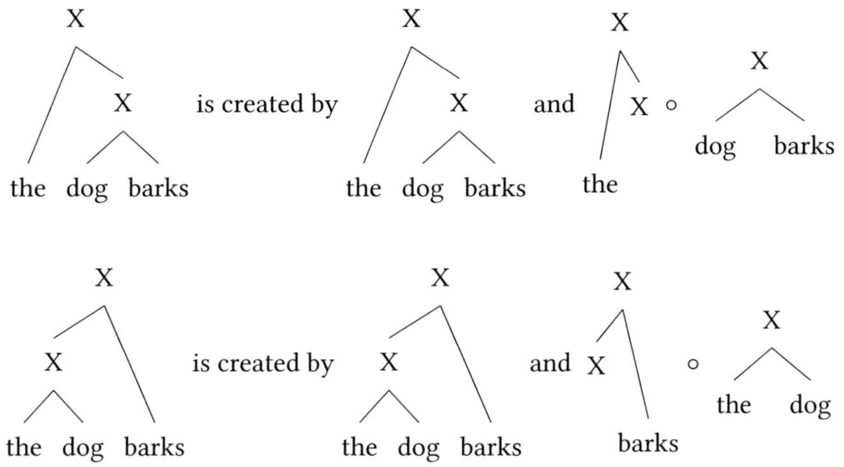

Figure 13.4: Analysis of *The dog barks* using subtrees from Figure 13.3

a lower weight. One can thereby also account for the fact that children do not have all sentences that they have ever heard available simultaneously. This extension makes the UDOP model more plausible for language acquisition.

In the example above, we did not assign categories to the words. If we were to do this, then we would get the tree in Figure 13.5 as a possible subtree. These kinds of

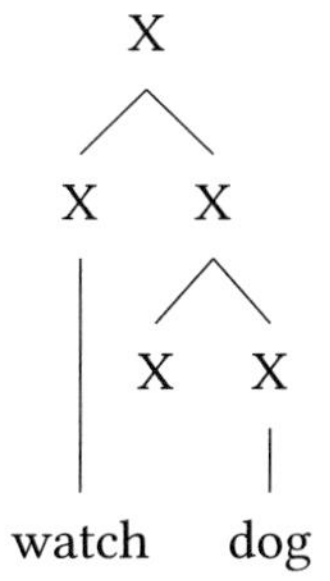

Figure 13.5: Discontinuous partial tree

discontinuous subtrees are important if one wants to capture dependencies between elements that occur in different subtrees of a given tree. Some examples are the following sentences:

(63) a. BA carried *more* people *than* cargo in 2005.
b. *What's* this scratch *doing* on the table?
c. Most software *companies* in Vietnam *are* small sized.

It is then also possible to learn auxiliary inversion in English with these kinds of discontinuous trees. All one needs are tree structures for the two sentences in (64) in order to prefer the correct sentence (65a) over the incorrect one (65b).

(64) a. The man who is eating is hungry.
  b. Is the boy hungry?

(65) a. Is the man who is eating hungry?
  b. * Is the man who eating is hungry?

U-DOP can learn the structures for (64) in Figure 13.6 from the sentences in (66):

(66) a. The man who is eating mumbled.
  b. The man is hungry.
  c. The man mumbled.
  d. The boy is eating.

Note that these sentences do not contain any instance of the structure in (65a). With

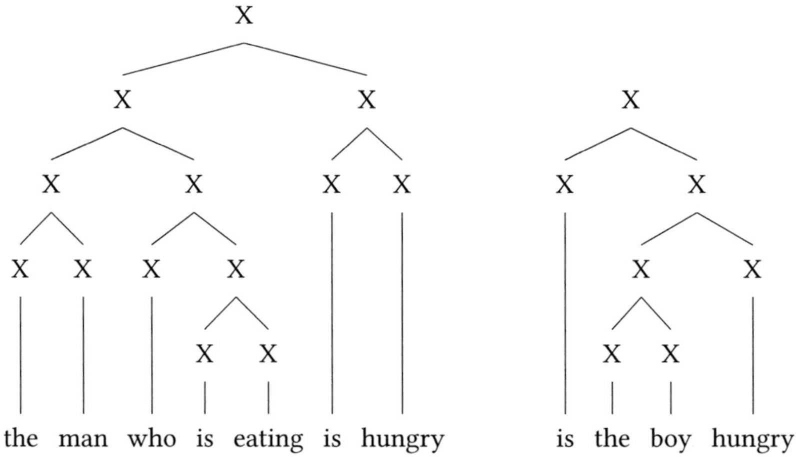

Figure 13.6: Structures that U-DOP learned from the examples in (64) and (66)

the structures learned here, it is possible to show that the shortest possible derivation for the position of the auxiliary is also the correct one: the correct order *Is the man who is eating hungry?* only requires that the fragments in Figure 13.7 on the following page are combined, whereas the structure for * *Is the man who eating is hungry?* requires at least four subtrees from Figure 13.6 to be combined with each other. This is shown by Figure 13.8 on the following page.

The motivation for always taking the derivation that consists of the least subparts is that one maximizes similarity to already known material.

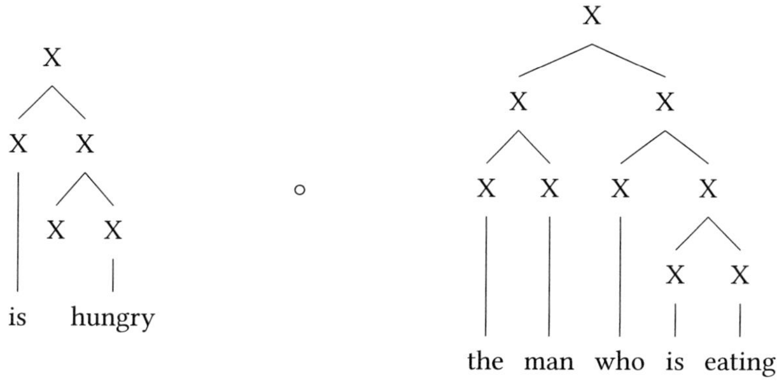

Figure 13.7: Derivation of the correct structure for combination with an auxiliary using two subtrees from Figure 13.6

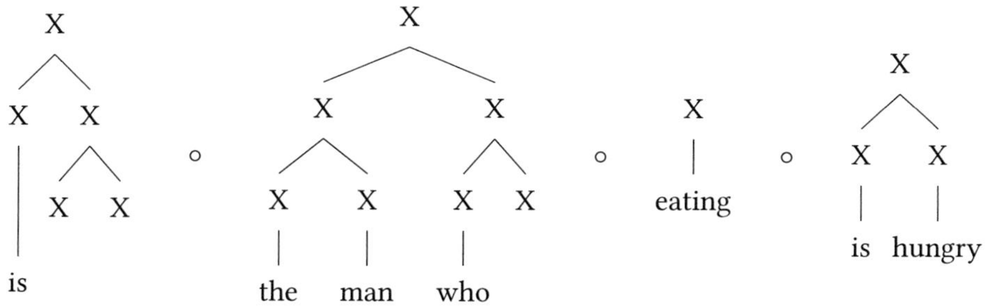

Figure 13.8: Derivation of the incorrect structure for the combination with an auxiliary using two subtrees from Figure 13.6

The tree for (67) containing one auxiliary too many can also be created from Figure 13.6 with just two subtrees (with the tree [$_X$ is$_X$ X] and the entire tree for *The man who is eating is hungry*).

(67) * Is the man who is eating is hungry?

Interestingly, children do produce this kind of incorrect sentences (Crain & Nakayama 1987: 530; Ambridge, Rowland & Pine 2008). However, if we consider the probabilities of the subtrees in addition to the the number of combined subparts, we get the correct result, namely (65a) and not (67). This is due to the fact that *the man who is eating* occurs in the corpus twice, in (65a) and in (66a). Thus, the probability of *the man who is eating* is just as high as the probability of *the man who is eating is hungry* and thus derivation in Figure 13.7 is preferred over the one for (67). This works for the constructed examples here, however one can imagine that in a realistic corpus, sequences of the form *the man who is eating* are more frequent than sequences with further words since *the man who is eating* can also occur in other contexts. Bod has applied this process to corpora of adult language (English, German and Chinese) as well as applying it to the Eve corpus from the CHILDES database in order to see whether analogy formation constitutes a plausible model for human acquisition of language. He was able to show that what we demonstrated for the sentences above also works for a larger corpus of naturally occurring language: although there were no examples for movement of an auxiliary across a complex NP in the Eve corpus, it is possible to learn by analogy that the auxiliary from a complex NP cannot be fronted.

It is therefore possible to learn syntactic structures from a corpus without any prior knowledge about parts of speech or abstract properties of language. The only assumption that Bod makes is that there are (binary-branching) structures. The assumption of binarity is not really necessary. But if one includes flat branching structures into the computation, the set of trees will become considerably bigger. Therefore, Bod only used binary-branching structures in his experiments. In his trees, X consists of two other X's or a word. We are therefore dealing with recursive structures. Therefore, Bod's work proposes a theory of the acquisition of syntactic structures that only requires recursion, something that is viewed by Hauser, Chomsky & Fitch (2002) as a basic property of language.

As shown in Section 13.1.8, there is evidence that recursion is not restricted to language and thus one can conclude that it is not necessary to assume innate linguistic knowledge in order to be able to learn syntactic structures from the given input.

Nevertheless, it is important to point out something here: what Bod shows is that syntactic structures can be learned. The information about the parts of speech of each word involved which are not yet included in his structures can also be derived using statistical methods (Redington et al. 1998; Clark 2000).[42] In all probability, the structures that can be learned correspond to structures that surface-oriented linguistic theories would also assume. However, not all aspects of the linguistic analysis are acquired. In Bod's model, only occurrences of words in structures are evaluated. Nothing is said about whether words stand in a particular regular relationship to one another or not (for example, a lexical rule connecting a passive participle and perfect participle). Furthermore, nothing is said about how the meaning of expressions arise (are they rather holistic in the sense of Construction Grammar or projected from the lexicon?). These are questions that still concern theoretical linguists (see Chapter 21) and cannot straightforwardly be derived from the statistic distribution of words and the structures computed from them (see Section 21.8.1 for more on this point).

A second comment is also needed: we have seen that statistical information can be used to derive the structure of complex linguistic expressions. This now begs the question of how this relates to Chomsky's earlier argumentation against statistical approaches (Chomsky 1957: 16). Abney (1996: Section 4.2) discusses this in detail. The problem with his earlier argumentation is that Chomsky referred to Markov models. These are statistical versions of finite automatons. Finite automatons can only describe type 3

[42] Computational linguistic algorithms for determining parts of speech often look at an entire corpus. But children are always dealing with just a particular part of it. The corresponding learning process must then also include a curve of forgetting. See Braine (1987: 67).

languages and are therefore not appropriate for analyzing natural language. However, Chomsky's criticism cannot be applied to statistical methods in general.

13.8.4 Negative evidence

In a number of works that assume innate linguistic knowledge, it is claimed that children do not have access to negative evidence, that is, nobody tells them that sentences such as (44e) – repeated here as (68) – are ungrammatical (Brown & Hanlon 1970: 42–52; Marcus 1993).

(68) * Is the dog that in the corner is hungry?

It is indeed correct that adults do not wake up their children with the ungrammatical sentence of the day, however, children do in fact have access to negative evidence of various sorts. For example, Chouinard & Clark (2003) have shown that English and French speaking parents correct the utterances of their children that are not well-formed. For example, they repeat utterances where the verb was inflected incorrectly. Children can deduce from the fact that the utterance was repeated and from what was changed in the repetition that they made a mistake and Chouinard and Clark also showed that they actually do this. The authors looked at data from five children whose parents all had an academic qualification. They discuss the parent-child relationship in other cultures, too (see Ochs (1982); Ochs & Schieffelin (1985) and Marcus (1993: 71) for an overview) and refer to studies of America families with lower socio-economic status (page 660).

A further form of negative evidence is indirect negative evidence, which Chomsky (1981a: 9) also assumes could play a role in acquisition. Goldberg (1995: Section 5.2) gives the utterance in (69a) as an example:[43]

(69) a. Look! The magician made the bird disappear.
b. * The magician disappeared the bird.

The child can conclude from the fact that adults use a more involved causative construction with *make* that the verb *disappear*, unlike other verbs such as *melt*, cannot be used transitively. An immediately instructive example for the role played by indirect negative evidence comes from morphology. There are certain productive rules that can however still not be applied if there is a word that blocks the application of the rule. An example is the *-er* nominalization suffix in German. By adding an *-er* to a verb stem, one can derive a noun that refers to someone who carries out a particular action (often habitually) (*Raucher* 'smoker', *Maler* 'painter', *Sänger* 'singer', *Tänzer* 'dancer'). However, *Stehler* 'stealer' is very unusual. The formation of *Stehler* is blocked by the existence of *Dieb* 'thief'. Language learners therefore have to infer from the non-existence of *Stehler* that the nominalization rule does not apply to *stehlen* 'to steal'.

Similarly, a speaker with a grammar of English that does not have any restrictions on the position of manner adverbs would expect that both orders in (70) are possible (Scholz & Pullum 2002: 206):

[43] Also, see Tomasello (2006a: 277).

(70) a. call the police immediately
b. * call immediately the police

Learners can conclude indirectly from the fact that verb phrases such as (70b) (almost) never occur in the input that these are probably not part of the language. This can be modeled using the relevant statistical learning algorithms.

The examples for the existence of negative evidence provided so far are more arguments from plausibility. Stefanowitsch (2008) has combined corpus linguistic studies on the statistical distribution with acceptability experiments and has shown that negative evidence gained from expected frequencies correlates with acceptability judgments of speakers. This process will be discussed now briefly: Stefanowitsch assumes the following principle:

(71) Form expectations about the frequency of co-occurrence of linguistic features or elements on the basis of their individual frequency of occurrence and check these expectations against the actual frequency of co-occurrence. (Stefanowitsch 2008: 518)

Stefanowitsch works with the part of the *International Corpus of English* that contains British English (ICE-GB). In this corpus, the verb *say* occurs 3,333 times and sentences with ditransitive verbs (Subj Verb Obj Obj) occur 1,824 times. The entire total of verbs in the corpus is 136,551. If all verbs occurred in all kinds of sentences with the same frequencies, then we would expect *say* to occur 44.52 times (X / 1,824 = 3,333 / 136,551 and hence X = 1,824 × 3,333 / 136,551) in the ditransitive construction. But the number of actual occurrences is actually 0 since, unlike (72b), sentences such as (72a) are not used by speakers of English.

(72) a. * Dad said Sue something nice.
b. Dad said something nice to Sue.

Stefanowitsch shows that the non-occurrence of *say* in the ditransitive sentence pattern is significant. Furthermore, he investigated how acceptability judgments compare to the frequent occurrence or non-occurrence of verbs in certain constructions. In a first experiment, he was able to show that the frequent non-occurrence of elements in particular constructions correlates with the acceptability judgments of speakers, whereas this is not the case for the frequent occurrence of a verb in a construction.

In sum, we can say that indirect negative evidence can be derived from linguistic input and that it seems to play an important role in language acquisition.

13.9 Summary

It follows from all this that not a single one of the arguments in favor of innate linguistic knowledge remains uncontroversial. This of course does not rule out there still being innate linguistic knowledge but those who wish to incorporate this assumption into their theories have to take more care than was previously the case to prove that what they assume to be innate is actually part of our linguistic knowledge and that it cannot be learned from the linguistic input alone.

Comprehension questions

1. Which arguments are there for the assumption of innate linguistic knowledge?

Further reading

Pinker's book (1994) is the best written book arguing for nativist models of language.

Elman, Bates, Johnson, Karmiloff-Smith, Parisi & Plunkett (1996) discuss all the arguments that have been proposed in favor of innate linguistic knowledge and show that the relevant phenomena can be explained differently. The authors adopt a connectionist view. They work with neuronal networks, which are assumed to model what is happening in our brains relatively accurately. The book also contains chapters about the basics of genetics and the structure of the brain, going into detail about why a direct encoding of linguistic knowledge in our genome is implausible.

Certain approaches using neuronal networks have been criticized because they cannot capture certain aspects of human abilities such as recursion or the multiple usage of the same words in an utterance. Pulvermüller (2010) discusses an architecture that has memory and uses this to analyze recursive structures. In his overview article, certain works are cited that show that the existence of more abstract rules or schemata of the kind theoretical linguists take for granted can be demonstrated on the neuronal level. Pulvermüller does not, however, assume that linguistic knowledge is innate (p. 173).

Pullum and Scholz have dealt with the Poverty-of-the-Stimulus argument in detail (Pullum & Scholz 2002; Scholz & Pullum 2002).

Goldberg (2006) and Tomasello (2003) are the most prominent proponents of Construction Grammar, a theory that explicitly tries to do without the assumption of innate linguistic knowledge.

14 Generative-enumerative vs. model-theoretic approaches

Generative-enumerative approaches assume that a grammar generates a set of sequences of symbols (strings of words). This is where the term Generative Grammar comes from. Thus, it is possible to use the grammar on page 53, repeated here as (1), to derive the string *er das Buch dem Mann gibt* 'he the book the man gives'.

(1)

NP → D, N	NP → er	N → Buch
S → NP, NP, NP, V	D → das	N → Mann
	D → dem	V → gibt

Beginning with the start symbol (S), symbols are replaced until one reaches a sequence of symbols only containing words. The set of all strings derived in this way is the language described by the grammar.

The following are classed as generative-enumerative approaches:

- all phrase structure grammars
- Transformational Grammars in almost all variants
- GPSG in the formalism of Gazdar, Klein, Pullum & Sag (1985)
- many variants of Categorial Grammar
- many variants of TAG
- Chomsky's Minimalist Grammars

LFG was also originally designed to be a generative grammar.

The opposite of such theories of grammar are model-theoretic or constraint-based approaches (MTA). MTAs formulate well-formedness conditions on the expressions that the grammar describes. In Section 6.7, we already discussed a model-theoretic approach for theories that use feature structures to model phenomena. To illustrate this point, I will discuss another HPSG example: (2) shows the lexical item for *kennst* 'know'. In the description of (2), it is ensured that the PHON value of the relevant linguistic sign is ⟨ *kennst* ⟩, that is, this value of PHON is constrained. There are parallel restrictions for the features given in (2): the SYNSEM value is given. In SYNSEM, there are restrictions on the LOC and NONLOC value. In CAT, there are individual restrictions for HEAD and SUBCAT. The value of SUBCAT is a list with descriptions of dependent elements. The descriptions are given as abbreviations here, which actually stand for complex feature descriptions

(2) Lexical item for *kennst*:

$$\begin{bmatrix} \text{PHON} & \langle \textit{kennst} \rangle \\ \text{SYNSEM} & \begin{bmatrix} \text{LOC} & \begin{bmatrix} \text{CAT} & \begin{bmatrix} \text{HEAD} & \begin{bmatrix} \textit{verb} & \\ \text{VFORM} & \textit{fin} \\ \text{DSL} & \textit{none}\end{bmatrix} \\ \text{SUBCAT} & \langle \text{NP}[\textit{nom}]_{\boxed{1}\,[\textit{second},\textit{sg}]}, \text{NP}[\textit{acc}]_{\boxed{2}} \rangle \end{bmatrix} \\ \text{CONT} & \begin{bmatrix} \text{IND} & \boxed{3} \\ \text{RELS} & \left\langle \begin{bmatrix} \textit{kennen} & \\ \text{EVENT} & \boxed{3} \\ \text{EXPERIENCER} & \boxed{1} \\ \text{THEME} & \boxed{2} \end{bmatrix} \right\rangle \end{bmatrix} \end{bmatrix} \\ \text{NONLOC} & \dots \end{bmatrix} \end{bmatrix}$$

that also consist of feature-value pairs. For the first argument of *kennst*, a HEAD value of type *noun* is required, the PER value in the semantic index has to be *second* and the NUM value has to be *sg*. The structure sharings in (2) are a special kind of constraint. Values that are not specified in the descriptions of lexical entries can vary in accordance with the feature geometry given by the type system. In (2), neither the SLASH value of the nominative NP nor the one of the accusative NP is fixed. This means that SLASH can either be an empty or non-empty list.

The constraints in lexical items such as (2) interact with further constraints that hold for the signs of type *phrase*. For instance, in head-argument structures, the non-head daughter must correspond to an element from the SUBCAT list of the head daughter.

Generative-enumerative and model-theoretic approaches view the same problem from different sides: the generative side only allows what can be generated by a given set of rules, whereas the model-theoretic approach allows everything that is not ruled out by constraints.[1]

Pullum & Scholz (2001: 19–20) and Pullum (2007) list the following model-theoretic approaches:[2]

- the non-procedural variant of Transformational Grammar of Lakoff, that formulates constraints on potential tree sequences,
- Johnson and Postal's formalization of Relational Grammar (1980),

[1] Compare this to an old joke: in dictatorships, everything that is not allowed is banned, in democracies, everything that is not banned is allowed and in France, everything that is banned is allowed. Generative-enumerative approaches correspond to the dictatorships, model-theoretic approaches are the democracies and France is something that has no correlate in linguistics.

[2] See Pullum (2007) for a historical overview of Model Theoretic Syntax (MTS) and for further references.

- GPSG in the variants developed by Gazdar et al. (1988), Blackburn et al. (1993) and Rogers (1997),
- LFG in the formalization of Kaplan (1995)[3] and
- HPSG in the formalization of King (1999).

Categorial Grammars (Bouma & van Noord 1994), TAG (Rogers 1994) and Minimalist approaches (Veenstra 1998) can be formulated in model-theoretic terms.

Pullum & Scholz (2001) point out various differences between these points of view. In the following sections, I will focus on two of these differences.[4] Section 14.3 deals with ten Hacken's objection to the model-theoretic view.

14.1 Graded acceptability

Generative-enumerative approaches differ from model-theoretic approaches in how they deal with the varying degrees of acceptability of utterances. In generative-enumerative approaches, a particular string is either included in the set of well-formed expressions or it is not. This means that it is not straightforwardly possible to say something about the degree of deviance: the first sentence in (3) is judged grammatical and the following three are equally ungrammatical.

(3) a. Du kennst diesen Aufsatz.
you know.2SG this.ACC essay

b. * Du kennen diesen Aufsatz.
you know.3PL this.ACC essay

c. * Du kennen dieser Aufsatz.
you know.3PL this.NOM essay

d. * Du kennen Aufsatz dieser.
you know.3PL essay this.NOM

At this point, critics of this view raise the objection that it is in fact possible to determine degrees of acceptability in (3b–d): in (3b), there is no agreement between the subject and the verb, in (3c), *dieser Aufsatz* 'this essay' has the wrong case in addition, and in (3d), *Aufsatz* 'essay' and *dieser* 'this' occur in the wrong order. Furthermore, the sentence in (4) violates grammatical rules of German, but is nevertheless still interpretable.

[3] According to Pullum (2013: Section 3.2), there seems to be a problem for model-theoretic formalizations of so-called *constraining equations*.

[4] The reader should take note here: there are differing views with regard to how generative-enumerative and MTS models are best formalized and not all of the assumptions discussed here are compatible with every formalism. The following sections mirror the important points in the general discussion.

(4) Studenten stürmen mit Flugblättern und Megafon die Mensa und rufen alle
students storm with flyers and megaphone the canteen and call all
auf zur Vollversammlung in der Glashalle *zum kommen*. *Vielen* bleibt das
up to plenary.meeting in the glass.hall to.the come many.DAT stays the
Essen im Mund stecken und *kommen sofort mit*.[5]
food in.the mouth stick and come immediately with
'Students stormed into the university canteen with flyers and a megaphone calling for everyone to come to a plenary meeting in the glass hall. For many, the food stuck in their throats and they immediately joined them.'

Chomsky (1975: Chapter 5; 1964b) tried to use a string distance function to determine the relative acceptability of utterances. This function compares the string of an ungrammatical expression with that of a grammatical expression and assigns an ungrammaticality score of 1, 2 or 3 according to certain criteria. This treatment is not adequate, however, as there are much more fine-grained differences in acceptability and the string distance function also makes incorrect predictions. For examples of this and technical problems with calculating the function, see Pullum & Scholz (2001: 29).

In model-theoretic approaches, grammar is understood as a system of well-formedness conditions. An expression becomes worse, the more well-formedness conditions it violates (Pullum & Scholz 2001: 26–27). In (3b), the person and number requirements of the lexical item for the verb *kennst* are violated. In addition, the case requirements for the object have not been fulfilled in (3c). There is a further violation of a linearization rule for the noun phrase in (3d).

Well-formedness conditions can be weighted in such a way as to explain why certain violations lead to more severe deviations than others. Furthermore, performance factors also play a role when judging sentences (for more on the distinction between performance and competence, see Chapter 15). As we will see in Chapter 15, constraint-based approaches work very well as performance-compatible grammar models. If we combine the relevant grammatical theory with performance models, we will arrive at explanations for graded acceptability differences owing to performance factors.

14.2 Utterance fragments

Pullum & Scholz (2001: Section 3.2) point out that generative-enumerative theories do not assign structure to fragments. For instance, neither the string *and of the* nor the string *the of and* would receive a structure since none of these sequences is well-formed as an utterance and they are therefore not elements of the set of sequences generated by the grammar. However, *and of the* can occur as part of the coordination of PPs in sentences such as (5) and would therefore have some structure in these cases, for example the one given in Figure 14.1 on the following page.

(5) That cat is afraid of the dog and of the parrot.

[5] Streikzeitung der Universität Bremen, 04.12.2003, p. 2. The emphasis is mine.

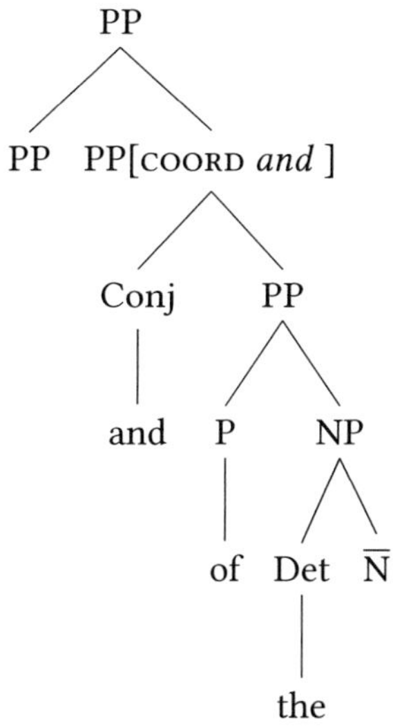

Figure 14.1: Structure of the fragment *and of the* following Pullum & Scholz (2001: 32)

As a result of the interaction of various constraints in a constraint-based grammar, it emerges that *the* is part of an NP and this NP is an argument of *of* and furthermore *and* is combined with the relevant *of*-PP. In symmetric coordination, the first conjunct has the same syntactic properties as the second, which is why the partial structure of *and of the* allows one to draw conclusions about the category of the conjunct despite it not being part of the string.

Ewan Klein noted that Categorial Grammar and Minimalist Grammars, which build up more complex expressions from simpler ones, can sometimes create this kind of fragments (Pullum 2013: 507). This is certainly the case for Categorial Grammars with composition rules, which allow one to combine any sequence of words to form a constituent. If one views derivations as logical proofs, as is common in some variants of Categorial Grammar, then the actual derivation is irrelevant. What matters is whether a proof can be found or not. However, if one is interested in the derived structures, then the argument brought forward by Pullum and Scholz is still valid. For some variants of Categorial Grammar that motivate the combination of constituents based on their prosodic and information-structural properties (Steedman 1991: Section 3), the problem persists since fragments have a structure independent of the structure of the entire utterance and independent of their information-structural properties within this complete structure. This structure of the fragment can be such that it is not possible to analyze it with type-raising rules and composition rules.

In any case, this argument holds for Minimalist theories since it is not possible to have a combination of *the* with a nominal constituent if this constituent was not already built up from lexical material by Merge.

14.3 A problem for model-theoretic approaches?

Ten Hacken (2007: 237–238) discusses the formal assumptions of HPSG. In HPSG, feature descriptions are used to describe feature structures. Feature structures must contain all the features belonging to a structure of a certain type. Additionally, the features have to have a maximally-specific value (see Section 6.7). Ten Hacken discusses gender properties of the English noun *cousin*. In English, gender is important in order to ensure the correct binding of pronouns (see page 270 for German):

(6) a. The man$_i$ sleeps. He$_i$ snores.
    b. The woman$_i$ sleeps. He$_{*i}$ snores.

While *he* in (6a) can refer to *man*, *woman* is not a possible antecedent. Ten Hacken's problem is that *cousin* is not marked with respect to gender. Thus, it is possible to use it to refer to both male and female relatives. As was explained in the discussion of the case value of *Frau* 'woman' in Section 6.7, it is possible for a value in a description to remain unspecified. Thus, in the relevant feature structures, any appropriate and maximally specific value is possible. The case of *Frau* can therefore be nominative, genitive, dative or accusative in an actual feature structure. Similarly, there are two possible genders for *cousin* corresponding to the usages in (7).

(7) a. I have a cousin$_i$. He$_i$ is very smart.
    b. I have a cousin$_i$. She$_i$ is very smart.

Ten Hacken refers to examples such as (8) and claims that these are problematic:

(8) a. Niels has two cousins.
    b. How many cousins does Niels have?

In plural usage, it is not possible to assume that *cousins* is feminine or masculine since the set of relatives can contain either women or men. It is interesting to note that (9a) is possible in English, whereas German is forced to use (9b) to express the same meaning.

(9) a. Niels and Odette are cousins.
    b. Niels und Odette sind Cousin und Cousine.
       Niels and Odette are cousin.M and cousin.F

Ten Hacken concludes that the gender value has to remain unspecified and this shows, in his opinion, that model-theoretic analyses are unsuited to describing language.

If we consider what exactly ten Hacken noticed, then it becomes apparent how one can account for this in a model-theoretic approach: Ten Hacken claims that it does not make sense to specify a gender value for the plural form of *cousin*. In a model-theoretic approach, this can be captured in two ways. One can either assume that there are no gender features for referential indices in the plural, or that one can add a gender value that plural nouns can have.

The first approach is supported by the fact that there are no inflectional differences between the plural forms of pronouns with regard to gender. There is therefore no reason to distinguish genders in the plural.

(10) a. Niels and Odette are cousins. They are very smart.
b. The cousins/brothers/sisters are standing over there. They are very smart.

No distinctions are found in plural when it comes to nominal inflection (*brothers, sisters, books*). In German, this is different. There are differences with both nominal inflection and the reference of (some) noun phrases with regard to the sexus of the referent. Examples of this are the previously mentioned examples *Cousin* 'male cousin' and *Cousine* 'female cousin' as well as forms with the suffix *-in* as in *Kindergärtnerin* 'female nursery teacher'. However, gender is normally a grammatical notion that has nothing to do with sexus. An example is the neuter noun *Mitglied* 'member', which can refer to both female and male persons.

The question that one has to ask when discussing Ten Hacken's problem is the following: does gender play a role for pronominal binding in German? If this is not the case, then the gender feature is only relevant within the morphology component, and here the gender value is determined for each noun in the lexicon. For the binding of personal pronouns, there is no gender difference in German.

(11) Die Schwestern / Brüder / Vereinsmitglieder / Geschwister stehen dort.
the sisters.F brothers.M club.members.N siblings stand there
Sie lächeln.
they smile.
'The sisters/brothers/club members/siblings are standing there. They are smiling.'

Nevertheless, there are adverbials in German that agree in gender with the noun to which they refer (Höhle 1983: Chapter 6):

(12) a. Die Fenster wurden eins nach dem anderen geschlossen.
the windows.N were one.N after the other closed
'The windows were closed one after the other.'
b. Die Türen wurden eine nach der anderen geschlossen.
the doors.F were one.F after the other closed
'The doors were closed one after the other.'
c. Die Riegel wurden einer nach dem anderen zugeschoben.
the bolts.M were one.M after the other closed
'The bolts were closed one after the other.'

For animate nouns, it is possible to diverge from the gender of the noun in question and use a form of the adverbial that corresponds to the biological sex:

(13) a. Die Mitglieder des Politbüros wurden eines / einer nach dem anderen
the members.N of.the politburo were one.N one.M after the other
aus dem Saal getragen.
out.of the hall carried
'The members of the politburo were carried out of the hall one after the other.'

b. Die Mitglieder des Frauentanzklubs verließen eines / eine nach dem
the members.N of.the women's.dance.club left one.N one.F after the.N
/ der anderen im Schutze der Dunkelheit den Keller.
the.F other in.the protection of.the dark the basement

'The members of the women's dance club left the basement one after the other under cover of darkness.'

This deviation from gender in favor of sexus can also be seen with binding of personal and relative pronouns with nouns such as *Weib* 'woman' (pej.) and *Mädchen* 'girl':

(14) a. „Farbe bringt die meiste Knete!“ verriet ein 14jähriges türkisches *Mädchen*,
color brings the most money revealed a 14-year.old Turkish girl.N
die die Mauerstückchen am Nachmittag am Checkpoint Charlie an
who.F the wall.pieces in.the afternoon at Checkpoint Charlie at
Japaner und US-Bürger verkauft.[6]
Japanese and US-citizens sells

' "Color gets the most money" said a 14-year old Turkish girl who sells pieces of the wall to Japanese and American citizens at Checkpoint Charlie.'

b. Es ist ein junges *Mädchen*, *die* auf der Suche nach CDs bei Bolzes
it is a young girl.N who.F on the search for CDs at Bolzes
reinschaut.[7]
stops.by

'It is a young girl looking for CDs that stops by Bolzes.'

For examples from Goethe, Kafka and Thomas Mann, see Müller (1999a: 417–418).

For inanimate nouns such as those in (12), agreement is obligatory. For the analysis of German, one therefore does in fact require a gender feature in the plural. In English, this is not the case since there are no parallel examples with pronouns inflecting for gender. One can therefore either assume that plural indices do not have a gender feature or that the gender value is *none*. In the latter case, the feature would have a value and hence fulfill the formal requirements. (15) shows the first solution: plural indices are modeled by feature structures of type *pl-ind* and the GENDER feature is just not appropriate for such objects.

(15) a. singular index:

$$\begin{bmatrix} \textit{sg-ind} & \\ \text{PER} & \textit{per} \\ \text{NUM} & \textit{sg} \\ \text{GEN} & \textit{gender} \end{bmatrix}$$

b. plural index:

$$\begin{bmatrix} \textit{pl-ind} & \\ \text{PER} & \textit{per} \\ \text{NUM} & \textit{pl} \end{bmatrix}$$

The second solution requires the type hierarchy in Figure 14.2 on the following page for the subtypes of *gender*. With such a type hierarchy *none* is a possible value of the GEN feature and no problem will arise.

[6] taz, 14.06.1990, p. 6.

[7] taz, 13.03.1996, p. 11.

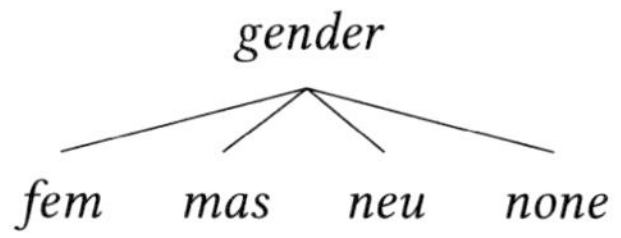

Figure 14.2: Type hierarchy for one of the solutions of ten Hacken's problem

In general, it is clear that cases such as the one constructed by ten Hacken will never be a problem since there are either values that make sense, or there are contexts for which there is no value that makes sense and one therefore does not require the features.

So, while ten Hacken's problem is a non-issue, there are certain problems of a more technical nature. I have pointed out one such technical problem in Müller (1999a: Section 14.4). I show that spurious ambiguities arise for a particular analysis of verbal complexes in German when one resolves the values of a binary feature (FLIP). I also show how this problem can be avoided by the complicated stipulation of a value in certain contexts.

15 The competence/performance distinction

The distinction between competence and performance (Chomsky 1965: Section 1.1), which is assumed by several theories of grammar, was already discussed in Section 12.6.3 about the analysis of scrambling and verbal complexes in TAG. Theories of competence are intended to describe linguistic knowledge and performance theories are assigned the task of explaining how linguistic knowledge is used as well as why mistakes are made in speech production and comprehension. A classic example in the competence/performance discussion are cases of center self-embedding. Chomsky & Miller (1963: 286) discuss the following example with recursively embedded relative clauses:

(1) (the rat (the cat (the dog chased) killed) ate the malt)

(2b) is a corresponding example in German:

(2) a. dass der Hund bellt, der die Katze jagt, die die Maus kennt, die
that the dog.M barks that.M the cat chases that.F the mouse knows who
im Keller lebt
in.the basement lives
'that the dog that chases the cat that knows the mouse who is living in the basement is barking'

b. dass er Hund, [$_1$ der die Katze, [$_2$ die die Maus, [$_3$ die im Keller
that the dog that the cat that the mouse who in.the basement
lebt, $_3$] kennt, $_2$] jagt $_1$] bellt
lives knows chases barks

The examples in (1) and (2b) are entirely incomprehensible for most people. If one rearranges the material somewhat, it is possible to process the sentences and assign a meaning to them.[1] For sentences such as (2b), it is often assumed that they fall within

[1] The sentence in (2a) can be continued following the pattern that was used to create the sentence. For instance by adding *die unter der Treppe lebte, die meine Freunde repariert haben* 'who lived under the staircase which my friends repaired'. This shows that a restriction of the number of elements that depend on one head to seven (Leiss 2003: 322) does not restrict the set of the sentences that are generated or licensed by a grammar to be finite. There are at most two dependents of each head in (2a). The extraposition of the relative clauses allows the hearer to group material into processable and reducible chunks, which reduces the cognitive burden during processing.

This means that the restriction to seven dependents does not cause a finitization of recursion ("Verendlichung von Rekursivität") as was claimed by Leiss (2003: 322). Leiss argued that Miller could not use his insights regarding short term memory, since he worked within Transformational Grammar rather than in Dependency Grammar. The discussion shows that dependency plays an important role, but that linear order is also important for processing.

our grammatical competence, that is, we possess the knowledge required to assign a structure to the sentence, although the processing of utterances such as (2b) exceeds language-independent abilities of our brain. In order to successfully process (2b), we would have to retain the first five noun phrases and corresponding hypotheses about the further progression of the sentence in our heads and could only begin to combine syntactic material when the verbs appear. Our brains become overwhelmed by this task. These problems do not arise when analyzing (2a) as it is possible to immediately begin to integrate the noun phrases into a larger unit.

Nevertheless, center self-embedding of relative clauses can also be constructed in such a way that our brains can handle them. Hans Uszkoreit (p. c. 2009) gives the following example:

(3) Die Bänke, [$_1$ auf denen damals die Alten des Dorfes, [$_2$ die allen
the benches on which back.then the old.people of.the village that all
Kindern, [$_3$ die vorbeikamen $_3$], freundliche Blicke zuwarfen $_2$], lange Stunden
children that came.by friendly glances gave long hours
schweigend nebeneinander saßen $_1$], mussten im letzten Jahr einem
silent next.to.each.other sat must in.the last year a
Parkplatz weichen.
car.park give.way.to

'The benches on which the older residents of the village, who used to give friendly glances to all the children who came by, used to sit silently next to one another for hours had to give way to a car park last year.'

Therefore, one does not wish to include in the description of our grammatical knowledge that relative clauses are not allowed to be included inside each other as in (2b) as this would also rule out (3).

We can easily accept the fact that our brains are not able to process structures past a certain degree of complexity and also that corresponding utterances then become unacceptable. The contrast in the following examples is far more fascinating:[2]

(4) a. # The patient [who the nurse [who the clinic had hired] admitted] met Jack.
b. * The patient who the nurse who the clinic had hired met Jack.

Although (4a) is syntactically well-formed and (4b) is not, Gibson & Thomas (1999) were able to show that (4b) is rated better by speakers than (4a). It does not occur to some people that an entire VP is missing. There are a number of explanations for this fact, all of which in some way make the claim that previously heard words are forgotten as soon as new words are heard and a particular degree of complexity is exceeded (Frazier 1985: 178; Gibson & Thomas 1999).

Instead of developing grammatical theories that treat (2b) and (4a) as unacceptable and (3) and (4b) as acceptable, descriptions have been developed that equally allow (2b),

[2] See Gibson & Thomas (1999: 227). Frazier (1985: 178) attributes the discovery of this kind of sentences to Janet Fodor.

(3), and (4a) (competence models) and then additionally investigate the way utterances are processed in order to find out what kinds of structures our brains can handle and what kinds of structures it cannot. The result of this research is then a performance model (see Gibson (1998), for example). This does not rule out that there are language-specific differences affecting language processing. For example, Vasishth, Suckow, Lewis & Kern (2010) have shown that the effects that arise in center self-embedding structures in German are different from those that arise in the corresponding English cases such as (4): due to the frequent occurrence of verb-final structures in German, speakers of German were able to better store predictions about the anticipated verbs into their working memory (p. 558).

Theories in the framework of Categorial Grammar, GB, LFG, GPSG and HPSG are theories about our linguistic competence.[3] If we want to develop a grammatical theory that directly reflects our cognitive abilities, then there should also be a corresponding performance model to go with a particular competence model. In the following two sections, I will recount some arguments from Sag & Wasow (2011) in favor of constraint-based theories such as GPSG, LFG and HPSG.

15.1 The derivational theory of complexity

The first point discussed by Sag & Wasow (2011) is the Derivational Theory of Complexity. In the early days of Transformational Grammar, it was assumed that transformations were cognitively real, that is, it is possible to measure the consumption of resources that transformations have. A sentence that requires more transformations than the analysis of another sentence should therefore also be more difficult for humans to process. The corresponding theory was dubbed the *Derivational Theory of Complexity* (DTC) and initial experiments seemed to confirm it (Miller & McKean 1964; Savin & Perchonock 1965; Clifton & Odom 1966), so that in 1968 Chomsky still assumed that the Derivational

[3] For an approach where the parser is equated with UG, see Abney & Cole (1986: Section 3.4). For a performance-oriented variant of Minimalism, see Phillips (2003).

In Construction Grammar, the question of whether a distinction between competence and performance would be justified at all is controversially discussed (see Section 10.6.4.5.1). Fanselow, Schlesewsky, Cavar & Kliegl (1999) also suggest a model – albeit for different reasons – where grammatical properties considerably affect processing properties. The aforementioned authors work in the framework of Optimality Theory and show that the OT constraints that they assume can explain parsing preferences. OT is not a grammatical theory on its own but rather a meta theory. It is assumed that there is a component GEN that creates a set of candidates. A further component EVAL then chooses the most optimal candidate from this set of candidates. GEN contains a generative grammar of the kind that we have seen in this book. Normally, a GP/MP variant or also LFG is assumed as the base grammar. If one assumes a transformational theory, then one automatically has a problem with the Derivational Theory of Complexity that we will encounter in the following section. If one wishes to develop OT parsing models, then one has to make reference to representational variants of GB as the aforementioned authors seem to.

Theory of Complexity was in fact correct (Chomsky 1976a: 249–250).[4] Some years later, however, most psycholinguists rejected the DTC. For discussion of several experiments that testify against the DTC, see Fodor, Bever & Garrett (1974: 320–328). One set of phenomena where the DTC makes incorrect predictions for respective analyses is that of elliptical constructions, for example (Fodor, Bever & Garrett 1974: 324): in elliptical constructions, particular parts of the utterance are left out or replaced by auxiliaries. In transformation-based approaches, it was assumed that (5b) is derived from (5a) by means of deletion of *swims* and (5c) is derived from (5b) by inserting *do.*

(5) a. John swims faster than Bob swims.
    b. John swims faster than Bob.
    c. John swims faster than Bob does.

The DTC predicts that (5b) should require more time to process than (5a), since the analysis of (5b) first requires to build up the structure in (5a) and then delete *swims.* This prediction was not confirmed.

Similarly, no difference could be identified for the pairs in (6) and (7) even though one of the sentences, given the relevant theoretical assumptions, requires more transformations for the derivation from a base structure (Fodor, Bever & Garrett 1974: 324).

(6) a. John phoned up the girl.
    b. John phoned the girl up.

(7) a. The bus driver was nervous after the wreck.
    b. The bus driver was fired after the wreck.

In (6), we are dealing with local reordering of the particle and the object. (7b) contains a passive clause that should be derived from an active clause under Transformational Grammar assumptions. If we compare this sentence with an equally long sentence with an adjective, like (7a), the passive clause should be more difficult to process. This is, however, not the case.

It is necessary to add two qualifications to Sag & Wasow's claims: if one has experimental data that show that the DTC makes incorrect predictions for a particular analysis, this does not necessarily mean that the DTC has been disproved. One could also try to find a different analysis for the phenomenon in question. For example, instead of a

[4] In the Transformational Grammar literature, transformations were later viewed as a metaphor (Lohnstein 2014: 170, also in Chomsky 2001: Footnote 4), that is, it was no longer assumed to have psycholinguistic reality. In *Derivation by phase* and *On phases,* Chomsky refers once again to processing aspects such as computational and memory load (Chomsky 2001: 11, 12, 15; 2007: 3, 12; 2008: 138, 145, 146, 155). See also Marantz (2005: 440) and Richards (2015).

A structure building operation that begins with words and is followed by transformations, as recently assumed by theories in the Minimalist Program, is psycholinguistically implausible for sentence parsing. See Labelle (2007) and Section 15.2 for more on incremental processing.

Chomsky (2007: 6) (written later than *On phases*) seems to adopt a constraint-based view. He writes that "a Merge-based system involves parallel operations" and compares the analysis of an utterance with a proof and explicitly mentions the competence/performance distinction.

transformation that deletes material, one could assume empty elements for the analysis of elliptical structures that are inserted directly into the structure without deleting any material (see page 68 for the assumption of an empty nominal head in structures with noun ellipsis in German). Data such as (5) would then be irrelevant to the discussion.[5] However, reordering such as (6b) and the passive in (7b) are the kinds of phenomena that are typically explained using transformations.

The second qualification pertains to analyses for which there is a representational variant: it is often said that transformations are simply metaphors (Jackendoff 2000: 22–23; 2007: 5, 20): for example, we have seen that extractions with a transformational grammar yield structures that are similar to those assumed in HPSG. Figure 15.1 shows cyclic movement in GB theory compared to the corresponding HPSG analysis.

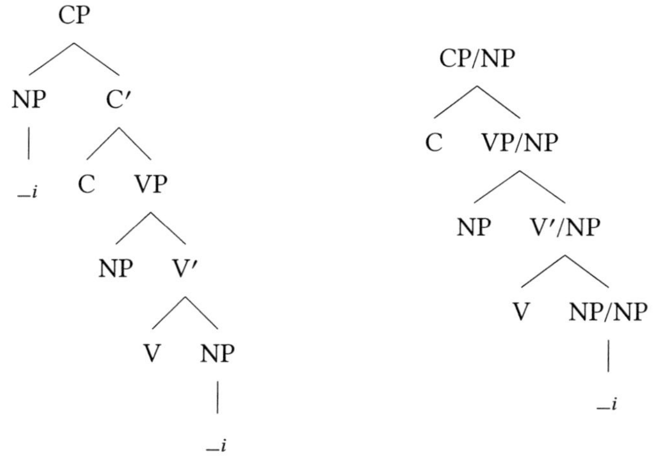

Figure 15.1: Cyclic movement vs. feature percolation

In GB, an element is moved to the specifier position of CP (SpecCP) and can then be moved from there to the next higher SpecCP position.

(8) a. Chris$_i$, we think [$_{CP}$ _$_i$ Anna claims [$_{CP}$ _$_i$ that David saw _$_i$]]. (GB)
 b. Chris$_i$, we think [$_{CP/NP}$ Anna claims [$_{CP/NP}$ that David saw _$_i$]]. (HPSG)

In HPSG, the same effect is achieved by structure sharing. Information about a long-distance dependency is not located in the specifier node but rather in the mother node of the projection itself. In Section 19.2, I will discuss various ways of eliminating empty elements from grammars. If we apply these techniques to structures such as the GB structure in Figure 15.1, then we arrive at structures where information about missing elements is integrated into the mother node (CP) and the position in SpecCP is unfilled.

[5] Culicover & Jackendoff (2005: Chapters 1 and 7) argue in favor of analyzing ellipsis as a semantic or pragmatic phenomenon rather than a syntactic one anyway.

This roughly corresponds to the HPSG structure in Figure 15.1.[6] It follows from this that there are classes of phenomena that can be spoken about in terms of transformations without expecting empirical differences with regard to performance when compared to transformation-less approaches. However, it is important to note that we are dealing with an S-structure in the left-hand tree in Figure 15.1. As soon as one assumes that this is derived by moving constituents out of other structures, this equivalence of approaches disappears.

15.2 Incremental processing

The next important point mentioned by Sag & Wasow (2011) is the fact that both comprehension and production of language take places incrementally. As soon as we hear or read even the beginning of a word, we begin to assign meaning and to create structure. In the same way, we sometimes start talking before we have finished planning the entire utterance. This is shown by interruptions and self-correction in spontaneous speech (Clark & Wasow 1998; Clark & Fox Tree 2002). When it comes to processing spoken speech, Tanenhaus et al. (1996) have shown that we access a word as soon as we have heard a part of it (see also Marslen-Wilson 1975). The authors of the study carried out an experiment where participants were instructed to pick up particular objects on a grid and reorganize them. Using eye-tracking measurements, Tanenhaus and colleagues could then show that the participants could identify the object in question earlier if the sound sequence at the beginning of the word was unambiguous than in cases where the initial sounds occurred in multiple words. An example for this is a configuration with a candle and candy: *candy* and *candle* both begin with *can* such that speakers could not yet decide upon hearing this sequence which lexical entry should be accessed. Therefore, there was a slight delay in accessing the lexical entry when compared to words where the objects in question did not contain the same segment at the start of the word (Tanenhaus et al. 1995: 1633).

If complex noun phrases were used in the instructions (*Touch the starred yellow square*), the participants' gaze fell on the object in question 250ms after it was unambiguously identifiable. This means that if there was only a single object with stars on it, then they looked at it after they heard *starred*. In cases where there were starred yellow blocks as well as squares, they looked at the square only after they had processed the word *square* (Tanenhaus et al. 1995: 1632). The planning and execution of a gaze lasts 200ms. From this, one can conclude that hearers combine words directly and as soon as enough information is available, they create sufficient structure in order to capture the (potential) meaning of an expression and react accordingly. This finding is incompatible with models that assume that one must have heard a complete noun phrase or even a complete utterance of even more complexity before it is possible to conclude anything about the meaning of a phrase/utterance. In particular, analyses in the Minimalist Program which assume that only entire phrases or so-called phases[7] are interpreted (see Chomsky 1999

[6] In Figure 15.1, additionally the unary branching of C′ to CP was omitted in the tree on the right so that C combines directly with VP/NP to form CP/NP.

[7] Usually, only CP and vP are assumed to be phases.

and also Marantz 2005: 441, who explicitly contrasts the MP to Categorial Grammar) must therefore be rejected as inadequate from a psycholinguistic perspective.[8,9]

With contrastive emphasis of individual adjectives in complex noun phrases (e.g., *the BIG blue triangle*), hearers assumed that there must be a corresponding counterpart to the reference object, e.g., a small blue triangle. The eye-tracking studies carried out by Tanenhaus et al. (1996) have shown that taking this kind of information into account results in objects being identified more quickly.

Similarly, Arnold et al. (2004) have shown, also using eye-tracking studies, that hearers tend to direct their gaze to previously unmentioned objects if the interlocutor interrupts their speech with *um* or *uh*. This can be traced back to the assumption that hearers assume that describing previously unmentioned objects is more complex than referring to objects already under discussion. The speaker can create more time for himself by using *um* or *uh*.

Examples such as those above constitute evidence for approaches that assume that when processing language, information from all available channels is used and that this information is also used as soon as it is available and not only after the structure of the entire utterance or complete phrase has been constructed. The results of experimental research therefore show that the hypothesis of a strictly modular organization of linguistic knowledge must be rejected. Proponents of this hypothesis assume that the output of one module constitutes the input of another without a given module having access to the inner states of another module or the processes taking place inside it. For example, the morphology module could provide the input for syntax and then this would be processed later by the semantic module. One kind of evidence for this kind of organization of linguistic knowledge that is often cited are so-called *garden path sentences* such as (9):

(9) a. The horse raced past the barn fell.
    b. The boat floated down the river sank.

The vast majority of English speakers struggle to process these sentences since their parser is led down a garden path as it builds up a complete structure for (10a) or (10b) only then to realize that there is another verb that cannot be integrated into this structure.

(10) a. The horse raced past the barn.
     b. The boat floated down the river.

[8] Sternefeld (2006: 729–730) points out that in theories in the Minimalist Program, the common assumption of uninterpretable features is entirely unjustified. Chomsky assumes that there are features that have to be deleted in the course of a derivation since they are only relevant for syntax. If they are not checked, the derivation crashes at the interface to semantics. It follows from this that NPs should not be interpretable under the assumptions of these theories since they contain a number of features that are irrelevant for the semantics and have to therefore be deleted (see Section 4.1.2 of this book and Richards 2015). As we have seen, these kinds of theories are incompatible with the facts.

[9] It is sometimes claimed that current Minimalist theories are better suited to explain production (generation) than perception (parsing). But these models are as implausible for generation as they are for parsing. The reason is that it is assumed that there is a syntax component that generates structures that are then shipped to the interfaces. This is not what happens in generation though. Usually speakers know what they want to say (at least partly), that is, they start with semantics.

However, the actual structure of (9) contains a reduced relative clause (*raced past the barn* or *floated down the river*). That is the sentences in (9a) are semantically equivalent to the sentences in (11):

(11) a. The horse that was raced past the barn fell.
     b. The boat that was floated down the river sank.

The failure of the parser in these cases was explained by assuming that syntactic processing such as constructing a sentence from NP and VP take place independently of the processing of other constraints. As Crain & Steedman (1985) and others have shown, yet there are data that make this explanation seem less plausible: if (9a) is uttered in a relevant context, the parser is not misled. In (12), there are multiple horses under discussion and each NP is clearly identified by a relative clause. The hearer is therefore prepared for a relative clause and can process the reduced relative clause without being led down the garden path, so to speak.

(12) The horse that they raced around the track held up fine. The horse that was raced down the road faltered a bit. And the horse raced past the barn fell.

By exchanging lexical material, it is also possible to modify (9a) in such way as to ensure that processing is unproblematic without having to add additional context. It is necessary to choose the material so that the interpretation of the noun as the subject of verb in the reduced relative clause is ruled out. Accordingly, *evidence* in (13) refers to an inanimate noun. It is therefore not a possible agent of *examined.* A hypothesis with *evidence* as the agent of *examined* is therefore never created when processing this sentence (Sag & Wasow 2011).

(13) The evidence examined by the judge turned out to be unreliable.

Since processing proceeds incrementally, it is sometimes assumed that realistic grammars should be obliged to immediately assign a constituent structure to previously heard material (Ades & Steedman 1982; Hausser 1992). Proponents of this view would assume a structure for the following sentence where every word forms a constituent with the preceding material:

(14) [[[[[[[[[[[[[[Das britische] Finanzministerium] stellt] dem] angeschlagenen]
     the British treasury provides the crippled
     Bankensystem] des] Landes] mindestens] 200] Milliarden] Pfund] zur]
     banking.system of.the country at.least 200 billion pounds to
     Verfügung].
     use
     'The British Treasury is making at least 200 billion pounds available to the crippled banking system.'

Pulman (1985), Stabler (1991) and Shieber & Johnson (1993: 301–308) have shown, however, that it is possible to build semantic structures incrementally, using the kind of phrase structure grammars we encountered in Chapter 2. This means that a partial semantic representation for the string *das britische* 'the British' can be computed without having to assume that the two words form a constituent in (14). Therefore, one does not necessarily need a grammar that licenses the immediate combination of words directly. Furthermore, Shieber & Johnson (1993) point out that from a purely technical point of view, synchronous processing is more costly than asynchronous processing since synchronous processing requires additional mechanisms for synchronization whereas asynchronous processing processes information as soon as it becomes available (p. 297–298). Shieber and Johnson do not clarify whether this also applies to synchronous/asynchronous processing of syntactic and semantic information. See Shieber & Johnson (1993) for incremental processing and for a comparison of Steedman's Categorial Grammar and TAG.

What kind of conclusions can we draw from the data we have previously discussed? Are there further data that can help to determine the kinds of properties a theory of grammar should have in order to count as psycholinguistically plausible? Sag, Wasow & Bender (2003) and Sag & Wasow (2011, 2015) list the following properties that a performance-compatible competence grammar should have:[10]

- surface-oriented
- model-theoretic and therefore constraint-based
- sign-based organization
- strictly lexicalist
- representational underspecification of semantic information

Approaches such as CG, GPSG, LFG, HPSG, CxG and TAG are surface-oriented since they do not assume a base structure from which other structures are derived via transformations. Transformational approaches, however, require additional assumptions.[11] This will be briefly illustrated in what follows. In Section 3.1.5, we encountered the following analysis of English interrogatives:

---

[10] Also, see Jackendoff (2007) for reflections on a performance model for a constraint-based, surface-oriented linguistic theory.

[11] An exception among transformational approaches is Phillips (2003). Phillips assumes that structures relevant for phenomena such as ellipsis, coordination and fronting are built up incrementally. These constituents are then reordered in later steps by transformations. For example, in the analysis of (i), the string *Wallace saw Gromit in* forms a constituent where *in* is dominated by a node with the label P(P). This node is then turned into a PP in a subsequent step (p. 43–44).

(i) Wallace saw Gromit in the kitchen.

While this approach is a transformation-based approach, the kind of transformation here is very idiosyncratic and incompatible with other variants of the theory. In particular, the modification of constituents contradicts the assumption of Structure Preservation when applying transformations as well as the *No Tampering Condition* of Chomsky (2008). Furthermore, the conditions under which an incomplete string such as *Wallace saw Gromit in* forms a constituent are not entirely clear.

(15) $[_{CP}$ What$_i$ $[_{C'}$ will$_k$ $[_{IP}$ Ann $[_{I'}$ $\_{}_k$ $[_{VP}$ read $\_{}_i]]]]]$.

This structure is derived from (16a) by two transformations (two applications of Move-α):

(16) a. Ann will read what?

b. * Will Ann read what

The first transformation creates the order in (16b) from (16a), and the second creates (15) from (16b).

When a hearer processes the sentence in (15), he begins to build structure as soon as he hears the first word. Transformations can, however, only be carried out when the entire utterance has been heard. One can, of course, assume that hearers process surface structures. However, since – as we have seen – they begin to access semantic knowledge early into an utterance, this begs the question of what we need a deep structure for at all.

In analyses such as those of (15), deep structure is superfluous since the relevant information can be reconstructed from the traces. Corresponding variants of GB have been proposed in the literature (see page 119). They are compatible with the requirement of being surface-oriented. Chomsky (1981a: 181; 1986a: 49) and Lasnik & Saito (1992: 59–60) propose analyses where traces can be deleted. In these analyses, the deep structure cannot be directly reconstructed from the surface structure and one requires transformations in order to relate the two. If we assume that transformations are applied 'online' during the analysis of utterances, then this would mean that the hearer would have to keep a structure derived from previously heard material as well as a list of possible transformations during processing in his working memory. In constraint-based grammars, entertaining hypotheses about potential upcoming transformation steps is not necessary since there is only a single surface structure that is processed directly. At present, it is still unclear whether it is actually possible to distinguish between these models empirically. But for Minimalist models with a large number of movements (see Figure 4.20 on page 144, for example), it should be clear that they are unrealistic since storage space is required to manage the hypotheses regarding such movements and we know that such short-term memory is very limited in humans.

Frazier & Clifton (1996: 27) assume that a transformation-based competence grammar yields a grammar with pre-compiled rules or rather templates that is then used for parsing. Therefore, theorems derived from UG are used for parsing and not axioms of UG directly. Johnson (1989) also suggests a parsing system that applies constraints from different sub-theories of GB as early as possible. This means that while he does assume the levels of representation D-Structure, S-Structure, LF and PF, he specifies the relevant constraints ($\overline{X}$ theory, Theta-Theory, Case Theory, …) as logical conditions that can be reorganized, then be evaluated in a different but logically equivalent order and be used for structure building.[12] Chomsky (2007: 6) also compares human parsing to working through a proof, where each step of the proof can be carried out in different orders. This view does not assume the psychological reality of levels of grammatical representation when processing language, but simply assumes that principles and structures play

[12] Stabler (1992: Section 15.7) also considers a constraint-based view, but arrives at the conclusion that parsing and other linguistic tasks should use the structural levels of the competence theory. This would again pose problems for the DTC.

a role when it comes to language acquisition. As we have seen, the question of whether we need UG to explain language acquisition was not yet decided in favor of UG-based approaches. Instead, all available evidence seems to point in the opposite direction. However, even if innate linguistic knowledge does exist, the question arises as to why one would want to represent this as several structures linked via transformations when it is clear that these do not play a role for humans (especially language learners) when processing language. Approaches that can represent this knowledge using fewer technical means, e.g., without transformations, are therefore preferable. For more on this point, see Kuhn (2007: 615).

The requirement for constraint-based grammars is supported by incremental processing and also by the ability to deduce what will follow from previously heard material. Stabler (1991) has pointed out that Steedman's argumentation with regard to incrementally processable grammars is incorrect, and instead argues for maintaining a modular view of grammar. Stabler has developed a constraint-based grammar where syntactic and semantic knowledge can be accessed at any time. He formulates both syntactic structures and the semantic representations attached to them as conjoined constraints and then presents a processing system that processes structures based on the availability of parts of syntactic and semantic knowledge. Stabler rejects models of performance that assume that one must first apply all syntactic constraints before the semantic ones can be applied. If one abandons this strict view of modularity, then we arrive at something like (17):

(17) $(\mathrm{Syn}_1 \wedge \mathrm{Syn}_2 \wedge \ldots \wedge \mathrm{Syn}_n) \wedge (\mathrm{Sem}_1 \wedge \mathrm{Sem}_2 \wedge \ldots \wedge \mathrm{Sem}_n)$

Syn_1–Syn_n stand for syntactic rules or constraints and Sem_1–Sem_n stand for semantic rules or constraints. If one so desires, the expressions in brackets can be referred to as modules. Since it is possible to randomly reorder conjoined expressions, one can imagine performance models that first apply some rules from the syntax module and then, when enough information is present, respective rules from the semantic module. The order of processing could therefore be as in (18), for example:

(18) $\mathrm{Syn}_2 \wedge \mathrm{Sem}_1 \wedge \mathrm{Syn}_1 \wedge \ldots \wedge \mathrm{Syn}_n \wedge \mathrm{Sem}_2 \wedge \ldots \wedge \mathrm{Sem}_n$

If one subscribes to this view of modularity, then theories such as HPSG or CxG also have a modular structure. In the representation assumed in the HPSG variant of Pollard & Sag (1987) and Sign-Based CxG (see Section 10.6.2), the value of SYN would correspond to the syntax module, the value of SEM to the semantic module and the value of PHON to the phonology module. If one were to remove the respective other parts of the lexical entries/dominance schemata, then one would be left with the part of the theory corresponding exactly to the level of representation in question.[13] Jackendoff (2000) argues for this form of modularity with the relevant interfaces between the modules for phonology, syntax, semantics and further modules from other areas of cognition. Exactly what

[13] In current theories in the Minimalist Program, an increasing amount of morphological, syntactic, semantic and information-structural information is being included in analyses (see Section 4.6.1). While there are suggestions for using feature-value pairs (Sauerland & Elbourne 2002: 290–291), a strict structuring of information as in GPSG, LFG, HPSG, CxG and variants of CG and TAG is not present. This means that there are the levels for syntax, Phonological Form and Logical Form, but the information relevant for these levels is an unstructured part of syntax, smeared all over syntactic trees.

there is to be gained from assuming these modules and how these could be proved empirically remains somewhat unclear to me. For skepticism with regard to the very concept of modules, see Jackendoff (2000: 22,27). For more on interfaces and modularization in theories such as LFG and HPSG, see Kuhn (2007).

Furthermore, Sag & Wasow (2015: 53–54) argue that listeners often leave semantic interpretation underspecified until enough information is present either in the utterance itself or the context. They do not commit to a certain reading early and run into garden paths or backtrack to other readings. This is modeled appropriately by theories that use a variant of underspecified semantics. For a concrete example of underspecification in semantics see Section 19.3.

In conclusion, we can say that surface-oriented, model-theoretic and strongly lexicalist grammatical theories such as CG, LFG, GPSG, HPSG, CxG and the corresponding GB/MP variants (paired with appropriate semantic representations) can plausibly be combined with processing models, while this is not the case for the overwhelming majority of GB/MP theories.

16 Language acquisition

Linguists and philosophers are fascinated by the human ability to acquire language. Assuming the relevant input during childhood, language acquisition normally takes place completely effortlessly. Chomsky (1965: 24–25) put forward the requirement that a grammatical theory must provide a plausible model of language acquisition. Only then could it actually explain anything and would otherwise remain descriptive at best. In this section, we will discuss theories of acquisition from a number of theoretical standpoints.

16.1 Principles & Parameters

A very influential explanation of language acquisition is Chomsky's Principles & Parameters model (1981a). Chomsky assumes that there is an innate Universal Grammar that contains knowledge that is equally relevant for all languages. Languages can then vary in particular ways. For every difference between languages in the area of core grammar, there is a feature with a specific value. Normally, the value of a parameter is binary, that is, the value is either '+' or '−'. Depending on the setting of a parameter, a language will have certain properties, that is, setting a parameter determines whether a language belongs to a particular class of languages. Parameters are assumed to influence multiple properties of a grammar simultaneously (Chomsky 1981a: 6). For example, Rizzi (1986) claims that the pro-drop parameter affects whether referential subjects can be omitted, the absence of expletives, subject extraction from clauses with complementizers (*that*-t contexts) and interrogatives and finally the possibility of realizing the subject postverbally in VO-languages (see Chomsky 1981a: Section 4.3; Meisel 1995: 12). It has been noted that there are counter-examples to all the correlations assumed.[1] Another example of a parameter is the Head Directionality Parameter discussed in Section 13.1.1. As was shown, there are languages where heads govern in different directions. In his overview article, Haider (2001) still mentions the parametrized Subjacency Principle but notes that subjacency is no longer assumed as a principle in newer versions of the theory (see Section 13.1.5.2 for more on subjacency).

Snyder (2001) discovered a correlation of various phenomena with productive root compounding as it is manifested for instance in compounding of two nouns. He argues

[1] See Haider (1994) and Haider (2001: Section 2.2) for an overview. Haider assumes that there is at least a correlation between the absence of expletive subjects and pro-drop. However, Galician is a pro-drop language with expletive subject pronouns (Raposo & Uriagereka 1990: Section 2.5). Franks (1995: 314) cites Upper and Lower Sorbian as pro-drop languages with expletive subjects. Scholz & Pullum (2002: 218) point out that there is an expletive pronoun *ci* in modern Italian although Italian is classed as a pro-drop language.

that the acquisition of complex predicate formation is connected to the acquisition of compound structures and that there is a parameter that is responsible for this type of compounding and simultaneously for the following set of phenomena:

(1) a. John painted the house red. (resultative)
b. Mary picked the book up/picked up the book. (verb-particle)
c. Fred made Jeff leave. (*make*-causative)
d. Fred saw Jeff leave. (perceptual report)
e. Bob put the book on the table. (*put*-locative)
f. Alice sent the letter to Sue. (*to*-dative)
g. Alice sent Sue the letter. (double-object dative)

Snyder examined languages from various language groups: Afroasiatic, Austroasiatic, Austronesian, Finno-Ugric, Indo-European (Germanic, Romance, Slavic), Japanese-Korean, Niger-Kordofanian (Bantu), and Sino-Tibetan, as well as American Sign Language and the language isolate Basque. The languages that were examined either had all of these phenomena or none. This was tested with native speakers of the respective languages. In addition the claim that these phenomena are acquired once noun-noun compounds are used productively was tested for English using CHILDES data. The result was positive with the exception of the double object construction, for which an explanation was provided. The correlation of the phenomena in (1) is interesting and was interpreted as proof of the existence of a parameter that correlates several phenomena in a language. However, Son (2007) and Son & Svenonius (2008) showed that Snyder's claims for Japanese were wrong and that there are further languages like Korean, Hebrew, Czech, Malayalam, Javanese in which some of the phenomena show no correlations.

Gibson & Wexler (1994) discuss the acquisition of constituent order and assume three parameters that concern the position of the verb relative to the subject (SV vs. VS) and relative to the object (VO vs. OV) as well as the V2-property. There is no consensus in the literature about which parameters determine the make-up of languages (see Newmeyer 2005: Section 3.2 and Haspelmath 2008 for an overview and critical discussion). Fodor (1998a: 346–347) assumes that there are 20 to 30 parameters, Gibson & Wexler (1994: 408) mention the number 40, Baker (2003: 349) talks of 10 to 20 and Roberts & Holmberg (2005: 541) of 50 to 100. There is no consensus in the literature as to which parameters one should assume, how they interact and what they predict. However, it is nevertheless possible to contemplate how a grammar of an individual language could be derived from a UG with parameters that need to be set. Chomsky's original idea (1986b: Section 3.5.1) was that the child sets the value of a parameter based on the language input as soon as the relevant evidence is present from the input (see also Gibson & Wexler 1994; Nowak, Komarova & Niyogi 2001). At a given point in time, the learner has a grammar with certain parameter settings that correspond to the input seen so far. In order to fully acquire a grammar, all parameters must be assigned a value. In theory, thirty utterances should be enough to acquire a grammar with thirty parameters if these utterances provide unambiguous evidence for a particular parameter value.

This approach has often been criticized. If setting a parameter leads to a learner using a different grammar, one would expect sudden changes in linguistic behavior. This is, however, not the case (Bloom 1993: 731). Fodor (1998a: 343–344) also notes the following three problems: 1) Parameters can affect things that are not visible from the perceptible constituent order. 2) Many sentences are ambiguous with regard to the setting of a particular parameter, that is, there are sometimes multiple combinations of parameters compatible with one utterance. Therefore, the respective utterances cannot be used to set any parameters (Berwick & Niyogi 1996; Fodor 1998b). 3) There is a problem with the interaction of parameters. Normally multiple parameters play a role in an utterance such that it can be difficult to determine which parameter contributes what and thus how the values should be determined.

Points 1) and 2) can be explained using the constituent order parameters of Gibson & Wexler: imagine a child hears sentences such as the English and the German examples in (2):

(2) a. Daddy drinks juice.

b. Papa trinkt Saft.
daddy drinks juice

These sentences look exactly the same, even though radically different structures are assumed for each. According to the theories under discussion, the English sentence has the structure shown in Figure 3.8 on page 97 given in abbreviated form in (3a). The German sentence, on the other hand, has the structure in Figure 3.13 on page 105 corresponding to (3b):

(3) a. [$_{\mathrm{IP}}$ [Daddy [$_{\mathrm{I'}}$ $\_{}_k$ [$_{\mathrm{VP}}$ drinks$_k$ juice]]].

b. [$_{\mathrm{CP}}$ Papa$_i$ [$_{\mathrm{C'}}$ trinkt$_k$ [$_{\mathrm{IP}}$ $\_{}_i$ [$_{\mathrm{I'}}$ [$_{\mathrm{VP}}$ Saft $\_{}_k$] $\_{}_k$]]]].

English has the basic constituent order SVO. The verb forms a constituent with the object (VP) and this is combined with the subject. The parameter setting must therefore be SV, VO and −V2. German, on the other had, is analyzed as a verb-final and verb-second language and the parameter values would therefore have to be SV, OV and +V2. If we consider the sentences in (2), we see that both sentences do not differ from one another with regard to the order of the verb and its arguments.

Fodor (1998a,b) concludes from this that one first has to build a structure in order to see what grammatical class the grammar licensing the structure belongs to since one first needs the structure in (3b) in order to be able to see that the verb in the partial constituent occurs after its argument in the VP (Saft $\_{}_k$). The question is now how one achieves this structure. A UG with 30 parameters corresponds to 2^{30} = 1,073,741,824 fully instantiated grammars. It is an unrealistic assumption that children try out these grammars successively or simultaneously.

Gibson & Wexler (1994) discuss a number of solutions for this problem: parameters have a default value and the learner can only change a parameter value if a sentence that could previously not be analyzed can then be analyzed with the new parameter setting (*Greediness Constraint*). In this kind of procedure, only one parameter can be changed at a time (*Single Value Constraint*), which aims at ruling out great leaps leading to extremely different grammars (see Berwick & Niyogi 1996: 612–613, however). This reduces the processing demands, however with 40 parameters, the worst case could still be that one has to test 40 parameter values separately, that is, try to parse a sentence with

40 different grammars. This processing feat is still unrealistic, which is why Gibson & Wexler (1994: 442) additionally assume that one hypothesis is tested per input sentence. A further modification of the model is the assumption that certain parameters only begin to play a role during the maturation of the child. At a given point in time, there could be only a few accessible parameters that also need to be set. After setting these parameters, new parameters could become available.

In their article, Gibson & Wexler show that the interaction between input and parameter setting is in no way trivial. In their example scenario with three parameters, a situation can arise in which a learner sets a parameter in order to analyze a new sentence, however setting this parameter leads to the fact that the target grammar cannot be acquired because only one value can be changed at a time and changes can only be made if more sentences can be analyzed than before. The learner reaches a so-called local maximum in these problematic cases.[2] Gibson & Wexler then suggest assigning a default value to particular parameters, whereby the default value is the one that will cause the learner to avoid problematic situations. For the V2 parameter, they assume '−' as the default value.

Berwick & Niyogi (1996) show that Gibson & Wexler calculated the problematic conditions incorrectly and that, if one shares their assumptions, it is even more frequently possible to arrive at parameter combinations from which it is not possible to reach the target grammar by changing individual parameter values. They show that one of the problematic cases not addressed by Gibson & Wexler is −V2 (p. 609) and that the assumption of a default value for a parameter does not solve the problem as both '+' and '−' can lead to problematic combinations of parameters.[3] In their article, Berwick and Niyogi show that learners in the example scenario above (with three parameters) learn the target grammar faster if one abandons the Greediness or else the Single Value Constraint. They suggest a process that simply randomly changes one parameter if a sentence cannot be analyzed (*Random Step*, p. 615–616). The authors note that this approach does not share the problems with the local maxima that Gibson & Wexler had in their example and that it also reaches its goal faster than theirs. However, the fact that *Random Step* converges more quickly has to do with the quality of the parameter space (p. 618). Since there is no consensus about parameters in the literature, it is not possible to assess how the entire system works.

Yang (2004: 453) has criticized the classic Principles & Parameters model since abrupt switching between grammars after setting a parameter cannot be observed. Instead, he proposes the following learning mechanism:

(4) For an input sentence, *s*, the child: (i) with probability P_i selects a grammar G_i, (ii) analyzes *s* with G_i, (iii) if successful, reward G_i by increasing P_i, otherwise punish G_i by decreasing P_i.

[2] If one imagines the acquisition process as climbing a hill, then the Greediness Constraint ensures that one can only go uphill. It could be the case, however, that one begins to climb the wrong hill and can no longer get back down.

[3] Kohl (1999, 2000) has investigated this acquisition model in a case with twelve parameters. Of the 4096 possible grammars, 2336 (57%) are unlearnable if one assumes the best initial values for the parameters.

Yang discusses the example of the pro-drop and topic drop parameters. In pro-drop languages (e.g., Italian), it is possible to omit the subject and in topic drop languages (e.g., Mandarin Chinese), it possible to omit both the subject and the object if it is a topic. Yang compares English-speaking and Chinese-speaking children noting that English children omit both subjects and objects in an early linguistic stage. He claims that the reason for this is that English-speaking children start off using the Chinese grammar.

The pro-drop parameter is one of the most widely discussed parameters in the context of Principles & Parameters theory and it will therefore be discussed in more detail here. It is assumed that speakers of English have to learn that all sentences in English require a subject, whereas speakers of Italian learn that subjects can be omitted. One can observe that children learning both English and Italian omit subjects (German children too in fact). Objects are also omitted notably more often than subjects. There are two possible explanations for this: a competence-based one and a performance-based one. In competence-based approaches, it is assumed that children use a grammar that allows them to omit subjects and then only later acquire the correct grammar (by setting parameters or increasing the rule apparatus). In performance-based approaches, by contrast, the omission of subjects is traced back to the fact that children are not yet capable of planning and producing long utterances due to their limited brain capacity. Since the cognitive demands are greatest at the beginning of an utterance, this leads to subjects beings increasingly left out. Valian (1991) investigated these various hypotheses and showed that the frequency with which children learning English and Italian respectively omit subjects is not the same. Subjects are omitted more often than objects. She therefore concludes that competence-based explanations are not empirically adequate. The omission of subjects should then be viewed more as a performance phenomenon (see also Bloom 1993). Another argument for the influence of performance factors is the fact that articles of subjects are left out more often than articles of objects (31% vs. 18%, see Gerken 1991: 440). As Bloom notes, no subject article-drop parameter has been proposed so far. If we explain this phenomenon as a performance phenomenon, then it is also plausible to assume that the omittance of complete subjects is due to performance issues.

Gerken (1991) shows that the metrical properties of utterances also play a role: in experiments where children had to repeat sentences, they omitted the subject/article of the subject more often than the object/article of the object. Here, it made a difference whether the intonation pattern was iambic (weak-strong) or trochaic (strong-weak). It can even be observed with individual words that children leave out weak syllables at the beginning of words more often than at the end of the word. Thus, it is more probable that “giRAFFE” is reduced to “RAFFE” than “MONkey” to “MON”. Gerken assumes the following for the metrical structure of utterances:

1. A metrical foot contains one and only one strong syllable.
2. Create maximally binary left-to-right feet.
3. Metrical structure is independent of syntactic structure.

Subject pronouns in English are sentence-initial and form a iambic foot with the following strongly emphasized verb as in (5a). Object pronouns, however, can form the weak syllable of a trochaic foot as in (5b).

(5) a. she KISSED + the DOG
    b. the DOG + KISSED her
    c. PETE + KISSED the + DOG

Furthermore, articles in iambic feet as in the object of (5a) and the subject of (5b) are omitted more often than in trochaic feet such as with the object of (5c).

It follows from this that there are multiple factors that influence the omission of elements and that one cannot simply take the behavior of children as evidence for switching between two grammars.

Apart from what has been discussed so far, the pro-drop parameter is of interest for another reason: there is a problem when it comes to setting parameters. The standard explanation is that learners identify that a subject must occur in all English sentences, which is suggested by the appearance of expletive pronouns in the input.

As discussed on page 511, there is no relation between the pro-drop property and the presence of expletives in a language. Since the pro-drop property does not correlate with any of the other putative properties either, only the existence of subject-less sentences in the input constitutes decisive evidence for setting a parameter. The problem is that there are grammatical utterances where there is no visible subject. Examples of this are imperatives such as (6), declaratives with a dropped subject as in (7a) and even declarative sentences without an expletive such as the example in (7b) found by Valian (1991: 32) in the New York Times.

(6) a. Give me the teddy bear!
    b. Show me your toy!

(7) a. She'll be a big hit. Sings like a dream.
    b. Seems like she always has something twin-related perking.

The following title of a Nirvana song also comes from the same year as Valian's article:

(8) Smells like Teen Spirit.

Teen Spirit refers to a deodorant and *smell* is a verb that, both in German and English, requires a referential subject but can also be used with an expletive *it* as subject. The usage that Kurt Cobain had in mind cannot be reconstructed[4], independent of the intended meaning, however, the subject in (8) is missing. Imperatives do occur in the input children have and are therefore relevant for acquisition. Valian (1991: 33) says the following about them:

[4] See http://de.wikipedia.org/wiki/Smells_Like_Teen_Spirit. 06.03.2016.

> What is acceptable in the adult community forms part of the child's input, and is also part of what children must master. The utterances that I have termed "acceptable" are not grammatical in English (since English does not have pro subjects, and also cannot be characterized as a simple VP). They lack subjects and therefore violate the extended projection principle (Chomsky 1981a), which we are assuming.
>
> Children are exposed to fully grammatical utterances without subjects, in the form of imperatives. They are also exposed to acceptable utterances which are not fully grammatical, such as [(7a)], as well as forms like, "Want lunch now?" The American child must grow into an adult who not only knows that overt subjects are grammatically required, but also knows when subjects can acceptably be omitted. The child must not only acquire the correct grammar, but also master the discourse conditions that allow relaxation of the grammar. (Valian 1991: 33)

This passage turns the relations on their head: we cannot conclude from the fact that a particular grammatical theory is not compatible with certain data, that these data should not be described by this theory, instead we should modify the incompatible grammar or, if this is not possible, we should reject it. Since utterances with imperatives are entirely regular, there is no reason to categorize them as utterances that do not follow grammatical rules. The quotation above represents a situation where a learner has to acquire two grammars: one that corresponds to the innate grammar and a second that partially suppresses the rules of innate grammar and also adds some additional rules.

The question we can pose at this point is: how does a child distinguish which of the data it hears are relevant for which of the two grammars?

Fodor (1998a: 347) pursues a different analysis that does not suffer from many of the aforementioned problems. Rather than assuming that learners try to find a correct grammar among a billion others, she instead assumes that children work with a single grammar that contains all possibilities. She suggests using parts of trees (*treelets*) rather than parameters. These treelets can also be underspecified and in extreme cases, a treelet can consist of a single feature (Fodor 1998b: 6). A language learner can deduce whether a language has a given property from the usage of a particular treelet. As an example, she provides a VP treelet consisting of a verb and a prepositional phrase. This treelet must be used for the analysis of the VP occurring in *Look at the frog*. Similarly, the analysis of an interrogative clause with a fronted *who* would make use of a treelet with a *wh*-NP in the specifier of a complementizer phrase (see Figure 3.7 on page 97). In Fodor's version of Principles and Parameters Theory, this treelet would be the parameter that licenses *wh*-movement in (overt) syntax. Fodor assumes that there are defaults that allow a learner to parse a sentence even when no or very few parameters have been set. This allows one to learn from utterances that one would have not otherwise been able to use since there would have been multiple possible analyses for them. Assuming a default can lead to misanalyses, however: due to a default value, a second parameter could be set because an utterance was analyzed with a treelet t_1 and t_3, for example, but t_1 was not suited to the particular language in question and the utterance should have instead been analyzed with the non-default treelet t_2 and the treelet t_{17}. In this acquisition model, there must therefore be the possibility to correct wrong decisions in the parameter setting process.

Fodor therefore assumes that there is a frequency-based degree of activation for parameters (p. 365): treelets that are often used in analyses have a high degree of activation, whereas those used less often have a lower degree of activation. In this way, it is not necessary to assume a particular parameter value while excluding others.

Furthermore, Fodor proposes that parameters should be structured hierarchically, that is, only if a parameter has a particular value does it then make sense to think about specific other parameter values.

Fodor's analysis is – as she herself notes (Fodor 2001: 385) – compatible with theories such as HPSG and TAG. Pollard & Sag (1987: 147) characterize UG as the conjunction of all universally applicable principles:

(9) $\mathrm{UG} = \mathrm{P}_1 \wedge \mathrm{P}_2 \wedge \ldots \wedge \mathrm{P}_n$

As well as principles that hold universally, there are other principles that are specific to a particular language or a class of languages. Pollard & Sag give the example of the constituent ordering principle that only holds for English. English can be characterized as follows if one assumes that P_{n+1}–P_m are language-specific principles, L_1–L_p a complete list of lexical entries and R_1–R_q a list of dominance schemata relevant for English.

(10) $\text{English} = \mathrm{P}_1 \wedge \mathrm{P}_2 \wedge \ldots \wedge \mathrm{P}_m \wedge (\mathrm{L}_1 \vee \ldots \vee \mathrm{L}_p \vee \mathrm{R}_1 \vee \ldots \vee \mathrm{R}_q)$

In Pollard & Sag's conception, only those properties of language that equally hold for all languages are part of UG. Pollard & Sag do not count the dominance schemata as part of this. However, one can indeed also describe UG as follows:

(11) $\mathrm{UG} = \mathrm{P}_1 \wedge \mathrm{P}_2 \wedge \ldots \wedge \mathrm{P}_n \wedge (\mathrm{R}_{\text{en-1}} \vee \ldots \vee \mathrm{R}_{\text{en-}q} \vee \mathrm{R}_{\text{de-1}} \vee \ldots \vee \mathrm{R}_{\text{de-}r} \vee \ldots)$

P_1–P_n are, as before, universally applicable principles and $\mathrm{R}_{\text{en-1}}$–$\mathrm{R}_{\text{en-}q}$ are the (core) dominance schemata of English and $\mathrm{R}_{\text{de-1}}$–$\mathrm{R}_{\text{de-}r}$ are the dominance schemata in German. The dominance schemata in (11) are combined by means of disjunctions, that is, not every disjunct needs to have a realization in a specific language. Principles can make reference to particular properties of lexical entries and rule out certain phrasal configurations. If a language only contains heads that are marked for final-position in the lexicon, then grammatical rules that require a head in initial position as their daughter can never be combined with these heads or their projections. Furthermore, theories with a type system are compatible with Fodor's approach to language acquisition because constraints can easily be underspecified. As such, constraints in UG do not have to make reference to all properties of grammatical rules: principles can refer to feature values, the language-specific values themselves do not have to already be contained in UG. Similarly, a supertype describing multiple dominance schemata that have similar but language-specific instantiations can also be part of UG, however the language-specific details remain open and are then deduced by the learner upon parsing (see Ackerman & Webelhuth 1998: Section 9.2). The differences in activation assumed by Fodor can be captured by weighting the constraints: the dominance schemata $\mathrm{R}_{\text{en-1}}$–$\mathrm{R}_{\text{en-}q}$ etc. are sets of feature-value pairs as well as path equations. As explained in Chapter 15, weights can be added to such constraints and also to sets of constraints. In Fodor's acquisition model, given a German input, the weights for the rules of English would be reduced and those for the German rules would be increased. Note that in Pollard & Sag's acquisition scenario, there are no triggers for parameter setting unlike in Fodor's model. Furthermore, properties that were previously disjunctively specified as part of UG will now be acquired directly. Using the treelet t_{17} (or rather a possibly underspecified dominance schema), it is not the case that the value '+' is set for a parameter P_5 but rather the activation potential of t_{17} is increased such that t_{17} will be prioritized for future analyses.

16.2 Principles and the lexicon

A variant of the UG-driven theory of language acquisition would be to assume that principles are so general that they hold for all languages and individual languages simply differ with regard to their lexicon. Principles then refer to properties of combined entities. Parameters therefore migrate from principles into the lexicon (Chomsky 1999: 2). See Mensching & Remberger (2011) for a study of Romance languages in this model and Son & Svenonius (2008: 395) for an analysis of Snyder's examples that were discussed in the previous subsection.

At this point, one can observe an interesting convergence in these approaches: most of the theories discussed here assume a very general structure for the combination of heads with their arguments. For example, in Categorial Grammar and the Minimalist Program, these are always binary functor-argument combinations. The way in which constituents can be ordered in a particular language depends on the lexical properties of the combined elements.

The question that is being discussed controversially at present is whether the spectrum of lexical properties is determined by UG (Chomsky 2007: 6–7) and whether all areas of the language can be described with the same general combinatorial possibilities (see Section 21.10 on phrasal constructions).

In Section 16.1, I have shown what theories of acquisition assuming innate language specific knowledge can look like and also that variants of such acquisition theories are compatible with all the theories of grammar we have discussed. During this discussion, one should bear in mind the question of whether it makes sense at all to assume that English children use parts of a Chinese grammar during some stages of their acquisition process (as suggested by Yang 2004: 453), or whether the relevant phenomena can be explained in different ways. In the following, I will present some alternative approaches that do not presuppose innate language specific knowledge, but instead assume that language can simply be acquired from the input. The following section will deal with pattern-based approaches and Section 16.4 will discuss the lexically-oriented variant of input-based language acquisition.

16.3 Pattern-based approaches

Chomsky (1981a: 7–8) proposed that languages can be divided into a core area and a periphery. The core contains all regular aspects of language. The core grammar of a language is seen as an instantiation of UG. Idioms and other irregular parts of language are then part of the periphery. Critics of the Principles & Parameters model have pointed out that idiomatic and irregular constructions constitute a relatively large part of our language and that the distinction, both fluid and somewhat arbitrary, is only motivated theory-internally (Jackendoff 1997: Chapter 7; Culicover 1999; Ginzburg & Sag 2000: 5; Newmeyer 2005: 48; Kuhn 2007: 619). For example, it is possible to note that there are interactions between various idioms and syntax (Nunberg, Sag & Wasow 1994). Most idioms in German with a verbal component allow the verb to be moved to initial position (12b), some allow that parts of idioms can be fronted (12c) and some can undergo passivization (12d).

(12) a. dass er ihm den Garaus macht
that he him the GARAUS makes
'that he finishes him off (kills him)'

b. Er macht ihm den Garaus.
he makes him the GARAUS
'He finishes him off.'

c. In Amerika sagte man der Kamera nach, die größte Kleinbildkamera der Welt zu sein. Sie war laut Schleiffer am Ende der Sargnagel der Mühlheimer Kameraproduktion.
Den Garaus machte ihr die Diskussion um die Standardisierung des
the GARAUS made her the discussion around the standardization of.the
16-Millimeter-Filmformats, an dessen Ende die DIN-Norm 19022 (Patrone
16-millimeter-film.format at whose end the DIN-norm 19022 cartridge
mit Spule für 16-Millimeter-Film) stand, die im März 1963 zur Norm
with coil for 16-millimeter-film stood that in March 1963 to.the norm
wurde.[5]
became
'In America, one says that this camera was the biggest compact camera in the world. According to Schleiffer, it was the last nail in the coffin for camera production in Mühlheim. What finished it off was the discussion about standardizing the 16 millimeter format, which resulted in the DIN-Norm 19022 (cartridge with coil for 16 millimeter film) that became the norm in March 1963.'

d. in Heidelberg wird „parasitären Elementen" unter den Professoren *der*
in Heidelberg are parasitic elements among the professors the
Garaus gemacht[6]
GARAUS made
'In Heidelberg, "parasitic elements" among professors are being killed off.'

It is assumed that the periphery and lexicon are not components of UG (Chomsky 1986b: 150–151; Fodor 1998a: 343) but rather are acquired using other learning methods – namely inductively directly from the input. The question posed by critics is now why these

[5] Frankfurter Rundschau, 28.06.1997, p. 2.

[6] Mannheimer Morgen, 28.06.1999, Sport; Schrauben allein genügen nicht.

methods should not work for regular aspects of the language as well (Abney 1996: 20; Goldberg 2003a: 222; Newmeyer 2005: 100; Tomasello 2006c: 36; 2006b: 20): the areas of the so-called 'core' are by definition more regular then components of the periphery, which is why they should be easier to learn.

Tomasello (2000, 2003) has pointed out that a Principles & Parameters model of language acquisition is not compatible with the observable facts. The Principles and Parameters Theory predicts that children should no longer make mistakes in a particular area of grammar once they have set a particular parameter correctly (see Chomsky 1986b: 146, Radford 1990: 21–22 and Lightfoot 1997: 175). Furthermore, it is assumed that a parameter is responsible for very different areas of grammar (see the discussion of the pro-drop parameter in Section 16.1). When a parameter value is set, then there should be sudden developments with regard to a number of phenomena (Lightfoot 1997: 174). This is, however, not the case. Instead, children acquire language from utterances in their input and begin to generalize from a certain age. Depending on the input, they can reorder certain auxiliaries and not others, although movement of auxiliaries is obligatory in English.[7] One argument put forward against these kinds of input-based theories is that children produce utterances that cannot be observed to a significant frequency in the input. One much discussed phenomenon of this kind are so called *root infinitives* (RI) or *optional infinitives* (OI) (Wexler 1998). These are infinitive forms that can be used in non-embedded clauses (*root sentences*) instead of a finite verb. Optional infinitives are those where children use both a finite (13a) and non-finite (13b) form (Wexler 1998: 59):

(13) a. Mary likes ice cream.
b. Mary like ice cream.

Wijnen, Kempen & Gillis (2001: 656) showed that Dutch children use the order object infinitive 90 % of the time during the two-word phase although these orders occur in less than 10 % of their mother's utterances that contained a verb. Compound verb forms, e.g., with a modal in initial position as in (14) that contain another instance of this pattern only occurred in 30 % of the input containing a verb (Wijnen, Kempen & Gillis 2001: 647).

(14) Willst du Brei essen?
want you porridge eat
'Do you want to eat porridge?'

At first glance, there seems to be a discrepancy between the input and the child's utterances. However, this deviation could also be explained by an utterance-final bias in learning (Wijnen et al. 2001; Freudenthal, Pine & Gobet 2006). A number of factors can be made responsible for the salience of verbs at the end of an utterance: 1) restrictions of the infant brain. It has been shown that humans (both children and adults) forget words during the course of an utterance, that is, the activation potential decreases. Since the cognitive capabilities of small children are restricted, it is clear why elements at the end of an utterance have an important status. 2) Easier segmentation at the end of an

[7] Here, Yang's suggestion to combine grammars with a particular probability does not help since one would have to assume that the child uses different grammars for different auxiliaries, which is highly unlikely.

utterance. At the end of an utterance, part of the segmentation problem for hearers disappears: the hearer first has to divide a sequence of phonemes into individual words before he can understand them and combine them to create larger syntactic entities. This segmentation is easier at the end of an utterance since the word boundary is already given by the end of the utterance. Furthermore according to Wijnen, Kempen & Gillis (2001: 637), utterance-final words have an above average length and do bear a pitch accent. This effect occurs more often in language directed at children.

Freudenthal, Pine, Aguado-Orea & Gobet (2007) have modeled language acquisition for English, German, Dutch, and Spanish. The computer model could reproduce differences between these languages based on input. At first glance, it is surprising that there are even differences between German and Dutch and between English and Spanish with regard to the use of infinitives as German and Dutch have a very similar syntax (SOV+V2). Similarly, English and Spanish are both languages with SVO order. Nevertheless, children learning English make OI mistakes, whereas this is hardly ever the case for children learning Spanish.

Freudenthal, Pine, Aguado-Orea & Gobet (2007) trace the differences in error frequencies back to the distributional differences in each language: the authors note that 75 % of verb-final utterances[8] in English consist of compound verbs (finite verb + dependent verb, e.g., *Can he go?*), whereas this is only the case 30 % of the time in Dutch.

German also differs from Dutch with regard to the number of utterance-final infinitives. Dutch has a progressive form that does not exist in Standard German:

(15) Wat ben je aan het doen?
what are you on it do.INF
'What are you doing?'

Furthermore, verbs such as *zitten* 'to sit', *lopen* 'to run' and *staan* 'to stand' can be used in conjunction with the infinitive to describe events happening in that moment:

(16) Zit je te spelen?
sit you to play
'Are you sitting and playing?'

Furthermore, there is a future form in Dutch that is formed with *ga* 'go'. These factors contribute to the fact that Dutch has 20 % more utterance-final infinitives than German.

Spanish differs from English in that it has object clitics:

(17) (Yo) Lo quiero.
I it want
'I want it.'

Short pronouns such as *lo* in (17) are realized in front of the finite verb so that the verb appears in final position. In English, the object follows the verb, however. Furthermore,

[8] For English, the authors only count utterances with a subject in third person singular since it is only in these cases that a morphological difference between the finite and infinitive form becomes clear.

there are a greater number of compound verb forms in the English input (70 %) than in Spanish (25 %). This is due to the higher frequency of the progressive in English and the presence of *do*-support in question formation.

The relevant differences in the distribution of infinitives are captured correctly by the proposed acquisition model, whereas alternative approaches that assume that children possess an adult grammar but use infinitives instead of the finite forms cannot explain the gradual nature of this phenomenon.

Freudenthal, Pine & Gobet (2009) could even show that input-based learning is superior to other explanations for the distribution of NPs and infinitives. They can explain why this order is often used with a modal meaning (e.g., *to want*) in German and Dutch (Ingram & Thompson 1996). In these languages, infinitives occur with modal verbs in the corresponding interrogative clauses. Alternative approaches that assume that the linguistic structures in question correspond to those of adults and only differ from them in that a modal verb is not pronounced cannot explain why not all utterances of object and verb done by children learning German and Dutch do have a modal meaning. Furthermore, the main difference to English cannot be accounted for: in English, the number of modal meanings is considerably less. Input-based models predict this exactly since English can use the dummy verb *do* to form questions:

(18) a. Did he help you?
  b. Can he help you?

If larger entities are acquired from the end of an utterance, then there would be both a modal and non-modal context for *he help you*. Since German and Dutch normally do not use the auxiliary *tun* 'do', the relevant endings of utterances are always associated with modals contexts. One can thereby explain why infinitival expressions have a modal meaning significantly more often in German and Dutch than in English.

Following this discussion of the arguments against input-based theories of acquisition, I will turn to Tomasello's pattern-based approach. According to Tomasello (2003: Section 4.2.1), a child hears a sentence such as (19) and realizes that particular slots can be filled freely (see also Dąbrowska (2001) for analogous suggestions in the framework of Cognitive Grammar).

(19) a. Do you want more juice/milk?
  b. Mommy is gone.

From these utterances, it is possible to derive so-called pivot schemata such as those in (20) into which words can then be inserted:

(20) a. more ___ → more juice/milk
  b. ___ gone → mommy/juice gone

In this stage of development (22 months), children do not generalize using these schemata, these schemata are instead construction islands and do not yet have any syntax (Tomasello et al. 1997). The ability to use previously unknown verbs with a subject and an object in an SVO order is acquired slowly between the age of three and four (Tomasello 2003: 128–129). More abstract syntactic and semantic relations only emerge with time: when confronted with multiple instantiations of the transitive construction, the child is then able to generalize:

(21) a. [$_{S}$ [$_{NP}$ The man/the woman] sees [$_{NP}$ the dog/the rabbit/it]].
b. [$_{S}$ [$_{NP}$ The man/the woman] likes [$_{NP}$ the dog/the rabbit/it]].
c. [$_{S}$ [$_{NP}$ The man/the woman] kicks [$_{NP}$ the dog/the rabbit/it]].

According to Tomasello (2003: 107), this abstraction takes the form [Sbj TrVerb Obj]. Tomasello's approach is immediately plausible since one can recognize how abstraction works: it is a generalization about reoccurring patterns. Each pattern is then assigned a semantic contribution. These generalizations can be captured in inheritance hierarchies (see page 201) (Croft 2001: 26). The problem with this kind of approach, however, is that it cannot explain the interaction between different areas of phenomena in the language: it is possible to represent simple patterns such as the use of transitive verbs in (21), but transitive verbs interact with other areas of the grammar such as negation. If one wishes to connect the construction one assumes for the negation of transitive verbs with the transitive construction, then one arrives at a problem since this is not possible in inheritance hierarchies.

(22) The woman did not kick the dog.

The problem is that the transitive construction has a particular semantic contribution but that negated transitive construction has the opposite meaning. The values of SEM features would therefore be contradictory. There are technical tricks to avoid this problem, however, since there are a vast number of these kinds of interactions between syntax and semantics, this kind of technical solution will result in something highly implausible from a cognitive perspective (Müller 2006, 2007c,b, 2010b; Müller & Wechsler 2014a). For discussion of Croft's analysis, see Section 21.4.1.

At this point, proponents of pattern-based analyses might try and argue that these kinds of problems are only the result of a poor/inadequate formalization and would rather do without a formalization (Goldberg 2009: Section 5). However, this does not help here as the problem is not the formalization itself, rather the formalization allows one to see the problem more clearly.

An alternative to an approach built entirely on inheritance is a TAG-like approach that allows one to insert syntactic material into phrasal constructions. Such a proposal was discussed in Section 10.6.3. Bergen & Chang (2005: 170) working in Embodied Construction Grammar suggest an Active-Ditransitive Construction with the form [RefExpr Verb RefExpr RefExpr], where RefExpr stands for a referential expression and the first RefExpr and the verb may be non-adjacent. In this way, it is possible to analyze (23a,b), while ruling out (23c):

(23) a. Mary tossed me a drink.
b. Mary happily tossed me a drink.
c. * Mary tossed happily me a drink.

While the compulsory adjacency of the verb and the object correctly predicts that (23c) is ruled out, the respective constraint also rules out coordinate structures such as (24):

(24) Mary tossed me a juice and Peter a water.

Part of the meaning of this sentence corresponds to what the ditransitive construction contributes to *Mary tossed Peter a water.* There is, however, a gap between *tossed* and *Peter.* Similarly, one can create examples where there is a gap between both objects of a ditransitive construction:

(25) He showed me and bought for Mary the book that was recommended in the Guardian last week.

In (25), *me* is not adjacent to *the book* …. It is not my aim here to request a coordination analysis. Coordination is a very complex phenomenon for which most theories do not have a straightforward analysis (see Section 21.6.2). Instead, I would simply like to point out that the fact that constructions can be realized discontinuously poses a problem for approaches that claim that language acquisition is exclusively pattern-based. The point is the following: in order to understand coordination data in a language, a speaker must learn that a verb which has its arguments somewhere in the sentence has a particular meaning together with these arguments. The actual pattern [Sbj V Obj1 Obj2] can, however, be interrupted in all positions. In addition to the coordination examples, there is also the possibility of moving elements out of the pattern either to the left or the right. In sum, we can say that language learners have to learn that there is a relation between functors and their arguments. This is all that is left of pattern-based approaches but this insight is also covered by the selection-based approaches that we will discuss in the following section.

A defender of pattern-based approaches could perhaps object that there is a relevant construction for (25) that combines all material. This means that one would have a construction with the form [Sbj V Obj1 Conj V PP Obj2]. It would then have to be determined experimentally or with corpus studies whether this actually makes sense. The generalization that linguists have found is that categories with the same syntactic properties can be coordinated (N, $\overline{\text{N}}$, NP, V, $\overline{\text{V}}$, VP, …). For the coordination of verbs or verbal projections, it must hold that the coordinated phrases require the same arguments:

(26) a. Er [arbeitet] und [liest viele Bücher].
he works and reads many books

b. Er [kennt und liebt] diese Schallplatte.
he knows and loves this record

c. Er [zeigt dem Jungen] und [gibt der Frau] die Punk-Rock-CD.
he shows the boy and gives the woman the punk rock CD

d. Er [liebt diese Schallplatte] und [schenkt ihr ein Buch].
he loves this record and gives her a book

In an approach containing only patterns, one would have to assume an incredibly large number of constructions and so far we are only considering coordinations that consist of exactly two conjuncts. However, the phenomenon discussed above is not only restricted to coordination of two elements. If we do not wish to abandon the distinction between competence and performance (see Chapter 15), then the number of conjuncts is not constrained at all (by the competence grammar):

(27) Er [kennt, liebt und verborgt] diese Schallplatte.
he knows loves and lends.out this record

It is therefore extremely unlikely that learners have patterns for all possible cases in their input. It is much more likely that they draw the same kind of generalizations as linguists from the data occurring in their input: words and phrases with the same syntactic properties can be coordinated. If this turns out to be true, then all that is left for pattern-based approaches is the assumption of discontinuously realized constructions and thus a dependency between parts of constructions that states that they do not have to be immediately adjacent to one another. The acquisition problem is then the same as for selection-based approaches that will be the topic of the following section: what ultimately has to be learned are dependencies between elements or valences (see Behrens (2009: 439), the author reaches the same conclusion following different considerations).

16.4 Selection-based approaches

I will call the alternative to pattern-based approaches *selection-based.* A selection-based approach has been proposed by Green (2011).

The generalizations about the pattern in (21) pertain to the valence class of the verb. In Categorial Grammar, the pattern [Sbj TrVerb Obj] corresponds to the lexical entry (s\np)/np (for the derivation of a sentence with this kind of lexical entry, see Figure 8.3 on page 239). A TAG tree for *likes* was given on page 406. Here, one can see quite clearly that lexical entries determine the structure of sentences in these models. Unlike pattern-based approaches, these analyses allow enough room for semantic embedding: the lexical entries in Categorial Grammar can be combined with adjuncts, and elementary trees in TAG also allow for adjunction to the relevant nodes.

Now, we face the question of how the jump from a pivot schema to a lexical entry with an argument structure takes place. In Tomasello's approach, there is no break between them. Pivot schemata are phrasal patterns and [Sbj TrVerb Obj] is also a phrasal pattern. Both schemata have open slots into which certain elements can be inserted. In selection-based approaches, the situation is similar: the elements that are fixed in the pivot schema are functors in the selection-based approach. Green (2011) proposes a theory of acquisition in HPSG that can do without UG. For the two-word phase, she assumes that *where's* is the head of an utterance such as (28) and that *where's* selects *Robin* as its argument.

(28) Where's Robin?

This means that, rather than assuming that there is a phrasal pattern *Where's* X? with an empty slot X for a person or thing, she assumes that there is a lexical entry *where's*, which contains the information that it needs to be combined with another constituent. What needs to be acquired is the same in each case: there is particular material that has to be combined with other material in order to yield a complete utterance.

In her article, Green shows how long-distance dependencies and the position of English auxiliaries can be acquired in later stages of development. The acquisition of grammar proceeds in a monotone fashion, that is, knowledge is added – for example, knowledge about the fact that material can be realized outside of the local context – and previous knowledge does not have to be revised. In her model, mistakes in the acquisition process are in fact mistakes in the assignment of lexical entries to valence classes. These mistakes have to be correctable.

In sum, one can say that all of Tomasello's insights can be applied directly to selection-based approaches and the problems with pattern-based approaches do not surface with selection-based approaches. It is important to point out explicitly once again here that the selection-based approach discussed here also is a construction-based approach. Constructions are just lexical and not phrasal. The important point is that, in both approaches, words and also more complex phrases are pairs of form and meaning and can be acquired as such.

In Chapter 21, we will discuss pattern-based approaches further and we will also explore areas of the grammar where phrasal patterns should be assumed.

16.5 Summary

We should take from the preceding discussion that models of language acquisition that assume that a grammar is chosen from a large set of grammars by setting binary parameters are in fact inadequate. All theories that make reference to parameters have in common that they are purely hypothetical since there is no non-trivial set of parameters that all proponents of the model equally agree on. In fact there is not even a trivial one.

In a number of experiments, Tomasello and his colleagues have shown that, in its original form, the Principles & Parameters model makes incorrect predictions and that language acquisition is much more pattern-based than assumed by proponents of P&P analyses. Syntactic competence develops starting from verb islands. Depending on the frequency of the input, certain verbal constructions can be mastered even though the same construction has not yet been acquired with less frequent verbs.

The interaction with other areas of grammar still remains problematic for pattern-based approaches: in a number of publications, it has been shown that the interaction of phenomena that one can observe in complex utterances can in fact not be explained with phrasal patterns since embedding cannot be captured in an inheritance hierarchy. This problem is not shared by selection-based approaches. All experimental results and insights of Tomasello can, however, be successfully extended to selection-based approaches.

Further reading

Meisel (1995) gives a very good overview of theories of acquisition in the Principles & Parameters model.

Adele Goldberg and Michael Tomasello are the most prominent proponents of Construction Grammar, a theory that explicitly tries to do without the assumption of innate linguistic knowledge. They published many papers and books about topics related to Construction Grammar and acquisition. The most important books probably are Goldberg (2006) and Tomasello (2003).

An overview of different theories of acquisition in German can be found in Klann-Delius (2008) an English overview is Ambridge & Lieven (2011).

17 Generative capacity and grammar formalisms

In several of the preceding chapters, the complexity hierarchy for formal languages was mentioned. The simplest languages are so-called regular languages (Type-3), they are followed by those described as context-free grammars (Type-2), then those grammars which are context-sensitive (Type-1) and finally we have unrestricted grammars (Type-0) that create recursively enumerable languages, which are the most complicated class. In creating theories, a conscious effort was made to use formal means that correspond to what one can actually observe in natural language. This led to the abandonment of unrestricted Transformational Grammar since this has generative power of Type-0 (see page 84). GPSG was deliberately designed in such a way as to be able to analyze just the context-free languages and not more. In the mid-80s, it was shown that natural languages have a higher complexity than context-free languages (Shieber 1985; Culy 1985). It is now assumed that so-called *mildly context sensitive* grammars are sufficient for analyzing natural languages. Researchers working on TAG are working on developing variants of TAG that fall into exactly this category. Similarly, it was shown for different variants of Stabler's *Minimalist Grammars* (see Section 4.6.4 and Stabler 2001, 2011b) that they have a mildly context-sensitive capacity (Michaelis 2001). Peter Hellwig's Dependency Unification Grammar is also mildly context-sensitive (Hellwig 2003: 595). LFG and HPSG, as well as Chomsky's theory in *Aspects*, fall into the class of Type-0 languages (Berwick 1982; Johnson 1988). The question at this point is whether it is an ideal goal to find a descriptive language that has exactly the same power as the object it describes. Carl Pollard (1996a) once said that it would be odd to claim that certain theories in physics were not adequate simply because they make use of tools from mathematics that are too powerful.[1] It is not the descriptive language that should constrain the theory but rather the theory contains the restrictions that must hold for the objects in question. This is the view that Chomsky (1981b: 277, 280) takes. Also, see Berwick (1982: Section 4), Kaplan & Bresnan (1982: Section 8) on LFG and Johnson (1988: Section 3.5) on the *Off-Line Parsability Constraint* in LFG and attribute-value grammars in general.

[1] If physicists required the formalism to constrain the theory:

Editor: Professor Einstein, I'm afraid we can't accept this manuscript of yours on general relativity.

Einstein: Why? Are the equations wrong?

Editor: No, but we noticed that your differential equations are expressed in the first-order language of set theory. This is a totally unconstrained formalism! Why, you could have written down ANY set of differential equations! (Pollard 1996a)

There is of course a technical reason to look for a grammar with the lowest level of complexity possible: we know that it is easier for computers to process grammars with lower complexity than more complex grammars. To get an idea about the complexity of a task, the so-called 'worst case' for the relevant computations is determined, that is, it is determined how long a program needs for an input of a certain length in the least favorable case to get a result for a grammar from a certain class. This begs the question if the worst case is actually relevant. For example, some grammars that allow discontinuous constituents perform less favorably in the worst case than normal phrase structure grammars that only allow for combinations of continuous strings (Reape 1991: Section 8). As I have shown in Müller (2004c), a parser that builds up larger units starting from words (a bottom-up parser) is far less efficient when processing a grammar assuming a verb movement analysis than is the case for a bottom-up parser that allows for discontinuous constituents. This has to do with the fact that verb traces do not contribute any phonological material and a parser cannot locate them without further machinery. It is therefore assumed that a verb trace exists in every position in the string and in most cases these traces do not contribute to an analysis of the complete input. Since the verb trace is not specified with regard to its valence information, it can be combined with any material in the sentence, which results in an enormous computational load. On the other hand, if one allows discontinuous constituents, then one can do without verb traces and the computational load is thereby reduced. In the end, the analysis using discontinuous constituents was eventually discarded for linguistic reasons (Müller 2005b,c, 2007b, 2015b), however, the investigation of the parsing behavior of both grammars is still interesting as it shows that worst case properties are not always informative.

I will discuss another example of the fact that language-specific restrictions can restrict the complexity of a grammar: Gärtner & Michaelis (2007: Section 3.2) assume that Stabler's Minimalist Grammars (see Section 4.6.4) with extensions for late adjunction and extraposition are actually more powerful than mildly context-sensitive. If one bans extraction from adjuncts (Frey & Gärtner 2002: 46) and also assumes the Shortest Move Constraint (see footnote 30 on page 160), then one arrives at a grammar that is mildly-context sensitive (Gärtner & Michaelis 2007: 178). The same is true of grammars with the Shortest Move Constraint and a constraint for extraction from specifiers.

Whether extraction takes place from a specifier or not depends on the organization of the particular grammar in question. In some grammars, all arguments are specifiers (Kratzer 1996: 120–123, also see Figure 18.4 on page 541). A ban on extraction from specifiers would imply that extraction out of arguments would be impossible. This is, of course, not true in general. Normally, subjects are treated as specifiers (also by Frey & Gärtner 2002: 44). It is often claimed that subjects are islands for extraction (see Grewendorf 1989: 35, 41; G. Müller 1996b: 220; 1998: 32, 163; Sabel 1999: 98; Fanselow 2001: 422). Several authors have noted, however, that extraction from subjects is possible in German (see Dürscheid 1989: 25; Haider 1993: 173; Pafel 1993; Fortmann 1996: 27; Suchsland 1997: 320; Vogel & Steinbach 1998: 87; Ballweg 1997: 2066; Müller 1999a: 100–101; De Kuthy 2002: 7). The following data are attested examples:

(1) a. [Von den übrigbleibenden Elementen]$_i$ scheinen [die Determinantien $\_{i}$] die
of the left.over elements seem the determinants the
wenigsten Klassifizierungsprobleme aufzuwerfen.[2]
fewest classification.problems to.throw.up
'Of the remaining elements, the determinants seem to pose the fewest problems for classification.'

b. [Von den Gefangenen]$_i$ hatte eigentlich [keine $\_{i}$] die Nacht der Bomben
of the prisoners had actually none the night of.the bombs
überleben sollen.[3]
survive should
'None of the prisoners should have actually survived the night of the bombings.'

c. [Von der HVA]$_i$ hielten sich [etwa 120 Leute $\_{i}$] dort in ihren Gebäuden
of the HVA held REFL around 120 people there in their buildings
auf.[4]
PRT
'Around 120 people from the HVA stayed there inside their buildings.'

d. [Aus dem „Englischen Theater"]$_i$ stehen [zwei Modelle $\_{i}$] in den Vitrinen.[5]
from the English theater stand two models in the cabinets
'Two models from the 'English Theater' are in the cabinets.'

e. [Aus der Fraktion]$_i$ stimmten ihm [viele $\_{i}$] zu darin, dass die
from the faction agreed him many PRT there.in that the
Kaufkraft der Bürger gepäppelt werden müsse, nicht die gute Laune
buying.power of.the citizens boosted become must not the good mood
der Wirtschaft.[6]
of.the economy
'Many of the fraction agreed with him that it is the buying power of citizens that needed to be increased, not the good spirits of the economy.'

f. [Vom Erzbischof Carl Theodor Freiherr von Dalberg]$_i$ gibt es
from archbishop Carl Theodor Freiherr from Dalberg gives it
beispielsweise [ein Bild $\_{i}$] im Stadtarchiv.[7]
for.example a picture in.the city.archives
'For example, there is a picture of archbishop Carl Theodor Freiherr of Dalberg in the city archives.'

[2] In the main text of Engel (1970: 102).
[3] Bernhard Schlink, *Der Vorleser*, Diogenes Taschenbuch 22953, Zürich: Diogenes Verlag, 1997, p. 102.
[4] Spiegel, 3/1999, p. 42.
[5] Frankfurter Rundschau, quoted from De Kuthy (2001: 52).
[6] taz, 16.10.2003, p. 5.
[7] Frankfurter Rundschau, quoted from De Kuthy (2002: 7).

g. [Gegen die wegen Ehebruchs zum Tod durch Steinigen verurteilte
against the because.of adultery to.the death by stoning sentenced
Amina Lawal]$_i$ hat gestern in Nigeria [der zweite Berufungsprozess $\_{i}$]
Amina Lawal has yesterday in Nigeria the second appeal.process
begonnen.[8]
begun
'The second appeal process began yesterday against Amina Lawal, who was sentenced to death by stoning for adultery.'

h. [Gegen diese Kahlschlagspolitik]$_i$ finden derzeit bundesweit
against this clear.cutting.politics happen at.the.moment statewide
[Proteste und Streiks $\_{i}$] statt.[9]
protests and strikes PRT
'At the moment, there are state-wide protests and strikes against this destructive politics.'

i. [Von den beiden, die hinzugestoßen sind], hat [einer $\_{i}$] eine Hacke, der
of the both that joined are has one a pickaxe the
andere einen Handkarren.[10]
other a handcart
'Of the two that joined, one had a pickaxe and the other a handcart.'

j. ein Plan, [gegen den]$_i$ sich nun [ein Proteststurm $\_{i}$] erhebt[11]
a plan against which REFL now a storm.of.protests rises
'a plan against which a storm of protests has now risen'

k. Dagegen$_i$ jedoch regt sich jetzt [Widerstand $\_{i}$]: […][12]
against however rises REFL now resistance
'Resistance to this is now rising, however:'

l. [Aus der Radprofiszene]$_i$ kennt ihn [keiner $\_{i}$] mehr.[13]
from the cycling.professional.scene knows him nobody anymore
'Nobody from the professional cycling scene acts like they know him anymore.'

m. [Über das chinesische Programm der Deutschen Welle] tobt dieser Tage
about the Chinese program of.the Deutsche Welle rages these days
[ein heftiger Streit $\_{i}$].[14]
a hefty controversy
'Recently, there has been considerable controversy about the Chinese program by the Deutsche Welle.'

[8] taz, 28.08.2003, p. 2.

[9] Streikaufruf, Universität Bremen, 03.12.2003, p. 1.

[10] Haruki Murakami, *Hard-boiled Wonderland und das Ende der Welt*, suhrkamp taschenbuch, 3197, 2000, Translation by Annelie Ortmanns and Jürgen Stalph, p. 414.

[11] taz, 30.12.2004, p. 6.

[12] taz, 02.09.2005, p. 18.

[13] taz, 04.07.2005, p. 5.

[14] taz, 21.10.2008, p. 12.

This means that a ban on extraction from specifiers cannot hold for German. As such, it cannot be true for all languages.

We have a situation that is similar to the one with discontinuous constituents: since it is not possible to integrate the ban on extraction discussed here into the grammar formalism, it is more powerful than what is required for describing natural language. However, the restrictions in actual grammars – in this case, the restrictions on extraction from specifiers in the relevant languages – ensure that the respective language-specific grammars have a mildly context-sensitive capacity.

18 Binary branching, locality, and recursion

This chapter discusses three points: section 18.1 deals with the question of whether all linguistic structures should be binary branching or not. Section 18.2 discusses the question what information should be available for selection, that is, whether governing heads can access the internal structure of selected elements or whether everything should be restricted to local selection. Finally, Section 18.3 discusses recursion and how/whether it is captured in the different grammar theories that are discussed in this book.

18.1 Binary branching

We have seen that the question of the kind of branching structures assumed has received differing treatments in various theories. Classical $\overline{\text{X}}$ theory assumes that a verb is combined with all its complements. In later variants of GB, all structures are strictly binary branching. Other frameworks do not treat the question of branching in a uniform way: there are proposals that assume binary branching structures and others that opt for flat structures.

Haegeman (1994: Section 2.5) uses learnability arguments (rate of acquisition, see Section 13.2 on this point). She discusses the example in (1) and claims that language learners have to choose one of eight structures if flat-branching structures can occur in natural language. If, on the other hand, there are only binary-branching structures, then the sentence in (1) cannot have the structures in Figure 18.1 to start with, and therefore a learner would not have to rule out the corresponding hypotheses.

(1) Mummy must leave now.

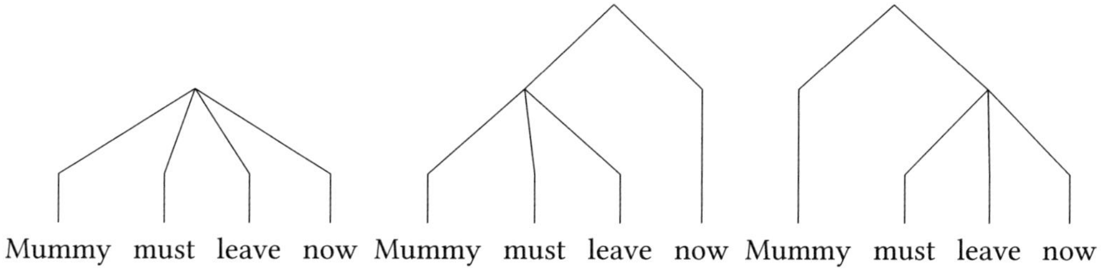

Figure 18.1: Structures with partial flat-branching

However, Haegeman (1994: 88) provides evidence for the fact that (1) has the structure in (2):

(2) [Mummy [must [leave now]]]

The relevant tests showing this include elliptical constructions, that is, the fact that it is possible to refer to the constituents in (2) with pronouns. This means that there is actually evidence for the structure of (1) that is assumed by linguists and we therefore do not have to assume that it is just hard-wired in our brains that only binary-branching structures are allowed. Haegeman (1994: 143) mentions a consequence of the binary branching hypothesis: if all structures are binary-branching, then it is not possible to straightforwardly account for sentences with ditransitive verbs in $\overline{\text{X}}$ theory. In $\overline{\text{X}}$ theory, it is assumed that a head is combined with all its complements at once (see Section 2.5). So in order to account for ditransitive verbs in $\overline{\text{X}}$ theory, an empty element (little *v*) has to be assumed (see Section 4.1.4).

It should have become clear in the discussion of the arguments for the Poverty of the Stimulus in Section 13.8 that the assumption that only binary-branching structures are possible is part of our innate linguistic knowledge is nothing more than pure speculation. Haegeman offers no kind of evidence for this assumption. As shown in the discussions of the various theories we have seen, it is possible to capture the data with flat structures. For example, it is possible to assume that, in English, the verb is combined with its complements in a flat structure (Pollard & Sag 1994: 39). There are sometimes theory-internal reasons for deciding for one kind of branching or another, but these are not always applicable to other theories. For example, Binding Theory in GB theory is formulated with reference to dominance relations in trees (Chomsky 1981a: 188). If one assumes that syntactic structure plays a crucial role for the binding of pronouns (see page 88), then it is possible to make assumptions about syntactic structure based on the observable binding relations. Binding data have, however, received a very different treatment in various theories. In LFG, constraints on f-structure are used for Binding Theory (Dalrymple 1993), whereas Binding Theory in HPSG operates on argument structure lists (valence information that are ordered in a particular way, see Section 9.6.1).

The opposite of Haegeman's position is the argumentation for flat structures put forward by Croft (2001: Section 1.6.2). In his Radical Construction Grammar FAQ, Croft observes that a phrasal construction such as the one in (3a) can be translated into a Categorial Grammar lexical entry like (3b).

(3) a. [$_{\text{VP}}$ V NP]
b. VP/NP

He claims that a disadvantage of Categorial Grammar is that it only allows for binary-branching structures and yet there exist constructions with more than two parts (p. 49). The exact reason why this is a problem is not explained, however. He even acknowledges himself that it is possible to represent constructions with more than two arguments in Categorial Grammar. For a ditransitive verb, the entry in Categorial Grammar of English would take the form of (4):

(4) ((s\np)/np)/np

If we consider the elementary trees for TAG in Figure 18.2, it becomes clear that it is equally possible to incorporate semantic information into a flat tree and a binary-branching tree. The binary-branching tree corresponds to a Categorial Grammar deriva-

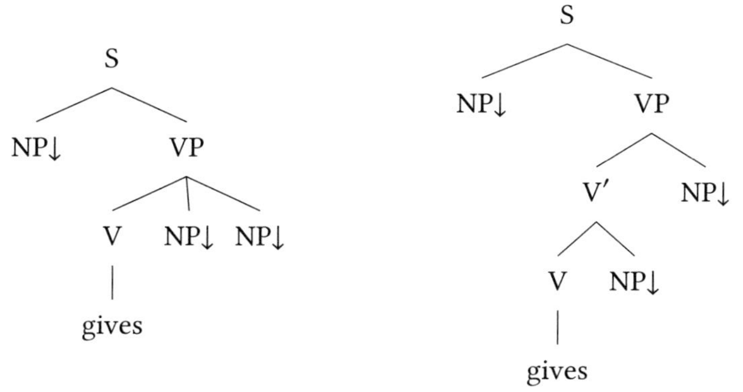

Figure 18.2: Flat and binary-branching elementary trees

tion. In both analyses in Figure 18.2, a meaning is assigned to a head that occurs with a certain number of arguments. Ultimately, the exact structure required depends on the kinds of restrictions on structures that one wishes to formulate. In this book, such restrictions are not discussed, but we have seen some theories model binding relations with reference to tree structures. Reflexive pronouns must be bound within a particular local domain inside the tree. In theories such as LFG and HPSG, these binding restrictions are formulated without any reference to trees. This means that evidence from binding data for one of the structures in Figure 18.2 (or for other tree structures) constitutes nothing more than theory-internal evidence.

Another reason to assume trees with more structure is the possibility to insert adjuncts on any node. In Chapter 9, an HPSG analysis for German that assumes binary-branching structures was proposed. With this analysis, it is possible to attach an adjunct to any node and thereby explain the free ordering of adjuncts in the middle field:

(5) a. [weil] der Mann der Frau das Buch *gestern* gab
because the man the woman the book yesterday gave
'because the man gave the woman the book yesterday'

b. [weil] der Mann der Frau *gestern* das Buch gab
because the man the woman yesterday the book gave

c. [weil] der Mann *gestern* der Frau das Buch gab
because the man yesterday the woman the book gave

d. [weil] *gestern* der Mann der Frau das Buch gab
because yesterday the man the woman the book gave

This analysis is not the only one possible, however. One could also assume an entirely flat structure where arguments and adjuncts are dominated by one node. Kasper (1994) suggests this kind of analysis in HPSG (see also Section 5.1.5 for GPSG analyses that make use of metarules for the introduction of adjuncts). Kasper requires complex relational constraints that create syntactic relations between elements in the tree and also compute the semantic contribution of the entire constituent using the meaning of both the verb and the adjuncts. The analysis with binary-branching structures is simpler than those with complex relational constraints and – in the absence of theory-external evidence for flat structures – should be preferred to the analysis with flat structures. At this point, one could object that adjuncts in English cannot occur in all positions between arguments and therefore the binary-branching Categorial Grammar analysis and the TAG analysis in Figure 18.2 are wrong. This is not correct, however, as it is the specification of adjuncts with regard to the adjunction site that is crucial in Categorial Grammar. An adverb has the category (s\np)\(s\np) or (s\np)/(s\np) and can therefore only be combined with constituents that correspond to the VP node in Figure 18.2. In the same way, an elementary tree for an adverb in TAG can only attach to the VP node (see Figure 12.3 on page 405). For the treatment of adjuncts in English, binary-branching structures therefore do not make any incorrect predictions.

18.2 Locality

The question of local accessibility of information has been treated in various ways by the theories discussed in this book. In the majority of theories, one tries to make information about the inner workings of phrases inaccessible for adjacent or higher heads, that is, *glaubt* 'believe' in (6) selects a sentential argument but it cannot "look inside" this sentential argument.

(6) a. Karl glaubt, dass morgen seine Schwester kommt.
Karl believes that tomorrow his sister comes
'Karl believes that his sister is coming tomorrow.'

b. Karl glaubt, dass seine Schwester morgen kommt.
Karl believes that his sister tomorrow comes

Thus for example, *glauben* cannot enforce that the subject of the verb has to begin with a consonant or that the complementizer has to be combined with a verbal projection starting with an adjunct. In Section 1.5, we saw that it is a good idea to classify constituents in terms of their distribution and independent of their internal structure. If we are talking about an NP box, then it is not important what this NP box actually contains. It is only of importance that a given head wants to be combined with an NP with a particular case marking. This is called *locality of selection*.

Various linguistic theories have tried to implement locality of selection. The simplest form of this implementation is shown by phrase structure grammars of the kind discussed in Chapter 2. The rule in (17) on page 59, repeated here as (7), states that a ditransitive verb can occur with three noun phrases, each with the relevant case:

(7) S → NP(Per1,Num1,nom)
NP(Per2,Num2,dat)
NP(Per3,Num3,acc)
V(Per1,Num1,ditransitive)

Since the symbols for NPs do not have any further internal structure, the verb cannot require that there has to be a relative clause in an NP, for example. The internal properties of the NP are not visible to the outside. We have already seen in the discussion in Chapter 2, however, that certain properties of phrases have to be outwardly visible. This was the information that was written on the boxes themselves. For noun phrases, at least information about person, number and case are required in order to correctly capture their relation to a head. The gender value is important in German as well, since adverbial phrases such as *einer nach dem anderen* 'one after the other' have to agree in gender with the noun they refer to (see example (12) on page 495). Apart from that, information about the length of the noun phrases is required, in order to determine their order in a clause. Heavy constituents are normally ordered after lighter ones, and are also often extraposed (cf. Behaghel's *Gesetz der wachsenden Glieder* 'Law of increasing constituents' (1909: 139; 1930: 86)).

Theories that strive to be as restrictive as possible with respect to locality therefore have to develop mechanisms that allow one to only access information that is required to explain the distribution of constituents. This is often achieved by projecting certain properties to the mother node of a phrase. In $\overline{\text{X}}$ theory, the part of speech a head belongs to is passed up to the maximal projection: if the head is an N, for example, then the maximal projection is an NP. In GPSG, HPSG and variants of CxG, there are Head Feature Principles responsible for the projection of features. Head Feature Principles ensure that an entire group of features, so-called head features, are present on the maximal projection of a head. Furthermore, every theory has to be capable of representing the fact that a constituent can lack one of its parts and this part is then realized via a long-distance dependency in another position in the clause. As previously discussed on page 293, there are languages in which complementizers inflect depending on whether their complement is missing a constituent or not. This means that this property must be somehow accessible. In GPSG, HPSG and variants of CxG, there are additional groups of features that are present at every node between a filler and a gap in a long-distance dependency. In LFG, there is f-structure instead. Using Functional Uncertainty, one can look for the position in the f-structure where a particular constituent is missing. In GB theory, movement proceeds cyclically, that is, an element is moved into the specifier of CP and can be moved from there into the next highest CP. It is assumed in GB theory that heads can look inside their arguments, at least they can see the elements in the specifier position. If complementizers can access the relevant specifier positions, then they can determine whether something is missing from an embedded phrase or not. In GB theory, there was also an analysis of case assignment in infinitive constructions in which the case-assigning verb governs into the embedded phrase and assigns case to the element in SpecIP. Figure 18.3 shows the relevant structure taken from Haegeman (1994: 170). Since the Case Principle is formulated in such a way that only finite I can assign

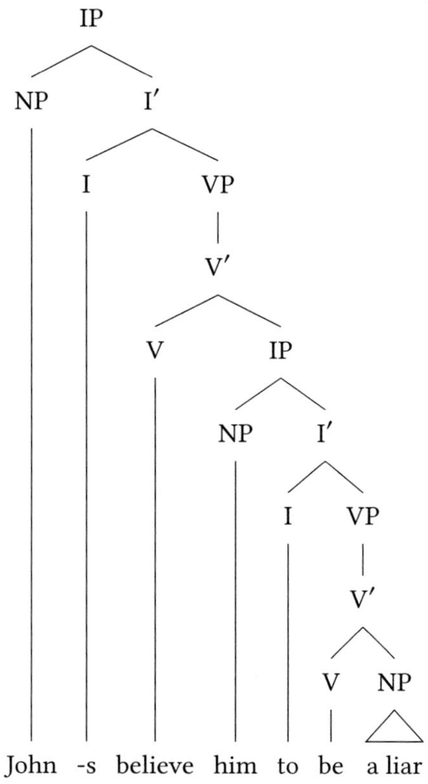

Figure 18.3: Analysis of the AcI construction with *Exceptional Case Marking*

case to the subject (cf. page 107), *him* does not receive case from I. Instead, it is assumed that the verb *believe* assigns case to the subject of the embedded infinitive.

Verbs that can assign case across phrase boundaries are referred to as ECM verbs, where ECM stands for *Exceptional Case Marking*. As the name suggests, this instance of case assignment into a phrase was viewed as an exception. In newer versions of the theory (e.g., Kratzer 1996: 120–123), all case assignment is to specifier positions. For example, the Voice head in Figure 18.4 on the following page assigns accusative to the DP in the specifier of VP. Since the Voice head governs into the VP, case assignment to a run-of-the-mill object in this theory is an instance of exceptional case assignment as well. The same is true in Adger's version of Minimalism, which was discussed in Chapter 4: Adger (2010) argues that his theory is more restrictive than LFG or HPSG since it is only one feature that can be selected by a head, whereas in LFG and HPSG complex feature bundles are selected. However, the strength of this kind of locality constraint is weakened by the operation Agree, which allows for nonlocal feature checking. As in Kratzer's proposal, case is assigned nonlocally by little *v* to the object inside the VP (see Section 4.1.5.2).

Adger discusses PP arguments of verbs like *depend* and notes that these verbs need specific PPs, that is, the form of the preposition in the PP has to be selectable. While

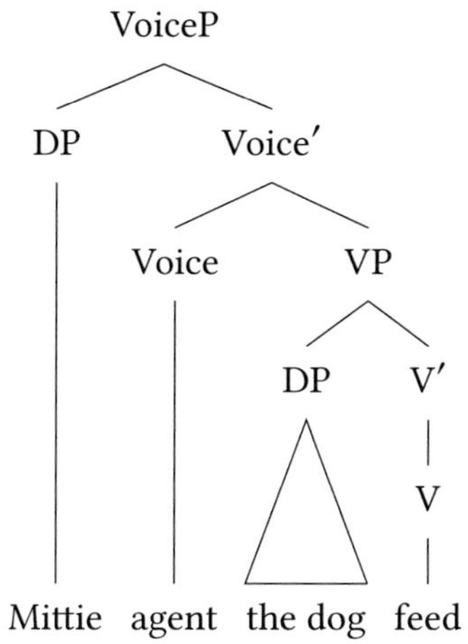

Figure 18.4: Analysis of structures with a transitive verb following Kratzer

this is trivial in Dependency Grammar, where the preposition is selected right away, the respective information is projected in theories like HPSG and is then selectable at the PP node. However, this requires that the governing verb can determine at least two properties of the selected element: its part of speech and the form of the preposition. This is not possible in Adger's system and he left this for further research. Of course it would be possible to assume an onP (a phrasal projection of *on* that has the category 'on'). Similar solutions have been proposed in Minimalist theories (see Section 4.6.1 on functional projections), but such a solution would obviously miss the generalization that all prepositional phrases have something in common, which would not be covered in a system with atomic categories that are word specific.

In theories such as LFG and HPSG, case assignment takes place locally in constructions such as those in (8):

(8) a. John believes him to be a liar.

b. Ich halte ihn für einen Lügner.
I hold him for a.ACC liar
'I take him to be a liar.'

c. Er scheint ein Lügner zu sein.
he seems a.NOM liar to be
'He seems to be a liar.'

d. Er fischt den Teich leer.
he fishes the.ACC pond empty
'He fishes (in) the pond (until it is) empty.'

Although *him*, *ihn* 'him', *er* 'he' and *den Teich* 'the pond' are not semantic arguments of the finite verbs, they are syntactic arguments (they are raised) and can therefore be assigned case locally. See Bresnan (1982a: 348–349 and Section 8.2) and Pollard & Sag

(1994: Section 3.5) for an analysis of raising in LFG and HPSG respectively. See Meurers (1999c), Przepiórkowski (1999b), and Müller (2007b: Section 17.4) for case assignment in HPSG and for its interaction with raising.

There are various phenomena that are incompatible with strict locality and require the projection of at least some information. For example, there are question tags in English that must match the subject of the clause with which they are combined:

(9) a. She is very smart, isn't she / * he?
  b. They are very smart, aren't they?

Bender & Flickinger (1999), Flickinger & Bender (2003) therefore propose making information about agreement or the referential index of the subject available on the sentence node.[1] In Sag (2007), all information about phonology, syntax and semantics of the subject is represented as the value of a feature XARG (EXTERNAL ARGUMENT). Here, *external argument* does not stand for what it does in GB theory, but should be understood in a more general sense. For example, it makes the possessive pronoun accessible on the node of the entire NP. Sag (2007) argues that this is needed to force coreference in English idioms:

(10) a. He$_i$ lost [his$_i$ / *her$_j$ marbles].
  b. They$_i$ kept/lost [their$_i$ / *our$_j$ cool].

The use of the XARG feature looks like an exact parallel to accessing the specifier position as we saw in the discussion of GB. However, Sag proposes that complements of prepositions in Polish are also made accessible by XARG since there are data suggesting that higher heads can access elements inside PPs (Przepiórkowski 1999a: Section 5.4.1.2).

In Section 10.6.2 about Sign-based Construction Grammar, we already saw that a theory that only makes the reference to one argument available on the highest node of a projection cannot provide an analysis for idioms of the kind given in (11). This is because the subject is made available with verbal heads, however, it is the object that needs to be accessed in sentences such as (11). This means that one has to be able to formulate constraints affecting larger portions of syntactic structure.

(11) a. Ich glaube, mich / # dich tritt ein Pferd.[2]
  I believes me you kicks a horse
  'I am utterly surprised.'
  b. Jonas glaubt, ihn tritt ein Pferd.[3]
  Jonas believes him kicks a horse
  'Jonas is utterly surprised.'
  c. # Jonas glaubt, dich tritt ein Pferd.
  Jonas believes you kicks a horse
  'Jonas believes that a horse kicks you.'

[1] See also Sag & Pollard (1991: 89).

[2] Richter & Sailer (2009: 311).

[3] http://www.machandel-verlag.de/der-katzenschatz.html, 06.07.2015.

Theories of grammar with extended locality domains do not have any problems with this kind of data.[4] An example for this kind of theory is TAG. In TAG, one can specify trees of exactly the right size (Abeillé 1988; Abeillé & Schabes 1989). All the material that is fixed in an idiom is simply determined in the elementary tree. Figure 18.5 shows the tree for *kick the bucket* as it is used in (12a).

(12) a. The cowboys kicked the bucket.
     b. Cowboys often kick the bucket.
     c. He kicked the proverbial bucket.

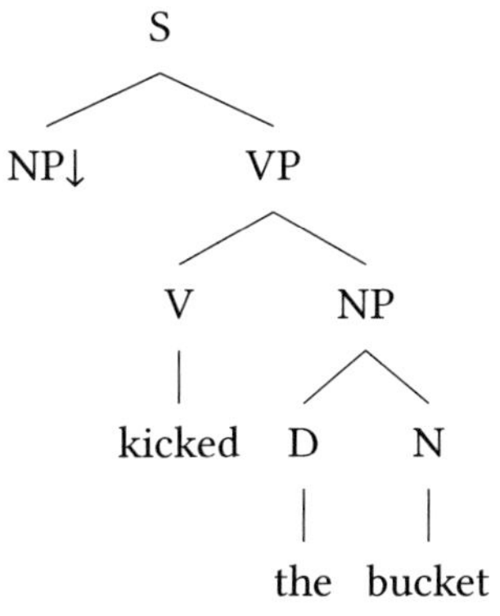

Figure 18.5: Elementary tree for *kick the bucket*

Since TAG trees can be split up by adjunction, it is possible to insert elements between the parts of an idiom as in (12b,c) and thus explain the flexibility of idioms with regard to adjunction and embedding.[5] Depending on whether the lexical rules for the passive and long-distance dependencies can be applied, the idiom can occur in the relevant variants.

---

4 Or more carefully put: they do not have any serious problems since the treatment of idioms in all their many aspects is by no means trivial (Sailer 2000).

5 Interestingly, variants of Embodied CxG are strikingly similar to TAG. The Ditransitive Construction that was discussed on page 332 allows for additional material to occur between the subject and the verb.

The problems that arise for the semantics construction are also similar. Abeillé & Schabes (1989: 9) assume that the semantics of *John kicked the proverbial bucket* is computed from the parts *John′*, *kick-the-bucket′* and *proverbial′*, that is, the added modifiers always have scope over the entire idiom. This is not adequate for all idioms (Fischer & Keil 1996):

(i) Er band ihr einen großen Bären auf.
    he tied her a big bear on
    'He pulled (a lot of) wool over her eyes.'

In the idiom in (i), *Bär* 'bear' actually means 'lie' and the adjective has to be interpreted accordingly. The relevant tree should therefore contain nodes that contribute semantic information and also say something about the composition of these features.

In the same way, when computing the semantics of noun phrases in TAG and Embodied Construction Grammar, one should bear in mind that the adjective that is combined with a discontinuous NP Construction (see page 330) or an NP tree can have narrow scope over the noun (*all alleged murderers*).

In cases where the entire idiom or parts of the idiom are fixed, it is possible to rule out adjunction to the nodes of the idiom tree. Figure 18.6 shows a pertinent example from Abeillé & Schabes (1989: 7). The ban on adjunction is marked by a subscript NA.

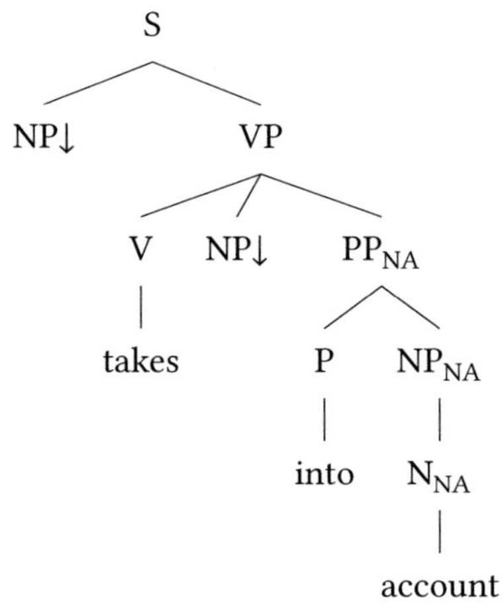

Figure 18.6: Elementary tree for *take into account*

The question that also arises for other theories is whether the efforts that have been made to enforce locality should be abandoned altogether. In our box model in Section 1.5, this would mean that all boxes were transparent. Since plastic boxes do not allow all of the light through, objects contained in multiple boxes cannot be seen as clearly as those in the topmost box (the path of Functional Uncertainty is longer). This is parallel to a suggestion made by Kay & Fillmore (1999) in CxG. Kay and Fillmore explicitly represent all the information about the internal structure of a phrase on the mother node and therefore have no locality restrictions at all in their theory. In principle, one can motivate this kind of theory in parallel to the argumentation in Chapter 17. The argument there made reference to the complexity of the grammatical formalism: the kind of complexity that the language of description has is unimportant, it is only important what one does with it. In the same way, one can say that regardless of what kind of information is in principle accessible, it is not accessed if this is not permitted. This was the approach taken by Pollard & Sag (1987: 143–145).

It is also possible to assume a world in which all the boxes contain transparent areas where it is possible to see parts of their contents. This is more or less the LFG world: the information about all levels of embedding contained in the f-structure is visible to both the inside and the outside. We have already discussed Nordlinger's (1998) LFG analysis of Wambaya on page 300. In Wambaya, words that form part of a noun phrase can be distributed throughout the clause. For example, an adjective that refers to a noun can occur in a separate position from it. Nordlinger models this by assuming that an adjective can make reference to an argument in the f-structure and then agrees with it in terms of case, number and gender. Bender (2008c) has shown that this analysis can be transferred to HPSG: instead of no longer representing an argument on the mother node after it has been combined with a head, simply marking the argument as realized allows us to keep it in the representation (Meurers 1999c; Przepiórkowski 1999b; Müller 2007b: Section 17.4). Detmar Meurers compares both of these HPSG approaches to different ways of working through a shopping list: in the standard approach taken by Pollard & Sag (1994), one tears away parts of the shopping list once the relevant item has been found. In the other case, the relevant item on the list is crossed out. At the end of the shopping trip, one ends up with a list of what has been bought as well as the items themselves.

I have proposed the crossing-out analysis for depictive predicates in German and English (Müller 2004a, 2008). Depictive predicates say something about the state of a person or object during the event expressed by a verb:

(13) a. Er sah sie nackt.[6]
he saw her naked
b. He saw her naked.

In (13), the depictive adjective can either refer to the subject or the object. However, there is a strong preference for readings where the antecedent noun precedes the depictive predicate (Lötscher 1985: 208). Figure 18.7 on the following page shows analyses for the sentences in (14):

(14) a. dass er$_i$ die Äpfel$_j$ ungewaschen$_{i/j}$ isst
that he the apples unwashed eats
'that he eats the apples unwashed'
b. dass er$_i$ ungewaschen$_{i/*j}$ die Äpfel$_j$ isst
that he unwashed the apples eats
'that he eats the apples (while he is) unwashed'

Arguments that have been realized are still represented on the upper nodes, however, they are crossed-out and thereby marked as "realized". In German, this preference for the antecedent noun can be captured by assuming a restriction that states that the antecedent noun must not yet have been realized.

It is commonly assumed for English that adjuncts are combined with a VP.

(15) a. John [[$_{VP}$ ate the apples$_i$] unwashed$_i$].
b. You can't [[$_{VP}$ give them$_i$ injections] unconscious$_i$].[7]

In approaches where the arguments of the verb are accessible at the VP node, it is possible to establish a relation between the depictive predicate and an argument although the antecedent noun is inside the VP. English differs from German in that depictives can refer to both realized (*them* in (15b)) and unrealized (*you* in (15b)) arguments.

[6] Haider (1985a: 94).
[7] Simpson (2005a: 17).

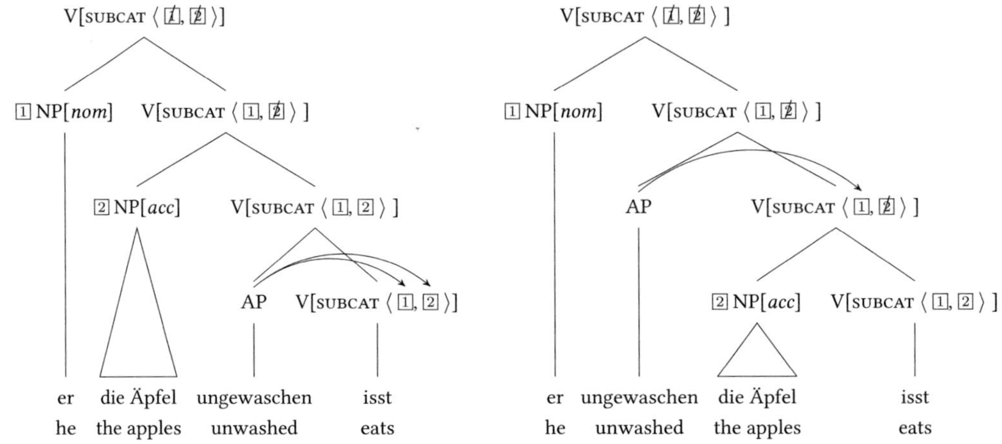

Figure 18.7: Analysis of *dass er die Äpfel ungewaschen isst* 'that he the apples unwashed eats' and *dass er ungewaschen die Äpfel isst* 'that he unwashed the apples eat'

Higginbotham (1985: 560) and Winkler (1997) have proposed corresponding non-cancellation approaches in GB theory. There are also parallel suggestions in Minimalist theories: checked features are not deleted, but instead marked as already checked (Stabler 2011b: 14). However, these features are still viewed as inaccessible.

Depending on how detailed the projected information is, it can be possible to see adjuncts and argument in embedded structures as well as their phonological, syntactic and semantic properties. In the CxG variant proposed by Kay and Fillmore, all information is available. In LFG, information about grammatical function, case and similar properties is accessible. However, the part of speech is not contained in the f-structure. If the part of speech does not stand in a one-to-one relation to grammatical function, it cannot be restricted using selection via f-structure. Nor is phonological information represented completely in the f-structure. If the analysis of idioms requires nonlocal access to phonological information or part of speech, then this has to be explicitly encoded in the f-structure (see Bresnan (1982b: 46–50) for more on idioms).

In the HPSG variant that I adopt, only information about arguments is projected. Since arguments are always represented by descriptions of type *synsem*, no information about their phonological realization is present. However, there are daughters in the structure so that it is still possible to formulate restrictions for idioms as in TAG or Construction Grammar (see Richter & Sailer (2009) for an analysis of the 'horse' example in (11a)). This may seem somewhat like overkill: although we already have the tree structure, we are still projecting information about arguments that have already been realized (unfortunately these also contain information about their arguments and so on). At this point, one could be inclined to prefer TAG or LFG since these theories only make use of one extension of locality: TAG uses trees of arbitrary or rather exactly the necessary size and LFG makes reference to a complete f-structure. However, things are not quite that simple: if one wants to create a relation to an argument when adjoining a depictive predicate in TAG, then one requires a list of possible antecedents. Syntactic factors (e.g., reference to dative vs. accusative noun phrases, to argument vs. adjuncts, coordination of verbs vs. nouns) play a role in determining the referent noun, this cannot be reduced to semantic relations. Similarly, there are considerably different restrictions for different kinds of idioms and these cannot all be formulated in terms of restrictions on f-structure since f-structure does not contain information about parts of speech.

One should bear in mind that some phenomena require reference to larger portions of structure. The majority of phenomena can be treated in terms of head domains and extended head domains, however, there are idioms that go beyond the sentence level. Every theory has to account for this somehow.

18.3 Recursion

Every theory in this book can deal with self-embedding in language as it was discussed on page 4. The example (2) is repeated here as (16):

(16) that Max thinks [that Julia knows [that Otto claims [that Karl suspects [that Richard confirms [that Friederike is laughing]]]]]

Most theories capture this directly with recursive phrase structure rules or dominance schemata. TAG is special with regard to recursion since recursion is factored out of the trees. The corresponding effects are created by an adjunction operation that allows any amount of material to be inserted into trees. It is sometimes claimed that Construction Grammar cannot capture the existence of recursive structure in natural language (e.g., Leiss 2009: 269). This impression is understandable since many analyses are extremely surface-oriented. For example, one often talks of a [Sbj TrVerb Obj] construction. However, the grammars in question also become recursive as soon as they contain a sentence embedding or relative clause construction. A sentence embedding construction could have the form [Sbj that-Verb that-S], where a that-Verb is one that can take a sentential complement and that-S stands for the respective complement. A *that*-clause can then be inserted into the that-S slot. Since this *that*-clause can also be the result of the application of this construction, the grammar is able to produce recursive structures such as those in (17):

(17) Otto claims [$_{\text{that-S}}$ that Karl suspects [$_{\text{that-S}}$ that Richard sleeps]].

In (17), both *Karl suspects that Richard sleeps* and the entire clause are instances of the [Sbj that-Verb that-S] construction. The entire clause therefore contains an embedded subpart that is licensed by the same construction as the clause itself. (17) also contains a constituent of the category *that*-S that is embedded inside of *that*-S. For more on recursion and self-embedding in Construction Grammar, see Verhagen (2010).

Similarly, every Construction Grammar that allows a noun to combine with a genitive noun phrase also allows for recursive structures. The construction in question could have the form [Det N NP[gen]] or [N NP[gen]]. The [Det N NP[gen]] construction licenses structures such as (18):

(18) [$_{NP}$ des Kragens [$_{NP}$ des Mantels [$_{NP}$ der Vorsitzenden]]]
the collar of.the coat of.the chairwoman

'the collar of the coat of the chairwoman'

Jurafsky (1996) and Bannard, Lieven & Tomasello (2009) use probabilistic context-free grammars (PCFG) for a Construction Grammar parser with a focus on psycholinguistic plausibility and modeling of acquisition. Context-free grammars have no problems with self-embedding structures like those in (18) and thus this kind of Construction Grammar itself does not encounter any problems with self-embedding.

Goldberg (1995: 192) assumes that the resultative construction for English has the following form:

(19) [SUBJ [V OBJ OBL]]

This corresponds to a complex structure as assumed for elementary trees in TAG. LTAG differs from Goldberg's approach in that every structure requires a lexical anchor, that is, for example (19), the verb would have to be fixed in LTAG. But in Goldberg's analysis, verbs can be inserted into independently existing constructions (see Section 21.1). In TAG publications, it is often emphasized that elementary trees do not contain any recursion. The entire grammar is recursive however, since additional elements can be added to the tree using adjunction and – as (17) and (18) show – insertion into substitution nodes can also create recursive structures.

19 Empty elements

This chapter deals with empty elements, I first discuss the general attitude of various research traditions towards empty elements and then show how they can be eliminated from grammars (Section 19.2). Section 19.3 discusses empty elements that have been suggested in order to facilitate semantic interpretation. Section 19.4 discusses possible motivation for empty elements with a special focus on cross-linguistic comparison and the final Section 19.5 shows that certain accounts with transformations, lexical rules, and empty elements can be translated into each other.

19.1 Views on empty elements

One point that is particularly controversial among proponents of the theories discussed in this book is the question of whether one should assume empty elements or not. The discussion of empty elements is quite old: there was already some investigation in 1961 with reference to phrase structure grammars (Bar-Hillel, Perles & Shamir 1961). The discussion of the status of empty elements has carried on ever since (see Löbner 1986; Wunderlich 1987, 1989; von Stechow 1989; Haider 1997a; Sag 2000; Bouma, Malouf & Sag 2001a; Levine & Hukari 2006; Müller 2014c; Arnold & Spencer 2015, for example). There are sometimes empirical differences between analyses that assume empty elements and those that do not (Arnold & Spencer 2015), but often this is not the case. Since empty elements often feature prominently in the argumentation for or against particular theories, I will discuss how they have been used in somewhat more detail here.

In GB theory, empty elements were assumed for traces of movement (verb movement and fronting of phrases) as well as for deleted elements in elliptical constructions. Starting with the analysis of Larson (1988), more and more empty heads have been introduced to ensure uniformity of structures and certain semantic interpretations (binding and scope, see Section 4.1.4 on little *v*). Other examples of an empty element that was introduced in order to maintain particular generalizations are the empty expletives of Coopmans (1989: 734) and Postal (2004: Chapter 1). These fill the subject position in inversion structures in English, where the position preceding the verb is occupied by a PP and not by an overt subject NP. Similarly, Grewendorf (1993: 1311) assumes that the subject position in impersonal passives and passives without subject movement is in fact occupied by an empty expletive. Also, see Newmeyer (2005: 91) and Lohnstein (2014: 180) for this assumption with regard to the passive in German. Sternefeld (2006: Section II.3.3.3) assumes that there is an empty expletive subject in impersonal passives and subjectless sentences such as (1).

(1) a. Mir graut.
me.DAT scares
'I am scared.'

b. Mich dürstet.
me.ACC is.thirsty
'I am thirsty.'

On page 161, we discussed Stabler's proposal for the analysis of sentences with intransitive verbs. Since, following Chomsky (2008: 146), the element that first merges with a head is the complement, intransitive verbs pose a problem for the theory. This problem is solved by Stabler by assuming that intransitive verbs are combined with an empty object (Veenstra 1998: 61, 124). Since these silent elements do not contribute to the meaning of an expression, we are also dealing with empty expletive pronouns.

In other theories, there are researchers that reject empty elements as well as those who assume them. In Categorial Grammar, Steedman suggests an analysis of nonlocal dependencies that does without empty elements (see Section 8.5), but as Pollard (1988) has shown, Steedman's analysis requires various kinds of type raising for NPs or a correspondingly high number of complex lexical items for relative pronouns (see Section 8.5.3). On the other hand, König (1999) uses traces. In GPSG, there is the traceless analysis of extraction by Uszkoreit (1987: 76–77) that we discussed in Section 5.4, but there is also the analysis of Gazdar, Klein, Pullum & Sag (1985: 143) that uses traces. In LFG, there are both analyses with traces (Bresnan 2001: 67) and those without (see Section 7.3 and Section 7.5). Many of the phrasal analyses in HPSG are born out of the wish to avoid empty elements (see Section 21.10). An example for this is the relative clause analysis by Sag (1997) that replaces the empty relativizer in Pollard & Sag (1994) with a corresponding phrasal rule. On the other hand we have Bender (2000) and Sag, Wasow & Bender (2003: 464), who assume a silent copula. Another attempt to eliminate empty elements from HPSG was to handle long-distance dependencies not by traces but rather in the lexicon (Bouma, Malouf & Sag 2001a). As Levine & Hukari (2006) could show, however, theories of extraction that introduce long-distance dependencies lexically have problems with the semantic interpretation of coordinate structures. For a suggestion of how to solve these problems, see Chaves (2009). There are many TAG analyses without silent elements in the lexicon (see Section 12.5 and Kroch (1987), for example), however there are variants of TAG such as that of Kallmeyer (2005: 194), where a trace is assumed for the reordering of constituents in sentences with a verbal complex. Rambow (1994: 10–11) assumes an empty head in every verb phrase (see Section 12.6.2 on V-TAG).[1] In Dependency Grammar, Mel'čuk (1988: 303; 2003: 219), Starosta (1988: 253), Eroms (2000: 471–472), Hudson (2007: Section 3.7; 2010b: 166) and Engel (2014) assume empty elements for determiners, nouns, ellipsis, imperatives, controlled infinitives, and for coordinate structures, but Groß & Osborne (2009: 73) reject empty elements (with the exception of ellipsis, Osborne 2016).

[1] Note that empty elements in TAG are slightly different from empty elements in other theories. In TAG the empty elements are usually part of elementary trees, that is, they are not lexical items that are combined with other material.

No empty elements are assumed in Construction Grammar (Michaelis & Ruppenhofer 2001: 49–50; Goldberg 2003a: 219; Goldberg 2006: 10), the related Simpler Syntax (Culicover & Jackendoff 2005) as well as in Cognitive Grammar.[2] The argumentation against empty elements runs along the following lines:

1. There is no evidence for invisible objects.

2. There is no innate linguistic knowledge.

3. Therefore, knowledge about empty elements cannot be learned, which is why they cannot be assumed as part of our grammar.

This begs the question of whether all the premises on which the conclusion is based actually hold. If we consider an elliptical construction such as (2), then it is clear that a noun has been omitted:

(2) Ich nehme den roten Ball und du den blauen.
I take the.ACC red.ACC ball and you the.ACC blue.ACC
'I'll take the red ball and you take the blue one.'

Despite there being no noun in *den blauen* 'the blue', this group of words behaves both syntactically and semantically just like a noun phrase. (2) is of course not necessarily evidence for there being empty elements, because one could simply say that *den blauen* is a noun phrase consisting only of an article and an adjective (Wunderlich 1987).

Similar to the fact that it is understood that a noun is missing in (2), speakers of English know that something is missing after *like*:

(3) Bagels, I like.

Every theory of grammar has to somehow account for these facts. It must be represented in some way that *like* in (3) behaves just like a verb phrase that is missing something. One possibility is to use traces. Bar-Hillel, Perles & Shamir (1961: 153, Lemma 4.1) have shown that it is possible to turn phrase structure grammars with empty elements into those without any. In many cases, the same techniques can be applied to the theories presented here and we will therefore discuss the point in more detail in the following section.

19.2 Eliminating empty elements from grammars

It is possible to turn a grammar with empty elements (also called *epsilon*) into a grammar without these by removing all categories that can be rewritten by an epsilon in every rule that uses such categories and then add the respective rules without the empty elements to the grammar. The following example has an epsilon rule for np. One therefore has to replace all rules containing the symbol np with new rules without this np symbol. (5) shows the result of this conversion of the grammar in (4):

[2] However, Fillmore (1988: 51) did not rule them out.

(4) $\overline{\text{v}} \rightarrow$ np, v
$\overline{\text{v}} \rightarrow$ np, pp, v
np $\rightarrow \epsilon$

(5) $\overline{\text{v}} \rightarrow$ np, v
$\overline{\text{v}} \rightarrow$ v
$\overline{\text{v}} \rightarrow$ np, pp, v
$\overline{\text{v}} \rightarrow$ pp, v

This can also lead to cases where all elements on the right-hand side of a rule are removed. Thus, what one has done is actually create a new empty category and then one has to apply the respective replacement processes again. We will see an example of this in a moment. Looking at the pair of grammars in (4)–(5), it is clear that the number of rules has increased in (5) compared to (4) despite the grammars licensing the same sequences of symbols. The fact that an NP argument can be omitted is not expressed directly in (5) but instead is implicitly contained in two rules.

If one applies this procedure to the HPSG grammar in Chapter 9, then the trace does not have a specific category such as NP. The trace simply has to be compatible with a non-head daughter. As the examples in (6) show, adjuncts, arguments and parts of verbal complexes can be extracted.

(6) a. Er_i liest t_i die Berichte.
he reads the reports

b. Oft_i liest er die Berichte t_i nicht.
often reads he the reports not
'Often, he does not read the reports.'

c. Lesen_i wird er die Berichte t_i müssen.
read will he the reports must
'He will have to read the reports.'

The relevant elements are combined with their head in a specific schema (Head-Argument Schema, Head-Adjunct Schema, Predicate Complex Schema). See Chapter 9 for the first two schemata; the Predicate Complex Schema is motivated in detail in Müller (2002a: Chapter 2; 2007b: Chapter 15). If one wishes to do without traces, then one needs further additional schemata for the fronting of adjuncts, of arguments and of parts of predicate complexes. The combination of a head with a trace is given in Figure 19.1 on the following page. The trace-less analysis is shown in Figure 19.2 on the following page. In Figure 19.1, the element in the SUBCAT list of *kennen* is identified with the SYNSEM value of the trace [4]. The lexical entry of the trace prescribes that the LOCAL value of the trace should be identical to the element in the INHER|SLASH list.

The Non-Local Feature Principle (page 291) ensures that the SLASH information is present on the mother node. Since an argument position gets saturated in Head-Argument structures, the accusative object is no longer contained in the SUBCAT list of the mother node.

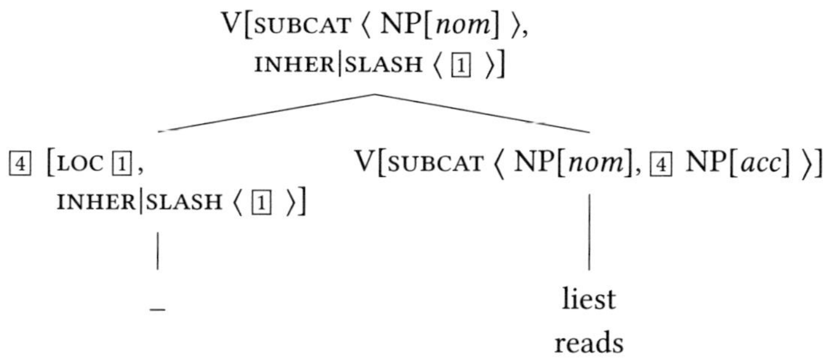

Figure 19.1: Introduction of information about long-distance dependencies with a trace

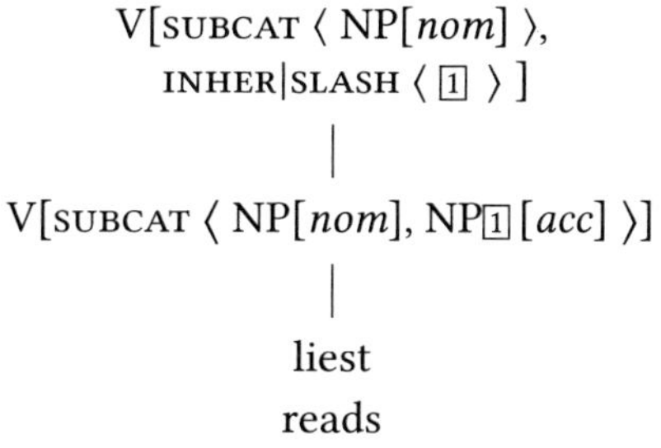

Figure 19.2: Introduction of information about long-distance dependencies using a unary projection

Figure 19.2 shows the parallel trace-less structure. The effect that one gets by combining a trace in argument position in Head-Argument structures is represented directly on the mother node in Figure 19.2: the LOCAL value of the accusative object was identified with the element in INHER|SLASH on the mother node and the accusative object does not occur in the valence list any more.

The grammar presented in Chapter 9 contains another empty element: a verb trace. This would then also have to be eliminated.

(7) a. Er$_i$ liest$_j$ t$_i$ die Berichte t$_j$.
he reads the reports

b. Oft$_i$ liest$_j$ er die Berichte t$_i$ nicht t$_j$.
often reads he the reports not
'Often, he does not read the reports.'

c. Lesen$_i$ wird$_j$ er die Berichte t$_i$ müssen t$_j$.
read will he the reports must
'He will have to read the reports.'

Figure 19.3 on the next page shows the combination of a verb trace with an accusative object. The verb trace is specified such that the DSL value is identical to the LOCAL value of

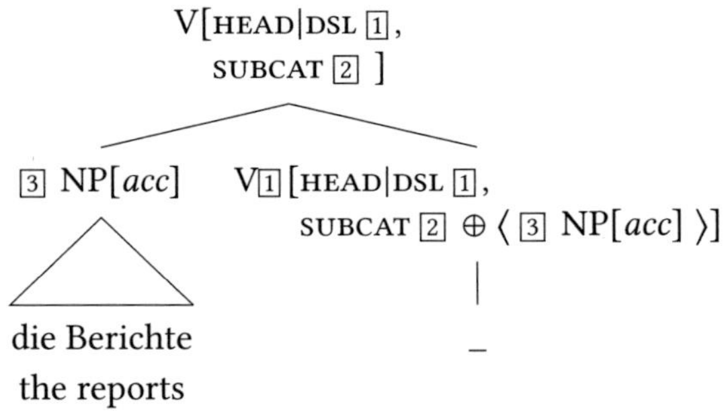

Figure 19.3: Analysis of verb position with verb trace

the trace (see p. 285). Since DSL is a head feature, the corresponding value is also present on the mother node. Figure 19.4 shows the structures that we get by omitting the empty node. This structure may look odd at first sight since a noun phrase is projected to a

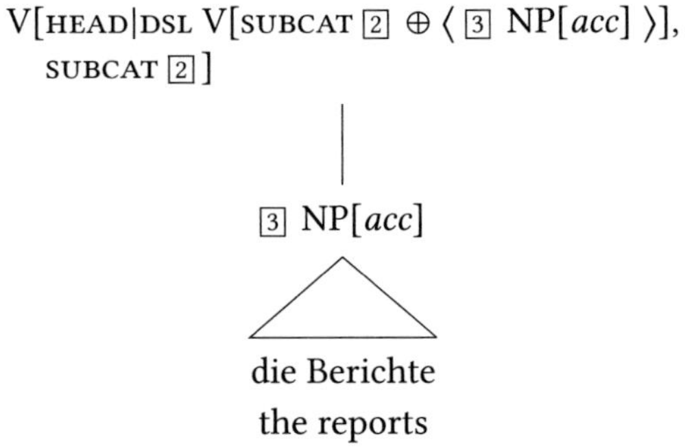

Figure 19.4: Analysis of verb position using a unary projection

verb (see page 227 for similar verb-less structures in LFG). The information about the fact that a verb is missing in the structure is equally contained in this structure as in the structure with the verb trace. It is the DSL value that is decisive for the contexts in which the structure in Figure 19.4 can appear. This is identical to the value in Figure 19.3 and contains the information that a verb that requires an accusative object is missing in the structure in question. Until now, we have seen that extraction traces can be removed from the grammar by stipulating three additional rules. Similarly, three new rules are needed for the verb trace. Unfortunately, it does not stop here as the traces for extraction and head movement can also interact. For example, the NP in the tree in Figure 19.4 could be an extraction trace. Therefore, the combination of traces can result in more empty elements that then also have to be eliminated. Since we have three schemata, we will have three new empty elements if we combine the non-head daughter with an extraction trace and the head daughter with a verb trace. (8) shows these cases:

(8) a. Er$_i$ [schläft$_j$ t$_i$ t$_j$]. (Extraction trace (argument) + verb trace)
he sleeps
'He is sleeping.'

b. Jetzt$_i$ [schlaf$_j$ t$_i$ t$_j$]! (Extraction trace (adjunct) + verb trace)
now sleep
'Go to sleep now!'

c. Geschlafen$_i$ [wird$_j$ t$_i$ t$_j$]! (Extraction trace (complex) + verb trace)
slept is
'Now is time to sleep!'

These three new traces can occur as non-head daughters in the Head-Argument Schema and thus one would require three new schemata for Head-Argument structures. Using these schemata, it then becomes possible to analyze the sentences in (8).

Six further schemata are required for the examples in (9) and (10) since the three new traces can each occur as heads in Head-Argument structures (9) and Head-Adjunct structures (10):

(9) a. Den Aufsatz$_i$ liest$_j$ [er t$_i$ t$_j$].
the essay reads he
'He is reading the essay.'

b. Oft$_i$ liest$_j$ er [ihn t$_i$ t$_j$].
often reads he it
'He often reads it.'

c. Lesen$_i$ wird$_j$ er [ihn t$_i$ t$_j$].
read will he it
'He will read it.'

(10) a. Den Aufsatz$_i$ liest$_j$ er [nicht t$_i$ t$_j$].
the essay reads he not
'He isn't reading the essay.'

b. Oft$_i$ liest$_j$ er ihn [nicht t$_i$ t$_j$].
often reads he it not
'He often doesn't read it'

c. Lesen$_i$ wird$_j$ er ihn [nicht t$_i$ t$_j$].
reads will he it not
'He won't read it.'

Eliminating two empty elements therefore comes at the price of twelve new rules. These rules are not particularly transparent and it is not immediately obvious why the mother node describes a linguistic object that follows general grammatical laws. For example, there are no heads in the structures following the pattern in Figure 19.4. Since there is no empirical difference between the theoretical variant with twelve additional schemata and the variant with two empty elements, one should prefer the theory that makes fewer assumptions (Occam's Razor) and that is the theory with two empty elements.

One might think that the problem discussed here is just a problem specific to HPSG not shared by trace-less analyses such as the LFG approach that was discussed in Section 7.5. If we take a closer look at the rule proposed by Dalrymple (2006: Section 2.2), we see that the situation in LFG grammars is entirely parallel. The brackets around the category symbols mark their optionality. The asterisk following the PP means that any number of PPs (zero or more) can occur in this position.

(11) V′ → (V) (NP) PP*

This means that (11) is a shorthand for rules such as those in (12):

(12) a. V′ → V
  b. V′ → V NP
  c. V′ → V NP PP
  d. V′ → V NP PP PP
  e. …
  f. V′ → NP
  g. V′ → NP PP
  h. V′ → NP PP PP
  i. …

Since all the elements on the right-hand side of the rule are optional, the rule in (11) also stands for (13):

(13) V′ → ϵ

Thus, one does in fact have an empty element in the grammar although the empty element is not explicitly listed in the lexicon. This follows from the optionality of all elements on the right-hand side of a rule. The rule in (12f) corresponds to the schema licensed by the structure in Figure 19.4. In the licensed LFG structure, there is also no head present. Furthermore, one has a large number of rules that correspond to exactly the schemata that we get when we eliminate empty elements from an HPSG grammar. This fact is, however, hidden in the representational format of the LFG rules. The rule schemata of LFG allow for handy abbreviations of sometimes huge sets of rules (even infinite sets when using '*').

Pollard (1988) has shown that Steedman's trace-less analysis of long-distance dependencies is not without its problems. As discussed in Section 8.5.3, a vast number of recategorization rules or lexical entries for relative pronouns are required.

19.3 Empty elements and semantic interpretation

In this section, I discuss an analysis that assumes empty elements in order to allow for different readings of particular sentences. I then show how one can use so-called underspecification approaches to do without empty elements.

Sentences such as (14) are interesting since they have multiple readings (see Dowty 1979: Section 5.6) and it is not obvious how these can be derived.

(14) dass Max alle Fenster wieder öffnete
that Max all windows again opened
'that Max opened all the windows again'

There is a difference between a repetitive and a restitutive reading: for the repetitive reading of (14), Max has to have opened every window at least once before, whereas the restitutive reading only requires that all windows were open at some point, that is, they could have been opened by someone else.

These different readings are explained by decomposing the predicate *open′* into at least two sub-predicates. Egg (1999) suggests the decomposition into CAUSE and *open′*:

(15) CAUSE(x, *open′*(y))

This means that there is a CAUSE operator that has scope over the relation *open′*. Using this kind of decomposition, it is possible to capture the varying scope of *wieder* 'again': in one of the readings, *wieder* scopes over CAUSE and it scopes over *open′* but below CAUSE in the other. If we assume that *öffnen* has the meaning in (15), then we still have to explain how the adverb can modify elements of a word's meaning, that is, how *wieder* 'again' can refer to *open′*. Von Stechow (1996: 93) developed the analysis in Figure 19.5 on the next page. AgrS and AgrO are functional heads proposed for subject and object agreement in languages like Basque and have been adopted for German (see Section 4.6). Noun phrases have to be moved from the VoiceP into the specifier position of the AgrS and AgrO heads in order to receive case. T stands for Tense and corresponds to Infl in the GB theory (see Section 3.1.5 and Section 4.1.5). What is important is that there is the Voice head and the separate representation of *offen* 'open' as the head of its own phrase. In the figure, everything below Voice′ corresponds to the verb *öffnen*. By assuming a separate Voice head that contributes causative meaning, it becomes possible to derive both readings in syntax: in the reading with narrow scope of *wieder* 'again', the adverb is adjoined to the XP and has scope over open(x). In the reading with wide scope, the adverb attaches to VoiceP or some higher phrase and therefore has scope over CAUSE(BECOME(open(x))).

Jäger & Blutner (2003) point out that this analysis predicts that sentences such as (16) only have the repetitive reading, that is, the reading where *wieder* 'again' has scope over CAUSE.

(16) dass Max wieder alle Fenster öffnete
that Max again all windows opened

This is because *wieder* precedes *alle Fenster* and therefore all heads that are inside VoiceP. Thus, *wieder* can only be combined with AgrOP or higher phrases and therefore has (too) wide scope. (16) does permit a restitutive reading, however: all windows were open at an earlier point in time and Max reestablishes this state.

Egg (1999) develops an analysis for these *wieder* cases using Constraint Language for Lambda-Structures (CLLS). CLLS is an underspecification formalism, that is, no logical formulae are given but instead expressions that describe logical formulae. Using this kind

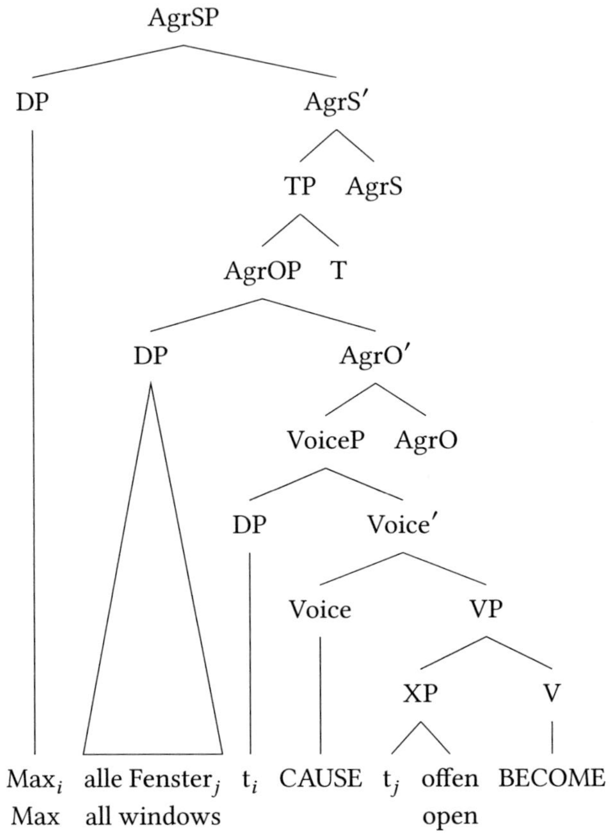

Figure 19.5: Decomposition in syntactic structures

of expressions, it is possible to leave scope relations underspecified. I have already mentioned Minimal Recursion Semantics (MRS) (Copestake, Flickinger, Pollard & Sag 2005) in several chapters of this book. As well as CLLS, MRS together with Underspecified Discourse Representation Theory (Reyle 1993; Frank & Reyle 1995) and Hole Semantics (Bos 1996; Blackburn & Bos 2005) all belong to the class of underspecification formalisms. See Baldridge & Kruijff (2002) for an underspecification analysis in Categorial Grammar and Nerbonne (1993) for an early underspecification analysis in HPSG. In the following, I will reproduce Egg's analysis in an MRS-like notation.

Before we turn to (14) and (16), let us consider the simpler sentence in (17):

(17) dass Max alle Fenster öffnete
that Max all windows opened
'that Max opened all the windows'

This sentence can mean that in a particular situation, it is true of all windows that Max opened them. A less readily accessible reading is the one in which Max causes all of the windows to be open. It is possible to force this reading if one rules out the first reading through contextual information (Egg 1999):

(18) Erst war nur die Hälfte der Fenster im Bus auf, aber dann öffnete Max
first was only the half of.the windows in.the bus open but then opened Max
alle Fenster.
all windows
'At first, only half of the windows in the bus were open, but then Max opened all of the windows.'

Both readings under discussion here differ with regard to the scope of the universal quantifier. The reading where Max opens all the windows himself corresponds to wide scope in (19a). The reading where some windows could have already been open corresponds to (19b):

(19) a. $\forall$ x *window′*(x) → CAUSE(*max′*, *open′*(x))
b. CAUSE(*max′*, $\forall$ x *window′*(x) → *open′*(x))

Using underspecification, both of these readings can be represented in one dominance graph such as the one given in Figure 19.6. Each relation in Figure 19.6 has a name that

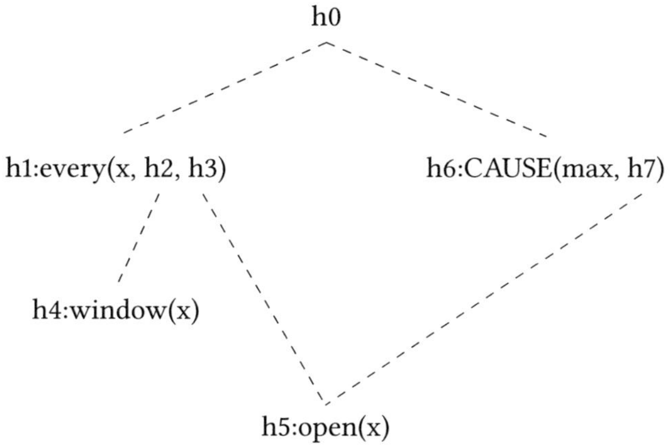

Figure 19.6: Dominance graph for *Max alle Fenster öffnete*

one can use to refer to the relation or "grasp" it. These names are referred to as *handle*. The dominance graph states that *h*0 dominates both *h*1 and *h*6 and that *h*2 dominates *h*4, *h*3 dominates *h*5, and *h*7 dominates *h*5. The exact scopal relations are underspecified: the universal quantifier can have scope over CAUSE or CAUSE can have scope over the universal quantifier. Figures 19.7 and 19.8 show the variants of the graph with resolved scope. The underspecified graph in Figure 19.6 does not say anything about the relation between *h*3 and *h*6. The only thing it says is that *h*3 somehow has to dominate *h*5. In Figure 19.7 every (*h*3) dominates CAUSE (*h*6) and CAUSE dominates open (*h*5). So, *every′* dominates *open′* indirectly. In Figure 19.8, CAUSE dominates *every′* and *every′*

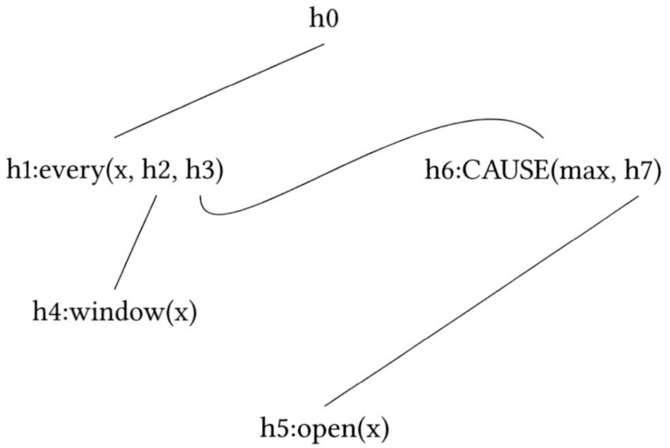

Figure 19.7: Dominance graph for the reading ∀ x window(x) → CAUSE(max,open(x)).

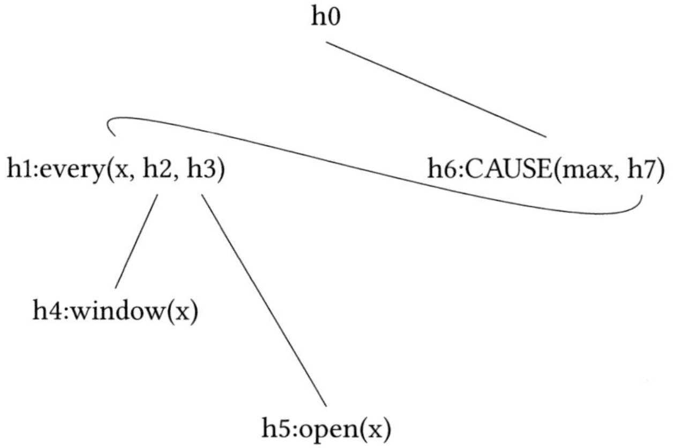

Figure 19.8: Graph for te reading CAUSE(max, ∀ x window(x) → open(x)).

dominates *open′*. Again the constraints of Figure 19.6 are fulfilled, but *h*7 dominates *h*5 only indirectly.

The fact that the quantifier dominates *h*4 is determined by the lexical entry of the quantifier. The fact that the quantifier dominates *h*5 does not have to be made explicit in the analysis since the quantifier binds a variable in the relation belonging to *h*5, namely x. The dominance relation between *h*7 and *h*5 is always determined in the lexicon since CAUSE and *open′* both belong to the semantic contribution of a single lexical entry.

The exact syntactic theory that one adopts for this analysis is, in the end, not of great importance. I have chosen HPSG here. As Figure 19.9 on the following page shows, the analysis of *alle Fenster öffnet* contains a simple structure with a verb and an object. This structure does not differ from the one that would be assumed for *alle Kinder kennt* 'all children know', involving the semantically simplex verb *kennen* 'to know'. The only

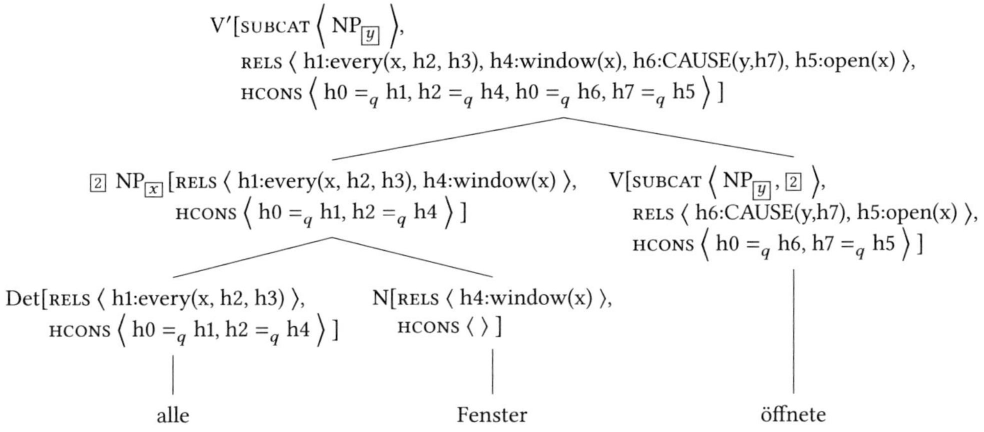

Figure 19.9: MRS analysis of *alle Fenster öffnete*

difference comes from the meaning of the individual words involved. As shown in Section 9.1.6, relations between individual words are passed on upwards. The same happens with scopal restrictions. These are also represented in lists. HCONS stands for *handle constraints.* $=_q$ in h0 $=_q$ h6 stand for the equality *modulo* quantifier scope.

Egg lists the following readings for the sentence in (16) – repeated here as (20):

(20) dass Max wieder alle Fenster öffnete
that Max again all windows opened
'that Max opened all the windows again'

1. Max opened every window and he had already done that at least once for each window (*again*′(∀(CAUSE(open))); repetitive)
2. Max caused every window to be open and he had done that at least once before (*again*′(CAUSE(∀(open))); repetitive)
3. At some earlier point in time, all windows were simultaneously open and Max re-established this state (CAUSE(*again*′(∀(open))); restitutive)

These readings correspond to the dominance graph in Figure 19.10 on the following page. Figure 19.11 on the next page shows the graph for (14) – repeated here as (21):

(21) dass Max alle Fenster wieder öffnete
that Max all windows again opened

To derive these dominance graphs from the ones without *wieder* 'again', all one has to do is add the expression h8:again(h9) and the dominance requirements that demand that *h*9 dominates quantifiers occurring to the right of *wieder* and that it is dominated by quantifiers to the left of *wieder*.

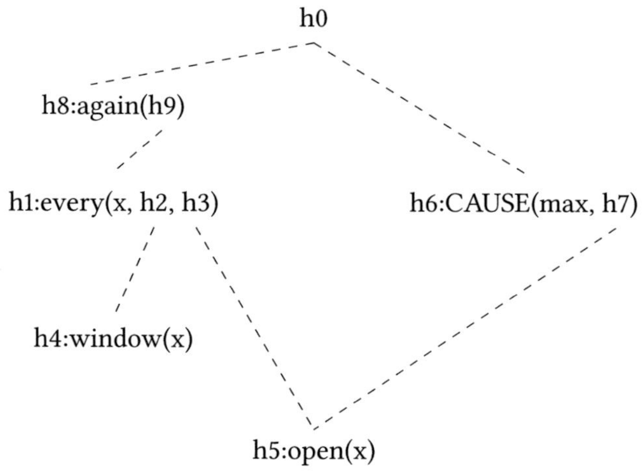

Figure 19.10: Dominance graph for *Max wieder alle Fenster öffnete* 'that Max opened all the windows again'

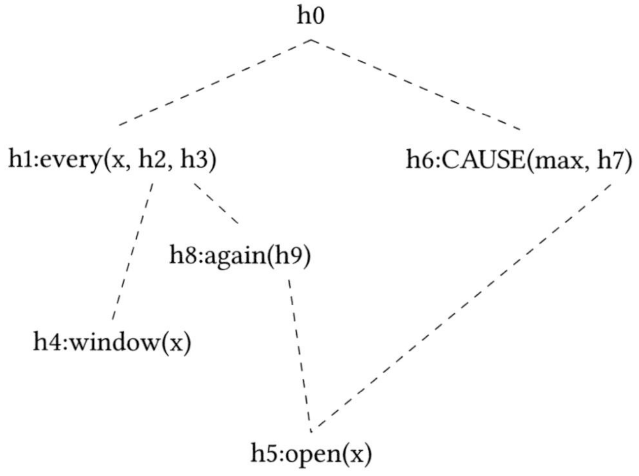

Figure 19.11: Dominance graph for *Max alle Fenster wieder öffnete* 'that Max opened all the windows again'

It is therefore unproblematic to derive the relevant readings for modification by *wieder* without empty elements for CAUSE and BECOME. The meaning of the word *öffnen* is decomposed in a similar way but the decomposed meaning is assigned to a single element, the verb. By underspecification of the scopal relations in the lexicon, the relevant readings can then be derived.

19.4 Evidence for empty elements

As previously discussed, grammarians agree that both linguists and speakers notice when there is a constituent missing from a string of words. For cases where it can be shown that analyses with or without traces are indistinguishable empirically, then one can assume empty elements. Nevertheless, the learnability argument put forward by Construction Grammarians has some validity: if one assumes that there is no or little innate linguistic knowledge, then it is not possible to motivate empty elements with data from other languages. This means that just because Basque shows object agreement, this does not mean that one can assume an empty head for object agreement (AgrO) in a grammar of German as for instance von Stechow (1996) and Meinunger (2000) do. Since there is no object agreement in German, there would be no way for the child to learn the fact that there is an AgrO head. Knowledge about AgrO must therefore be innate. Since the assumption of innate linguistic knowledge is controversial (see Chapter 13), any theory that uses cross-linguistic data to motivate the use of empty elements is on shaky ground.

Cross-linguistic considerations can only be drawn upon if there are no empirical differences between multiple alternative analyses compatible and motivated by the language under consideration. In this case, one should follow Occam's Razor and choose the analysis which is compatible with analyses of other languages (see Müller 2015a and Chapter 22.2).

19.5 Transformations, lexical rules, and empty elements

In the discussion of the passive in the framework of TAG, it became clear that lexical rules correspond to particular transformations, namely those which have some relation to a lexical item (lexically governed transformations, Dowty 1978; for the discussion of transformations and lexical rules, see Bresnan (1978) and Bresnan & Kaplan (1982)). In the respective variants of TAG, lexical rules establish a relation between a lexical item for an active tree with a lexical item of a passive tree. Both the active and passive tree can be extended by adjunction.

In theories such as Categorial Grammar, the situation is similar: since the direction in which a functor expects to find its argument is fixed for languages such as English, the lexical item stands for an entire tree. Only the attachment of adjuncts is not yet specified in lexical items. The positions in the tree where the adjuncts can occur depend on the properties of the adjuncts. In Section 8.4, we have seen suggestions for treatments of languages with free constituent order. If the direction of combination is not fixed in the lexicon, then the lexical item can occur in a number of trees. If we compare lexical rules that can be applied to this kind of lexical items with transformations, we see that lexical rules create relations between different sets of trees.

In HPSG analyses, this works in a similar way: lexical rules relate lexical items with differing valence properties to each other. In HPSG grammars of English, there is normally a schema that licenses a VP containing the verb and all its complements as well as a schema that connects the subject to the VP (Pollard & Sag 1994: 39). In the lexical items for finite verbs, it is already determined what the tree will look like in the end. As in Categorial Grammar, adjuncts in HPSG can be combined with various intermediate projections. Depending on the dominance schemata used in a particular grammar, the lexical item will determine the constituent structure in which it can occur or allow for multiple structures. In the grammar of German proposed in Chapter 9, it is possible to analyze six different sequences with a lexical item for a ditransitive verb, that is, the lexical item can – putting adjuncts aside – occur in six different structures with verb-final order. Two sequences can be analyzed with the passive lexical item, which only has two arguments. As in Categorial Grammar, sets of licensed structures are related to other sets of licensed structures. In HPSG theorizing and also in Construction Grammar, there have been attempts to replace lexical rules with other mechanisms since their "status is dubious and their interaction with other analyses is controversial" (Bouma, Malouf & Sag 2001a: 19). Bouma et al. (2001a) propose an analysis for extraction that, rather than connecting lexical items with differing valence lists, establishes a relation between a subset of a particular list in a lexical item and another list in the same lexical item. The results of the two alternative analyses are shown in (22) and (23), respectively:

(22) a. $\begin{bmatrix} \textsc{subcat} & \langle \text{NP}[\textit{nom}], \text{NP}[\textit{acc}] \rangle \\ \textsc{slash} & \langle\rangle \end{bmatrix}$

b. $\begin{bmatrix} \textsc{subcat} & \langle \text{NP}[\textit{nom}] \rangle \\ \textsc{slash} & \langle \text{NP}[\textit{acc}] \rangle \end{bmatrix}$

In (22), (22a) is the basic entry and (22b) is related to (22a) via a lexical rule. The alternative analysis would only involve specifying the appropriate value of the ARG-ST feature[3] and the SUBCAT and SLASH value is then derived from the ARG-ST value using the relevant constraints. (23) shows two of the licensed lexical items.

(23) a. $\begin{bmatrix} \textsc{arg-st} & \langle \text{NP}[\textit{nom}], \text{NP}[\textit{acc}] \rangle \\ \textsc{subcat} & \langle \text{NP}[\textit{nom}], \text{NP}[\textit{acc}] \rangle \\ \textsc{slash} & \langle\rangle \end{bmatrix}$

b. $\begin{bmatrix} \textsc{arg-st} & \langle \text{NP}[\textit{nom}], \text{NP}[\textit{acc}] \rangle \\ \textsc{subcat} & \langle \text{NP}[\textit{nom}] \rangle \\ \textsc{slash} & \langle \text{NP}[\textit{acc}] \rangle \end{bmatrix}$

[3] ARG-ST stands for *Argument Structure*. The value of ARG-ST is a list containing all the arguments of a head. For more on ARG-ST, see Section 9.6.1.

If we want to eliminate lexical rules entirely in this way, then we would require an additional feature for each change.[4] Since there are many interacting valence-changing processes, things only work out with the stipulation of a large number of auxiliary features. The consequences of assuming such analyses have been discussed in detail in Müller (2007b: Section 7.5.2.2). The problems that arise are parallel for inheritance-based approaches for argument structure-changing processes: they also require auxiliary features since it is not possible to model embedding and multiple changes of valence information with inheritance. See Section 10.2.

Furthermore, the claim that the status of lexical rules is dubious must be rejected: there are worked-out formalizations of lexical rules (Meurers 2001; Copestake & Briscoe 1992; Lascarides & Copestake 1999) and their interaction with other analyses is not controversial. Most HPSG implementations make use of lexical rules and the interaction of a number of rules and constraints can be easily verified by experiments with implemented fragments.

Jackendoff (1975) presents two possible conceptions of lexical rules: in one variant, the lexicon contains all words in a given language and there are just redundancy rules saying something about how certain properties of lexical entries behave with regard to properties of other lexical entries. For example, *les-* 'read-' and *lesbar* 'readable' would both have equal status in the lexicon. In the other way of thinking of lexical rules, there are a few basic lexical entries and the others are derived from these using lexical rules. The stem *les-* 'read-' would be the basic entry and *lesbar* would be derived from it. In HPSG, the second of the two variants is more often assumed. This is equivalent to the assumption of unary rules. In Figure 9.8 on page 281, this has been shown accordingly: the verb *kennt* 'knows' is mapped by a lexical rule to a verb that selects the projection of an empty verbal head. With this conception of lexical rules, it is possible to remove lexical rules from the grammar by assuming binary-branching structures with an empty head rather than unary rules. For example, in HPSG analyses of resultative constructions such as (24), lexical rules have been proposed (Verspoor 1997; Wechsler 1997; Wechsler & Noh 2001; Müller 2002a: Chapter 5).

(24) [dass] Peter den Teich leer fischt
that Peter the pond empty fishes
'that Peter fishes the pond empty'

In my own analysis, a lexical rule connects a verb used intransitively to a verb that selects an accusative object and a predicate. Figure 19.12 on the following page shows the corresponding tree. If we consider what (24) means, then we notice that the fishing act causes the pond to become empty. This causation is not contained in any of the basic lexical items for the words in (24). In order for this information to be present in the semantic representation of the entire expression, it has to be added by means of a lexical rule. The lexical rule says: if a verb is used with an additional predicate and accusative object, then the entire construction has a causative meaning.

[4] Alternatively, one could assume a very complex relation that connects ARG-ST and SUBCAT. But this would then have to deliver the result of an interaction of a number of phenomena and the interaction of these phenomena would not be captured in a transparent way.

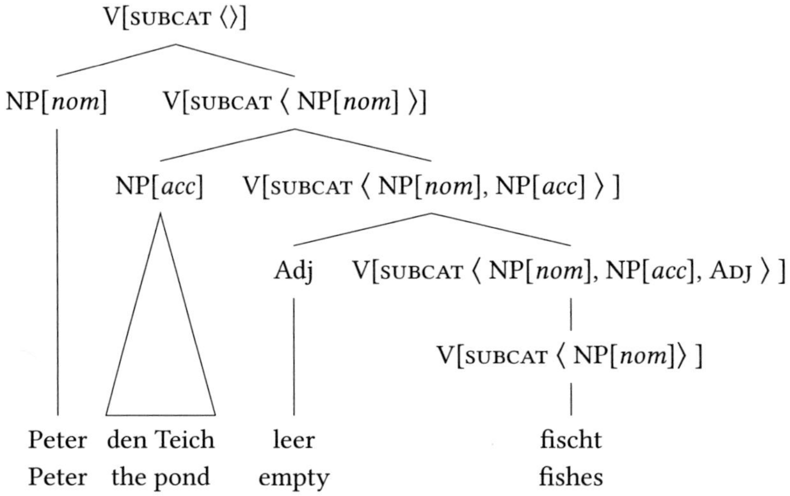

Figure 19.12: Analysis of the resultative construction with a lexical rule

Figure 19.13 on the following page shows how a lexical rule can be replaced by an empty head. The empty head requires the intransitive verb and additionally an adjective, an accusative object and a subject. The subject of *fischt* 'fishes' must of course be identical to the subject that is selected by the combination of *fischt* and the empty head. This is not shown in the figure. It is possible, however, to establish this identity (see Hinrichs & Nakazawa 1994). The causative semantics is contributed by the empty head in this analysis. The trick that is being implemented here is exactly what was done in Section 19.2, just in the opposite direction: in the previous section, binary-branching structures with an empty daughter were replaced by unary-branching structures. In this section, we have replaced unary-branching structures with binary-branching structures with an empty daughter.[5]

We have therefore seen that certain transformations can be replaced by lexical rules and also that lexical rules can be replaced by empty heads. The following chapter deals with the question of whether phenomena like extraction, scrambling, and passive should be described with the same tool as in GB/Minimalism or with different tools as in LFG and HPSG.

[5] Here, we are discussing lexical rules, but this transformation trick can also be applied to other unary rules. Semanticists often use such rules for type shifting. For example, a rule that turns a referential NP such as *a trickster* in (i.a) into a predicative one (i.b) (Partee 1987).

(i) a. A trickster laughs.
    b. He is a trickster.

These changes can be achieved by a unary rule that is applied to an NP or with a special empty head that takes an NP as its argument. In current Minimalist approaches, empty heads are used (Ramchand 2005: 370), in Categorial Grammar and HPSG unary-branching rules are more common (Flickinger 2008: 91–92; Müller 2009c, 2012a).

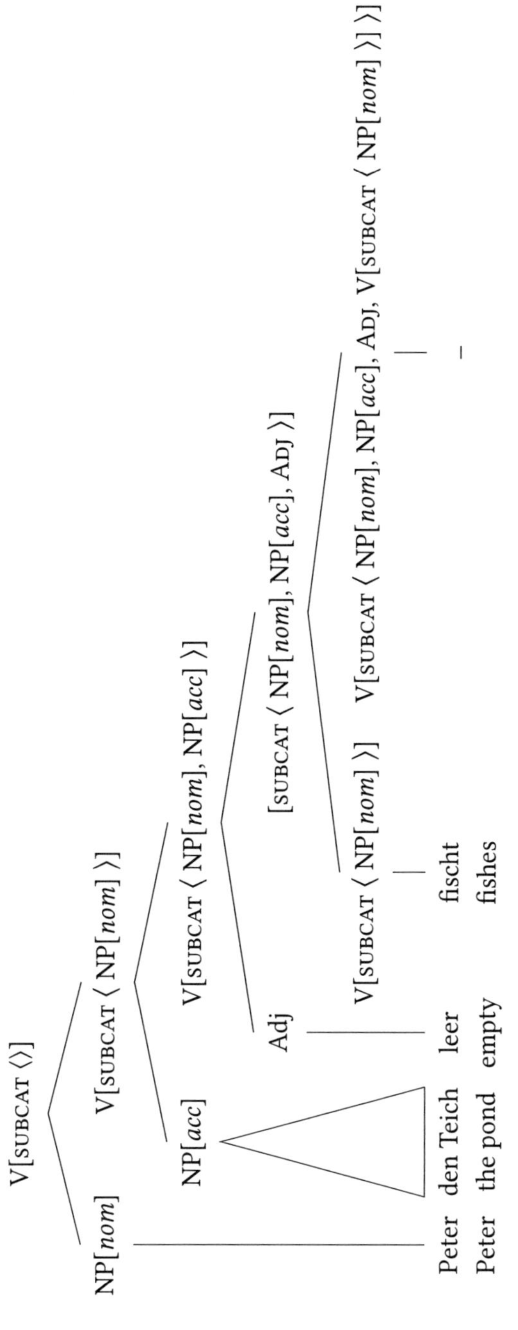

Figure 19.13: Analysis of the resultative construction with an empty head

20 Extraction, scrambling, and passive: one or several descriptive devices?

An anonymous reviewer suggested discussing one issue in which transformational theories differ from theories like LFG and HPSG. The reviewer claimed that Transformational Grammars use just one tool for the description of active/passive alternations, scrambling, and extraction, while theories like LFG and HPSG use different techniques for all three phenomena. If this claim were correct and if the analyses made correct predictions, the respective GB/Minimalism theories would be better than their competitors, since the general aim in science is to develop theories that need a minimal set of assumptions. I already commented on the analysis of passive in GB in Section 3.4, but I want to extend this discussion here and include a Minimalist analysis and one from Dependency Grammar.

The task of any passive analysis is to explain the difference in argument realization in examples like (1):

(1) a. She beats him.
    b. He was beaten.

In these examples about chess, the accusative object of *beat* is realized as the nominative in (1b). In addition, it can be observed that the position of the elements is different: while *him* is realized postverbally in object position in (1a), it is realized preverbally in (1b). In GB this is explained by a movement analysis. It is assumed that the object does not get case in passive constructions and hence has to move into the subject position where case is assigned by the finite verb. This analysis is also assumed in Minimalist work as in David Adger's textbook (2003), for instance. Figure 20.1 on the following page shows his analysis of (2):

(2) Jason was killed.

TP stands for Tense Phrase and corresponds to the IP that was discussed in Chapter 3. PassP is a functional head for passives. *v*P is a special category for the analysis of verb phrases that was originally introduced for the analysis of ditransitives (Larson 1988) and VP is the normal VP that consists of verb and object. In Adger's analysis, the verb *kill* moves from the verb position in VP to the head position of *v*, the passive auxiliary *be* moves from the head position of PassP to the head position of the Tense Phrase. Features like Infl are 'checked' in combination with such movements. The exact implementation of these checking and valuing operations does not matter here. What is important is that *Jason* moves from the object position to a position that was formerly known as the

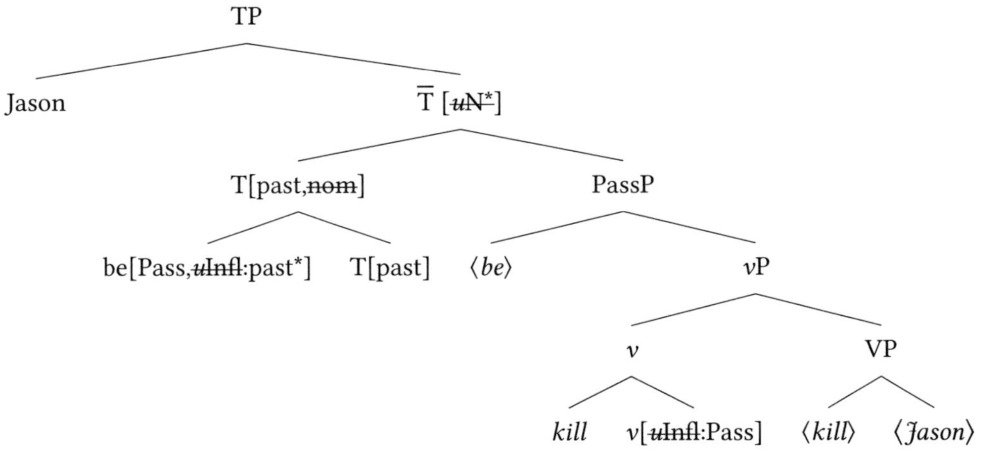

Figure 20.1: Adger's Minimalist movement-based analysis of the passive (p. 231)

specifier position of T (see Footnote 26 on page 156 on the notion of specifier). All these analyses assume that the participle cannot assign accusative to its object and that the object has to move to another position to get case or check features. How exactly one can formally represents the fact that the participle cannot assign case is hardly ever made explicit in the GB literature. The following is a list of statements that can be found in the literature:

(3) a. We shall assume that a passivized verb loses the ability to assign structural ACCUSATIVE case to its complement. (Haegeman 1994: 183)

b. das Objekt des Aktivsatzes wird zum Subjekt des Passivsatzes, weil die passivische Verbform keinen Akkusativ-Kasus regieren kann (Akk-Kasus-Absorption). (Lohnstein 2014: 172)

In addition, it is sometimes said that the external theta-role is absorbed by the verb morphology (Jaeggli 1986; Haegeman 1994: 183). Now, what would it entail if we made this explicit? There is some lexical item for verbs like *beat*. The active form has the ability to assign accusative to its object, but the passive form does not. Since this is a property that is shared by all transitive verbs (by definition of the term transitive verb), this is some regularity that has to be captured. One way to capture this is the assumption of a special passive morpheme that suppresses the agent and changes something in the case specification of the stem it attaches too. How this works in detail was never made explicit. Let us compare this morpheme-based analysis with lexical rule-based analyses: as was explained in Section 19.5, empty heads can be used instead of lexical rules in those cases in which the phonological form of the input and the output do not differ. So for example, lexical rules that license additional arguments as in resultative constructions, for instance, can be replaced by an empty head. However, as was explained in Section 9.2, lexical rules are also used to model morphology. This is also true for Construction Grammar (see Gert Booij's work on Construction Morphology (2010), which is in many ways similar to Riehemann's work in HPSG (1993; 1998)). In the case of the passive lexical rule, the participle morphology is combined with the stem and the subject is suppressed in the corresponding valence list. This is exactly what is described in the GB/MP literature. The respective lexical rule for the analysis of *ge-lieb-t* 'loved' is depicted in Figure 20.2 to the left. The morpheme-based analysis is shown to the right. To keep things simple, I

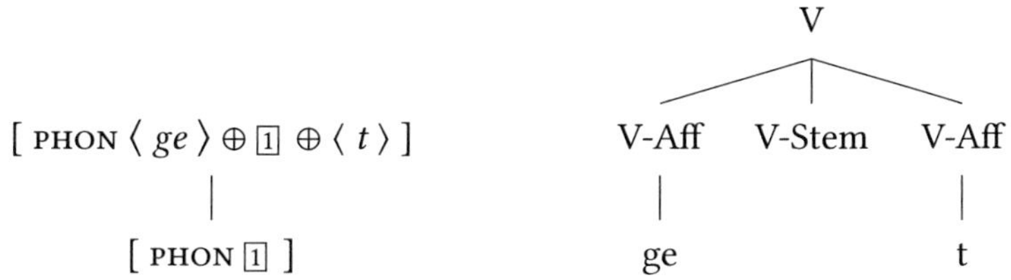

Figure 20.2: Lexical rule-based/constructionist vs. morpheme-based analysis

assume a flat analysis, but those who insist on binary branching structures would have to come up with a way of deciding whether the *ge-* or the *-t* is combined first with the stem and in which way selection and percolation of features takes place. Independent of how morphology is done, the fact that the inflected form (the top node in both figures) has different properties than the verb stem has to be represented somehow. In the morpheme-based world, the morpheme is responsible for suppressing the agent and changing the case assignment properties, in the lexical rule/construction world this is done by the respective lexical rule. There is no difference in terms of needed tools and necessary stipulations.

The situation in Minimalist theories is a little bit different. For instance, (Adger 2003: 229, 231) writes the following:

> Passives are akin to unaccusatives, in that they do not assign accusative case to their object, and they do not appear to have a thematic subject. [...] Moreover, the idea that the function of this auxiliary is to select an unaccusative little *v*P simultaneously explains the lack of accusative case and the lack of a thematic subject. (Adger 2003: 229, 231)

So this is an explicit statement. The relation between a stem and a passive participle form that was assumed in GB analyses is now a verb stem that is combined with two different versions of little *v*. Which *v* is chosen is determined by the governing head, a functional Perf head or a Pass head. This can be depicted as in Figure 20.3 on the following page. When *kill* is used in the perfect or the passive, it is spelled out as *killed.* If it is used in the active with a 3rd person singular subject it is spelled out as *kills.* This can be compared with a lexical analysis, for instance the one assumed in HPSG. The analysis is shown in Figure 20.4 on the next page. The left figure shows a lexical item that is licensed by a lexical rule that is applied to the stem *kill-*. The stem has two elements in its argument structure list and for the active forms the complete argument structure list

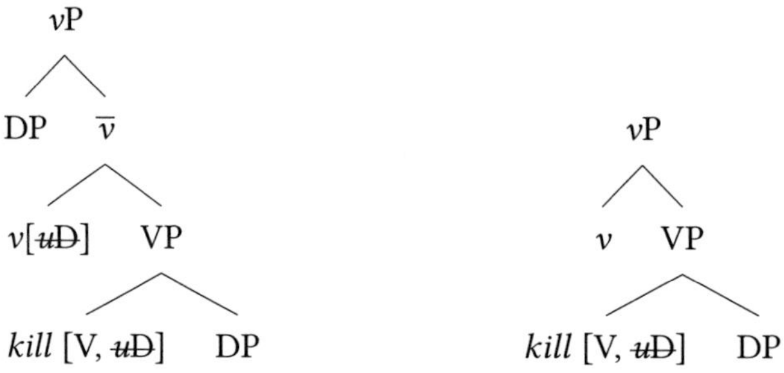

Figure 20.3: Analysis of the passive and the perfect and the passive in a Minimalist theory involving two different versions of little *v*

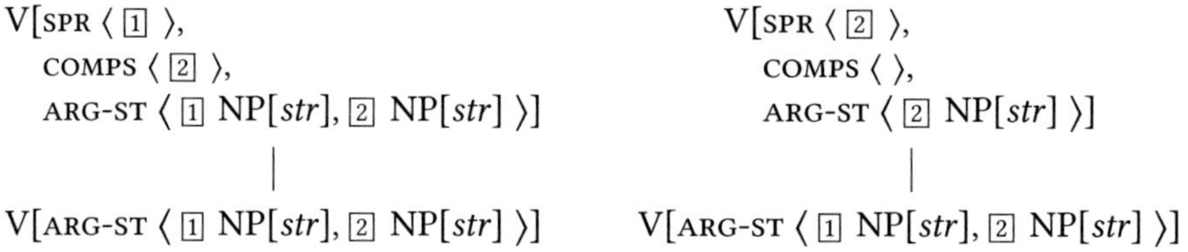

Figure 20.4: Lexical rule-based analysis of the perfect and the passive in HPSG

is shared between the licensed lexical item and the stem. The first element of the ARG-ST list is mapped to SPR and the other elements to COMPS (in English). Passive is depicted in the right figure: the first element of the ARG-ST with structural case is suppressed and since the element that was the second element in the ARG-ST list of the stem (2) is now the first element, this item is mapped to SPR. See Section 9.2 for passive in HPSG and Section 9.6.1 for comments on ARG-ST and the differences between German and English.

The discussion of Figures 20.3 and 20.4 are a further illustration of a point made in Section 19.5: lexical rules can be replaced by empty heads and vice versa. While HPSG says there are stems that are related to inflected forms and corresponding to the inflection the arguments are realized in a certain way, Minimalist theories assume two variants of little *v* that differ in their selection of arguments. Now, the question is: are there empirical differences between the two approaches? I think there are differences if one considers the question of language acquisition. What children can acquire from data is that there are various inflected forms and that they are related somehow. What remains questionable is whether they really would be able to detect empty little *v*s. One could claim of course that children operate with chunks of structures such as the ones in Figure 20.3. But then a verb would be just a chunk consisting of little *v* and V and having some open slots. This would be indistinguishable from what the HPSG analysis assumes.

As far as the "lexical rules as additional tool" aspect is concerned, the discussion is closed, but note that the standard GB/Minimalism analyses differ in another way from LFG and HPSG analyses, since they assume that passive has something to do with movement, that is, they assume that the same mechanisms are used that are used for nonlocal dependencies.[1] This works for languages like English in which the object has to be realized in postverbal position in the active and in preverbal position in the passive, but it fails for languages like German in which the order of constituents is more free. Lenerz (1977: Section 4.4.3) discussed the examples in (44) on page 109 – which are repeated here as (4) for convenience:

(4) a. weil das Mädchen dem Jungen den Ball schenkt
because the girl the.DAT boy the.ACC Ball gives
'because the girl gives the ball to the boy'

b. weil dem Jungen der Ball geschenkt wurde
because the.DAT boy the.NOM ball given was

c. weil der Ball dem Jungen geschenkt wurde
because the.NOM ball the.DAT boy given was
'because the ball was given to the boy'

While both orders in (4b) and (4c) are possible, the one with dative–nominative order in (4b) is the unmarked one. There is a strong linearization preference in German demanding that animate NPs be serialized before inanimate ones (Hoberg 1981: 46). This linearization rule is unaffected by passivization. Theories that assume that passive is movement either have to assume that the passive of (4a) is (4c) and (4b) is derived from (4c) by a further reordering operation (which would be implausible since usually one assumes that more marked constructions require more transformations), or they would have to come up with other explanations for the fact that the subject of the passive sentence has the same position as the object in active sentences. As was already explained in Section 3.4, one such explanation is to assume an empty expletive subject that is placed in the position where nominative is assigned and to somehow connect this expletive element to the subject in object position. While this somehow works, it should be clear that the price for rescuing a movement-based analysis of passive is rather high: one has to assume an empty expletive element, that is, something that neither has a form nor a meaning. The existence of such an object could not be inferred from the input unless it is assumed that the structures in which it is assumed are given. Thus, a rather rich UG would have to be assumed.

The question one needs to ask here is: why does the movement-based analysis have these problems and why does the valence-based analysis not have them? The cause of the problem is that the analysis of the passive mixes two things: the fact that SVO languages like English encode subjecthood positionally, and the fact that the subject is suppressed in passives. If these two things are separated the problem disappears. The fact that the object of the active sentence in (1a) is realized as the subject in (1b) is explained

[1] There is another option in Minimalist theories. Since Agree can check features nonlocally, T can assign nominative to an embedded element. So, in principle the object may get nominative in the VP without moving to T. However, Adger (2003: 368) assumes that German has a strong EPP feature on T, so that the underlying object has to move to the specifier of T. This is basically the old GB analysis of passive in German with all its conceptual problems and disadvantages.

by the assumption that the first NP on the argument structure list with structural case is realized as subject and mapped to the respective valence feature: SPR in English. Such mappings can be language specific (see Section 9.6.1 and Müller (2016a) where I discuss Icelandic, which is an SVO language with subjects with lexical case).

In what follows, I discuss another set of examples that are sometimes seen as evidence for a movement-based analysis. The examples in (5) are instances of the so-called remote passive (Höhle 1978: 175–176).[2]

(5) a. daß er auch von mir zu überreden versucht wurde[3]
that he.NOM also from me to persuade tried got
'that an attempt to persuade him was also made by me'

b. weil der Wagen oft zu reparieren versucht wurde
because the car.NOM often to repair tried was
'because many attempts were made to repair the car'

What is interesting about these examples is that the subject is the underlying object of a deeply embedded verb. This seems to suggest that the object is extracted out of the verb phrase. So the analysis of (5b) would be (6):

(6) weil [$_{IP}$ der Wagen$_i$ [$_{VP}$ oft [$_{VP}$ [$_{VP}$ [$_{VP}$ _$_i$ zu reparieren] versucht] wurde]
because the car.NOM often to repair tried was

While this is a straight-forward explanation of the fact that (5b) is grammatical, another explanation is possible as well. In the HPSG analysis of German (and Dutch) it is assumed that verbs like those in (5b) form a verbal complex, that is, *zu reparieren versucht wurde* 'to repair tried was' forms one unit. When two or more verbs form a complex, the highest verb attracts the arguments from the verb it embeds (Hinrichs & Nakazawa 1989b, 1994; Bouma & van Noord 1998). A verb like *versuchen* 'to try' selects a subject, an infinitive with *zu* 'to' and all complements that are selected by this infinitive. In the analysis of (7), *versuchen* 'to try' selects for its subject, the object of *reparieren* 'to repair' and for the verb *zu reparieren* 'to repair'.

(7) weil er den Wagen zu reparieren versuchen will
because he.NOM the.ACC car to repair try wants
'because he wants to try to repair the car'

Now if the passive lexical rule applies to *versuch-*, it suppresses the first argument of *versuch-* with structural case, which is the subject of *versuch-*. The next argument of *versuch-* is the object of *zu reparieren*. Since this element is the first NP with structural case, it gets nominative as in (5b). So, this shows that there is an analysis of the remote passive that does not rely on movement. Since movement-based analyses were shown to be problematic and since there are no data that cannot be explained without movement, analyses without movement have to be preferred.

[2] See Müller (2002a: Section 3.1.4.1) and Wurmbrand (2003b) for corpus examples.

[3] Oppenrieder (1991: 212).

This leaves us with movement-based accounts of local reordering (scrambling). The reviewer suggested that scrambling, passive, and nonlocal extraction may be analyzed with the same mechanism. It was long thought that scope facts made the assumption of movement-based analyses of scrambling necessary, but it was pointed out by Kiss (2001: 146) and Fanselow (2001: Section 2.6) that the reverse is true: movement-based accounts of scrambling make wrong predictions with regard to available quantifier scopings. I discussed the respective examples in Section 3.5 already and will not repeat the discussion here. The conclusion that has to be drawn from this is that passive, scrambling, and long distance extraction are three different phenomena that should be treated differently. The solution for the analysis of the passive that is adopted in HPSG is based on an analysis by Haider (1986a), who worked within the GB framework. The "scrambling-as-base generation" approach to local reordering that was used in HPSG right from the beginning (Gunji 1986) is also adopted by some practitioners of GB/Minimalism, e.g., Fanselow (2001).

Having discussed the analyses in GB/Minimalism, I now turn to Dependency Grammar. Groß & Osborne (2009) suggest that *w*-fronting, topicalization, scrambling, extraposition, splitting, and also the remote passive should be analyzed by what they call *rising*. The concept was already explained in Section 11.5. The Figures 20.5 and 20.6 show examples for the fronting and the scrambling of an object. Groß and Osborne assume

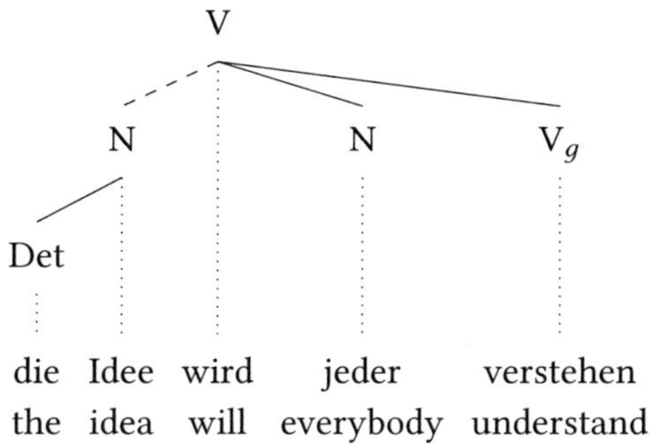

Figure 20.5: Analysis of *Die Idee wird jeder verstehen.* 'Everybody will understand the idea.' involving rising

that the object depends on the main verb in sentences with auxiliary verbs, while the subject depends on the auxiliary. Therefore, the object *die Idee* 'the idea' and the object *sich* 'himself' have to rise to the next higher verb in order to keep the structures projective. Figure 20.7 on the following page shows the analysis of the remote passive. The object of *zu reparieren* 'to repair' rises to the auxiliary *wurde* 'was'.

Groß and Osborne use the same mechanism for all these phenomena, but it should be clear that there have to be differences in the exact implementation. Groß and Osborne say that English does not have scrambling, while German does. If this is to be captured, there must be a way to distinguish the two phenomena, since if this were not possible, one would predict that English has scrambling as well, since both German and English

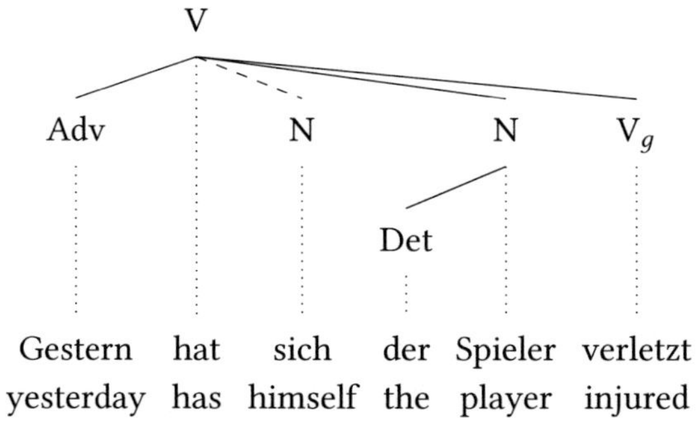

Figure 20.6: Analysis of *Gestern hat sich der Spieler verletzt.* 'Yesterday, the player injured himself.' involving rising of the object of the main verb *verletzt* 'injured'

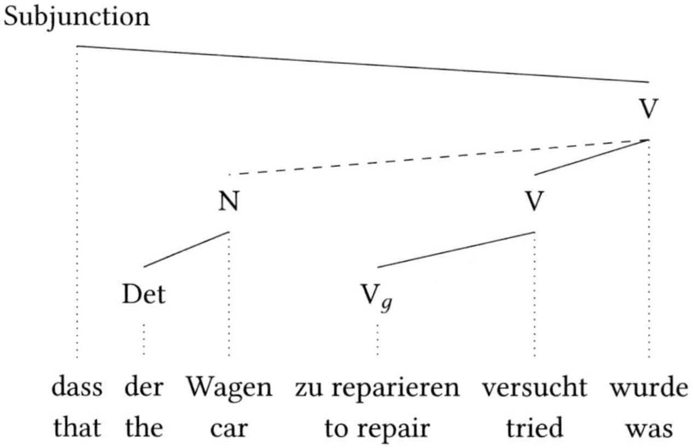

Figure 20.7: Analysis of the remote passive *dass der Wagen zu reparieren versucht wurde* 'that it was tried to repair the car' involving rising

allow long distance fronting. Groß & Osborne (2009: 58) assume that object nouns that rise must take the nominative. But if the kind of rising that they assume for remote passives is identical to the one that they assume for scrambling, they would predict that *den Wagen* gets nominative in (8) as well:

(8) dass den Wagen niemand repariert hat
that the.ACC car nobody.NOM repaired has
'that nobody repaired the car'

Since *den Wagen* 'the car' and *repariert* 'repaired' are not adjacent, *den Wagen* has to rise to the next higher head in order to allow for a projective realization of elements. So in order to assign case properly, one has to take into account the arguments that are governed by the head to which a certain element rises. Since the auxiliary *hat* 'has' already governs a nominative, the NP *den Wagen* has to be realized in the accusative. An analysis that assumes that both the accusative and nominative depend on *hat* 'has' in (8) is basically the verbal complex analysis assumed in HPSG and some GB variants.

Note, however, that this does not extend to nonlocal dependencies. Case is assigned locally by verbs or verbal complexes, but not to elements that come from far away. The long distance extraction of NPs is more common in southern variants of German and there are only a few verbs that do not take a nominative argument themselves. The examples below involve *dünken* 'to think', which governs an accusative and a sentential object and *scheinen* 'to seem', which governs a dative and a sentential object. If (9a) is analyzed with *den Wagen* rising to *dünkt*, one might expect that *den Wagen* 'the car' gets nominative since there is no other element in the nominative. However, (8b) is entirely out.

(9) a. Den Wagen dünkt mich, dass er repariert.
the.ACC car thinks me.ACC that he.NOM repairs
'I think that he repairs the car'

b. * Der Wagen dünkt mich, dass er repariert.
the.NOM car thinks me.ACC that he.NOM repairs

Similarly there is no agreement between the fronted element and the verb to which it attaches:

(10) a. Mir scheint, dass die Wagen ihm gefallen.
me.DAT.1PL seems.3SG that the cars.3PL him please.3PL
'He seems to me to like the cars.'

b. Die Wagen scheint mir, dass ihm gefallen.
the cars.3PL seem.3SG me.DAT that him please.3PL
'The cars, he seems to me to like.'

c. * Die Wagen scheinen mir, dass ihm gefällt.
the cars.3PL seem.3PL me.DAT that him pleases.3SG

d. * Die Wagen scheinen mir, dass ihm gefallen.
the cars.3PL seem.3PL me.DAT that him please.3PL

This shows that scrambling/remote passive and extraction should not be dealt with by the same mechanism or if they are dealt with by the same mechanism one has to make sure that there are specialized variants of the mechanism that take the differences into account. I think what Groß and Osborne did is simply recode the attachment relations of phrase structure grammars. *die Idee* 'the idea' has some relation to *wird jeder verstehen* 'will everybody understand' in Figure 20.5, as it does in GB, LFG, GPSG, HPSG, and other similar frameworks. In HPSG, *die Idee* 'the idea' is the filler in a filler-head configuration. The remote passive and local reorderings of arguments of auxiliaries, modal verbs, and other verbs that behave similarly are explained by verbal complex formation where all non-verbal arguments depend on the highest verb (Hinrichs & Nakazawa 1994).

Concluding this chapter, it can be said that local reorderings and long-distance dependencies are two different things that should be described with different tools (or there should be further constraints that differ for the respective phenomena when the same tool is used). Similarly, movement-based analyses of the passive are problematic since passive does not necessarily imply reordering.

21 Phrasal vs. lexical analyses

coauthored with Stephen Wechsler

This section deals with a rather crucial aspect when it comes to the comparison of the theories described in this book: valence and the question whether sentence structure, or rather syntactic structure in general, is determined by lexical information or whether syntactic structures have an independent existence (and meaning) and lexical items are just inserted into them. Roughly speaking, frameworks like GB/Minimalism, LFG, CG, HPSG, and DG are lexical, while GPSG and Construction Grammar (Goldberg 1995, 2003a; Tomasello 2003, 2006b; Croft 2001) are phrasal approaches. This categorization reflects tendencies, but there are non-lexical approaches in Minimalism (Borer's exoskeletal approach, 2003) and LFG (Alsina 1996; Asudeh et al. 2008, 2013) and there are lexical approaches in Construction Grammar (Sign-Based Construction Grammar, see Section 10.6.2). The phrasal approach is wide-spread also in frameworks like Cognitive Grammar (Dąbrowska 2001; Langacker 2009: 169) and Simpler Syntax (Culicover & Jackendoff 2005; Jackendoff 2008) that could not be discussed in this book.

The question is whether the meaning of an utterance like (1a) is contributed by the verb *give* and the structure needed for the NPs occurring together with the verb does not contribute any meaning or whether there is a phrasal pattern [X Verb Y Z] that contributes some "ditransitive meaning" whatever this may be.[1]

(1) a. Peter gives Mary the book.
    b. Peter fishes the pond empty.

Similarly, there is the question of how the constituents in (1b) are licensed. This sentence is interesting since it has a resultative meaning that is not part of the meaning of the verb *fish*: Peter's fishing causes the pond to become empty. Nor is this additional meaning part of the meaning of any other item in the sentence. On the lexical account, there is a lexical rule that licenses a lexical item that selects for *Peter*, *the pond*, and *empty*. This lexical item also contributes the resultative meaning. On the phrasal approach, it is

[1] Note that the prototypical meaning is a transfer of possession in which Y receives Z from X, but the reverse holds in (i.b):

(i) a. Er gibt ihr den Ball.
       he.NOM gives her.DAT the.ACC ball
    b. Er stiehlt ihr den Ball.
       he.NOM steals her.DAT the.ACC ball
       'He steals the ball from her.'

assumed that there is a pattern [Subj V Obj Obl]. This pattern contributes the resultative meaning, while the verb that is inserted into this pattern just contributes its prototypical meaning, e.g., the meaning that *fish* would have in an intransitive construction. I call such phrasal approaches *plugging approaches*, since lexical items are plugged into ready-made structures that do most of the work.

In what follows I will examine these proposals in more detail and argue that the lexical approaches to valence are the correct ones. The discussion will be based on earlier work of mine (Müller 2006, 2007c, 2010b) and work that I did together with Steve Wechsler (Müller & Wechsler 2014a,b). Some of the sections in Müller & Wechsler (2014a) started out as translations of Müller (2013b), but the material was reorganized and refocused due to intensive discussion with Steve Wechsler. So rather than using a translation of Section 11.11 of Müller (2013b), I use parts of Müller & Wechsler (2014a) here and add some subsections that had to be left out of the article due to space restrictions (Subsections 21.3.6 and 21.7.3). Because there have been misunderstandings in the past (e.g., Boas (2014), see Müller & Wechsler (2014b)), a disclaimer is necessary here: this section is not an argument against Construction Grammar. As was mentioned above Sign-Based Construction Grammar is a lexical variant of Construction Grammar and hence compatible with what I believe to be correct. This section is also not against phrasal constructions in general, since there are phenomena that seem to be best captured with phrasal constructions. These are discussed in detail in Subsection 21.10. What I will argue against in the following subsections is a special kind of phrasal construction, namely phrasal argument structure constructions (phrasal ASCs). I believe that all phenomena that have to do with valence and valence alternations should be treated lexically.

21.1 Some putative advantages of phrasal models

In this section we examine certain claims to purported advantages of phrasal versions of Construction Grammar over lexical rules. Then in the following section, we will turn to positive arguments for lexical rules.

21.1.1 Usage-based theories

For many practitioners of Construction Grammar, their approach to syntax is deeply rooted in the ontological strictures of *usage-based* theories of language (Langacker 1987; Goldberg 1995; Croft 2001; Tomasello 2003). Usage-based theorists oppose the notion of "linguistic rules conceived of as algebraic procedures for combining symbols that do not themselves contribute to meaning" (Tomasello 2003: 99). All linguistic entities are symbolic of things in the realm of denotations; "all have communicative significance because they all derive directly from language use" (*ibid*). Although the formatives of language may be rather abstract, they can never be divorced from their functional origin as a tool of communication. The usage-based view of constructions is summed up well in the following quote:

> The most important point is that constructions are nothing more or less than patterns of usage, which may therefore become relatively abstract if these patterns

include many different kinds of specific linguistic symbols. But never are they empty rules devoid of semantic content or communicative function. (Tomasello 2003: 100)

Thus constructions are said to differ from grammatical rules in two ways: they must carry meaning; and they reflect the actual "patterns of usage" fairly directly.

Consider first the constraint that every element of the grammar must carry meaning, which we call the *semiotic dictum*. Do lexical or phrasal theories hew the most closely to this dictum? Categorial Grammar, the paradigm of a lexical theory (see Chapter 8), is a strong contender: it consists of meaningful words, with only a few very general combinatorial rules such as $X/Y * Y = X$. Given the rule-to-rule assumption, those combinatorial rules specify the meaning of the whole as a function of the parts. Whether such a rule counts as meaningful in itself in Tomasello's sense is not clear.

What does seem clear is that the combinatorial rules of Construction Grammar, such as Goldberg's Correspondence Principle for combining a verb with a construction (1995: 50), have the same status as those combinatorial rules:

(2) The Correspondence Principle: each participant that is lexically profiled and expressed must be fused with a profiled argument role of the construction. If a verb has three profiled participant roles, then one of them may be fused with a non-profiled argument role of a construction. (Goldberg 1995: 50)

Both verbs and constructions are specified for participant roles, some of which are *profiled*. Argument profiling for verbs is "lexically determined and highly conventionalized" (Goldberg 1995: 46). Profiled argument roles of a construction are mapped to direct grammatical functions, i. e., SUBJ, OBJ, or OBJ2. By the Correspondence Principle the lexically profiled argument roles must be direct, unless there are three of them, in which case one may be indirect.[2] With respect to the semiotic dictum, the Correspondence Principle has the same status as the Categorial Grammar combinatorial rules: a meaningless algebraic rule that specifies the way to combine meaningful items.

Turning now to the lexicalist syntax we favor, some elements abide by the semiotic dictum while others do not. Phrase structure rules for intransitive and transitive VPs (or the respective HPSG ID schema) do not. Lexical valence structures clearly carry meaning since they are associated with particular verbs. In an English ditransitive, the first object expresses the role of "intended recipient" of the referent of the second object. Hence *He carved her a toy* entails that he carved a toy with the intention that she receive it. So the lexical rule that adds a benefactive recipient argument to a verb adds meaning. Alternatively, a phrasal ditransitive construction might contribute that "recipient" meaning.[3] Which structures have meaning is an empirical question for us.

In Construction Grammar, however, meaning is assumed for all constructions *a priori*. But while the ditransitive construction plausibly contributes meaning, no truth-

[2] We assume that the second sentence of (2) provides for exceptions to the first sentence.

[3] In Section 21.2.1 we argue that the recipient should be added in the lexical argument structure, not through a phrasal construction. See Wechsler (1991: 111–113; 1995: 88–89) for an analysis of English ditransitives with elements of both constructional and lexical approaches. It is based on Kiparsky's notion of a *thematically restricted positional linker* (1987; 1988).

conditional meaning has yet been discovered for either the intransitive or bivalent transitive constructions. Clearly the constructionist's evidence for the meaningfulness of *certain* constructions such as the ditransitive does not constitute evidence that *all* phrasal constructions have meaning. So the lexical and phrasal approaches seem to come out the same, as far as the semiotic dictum is concerned.

Now consider the second usage-based dictum, that the elements of the grammar directly reflect patterns of usage, which we call *the transparency dictum*. The Construction Grammar literature often presents their constructions informally in ways that suggest that they represent surface constituent order patterns: the transitive construction is "[X VERB Y]" (Tomasello) or "[Subj V Obj]" (Goldberg 1995, 2006)[4]; the passive construction is "X *was* VERB*ed by* Y" (Tomasello 2003: 100) or "Subj aux Vpp (PPby)" (Goldberg 2006: 5). But a theory in which constructions consist of surface patterns was considered in detail and rejected by Müller (2006: Section 2), and does not accurately reflect Goldberg's actual theory.[5] The more detailed discussions present *argument structure constructions*, which are more abstract and rather like the lexicalists' grammatical elements (or perhaps an LFG f-structure): the transitive construction resembles a transitive valence structure (minus the verb itself); the passive construction resembles the passive lexical rule.

With respect to fulfilling the desiderata of usage-based theorists, we do not find any significant difference between the non-lexical and lexical approaches.

21.1.2 Coercion

Researchers working with plugging proposals usually take coercion as an indication of the usefulness of phrasal constructions. For instance, Anatol Stefanowitsch (Lecture in the lecture series *Algorithmen und Muster -- Strukturen in der Sprache*, 2009) discussed the example in (3):

(3) Das Tor zur Welt Hrnglb öffnete sich ohne Vorwarnung und verschlang [sie] ... die Welt Hrnglb wird von Magiern erschaffen, die Träume zu Realität formen können, aber nicht in der Lage sind zu träumen. Haltet aus, Freunde. Und ihr da draußen, bitte träumt ihnen ein Tor.[6]

The crucial part is *bitte träumt ihnen ein Tor* 'Dream a gate for them'. In this fantasy context the word *träumen*, which is intransitive, is forced into the ditransitive construction and therefore gets a certain meaning. This forcing of a verb corresponds to overwriting or rather extending properties of the verb by the phrasal construction.

---

[4] Goldberg et al. (2004: 300) report about a language acquisition experiment that involves an SOV pattern. The SOV order is mentioned explicitly and seen as part of the construction.

[5] This applies to argument structure constructions only. In some of her papers Goldberg assumes that very specific phrase structural configurations are part of the constructions. For instance in her paper on complex predicates in Persian (Goldberg 2003b) she assigns V^0 and $\overline{V}$ categories. See Müller (2010b: Section 4.9) for a critique of that analysis.

[6] http://www.elbenwaldforum.de/showflat.php?Cat=&Board=Tolkiens_Werke&Number=1457418&page=3&view=collapsed&sb=5&o=&fpart=16, 27.02.2010.

'The gate to the world Hrnglb opened without warning and swallowed them. The world Hrnglb is created by magicians that can form reality from dreams but cannot dream themselves. Hold out, friends! And you out there, please, dream a gate for them.'

In cases in which the plugging proposals assume that information is overwritten or extended, lexical approaches assume mediating lexical rules. Briscoe & Copestake (1999: Section 4) have worked out a lexical approach in detail.[7] They discuss the ditransitive sentences in (4), which either correspond to the prototypical ditransitive construction (4a) or deviate from it in various ways.

(4) a. Mary gave Joe a present.
    b. Joe painted Sally a picture.
    c. Mary promised Joe a new car.
    d. He tipped Bill two pounds.
    e. The medicine brought him relief.
    f. The music lent the party a festive air.
    g. Jo gave Bob a punch.
    h. He blew his wife a kiss.
    i. She smiled herself an upgrade.

For the non-canonical examples they assume lexical rules that relate transitive (*paint*) and intransitive (*smile*) verbs to ditransitive ones and contribute the respective semantic information or the respective metaphorical extension. The example in (4i) is rather similar to the *träumen* example discussed above and is also analyzed with a lexical rule (page 509). Briscoe and Copestake note that this lexical rule is much more restricted in its productivity than the other lexical rules they suggest. They take this as motivation for developing a representational format in which lexical items (including those that are derived by lexical rules) are associated with probabilities, so that differences in productivity of various patterns can be captured.

Looking narrowly at such cases, it is hard to see any rational grounds for choosing between the phrasal analysis and the lexical rule. But if we broaden our view, the lexical rule approach can be seen to have a much wider application. Coercion is a very general pragmatic process, occurring in many contexts where no construction seems to be responsible (Nunberg 1995). Nunberg cites many cases such as the restaurant waiter asking *Who is the ham sandwich?* (Nunberg 1995: 115). Copestake & Briscoe (1992: 116) discuss the conversion of terms for animals to mass nouns (see also Copestake & Briscoe (1995: 36–43)). Example (5) is about a substance, not about a cute bunny.

(5) After several lorries had run over the body, there was rabbit splattered all over the road.

The authors suggest a lexical rule that maps a count noun onto a mass noun. This analysis is also assumed by Fillmore (1999: 114–115). Such coercion can occur without any syntactic context: one can answer the question *What's that stuff on the road?* or *What are you eating?* with the one-word utterance *Rabbit.* Some coercion happens to affect the complement structure of a verb, but this is simply a special case of a more general phenomenon that has been analyzed by rules of systematic polysemy.

[7] Kay (2005), working in the framework of CxG, also suggests unary constructions.

21.1.3 Aspect as a clause level phenomenon

Alsina (1996), working in the framework of LFG, argues for a phrasal analysis of resultative constructions based on the aspectual properties of sentences, since aspect is normally viewed as a property that is determined by the sentence syntax. Intransitive verbs such as *bark* refer to activities, a resultative construction with the same verb, however, stands for an accomplishment (an extended change of state). Alsina supports this with the following data:

(6) a. (*) The dog barked in five minutes.
    b. The dog barked the neighbors awake in five minutes.

The latter sentence means that the *barking* event was completed after five minutes. A reading referring to the time span of the event is not available for (6a). If (6a) is grammatical at all, then a claim is being made about the time frame in which the event begun.

If we now consider examples such as (7c), however, we see that Alsina's argumentation is not cogent since the resultative meaning is already present at the word-level in nominalizations. As the examples in (7) show, this contrast can be observed in nominal constructions and is therefore independent of the sentence syntax:

(7) a. weil sie die Nordsee in fünf Jahren leer fischten
    because they the North.Sea in five years empty fished
    'because they fished the North Sea (until it was) empty in five years'
  b. # weil sie in fünf Jahren fischten
    because they in five years fished
  c. das Leerfischen der Nordsee in fünf Jahren
    the empty.fishing of.the North.Sea in five years
  d. # das Fischen in fünf Jahren
    the fishing in five years

In a lexical approach there is a verb stem selecting for two NPs and a resultative predicate. This stem has the appropriate meaning and can be inflected or undergo derivation und successive inflection. In both cases we get words that contain the resultative semantics and hence are compatible with respective adverbials.

21.1.4 Simplicity and polysemy

Much of the intuitive appeal of the plugging approach stems from its apparent simplicity relative to the use of lexical rules. But the claim to greater simplicity for Construction Grammar is based on misunderstandings of both lexical rules and Construction Grammar (specifically of Goldberg's (1995; 2006) version). It draws the distinction in the wrong place and misses the real differences between these approaches. This argument from simplicity is often repeated and so it is important to understand why it is incorrect.

Tomasello (2003) presents the argument as follows. Discussing first the lexical rules approach, Tomasello (2003: 160) writes that

> One implication of this view is that a verb must have listed in the lexicon a different meaning for virtually every different construction in which it participates [...]. For example, while the prototypical meaning of *cough* involves only one participant, the cougher, we may say such things as *He coughed her his cold*, in which there are three core participants. In the lexical rules approach, in order to produce this utterance the child's lexicon must have as an entry a ditransitive meaning for the verb *cough*. (Tomasello 2003: 160)

Tomasello (2003: 160) then contrasts a Construction Grammar approach, citing Fillmore et al. (1988), Goldberg (1995), and Croft (2001). He concludes as follows:

> The main point is that if we grant that constructions may have meaning of their own, in relative independence of the lexical items involved, then we do not need to populate the lexicon with all kinds of implausible meanings for each of the verbs we use in everyday life. The construction grammar approach in which constructions have meanings is therefore both much simpler and much more plausible than the lexical rules approach. (Tomasello 2003: 161)

This reflects a misunderstanding of lexical rules, as they are normally understood. There is no implausible sense populating the lexicon. The lexical rule approach to *He coughed her his cold* states that when the word *coughed* appears with two objects, the whole complex has a certain meaning (see Müller 2006: 876). Furthermore we explicitly distinguish between listed elements (lexical entries) and derived ones. The general term subsuming both is *lexical item*.

The simplicity argument also relies on a misunderstanding of a theory Tomasello advocates, namely the theory due to Goldberg (1995, 2006). For his argument to go through, Tomasello must tacitly assume that verbs can combine freely with constructions, that is, that the grammar does not place extrinsic constraints on such combinations. If it is necessary to also stipulate which verbs can appear in which constructions, then the claim to greater simplicity collapses: each variant lexical item with its "implausible meaning" under the lexical rule approach corresponds to a verb-plus-construction combination under the phrasal approach.

Passages such as the following may suggest that verbs and constructions are assumed to combine freely:[8]

> Constructions are combined freely to form actual expressions as long as they can be construed as not being in conflict (invoking the notion of construal is intended to allow for processes of accommodation or coercion). [...] Allowing constructions to combine freely as long as there are no conflicts, allows for the infinitely creative potential of language. [...] That is, a speaker is free to creatively combine constructions as long as constructions exist in the language that can be combined suitably to categorize the target message, given that there is no conflict among the constructions. (Goldberg 2006: 22)

[8] The context of these quotes makes clear that the verb and the argument structure construction are considered constructions. See Goldberg (2006: 21, ex. (2)).

But in fact Goldberg does not assume free combination, but rather that a verb is "conventionally associated with a construction" (Goldberg 1995: 50): verbs specify their participant roles and which of those are obligatory direct arguments (*profiled*, in Goldberg's terminology). In fact, Goldberg herself (2006: 211) argues against Borer's putative assumption of free combination (2003) on the grounds that Borer is unable to account for the difference between *dine* (intransitive), *eat* (optionally transitive), and *devour* (obligatorily transitive).[9] Despite Tomasello's comment above, Construction Grammar is no simpler than the lexical rules.

The resultative construction is often used to illustrate the simplicity argument. For example, Goldberg (1995: Chapter 7) assumes that the same lexical item for the verb *sneeze* is used in (8a) and (8b). It is simply inserted into different constructions:

(8) a. He sneezed.
    b. He sneezed the napkin off the table.

The meaning of (8a) corresponds more or less to the verb meaning, since the verb is used in the Intransitive Construction. But the Caused-Motion Construction in (8b) contributes additional semantic information concerning the causation and movement: his sneezing caused the napkin to move off the table. *sneeze* is plugged into the Caused-Motion Construction, which licenses the subject of *sneeze* and additionally provides two slots: one for the theme (*napkin*) and one for the goal (*off the table*). The lexical approach is essentially parallel, except that the lexical rule can feed further lexical processes like passivization (*The napkin was sneezed off the table*), and conversion to nouns or adjectives (see Sections 21.2.2 and 21.6).

In a nuanced comparison of the two approaches, Goldberg (1995: 139–140) considers again the added recipient argument in *Mary kicked Joe the ball*, where *kick* is lexically a 2-place verb. She notes that on the constructional view, "the composite fused structure involving both verb and construction is stored in memory". The verb itself retains its original meaning as a 2-place verb, so that "we avoid implausible verb senses such as 'to cause to receive by kicking'." The idea seems to be that the lexical approach, in contrast, must countenance such implausible verb senses since a lexical rule adds a third argument.

But the lexical and constructional approaches are actually indistinguishable on this point. The lexical rule does not produce a verb with the "implausible sense" in (9a). Instead it produces the sense in (9b):

(9) a. cause-to-receive-by-kicking(x, y, z)
    b. cause(kick(x, y),receive(z,y))

The same sort of "composite fused structure" is assumed under either view. With respect to the semantic structure, the number and plausibility of senses, and the polyadicity of the semantic relations, the two theories are identical. They mainly differ in the way this representation fits into the larger theory of syntax. They also differ in another respect: on the lexical view, the derived three-argument valence structure is associated with the phonological string *kicked*. Next, we present evidence for this claim.

[9] Goldberg's critique cites a 2001 presentation by Borer with the same title as Borer (2003). See Section 21.3.4 for more discussion of this issue. As far as we know, the *dine / eat / devour* minimal triplet originally came from Dowty (1989: 89–90).

21.2 Evidence for lexical approaches

21.2.1 Valence and coordination

On the lexical account, the verb *paint* in (4b), for example, is lexically a 2-argument verb, while the unary branching node immediately dominating it is effectively a 3-argument verb. On the constructional view there is no such predicate seeking three arguments that dominates only the verb. Coordination provides evidence for the lexical account.

A generalization about coordination is that two constituents which have compatible syntactic properties can be coordinated and that the result of the coordination is an object that has the syntactic properties of each of the conjuncts. This is reflected by the Categorial Grammar analysis which assumes the category (X\X)/X for the conjunction: the conjunction takes an X to the right, an X to the left and the result is an X.

For example, in (10a) we have a case of the coordination of two lexical verbs. The coordination *know and like* behaves like the coordinated simplex verbs: it takes a subject and an object. Similarly, two sentences with a missing object are coordinated in (10b) and the result is a sentence with a missing object.

(10) a. I know and like this record.
b. Bagels, I like and Ellison hates.

The German examples in (11) show that the case requirement of the involved verbs has to be respected. In (11b,c) the coordinated verbs require accusative and dative respectively and since the case requirements are incompatible with unambiguously case marked nouns both of these examples are out.

(11) a. Ich kenne und unterstütze diesen Mann.
I know and support this.ACC man
b. * Ich kenne und helfe diesen Mann.
I know and help this.ACC man
c. * Ich kenne und helfe diesem Mann.
I know and help this.DAT man

Interestingly, it is possible to coordinate basic ditransitive verbs with verbs that have additional arguments licensed by the lexical rule. (12) provides examples in English and German ((12b) is quoted from Müller (2013b: 420)):

(12) a. She then offered and made me a wonderful espresso – nice.[10]
b. ich hab ihr jetzt diese Ladung Muffins mit den Herzchen drauf
I have her now this load Muffins with the little.heart there.on
gebacken und gegeben.[11]
baked and given
'I have now baked and given her this load of muffins with the little heart on top.'

[10] http://www.thespinroom.com.au/?p=102 07.07.2012
[11] http://www.musiker-board.de/diverses-ot/35977-die-liebe-637-print.html. 08.06.2012

These sentences show that both verbs are 3-argument verbs at the V^0 level, since they involve V^0 coordination:

(13) $[_{V^0}$ offered and made$]$ $[_{NP}$ me$]$ $[_{NP}$ a wonderful espresso$]$

This is expected under the lexical rule analysis but not the non-lexical constructional one.[12]

Summarizing the coordination argument: coordinated verbs generally must have compatible syntactic properties like valence properties. This means that in (12b), for example, *gebacken* 'baked' and *gegeben* 'given' have the same valence properties. On the lexical approach the creation verb *gebacken*, together with a lexical rule, licenses a ditransitive verb. It can therefore be coordinated with *gegeben*. On the phrasal approach however, the verb *gebacken* has two argument roles and is not compatible with the verb *gegeben*, which has three argument roles. In the phrasal model, *gebacken* can only realize three arguments when it enters the ditransitive phrasal construction or argument structure construction. But in sentences like (12) it is not *gebacken* alone that enters the phrasal syntax, but rather the combination of *gebacken* and *gegeben*. On this view, the verbs are incompatible as far as the semantic roles are concerned.

To fix this under the phrasal approach, one could posit a mechanism such that the semantic roles that are required for the coordinate phrase *baked and given* are shared by each of its conjunct verbs and that they are therefore compatible. But this would amount to saying that there are several verb senses for *baked*, something that the anti-lexicalists claim to avoid, as discussed in the next section.

A reviewer of Theoretical Linguistics correctly observes that a version of the (phrasal) ASC approach could work in the exactly same way as our lexical analysis. Our ditransitive lexical rule would simply be rechristened as a "ditransitive ASC". This construction would combine with *baked*, thus adding the third argument, prior to its coordination with *gave*. As long as the ASC approach is a non-distinct notational variant of the lexical rule approach then of course it works in exactly the same way. But the literature on the ASC approach represents it as a radical alternative to lexical rules, in which constructions are combined through inheritance hierarchies, instead of allowing lexical rules to alter the argument structure of a verb prior to its syntactic combination with the other words and phrases.

The reviewer also remarked that examples like (14) show that the benefactive argument has to be introduced on the phrasal level.

(14) I designed and built him a house.

[12] One might wonder whether these sentences could be instances of Right Node Raising (RNR) out of coordinated VPs (Bresnan 1974; Abbott 1976):

(i) She [offered ___] and [made me ___] a wonderful espresso.

But this cannot be correct. Under such an analysis the first verb has been used without a benefactive or recipient object. But *me* is interpreted as the recipient of both the offering and making. Secondly, the second object can be an unstressed pronoun (*She offered and made me it*), which is not possible in RNR. Note that *offered and made* cannot be a pseudo-coordination meaning 'offered to make'. This is possible only with stem forms of certain verbs such as *try*.

Both *designed* and *built* are bivalent verbs and *him* is the benefactive that extends both *designed* and *built.* However, we assume that sentences like (14) can be analyzed as coordination of two verbal items that are licensed by the lexical rule that introduces the benefactive argument. That is, the benefactive is introduced before the coordination.

The coordination facts illustrate a more general point. The output of a lexical rule such as the one that would apply in the analysis of *gebacken* in (12b) is just a word (an X^0), so it has the same syntactic distribution as an underived word with the same category and valence feature. This important generalization follows from the lexical account while on the phrasal view, it is mysterious at best. The point can be shown with any of the lexical rules that the anti-lexicalists are so keen to eliminate in favor of phrasal constructions. For example, active and passive verbs can be coordinated, as long as they have the same valence properties, as in this Swedish example:

(15) Golfklubben begärde och beviljade-s marklov för banbygget efter
golf.club.DEF requested and granted-PASS ground.permit for track.build.DEF after
en hel del förhandlingar och kompromisser med Länsstyrelsen och
a whole part negotiations and compromises with county.board.DEF and
Naturvårdsverket.[13]
nature.protection.agency.DEF
'The golf club requested and was granted a ground permit for fairlane construction after a lot of negotiations and compromises with the County Board and the Environmental Protection Agency.'

(English works the same way, as shown by the grammatical translation line.) The passive of the ditransitive verb *bevilja* 'grant' retains one object, so it is effectively transitive and can be coordinated with the active transitive *begära* 'request'.

Moreover, the English passive verb form, being a participle, can feed a second lexical rule deriving adjectives from verbs. All categories of English participles can be converted to adjectives (Bresnan, 1982b, 2001: Chapter 3):

(16) a. active present participles (cf. The leaf is falling): *the falling leaf*
b. active past participles (cf. The leaf has fallen): *the fallen leaf*
c. passive participles (cf. The toy is being broken (by the child).): *the broken toy*

That the derived forms are adjectives, not verbs, is shown by a host of properties, including negative *un-* prefixation: *unbroken* means 'not broken', just as *unkind* means 'not kind', while the *un-* appearing on verbs indicates, not negation, but action reversal, as in *untie* (Bresnan, 1982b: 21, 2001: Chapter 3). Predicate adjectives preserve the subject of predication of the verb and for prenominal adjectives the rule is simply that the role that would be assigned to the subject goes to the modified noun instead (*The toy remained (un-)broken.*; *the broken toy*). Being an A^0, such a form can be coordinated with another A^0, as in the following:

[13] http://www.lyckselegolf.se/index.asp?Sida=82

(17) a. The suspect should be considered [armed and dangerous].
b. any [old, rotting, or broken] toys

In (17b), three adjectives are coordinated, one underived (*old*), one derived from a present participle (*rotting*), and one from a passive participle (*broken*). Such coordination is completely mundane on a lexical theory. Each A^0 conjunct has a valence feature (in HPSG it would be the SPR feature for predicates or the MOD feature for the prenominal modifiers), which is shared with the mother node of the coordinate structure. But the point of the phrasal (or ASC) theory is to deny that words have such valence features.

The claim that lexical derivation of valence structure is distinct from phrasal combination is further supported with evidence from deverbal nominalization (Wechsler 2008a). To derive nouns from verbs, *-ing* suffixation productively applies to all inflectable verbs (*the shooting of the prisoner*), while morphological productivity is severely limited for various other suffixes such as *-(a)tion* (** the shootation of the prisoner*). So forms such as *destruction* and *distribution* must be retrieved from memory while *-ing* nouns such as *looting* or *growing* could be (and in the case of rare verbs or neologisms, must be) derived from the verb or the root through the application of a rule (Zucchi 1993). This difference explains why *-ing* nominals always retain the argument structure of the cognate verb, while other forms show some variation. A famous example is the lack of the agent argument for the noun *growth* versus its retention by the noun *growing*: **John's growth of tomatoes* versus *John's growing of tomatoes* (Chomsky 1970).[14]

But what sort of rule derives the *-ing* nouns, a lexical rule or a phrasal one? In Marantz's (1997) phrasal analysis, a phrasal construction (notated as *v*P) is responsible for assigning the agent role of *-ing* nouns such as *growing*. For him, none of the words directly selects an agent via its argument structure. The *-ing* forms are permitted to appear in the *v*P construction, which licenses the possessive agent. Non-*ing* nouns such as *destruction* and *growth* do not appear in *v*P. Whether they allow expression of the agent depends on semantic and pragmatic properties of the word: *destruction* involves external causation so it does allow an agent, while *growth* involves internal causation so it does not allow an agent.

However, a problem for Marantz is that these two types of nouns can coordinate and share dependents (example (18a) is from Wechsler (2008a: Section 7)):

(18) a. With nothing left after the soldier's [destruction and looting] of their home, they reboarded their coach and set out for the port of Calais.[15]
b. The [cultivation, growing or distribution] of medical marijuana within the County shall at all times occur within a secure, locked, and fully enclosed structure, including a ceiling, roof or top, and shall meet the following requirements.[16]

On the phrasal analysis, the nouns *looting* and *growing* occur in one type of syntactic environment (namely *v*P), while forms *destruction*, *cultivation*, and *distribution* occur in

[14] See Section 21.3.3 for further discussion.
[15] http://www.amazon.com/review/R3IG4M3Q6YYNFT, 21.07.2012
[16] http://www.scribd.com/doc/64013640/Tulare-County-medical-cannabis-cultivation-ordinance, 05.03.2016

a different syntactic environment. This places contradictory demands on the structure of coordinations like those in (18). As far as we know, neither this problem nor the others raised by Wechsler (2008a) have even been addressed by advocates of the phrasal theory of argument structure.

Consider one last example. In an influential phrasal analysis, Hale and Keyser (1993) derived denominal verbs like *to saddle* through noun incorporation out of a structure akin to [PUT a saddle ON x]. Again, verbs with this putative derivation routinely coordinate and share dependents with verbs of other types:

(19) Realizing the dire results of such a capture and that he was the only one to prevent it, he quickly [saddled and mounted] his trusted horse and with a grim determination began a journey that would become legendary.[17]

As in all of these X^0 coordination cases, under the phrasal analysis the two verbs place contradictory demands on a single phrase structure.

A lexical valence structure is an abstraction or generalization over various occurrences of the verb in syntactic contexts. To be sure, one key use of that valence structure is simply to indicate what sort of phrases the verb must (or can) combine with, and the result of semantic composition; if that were the whole story then the phrasal theory would be viable. But it is not. As it turns out, this lexical valence structure, once abstracted, can alternatively be used in other ways: among other possibilities, the verb (crucially including its valence structure) can be coordinated with other verbs that have similar valence structures; or it can serve as the input to lexical rules specifying a new word bearing a systematic relation to the input word. The coordination and lexical derivation facts follow from the lexical view, while the phrasal theory at best leaves these facts as mysterious and at worst leads to irreconcilable contradictions for the phrase structure.

21.2.2 Valence and derivational morphology

Goldberg & Jackendoff (2004), Alsina (1996), and Asudeh, Dalrymple & Toivonen (2008, 2013) suggest analyzing resultative constructions and/or caused-motion constructions as phrasal constructions.[18] As was argued in Müller (2006) this is incompatible with the assumption of lexical integrity. Lexical integrity means that word formation happens before syntax and that the morphological structure is inaccessible to syntactic processes (Bresnan & Mchombo 1995).[19] Let us consider a concrete example, such as (20):

[17] http://www.jouetthouse.org/index.php?option=com_content&view=article&id=56&Itemid=63, 21.07.2012

[18] Asudeh & Toivonen (2014: Section 2.3) argue that their account is not constructional. If a construction is a form-meaning pair, their account is constructional, since a certain c-structure is paired with a semantic contribution. Asudeh and Toivonen compare their approach with approaches in Constructional HPSG (Sag 1997) and Sign-Based Construction Grammar (see Section 10.6.2), which they term constructional. The only difference between these approaches and the approach by Asudeh, Dalrymple & Toivonen is that the constructions in the HPSG-based theories are modeled using types and hence have a name.

[19] Asudeh et al. (2013: 14) claim that the Swedish Directed Motion Construction does not interact with derivational morphology. However, the parallel German construction does interact with derivational morphology. The absence of this interaction in Swedish can be explained by other factors of Swedish grammar and given this I believe it to be more appropriate to assume an analysis that captures both the German and the Swedish data in the same way.

(20) a. Er tanzt die Schuhe blutig / in Stücke.
he dances the shoes bloody into pieces

b. die in Stücke / blutig getanzten Schuhe
the into pieces bloody danced shoes

c. * die getanzten Schuhe
the danced shoes

The shoes are not a semantic argument of *tanzt.* Nevertheless the referent of the NP that is realized as accusative NP in (20a) is the element the adjectival participle in (20b) predicates over. Adjectival participles like the one in (20b) are derived from a passive participle of a verb that governs an accusative object. If the accusative object is licensed phrasally by configurations like the one in (20a), then it is not possible to explain why the participle *getanzten* can be formed despite the absence of an accusative object in the valence specification of the verb. See Müller (2006: Section 5) for further examples of the interaction of resultatives and morphology. The conclusion drawn by Dowty (1978: 412) and Bresnan (1982b: 21) in the late 70s and early 80s is that phenomena which feed morphology should be treated lexically. The natural analysis in frameworks like HPSG, CG, CxG, and LFG is therefore one that assumes a lexical rule for the licensing of resultative constructions. See Verspoor (1997), Wechsler (1997), Wechsler & Noh (2001), Wunderlich (1992: 45; 1997: 120–126), Kaufmann & Wunderlich (1998), Müller (2002a: Chapter 5), Kay (2005), and Simpson (1983) for lexical proposals in some of these frameworks.

This argument is similar to the one that was discussed in connection with the GPSG representation of valence in Section 5.5: morphological processes have to be able to see the valence of the element they apply to. This is not the case if arguments are introduced by phrasal configurations after the level of morphology.

Asudeh, Dalrymple & Toivonen's papers are about the concept of lexical integrity and about constructions. Asudeh & Toivonen (2014) replied to our target article and pointed out (again) that their template approach makes it possible to specify the functional structure of words and phrases alike. In the original paper they discussed the Swedish word *vägen,* which is the definite form of *väg* 'way'. They showed that the f-structure is parallel to the f-structure for the English phrase *the way.* In our reply (2014b), we gave in too early, I believe. Since the point is not about being able to provide the f-structure of words, the point is about morphology, that is – in LFG terms – about deriving the f-structure by a morphological analysis. More generally speaking, one wants to derive all properties of the involved words, that is, their valence, their meaning, and the linking of this meaning to their dependents. What we used in our argument based on the sentences in (20) was parallel to what Bresnan (1982b: 21; 2001: 31) used in her classical argument for a lexical treatment of the passive. So either Bresnan's argument (and ours) is invalid or both arguments are valid and there is a problem for Asudeh, Dalrymple & Toivonen's approach and for phrasal approaches in general. I want to give another example that was already discussed in Müller (2006: 869) but was omitted in Müller & Wechsler (2014a) due to space limitations. I will first point out why this example is problematic for phrasal approaches and then explain why it is not sufficient to be able to assign certain f-structures to words: in (21a), we are dealing with a resultative construction. According to the plugging approach, the resultative meaning is contributed by a phrasal construction into which the verb *fischt* is inserted. There is no lexical item that requires a resultative predicate as its argument. If no such lexical item exists, then it is unclear how the relation between (21a) and (21b) can be established:

(21) a. [dass] jemand die Nordsee leer fischt
that somebody the North.Sea empty fishes
'that somebody fishes the North Sea empty'

b. wegen der *Leerfischung* der Nordsee[20]
because of.the empty.fishing of.the North.Sea
'because of the fishing that resulted in the North Sea being empty'

As Figure 21.1 shows, both the arguments selected by the heads and the structures are completely different. In (21b), the element that is the subject of the related construction in (21a) is not realized. As is normally the case in nominalizations, it is possible to realize it in a PP with the preposition *durch* 'by':

(22) wegen der Leerfischung der Nordsee durch die Anrainerstaaten
because of.the empty.fishing of.the North.Sea by the neighboring.states
'because of the fishing by the neighboring states that resulted in the North Sea being empty'

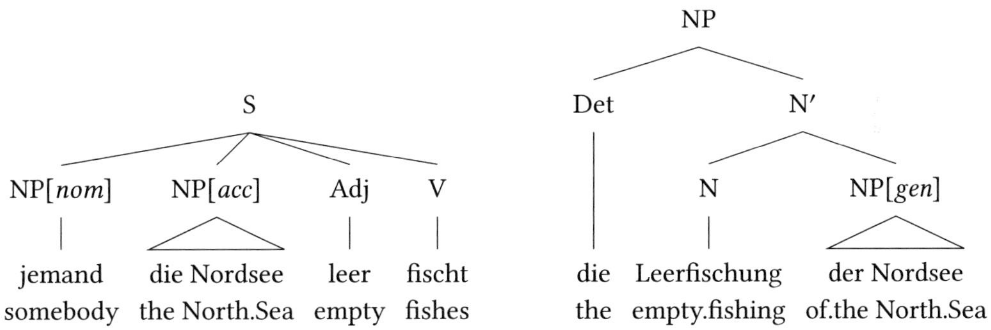

Figure 21.1: Resultative construction and nominalization

If one assumes that the resultative meaning comes from a particular configuration in which a verb is realized, there would be no explanation for (21b) since no verb is involved in the analysis of this example. One could of course assume that a verb stem is inserted into a construction both in (21a) and (21b). The inflectional morpheme *-t* and the derivational morpheme *-ung* as well as an empty nominal inflectional morpheme would then be independent syntactic components of the analysis. However, since Goldberg (2003b: 119) and Asudeh et al. (2013) assume lexical integrity, only entire words can

[20] taz, 20.06.1996, p. 6.

be inserted into syntactic constructions and hence the analysis of the nominalization of resultative constructions sketched here is not an option for them.

One might be tempted to try and account for the similarities between the phrases in (21) using inheritance. One would specify a general resultative construction standing in an inheritance relation to the resultative construction with a verbal head and the nominalization construction. I have discussed this proposal in more detail in Müller (2006: Section 5.3). It does not work as one needs embedding for derivational morphology and this cannot be modeled in inheritance hierarchies (Krieger & Nerbonne (1993), see also Müller (2006) for a detailed discussion).

It would also be possible to assume that both constructions in (23), for which structures such as those in Figure 21.1 would have to be assumed, are connected via metarules.[21, 22]

(23) a. [Sbj Obj Obl V]
  b. [Det [[Adj V -ung]] NP[*gen*]]

The construction in (23b) corresponds to Figure 21.2.[23] The genitive NP is an argument

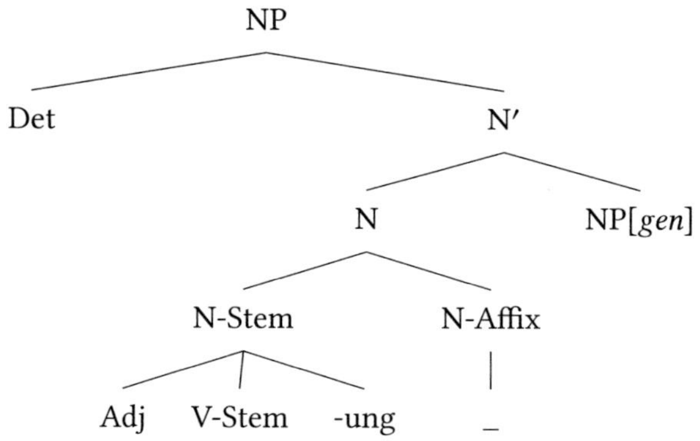

Figure 21.2: Resultative construction and nominalization

of the adjective. It has to be linked semantically to the subject slot of the adjective. Alternatively, one could assume that the construction only has the form [Adj V *-ung*], that is, that it does not include the genitive NP. But then one could also assume that the verbal variant of the resultative construction has the form [OBL V] and that Sbj and Obj are only represented in the valence lists. This would almost be a lexical analysis, however.

[21] Goldberg (p. c. 2007, 2009) suggests connecting certain constructions using GPSG-like metarules. Deppermann (2006: 51), who has a more Croftian view of CxG, rules this out. He argues for active/passive alternations that the passive construction has other information structural properties. Note also that GPSG metarules relate phrase structure rules, that is, local trees. The structure in Figure 21.2, however, is highly complex.

[22] The structure in (23b) violates a strict interpretation of lexical integrity as is commonly assumed in LFG. Booij (2005, 2009), working in Construction Grammar, subscribes to a somewhat weaker version, however.

[23] I do not assume zero affixes for inflection. The respective affix in Figure 21.2 is there to show that there is structure. Alternatively one could assume a unary branching rule/construction as is common in HPSG/Construction Morphology.

Turning to lexical integrity again, I want to point out that all that Asudeh & Toivonen can do is assign some f-structure to the N in Figure 21.2. What is needed, however, is a principled account of how this f-structure comes about and how it is related to the resultative construction on the sentence level.

Before I turn to approaches with radical underspecification of argument structure in the next section, I want to comment on a more recent paper by Asudeh, Giorgolo & Toivonen (2014). The authors discuss the phrasal introduction of cognate objects and benefactives. (24a) is an example of the latter construction.

(24) a. The performer sang the children a song.
b. The children were sung a song.

According to the authors, the noun phrase *the children* is not an argument of *sing* but contributed by the c-structure rule that optionally licenses a benefactive.

(25) $\mathrm{V}' \rightarrow \underset{(\ @\textsc{Benefactive}\ )}{\underset{\uparrow = \downarrow}{\mathrm{V}}} \quad \underset{(\uparrow \mathrm{OBJ}) = \downarrow}{\mathrm{DP}} \quad \underset{(\uparrow \mathrm{OBJ}_\theta) = \downarrow}{\mathrm{DP}}$

Whenever this rule is evoked, the template Benefactive can add a benefactive role and the respective semantics of this is compatible with the verb that is inserted into the structure. The authors show how the mappings for the passive example in (24b) work, but they do not provide the c-structure that licenses such examples. In order to analyze these examples one would need a c-structure rule for passive VPs and this rule has to license a benefactive as well. So it would be:

(26) $\mathrm{V}' \rightarrow \underset{(\ @\textsc{Benefactive}\ )}{\underset{\uparrow = \downarrow}{\mathrm{V[pass]}}} \quad \underset{(\uparrow \mathrm{OBJ}_\theta) = \downarrow}{\mathrm{DP}}$

Note that a benefactive cannot be added to any verb: adding a benefactive to an intransitive verb as in (27a) is out and the passive that would correspond to (27a) is ungrammatical as well, as (27b) shows:

(27) a. * He laughed the children.
b. * The children were laughed.

So one could not just claim that all c-structure rules optionally introduce a benefactive argument. Therefore there is something special about the two rules in (25) and (26). The problem is that there is no relation between these rules. They are independent statements saying that there can be a benefactive in the active and that there can be one in the passive. This is what Chomsky (1957: 43) criticized in 1957 and this was the reason for the introduction of transformations (see Section 3.1.1 of this book). Bresnan-style LFG captured the generalizations by lexical rules and later by Lexical Mapping Theory. But if elements are added outside the lexical representations, the representations where these elements are added have to be related too. One could say that our knowledge about formal tools has changed since 1957. We now can use inheritance hierarchies to capture generalizations. So one can assume a type (or a template) that is the supertype of all those c-structure rules that introduce a benefactive. But since not all rules allow for the introduction of a benefactive element, this basically amounts to saying: c-structure rule A, B, and C allow for the introduction of a benefactive. In comparison, lexical rule-based approaches have one statement introducing the benefactive. The lexical rule states what verbs are appropriate for adding a benefactive and syntactic rules are not affected.

In Müller & Wechsler (2014a) we argued that the approach to Swedish Caused-Motion Constructions in Asudeh et al. (2008, 2013) would not carry over to German since the German construction interacts with derivational morphology. Asudeh & Toivonen (2014) argued that Swedish is different from German and hence there would not be a problem. However, the situation is different with the benefactive constructions. Although English and German do differ in many respects, both languages have similar dative constructions:

(28) a. He baked her a cake.
  b. Er buk ihr einen Kuchen.
  he baked her.DAT a.ACC cake

Now, the analysis of the free constituent order was explained by assuming binary branching structures in which a VP node is combined with one of its arguments or adjuncts (see Section 7.4). The c-structure rule is repeated in (29):

(29) $\text{VP} \rightarrow \underset{(\uparrow \text{SUBJ} | \text{OBJ} | \text{OBJ}_\theta) = \downarrow}{\text{NP}} \quad \underset{\uparrow = \downarrow}{\text{VP}}$

The dependent elements contribute to the f-structure of the verb and coherence/completeness ensure that all arguments of the verb are present. One could add the introduction of the benefactive argument to the VP node of the right-hand side of the rule. However, since the verb-final variant of (28b) would have the structure in (30), one would get spurious ambiguities, since the benefactive could be introduced at every node:

(30) weil [$_{VP}$ er [$_{VP}$ ihr [$_{VP}$ einen Kuchen [$_{VP}$ [$_{V}$ buk]]]]]
  because he her a cake baked

So the only option seems to be to introduce the benefactive at the rule that got the recursion going, namely the rule that projected the lexical verb to the VP level. The rule (39) from page 228 is repeated as (31) for convenience.

(31) $\text{VP} \rightarrow \underset{\uparrow = \downarrow}{\text{(V)}}$

Note also that benefactive datives appear in adjectival environments as in (32):

(32) a. der seiner Frau einen Kuchen backende Mann
  the his.DAT wife a.ACC cake baking man
  'the man who is baking a cake for her'
  b. der einen Kuchen seiner Frau backende Mann
  the a.ACC cake his.DAT wife baking man
  'the man who is baking a cake for her'

In order to account for these datives one would have to assume that the adjective-to-AP rule that would be parallel to (31) introduces the dative. The semantics of the benefactive template would have to somehow make sure that the benefactive argument is not added to intransitive verbs like *lachen* 'to laugh' or participles like *lachende* 'laughing'. While this may be possible, I find the overall approach unattractive. First it does not have anything to do with the original constructional proposal but just states that the benefactive may be introduced at several places in syntax, second the unary branching syntactic rule is applying to a lexical item and hence is very similar to a lexical rule and third the analysis does not capture cross-linguistic commonalities of the construction. In a lexical rule-based approach as the one that was suggested by Briscoe & Copestake (1999: Section 5), a benefactive argument is added to certain verbs and the lexical rule is parallel in all languages that have this phenomenon. The respective languages differ simply in the way the arguments are realized with respect to their heads. In languages that have adjectival participles, these are derived from the respective verbal stems. The morphological rule is the same independent of benefactive arguments and the syntactic rules for adjectival phrases do not have to mention benefactive arguments.

21.3 Radical underspecification: the end of argument structure?

21.3.1 Neo-Davidsonianism

In the last section we examined proposals that assume that verbs come with certain argument roles and are inserted into prespecified structures that may contribute additional arguments. While we showed that this is not without problems, there are even more radical proposals that the construction adds all agent arguments, or even all arguments. The notion that the agent argument should be severed from its verbs is put forth by Marantz (1984, 1997), Kratzer (1996), Embick (2004) and others. Others suggest that no arguments are selected by the verb. Borer (2003) calls such proposals *exoskeletal* since the structure of the clause is not determined by the predicate, that is, the verb does not project an inner "skeleton" of the clause. Counter to such proposals are *endoskeletal* approaches, in which the structure of the clause is determined by the predicate, that is, lexical proposals. The radical exoskeletal approaches are mainly proposed in Mainstream Generative Grammar (Borer 1994, 2003, 2005; Schein 1993; Hale & Keyser 1997; Lohndal 2012) but can also be found in HPSG (Haugereid 2009). We will not discuss these proposals in detail here, but we review the main issues insofar as they relate to the question of lexical argument structure.[24] We conclude that the available empirical evidence favors the lexical argument structure approach over such alternatives.

Exoskeletal approaches usually assume some version of Neo-Davidsonianism. Davidson (1967) argued for an event variable in the logical form of action sentences (33a). Dowty (1989) coined the term *neo-Davidsonian* for the variant in (33b), in which the verb translates to a property of events, and the subject and complement dependents

[24] See Müller (2010a: Section 11.11.3) for a detailed discussion of Haugereid's approach.

are translated as arguments of secondary predicates such as *agent* and *theme*.[25] Kratzer (1996) further noted the possibility of mixed accounts such as (33c), in which the agent (subject) argument is severed from the *kill′* relation, but the theme (object) remains an argument of the *kill′* relation.[26]

(33) a. *kill*: $\lambda y \lambda x \exists e[kill(e, x, y)]$ (Davidsonian)
b. *kill*: $\lambda y \lambda x \exists e[kill(e) \wedge agent(e, x) \wedge theme(e, y)]$ (neo-Davidsonian)
c. *kill*: $\lambda y \lambda x \exists e[kill(e, y) \wedge agent(e, x)]$ (mixed)

Kratzer (1996) observed that a distinction between Davidsonian, neo-Davidsonian and mixed can be made either "in the syntax" or "in the conceptual structure" (Kratzer 1996: 110–111). For example, on a lexical approach of the sort we advocate here, any of the three alternatives in (33) could be posited as the semantic content of the verb *kill*. A lexical entry for *kill* in the mixed model is given in (34).

(34) $\begin{bmatrix} \text{PHON} & \langle \textit{kill} \rangle \\ \text{ARG-ST} & \langle \text{NP}_x, \text{NP}_y \rangle \\ \text{CONTENT} & \textit{kill(e, y)} \wedge \textit{agent(e, x)} \end{bmatrix}$

In other words, the lexical approach is neutral on the question of the "conceptual structure" of eventualities, as noted already in a different connection in Section 21.1.4. For this reason, certain semantic arguments for the neo-Davidsonian approach, such as those put forth by Schein (1993: Chapter 4) and Lohndal (2012), do not directly bear upon the issue of lexicalism, as far as we can tell.

But Kratzer (1996), among others, has gone further and argued for an account that is neo-Davidsonian (or rather, mixed) "in the syntax". Kratzer's claim is that the verb specifies only the internal argument(s), as in (35a) or (35b), while the agent (external argument) role is assigned by the phrasal structure. On the "neo-Davidsonian in the syntax" view, the lexical representation of the verb has no arguments at all, except the event variable, as shown in (35c).

(35) a. *kill*: $\lambda y \lambda e[kill(e, y)]$ (agent is severed)
b. *kill*: $\lambda y \lambda e[kill(e) \wedge theme(e, y)]$ (agent is severed)
c. *kill*: $\lambda e[kill(e))]$ (all arguments severed)

On such accounts, the remaining dependents of the verb receive their semantic roles from silent secondary predicates, which are usually assumed to occupy the positions of functional heads in the phrase structure. An Event Identification rule identifies the event variables of the verb and the silent light verb (Kratzer 1996: 22); this is why the existential quantifiers in (33) have been replaced with lambda operators in (35). A standard term for the agent-assigning silent predicate is "little *v*" (see Section 4.1.4 on little *v*). These

[25] Dowty (1989) called the system in (33a) an *ordered argument system*.

[26] The event variable is shown as existentially bound, as in Davidson's original account. As discussed below, in Kratzer's version it must be bound by a lambda operator instead.

extra-lexical dependents are the analogs of the ones contributed by the constructions in Construction Grammar.

In the following subsections we address arguments that have been put forth in favor of the little *v* hypothesis, from idiom asymmetries (Section 21.3.2) and deverbal nominals (Section 21.3.3). We argue that the evidence actually favors the lexical view. Then we turn to problems for exoskeletal approaches, from idiosyncratic syntactic selection (Section 21.3.4) and expletives (Section 21.3.5). We conclude with a look at the treatment of idiosyncratic syntactic selection under Borer's exoskeletal theory (Section 21.3.7), and a summary (Section 21.3.8).

21.3.2 Little *v* and idiom asymmetries

Marantz (1984) and Kratzer (1996) argued for severing the agent from the argument structure as in (35a), on the basis of putative idiom asymmetries. Marantz (1984) observed that while English has many idioms and specialized meanings for verbs in which the internal argument is the fixed part of the idiom and the external argument is free, the reverse situation is considerably rarer. To put it differently, the nature of the role played by the subject argument often depends on the filler of the object position, but not vice versa. To take Kratzer's examples (Kratzer 1996: 114):

(36) a. kill a cockroach
  b. kill a conversation
  c. kill an evening watching TV
  d. kill a bottle (i.e. empty it)
  e. kill an audience (i.e., wow them)

On the other hand, one does not often find special meanings of a verb associated with the choice of subject, leaving the object position open (examples from Marantz (1984: 26)):

(37) a. Harry killed NP.
  b. Everyone is always killing NP.
  c. The drunk refused to kill NP.
  d. Silence certainly can kill NP.

Kratzer observes that a mixed representation of *kill* as in (38a) allows us to specify varying meanings that depend upon its sole NP argument.

(38) a. *kill*: $\lambda y \lambda e[kill(e, y)]$
  b. If *a* is a time interval, then $kill(e, a) = truth$ if *e* is an event of wasting *a*
  If *a* is animate, then $kill(e, a) = truth$ if *e* is an event in which *a* dies
  ... etc.

On the polyadic (Davidsonian) theory, the meaning could similarly be made to depend upon the filler of the agent role. On the polyadic view, "there is no technical obstacle" (Kratzer 1996: 116) to conditions like those in (38b), except reversed, so that it is the filler of the agent role instead of the theme role that affects the meaning. But, she writes, this could not be done if the agent is not an argument of the verb. According to Kratzer, the agent-severed representation (such as (38a)) disallows similar constraints on the meaning that depend upon the agent, thereby capturing the idiom asymmetry.

But as noted by Wechsler (2005), "there is no technical obstacle" to specifying agent-dependent meanings even if the Agent has been severed from the verb as Kratzer proposes. It is true that there is no variable for the agent in (38a). But there is an event variable *e*, and the language user must be able to identify the agent of *e* in order to interpret the sentence. So one could replace the variable *a* with "the agent of *e*" in the expressions in (38b), and thereby create verbs that violate the idiom asymmetry.

While this may seem to be a narrow technical or even pedantic point, it is nonetheless crucial. Suppose we try to repair Kratzer's argument with an additional assumption: that modulations in the meaning of a polysemous verb can only depend upon arguments of the *relation* denoted by that verb, and not on other participants in the event. Under that additional assumption, it makes no difference whether the agent is severed from the lexical entry or not. For example, consider the following (mixed) neo-Davidsonian representation of the semantic content in the lexical entry of *kill*:

(39) *kill*: $\lambda y \lambda x \lambda e[kill(e, y) \wedge agent(e, x)]$

Assuming that sense modulations can only be affected by arguments of the *kill(e,y)* relation, we derive the idiom asymmetry, even if (39) is the lexical entry for *kill*. So suppose that we try to fix Kratzer's argument with a different assumption: that modulations in the meaning of a polysemous verb can only depend upon an argument of the lexically denoted function. Kratzer's "neo-Davidsonian in the syntax" lexical entry in (35a) lacks the agent argument, while the lexical entry in (39) clearly has one. But Kratzer's entry still fails to predict the asymmetry because, as noted above, it has the *e* argument and so the sense modulation can be conditioned on the "agent of *e*". As noted above, that event argument cannot be eliminated (for example through existential quantification) because it is needed in order to undergo event identification with the event argument of the silent light verb that introduces the agent (Kratzer 1996: 22).

Moreover, recasting Kratzer's account in lexicalist terms allows for verbs to vary. This is an important advantage, because the putative asymmetry is only a tendency. The following are examples in which the subject is a fixed part of the idiom and there are open slots for non-subjects:[27]

(40)
a. A little bird told X that S.
   'X heard the rumor that S.'
b. The cat's got X's tongue.
   'X cannot speak.'
c. What's eating X?
   'Why is X so galled?'

[27] (40a) is from Nunberg, Sag & Wasow (1994: 526), (40b) from Bresnan (1982a: 349–350), and (40c) from Bresnan (1982a: 349–350).

Further data and discussion of subject idioms in English and German can be found in Müller (2007b: Section 3.2.1).

The tendency towards a subject-object asymmetry plausibly has an independent explanation. Nunberg, Sag & Wasow (1994) argue that the subject-object asymmetry is a side-effect of an animacy asymmetry. The open positions of idioms tend to be animate while the fixed positions tend to be inanimate. Nunberg et al. (1994) derive these animacy generalizations from the figurative and proverbial nature of the metaphorical transfers that give rise to idioms. If there is an independent explanation for this tendency, then a lexicalist grammar successfully encodes those patterns, perhaps with a mixed neo-Davidsonian lexical decomposition, as explained above (see Wechsler (2005) for such a lexical account of the verbs *buy* and *sell*). But the little *v* hypothesis rigidly predicts this asymmetry for all agentive verbs, and that prediction is not borne out.

21.3.3 Deverbal nominals

An influential argument against lexical argument structure involves English deverbal nominals and the causative alternation. It originates from a mention in Chomsky (1970), and is developed in detail by Marantz (1997); see also Pesetsky (1996) and Harley & Noyer (2000). The argument is often repeated, but it turns out that the empirical basis of the argument is incorrect, and the actual facts point in the opposite direction, in favor of lexical argument structure (Wechsler 2008b,a).

Certain English causative alternation verbs allow optional omission of the agent argument (41), while the cognate nominal disallows expression of the agent (42):

(41) a. that John grows tomatoes
  b. that tomatoes grow

(42) a. * John's growth of tomatoes
  b. the tomatoes' growth, the growth of the tomatoes

In contrast, nominals derived from obligatorily transitive verbs such as *destroy* allow expression of the agent, as shown in (44a):

(43) a. that the army destroyed the city
  b. * that the city destroyed

(44) a. the army's destruction of the city
  b. the city's destruction

Following a suggestion by Chomsky (1970), Marantz (1997) argued on the basis of these data that the agent role is lacking from lexical entries. In verbal projections like (41) and (43) the agent role is assigned in the syntax by little *v*. Nominal projections like (42) and (44) lack little *v*. Instead, pragmatics takes over to determine which agents can be expressed by the possessive phrase: the possessive can express "the sort of agent implied by an event with an external rather than an internal cause" because only the former can "easily be reconstructed" (quoted from Marantz (1997: 218)). The destruction of a city has a cause external to the city, while the growth of tomatoes is internally caused by the tomatoes themselves (Smith 1970). Marantz points out that this explanation is unavailable if the noun is derived from a verb with an argument structure specifying its agent, since the deverbal nominal would inherit the agent of a causative alternation verb.

The empirical basis for this argument is the putative mismatch between the allowability of agent arguments, across some verb-noun cognate pairs: e.g., *grow* allows the agent but *growth* does not. But it turns out that the *grow/growth* pattern is rare. Most deverbal nominals precisely parallel the cognate verb: if the verb has an agent, so does the noun. Moreover, there is a ready explanation for the exceptional cases that exhibit the *grow/growth* pattern (Wechsler 2008a). First consider non-alternating theme-only intransitives (unaccusatives), as in (45) and non-alternating transitives as in (46). The pattern is clear: if the verb is agentless, then so is the noun:

(45) *arriv(al), disappear(ance), fall* etc.:
  a. A letter arrived.
  b. the arrival of the letter
  c. * The mailman arrived a letter.
  d. * the mailman's arrival of the letter

(46) *destroy/destruction, construct(ion), creat(ion), assign(ment)* etc.:
  a. The army is destroying the city.
  b. the army's destruction of the city

This favors the view that the noun inherits the lexical argument structure of the verb. For the anti-lexicalist, the badness of (45c) and (45d), respectively, would have to receive independent explanations. For example, on Harley and Noyer's 2000 proposal, (45c) is disallowed because a feature of the root ARRIVE prevents it from appearing in the context of *v*, but (45d) is instead ruled out because the cause of an event of arrival cannot be easily reconstructed from world knowledge. This exact duplication in two separate components of the linguistic system would have to be replicated across all non-alternating intransitive and transitive verbs, a situation that is highly implausible.

Turning to causative alternation verbs, Marantz's argument is based on the implicit generalization that noun cognates of causative alternation verbs (typically) lack the agent argument. But apart from the one example of *grow/growth*, there do not seem to be any clear cases of this pattern. Besides *grow(th)*, Chomsky (1970: examples (7c) and (8c)) cited two experiencer predicates, *amuse* and *interest*: *John amused (interested) the children with his stories* versus **John's amusement (interest) of the children with his stories.* But this was later shown by Rappaport (1983) and Dowty (1989) to have an independent aspectual explanation. Deverbal experiencer nouns like *amusement* and *interest* typically denote a mental state, where the corresponding verb denotes an event in which such a mental state comes about or is caused. These result nominals lack not only the agent but all the eventive arguments of the verb, because they do not refer to events. Exactly to the extent that such nouns can be construed as representing events, expression of the agent becomes acceptable.

In a response to Chomsky (1970), Carlota Smith (1972) surveyed Webster's dictionary and found no support for Chomsky's claim that deverbal nominals do not inherit agent arguments from causative alternation verbs. She listed many counterexamples, including "*explode, divide, accelerate, expand, repeat, neutralize, conclude, unify*, and so on at length." (Smith 1972: 137). Harley and Noyer (2000) also noted many so-called "exceptions": *explode, accumulate, separate, unify, disperse, transform, dissolve/dissolution, detach(ment), disengage-(ment)*, and so on. The simple fact is that these are not exceptions because there is no generalization to which they can be exceptions. These long lists of verbs represent the norm, especially for suffix-derived nominals (in *-tion*, *-ment*, etc.). Many zero-derived nominals from alternating verbs also allow the agent, such as *change, release*, and *use*: *my constant change of mentors from 1992–1997*; *the frequent release of the prisoners by the governor*; *the frequent use of sharp tools by underage children* (examples from Borer (2003: fn. 13)).[28]

Like the experiencer nouns mentioned above, many zero-derived nominals lack event readings. Some reject all the arguments of the corresponding eventive verb, not just the agent: * *the freeze of the water*, * *the break of the window*, and so on. According to Stephen Wechsler, *his drop of the ball* is slightly odd, but *the drop of the ball* has exactly the same degree of oddness. The locution *a drop in temperature* matches the verbal one *The temperature dropped*, and both verbal and nominal forms disallow the agent: * *The storm dropped the temperature.* * *the storm's drop of the temperature.* In short, the facts seem to point in exactly the opposite direction from what has been assumed in this oft-repeated argument against lexical valence. Apart from the one isolated case of *grow/growth*, event-denoting deverbal nominals match their cognate verbs in their argument patterns.

Turning to *grow/growth* itself, we find a simple explanation for its unusual behavior (Wechsler 2008a). When the noun *growth* entered the English language, causative (transitive) *grow* did not exist. The OED provides these dates of the earliest attestations of *grow* and *growth*:

(47)	a. intransitive *grow*:	c725	'be verdant' ... 'increase' (intransitive)
	b. the noun *growth*:	1587	'increase' (intransitive)
	c. transitive *grow*:	1774	'cultivate (crops)'

Thus *growth* entered the language at a time when transitive *grow* did not exist. The argument structure and meaning were inherited by the noun from its source verb, and then preserved into present-day English. This makes perfect sense if, as we claim, words have predicate argument structures. Nominalization by *-th* suffixation is not productive in English, so *growth* is listed in the lexicon. To explain why *growth* lacks the agent we need only assume that a lexical entry's predicate argument structure dictates whether

[28] Pesetsky (1996: 79, ex. (231)) assigns a star to *the thief's return of the money*, but it is acceptable to many speakers. The *Oxford English Dictionary* lists a transitive sense for the noun *return* (definition 11a), and corpus examples like *her return of the spoils* are not hard to find.

it takes an agent argument or not. So even this one word provides evidence for lexical argument structure.

21.3.4 Idiosyncratic syntactic selections

The notion of lexical valence structure immediately explains why the argument realization patterns are strongly correlated with the particular lexical heads selecting those arguments. It is not sufficient to have general lexical items without valence information and let the syntax and world knowledge decide about argument realizations, because not all realizational patterns are determined by the meaning. The form of the preposition of a prepositional object is sometimes loosely semantically motivated but in other cases arbitrary. For example, the valence structure of the English verb *depend* captures the fact that it selects an *on*-PP to express one of its semantic arguments:

(48) a. John depends on Mary. (*counts, relies,* etc.)
b. John trusts (*on) Mary.
c. $\begin{bmatrix} \text{PHON} & \langle \textit{depend} \rangle \\ \text{ARG-ST} & \langle \text{NP}_x \text{ , PP}[\textit{on}]_y \rangle \\ \text{CONTENT} & \textit{depend(x,y)} \end{bmatrix}$

Such idiosyncratic lexical selection is utterly pervasive in human language. The verb or other predicator often determines the choice between direct and oblique morphology, and for obliques, it determines the choice of adposition or oblique case. In some languages such as Icelandic even the subject case can be selected by the verb (Zaenen, Maling & Thráinsson 1985).

Selection is language-specific. English *wait* selects *for* (German *für*) while German *warten* selects *auf* 'on' with an accusative object:

(49) a. I am waiting for my man.
b. Ich warte auf meinen Mann.
I wait on my man.ACC

It is often impossible to find semantic motivation for case. In German there is a tendency to replace genitive (50a) with dative (50b) with no apparent semantic motivation:

(50) a. dass der Opfer gedacht werde
that the victims.GEN remembered is
'that the victims would be remembered'
b. daß auch hier den Opfern des Faschismus gedacht werde [...][29]
that also here the victims.DAT of.the fascism remembered is
'that the victims of fascism would be remembered here too'

[29] Frankfurter Rundschau, 07.11.1997, p. 6.

The synonyms *treffen* and *begegnen* 'to meet' govern different cases (example from Pollard & Sag (1987: 126)).

(51) a. Er traf den Mann.
he.NOM met the.ACC man

b. Er begegnete dem Mann.
he.NOM met the.DAT man

One has to specify the case that the respective verbs require in the lexical items of the verbs.[30]

A radical variant of the plugging approach is suggested by Haugereid (2009).[31] Haugereid (pages 12–13) assumes that the syntax combines a verb with an arbitrary combination of a subset of five different argument roles. Which arguments can be combined with a verb is not restricted by the lexical item of the verb.[32] A problem for such views is that the meaning of an ambiguous verb sometimes depends on which of its arguments are expressed. The German verb *borgen* has the two translations 'borrow' and 'lend', which basically are two different perspectives on the same event (see Kunze (1991, 1993) for an extensive discussion of verbs of exchange of possession). Interestingly, the dative object is obligatory only with the 'lend' reading (Müller 2010a: 403):

(52) a. Ich borge ihm das Eichhörnchen.
I lend him the squirrel
'I lend the squirrel to him.'

b. Ich borge (mir) das Eichhörnchen.
I borrow me the squirrel
'I borrow the squirrel.'

If we omit it, we get only the 'borrow' reading. So the grammar must specify for specific verbs that certain arguments are necessary for a certain verb meaning or a certain perspective on an event.

Synonyms with differing valence specifications include the minimal triplet mentioned earlier: *dine* is obligatorily intransitive (or takes an *on*-PP), *devour* is transitive, and *eat* can be used either intransitively or transitively (Dowty 1989: 89–90). Many other examples are given in Levin (1993) and Levin & Rappaport Hovav (2005).

In a phrasal constructionist approach one would have to assume phrasal patterns with the preposition or case, into which the verb is inserted. For (49b), the pattern includes a prepositional object with *auf* and an accusative NP, plus an entry for *warten* specifying that it can be inserted into such a structure (see Kroch & Joshi (1985: Section 5.2) for such a proposal in the framework of TAG). Since there are generalizations regarding

[30] Or at least mark the fact that *treffen* takes an object with the default case for objects and *begegnen* takes a dative object in German. See Haider (1985a), Heinz & Matiasek (1994), and Müller (2001) on structural and lexical case.

[31] Technical aspects of Haugereid's approach are discussed in Section 21.3.6.

[32] Haugereid has the possibility to impose valence restrictions on verbs, but he claims that he uses this possibility just in order to get a more efficient processing of his computer implementation (p. 13).

verbs with such valence representations, one would be forced to have two inheritance hierarchies: one for lexical entries with their valence properties and another one for specific phrasal patterns that are needed for the specific constructions in which these lexical items can be used.

More often, proponents of neo-constructionist approaches either make proposals that are difficult to distinguish from lexical valence structures (see Section 21.3.7 below) or simply decline to address the problem. For instance, Lohndal (2012) writes:

> An unanswered question on this story is how we ensure that the functional heads occur together with the relevant lexical items or roots. This is a general problem for the view that Case is assigned by functional heads, and I do not have anything to say about this issue here. (Lohndal 2012)

We think that getting case assignment right in simple sentences, without vast overgeneration of ill-formed word sequences, is a minimal requirement for a linguistic theory.

21.3.5 Expletives

A final example for the irreducibility of valence to semantics are verbs that select for expletives and reflexive arguments of inherently reflexive verbs in German:

(53) a. weil es regnet
because it rains

b. weil (es) mir (vor der Prüfung) graut
because EXPL me.DAT before the exam dreads
'because I am dreading the exam'

c. weil er es bis zum Professor bringt
because he EXPL until to.the professor brings
'because he made it to professor'

d. weil es sich um den Montag handelt
because EXPL REFL around the Monday trades
'because it is about the Monday'

e. weil ich mich (jetzt) erhole
because I myself now recreate
'because I am relaxing now'

The lexical heads in (53) need to contain information about the expletive subjects/objects and/or reflexive pronouns that do not fill semantic roles. Note that German allows for subjectless predicates and hence the presence of expletive subjects cannot be claimed to follow from general principles. (53c) is an example with an expletive object. Explanations referring to the obligatory presence of a subject would fail on such examples in any case. Furthermore it has to be ensured that *erholen* is not realized in the [Sbj IntrVerb] construction for intransitive verbs or respective functional categories in a Minimalist setting although the relation *erholen′* (*relax′*) is a one-place predicate and hence *erholen* is semantically compatible with the construction.

21.3.6 An exoskeletal approach

In what follows I discuss Haugereid's proposal (2007) in more detail. His analysis has all the high-level problems that were mentioned in the previous subsections, but since it is worked out in detail it is interesting to see its predictions.

Haugereid (2007), working in the framework of HPSG, suggests an analysis along the lines of Borer (2005) where the meaning of an expression is defined as depending on the arguments that are present. He assumes that there are five argument slots that are assigned to semantic roles as follows:

- Arg1: agent or source
- Arg2: patient
- Arg3: benefactive or recipient
- Arg4: goal
- Arg5: antecedent

Here, antecedent is a more general role that stands for instrument, comitative, manner and source. The roles Arg1–Arg3 correspond to subject and objects. Arg4 is a resultative predicate of the end of a path. Arg4 can be realized by a PP, an AP or an NP. (54) gives examples for the realization of Arg4:

(54) a. John smashed the ball *out of the room.*
b. John hammered the metal *flat.*
c. He painted the car *a brilliant red.*

Whereas Arg4 follows the other participants in the causal chain of events, the antecedent precedes the patient in the order of events. It is realized as a PP. (55) is an example of the realization of Arg5:

(55) John punctured the balloon *with a needle.*

Haugereid now assumes that argument frames consist of these roles. He provides the examples in (56):

(56) a. John smiles. (arg1-frame)
b. John smashed the ball. (arg12-frame)
c. The boat arrived. (arg2-frame)
d. John gave Mary a book. (arg123-frame)
e. John gave a book to Mary. (arg124-frame)
f. John punctured the ball with a needle. (arg125-frame)

Haugereid points out that multiple verbs can occur in multiple argument frames. He provides the variants in (57) for the verb *drip*:

(57) a. The roof drips. (arg1-frame)
b. The doctor drips into the eyes. (arg14-frame)
c. The doctor drips with water. (arg15-frame)
d. The doctor drips into the eyes with water. (arg145-frame)
e. The roof drips water. (arg12-frame)
f. The roof drips water into the bucket. (arg124-frame)
g. The doctor dripped the eyes with water. (arg125-frame)
h. The doctor dripped into the eyes with water. (arg145-frame)
i. John dripped himself two drops of water. (arg123-frame)
j. John dripped himself two drops of water into his eyes. (arg1234-frame)
k. John dripped himself two drops of water into his eyes with a drop counter. (arg12345-frame)
l. Water dripped. (arg2-frame)
m. It drips. (arg0-frame)

He proposes the inheritance hierarchy in Figure 21.3 in order to represent all possible argument combinations. The Arg5 role is omitted due to space considerations.

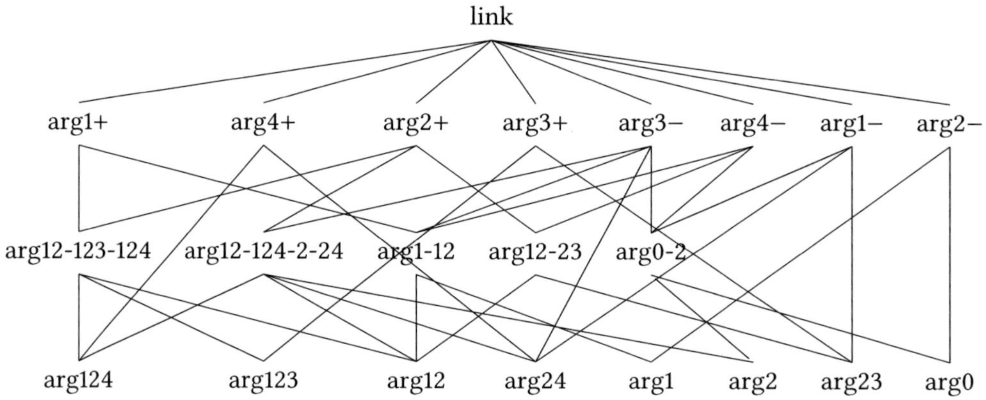

Figure 21.3: Hierarchy of argument frames following Haugereid (2007)

Haugereid assumes binary-branching structures where arguments can be combined with a head in any order. There is a dominance schema for each argument role. The schema realizing the argument role 3 provides a link value *arg3+*. If the argument role 2 is provided by another schema, we arrive at the frame *arg23*. For unergative intransitive verbs, it is possible to determine that it has an argument frame of *arg1*. This frame is only compatible with the types *arg1+*, *arg2−*, *arg3−* and *arg4−*. Verbs that have an optional object are assigned to *arg1-12* according to Haugereid. This type allows for the following combinations: *arg1+*, *arg2−*, *arg3−* and *arg4−* such as *arg1+*, *arg2+*, *arg3−* and *arg4−*.

This approach comes very close to an idea by Goldberg: verbs are underspecified with regard to the sentence structures in which they occur and it is only the actual realization of arguments in the sentence that decides which combinations of arguments are realized. One should bear in mind that the hierarchy in Figure 21.3 corresponds to a considerable disjunction: it lists all possible realizations of arguments. If we say that *essen* 'to eat' has the type *arg1-12*, then this corresponds to the disjunction *arg1* ∨ *arg12*. In addition to the information in the hierarchy above, one also requires information about the syntactic properties of the arguments (case, the form of prepositions, verb forms in verbal complements). Since this information is in part specific to each verb (see Section 21.1), it cannot be present in the dominance schemata and must instead be listed in each individual lexical entry. For the lexical entry for *warten auf* 'wait for', there must be information about the fact that the subject has to be an NP and that the prepositional object is an *auf*-PP with accusative. The use of a type hierarchy then allows one to elegantly encode the fact that the prepositional object is optional. The difference to a disjunctively specified SUBCAT list with the form of (58) is just a matter of formalization.

(58) SUBCAT ⟨ NP[*str*] ⟩ ∨ ⟨ NP[*str*], PP[*auf*, *acc*] ⟩

Since Haugereid's structures are binary-branching, it is possible to derive all permutations of arguments (59a–b), and adjuncts can be attached to every branching node (59c–d).

(59) a. dass [$_{arg1}$ keiner [$_{arg2}$ Pizza isst]]
that nobody pizza eats
'that nobody eats pizza'

b. dass [$_{arg2}$ Pizza [$_{arg1}$ keiner isst]]
that pizza nobody eats

c. dass [$_{arg1}$ keiner [gerne [$_{arg2}$ Pizza isst]]]
that nobody gladly pizza eats
'that nobody eats pizza gladly'

d. dass [[hier [$_{arg1}$ keiner [$_{arg2}$ Pizza isst]]]
that here nobody pizza eats
'that nobody eats pizza here'

Haugereid has therefore found solutions for some of the problems in Goldberg's analysis that were pointed out in Müller (2006). Nevertheless, there are a number of other problems, which I will discuss in what follows. In Haugereid's approach, nothing is said about the composition of meaning. He follows the so-called Neo-Davidsonian approach. In this kind of semantic representation, arguments of the verb are not directly represented on the verb. Instead, the verb normally has an event argument and the argument roles belonging to the event in question are determined in a separate predication. (60) shows two alternative representations, where *e* stands for the event variable.

(60) a. Der Mann isst eine Pizza.
the man eats a pizza
'The man is eating a pizza'

b. *eat′*(e, x, y) ∧ *man′*(x) ∧ *pizza′*(y)

c. *eat′*(e) ∧ *agent*(e,x) ∧ *theme*(e,y) ∧ *man′*(x) ∧ *pizza′*(y)

Haugereid adopts Minimal Recursion Semantics (MRS) as his semantic formalism (see also Section 9.1.6 and 19.3). The fact that arguments belong to a particular predicate is represented by the fact that the relevant predicates have the same handle. The representation in (60c) corresponds to (61):

(61) h1:*essen′*(e), h1:*arg1*(x), h1:*arg2*(y), h2:*mann′*(x), h3:*pizza′*(y)

This analysis captures Goldberg's main idea: meaning arises from particular constituents being realized together with a head.

For the sentence in (62a), Haugereid (2007, p. c.) assumes the semantic representation in (62b):[33]

(62) a. der Mann den Teich leer fischt
the man the pond empty fishes

b. h1:*mann′*(x), h2:*teich′*(y), h3:*leer′*(e),
h4:*fischen′*(e2), h4:*arg1*(x), h4:*arg2*(y), h4:*arg4*(h3)

In (62b), the *arg1*, *arg2* and *arg4* relations have the same handle as *fischen′*. Following Haugereid's definitions, this means that *arg2* is the patient of the event. In the case of (62a), this makes incorrect predictions since the accusative element is not a semantic argument of the main verb. It is a semantic argument of the secondary predicate *leer* 'empty' and has been raised to the object of the resultative construction. Depending on the exact analysis assumed, the accusative object is either a syntactic argument of the verb or of the adjective, however, it is never a semantic argument of the verb. In addition to this problem, the representation in (62b) does not capture the fact that *leer* 'empty' predicates over the object. Haugereid (2007, p.c.) suggests that this is implicit in the representation and follows from the fact that all *arg4*s predicate over all *arg2*s. Unlike Haugereid's analysis, analyses using lexical rules that relate a lexical item of a verb to another verbal item with a resultative meaning allow for a precise specification of the semantic representation that then captures the semantic relation between the predicates involved. In addition, the lexical rule-based analysis makes it possible to license lexical items that do not establish a semantic relation between the accusative object and the verb (Wechsler 1997; Wechsler & Noh 2001; Müller 2002a: Chapter 5).

[33] See Haugereid (2009: 165) for an analysis of the Norwegian examples in (i).

(i) Jon maler veggen rød.
Jon paints wall.DEF red
'Jon paints the wall red.'

Haugereid sketches an analysis of the syntax of the German clause and tackles active/passive alternations. However, certain aspects of the grammar are not elaborated on. In particular, it remains unclear how complex clauses containing AcI verbs such as *sehen* 'to see' and *lassen* 'to let' should be analyzed. Arguments of embedded and embedding verbs can be permuted in these constructions. Haugereid (2007, p. c.) assumes special rules that allow to saturate arguments of more deeply embedded verbs, for example, a special rule that combines an *arg2* argument of an argument with a verb. In order to combine *das Nilpferd* and *nicht füttern helfen lässt* in sentences such as (63), he is forced to assume a special grammatical rule that combines an argument of a doubly embedded verb with another verb:

(63) weil Hans Cecilia John das Nilpferd nicht füttern helfen lässt
because Hans Cecilia John the hippo not feed help let
'because Hans is not letting Cecilia help John feed the hippo.'

In Müller (2004c: 220), I have argued that embedding under complex-forming predicates is only constrained by performance factors (see also Section 12.6.3). In German, verbal complexes with more than four verbs are barely acceptable. Evers (1975: 58–59) has pointed out, however, that the situation in Dutch is different since Dutch verbal complexes have a different branching: in Dutch, verbal complexes with up to five verbs are possible. Evers attributes this difference to a greater processing load for German verbal complexes (see also Gibson 1998: Section 3.7). Haugereid would have to assume that there are more rules for Dutch than for German. In this way, he would give up the distinction between competence and performance and incorporate performance restrictions directly into the grammar. If he wanted to maintain a distinction between the two, then Haugereid would be forced to assume an infinite number of schemata or a schema with functional uncertainty since depth of embedding is only constrained by performance factors. Existing HPSG approaches to the analysis of verbal complexes do without functional uncertainty (Hinrichs & Nakazawa 1994). Since such raising analyses are required for object raising anyway (as discussed above), they should be given preference.

Summing up, it must be said that Haugereid's exoskeletal approach does account for different orderings of arguments, but it neither derives the correct semantic representations nor does it offer a solution for the problem of idiosyncratic selection of arguments and the selection of expletives.

21.3.7 Is there an alternative to lexical valence structure?

The question for theories denying the existence of valence structure is what replaces it to explain idiosyncratic lexical selection. In her exoskeletal approach, Borer (2005) explicitly rejects lexical valence structures. But she posits post-syntactic interpretive rules that are difficult to distinguish from them. To explain the correlation of *depend* with an *on*-PP, she posits the following interpretive rule (Borer 2005: Vol. II, p. 29):

(64) MEANING $\Leftrightarrow \pi_9 + [\langle e^{on} \rangle]$

Borer refers to all such cases of idiosyncratic selection as idioms. In a rule such as (64), "MEANING is whatever the relevant idiom means" (Borer 2005: Vol. II, p. 27). In (64), π_9 is the "phonological index" of the verb *depend* and e^{on} "corresponds to an open value that must be assigned range by the f-morph *on*" (Borer 2005: Vol. II, p. 29), where f-morphs are function words or morphemes. Hence this rule brings together much the same information as the lexical valence structure in (48c). Discussing such "idiom" rules, Borer writes

> Although by assumption a listeme cannot be associated with any grammatical properties, one device used in this work has allowed us to get around the formidable restrictions placed on the grammar by such a constraint – the formation of idioms. [...] Such idiomatic specification could be utilized, potentially, not just for *arrive* and *depend on*, but also for obligatorily transitive verbs [...], for verbs such as *put*, with their obligatory locative, and for verbs which require a sentential complement.
>
> The reader may object that subcategorization, of sorts, is introduced here through the back door, with the introduction, in lieu of lexical syntactic annotation, of an articulated listed structure, called an *idiom*, which accomplishes, de facto, the same task. The objection of course has some validity, and at the present state of the art, the introduction of idioms may represent somewhat of a concession.
> (Borer 2005: Vol. II, p. 354–355)

Borer goes on to pose various questions for future research, related to constraining the class of possible idioms. With regard to that research program it should be noted that a major focus of lexicalist research has been narrowing the class of subcategorization and extricating derivable properties from idiosyncratic subcategorization. Those are the functions of HPSG lexical hierarchies, for example.

21.3.8 Summary

In Sections 21.3.2–21.3.5 we showed that the question of which arguments must be realized in a sentence cannot be reduced to semantics and world knowledge or to general facts about subjects. The consequence is that valence information has to be connected to lexical items. One therefore must either assume a connection between a lexical item and a certain phrasal configuration as in Croft's approach (2003) and in LTAG or assume our lexical variant. In a Minimalist setting the right set of features must be specified lexically to ensure the presence of the right case assigning functional heads. This is basically similar to the lexical valence structures we are proposing here, except that it needlessly introduces various problems discussed above, such as the problem of coordination raised in Section 21.2.1.

21.4 Relations between constructions

On the lexical rules approach, word forms are related by lexical rules: a verb stem can be related to a verb with finite inflection and to a passive verb form; verbs can be converted to adjectives or nouns; and so on. The lexical argument structure accompanies the word and can be manipulated by the lexical rule. In this section we consider what can replace such rules within a phrasal or ASC approach.

21.4.1 Inheritance hierarchies for constructions

For each valence structure that the lexicalist associates with a root lexeme (transitive, ditransitive, etc.), the phrasal approach requires multiple phrasal constructions, one to replace each lexical rule or combination of lexical rules that can apply to the word. Taking ditransitives, for example, the phrasal approach requires an active-ditransitive construction, a passive-ditransitive construction, and so on, to replace the output of every lexical rule or combination of lexical rules applied to a ditransitive verb. (Thus Bergen & Chang (2005: 169–170) assume an active-ditransitive and a passive-ditransitive construction and Kallmeyer & Osswald (2012: 171–172) assume active and passive variants of the transitive construction.) On that view some of the active voice constructions for German would be:

(65) a. Nom V
b. Nom Acc V
c. Nom Dat V
d. Nom Dat Acc V

The passive voice constructions corresponding to (65) would be:

(66) a. V V-Aux
b. Nom V V-Aux
c. Dat V V-Aux
d. Dat Nom V V-Aux

Merely listing all these constructions is not only uneconomical but fails to capture the obvious systematic relation between active and passive constructions. Since phrasalists reject both lexical rules and transformations, they need an alternative way to relate phrasal configurations and thereby explain the regular relation between active and passive. The only proposals to date involve the use of inheritance hierarchies, so let us examine them.

Researchers working in various frameworks, both with lexical and phrasal orientation, have tried to develop inheritance-based analyses that could capture the relation between valence patterns such as those in (65) and (66) (see for instance Kay & Fillmore 1999: 12; Michaelis & Ruppenhofer 2001: Chapter 4; Candito 1996; Clément & Kinyon 2003: 188; Kallmeyer & Osswald 2012: 171–172; Koenig 1999: Chapter 3; Davis & Koenig 2000; Kordoni 2001 for proposals in CxG, TAG, and HPSG). The idea is that a single representation (lexical or phrasal, depending on the theory) can inherit properties from multiple constructions. In a phrasal approach the description of the pattern in (65b) inherits from the transitive and the active construction and the description of (66b) inherits from both the transitive and the passive constructions. Figure 21.4 illustrates the inheritance-based lexical approach: a lexical entry for a verb such as *read* or *eat* is combined with either an active or passive representation. The respective representations for the active and passive are responsible for the expression of the arguments.

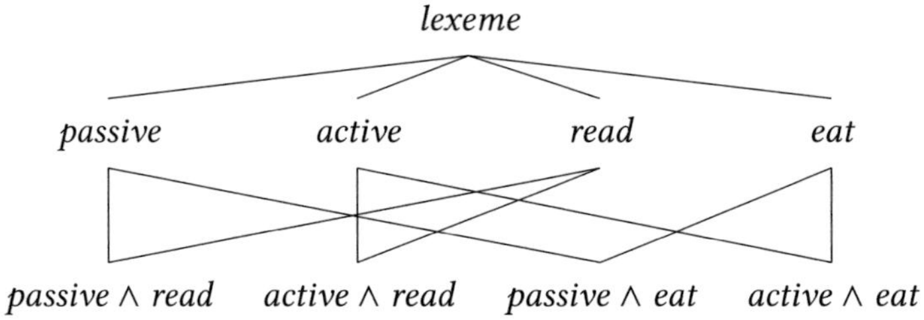

Figure 21.4: Inheritance Hierarchy for active and passive

As was already discussed in Section 10.2, inheritance-based analyses cannot account for multiple changes in valence as for instance the combination of passive and impersonal construction that can be observed in languages like Lithuanian (Timberlake 1982: Section 5), Irish (Noonan 1994), and Turkish (Özkaragöz 1986). Özkaragöz's Turkish examples are repeated here with the original glossing as (67) for convenience:

(67) a. Bu şato-da boğ-ul-un-ur. (Turkish)
this château-LOC strangle-PASS-PASS-AOR
'One is strangled (by one) in this château.'

b. Bu oda-da döv-ül-ün-ür.
this room-LOC hit-PASS-PASS-AOR
'One is beaten (by one) in this room.'

c. Harp-te vur-ul-un-ur.
war-LOC shoot-PASS-PASS-AOR
'One is shot (by one) in war.'

Another example from Section 10.2 that cannot be handled with inheritance is multiple causativization in Turkish. Turkish allows double and even triple causativization (Lewis 1967: 146):

(68) Öl-dür-t-tür-t- (Turkish)
'to cause somebody to cause somebody to kill somebody'

An inheritance-based analysis would not work, since inheriting the same information several times does not add anything new. Krieger & Nerbonne (1993) make the same point with respect to derivational morphology in cases like *preprepreversion*: inheriting information about the prefix *pre-* twice or more often, does not add anything.

So assuming phrasal models, the only way to capture the generalization with regard to (65) and (66) seems to be to assume GPSG-like metarules that relate the constructions in (65) to the ones in (66). If the constructions are lexically linked as in LTAG, the respective mapping rules would be lexical rules. For approaches that combine LTAG with the Goldbergian plugging idea such as the one by Kallmeyer & Osswald (2012) one would have to have extended families of trees that reflect the possibility of having additional arguments and would have to make sure that the right morphological form is inserted into the respective trees. The morphological rules would be independent of the syntactic structures in which the derived verbal lexemes could be used. One would have to assume two independent types of rules: GPSG-like metarules that operate on trees and morphological rules that operate on stems and words. We believe that this is an unnecessary complication and apart from being complicated the morphological rules would not be acceptable as form-meaning pairs in the CxG sense since one aspect of the form namely that additional arguments are required is not captured in these morphological rules. If such morphological rules were accepted as proper constructions then there would not be any reason left to require that the arguments have to be present in a construction in order for it to be recognizable, and hence, the lexical approach would be accepted.[34]

Inheritance hierarchies are the main explanatory device in Croft's Radical Construction Grammar (Croft 2001). He also assumes phrasal constructions and suggests representing these in a taxonomic network (an inheritance hierarchy). He assumes that every idiosyncrasy of a linguistic expression is represented on its own node in this kind of network. Figure 21.5 shows part of the hierarchy he assumes for sentences. There are

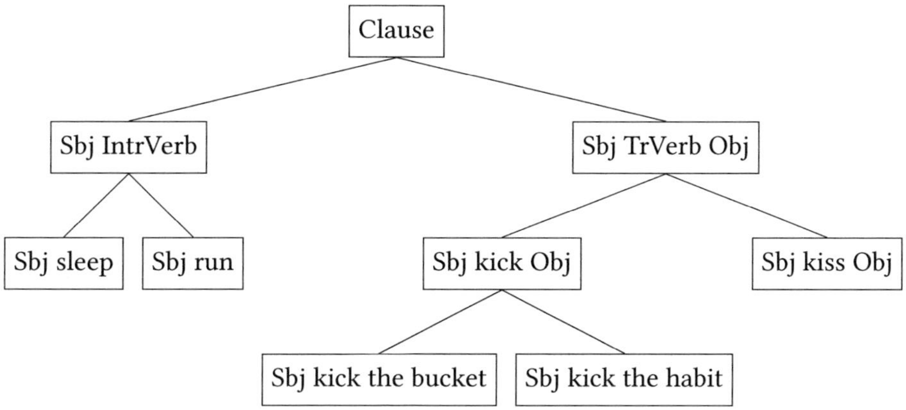

Figure 21.5: Classification of phrasal patterns in Croft (2001: 26)

sentences with intransitive verbs and sentences with transitive verbs. Sentences with the form [Sbj kiss Obj] are special instances of the construction [Sbj TrVerb Obj]. The [Sbj kick Obj] construction also has further sub-constructions, namely the constructions [Sbj kick the bucket] and [Subj kick the habit]. Since constructions are always pairs of form and meaning, this gives rise to a problem: in a normal sentence with *kick*, there is a kicking relation between the subject and the object of *kick*. This is not the case for the idiomatic use of *kick* in (69):

[34] Compare the discussion of *Totschießen* 'shoot dead' in example (81) below.

(69) He kicked the bucket.

This means that there cannot be a normal inheritance relation between the [Sbj kick Obj] and the [Sbj kick the bucket] construction. Instead, only parts of the information may be inherited from the [Sbj kick Obj] construction. The other parts are redefined by the sub-construction. This kind of inheritance is referred to as *default inheritance.*

kick the bucket is a rather fixed expression, that is, it is not possible to passivize it or front parts of it without losing the idiomatic reading (Nunberg, Sag & Wasow 1994: 508). However, this is not true for all idioms. As Nunberg, Sag & Wasow (1994: 510) have shown, there are idioms that can be passivized (70a) as well as realizations of idioms where parts of idioms occur outside of the clause (70b).

(70) a. The beans were spilled by Pat.
b. The strings [that Pat pulled] got Chris the job.

The problem is now that one would have to assume two nodes in the inheritance hierarchy for idioms that can undergo passivization since the realization of the constituents is different in active and passive variants but the meaning is nevertheless idiosyncratic. The relation between the active and passive form would not be captured. Kay (2002) has proposed an algorithm for computing objects (Construction-like objects = CLOs) from hierarchies that then license active and passive variants. As I have shown in Müller (2006: Section 3), this algorithm does not deliver the desired results and it is far from straightforward to improve it to the point that it actually works. Even if one were to adopt the changes I proposed, there are still phenomena that cannot be described using inheritance hierarchies (see Section 10.2 in this book).

A further interesting point is that the verbs have to be explicitly listed in the constructions. This begs the question of how constructions should be represented where the verbs are used differently. If a new node in the taxonomic network is assumed for cases like (71), then Goldberg's criticism of lexical analyses that assume several lexical entries for a verb that can appear in various constructions[35] will be applicable here: one would have to assume constructions for every verb and every possible usage of that verb.

(71) He kicked the bucket into the corner.

For sentences with negation, Croft assumes the hierarchy with multiple inheritance given in Figure 21.6 on the following page. The problem with this kind of representation is that it remains unclear as to how the semantic embedding of the verb meaning under negation can be represented. If all constructions are pairs of form and meaning, then there would have to be a semantic representation for [Sbj IntrVerb] (CONT value or SEM value). Similarly, there would have to be a meaning for [Sbj Aux-n't Verb]. The problem now arises that the meaning of [Sbj IntrVerb] has to be embedded under the meaning of the negation and this cannot be achieved directly using inheritance since X and not(X) are incompatible. There is a technical solution to this problem using auxiliary

[35] Note the terminology: I used the word *lexical entry* rather than *lexical item.* The HPSG analysis uses lexical rules that correspond to Goldberg's templates. What Goldberg criticizes is lexical rules that relate lexical entries, not lexical rules that licence new lexical items, which may be stored or not. HPSG takes the latter approach to lexical rules. See Section 9.2.

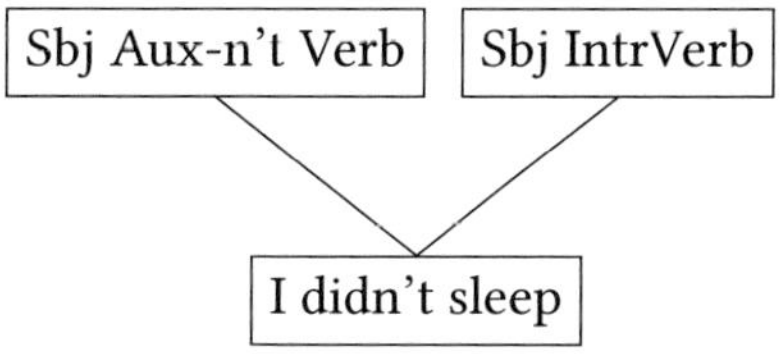

Figure 21.6: Interaction of phrasal patterns following Croft (2001: 26)

features. Since there are a number of interactions in grammars of natural languages, this kind of analysis is highly implausible if one claims that features are a direct reflection of observable properties of linguistic objects. For a more detailed discussion of approaches with classifications of phrasal patterns, see Müller (2010b) as well as Müller (2007b: Section 18.3.2.2) and for the use of auxiliary features in inheritance-based analyses of the lexicon, see Müller (2007b: Section 7.5.2.2).

21.4.2 Mappings between different levels of representations

Culicover & Jackendoff (2005: Chapter 6.3) suggest that passive should be analyzed as one of several possible mappings from the Grammatical Function tier to the surface realization of arguments. Surface realizations of referential arguments can be NPs in a certain case, with certain agreement properties, or in a certain position. While such analyses that work by mapping elements with different properties onto different representations are common in theories like LFG and HPSG (Koenig 1999; Bouma, Malouf & Sag 2001a), a general property of these analyses is that one needs one level of representation per interaction of phenomena (ARG-ST, SEM-ARG, ADD-ARG in Koenig's proposal, ARG-ST, DEPS, SPR, COMPS in Bouma, Malouf and Sag's proposal). This was discussed extensively in Müller (2007b: Section 7.5.2.2) with respect to extensions that would be needed for Koenig's analysis.

Since Culicover and Jackendoff argue for a phrasal model, we will discuss their proposal here. Culicover and Jackendoff assume a multilayered model in which semantic representations are linked to grammatical functions, which are linked to tree positions. Figure 21.7 shows an example for an active sentence. GF stands for Grammatical Func-

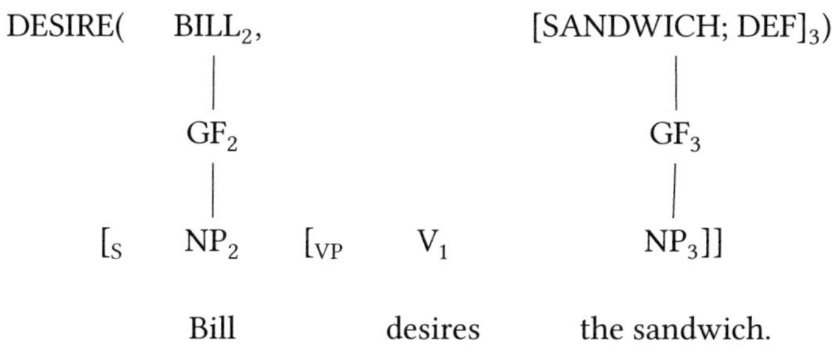

Figure 21.7: Linking grammatical functions to tree positions: active

tion. Culicover & Jackendoff (2005: 204) explicitly avoid names like Subject and Object since this is crucial for their analysis of the passive to work. They assume that the first GF following a bracket is the subject of the clause the bracket corresponds to (p. 195–196) and hence has to be mapped to an appropriate tree position in English. Note that this view of grammatical functions and obliqueness does not account for subjectless sentences that are possible in some languages, for instance in German.[36]

Regarding the passive, the authors write:

> we wish to formulate the passive not as an operation that deletes or alters part of the argument structure, but rather as a piece of structure in its own right that can be unified with the other independent pieces of the sentence. The result of the unification is an alternative licensing relation between syntax and semantics. (Culicover & Jackendoff 2005: 203)

They suggest the following representation of the passive:

(72) $[GF_i > [GF \ldots]]_k \Leftrightarrow [\ \ldots \mathrm{V}_k + \mathrm{pass} \ldots (\mathrm{by}\ \mathrm{NP}_i) \ldots]_k$

The italicized parts are the normal structure of the sentence and the non-italicized parts are an overlay on the normal structure, that is, additional constraints that have to hold in passive sentences. Figure 21.8 shows the mapping of the example discussed above that corresponds to the passive.

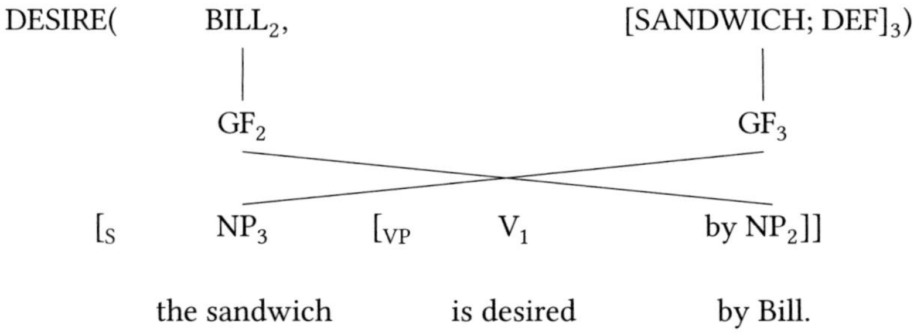

Figure 21.8: Linking grammatical functions to tree positions: passive

Although Culicover and Jackendoff emphasize the similarity between their approach and Relational Grammar (Perlmutter 1983), there is an important difference: in Relational Grammar additional levels (strata) can be stipulated if additional remappings are needed. In Culicover and Jackendoff's proposal there is no additional level. This causes problems for the analysis of languages which allow for multiple argument alternations. Examples from Turkish were provided in (67). Approaches that assume that the personal passive is the unification of a general structure with a passive-specific structure will not be able

[36] Of course one could assume empty expletive subjects, as was suggested by Grewendorf (1993: 1311), but empty elements and especially those without meaning are generally avoided in the constructionist literature. See Müller (2010a: Section 3.4, Section 11.1.1.3) for further discussion.

to capture this, since they committed to a certain structure too early. The problem for approaches that state syntactic structure for the passive is that such a structure, once stated, cannot be modified. Culicover and Jackendoff's proposal works in this respect since there are no strong constraints in the right-hand side of their constraint in (72). But there is a different problem: when passivization is applied the second time, it has to apply to the innermost bracket, that is, the result of applying (72) should be:

(73) $[GF_i > [GF_j \ldots]]_k \Leftrightarrow [\ \ldots \mathrm{V}_k + \mathrm{pass} \ldots (\mathrm{by\ NP}_i) \ldots (\mathrm{by\ NP}_j) \ldots]_k$

This cannot be done with unification, since unification checks for compatibility and since the first application of passive was possible it would be possible for the second time as well. Dots in representations are always dangerous and in the example at hand one would have to make sure that NP_i and NP_j are distinct, since the statement in (72) just says there has to be a *by*-PP somewhere. What is needed instead of unification would be something that takes a GF representation and searches for the outermost bracket and then places a bracket to the left of the next GF. But this is basically a rule that maps one representation onto another one, just like lexical rules do.

If Culicover and Jackendoff want to stick to a mapping analysis, the only option to analyze the data seems to be to assume an additional level for impersonal passives from which the mapping to phrase structure is done. In the case of Turkish sentences like (74), which is a personal passive, the mapping to this level would be the identity function.

(74) Arkadaş-ım bu oda-da döv-ül-dü.
friend-my this room-LOC hit-PASS-AOR
'My friend is beaten (by one) in this room.'

In the case of passivization + impersonal construction, the correct mappings would be implemented by two mappings between the three levels that finally result in a mapping as the one that is seen in (67b), repeated here as (75) for convenience.

(75) Bu oda-da döv-ül-ün-ür.
this room-LOC hit-PASS-PASS-AOR
'One is beaten (by one) in this room.'

Note that passivization + impersonal construction is also problematic for purely inheritance based approaches. What all these approaches can suggest though is that they just stipulate four different relations between argument structure and phrase structure: active, passive, impersonal construction, passive + impersonal construction. But this misses the fact that (75) is an impersonal variant of the passive in (74).

In contrast, the lexical rule-based approach suggested by Müller (2003b) does not have any problems with such multiple alternations: the application of the passivization lexical rule suppresses the least oblique argument and provides a lexical item with the argument structure of a personal passive. Then the impersonal lexical rule applies and suppresses the now least oblique argument (the object of the active clause). The result is impersonal constructions without any arguments as the one in (75).

21.4.3 Is there an alternative to lexical rules?

In this section we have reviewed the attempts to replace lexical rules with methods of relating constructions. These attempts have not been successful, in our assessment. We believe that the essential problem with them is that they fail to capture the derivational character of the relationship between certain word forms. Alternations signaled by passive voice and causative morphology are relatively simple and regular when formulated as operations on lexical valence structures that have been abstracted from their phrasal context. But non-transformational rules or systems formulated on the phrasal structures encounter serious problems that have not yet been solved.

21.5 Further problems for phrasal approaches

Müller (2006) discussed the problems shared by proposals that assume phrasal constructions to be a fixed configuration of adjacent material as for instance the one by Goldberg & Jackendoff (2004). I showed that many argument structure constructions allow great flexibility as far as the order of their parts is concerned. Back then I discussed resultative constructions in their interaction with free datives, passive and other valence changing phenomena and showed that for all these constructions licensed by such interactions the construction parts can be scrambled, the verb can appear in different positions, arguments can be extracted and so on. The following subsection discusses particle verbs, which pose similar problems for theories that assume a phrasal construction with fixed order of verb and particle.

21.5.1 Particle verbs and commitment to phrase structure configurations

A general problem of approaches that assume phrase structure configurations paired with meaning is that the construction may appear in different contexts: the construction parts may be involved in derivational morphology (as discussed in the previous subsection) or the construction parts may be involved in dislocations. A clear example of the latter type is the phrasal analysis of particle verbs that was suggested by Booij (2002: Section 2; 2012) and Blom (2005), working in the frameworks of Construction Grammar and LFG, respectively. The authors working on Dutch and German assume that particle verbs are licensed by phrasal constructions (pieces of phrase structure) in which the first slot is occupied by the particle.

(76) $[\,X\,[\,]_{V}\,]_{V'}$ where X = P, Adv, A, or N

Examples for specific Dutch constructions are:

(77) a. $[\,\text{af}\,[\,]_{V}\,]_{V'}$
b. $[\,\text{door}\,[\,]_{V}\,]_{V'}$
c. $[\,\text{op}\,[\,]_{V}\,]_{V'}$

This suggestion comes with the claim that particles cannot be fronted. This claim is made frequently in the literature, but it is based on introspection and wrong for languages like Dutch and German. On Dutch see Hoeksema (1991: 19), on German, Müller (2002a,c, 2003c, 2007d).[37] A German example is given in (78); several pages of attested examples can be found in the cited references and some more complex examples will also be discussed in Section 21.7.3 on page 633.

(78) *Los* damit *geht* es schon am 15. April.[38]
PART there.with goes it already at.the 15 April
'It already starts on April the 15th.'

Particle verbs are mini-idioms. So the conclusion is that idiomatic expressions that allow for a certain flexibility in order should not be represented as phrasal configurations describing adjacent elements. For some idioms, a lexical analysis along the lines of Sag (2007) seems to be required.[39] The issue of particle verbs will be taken up in Section 21.7.3 again, where we discuss evidence for/against phrasal analyses from neuroscience.

21.6 Arguments from language acquisition

The question whether language acquisition is pattern-based and hence can be seen as evidence for the phrasal approach has already been touched upon in the Sections 16.3 and 16.4. It was argued that constructions can be realized discontinuously in coordinations and hence it is the notion of dependency that has to be acquired; acquiring simple continuous patterns is not sufficient.

Since the present discussion about phrasal and lexical approaches deals with specific proposals, I would like to add two more special subsections: Section 21.6.1 deals with the recognizability of constructions and Section 21.6.2 discusses specific approaches to coordination in order to demonstrate how frameworks deal with the discontinuous realization of constructions.

21.6.1 Recognizability of constructions

I think that a purely pattern-based approach is weakened by the existence of examples like (79):

(79) a. John tried to sleep.
b. John tried to be loved.

[37] Some more fundamental remarks on introspection and corpus data with relation to particle verbs can also be found in Müller (2007d) and Meurers & Müller (2009).

[38] taz, 01.03.2002, p. 8, see also Müller (2005c: 313).

[39] Note also that the German example is best described as a clause with a complex internally structured constituent in front of the finite verb and it is doubtful whether linearization-based proposals like the ones in Kathol (1995: 244–248) or Wetta (2011) can capture this. See also the discussion of multiple frontings in connection to Dependency Grammar in Section 11.7.1.

Although no argument of *sleep* is present in the phrase *to sleep* and neither a subject nor an object is realized in the phrase *to be loved*, both phrases are recognized as phrases containing an intransitive and a transitive verb, respectively.[40]

The same applies to arguments that are supposed to be introduced/licensed by a phrasal construction: in (80) the resultative construction is passivized and then embedded under a control verb, resulting in a situation in which only the result predicate (*tot* 'dead') and the matrix verb (*geschossen* 'shot') are realized overtly within the local clause, bracketed here:

(80) Der kranke Mann wünschte sich, [totgeschossen zu werden].[41]
the sick man wished SELF dead.shot to be
'The sick man wanted to be shot dead.'

Of course passivization and control are responsible for these occurrences, but the important point here is that arguments can remain unexpressed or implicit and nevertheless a meaning usually connected to some overt realization of arguments is present (Müller 2007c: Section 4). So, what has to be acquired by the language learner is that when a result predicate and a main verb are realized together, they contribute the resultative meaning. To take another example, NP arguments that are usually realized in active resultative constructions may remain implicit in nominalizations like the ones in (81):

(81) a. dann scheint uns das Totschießen mindestens ebensoviel Spaß zu machen[42]
then seems us the dead-shooting at.least as.much fun to make
'then the shooting dead seems to us to be as least as much fun'

b. Wir lassen heut das Totgeschieße,
we let today the annoying.repeated.shooting.dead
Weil man sowas heut nicht tut.
since one such.thing today not does
Und wer einen Tag sich ausruht,
and who a day SELF rests
Der schießt morgen doppelt gut.[43]
this shoots tomorrow twice good
'We do not shoot anybody today, since one does not do this today, and those who rest a day shoot twice as well tomorrow.'

The argument corresponding to the patient of the verb (the one who is shot) can remain unrealized, because of the syntax of nominalizations. The resultative meaning is still

[40] Constructionist theories do not assume empty elements. Of course, in the GB framework the subject would be realized by an empty element. So it would be in the structure, although inaudible.

[41] Müller (2007c: 387).

[42] https://www.elitepartner.de/forum/wie-gehen-die-maenner-mit-den-veraenderten-anspruechen-der-frauen-um-26421-6.html. 26.03.0212.

[43] Gedicht für den Frieden, Oliver Kalkofe, http://www.golyr.de/oliver-kalkofe/songtext-gedicht-fuer-den-frieden-417329.html. 04.03.2016.

understood, which shows that it does not depend upon the presence of a resultative construction involving Subj V Obj and Obl.

21.6.2 Coordination and discontinuousness

The following subsection deals with analyses of coordination in some of the frameworks that were introduced in this book. The purpose of the section is to show that simple phrasal patterns have to be broken up in coordination structures. This was already mentioned in Section 16.3, but I think it is illuminative to have a look at concrete proposals.

In Categorial Grammar, there is a very elegant treatment of coordination (see Steedman 1991). A generalization with regard to so-called symmetric coordination is that two objects with the same syntactic properties are combined to an object with those properties. We have already encountered the relevant data in the discussion of the motivation for feature geometry in HPSG on page 263. Their English versions are repeated below as (82):

(82) a. the man and the woman
b. He knows and loves this record.
c. He is dumb and arrogant.

Steedman (1991) analyzes examples such as those in (82) with a single rule:

(83) X conj X ⇒ X

This rule combines two categories of the same kind with a conjunction in between to form a category that has the same category as the conjuncts.[44] Figure 21.9 shows the analysis of (82a) and Figure 21.10 on the next page gives an analysis of the corresponding English example of (82b).

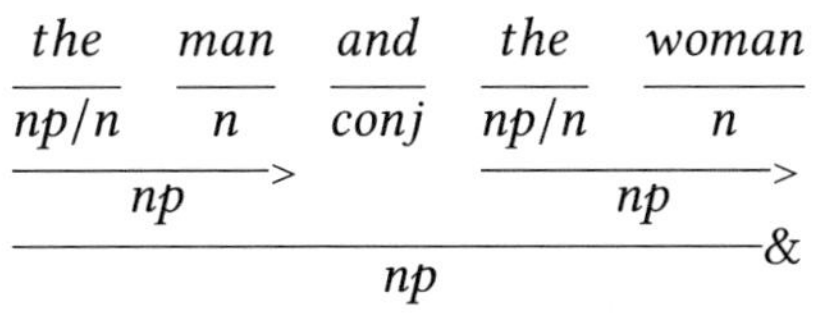

Figure 21.9: Coordination of two NPs in Categorial Grammar

If we compare this analysis to the one that would have to be assumed in traditional phrase structure grammars, it becomes apparent what the advantages are: one rule was required for the analysis of NP coordination where two NPs are coordinated to form

[44] Alternatively, one could analyze all three examples using a single lexical entry for the conjunction *and*: *and* is a functor that takes a word or phrase of any category to its right and after this combination then needs to be combined with an element of the same category to its left in order to form the relevant category after combining with this second element. This means that the category for *und* would have the form (X\X)/X. This analysis does not require any coordination rules. If one wants to assume, as is common in GB/MP, that every structure has a head, then a headless analysis that assumes a special rule for coordination like the one in (83) would be ruled out.

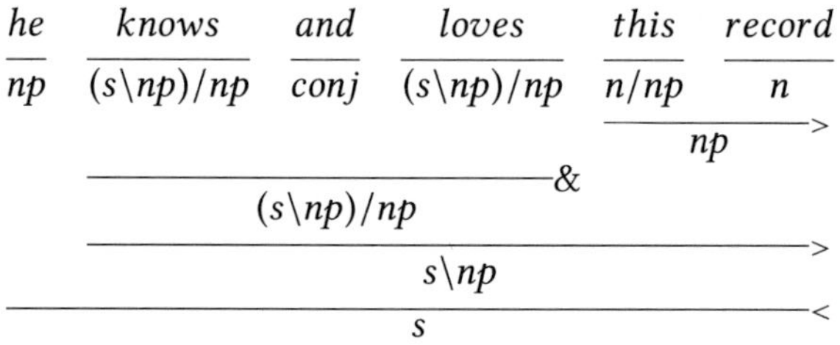

Figure 21.10: Coordination of two transitive verbs in Categorial Grammar

an NP and another was required for the analysis of V coordination. This is not only undesirable from a technical point of view, neither does it capture the basic property of symmetric coordination: two symbols with the same syntactic category are combined with each other.

It is interesting to note that it is possible to analyze phrases such as (84) in this way:

(84) give George a book and Martha a record

In Section 1.3.2.4, we have seen that this kind of sentences is problematic for constituent tests. However, in Categorial Grammar, it is possible to analyze them without any problems if one adopts rules for type raising and composition as Dowty (1988) and Steedman (1991) do. In Section 8.5, we have already seen forward type raising as well as forward and backward composition. In order to analyze (84), one would require backward type raising repeated in (85) and backward composition repeated in (86):

(85) Backward type raising (< T)
X ⇒ T\(T/X)

(86) Backward composition (< B)
Y\Z ∗ X\Y = X\Z

Dowty's analysis of (84) is given in Figure 21.11. vp stands for s\np.

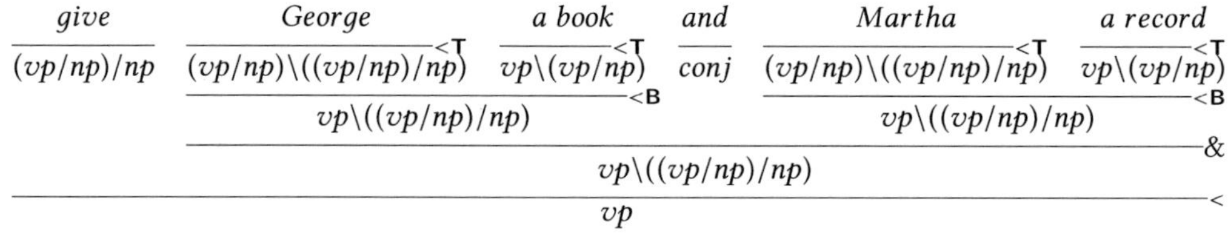

Figure 21.11: Gapping in Categorial Grammar

This kind of type-raising analysis was often criticized because raising categories leads to many different analytical possibilities for simple sentences. For example, one could first combine a type-raised subject with the verb and then combine the resulting constituent with the object. This would mean that we would have a [[S V] O] in addition to the standard [S [V O]] analysis. Steedman (1991) argues that both analyses differ in terms of information structure and it is therefore valid to assume different structures for the sentences in question.

I will not go into these points further here. However, I would like to compare Steedman's lexical approach to phrasal analyses: all approaches that assume that the ditransitive construction represents a continuous pattern encounter a serious problem with the examples discussed above. This can be best understood by considering the TAG analysis of coordination proposed by Sarkar & Joshi (1996). If one assumes that [Sbj TransVerb Obj] or [S [V O]] constitutes a fixed unit, then the trees in Figure 21.12 form the starting point for the analysis of coordination.

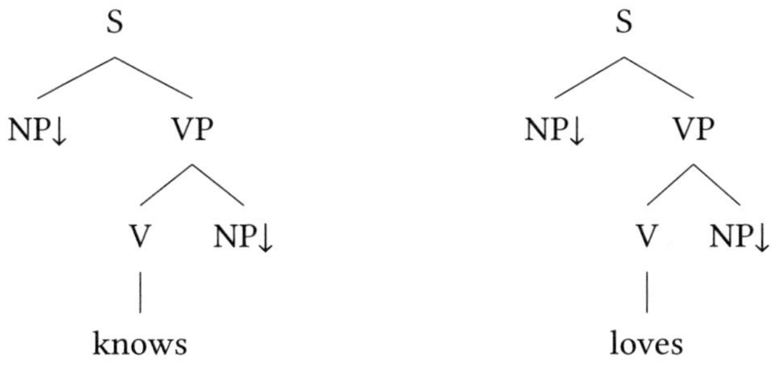

Figure 21.12: Elementary trees for *knows* and *loves*

If one wants to use these trees/constructions for the analysis of (87), there are in principle two possibilities: one assumes that two complete sentences are coordinated or alternatively, one assumes that some nodes are shared in a coordinated structure.

(87) He knows and loves this record.

Abeillé (2006) has shown that it is not possible to capture all the data if one assumes that cases of coordination such as those in (87) always involve the coordination of two complete clauses. It is also necessary to allow for lexical coordination of the kind we saw in Steedman's analysis (see also Section 4.6.3). Sarkar & Joshi (1996) develop a TAG analysis in which nodes are shared in coordinate structures. The analysis of (87) can be seen in Figure 21.13 on the next page. The subject and object nodes are only present once in this figure. The S nodes of both elementary trees both dominate the *he* NP. In the same way, the object NP node belongs to both VPs. The conjunction connects two verbs indicated by the thick lines. Sarkar and Joshi provide an algorithm that determines which nodes are to be shared. The structure may look strange at first, but for TAG purposes, it is not the derived tree but rather the derivation tree that is important, since this is the one that is used to compute the semantic interpretation. The authors show that the derivation trees for the example under discussion and even more complex examples can be constructed correctly.

In theories such as HPSG and LFG where structure building is, as in Categorial Grammar, driven by valence, the above sentence is unproblematic: both verbs are conjoined

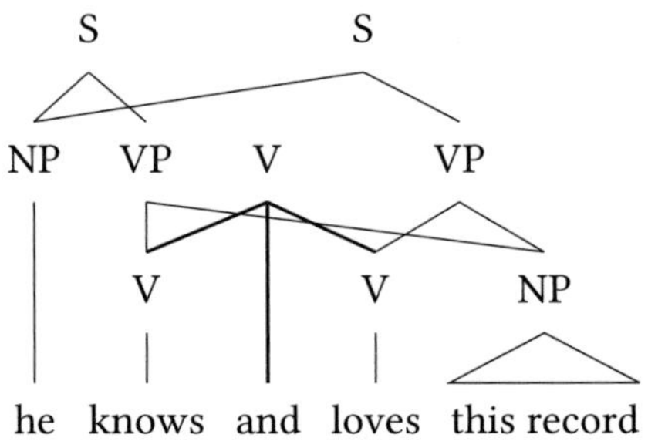

Figure 21.13: TAG analysis of *He knows and loves this record.*

and then the combination behaves like a simple verb. The analysis of this is given in Figure 21.14. This analysis is similar to the Categorial Grammar analysis in Figure 21.10.[45]

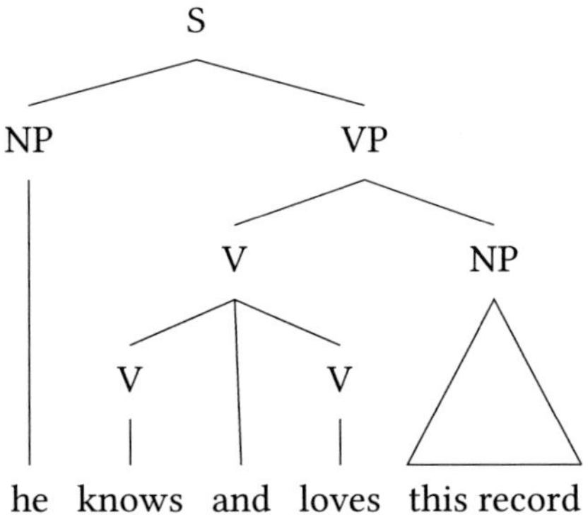

Figure 21.14: Selection-based analysis of *He knows and loves this record.* in tree notation

With Goldberg's plugging analysis one could also adopt this approach to coordination: here, *knows* and *loves* would first be plugged into a coordination construction and the result would then be plugged into the transitive construction. Exactly how the semantics of *knows and loves* is combined with that of the transitive construction is unclear since the meaning of this phrase is something like *and′*(*know′*(x, y), *love′*(x, y)), that is, a complex event with at least two open argument slots x and y (and possibly additionally an event and a world variable depending on the semantic theory that is used). Goldberg

[45] A parallel analysis in Dependency Grammar is possible as well. Tesnière's original analysis was different though. See Section 11.6.2.1 for discussion.

would probably have to adopt an analysis such as the one in Figure 21.13 in order to maintain the plugging analysis.

Croft would definitely have to adopt the TAG analysis since the verb is already present in his constructions. For the example in (84), both Goldberg and Croft would have to draw from the TAG analysis in Figure 21.15.

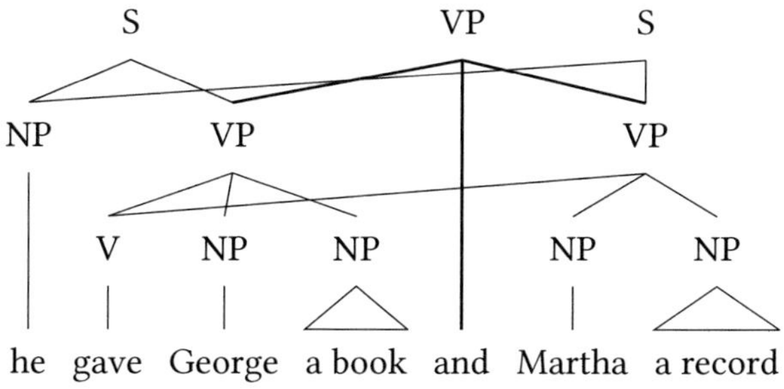

Figure 21.15: TAG analysis of *He gave George a book and Martha a record.*

The consequence of this is that one requires discontinuous constituents. Since coordination allows a considerable number of variants, there can be gaps between all arguments of constructions. An example with a ditransitive verb is given in (88):

(88) He gave George and sent Martha a record.

See Crysmann (2008) and Beavers & Sag (2004) for HPSG analyses that assume discontinuous constituents for particular coordination structures.

The result of these considerations is that the argument that particular elements occur next to each other and that this occurrence is associated with a particular meaning is considerably weakened. What competent speakers do acquire is the knowledge that heads must occur with their arguments somewhere in the utterance and that all the requirements of the heads involved have to somehow be satisfied (θ-Criterion, coherence/completeness, empty SUBCAT list). The heads themselves need not necessarily occur directly adjacent to their arguments. See the discussion in Section 16.3 about pattern-based models of language acquisition.

The computation of the semantic contribution of complex structures such as those in Figure 21.15 is by no means trivial. In TAG, there is the derivation tree in addition to the derived tree that can then be used to compute the semantic contribution of a linguistic object. Construction Grammar does not have this separate level of representation. The question of how the meaning of the sentences discussed here is derived from their component parts still remains open for phrasal approaches.

Concluding the section on language acquisition, we assume that a valence representation is the result of language acquisition, since this is necessary for establishing the dependency relations in various possible configurations in an utterance. See also Behrens (2009: 439) for a similar conclusion.

21.7 Arguments from psycho- and neurolinguistics

This section has three parts: in the first part we compare approaches which assume that valence alternations are modeled by lexical rules, underspecification, or disjunctions with phrasal approaches. In Subsection 21.7.2 part we discuss approaches to light verb constructions and Subsection 21.7.3 is devoted to neurolinguistic findings.

21.7.1 Lexical rules vs. phrasal constructions

Goldberg (1995: Section 1.4.5) uses evidence from psycholinguistic experiments to argue against lexical approaches that use lexical rules to account for argument structure alternations: Carlson & Tanenhaus (1988) showed that sentences with true lexical ambiguity like those in (89) and sentences with two verbs with the same core meaning have different processing times.

(89) a. Bill set the alarm clock onto the shelf.
     b. Bill set the alarm clock for six.

(90) a. Bill loaded the truck onto the ship.
     b. Bill loaded the truck with bricks.

Errors due to lexical ambiguity cause a bigger increase in processing time than errors in the use of the same verb. Experiments showed that there was a bigger difference in processing times for the sentences in (89) than for the sentences in (90). The difference in processing times between (90a) and (90b) would be explained by different preferences for phrasal constructions. In a lexicon-based approach one could explain the difference by assuming that one lexical item is more basic, that is, stored in the mental dictionary and the other is derived from the stored one. The application of lexical rules would be time consuming, but since the lexical items are related, the overall time consumption is smaller than the time needed to process two unrelated items (Müller 2002a: 405).

Alternatively one could assume that the lexical items for both valence patterns are the result of lexical rule applications. As with the phrasal constructions, the lexical rules would have different preferences. This shows that the lexical approach can explain the experimental results as well, so that they do not force us to prefer phrasal approaches.

Goldberg (1995: 18) claims that lexical approaches have to assume two variants of *load* with different meaning and that this would predict that *load* alternations would behave like two verbs that really have absolutely different meanings. The experiments discussed above show that such predictions are wrong and hence lexical analyses would be falsified. However, as was shown in Müller (2010a: Section 11.11.8.2), the argumentation contains two flaws: let's assume that the construction meaning of the construction that licenses (90a) is C_1 and the construction meaning of the construction that licenses (90b) is C_2. Under such assumptions the semantic contribution of the two lexical items in the lexical analysis would be (91). load(…) is the contribution of the verb that would be assumed in phrasal analyses.

(91) a. load (onto): $C_1 \wedge$ load(…)
b. load (with): $C_2 \wedge$ load(…)

(91) shows that the lexical items partly share their semantic contribution. We hence predict that the processing of the dispreferred argument realization of *load* is simpler than the dispreferred meaning of *set*: in the latter case a completely new verb has to be activated while in the first case parts of the meaning are activated already.[46]

Goldberg (1995: 107) argues against lexical rule-based approaches for locative alternations like (92), since according to her such approaches have to assume that one of the verb forms has to be the more basic form.

(92) a. He loaded hay onto the wagon.
b. He loaded the wagon with hay.

She remarks that this is problematic since we do not have clear intuitions about what the basic and what the derived forms are. She argues that the advantage of phrasal approaches is that various constructions can be related to each other without requiring the assumption that one of the constructions is more basic than the other. There are two phrasal patterns and the verb is used in one of the two patterns. This criticism can be addressed in two ways: first one could introduce two lexical types (for instance *onto-verb* and *with-verb*) into a type hierarchy. The two types correspond to two valence frames that are needed for the analysis of (92a) and (92b). These types can have a common supertype (*onto-with-verb*) which is relevant for all *spray/load* verbs. One of the subtypes or the respective lexical item of the verb is the preferred one. This corresponds to a disjunction in the lexicon, while the phrasal approach assumes a disjunction in the set of phrasal constructions.

A variant of this approach is to assume that the lexical description of *load* just contains the supertype describing all *spray/load* verbs. Since model theoretic approaches assume that all structures that are models of utterances contain only maximally specific types (see for instance King (1999) and Pollard & Sag (1994: 21)), it is sufficient to say about verbs like *load* that they are of type *onto-with-verb*. As this type has exactly two subtypes, *load* has to be either *onto-verb* or *with-verb* in an actual model.[47]

A second option is to stick with lexical rules and to assume a single representation for the root of a verb that is listed in the lexicon. In addition, one assumes two lexical rules

[46] See also Croft (2003: 64–65) for a brief rejection of Goldberg's interpretation of the experiment that corresponds to what is said here.

[47] This analysis does not allow the specification of verb specific preferences for one of the realization patterns since the lexicon contains the general type only.

that map this basic lexical item onto other items that can be used in syntax after being inflected. The two lexical rules can be described by types that are part of a type hierarchy and that have a common supertype. This would capture commonalities between the lexical rules. We therefore have the same situation as with phrasal constructions (two lexical rules vs. two phrasal constructions). The only difference is that the action is one level deeper in the lexical approach, namely in the lexicon (Müller 2002a: 405–406).

The argumentation with regard to the processing of resultative constructions like (93c) is parallel:

(93) a. He drinks.
b. He drinks the milk.
c. He drinks the pub empty.

When humans parse a sentence they build up structure incrementally. If one hears a word that is incompatible with the current hypothesis, the parsing process breaks down or the current hypothesis is revised. In (93c) *the pub* does not correspond to the normal transitive use of *drink*, so the respective hypothesis has to be revised. In the phrasal approach the resultative construction would have to be used instead of the transitive construction. In the lexical analysis the lexical item that is licensed by the resultative lexical rule would have to be used rather than the bivalent one. Building syntactic structure and lexicon access in general place different demands on our processing capacities. However, when (93c) is parsed, the lexical items for *drink* are active already, we only have to use a different one. It is currently unclear to us whether psycholinguistic experiments can differentiate between the two approaches, but it seems to be unlikely.

21.7.2 Light verbs

Wittenberg, Jackendoff, Kuperberg, Paczynski, Snedeker & Wiese (2014) report on a number of experiments that test predictions made by various approaches to light verb constructions. (94a) shows a typical light verb construction: *take* is a light verb that is combined with the nominal that provides the main predication.

(94) a. take a walk to the park
b. walk to the park

Wittenberg & Piñango (2011) examined two psychologically plausible theories of light verb constructions. The phrasal approach assumes that light verb constructions are stored objects associated with semantics (Goldberg 2003b). The alternative compositional view assumes that the semantics is computed as a fusion of the semantics of the event noun and the semantics of the light verb (Grimshaw 1997; Butt 2003; Jackendoff 2002; Culicover & Jackendoff 2005; Müller 2010b; Beavers et al. 2008). Since light verb constructions are extremely frequent (Piñango, Mack & Jackendoff 2006; Wittenberg & Piñango 2011: 399), the phrasal approaches assuming that light verb constructions are stored items with the object and verb fixed predict that light verb constructions should be retrievable faster than non-light verb constructions like (95) (Wittenberg & Piñango 2011: 396).

(95) take a frisbee to the park

This is not the case. As Wittenberg and Piñango found, there is no difference in processing at the licensing condition (the noun in VO languages like English and the verb in OV languages like German).

However, Wittenberg & Piñango (2011) found an increased processing load 300ms *after* the light verb construction is processed. The authors explain this by assuming that semantic integration of the noun with the verbal meaning takes place after the syntactic combination. While the syntactic combination is rather fast, the semantic computation takes additional resources and this is measurable at 300ms. The verb contributes aspectual information and integrates the meaning of the nominal element. The semantic roles are fused. The resource consumption effect would not be expected if the complete light verb construction were a stored item that is retrieved together with the complete meaning (p. 404). We can conclude that Wittenberg and Piñango's results are compatible with the lexical proposal, but are incompatible with the phrasal view.

21.7.3 Arguments from neurolinguistics

Pulvermüller, Cappelle & Shtyrov (2013) discuss neurolinguistic facts and relate them to the CxG view of grammar theory. One important finding is that deviant words (lexical items) cause brain responses that differ in polarity from brain responses on incorrect strings of words, that is, syntactic combinations. This suggests that there is indeed an empirical basis for deciding the issue.

Concerning the standard example of the Caused-Motion Construction in (96) the authors write the following:

(96) She sneezed the foam off the cappuccino.[48]

> this constellation of brain activities may initially lead to the co-activation of the verb *sneeze* with the DCNAs for *blow* and thus to the sentence mentioned. Ultimately, such co-activation of a one-place verb and DCNAs associated with other verbs may result in the former one-place verb being subsumed into a three-place verb category and DCNA set, a process which arguably has been accomplished for the verb *laugh* as used in the sequence *laugh NP off the stage.* (Pulvermüller, Cappelle & Shtyrov 2013)

A DCNA is a discrete combinatorial neuronal assembly. Regarding the specifics of DCNAs the authors write that

> Apart from linking categories together, typical DCNAs establish a temporal order between the category members they bind to. DCNAs that do not impose temporal

[48] Goldberg (2006: 42).

order (thus acting, in principle, as AND units for two constituents) are thought to join together constituents whose sequential order is free or allow for scrambling. (Pulvermüller, Cappelle & Shtyrov 2013: 404)

I believe that this view is entirely compatible with the lexical view outlined above: the lexical item or DCNA requires certain arguments to be present. A lexical rule that relates an intransitive verb to one that can be used in the Caused-Motion Construction is an explicit representation of what it means to activate the valence frame of *blow*.

The authors cite earlier work (Cappelle, Shtyrov & Pulvermüller 2010) and argue that particle verbs are lexical objects, admitting for a discontinuous realization despite their lexical status (p. 21). They restrict their claim to frequently occurring particle verbs. This claim is of course compatible with our assumptions here, but the differences in brain behavior are interesting when it comes to fully productive uses of particle verbs. For instance any semantically appropriate monovalent verb in German can be combined with the aspectual particle *los*: *lostanzen* 'start to dance', *loslachen* 'start to laugh', *lossingen* 'start to sing', ... Similarly, the combination of monovalent verbs with the particle *an* with the reading *directed-towards* is also productive: *anfahren* 'drive towards', *anlachen* 'laugh in the direction of', *ansegeln* 'sail towards', ... (see Stiebels (1996) on various productive patterns). The interesting question is how particle verbs behave that follow these patterns but occur with low frequency. This is still an open question as far as the experimental evidence is concerned, but as I argue below lexical proposals to particle verbs as the one suggested by Müller (2003c) are compatible with both possible outcomes.

Summarizing the discussion so far, lexical approaches are compatible with the accumulated neurobiological evidence and as far as particle verbs are concerned they seem to be better suited than the phrasal proposals by Booij (2002: Section 2) and Blom (2005) (See Section 21.5.1 for discussion). However, in general, it remains an open question what it means to be a discontinuous lexical item. The idea of discontinuous words is pretty old (Wells 1947), but there have not been many formal accounts of this idea. Nunberg, Sag & Wasow (1994) suggest a representation in a linearization-based framework of the kind that was proposed by Reape (1994) and Kathol (1995: 244–248) and Crysmann (2002) worked out such analyses in detail. Kathol's lexical item for *aufwachen* 'to wake up' is given in (97):

(97) *aufwachen* (following Kathol 1995: 246):

$$\begin{bmatrix} \ldots|\text{HEAD}\ \boxed{1}\ \textit{verb} \\ \ldots|\text{VCOMP}\ \langle\rangle \\ \text{DOM}\ \left\langle \begin{bmatrix} \langle\ \textit{wachen}\ \rangle \\ \ldots|\text{HEAD}\ \boxed{1} \\ \ldots|\text{VCOMP}\ \langle\ \boxed{2}\ \rangle \end{bmatrix} \right\rangle \bigcirc \left\langle \begin{bmatrix} \textit{vc} \\ \langle\ \textit{auf}\ \rangle \\ \text{SYNSEM}\ \boxed{2}\ \begin{bmatrix} \ldots|\text{HEAD} \begin{bmatrix} \textit{sepref} \\ \text{FLIP}\ - \end{bmatrix} \end{bmatrix} \end{bmatrix} \right\rangle \end{bmatrix}$$

The lexical representation contains the list-valued feature DOM that contains a description of the main verb and the particle (see Section 11.7.2.2 for details). The DOM list is a list that contains the dependents of a head. The dependents can be ordered in any order provided no linearization rule is violated (Reape 1994). The dependency between the particle and the main verb was characterized by the value of the VCOMP feature, which is a valence feature for the selection of arguments that form a complex predicate with their head. The shuffle operator ○ concatenates two lists without specifying an order between the elements of the two lists, that is, both *wachen, auf* and *auf, wachen* are possible. The little marking *vc* is an assignment to a topological field in the clause.

I criticized such linearization-based proposals since it is unclear how analyses that claim that the particle is just linearized in the domain of its verb can account for sentences like (98), in which complex syntactic structures are involved (Müller 2007c). German is a V2 language and the fronting of a constituent into the position before the finite verb is usually described as some sort of nonlocal dependency; that is, even authors who favor linearization-based analyses do not assume that the initial position is filled by simple reordering of material (Kathol 2000; Müller 1999a, 2002a; Bjerre 2006).[49]

(98) a. [$_{vf}$ [$_{mf}$ Den Atem] [$_{vc}$ an]] hielt die ganze Judenheit.[50]
the breath PART held the whole Jewish.community
'The whole Jewish community held their breath.'

b. [$_{vf}$ [$_{mf}$ Wieder] [$_{vc}$ an]] treten auch die beiden Sozialdemokraten.[51]
again PART kick also the two Social.Democrats
'The two Social Democrats are also running for office again.'

c. [$_{vf}$ [$_{vc}$ Los] [$_{nf}$ damit]] geht es schon am 15. April.[52]
PART there.with went it already at.the 15 April
'It already starts on April the 15th.'

The conclusion that has to be drawn from examples like (98) is that particles interact in complex ways with the syntax of sentences. This is captured by the lexical treatment that was suggested in Müller (2002a: Chapter 6) and Müller (2003c): the main verb selects for the verbal particle. By assuming that *wachen* selects for *auf*, the tight connection between verb and particle is represented.[53] Such a lexical analysis provides an easy way

[49] Kathol (1995: Section 6.3) working in HPSG suggested such an analysis for simple sentences, but later changed his view. Wetta (2011) also working in HPSG assumes a purely linearization-based approach. Similarly Groß & Osborne (2009) working in Dependency Grammar assume that there is a simple dependency structure in simple sentences while there are special mechanisms to account for extraction out of embedded clauses. I argue against such proposals in Müller (2015b) referring to the scope of adjuncts, coordination of simple with complex sentences and Across the Board Extraction and apparent multiple frontings. See also Section 11.7.1.

[50] Lion Feuchtwanger, *Jud Süß*, p. 276, quoted from Grubačić (1965: 56).

[51] taz, bremen, 24.05.2004, p. 21.

[52] taz, 01.03.2002, p. 8.

[53] Cappelle et al. (2010: 197) write: "the results provide neurophysiological evidence that phrasal verbs are lexical items. Indeed, the increased activation that we found for existing phrasal verbs, as compared to infelicitous combinations, suggests that a verb and its particle together form one single lexical representation, i. e. a single lexeme, and that a unified cortical memory circuit exists for it, similar to that encoding a single word". I believe that my analysis is compatible with this statement.

to account for fully nontransparent particle verbs like *an-fangen* 'to begin'. However, I also argued for a lexical treatment of transparent particle verbs like *losfahren* 'to start to drive' and *jemanden/etwas anfahren* 'drive directed towards somebody/something'. The analysis involves a lexical rule that licenses a verbal item selecting for an adjunct particle. The particles *an* and *los* can modify verbs and contribute arguments (in the case of *an*) and the particle semantics. This analysis can be shown to be compatible with the neuro-mechanical findings: if it is the case that even transparent particle verb combinations with low frequency are stored, then the rather general lexical rule that I suggested in the works cited above is the generalization of the relation between a large amount of lexical particle verb items and their respective main verb. The individual particle verbs would be special instantiations that have the form of the particle specified as it is also the case for non-transparent particle verbs like *anfangen.* If it should turn out that productive combinations with particle verbs of low frequency cause syntactic reflexes in the brain, this could be explained as well: the lexical rule licenses an item that selects for an adverbial element. This selection would then be seen as parallel to the relation between the determiner and the noun in the NP *der Mut* 'the courage', which Cappelle et al. (2010: 191) discuss as an example of a syntactic combination. Note that this analysis is also compatible with another observation made by Shtyrov, Pihko & Pulvermüller (2005): morphological affixes also cause the lexical reflexes. In my analysis the stem of the main verb is related to another stem that selects for a particle. This stem can be combined with (derivational and inflectional) morphological affixes causing the lexical activation pattern in the brain. After this combination the verb is combined with the particle and the dependency can be either a lexical or a syntactic one, depending on the results of the experiments to be carried out. The analysis is compatible with both results.

Note that my analysis allows the principle of lexical integrity to be maintained. I therefore do not follow Cappelle, Shtyrov & Pulvermüller (2010: 198), who claim that they "provide proof that potentially separable multi-word items can nonetheless be word-like themselves, and thus against the validity of a once well-established linguistic principle, the Lexical Integrity Principle". I agree that non-transparent particle verbs are multi-word lexemes, but the existence of multi-word lexemes does not show that syntax has access to the word-internal morphological structure. The parallel between particle verbs and clearly phrasal idioms was discussed in Müller (2002a,c) and it was concluded that idiom-status is irrelevant for the question of wordhood. Since the interaction of clearly phrasal idioms with derivational morphology as evidenced by examples like (99) did not force grammarians to give up on lexical integrity, it can be argued that particle verbs are not convincing evidence for giving up the Lexical Integrity Principle either.[54]

(99) a. Er hat ins Gras gebissen.
he has in.the grass bit
'He bit the dust.'

[54] However, see Booij (2009) for some challenges to lexical integrity.

b. „Heath Ledger“ kann ich nicht einmal schreiben, ohne dass mir sein ins
Heath Ledger can I not even write without that me his in.the
Gras-Gebeiße wieder so wahnsinnig leid tut[55]
grass.biting again so crazy sorrow does
'I cannot even write "Heath Ledger" without being sad again about his biting the dust.'

The example in (99b) involves the discontinuous derivation with the circumfix *Ge- -e* (Lüdeling 2001: Section 3.4.3; Müller 2002a: 324–327, 372–377; Müller 2003c: Section 2.2.1, Section 5.2.1). Still the parts of the idiom *ins Gras beiß-* 'bite the dust' are present and with them the idiomatic reading. See Sag (2007) for a lexical analysis of idioms that can explain examples like (99).

So, while I think that it is impossible to distinguish phrasal and lexical approaches for phenomena where heads are used with different valence patterns (Section 21.7.1), there seem to be ways to test whether patterns with high frequency and strong collocations should be analyzed as one fixed chunk of material with a fixed form and a fixed meaning or whether they should be analyzed compositionally.

21.8 Arguments from statistical distribution

In this section, we want to look at arguments from statistics that have been claimed to support a phrasal view. We first look at data-oriented parsing, a technique that was successfully used by Bod (2009b) to model language acquisition and then we turn to the collostructional analysis by Stefanowitsch & Gries (2009). Lastly, we argue that these distributional analyses cannot decide the question whether argument structure constructions are phrasal or lexical.

21.8.1 Unsupervised Data-Oriented Parsing

In Section 13.8.3, we saw Bod's approach to the structuring of natural language utterances (2009b). If one assumes that language is acquired from the input without innate knowledge, the structures that Bod extracts from the distribution of words would have to be the ones that children also learn (parts of speech, meaning, and context would also have to be included). These structures would then also have to be the ones assumed in linguistic theories. Since Bod does not have enough data, he carried out experiments under the assumption of binary-branching trees and, for this reason, it is not possible to draw any conclusions from his work about whether rules license flat or binary-branching structures. There will almost certainly be interesting answers to this question in the future. What can certainly not be determined in a distribution-based analysis is the exact node in the tree where meaning is introduced. Bod (2009a: 132) claims that his approach constitutes "a testable realization of CxG" in the Goldbergian sense, but the trees that he

[55] http://www.coffee2watch.at/egala. 23.03.2012

can construct do not help us to decide between phrasal or lexical analyses or analyses with empty heads. These alternative analyses are represented in Figure 21.16.[56] The first

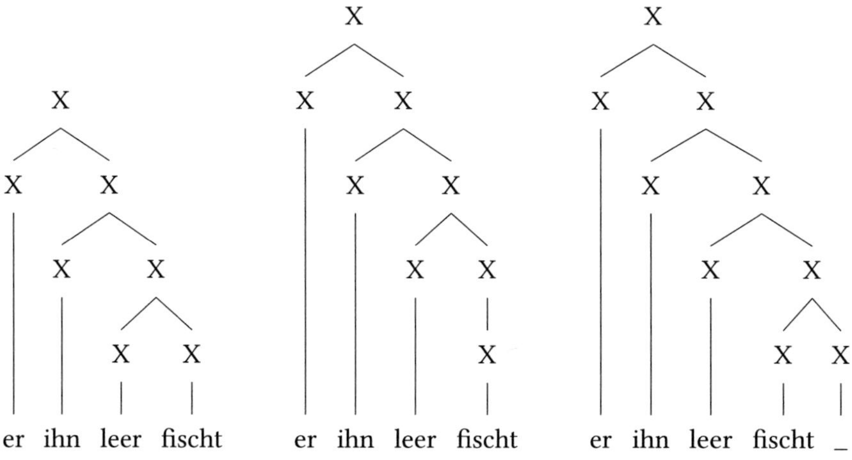

Figure 21.16: Three possible analyses for resultative construction: holistic construction, lexical rule, empty head

figure stands for a complex construction that contributes the meaning as a whole. The second figure corresponds to the analysis with a lexical rule and the third corresponds to the analysis with an empty head. A distributional analysis cannot decide between these theoretical proposals. Distribution is computed with reference to words; what the words actually mean is not taken into account. As such, it is only possible to say that the word *fischt* 'fishes' occurs in a particular utterance, however it is not possible to see if this word contains resultative semantics or not. Similarly, a distributional analysis does not help to distinguish between theoretical analyses with or without a lexical head. The empty head is not perceptible in the signal. It is a theoretical construct and, as we have seen in Section 19.5, it is possible to translate an analysis using an empty head into one

[56] The discussion is perhaps easier to follow if one assumes flat structures rather than binary-branching ones.

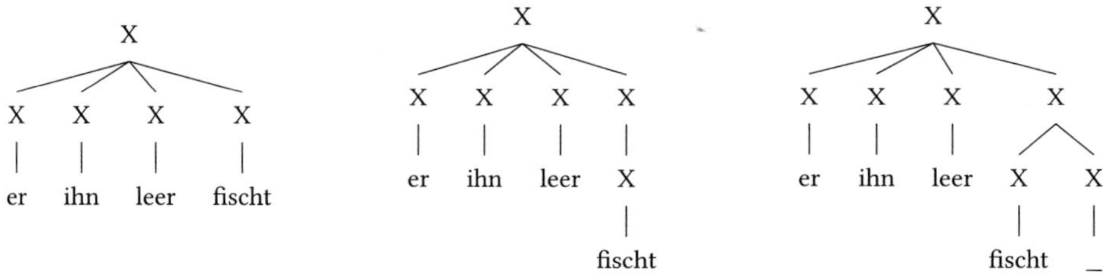

The first figure corresponds to the Goldbergian view of phrasal constructions where the verb is inserted into the construction and the meaning is present at the topmost node. In the second figure, there is a lexical rule that provides the resultative semantics and the corresponding valence information. In the third analysis, there is an empty head that combines with the verb and has ultimately the same effect as the lexical rule.

with a lexical rule. For the present example, any argumentation for a particular analysis will be purely theory-internal.

Although Unsupervised Data-Oriented Parsing (U-DOP) cannot help us to decide between analyses, there are areas of grammar for which these structures are of interest: under the assumption of binary-branching structures, there are different branching possibilities depending on whether one assumes an analysis with verb movement or not. This means that although one does not see an empty element in the input, there is a reflex in statistically-derived trees. The left tree in Figure 21.17 shows a structure that one would expect from an analysis following Steedman (2000: 159), see Section 8.3. The tree on the right shows a structure that would be expected from a GB-type verb movement analysis (see Section 3.2). But at present, there is no clear finding in this regard (Bod, p. c.

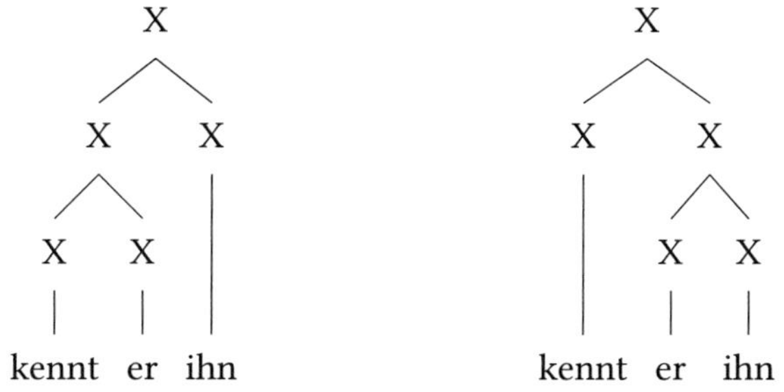

Figure 21.17: Structures corresponding to analyses with or without verb movement

2009). There is a great deal of variance in the U-DOP trees. The structure assigned to an utterance depends on the verb (Bod, referring to the Wall Street Journal). Here, it would be interesting to see if this changes with a larger data sample. In any case, it would be interesting to look at how all verbs as well as particular verb classes behave. The U-DOP procedure applies to trees containing at least one word each. If one makes use of parts of speech in addition, this results in structures that correspond to the ones we have seen in the preceding chapters. Sub-trees would then not have two Xs as their daughters but rather NP and V, for example. It is also possible to do statistic work with this kind of subtrees and use the part of speech symbols of words (the preterminal symbols) rather than the words themselves in the computation. For example, one would get trees for the symbol V instead of many trees for specific verbs. So instead of having three different trees for *küssen* 'kiss', *kennen* 'know' and *sehen* 'see', one would have three identical trees for the part of speech "verb" that corresponds to the trees that are needed for transitive verbs. The probability of the V tree is therefore higher than the probabilities of the trees for the individual verbs. Hence one would have a better set of data to compute structures for utterances such as those in Figure 21.17. I believe that there are further results in this area to be found in the years to come.

Concluding this subsection, we contend that Bod's paper is a milestone in the Poverty of the Stimulus debate, but it does not and cannot show that a particular version of constructionist theories, namely the phrasal one, is correct.

21.8.2 Collostructions

Stefanowitsch & Gries (2009: Section 5) assume a plugging analysis: "words occur in (slots provided by) a given construction if their meaning matches that of the construction". The authors claim that their *collostructional analysis has confirmed* [*the plugging analysis*] *from various perspectives.* Stefanowitsch and Gries are able to show that certain verbs occur more often than not in particular constructions, while other verbs never occur in the respective constructions. For instance, *give, tell, send, offer* and *show* are attracted by the Ditransitive Construction, while *make* and *do* are repelled by this construction, that is they occur significantly less often in this construction than what would be expected given the overall frequency of verbs in the corpus. Regarding this distribution the authors write:

> These results are typical for collexeme analysis in that they show two things. First, there are indeed significant associations between lexical items and grammatical structures. Second, these associations provide clear evidence for semantic coherence: the strongly attracted collexemes all involve a notion of 'transfer', either literally or metaphorically, which is the meaning typically posited for the ditransitive. This kind of result is typical enough to warrant a general claim that collostructional analysis can in fact be used to identify the meaning of a grammatical construction in the first place. (Stefanowitsch & Gries 2009: 943)

We hope that the preceding discussion has made clear that the distribution of words in a corpus cannot be seen as evidence for a phrasal analysis. The corpus study shows that *give* usually is used with three arguments in a certain pattern that is typical for English (Subject Verb Object1 Object2) and that this verb forms a cluster with other verbs that have a transfer component in their meaning. The corpus data do not show whether this meaning is contributed by a phrasal pattern or by lexical entries that are used in a certain configuration.

21.9 Conclusion

The essence of the lexical view is that a verb is stored with a valence structure indicating how it combines semantically and syntactically with its dependents. Crucially, that structure is abstracted from the actual syntactic context of particular tokens of the verb. Once abstracted, that valence structure can meet other fates besides licensing the phrasal structure that it most directly encodes: it can undergo lexical rules that manipulate that structure in systematic ways; it can be composed with the valence structure of another predicate; it can be coordinated with similar verbs; and so on. Such an abstraction allows for simple explanations of a wide range of robust, complex linguistic phenomena. We have surveyed the arguments against the lexical valence approach and in favor of a phrasal representation instead. We find the case for a phrasal representation of argument structure to be unconvincing: there are no compelling arguments in favor of such approaches, and they introduce a number of problems:

- They offer no account for the interaction of valence changing processes and derivational morphology.
- They offer no account for the interaction of valence changing processes and coordination of words.
- They offer no account for the iteration of valence changing processes.
- They overgenerate, unless a link between lexical items and phrasal constructions is assumed.
- They offer no account for distribution of arguments in partial fronting examples.

Assuming a lexical valence structure allows us to solve all the problems that arise with phrasal approaches.

21.10 Why (phrasal) constructions?

In previous sections, I have argued against assuming too much phrasality in grammatical descriptions. If one wishes to avoid transformations in order to derive alternative patterns from a single base structure, while still maintaining lexical integrity, then phrasal analyses become untenable for analyzing all those phenomena where changes in valence and derivational morphology interact. There are, however, some areas in which these two do not interact. In these cases, there is mostly a choice between analyses with silent heads and those with phrasal constructions. In this section, I will discuss some of these cases.

21.10.1 Verbless directives

Jacobs (2008) showed that there are linguistic phenomena where it does not make sense to assume that there is a head in a particular group of words. These configurations are best described as phrasal constructions, in which the adjacency of particular constituents leads to a complete meaning that goes beyond the sum of its parts. Examples of the phenomena that are discussed by Jacobs are phrasal templates such as those in (100) and verbless directives as in (105):

(100) $\text{Pro}_{\text{+w,caus/purp}}$ NP

a. Wozu Konstruktionen?
   why constructions
   'Why constructions?'

b. Warum ich?
   why I
   'Why me?'

(101) NP_{acc} $Y_{PP/A/Adv}$
Den Hut in der Hand (kam er ins Zimmer).
the hat in the hand came he into.the room
'(He came into the room) hat in hand.'

In (100), we are dealing with abbreviated questions:

(102) a. Wozu braucht man Konstruktionen? / Wozu sollte man Konstruktionen annehmen?
to.what needs one constructions to.what should one constructions assume
'Why do we need constructions?' / 'Why should we assume constructions?'

b. Warum soll ich das machen? / Warum wurde ich ausgewählt? / Warum passiert mir sowas?
why should I that do why was I chosen why happens me something.like.that
'Why should I do that?' / 'Why was I chosen?' / 'Why do things like that happen to me?'

In (101), a participle has been omitted:

(103) Den Hut in der Hand haltend kam er ins Zimmer.
the hat.ACC in the hand holding came he in.the room
'He came into the room hat in hand.'

Cases such as (101) can be analyzed with an empty head that corresponds to *haltend* 'holding'. For (100), on the other hand, one would require either a syntactic structure with multiple empty elements, or an empty head that selects both parts of the construction and contributes the components of meaning that are present in (102). If one adopts the first approach with multiple silent elements, then one would have to explain why these elements cannot occur in other constructions. For example, it would be necessary to assume an empty element corresponding to *man* 'one'/'you'. But such an empty element could never occur in embedded clauses since subjects cannot simply be omitted there:

(104) * weil dieses Buch gerne liest
because this book gladly reads
Intended: 'because he/she/it likes to read this book'

If one were to follow the second approach, one would be forced to assume an empty head with particularly odd semantics.

The directives in (105) and (106) are similarly problematic (see also Jackendoff & Pinker (2005: 220) for parallel examples in English):

(105) a. Her mit dem Geld / dem gestohlenen Geld!
here with the money the stolen money
'Hand over the (stolen) money!'

b. Weg mit dem Krempel / dem alten Krempel!
away with the junk the old junk
'Get rid of this (old) junk!'

c. Nieder mit den Studiengebühren / den sozialfeindlichen Studiengebühren!
down with the tuition.fees the antisocial tuition.fees
'Down with (antisocial) tuition fees!'

(106) a. In den Müll mit diesen Klamotten!
in the trash with these clothes
'Throw these clothes into the trash!'

b. Zur Hölle mit dieser Regierung!
to.the hell with this government
'To hell with this government!'

Here, it is also not possible to simply identify an elided verb. It is, of course, possible to assume an empty head that selects an adverb or a *mit*-PP, but this would be *ad hoc*. Alternatively, it would be possible to assume that adverbs in (105) select the *mit*-PP. Here, one would have to disregard the fact that adverbs do not normally take any arguments. The same is true of Jacobs's examples in (106). For these, one would have to assume that *in* and *zur* 'to the' are the respective heads. Each of the prepositions would then have to select a noun phrase and a *mit*-PP. While this is technically possible, it is as unattractive as the multiple lexical entries that Categorial Grammar has to assume for pied-piping constructions (see Section 8.6).

A considerably more complicated analysis has been proposed by G. Müller (2009a). Müller treats verbless directives as antipassive constructions. Antipassive constructions involve either the complete suppression of the direct object or its realization as an oblique element (PP). There can also be morphological marking on the verb. The subject is normally not affected by the antipassive but can, however, receive a different case in ergative case systems due to changes in the realization of the object. According to G. Müller, there is a relation between (107a) and (107b) that is similar to active-passive pairs:

(107) a. [dass] jemand diese Klamotten in den Müll schmeißt
that somebody these clothes in the trash throws
'that somebody throws these clothes into the thrash'

b. In den Müll mit diesen Klamotten!
in the trash with these clothes
'Throw these clothes into the trash!'

An empty passive morpheme absorbs the capability of the verb to assign accusative (see also Section 3.4 on the analysis of the passive in GB theory). The object therefore has to be realized as a PP or not at all. It follows from Burzio's Generalization that as the accusative object has been suppressed, there cannot be an external argument. G. Müller assumes, like proponents of Distributed Morphology (e.g., Marantz 1997), that lexical entries are inserted into complete trees post-syntactically. The antipassive morpheme creates a feature bundle in the relevant tree node that is not compatible with German verbs such as *schmeißen* 'throw' and this is why only a null verb with the corresponding specifications can be inserted. Movement of the directional PP is triggered by mechanisms that cannot be discussed further here. The antipassive morpheme forces an obligatory reordering of the verb in initial position (to C, see Section 3.2 and Section 4.2). By stipulation, filling the prefield is only possible in sentences where the C position is filled by a visible verb and this is why G. Müller's analysis does only derive V1 clauses. These are interpreted as imperatives or polar questions. Figure 21.18 gives the analysis of (107b). Budde (2010)

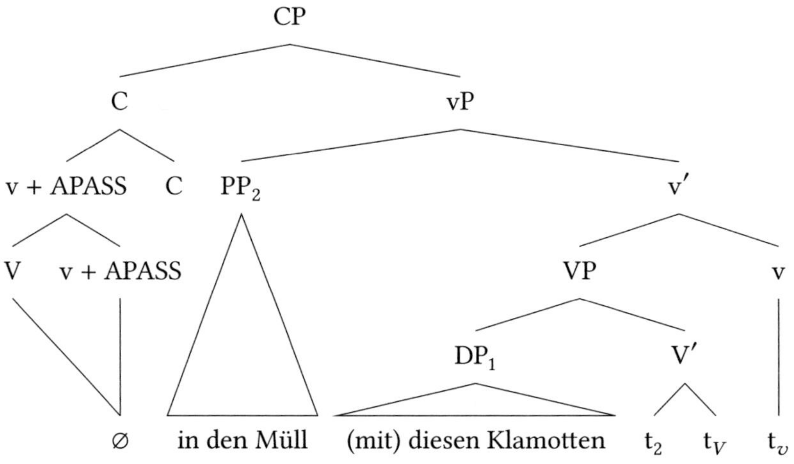

Figure 21.18: *In den Müll mit diesen Klamotten* 'in the trash with these clothes' as an antipassive following G. Müller (2009a)

and Maché (2010) note that the discussion of the data has neglected the fact that there are also interrogative variants of the construction:

(108) a. Wohin mit den Klamotten?
where.to with the clothes
'Where should the clothes go?'

b. Wohin mit dem ganzen Geld?
where.to with the entire money
'Where should all this money go?'

Since these questions correspond to V2 sentences, one does not require the constraint that the prefield can only be filled if the C position is filled.

One major advantage of this analysis is that it derives the different sentence types that are possible with this kind of construction: the V1-variants correspond to polar questions and imperatives, and the V2-variants with a question word correspond to *wh*-questions. A further consequence of the approach pointed out by G. Müller is that no further explanation is required for other interactions with the grammar. For example, the way in which the constructions interact with adverbs follows from the analysis:

(109) a. Schmeiß den Krempel weg!
throw the junk away

b. Schmeiß den Krempel schnell weg!
throw the junk quickly away

c. ?* Schmeiß den Krempel sorgfältig weg!
throw the junk carefully away

(110) a. Weg mit dem Krempel!
away with the junk

b. Schnell weg mit dem Krempel!
quickly away with the junk

c. ?* Sorgfältig weg mit dem Krempel!
carefully away with the junk

Nevertheless one should still bear the price of this analysis in mind: it assumes an empty antipassive morpheme that is otherwise not needed in German. It would only be used in constructions of the kind discussed here. This morpheme is not compatible with any verb and it also triggers obligatory verb movement, which is something that is not known from any other morpheme used to form verb diatheses.

The costs of this analysis are, of course, less severe if one assumes that humans already have this antipassive morpheme anyway, that is, this morpheme is part of our innate Universal Grammar. But if one follows the argumentation from the earlier sections of this chapter, then one should only assume innate linguistic knowledge if there is no alternative explanation.

G. Müller's analysis can be translated into HPSG. The result is given in (111):

(111)
$$\begin{bmatrix} \textit{verb-initial-lr} \\ \text{RELS} \left\langle \begin{bmatrix} \textit{imperative-or-interrogative} \\ \text{EVENT } \boxed{2} \end{bmatrix} \right\rangle \oplus \boxed{} \\ \text{LEX-DTR} \begin{bmatrix} \text{PHON } \langle\rangle \\ \text{SS|LOC} \begin{bmatrix} \text{CAT} \begin{bmatrix} \text{HEAD|MOD } \textit{none} \\ \text{SUBCAT} \left\langle \text{XP[MOD} \ldots \text{IND } \boxed{1}\text{]}, (\text{PP}[\textit{mit}]_{\boxed{1}}) \right\rangle \end{bmatrix} \\ \text{CONT} \begin{bmatrix} \text{IND } \boxed{2} \\ \text{RELS} \left\langle \begin{bmatrix} \textit{directive} \\ \text{EVENT } \boxed{2} \\ \text{PATIENT } \boxed{1} \end{bmatrix} \right\rangle \end{bmatrix} \end{bmatrix} \end{bmatrix} \end{bmatrix}$$

(111) contains a lexical entry for an empty verb in verb-initial position. *directive′* is a placeholder for a more general relation that should be viewed as a supertype of all possible meanings of this construction. These subsume both *schmeißen* 'to throw' and cases such as (112) that were pointed out to me by Monika Budde:

(112) Und mit dem Klavier ganz langsam durch die Tür!
and with the piano very slowly through the door
'Carry the piano very slowly through the door!'

Since only verb-initial and verb-second orders are possible in this construction, the application of the lexical rule for verb-initial position (see page 284) is obligatory. This can be achieved by writing the result of the application of this lexical rule into the lexicon, without having the object to which the rule should have applied actually being present in the lexicon itself. Koenig (1999: Section 3.4.2, 5.3) proposed something similar for English *rumored* 'it is rumored that …' and *aggressive*. There is no active variant of the verb *rumored*, a fact that can be captured by the assumption that only the result of applying a passive lexical rule is present in the lexicon. The actual verb or verb stem from which the participle form has been derived exists only as the daughter of a lexical rule but not as an independent linguistic object. Similarly, the verb **aggress* only exists as the daughter of a (non-productive) adjective rule that licenses *aggressive* and a nominalization rule licensing *aggression*.

The optionality of the *mit*-PP is signaled by the brackets in (111). If one adds the information inherited from the type *verb-initial-lr* under SYNSEM, then the result is (113).

(113)
$$\begin{bmatrix} \textit{verb-initial-lr} \\ \text{SYNSEM|LOC} \begin{bmatrix} \text{HEAD} \begin{bmatrix} \textit{verb} \\ \text{VFORM} & \textit{fin} \\ \text{INITIAL} & + \\ \text{DSL} & \textit{none} \end{bmatrix} \\ \text{SUBCAT} \left\langle \begin{bmatrix} \text{LOC|CAT} \begin{bmatrix} \text{HEAD} \begin{bmatrix} \textit{verb} \\ \text{DSL} \ \boxed{3} \end{bmatrix} \\ \text{SUBCAT} \ \langle\rangle \end{bmatrix} \end{bmatrix} \right\rangle \end{bmatrix} \\ \text{RELS} \left\langle \begin{bmatrix} \textit{imperative-or-interrogative} \\ \text{EVENT} \ \boxed{2} \end{bmatrix} \right\rangle \oplus \boxed{4} \\ \text{LEX-DTR} \begin{bmatrix} \text{PHON} \ \langle\rangle \\ \text{SS|LOC} \ \boxed{3} \begin{bmatrix} \text{CAT} \begin{bmatrix} \text{HEAD|MOD} \ \textit{none} \\ \text{SUBCAT} \left\langle \text{XP[MOD} \ldots \text{IND} \ \boxed{1}\text{]}, (\text{PP}[\textit{mit}]_{\boxed{1}}) \right\rangle \end{bmatrix} \\ \text{CONT} \begin{bmatrix} \text{IND} \ \boxed{2} \\ \text{RELS} \ \boxed{4} \left\langle \begin{bmatrix} \textit{directive} \\ \text{EVENT} \ \boxed{2} \\ \text{PATIENT} \ \boxed{1} \end{bmatrix} \right\rangle \end{bmatrix} \end{bmatrix} \end{bmatrix} \end{bmatrix}$$

The valence properties of the empty verb in (113) are to a large extent determined by the lexical rule for verb-initial order: the V1-LR licenses a verbal head that requires a VP to its right that is missing a verb with the local properties of the LEX-DTR ([3]).

Semantic information dependent on sentence type (assertion, imperative or question) is determined inside the V1-LR depending on the morphological make-up of the verb and the SLASH value of the selected VP (see Müller 2007b: Section 10.3; 2016b; 2015b). Setting the semantics to *imperative-or-interrogative* rules out *assertion* as it occurs in V2-clauses. Whether this type is resolved in the direction of *imperative* or *interrogative* is ultimately decided by further properties of the utterance such as intonation or the use of interrogative pronouns.

The valence of the lexical daughters in (113) as well as the connection to the semantic role (the linking to the patient role) are simply stipulated. Every approach has to stipulate that an argument of the verb has to be expressed as a *mit*-PP. Since there is no antipassive in German, the effect that could be otherwise achieved by an antipassive lexical rule in (113) is simply written into the LEX-DTR of the verb movement rule.

The SUBCAT list of LEX-DTR contains a modifier (adverb, directional PP) and the *mit*-PP. This *mit*-PP is co-indexed with the patient of *directive′* and the modifier refers to the referent of the *mit*-PP. The agent of *directive′* is unspecified since it depends on the context (speaker, hearer, third person).

This analysis is shown in Figure 21.19. Here, V[LOC [2]] corresponds to the LEX-DTR in

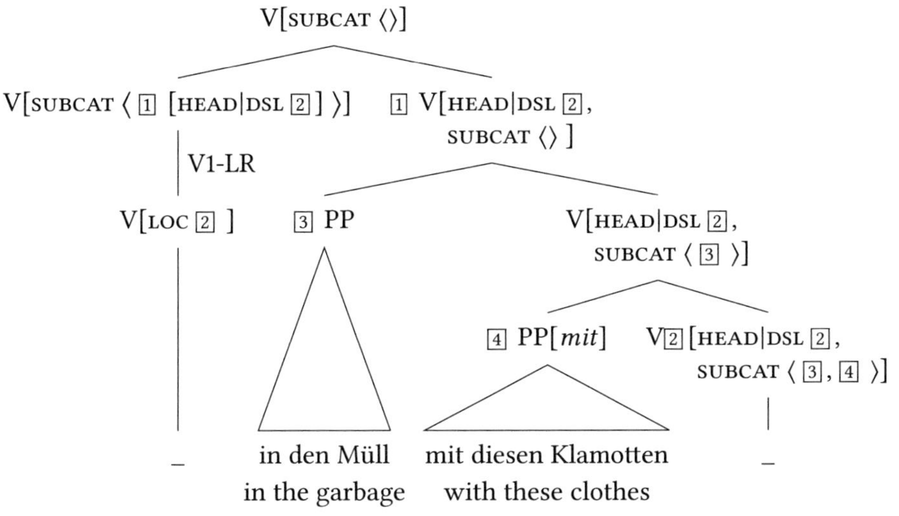

Figure 21.19: HPSG variant of the analysis of *In den Müll mit diesen Klamotten!/?*

(113). The V1-LR licenses an element that requires a maximal verb projection with that exact DSL value [2]. Since DSL is a head feature, the information is present along the head path. The DSL value is identified with the LOCAL value ([2] in Figure 21.19) in the verb movement trace (see page 285). This ensures that the empty element at the end of sentence has exactly the same local properties that the LEX-DTR in (113) has. Thus, both the correct syntactic and semantic information is present on the verb trace and structure building involving the verb trace follows the usual principles. The structures correspond to the structures that were assumed for German sentences in Chapter 9. Therefore, there are the usual possibilities for integrating adjuncts. The correct derivation of the semantics, in particular embedding under imperative or interrogative semantics, follows automatically (for the semantics of adjuncts in conjunction with verb position, see Müller (2007b: Section 9.4)). Also, the ordering variants with the *mit*-PP preceding the direction (112) and direction preceding the *mit*-PP (107b) follow from the usual mechanisms.

If one rejects the analyses discussed up to this point, then one is only really left with phrasal constructions or dominance schemata that connect parts of the construction and contribute the relevant semantics. Exactly how one can integrate adjuncts into the phrasal construction in a non-stipulative way remains an open question; however, there are already some initial results by Jakob Maché (2010) suggesting that directives can still be sensibly integrated into the entire grammar provided an appropriate phrasal schema is assumed.

21.10.2 Serial verbs

There are languages with so-called serial verbs. For example, it is possible to form sentences in Mandarin Chinese where there is only one subject and several verb phrases (Li & Thompson 1981: Chapter 21). There are multiple readings depending on the distribution of aspect marking inside the VP:[57] if the first VP contains a perfect marker, then we have the meaning 'VP1 in order to do/achieve VP2' (114a). If the second VP contains a perfect marker, then the entire construction means 'VP2 because VP1' (114b), and if the first VP contains a durative marker and the verb *hold* or *use*, then the entire construction means 'VP2 using VP1' (114c).

(114) a. Ta1 qu3 le qian2 qu4 guang1jie1.
he withdraw PRF money go shop
'He withdrew money to go shopping.'

b. Ta1 zhu4 Zhong1guo2 xue2 le Han4yu3.
he live China learn PRF Chinese
'He learned Chinese because he lived in China.'

c. Ta1 na2 zhe kuai4zi chi1 fan4.
he take DUR chopsticks eat food
'He eats with chopsticks.'

If we consider the sentences, we only see two adjacent VPs. The meanings of the entire sentences, however, contain parts of meaning that go beyond the meaning of the verb phrases. Depending on the kind of aspect marking, we arrive at different interpretations with regard to the semantic combination of verb phrases. As can be seen in the transla-

[57] See Müller & Lipenkova (2009) for a detailed discussion and further references.

tions, English sometimes uses conjunctions in order to express relations between clauses or verb phrases.

There are three possible ways to capture these data:

1. One could claim that speakers of Chinese simply deduce the relation between the VPs from the context,
2. one could assume that there are empty heads in Chinese corresponding to *because* or *to*, or
3. one could assume a phrasal construction for serial verbs that contributes the correct semantics for the complete meaning depending on the aspect marking inside the VPs.

The first approach is unsatisfactory because the meaning does not vary arbitrarily. There are grammaticalized conventions that should be captured by a theory. The second solution has a stipulative character and thus, if one wishes to avoid empty elements, only the third solution remains. Müller & Lipenkova (2009) have presented a corresponding analysis.

21.10.3 Relative and interrogative clauses

Sag (1997) develops a phrasal analysis of English relative clauses as have Ginzburg & Sag (2000) for interrogative clauses. Relative and interrogative clauses consist of a fronted phrase and a clause or a verb phrase missing the fronted phrase. The fronted phrase contains a relative or interrogative pronoun.

(115) a. the man [who] sleeps
b. the man [who] we know
c. the man [whose mother] visited Kim
d. a house [in which] to live

(116) a. I wonder [who] you know.
b. I want to know [why] you did this.

The GB analysis of relative clauses is given in Figure 21.20. In this analysis, an empty head is in the C position and an element from the IP is moved to the specifier position.

The alternative analysis shown in Figure 21.21 on the following page involves combining the subparts directly in order to form a relative clause. Borsley (2006) has shown that one would require six empty heads in order to capture the various types of relative clauses possible in English if one wanted to analyze them lexically. These heads can be avoided and replaced by corresponding schemata (see Chapter 19 on empty elements). A parallel argument can also be found in Webelhuth (2011) for German: grammars of German would also have to assume six empty heads for the relevant types of relative clause.

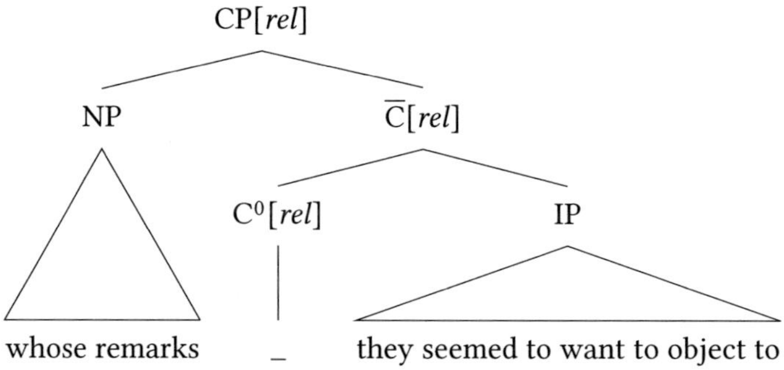

Figure 21.20: Analysis of relative clauses in GB theory

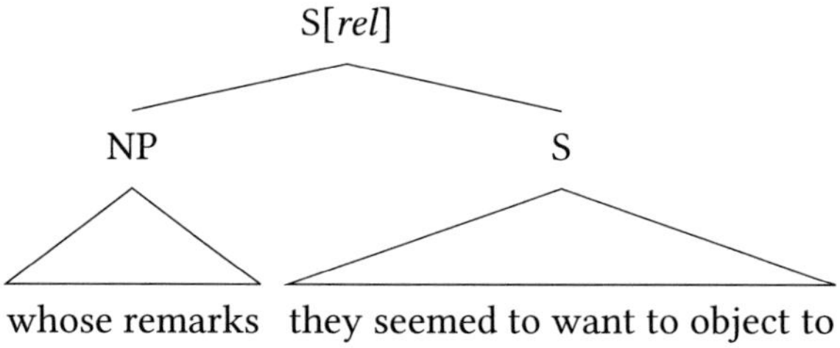

Figure 21.21: Analysis of relative clauses in HPSG following Sag (1997)

Unlike the resultative constructions that were already discussed, there is no variability among interrogative and relative clauses with regard to the order of their parts. There are no changes in valence and no interaction with derivational morphology. Thus, nothing speaks against a phrasal analysis. If one wishes to avoid the assumption of empty heads, then one should opt for the analysis of relative clauses by Sag, or the variant in Müller (1999a: Chapter 10; 2007b: Chapter 11). The latter analysis does without a special schema for noun-relative clause combinations since the semantic content of the relative clause is provided by the relative clause schema.

Sag (2010) discusses long-distance dependencies in English that are subsumed under the term *wh*-movement in GB theory and the Minimalist Program. He shows that this is by no means a uniform phenomenon. He investigates *wh*-questions (117), *wh*-exclamatives (118), topicalization (119), *wh*-relative clauses (120) and *the*-clauses (121):

(117) a. How foolish is he?
b. I wonder *how foolish he is.*

(118) a. What a fool he is!
b. It's amazing *how odd it is.*

(119) The bagels, I like.

(120) a. I met the person *who they nominated.*
b. I'm looking for a bank *in which to place my trust.*

(121) a. The more people I met, *the happier I became.*
b. *The more people I met,* the happier I became.

These individual constructions vary in many respects. Sag lists the following questions that have to be answered for each construction:

- Is there a special *wh*-element in the filler daughter and, if so, what kind of element is it?
- Which syntactic categories can the filler daughters have?
- Can the head-daughter be inverted or finite? Is this obligatory?
- What is the semantic and/or syntactic category of the mother node?
- What is the semantic and/or syntactic category of the head-daughter?
- Is the sentence an island? Does it have to be an independent clause?

The variation that exists in this domain has to be captured somehow by a theory of grammar. Sag develops an analysis with multiple schemata that ensure that the category and semantic contribution of the mother node correspond to the properties of both daughters. The constraints for both classes of constructions and specific constructions are represented in an inheritance hierarchy so that the similarities between the constructions can be accounted for. The analysis can of course also be formulated in a GB-style using empty heads. One would then have to find some way of capturing the generalizations pertaining to the construction. This is possible if one represents the constraints on empty heads in an inheritance hierarchy. Then, the approaches would simply be notational variants of one another. If one wishes to avoid empty elements in the grammar, then the phrasal approach would be preferable.

21.10.4 The N-P-N construction

Jackendoff (2008) discusses the English N-P-N construction. Examples of this construction are given in (122):

(122) a. day by day, paragraph by paragraph, country by country
b. dollar for dollar, student for student, point for point
c. face to face, bumper to bumper
d. term paper after term paper, picture after picture
e. book upon book, argument upon argument

This construction is relatively restricted: articles and plural nouns are not allowed. The phonological content of the first noun has to correspond to that of the second. There are also similar constructions in German:

(123) a. Er hat Buch um Buch verschlungen.
he has book around book swallowed
'He binge-read book after book.'

b. Zeile für Zeile[58]
line for line
'line by line'

Determining the meaning contribution of this kind of N-P-N construction is by no means trivial. Jackendoff suggests the meaning *many Xs in succession* as an approximation.

Jackendoff points out that this construction is problematic from a syntactic perspective since it is not possible to determine a head in a straightforward way. It is also not clear what the structure of the remaining material is if one is working under assumptions of $\overline{\text{X}}$ theory. If the preposition *um* were the head in (123a), then one would expect that it is combined with an NP, however this is not possible:

(124) a. * Er hat dieses Buch um jenes Buch verschlungen.
he has this book around this book swallowed

b. * Er hat ein Buch um ein Buch verschlungen.
he has a book around a book swallowed

For this kind of structures, it would be necessary to assume that a preposition selects a noun to its right and, if it find this, it then requires a second noun of this exact form to its left. For N-*um*-N and N-*für*-N, it is not entirely clear what the entire construction has to do with the individual prepositions. One could also try to develop a lexical analysis for this phenomenon, but the facts are different to those for resultative constructions: in resultative constructions, the semantics of simplex verbs clearly plays a role. Furthermore, unlike with the resultative construction, the order of the component parts of the construction is fixed in the N-P-N construction. It is not possible to extract a noun or place the preposition in front of both nouns. Syntactically, the N-P-N combination with some prepositions behaves like an NP (Jackendoff 2008: 9):

(125) Student after/upon/*by student flunked.

This is also strange if one wishes to view the preposition as the head of the construction.

Instead of a lexical analysis, Jackendoff proposes the following phrasal construction for N-*after*-N combinations:

(126) Meaning: MANY X_is IN SUCCESSION [or however it is encoded]
Syntax: $[_{NP}\ N_i\ P_j\ N_i]$
Phonology: Wd_i $after_j$ Wd_i

The entire meaning as well as the fact that the N-P-N has the syntactic properties of an NP would be captured on the construction level.

I already discussed examples by Bragmann (2015) in Section 11.7.2.4 that show that N-P-N constructions may be extended by further P-N combinations:

[58] *Zwölf Städte*. Einstürzende Neubauten. Fünf auf der nach oben offenen Richterskala, 1987.

(127) Day after day after day went by, but I never found the courage to talk to her.

So rather than an N-P-N pattern Bragmann suggests the pattern in (128), where '+' stands for at least one repetition of a sequence.

(128) N (P N)+

As was pointed out on page 401 this pattern is not easy to cover in selection-based approaches. One could assume that an N takes arbitrarily many P-N combinations, which would be very unusual for heads. Alternatively, one could assume recursion, so N would be combined with a P and with an N-P-N to yield N-P-N-P-N. But such an analysis would make it really difficult to enforce the restrictions regarding the identity of the nouns in the complete construction. In order to enforce such an identity the N that is combined with N-P-N would have to impose constraints regarding deeply embedded nouns inside the embedded N-P-N object (see also Section 18.2).

G. Müller (2011) proposes a lexical analysis of the N-P-N construction. He assumes that prepositions can have a feature REDUP. In the analysis of *Buch um Buch* 'book after book', the preposition is combined with the right noun *um Buch*. In the phonological component, reduplication of *Buch* is triggered by the REDUP feature, thereby yielding *Buch um Buch*. This analysis also suffers from the problems pointed out by Jackendoff: in order to derive the semantics of the construction, the semantics would have to be present in the lexical entry of the reduplicating preposition (or in a relevant subsequent component that interprets the syntax). Furthermore it is unclear how a reduplication analysis would deal with the Bragmann data.

22 Universal Grammar and doing comparative linguistics without an a priori assumption of a (strong) UG

The following two sections deal with the tools that I believe to be necessary to capture generalizations and the way one can derive such generalizations.

22.1 Formal tools for capturing generalizations

In Chapter 13, it was shown that all the evidence that has previously been brought forward in favor of innate linguistic knowledge is in fact controversial. In some cases, the facts are irrelevant to the discussion and in other cases, they could be explained in other ways. Sometimes, the chains of argumentation are not logically sound or the premises are not supported. In other cases, the argumentation is circular. As a result, the question of whether there is innate linguistic knowledge still remains unanswered. All theories that presuppose the existence of this kind of knowledge are making very strong assumptions. If one assumes, as Kayne (1994) for example, that all languages have the underlying structure [specifier [head complement]] and that movement is exclusively to the left, then these two basic assumptions must be part of innate linguistic knowledge since there is no evidence for the assumption that utterances in all natural languages have the structure that Kayne suggests. As an example, the reader may check Laenzlinger's proposal for German (2004: 224), which is depicted in Figure 4.20 on page 144. According to Laenzlinger, (1a) is derived from the underlying structure in (1b):

(1) a. weil der Mann wahrscheinlich diese Sonate nicht oft gut gespielt hat
because the man probably this sonata not often well played has
'because the man probably had not played this sonata well often'

b. * weil der Mann wahrscheinlich nicht oft gut hat gespielt diese Sonate
because the man probably not often well has played this sonata

(1b) is entirely unacceptable, so the respective structure cannot be acquired from input and hence the principles and rules that license it would have to be innate.

As we have seen, there are a number of alternative theories that are much more surface-oriented than most variants of Transformational Grammar. These alternative theories often differ with regard to particular assumptions that have been discussed in the preceding sections. For example, there are differences in the treatment of long-distance dependencies that have led to a proliferation of lexical items in Categorial Grammar (see Section 8.6). As has been shown by Jacobs (2008), Jackendoff (2008) and others, approaches such as Categorial Grammar that assume that every phrase must have a functor/head cannot explain certain constructions in a plausible way. Inheritance-based phrasal analyses that only list heads with a core meaning in the lexicon and have the constructions in which the heads occur determine the meaning of a complex expression turn out to have difficulties with derivational morphology and with accounting for alternative ways of argument realization (see Section 21.2.2, 21.4.1, and 21.4.2). We therefore need a theory that handles argument structure changing processes in the lexicon and still has some kind of phrase structure or relevant schemata. Some variants of GB/MP as well as LFG, HPSG, TAG and variants of CxG are examples of this kind of theory. Of these theories, only HPSG and some variants of CxG make use of the same descriptive tools ((typed) feature descriptions) for roots, stems, words, lexical rules and phrases. By using a uniform description for all these objects, it is possible to formulate generalizations over the relevant objects. It is therefore possible to capture what particular words have in common with lexical rules or phrases. For example, the *-bar* 'able' derivation corresponds to a complex passive construction with a modal verb. (2) illustrates.

(2) a. Das Rätsel ist lösbar.
the puzzle is solvable

b. Das Rätsel kann gelöst werden.
the puzzle can solved be
'The puzzle can be solved.'

By using the same descriptive inventory for syntax and morphology, it is possible to capture cross-linguistic generalizations: something that is inflection/derivation in one language can be syntax in another.

It is possible to formulate principles that hold for both words and phrases and furthermore, it is possible to capture cross-linguistic generalizations or generalizations that hold for certain groups of languages. For example, languages can be divided into those with fixed constituent order and those with more flexible or completely free constituent order. The corresponding types can be represented with their constraints in a type hierarchy. Different languages can use a particular part of the hierarchy and also formulate different constraints for each of the types (see Ackerman & Webelhuth 1998: Section 9.2). HPSG differs from theories such as LFG and TAG in that phrases are not ontologically different from words. This means that there are no special c-structures or tree structures. Descriptions of complex phrases simply have additional features that say something about their daughters. In this way, it is possible to formulate cross-linguistic generalizations about dominance schemata. In LFG, the c-structure rules are normally specified separately for each language. Another advantage of consistent description is that one can capture similarities between words and lexical rules, as well as between words and phrases. For example, a complementizer such as *dass* 'that' shares a number of properties with a simple verb or with coordinated verbs in initial position:

(3) a. [dass] Maria die Platte kennt und liebt
that Maria the record knows and loves
'that Maria knows and loves the record'

b. [Kennt und liebt] Maria die Platte?
knows and loves Maria the record
'Does Mary know and love the record?'

The difference between the two linguistic objects mainly lies in the kind of phrase they select: the complementizer requires a sentence with a visible finite verb, whereas the verb in initial position requires a sentence without a visible finite verb.

In Section 9.1.5, a small part of an inheritance hierarchy was presented. This part contains types that probably play a role in the grammars of all natural languages: there are head-argument combinations in every language. Without this kind of combinatorial operation, it would not be possible to establish a relation between two concepts. The ability to create relations, however, is one of the basic properties of language.

In addition to more general types, the type hierarchy of a particular language contains language-specific types or those specific to a particular class of languages. All languages presumably have one and two-place predicates and for most languages (if not all), it makes sense to talk about verbs. It is then possible to talk about one and two-place verbs. Depending on the language, these can then be subdivided into intransitive and transitive. Constraints are formulated for the various types that can either hold generally or be language-specific. In English, verbs have to occur before their complements and therefore have the INITIAL value +, whereas verbs in German have the INITIAL value − and it is the lexical rule for initial position that licenses a verb with an INITIAL value +.

The differing settings of the INITIAL value for German and English is reminiscent of parameters from GB-Theory. There is one crucial difference, however: it is not assumed that a language learner sets the INITIAL value for all heads once and for all. The use of an INITIAL value is compatible with models of acquisition that assume that learners learn individual words with their positional properties. It is certainly possible for the respective words to exhibit different values for a particular feature. Generalizations about the position of entire word classes are only learned at a later point in the acquisition process.

A hierarchy analogous to the one proposed by Croft (see Section 21.4.1) is given in Figure 22.1 on the next page. For inflected words, the relevant roots are in the lexicon. Examples of this are *schlaf-* 'sleep', *lieb-* 'love' and *geb-* 'give'. In Figure 22.1, there are different subtypes of *root*, the general type for roots: e.g., *intrans-verb* for intransitive verbs and *trans-verb* for transitive verbs. Transitive verbs can be further subdivided into strictly transitive verbs (those with nominative and accusative arguments) and ditransitive verbs (those with nominative and both accusative and dative arguments). The hierarchy above would of course have to be refined considerably as there are even further sub-classes for both transitive and intransitive verbs. For example, one can divide intransitive verbs into unaccusative and unergative verbs and even strictly transitive verbs would have to be divided into further sub-classes (see Welke 2009: Section 2).

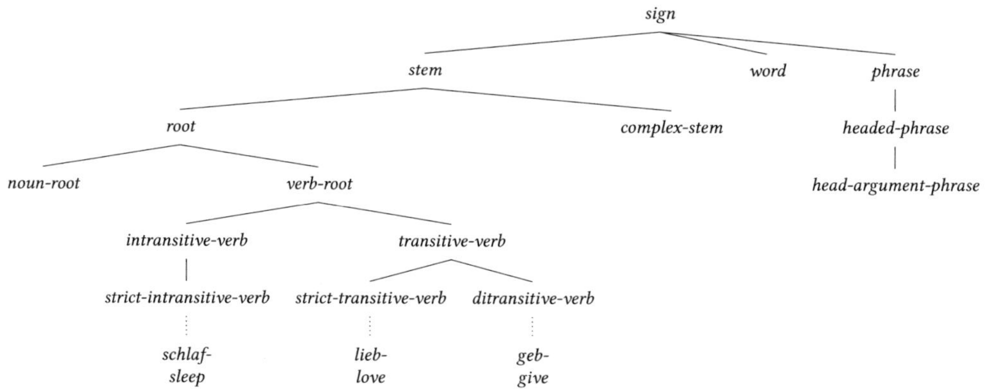

Figure 22.1: Section of an inheritance hierarchy with lexical entries and dominance schemata

In addition to a type for roots, the above figure contains types for stems and words. Complex stems are complex objects that are derived from simple roots but still have to be inflected (*lesbar-* 'readable', *besing-* 'to sing about'). Words are objects that do not inflect. Examples of these are the pronouns *er* 'he', *sie* 'she' etc. as well as prepositions. An inflected form can be formed from a verbal stem (*geliebt* 'loved', *besingt* 'sings about'). Relations between inflected words and (complex) stems can be formed again using derivation rules. In this way, *geliebt* 'loved' can be recategorized as an adjective stem that must then be combined with adjectival endings (*geliebt-e*). The relevant descriptions of complex stems/words are subtypes of *complex-stem* or *word*. These subtypes describe the form that complex words such as *geliebte* must have. For a technical implementation of this, see Müller (2002a: Section 3.2.7). Using dominance schemata, all words can be combined to form phrases. The hierarchy given here is of course by no means complete. There are a number of additional valence classes and one could also assume more general types that simply describe one, two and three-place predicates. Such types are probably plausible for the description of other languages. Here, we are only dealing with a small part of the type hierarchy in order to have a comparison to the Croftian hierarchy: in Figure 22.1, there are no types for sentence patterns with the form [Sbj IntrVerb], but rather types for lexical objects with a particular valence (V[SUBCAT ⟨ NP[*str*] ⟩]). Lexical rules can then be applied to the relevant lexical objects that license objects with another valence or introduce information about inflection. Complete words can be combined in the syntax with relatively general rules, for example in head-argument structures. The problems from which purely phrasal approaches suffer are thereby avoided. Nevertheless generalizations about lexeme classes and the utterances that can be formed can be captured in the hierarchy.

There are also principles in addition to inheritance hierarchies: the Semantics Principle presented in Section 9.1.6 holds for all languages. The Case Principle that we also saw is a constraint that only applies to a particular class of languages, namely nominative-accusative languages. Other languages have an ergative-absolutive system.

The assumption of innate linguistic knowledge is not necessary for the theory of language sketched here. As the discussion in Section 13 has shown, the question of whether this kind of knowledge exists has still not been answered conclusively. Should it turn out that this knowledge actually exists, the question arises of what exactly is innate. It would be a plausible assumption that the part of the inheritance hierarchy that is relevant for all languages is innate together with the relevant principles (e.g., the constraints on Head-Argument structures and the Semantics Principle). It could, however, also be the case that only a part of the more generally valid types and principles is innate since something being innate does not follow from the fact that it is present in all languages (see also Section 13.1.9).

In sum, one can say that theories that describe linguistic objects using a consistent descriptive inventory and make use of inheritance hierarchies to capture generalizations are the ones best suited to represent similarities between languages. Furthermore, this kind of theory is compatible with both a positive and a negative answer to the question of whether there is innate linguistic knowledge.

22.2 How to develop linguistic theories that capture cross-linguistic generalizations

In the previous section I argued for a uniform representation of linguistic knowledge at all descriptive levels and for type hierarchies as a good tool for representing generalizations. This section explores a way to develop grammars that are motivated by facts from several languages.

If one looks at the current practice in various linguistic schools one finds two extreme ways of approaching language. On the one hand, we have the Mainstream Generative Grammar (MGG) camp and, on the other hand, we have the Construction Grammar/Cognitive Grammar camp. I hasten to say that what I state here does not hold for all members of these groups, but for the extreme cases. The caricature of the MGG scientist is that he is looking for underlying structures. Since these have to be the same for all languages (poverty of the stimulus), it is sufficient to look at one language, say English. The result of this research strategy is that one ends up with models that were suggested by the most influential linguist for English and that others then try to find ways to accommodate other languages. Since English has an NP VP structure, all languages have to have it. Since English reorders constituents in passive sentences, passive is movement and all languages have to work this way. I discussed the respective analyses of German in more detail in Section 3.4.2 and in Chapter 20 and showed that the assumption that passive is movement makes unwanted predictions for German, since the subject of passives stays in the object position in German. Furthermore, this analysis requires the assumption of invisible expletives, that is, entities that cannot be seen and do not have any meaning.

On the other extreme of the spectrum we find people working in Construction Grammar or without any framework at all (see footnote 1 on page 1 for discussion) who claim that all languages are so different that we cannot even use the same vocabulary to analyze them. Moreover, within languages, we have so many different objects that it is impossible (or too early) to state any generalizations. Again, what I describe here are extreme positions and clichés.

In what follows, I sketch the procedure that we apply in the CoreGram project[1] (Müller 2013a, 2015a). In the CoreGram project we work on a set of typologically diverse languages in parallel:

- German (Müller 2007b, 2009c, 2012a; Müller & Ørsnes 2011, 2013a; Müller 2014b, 2015b)
- Danish (Ørsnes 2009b; Müller 2009c, 2012a; Müller & Ørsnes 2011, 2013a,b, 2015)
- Persian (Müller 2010b; Müller & Ghayoomi 2010)
- Maltese (Müller 2009b)
- Mandarin Chinese (Lipenkova 2009; Müller & Lipenkova 2009, 2013, 2016)
- Yiddish (Müller & Ørsnes 2011)
- English (Müller 2009c, 2012a; Müller & Ørsnes 2013a)
- Hindi
- Spanish (Machicao y Priemer 2015)
- French

These languages belong to diverse language families (Indo-European, Afro-Asiatic, Sino-Tibetan) and among the Indo-European languages the languages belong to different groups (Germanic, Romance, Indo-Iranian). Figure 22.2 provides an overview. We work out fully formalized, computer-processable grammar fragments in the framework of HPSG that have a semantics component. The details will not be discussed here, but the interested reader is referred to Müller (2015a).

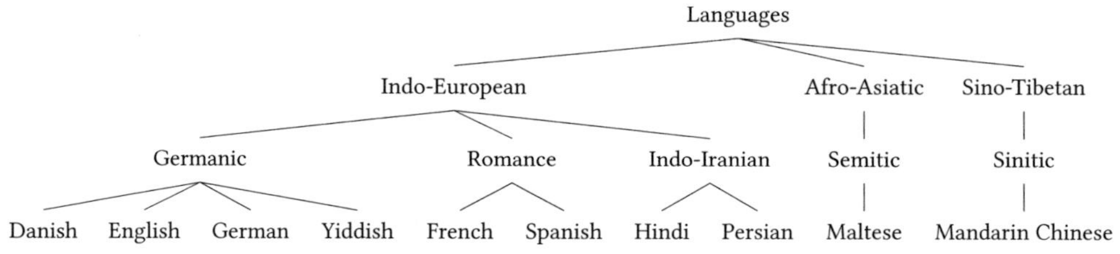

Figure 22.2: Language families and groups of the languages covered in the CoreGram project

[1] http://hpsg.fu-berlin.de/Projects/CoreGram.html, March 11, 2016.

As was argued in previous sections, the assumption of innate language-specific knowledge should be kept to a minimum. This is also what Chomsky suggested in his Minimalist Program. There may even be no language-specific innate knowledge at all, a view taken in Construction Grammar/Cognitive Grammar. So, instead of imposing constraints from one language onto other languages, a bottom-up approach seems to be more appropriate: grammars for individual languages should be motivated language-internally. Grammars that share certain properties can be grouped in classes. This makes it possible to capture generalizations about groups of languages and natural language as such. Let us consider a few example languages: German, Dutch, Danish, English and French. If we start developing grammars for German and Dutch, we find that they share a lot of properties: for instance, both are SOV and V2 languages and both have a verbal complex. One main difference is the order of elements in the verbal complex. The situation can be depicted as in Figure 22.3. There are some properties that are shared

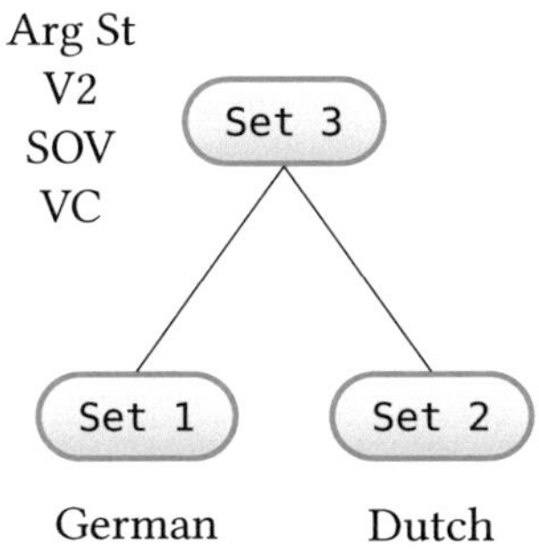

Figure 22.3: Shared properties of German and Dutch

between German and Dutch (Set 3). For instance, the argument structure of lexical items, a list containing descriptions of syntactic and semantic properties of arguments and the linking of these arguments to the meaning of the lexical items, is contained in Set 3. In addition to the constraints for SOV languages, the verb position and the fronting of a constituent in V2 clauses are contained in Set 3. The respective constraints are shared between the two grammars. Although these sets are arranged in a hierarchy in Figure 22.3 and the following figures this has nothing to do with the type hierarchies that have been discussed in the previous subsection. These type hierarchies are part of our linguistic theories and various parts of such hierarchies can be in different sets: those parts of the type hierarchy that concern more general aspects can be in Set 3 in Figure 22.3 and those that are specific to Dutch or German are in the respective other sets. When we add another language, say Danish, we get further differences. While German and Dutch are SOV, Danish is an SVO language. Figure 22.4 on the next page shows the resulting situation: the topmost node represents constraints that hold for all the languages considered so far (for instance the argument structure constraints, linking and V2) and the node below it

(Set 4) contains constraints that hold for German and Dutch only.[2] For instance, Set 4 contains constraints regarding verbal complexes and SOV order. The union of Set 4 and Set 5 is Set 3 of Figure 22.3.

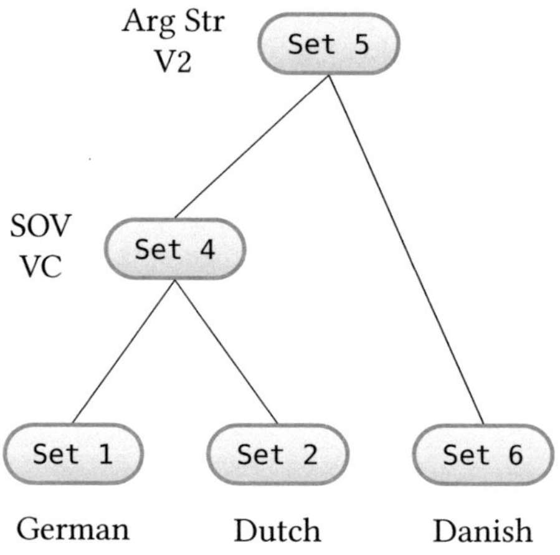

Figure 22.4: Shared properties of German, Dutch, and Danish

If we add further languages, further constraint sets will be distinguished. Figure 22.5 on the following page shows the situation that results when we add English and French. Again, the picture is not complete since there are constraints that are shared by Danish and English but not by French, but the general idea should be clear: by systematically working this way, we should arrive at constraint sets that directly correspond to those that have been established in the typological literature.

The interesting question is what will be the topmost set if we consider enough languages. At first glance, one would expect that all languages have valence representations and linkings between these and the semantics of lexical items (argument structure lists in the HPSG framework). However, Koenig & Michelson (2012) argue for an analysis of Oneida (a Northern Iroquoian language) that does not include a representation of syntactic valence. If this analysis is correct, syntactic argument structure would not be universal. It would, of course, be characteristic of a large number of languages, but it would not be part of the topmost set. So this leaves us with just one candidate for the topmost set from the area of syntax: the constraints that license the combination of two or more linguistic objects. This is basically Chomsky's External Merge without the binarity restriction[3]. In addition, the topmost set would, of course, contain the basic

[2] In principle, there could be constraints that hold for Dutch and Danish, but not for German or for German and Danish, but not for Dutch. These constraints would be removed from Set 1 and Set 2, respectively, and inserted into another constraint set higher up in the hierarchy. These sets are not illustrated in the figure and I keep the names Set 1 and Set 2 from Figure 22.3 for the constraint sets for German and Dutch.

[3] Note that binarity is more restrictive than flat structures: there is an additional constraint that there have to be exactly two daughters. As was argued in Section 21.10.4 one needs phrasal constructions with more than two constituents.

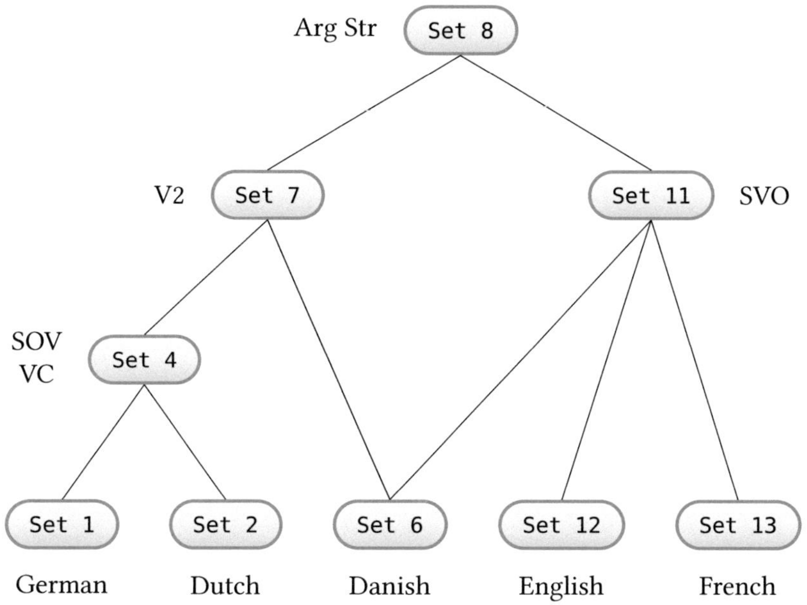

Figure 22.5: Languages and language classes

machinery for representing phonology and semantics.

It should be clear from what has been said so far that the goal of every scientist who works this way is to find generalizations and to describe a new language in a way that reuses theoretical constructs that have been found useful for a language that is already covered. However, as was explained above, the resulting grammars should be motivated by data of the respective languages and not by facts from other languages. In situations where more than one analysis would be compatible with a given dataset for language X, the evidence from language Y with similar constructs is most welcome and can be used as evidence in favor of one of the two analyses for language X. I call this approach the *bottom-up approach with cheating*: unless there is contradicting evidence, we can reuse analyses that have been developed for other languages.

Note that this approach is compatible with the rather agnostic view advocated by Haspelmath (2010a), Dryer (1997), Croft (2001: Section 1.4.2–1.4.3), and others, who argue that descriptive categories should be language-specific, that is, the notion of *subject* for Tagalog is different from the one for English, the category *noun* in English is different from the category *noun* in Persian and so on. Even if one follows such extreme positions, one can still derive generalizations regarding constituent structure, head-argument relations and so on. However, I believe that some categories can fruitfully be used cross-linguistically; if not universally, then at least for language classes. As Newmeyer (2010: 692) notes with regard to the notion of *subject*: calling two items *subject* in one language does not entail that they have identical properties. The same is true for two linguistic items from different languages: calling a Persian linguistic item *subject* does not entail that it has exactly the same properties as an English linguistic item that is called *subject*. The same is, of course, true for all other categories and relations, for instance, parts of speech: Persian nouns do not share all properties with English nouns.[4] Haspelmath (2010c: 697) writes: "Generative linguists try to use as many crosslinguistic categories in the description of individual languages as possible, and this often leads to insurmountable problems." If the assumption of a category results in problems, they have to be solved. If this is not possible with the given set of categories/features, new ones have to be assumed. This is not a drawback of the methodology, quite the opposite is true: if we have found something that does not integrate nicely into what we already have, this is a sign that we have discovered something new and exciting. If we stick to language-particular categories and features, it is much harder to notice that a special phenomenon is involved, since all categories and features are specific to one language anyway. Note also that not all speakers of a language community have exactly the same categories. If one were to take the idea of language-particular category symbols to an extreme, one would end up with person specific category symbols like *Klaus-English-noun*.

After my talk at the MIT in 2013, members of the linguistics department objected to the approach taken in the CoreGram project and claimed that it would not make any predictions as far as possible/impossible languages are concerned. Regarding predictions two things must be said: firstly, predictions are being made on a language particular basis. As an example consider the following sentences from Netter (1991):

(4) a. [Versucht, zu lesen], hat er das Buch nicht.
tried to read has he.NOM the.ACC book not
'He did not try to read the book.'

b. [Versucht, einen Freund vorzustellen], hat er ihr noch nie.
tried a.ACC friend to.introduce has he.NOM her.DAT yet never
'He never before tried to introduce a friend to her.'

When I first read these sentences I had no idea about their structure. I switched on my computer and typed them in and within milliseconds I got an analysis of the sentences and by inspecting the result I realized that these sentences are combinations of partial verb phrase fronting and the so-called third construction (Müller 1999a: 439). I had previously implemented analyses of both phenomena but had never thought about

[4] Note that using labels like *Persian Noun* and *English Noun* (see for instance Haspelmath 2010a: Section 2 for such a suggestion regarding case, e.g., Russian Dative, Korean Dative, …) is somehow strange since it implies that both Persian nouns and English nouns are somehow nouns. Instead of using the category *Persian Noun* one could assign objects of the respective class to the class *noun* and add a feature LANGUAGE with the value *persian*. This simple trick allows one to assign both objects of the type *Persian Noun* and objects of the type *English Noun* to the class *noun* and still maintain the fact that there are differences. Of course, no theoretical linguist would introduce the LANGUAGE feature to differentiate between Persian and English nouns, but nouns in the respective languages have other features that make them differ. So the part of speech classification as noun is a generalization over nouns in various languages and the categories *Persian Noun* and *English Noun* are feature bundles that contain further, language-specific information.

the interaction of the two. The grammar predicted that examples like (4) are grammatical. Similarly the constraints of the grammar can interact to rule out certain structures. So predictions about ungrammaticality/impossible structures are in fact made as well.

Secondly, the topmost constraint set holds for all languages seen so far. It can be regarded as a hypothesis about properties that are shared by all languages. This constraint set contains constraints about the connection between syntax and information structure and such constraints allow for V2 languages but rule out languages with the verb in penultimate position (see Kayne 1994: 50 for the claim that such languages do not exist. Kayne develops a complicated syntactic system that predicts this). Of course, if a language is found that places the verb in penultimate position for the encoding of sentence types or some other communicative effect, a more general topmost set has to be defined. But this is parallel for Minimalist theories: if languages are found that are incompatible with basic assumptions, the basic assumptions have to be revised. As with the language particular constraints, the constraints in the topmost set make certain predictions about what can be and what cannot be found in languages.

Frequently discussed examples such as those languages that form questions by reversing the order of the words in a string (Musso et al. 2003) need not be ruled out by the grammar, since they are ruled out by language external constraints: we simply lack the working memory to do such complex computations.

A variant of this argument comes from David Pesetsky and was raised in Facebook discussions of an article by Paul Ibbotson and Michael Tomasello published in The Guardian[5]. Pesetsky claimed that Tomasello's theory of language acquisition could not explain why we find V2 languages but no V3 languages. First, I do not know of anything that blocks V3 languages in current Minimalist theories. So per se the fact that V3 languages may not exist cannot be used to support any of the competing approaches. Of course, the question could be asked whether the V3 pattern would be useful for reaching our communicative goals and whether it can be easily acquired. Now, with V2 as a pattern it is clear that we have exactly one position that can be used for special purposes in the V2 sentence (topic or focus). For monovalent and bivalent verbs we have an argument that can be placed in initial position. The situation is different for the hypothetical V3 languages, though: If we have monovalent verbs like *sleep*, there is nothing for the second position. As Pesetsky pointed out in the answer to my comment on a blog post, languages solve such problems by using expletives. For instance some languages insert an expletive to mark subject extraction in embedded interrogative sentences, since otherwise the fact that the subject is extracted would not be recognizable by the hearer. So the expletive helps to make the structure transparent. V2 languages also use expletives to fill the initial position if speakers want to avoid something in the special, designated position:

(5) Es kamen drei Männer zum Tor hinein.
EXPL came three man to.the gate in
'Three man came through the gate.'

[5] *The roots of language: What makes us different from other animals?* Published 05.11.2015. http://www.theguardian.com/science/head-quarters/2015/nov/05/roots-language-what-makes-us-different-animals

In order to do the same in V3 languages one would have to put two expletives in front of the verb. So there seem to be many disadvantages of a V3 system that V2 systems do not have and hence one would expect that V3 systems are less likely to come into existence. If they existed, they would be expected to be subject to change in the course of time; e.g., omission of the expletive with intransitives, optional V2 with transitives and finally V2 in general. With the new modeling techniques for language acquisition and agent-based community simulation one can actually simulate such processes and I guess in the years to come, we will see exciting work in this area.

Cinque (1999: 106) suggested a cascade of functional projections to account for reoccurring orderings in the languages of the world. He assumes elaborate tree structures to play a role in the analysis of all sentences in all languages even if there is no evidence for respective morphosyntactic distinctions in a particular language (see also Cinque & Rizzi 2010: 55). In the latter case, Cinque assumes that the respective tree nodes are empty. Cinque's results could be incorporated in the model advocated here. We would define part of speech categories and morpho-syntactic features in the topmost set and state linearization constraints that enforce the order that Cinque encoded directly in his tree structure. In languages in which such categories are not manifested by lexical material, the constraints would never apply. Neither empty elements nor elaborate tree structures would be needed. Thus Cinque's data could be covered in a better way in an HPSG with a rich UG but I, nevertheless, refrain from introducing 400 categories (or features) into the theories of all languages and, again, I point out that such a rich and language-specific UG is implausible from a genetic point of view. Therefore, I wait for other, probably functional, explanations of the Cinque data.

Note also that implicational universals can be derived from hierarchically organized constraint sets as the ones proposed here. For instance, one can derive from Figure 22.5 the implicational statement that all SVO languages are V2 languages, since there is no language that has constraints from Set 4 that does not also have the constraints of Set 7. Of course, this implicational statement is wrong, since there are lots and lots of SOV languages and just exceptionally few V2 languages. So, as soon as we add other languages as for instance Persian or Japanese, the picture will change.

The methodology suggested here differs from what is done in MGG, since MGG stipulates the general constraints that are supposed to hold for all languages on the basis of general specualtions about language. In the best case, these general assumptions are fed by a lot of experience with different languages and grammars, in the worst case they are derived from insights gathered from one or more Indo-European languages. Quite often impressionistic data is used to motivate rather far-reaching fundamental design decisions (Fanselow 2009; Sternefeld & Richter 2012; Haider 2014). It is interesting to note that this is exactly what members of the MGG camp reproach typologists for. Evans & Levinson (2009a) pointed out that counterexamples can be found for many alleged universals. A frequent response to this is that unanalyzed data cannot refute grammatical hypotheses (see, for instance, Freidin 2009: 454). In the very same way it has to be said that unanalyzed data should not be used to build theories on (Fanselow 2009). In the CoreGram project, we aim to develop broad-coverage grammars of several languages, so those constraints that make it to the top node are motivated and not stipulated on the basis of intuitive implicit knowledge about language.

Since it is data-oriented and does not presuppose innate language-specific knowledge, this research strategy is compatible with work carried out in Construction Grammar (see Goldberg 2013b: 481 for an explicit statement to this end) and in any case it should also be compatible with the Minimalist world.

23 Conclusion

The analyses discussed in this book show a number of similarities. All frameworks use complex categories to describe linguistic objects. This is most obvious for GPSG, LFG, HPSG, CxG and FTAG, however, GB/Minimalism and Categorial Grammar also talk about NPs in third person singular and the relevant features for part of speech, person and number form part of a complex category. In GB, there are the feature N and V with binary values (Chomsky 1970: 199), Stabler (1992: 119) formalizes *Barriers* with feature-value pairs and Sauerland & Elbourne (2002: 290–291) argue for the use of feature-value pairs in a Minimalist theory. Also, see Veenstra (1998) for a constraint-based formalization of a Minimalist analysis using typed feature descriptions. Dependency Grammar dialects like Hellwig's Dependency Unification Grammar also use feature-value pairs (Hellwig 2003: 612).

Furthermore, there is a consensus in all current frameworks (with the exception of Construction Grammar and Dependency Grammar) about how the sentence structure of German should be analyzed: German is an SOV and V2 language. Clauses with verb-initial order resemble verb-final ones in terms of structure. The finite verb is either moved (GB) or stands in a relation to an element in verb-final position (HPSG). Verb-second clauses consist of verb-initial clauses out of which one constituent has been extracted. It is also possible to see some convergence with regard to the analysis of the passive: some ideas originally formulated by Haider (1984, 1985a, 1986a) in the framework of GB have been adopted by HPSG. Some variants of Construction Grammar also make use of a specially marked 'designated argument' (Michaelis & Ruppenhofer 2001: 55–57).

If we consider new developments in the individual frameworks, it becomes clear that the nature of the proposed analyses can sometimes differ drastically. Whereas CG, LFG, HPSG and CxG are surface-oriented, sometimes very abstract structures are assumed in Minimalism and in some cases, one tries to trace all languages back to a common base structure (Universal Base Hypothesis).[1] This kind of approach only makes sense if one assumes that there is innate linguistic knowledge about this base structure common to all languages as well as about the operations necessary to derive the surface structures. As was shown in Chapter 13, all arguments for the assumption of innate linguistic knowledge are either not tenable or controversial at the very least. The acquisition of linguistic abilities can to a large extent receive an input-based explanation (Section 13.8.3, Section 16.3 and Section 16.4). Not all questions about acquisition have been settled once and for all, but input-based approaches are at least plausible enough for one to be very cautious about any assumption of innate linguistic knowledge.

[1] It should be noted that there are currently many subvariants and individual opinions in the Minimalist community so that it is only possible – as with CxG – to talk about tendencies.

Models such as LFG, CG, HPSG, CxG and TAG are compatible with performance data, something that is not true of certain transformation-based approaches, which are viewed as theories of competence that do not make any claims about performance. In MGG, it is assumed that there are other mechanisms for working with linguistic knowledge, for example, mechanisms that combine 'chunks' (fragments of linguistic material). If one wishes to make these assumptions, then it is necessary to explain how chunks and the processing of chunks are acquired and not how a complex system of transformations and transformation-comparing constraints is acquired. This means that the problem of language acquisition would be a very different one. If one assumes a chunk-based approach, then the innate knowledge about a universal transformational base would only be used to derive a surface-oriented grammar. This then poses the question of what exactly the evidence for transformations in a competence grammar is and if it would not be preferable to simply assume that the competence grammar is of the kind assumed by LFG, CG, HPSG, CxG or TAG. One can therefore conclude that constraint-based analyses and the kind of transformational approaches that allow a constraint-based reformulation are the only approaches that are compatible with the current facts, whereas all other analyses require additional assumptions.

A number of works in Minimalism differ from those in other frameworks in that they assume structures (sometimes also invisible structures) that can only be motivated by evidence from other languages. This can streamline the entire apparatus for deriving different structures, but the overall costs of the approach are not reduced: some amount of the cost is just transferred to the UG component. The abstract grammars that result cannot be learned from the input.

One can take from this discussion that only constraint-based, surface-oriented models are adequate and explanatory: they are also compatible with psycholinguistic facts and plausible from the point of view of acquisition.

If we now compare these approaches, we see that a number of analyses can be translated into one another. LFG (and some variants of CxG and DG) differ from all other theories in that grammatical functions such as subject and object are primitives of the theory. If one does not want this, then it is possible to replace these labels with Argument1, Argument2, etc. The numbering of arguments would correspond to their relative obliqueness. LFG would then move closer to HPSG. Alternatively, one could mark arguments in HPSG and CxG with regard to their grammatical function additionally. This is what is done for the analysis of the passive (DESIGNATED ARGUMENT).

LFG, HPSG, CxG and variants of Categorial Grammar (Moens et al. 1989; Briscoe 2000; Villavicencio 2002) possess means for the hierarchical organization of knowledge, which is important for capturing generalizations. It is, of course, possible to expand any other framework in this way, but this has never been done explicitly, except in computer implementations and inheritance hierarchies do not play an active role in theorizing in the other frameworks.

In HPSG and CxG, roots, stems, words, morphological and syntactic rules are all objects that can be described with the same means. This then allows one to make generalizations that affect very different objects (see Chapter 22). In LFG, c-structures are viewed as something fundamentally different, which is why this kind of generalization is not possible. In cross-linguistic work, there is an attempt to capture similarities in the f-structure, the c-structure is less important and is not even discussed in a number of works. Furthermore, its implementation from language to language can differ enormously. For this reason, my personal preference is for frameworks that describe all linguistic objects using the same means, that is, HPSG and CxG. Formally, nothing stands in the way of a description of the c-structure of an LFG grammar using feature-value pairs so that in years to come there could be even more convergence between the theories. For hybrid forms of HPSG and LFG, see Ackerman & Webelhuth (1998) and Hellan & Haugereid (2003), for example.

If one compares CxG and HPSG, it becomes apparent that the degree of formalization in CxG works is relatively low and a number of questions remain unanswered. The more formal approaches in CxG (with the exception of Fluid Construction Grammar) are variants of HPSG. There are relatively few precisely worked-out analyses in Construction Grammar and no description of German that would be comparable to the other approaches presented in this book. To be fair, it must be said that Construction Grammar is the youngest of the theories discussed here. Its most important contributions to linguistic theory have been integrated into frameworks such as HPSG and LFG.

The theories of the future will be a fusion of surface-oriented, constraint-based and model-theoretic approaches like CG, LFG, HPSG, Construction Grammar, equivalent variants of TAG and GB/Minimalist approaches that will be reformulated as constraint-based. (Variants of) Minimalism and (variants of) Construction Grammar are the most widely adopted approaches at present. I actually suspect the truth to lie somewhere in the middle. The linguistics of the future will be data-oriented. Introspection as the sole method of data collection has proven unreliable (Müller 2007d; Meurers & Müller 2009) and is being increasingly complemented by experimental and corpus-based analyses.

Statistical information and statistical processes play a very important role in machine translation and are becoming more important for linguistics in the narrow sense (Abney 1996). We have seen that statistical information is important in the acquisition process and Abney discusses cases of other areas of language such as language change, parsing preferences and gradience with grammaticality judgments. Following a heavy focus on statistical procedures, there is now a transition to hybrid forms in computational linguistics,[2] since it has been noticed that it is not possible to exceed certain levels of quality with statistical methods alone (Steedman 2011; Church 2011; Kay 2011). The same holds here as above: the truth is somewhere in between, that is, in combined systems. In order to have something to combine, the relevant linguistic theories first need to be developed. As Manfred Pinkal said: "It is not possible to build systems that understand language without understanding language."

[2] See Kaufmann & Pfister (2007) and Kaufmann (2009) for the combination of a speech recognizer with a HPSG grammar.

24 Solutions to the exercises

24.1 Introduction and basic terms

(1) a. $\underbrace{\text{Karl}}_{\text{VF}}\ \underbrace{\text{isst}}_{\text{LS}}\ .$

b. $\underbrace{\text{Der Mann}}_{\text{VF}}\ \underbrace{\text{liebt}}_{\text{LS}}\ \underbrace{\text{eine Frau,}}_{\text{MF}}\ \underbrace{\underbrace{\text{den}}_{\text{VF}}\ \underbrace{\text{Peter}}_{\text{MF}}\ \underbrace{\text{kennt.}}_{\text{RS}}}_{\text{NF}}$

c. $\underbrace{\text{Der Mann}}_{\text{VF}}\ \underbrace{\text{liebt}}_{\text{LS}}\ \underbrace{\text{eine Frau,}\ \underbrace{\text{die}}_{\text{VF}}\ \underbrace{\text{Peter}}_{\text{MF}}\ \underbrace{\text{kennt.}}_{\text{RS}}}_{\text{MF}}$

d. $\underbrace{\text{Die Studenten}}_{\text{VF}}\ \underbrace{\text{haben}}_{\text{LS}}\ \underbrace{\text{behauptet,}}_{\text{RS}}\ \underbrace{\underbrace{\text{nur wegen der Hitze}}_{\text{MF}}\ \underbrace{\text{einzuschlafen.}}_{\text{RS}}}_{\text{NF}}$

e. $\underbrace{\underbrace{\text{Dass}}_{\text{LS}}\ \underbrace{\text{Peter nicht}}_{\text{MF}}\ \underbrace{\text{kommt,}}_{\text{RS}}}_{\text{VF}}\ \underbrace{\text{ärgert}}_{\text{LS}}\ \underbrace{\text{Klaus.}}_{\text{MF}}$

f. $\underbrace{\underbrace{\text{Einen Mann}}_{\text{MF}}\ \underbrace{\text{küssen,}}_{\text{RS}}\ \underbrace{\underbrace{\text{der}}_{\text{VF}}\ \underbrace{\text{ihr nicht}}_{\text{MF}}\ \underbrace{\text{gefällt,}}_{\text{RS}}}_{\text{NF}}}_{\text{VF}}\ \underbrace{\text{würde}}_{\text{LS}}\ \underbrace{\text{sie nie.}}_{\text{MF}}$

On (1c): theoretically, this could also be a case of extraposition of the relative clause to the postfield. Since *eine Frau, die Peter kennt* is a constituent, however, it is assumed that no reordering of the relative clause has taken place. Instead, we have a simpler structure with *eine Frau, die Peter kennt* as a complete NP in the middle field.

24.2 Phrase structure grammars

1. For any grammar, it is possible to assume additional symbols and rules that create unnecessary structure or are simply never used because there are no words or phrases that could be used on the right-hand side of the rule. If we were to add

the following rule to our grammar, for example, we would have a more complex grammar that can still analyze the same fragment of the language.

(2) Tralala → Trulla Trololo

2. In general, it is assumed that the grammar with the fewest rules is the best one. Therefore, we can reject grammars that contain unnecessary rules such as (2).

   One should bear in mind what the aim of a theory of grammar is. If our goal is to describe the human language capacity, then a grammar with more rules could be better than other grammars with less rules. This is because psycholinguistic research has shown that highly-frequent units are simply stored in our brains and not built up from their individual parts each time, although we would of course be able to do this.

3. The problem here is the fact that it is possible to derive a completely empty noun phrase (see Figure 24.1). This noun phrase could be inserted in all positions where

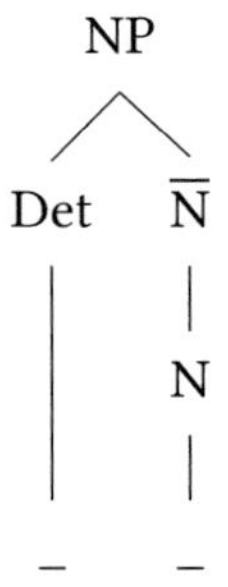

Figure 24.1: Noun phrases without a visible determiner and noun

   an otherwise filled NP would have to stay. Then, we would be able to analyze sequences of words such as (3), where the subject of *schläft* 'sleeps' is realized by an empty NP:

   (3) * Ich glaube, dass schläft.
   I believe that sleeps

   This problem can be solved using a feature that determines whether the left periphery of the $\overline{\mathrm{N}}$ is empty. Visible Ns and $\overline{\mathrm{N}}$ with at least an adjective would have the value '–' and all others '+'. Empty determiners could then only be combined with $\overline{\mathrm{N}}$s that have the value '–'. See Netter (1994).

4. If *Bücher* 'books' were an NP in the lexicon, then adjectives such as *interessant* 'interesting' would have to modify NPs in order for phrases such as (4) to be analyzed.

(4) interessante Bücher
interesting books

If adjectives are combined with NPs, however, it still has to be explained why (5) is ungrammatical.

(5) * interessante die Bücher
interesting the books

For a detailed discussions of this topic, see Müller (2007b: Section 6.6.2).

5. This kind of rule cannot analyze noun phrases such as those in (6):

(6) a. interessante [Aufsätze und Bücher]
interesting essays and books

b. interessante [Aufsätze und Bücher aus Stuttgart]
interesting essays and books from Stuttgart

Since adjectives can only be combined directly with nouns, these phrases cannot be analyzed. *Bücher* 'books' or *Bücher aus Stuttgart* 'books from Stuttgart' would be complete NPs. Since it is assumed that coordinated elements always have the same syntactic category, then *Aufsätze* 'essays' would have to be an NP. *Aufsätze und Bücher* and *Aufsätze und Bücher aus Stuttgart* would then also be NPs and it remains unexplained how an adjective can be combined with this NP. Because of (5), we must rule out analyses that assume that full NPs combine with adjectives.

See Chapter 19 for a general discussion of empty elements.

6. If a specific determiner or just any determiner were to be combined with an adjective to form a complete NP, there would be no room for the integration of postnominal modifiers like modifying genitives, PPs and relative clauses. For PPs and relative clauses, analyses have been suggested in which these postnominal modifiers attach to complete NPs (Kiss 2005), but modifying genitives usually attach to smaller units. But even if one admits postnominal modifiers to attach to complete NPs, one cannot account for the iteration of adjectives and for arguments that depend on the elided noun.

So, the simplest way to cope with the German data is the assumption of an empty noun. Alternatively one could assume that an adjective is directly projected to an $\overline{\text{N}}$. This $\overline{\text{N}}$ then can be modified by further adjectives or postnominal modifiers. The $\overline{\text{N}}$ is combined with a determiner to form a full NP. For phrases that involve elided relational nouns, one would have to assume the projection of an argument like *vom Gleimtunnel* 'of the Gleimtunnel' to $\overline{\text{N}}$. The $\overline{\text{N}}$ could be further modified or combined with a determiner directly.

7. Adjective phrases such as those in (7) cannot be analyzed since the degree modifier occurs between the complement and the adjective:

(7) der auf seinen Sohn sehr stolze Vater
the on his son very proud father
'the father very proud of his son'

One would either have to allow for specifiers to be combined with their heads before complements or allow crossing lines in trees. Another assumption could be that German is like English, however then adjectival complements would have to be obligatorily reordered before their specifier. For a description of this kind of reordering, see Chapter 3. See Section 13.1.2 for a discussion of $\overline{\text{X}}$-Theory.

8. Write a phrase structure grammar that can analyze the sentences in (8), but does not allow the strings of words in (9).

(8) a. Der Mann hilft der Frau.
the.NOM man helps the.DAT woman
'The man helps the woman.'

b. Er gibt ihr das Buch.
he.NOM gives her.DAT the.ACC book
'He gives her the book.'

c. Er wartet auf ein Wunder.
he.NOM waits on a miracle.ACC
'He is waiting for a miracle.'

(9) a. * Der Mann hilft er.
the.NOM man helps he.NOM

b. * Er gibt ihr den Buch.
he.NOM gives her.DAT the.ACC book

In order to rule out the last two sentences, the grammar has to contain information about case. The following grammar will do the job:

(10) a. s → np(nom) v(nom_dat), np(dat)
b. s → np(nom), v(nom_dat_acc), np(dat), np(acc)
c. s → np(nom), v(nom_pp_auf), pp(auf,acc)
d. pp(Pform,Case) → p(Pform,Case), np(Case)
e. np(Case) → d(Case), n(Case)
f. v(nom_dat) → hilft
g. v(nom_dat_acc) → gibt
h. v(nom_pp_auf) → wartet
i. np(nom) → er
j. np(dat) → ihr

k. d(nom) → der
l. d(dat) → der
m. d(acc) → das
n. d(acc) → ein
o. n(nom) → Mann
p. n(dat) → Frau
q. n(acc) → Buch
r. n(acc) → Wunder
s. p(auf,acc) → auf

24.3 Transformational Grammar – Government & Binding

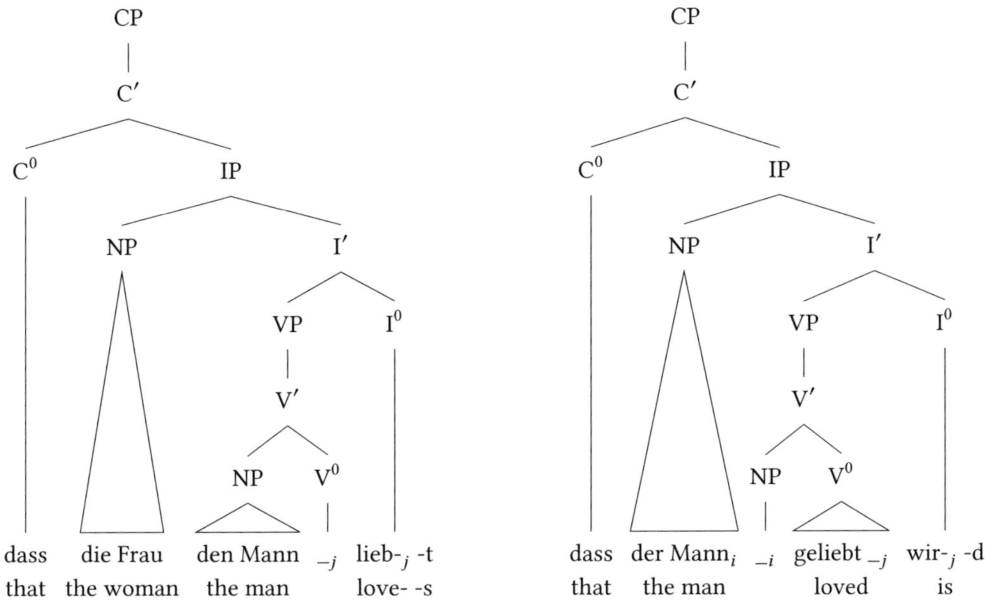

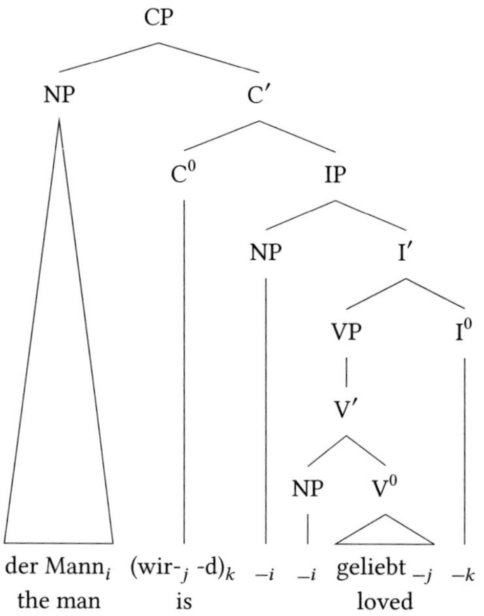
CP
NP
C′
C0
IP
NP
I′
VP
I0
V′
NP
V0
der Manni (wir-j -d)k –i –i geliebt –j –k
the man is loved

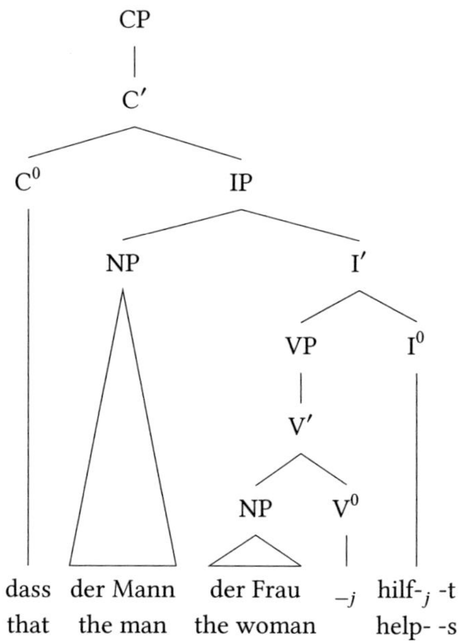
CP
C′
C0
IP
NP
I′
VP
I0
V′
NP
V0
dass der Mann der Frau –j hilf-j -t
that the man the woman help- -s

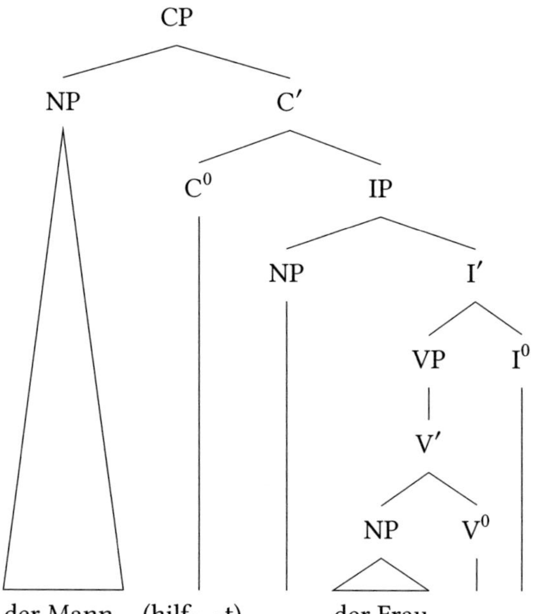
CP
NP
C′
C0
IP
NP
I′
VP
I0
V′
NP
V0
der Manni (hilf-j -t)k –i der Frau –j –k
the man help- -s the woman

24.4 Generalized Phrase Structure Grammar

In order to analyze the sentences in (11), one requires a rule for transitive verbs and a metarule for the extraction of an element. Furthermore, rules for the combination of elements in the noun phrase are required.

(11) a. [dass] der Mann ihn liest
that the man it reads
'that the man reads it'

b. [dass] ihn der Mann liest
that it the man reads
'that the man reads it'

c. Der Mann liest ihn.
the man reads it
'The man reads it.'

It is possible to analyze the sentences in (11a,b) using the rules in (12) and the lexical entries in (13).

(12) a. V3 → H[6], N2[CASE nom], N2[CASE acc]
b. N2 → Det[CASE CAS], H1[CASE CAS]
c. N1 → H[27]

(13) a. Det[CASE nom] → der
b. N[27] → Mann
c. V[6, +FIN] → liest
d. N2[CASE acc] → ihn

The rules (12b,c) correspond to $\overline{\text{X}}$-rules that we encountered in Section 2.4.1. They only differ from these rules in that the part of speech of the head is not given on the right-hand side of the rule. The part of speech is determined by the Head Feature Convention. The part of speech of the head is identical to that on the left-hand side of the rule, that is, it must be N in (12b,c). It also follows from the Head Feature Convention that the whole NP has the same case as the head and therefore does not have to be mentioned additionally in the rule above. 27 is the SUBCAT value. This number is arbitrary.

In order for the verb to appear in the correction position, we need linearization rules:

(14) V[+MC] < X
X < V[−MC]

The fact that the determiner precedes the noun is ensured by the following LP-rule:

(15) Det < X

The Extraction Metarule in (16) is required in order to analyze (11c):

(16) V3 → W, X ↦
V3/X → W

Among others, this metarule licenses the rule in (17) for (12a):

(17) V3/N2[CASE nom] → H[6], N2[CASE acc]

The rule in (18) is used to bind off long-distance dependencies.

(18) V3[+FIN] → X[+TOP], V3[+MC]/X

The following linearization rule ensures that the +TOP-constituent precedes the sentence in which it is missing:

(19) [+TOP] < X

Figure 24.2 shows the structure licensed by the grammar. In sum, one can say that the

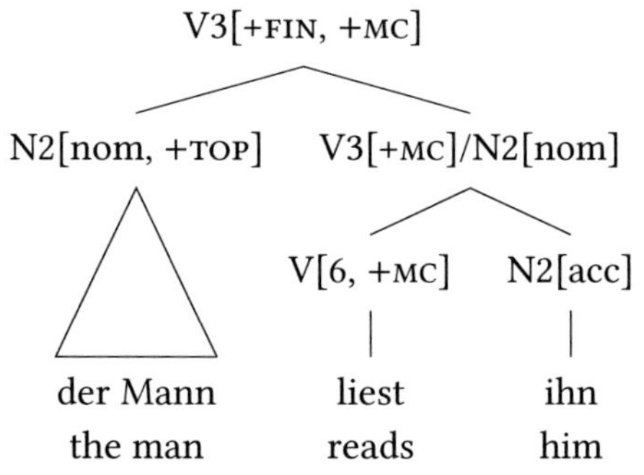

Figure 24.2: Analysis of *Der Mann liest ihn.* 'The man reads it.'

grammar that licenses the sentences in (11) should have (at least) the following parts:

1. ID rules:

   (20) a. V3 → H[6], N2[CASE nom], N2[CASE acc]
   b. N2 → Det[CASE CAS], H1[CASE CAS]
   c. N1 → H[27]

2. LP rules:

   (21) V[+MC] < X
   X < V[−MC]
   Det < X
   [+TOP] < X

3. Metarules:

(22) V3 → W, X ↦
V3/X → W

4. Lexical entries

(23)
a. Det[CASE nom] → der
b. N[27] → Mann
c. V[6, +FIN] → liest
d. N2[CASE acc] → ihn

24.5 Feature descriptions

1. For the class [+V], the type *verbal* is assumed with the subtypes *adjective* and *verb*. For the class [−V] there is the type *non-verbal* and its subtypes *noun* and *preposition*. This is analogous for the N values. The corresponding hierarchy is given in the following figure:

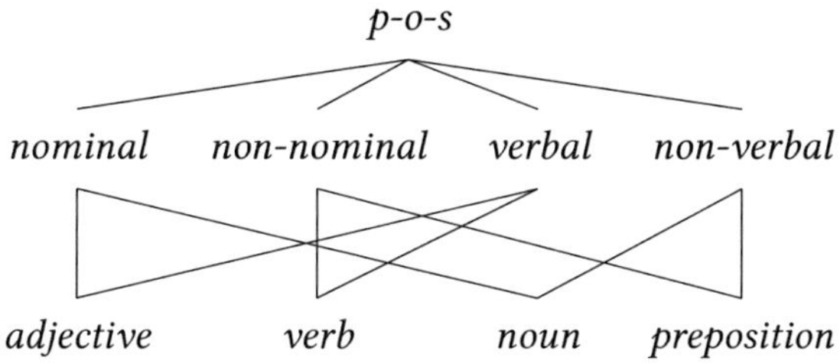

2. Lists can be described using recursive structures that consist of both a list beginning and a rest. The rest can either be a non-empty list (*ne_list*) or the empty list (*e_list*). The list ⟨ *a*, *b*, *c* ⟩ can be represented as follows:

(24)
$$\begin{bmatrix} \textit{ne\_list} & \\ \text{FIRST} & a \\ \text{REST} & \begin{bmatrix} \textit{ne\_list} & \\ \text{FIRST} & b \\ \text{REST} & \begin{bmatrix} \textit{ne\_list} & \\ \text{FIRST} & c \\ \text{REST} & \textit{e\_list} \end{bmatrix} \end{bmatrix} \end{bmatrix}$$

3. If we extend the data structure in (24) by two additional features, it is possible to do without *append*. The keyword is *difference list*. A difference list consists of a list and a pointer to the end of the list.

(25)
$$\begin{bmatrix} \textit{diff-list} & \\ \text{LIST} & \begin{bmatrix} \textit{ne\_list} & \\ \text{FIRST} & a \\ \text{REST} & \begin{bmatrix} \textit{ne\_list} & \\ \text{FIRST} & b \\ \text{REST} & \boxed{1}\ \textit{list} \end{bmatrix} \end{bmatrix} \\ \text{LAST} & \boxed{1} \end{bmatrix}$$

Unlike the list representation in (24), the REST value of the end of the list is not *e_list*, but rather simply *list*. It is then possible to extend a list by adding another list to the point where it ends. The concatenation of (25) and (26a) is (26b).

(26) a.
$$\begin{bmatrix} \textit{diff-list} & \\ \text{LIST} & \begin{bmatrix} \textit{ne\_list} & \\ \text{FIRST} & c \\ \text{REST} & \boxed{2}\ \textit{list} \end{bmatrix} \\ \text{LAST} & \boxed{2} \end{bmatrix}$$

b.
$$\begin{bmatrix} \textit{diff-list} & \\ \text{LIST} & \begin{bmatrix} \textit{ne\_list} & \\ \text{FIRST} & a \\ \text{REST} & \begin{bmatrix} \textit{ne\_list} & \\ \text{FIRST} & b \\ \text{REST} & \begin{bmatrix} \textit{ne\_list} & \\ \text{FIRST} & c \\ \text{REST} & \boxed{2}\ \textit{list} \end{bmatrix} \end{bmatrix} \end{bmatrix} \\ \text{LAST} & \boxed{2} \end{bmatrix}$$

In order to combine the lists, the LIST value of the second list has to be identified with the LAST value of the first list. The LAST value of the resulting list then corresponds to the LAST value of the second list ($\boxed{2}$ in the example.)

Information about the encoding of difference lists can be found by searching for the keywords *list*, *append*, and *feature structure*. In the search results, one can find pages on developing grammars that explain difference lists.

24.6 Lexical Functional Grammar

1. *kannte* 'knew' is a transitive verb:

(27) *kannte* V (↑ PRED) = 'KENNEN⟨SUBJ, OBJ ⟩'
(↑ SUBJ AGR CAS = NOM)
(↑ OBJ AGR CAS = ACC)
(↑ TENSE) = PAST

2. In the sentence (28), the object of *verschlingen* 'devour' is in the prefield.

(28) Den Apfel verschlingt David.
the.ACC apple devours David.NOM
'David is devouring the apple.'

The analysis is a combination of the analysis in Figure 7.2 on page 227 and the analysis of long-distance dependencies that was presented in Section 7.5. The object is not realized inside the VP, but rather in the prefield.

The necessary c-structure rules are given in (29):

(29) a. VP → NP (↑SUBJ |OBJ) = ↓ VP ↑= ↓
b. VP → (V) ↑= ↓
c. C′ → C ↑= ↓ VP ↑= ↓
d. CP → XP (↑DF) = ↓ (↑DF) = (↑COMP* GF) C′ ↑=↓

These rules allow two f-structures for the example in question: one in which the NP *den Apfel* 'the apple' is the topic and another in which this NP is the focus. Figure 24.3 shows the analysis with a topicalized constituent in the prefield.

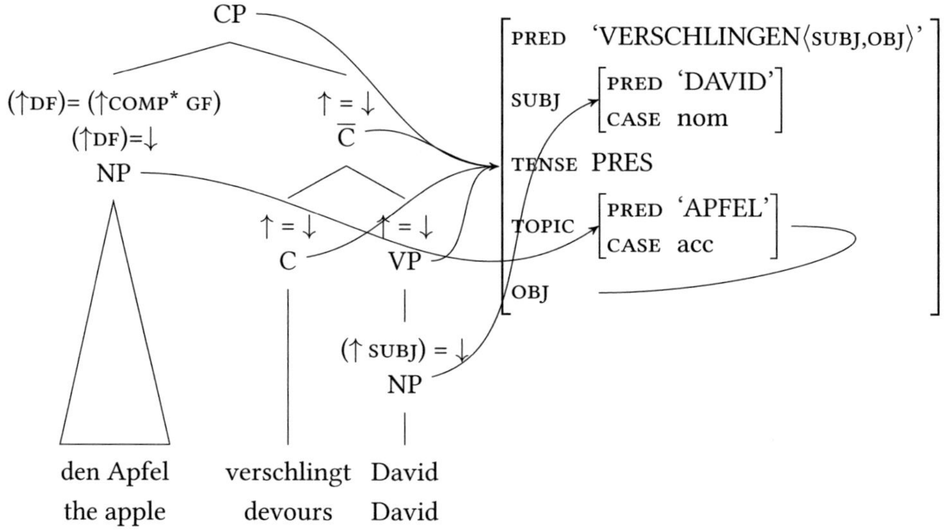

Figure 24.3: Analysis of verb second

24.7 Categorial Grammar

1. The analysis of *The children in the room laugh loudly.* is given in Figure 24.4.

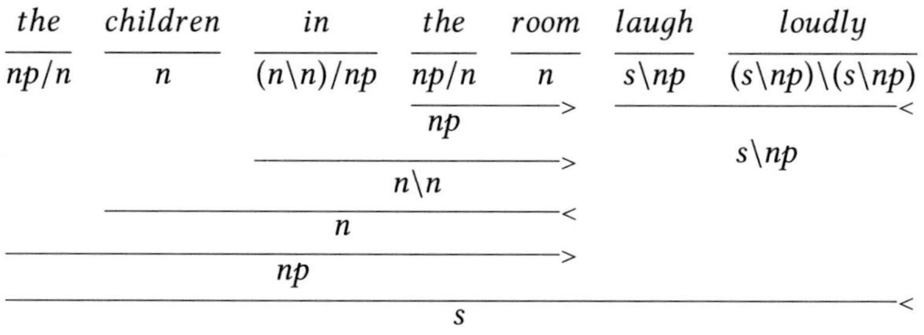

Figure 24.4: Categorial Grammar analysis of *The children in the room laugh loudly.*

2. The analysis of *the picture of Mary* is given in Figure 24.5. n/pp corresponds to N^0, n corresponds to $\overline{N}$ and np corresponds to NP.

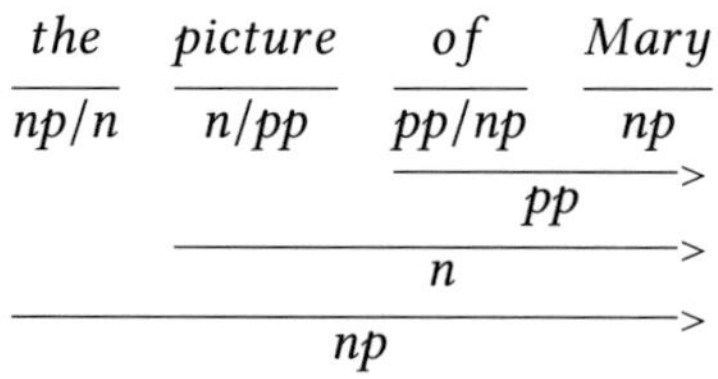

Figure 24.5: Categorial Grammar analysis of *the picture of Mary*

24.8 Head-Driven Phrase Structure Grammar

1. The solution is:

```
[head-argument-phrase
 PHON ⟨ Max lacht ⟩
 SYNSEM|LOC [CAT  [HEAD   [1]
                   SUBCAT [2] ⟨⟩]
             CONT [IND  [3]
                   RELS ⟨ [4], [5] ⟩]]
 HEAD-DTR [word
           PHON ⟨ lacht ⟩
           SYNSEM|LOC [CAT  [HEAD   [1] [verb
                                         INITIAL −
                                         VFORM   fin]
                             SUBCAT [2] ⊕ ⟨ [6] ⟩]
                       CONT [IND  [3] event
                             RELS ⟨ [4] [lachen
                                         EVENT [3]
                                         AGENS [7]] ⟩]]]
 NON-HEAD-DTRS ⟨ [word
                  PHON ⟨ Max ⟩
                  SYNSEM [6] [LOC [CAT  [HEAD   [noun
                                                 CAS nom]
                                         SUBCAT ⟨⟩]
                                   CONT [IND  [7] [PER 3
                                                   NUM sg
                                                   GEN mas]
                                         RELS ⟨ [5] [named
                                                     NAME max
                                                     INST [7]] ⟩]]]] ⟩]
```

2. An analysis of the difference in (30) has to capture the fact that the case of the adjective has to agree with that of the noun. In (30a), the genitive form of *interessant* 'interesting' is used, whereas (30b) contains a form that is incompatible with the genitive singular.

(30) a. eines interessanten Mannes
one.GEN interesting.GEN man.GEN

b. * eines interessanter Mannes
one.GEN interesting.NOM man.GEN

(31) shows the CAT value of *interessanten.*

(31) CAT value of *interessanten* 'interesting' with case information:

$$\left[\begin{array}{ll} \text{HEAD} & \left[\begin{array}{l} \textit{adj} \\ \text{MOD}\ \ \overline{\text{N}}\,[\text{CASE}\ \boxed{1}\,] \\ \text{CASE}\ \ \boxed{1}\ \textit{gen} \end{array}\right] \\ \text{SUBCAT} & \langle\rangle \end{array}\right]$$

The structure sharing of the case value of the adjective with the case value of the $\overline{\text{N}}$ under MOD identifies the case values of the noun and the adjective. *interessanten* can therefore be combined with *Mannes*, but not with *Mann*. Similarly, *interessanter* can only be combined with the nominative *Mann*, but not with the genitive *Mannes*.

For a refinement of the analysis of agreement inside the noun phrase, see Müller (2007b: Abschnitt 13.2).

24.9 Construction Grammar

Idioms can be found by reading the newspaper carefully. The less exciting method is to look them up a dictionary of idioms such as the Free Dictionary of Idioms and Phrases[1].

[1] http://idioms.thefreedictionary.com/, 04.03.2015.

24.10 Dependency Grammar

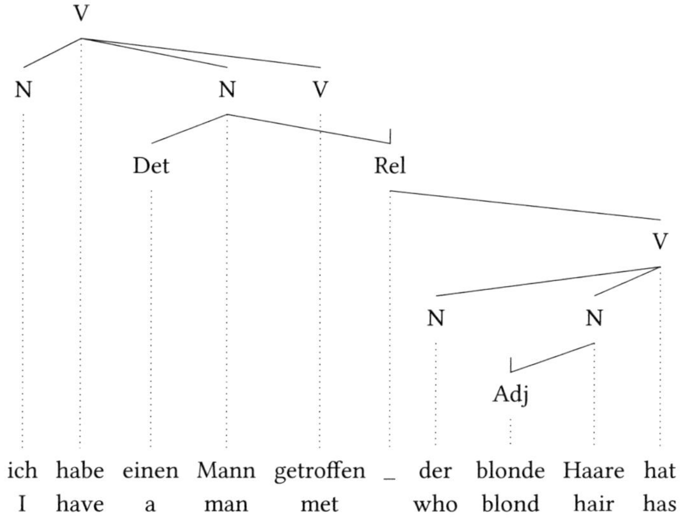

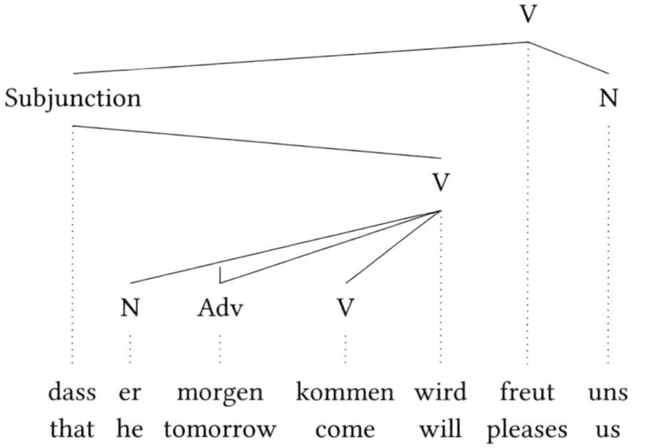

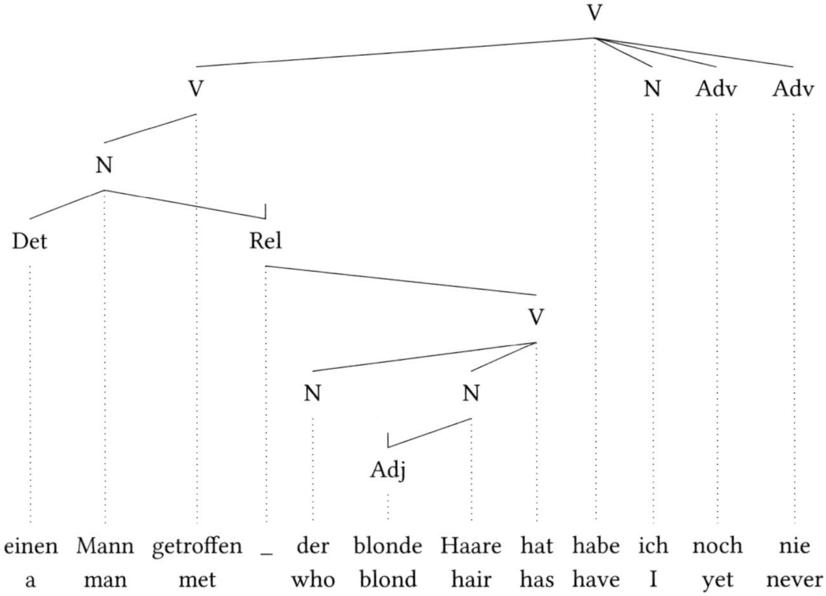

24.11 Tree Adjoining Grammar

The elementary trees in Figure 24.6 are needed for the analysis of (32).

(32) der dem König treue Diener
the.NOM the.DAT king loyal servant
'the servant loyal to the king'

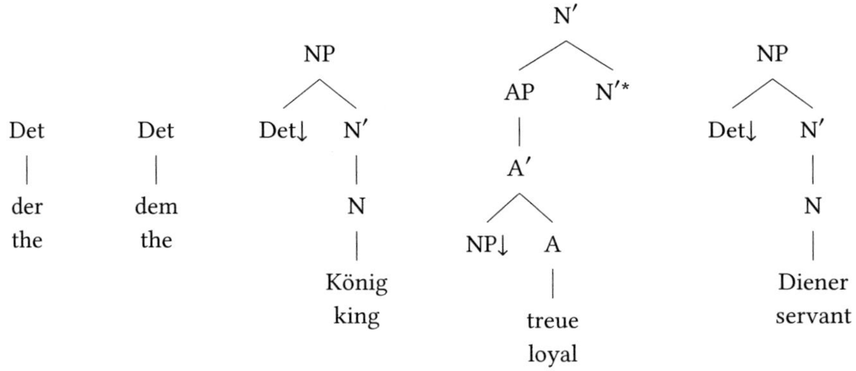

Figure 24.6: Elementary trees for *der dem König treue Diener*

By substituting the tree for *dem* 'the' in the substitution node of *König* 'king', one then arrives at a full NP. This can then be inserted into the substitution node of *treue* 'loyal'.

Similarly, the tree for *der* 'the' can be combined with the one for *Diener*. One then has both of the trees in Figure 24.7.

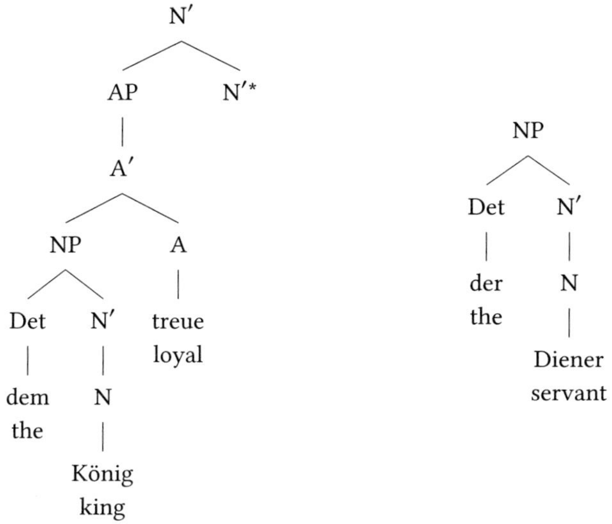

Figure 24.7: Trees for *der dem König treue* and *der Diener* after substitution

The adjective tree can then be adjoined to the N′-node of *der Diener*, which yields the structure in Figure 24.8 on the next page.

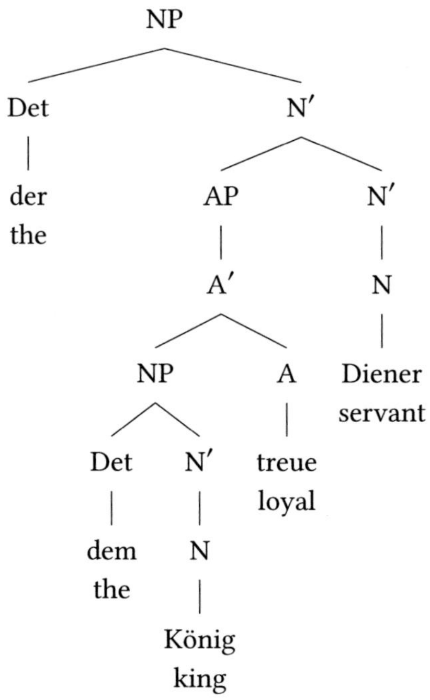

Figure 24.8: Result of adjunction of the AP to the N′-node

Bibliography

Abbott, Barbara. 1976. Right node raising as a test for constituenthood. *Linguistic Inquiry* 7(4). 639–642.

Abeillé, Anne. 1988. Parsing French with Tree Adjoining Grammar: Some linguistic accounts. In Dénes Vargha (ed.), *Proceedings of COLING 88*, 7–12. University of Budapest: Association for Computational Linguistics. http://www.aclweb.org/anthology/C/C88/C88-1002.pdf.

Abeillé, Anne. 2006. In defense of lexical coordination. In Olivier Bonami & Patricia Cabredo Hofherr (eds.), *Empirical issues in formal syntax and semantics*, vol. 6, 7–36. Paris: CNRS. http://www.cssp.cnrs.fr/eiss6/.

Abeillé, Anne & Owen Rambow (eds.). 2000. *Tree Adjoining Grammars: Formalisms, linguistic analysis and processing* (CSLI Lecture Notes 156). Stanford, CA: CSLI Publications.

Abeillé, Anne & Yves Schabes. 1989. Parsing idioms in Lexicalized TAG. In Harold Somers & Mary McGee Wood (eds.), *Proceedings of the Fourth Conference of the European Chapter of the Association for Computational Linguistics*, 1–9. Manchester, England: Association for Computational Linguistics.

Abney, Steven P. 1987. *The English noun phrase in its sentential aspect*. Cambridge, MA: MIT dissertation. http://www.vinartus.net/spa/87a.pdf.

Abney, Steven P. 1996. Statistical methods and linguistics. In Judith L. Klavans & Philip Resnik (eds.), *The balancing act: Combining symbolic and statistical approaches to language* (Language, Speech, and Communication), 1–26. London, England/Cambridge, MA: MIT Press.

Abney, Steven P. & Jennifer Cole. 1986. A Government-Binding parser. In S. Berman, J-W. Choe & J. McDonough (eds.), *Proceedings of NELS 16*, 1–17. University of Massachusetts, Amherst: GLSA.

Abraham, Werner. 1995. *Deutsche Syntax im Sprachenvergleich: Grundlegung einer typologischen Syntax des Deutschen* (Studien zur deutschen Grammatik 41). Tübingen: Stauffenburg Verlag.

Abraham, Werner. 2003. The syntactic link between thema and rhema: The syntax-discourse interface. *Folia Linguistica* 37(1–2). 13–34.

Abraham, Werner. 2005. *Deutsche Syntax im Sprachenvergleich: Grundlegung einer typologischen Syntax des Deutschen* (Studien zur deutschen Grammatik 41). Tübingen: Stauffenburg Verlag 2nd edn.

Abzianidze, Lasha. 2011. *An HPSG-based formal grammar of a core fragment of Georgian implemented in TRALE*. Charles University in Prague MA thesis.

Ackerman, Farrell & Gert Webelhuth. 1998. *A theory of predicates* (CSLI Lecture Notes 76). Stanford, CA: CSLI Publications.

Adams, Marianne. 1984. Multiple interrogation in Italian. *The Linguistic Review* 4(1). 1–27.

Ades, Anthony E. & Mark J. Steedman. 1982. On the order of words. *Linguistics and Philosophy* 4(4). 517–558.

Adger, David. 2003. *Core syntax: A Minimalist approach* (Oxford Core Linguistics 1). Oxford: Oxford University Press Oxford.

Adger, David. 2010. A Minimalist theory of feature structure. In Anna Kibort & Greville G. Corbett (eds.), *Features: Perspectives on a key notion in linguistics* (Oxford Linguistics), 185–218. Oxford: Oxford University Press.

Adger, David. 2013. Constructions and grammatical explanation: Comments on Goldberg. *Mind and Language* 28(4). 466–478.

Ágel, Vilmos. 2000. *Valenztheorie* (Narr Studienbücher). Tübingen: Gunter Narr Verlag.

Ágel, Vilmos, Ludwig M. Eichinger, Hans Werner Eroms, Peter Hellwig, Hans Jürgen Heringer & Henning Lobin (eds.). 2003. *Dependenz und Valenz / Dependency and valency: Ein internationales Handbuch der zeitgenössischen Forschung / An international handbook of contemporary research*, vol. 25.1 (Handbücher zur Sprach- und Kommunikationswissenschaft). Berlin: Walter de Gruyter.

Ágel, Vilmos, Ludwig M. Eichinger, Hans Werner Eroms, Peter Hellwig, Hans Jürgen Heringer & Henning Lobin (eds.). 2006. *Dependenz und Valenz / Dependency and valency: Ein internationales Handbuch der zeitgenössischen Forschung / An international handbook of contemporary research*, vol. 25.2 (Handbücher zur Sprach- und Kommunikationswissenschaft). Berlin: Walter de Gruyter.

Ágel, Vilmos & Klaus Fischer. 2010. 50 Jahre Valenztheorie und Dependenzgrammatik. *Zeitschrift für Germanistische Linguistik* 38(2). 249–290.

Ajdukiewicz, Kasimir. 1935. Die syntaktische Konnexität. *Studia Philosophica* 1. 1–27.

de Alencar, Leonel. 2004. Complementos verbais oracionais – uma análise léxicofuncional. *Lingua(gem)* 1(1). 173–218.

de Alencar, Leonel. 2013. BrGram: uma gramática computacional de um fragmento do português brasileiro no formalismo da LFG. In *Proceedings of the 9th Brazilian Symposium in Information and Human Language Technology. Fortaleza, Ceará, Brazil, October 20–24*, 183–188. Fortaleza, Ceará: Sociedade Brasileira de Computação. http://www.aclweb.org/anthology/W13-4823.

Alsina, Alex. 1996. Resultatives: A joint operation of semantic and syntactic structures. In Miriam Butt & Tracy Holloway King (eds.), *Proceedings of the LFG '96 conference, Rank Xerox, Grenoble*, Stanford, CA: CSLI Publications. http://csli-publications.stanford.edu/LFG/1/.

Alsina, Alex, KP Mohanan & Tara Mohanan. 2005. How to get rid of the COMP. In Miriam Butt & Tracy Holloway King (eds.), *Proceedings of the LFG 2005 conference*, Stanford, CA: CSLI Publications. http://csli-publications.stanford.edu/LFG/10/lfg05amm.pdf.

Altmann, Hans & Ute Hofman. 2004. *Topologie fürs Examen: Verbstellung, Klammerstruktur, Stellungsfelder, Satzglied- und Wortstellung* (Linguistik fürs Examen 4). Wiesbaden: VS Verlag für Sozialwissenschaften/GWV Fachverlage GmbH.

Ambridge, Ben & Adele E. Goldberg. 2008. The island status of clausal complements: Evidence in favor of an information structure explanation. *Cognitive Linguistics* 19. 349–381.

Ambridge, Ben & Elena V. M. Lieven. 2011. *Child language acquisition: Contrasting theoretical approaches*. Cambridge, UK: Cambridge University Press.

Ambridge, Ben, Caroline F. Rowland & Julian M. Pine. 2008. Is structure dependence an innate constraint? New experimental evidence from children's complex-question production. *Cognitive Science: A Multidisciplinary Journal* 32(1). 222–255.

Anderson, John M. 1971. *The grammar of case: Towards a localistic theory*, vol. 4 (Cambridge Studies in Linguistics). Cambridge, UK: Cambridge University Press.

Anderson, Stephen R. 1992. *A-morphous morphology* (Cambridge Studies in Linguistics 62). Cambridge: Cambridge University Press.

Aoun, Joseph & David W. Lightfoot. 1984. Government and contraction. *Linguistic Inquiry* 15(3). 465–473.

Aoun, Joseph & Dominique Sportiche. 1983. On the formal theory of government. *The Linguistic Review* 2(3). 211–236.

Arad Greshler, Tali, Livnat Herzig Sheinfux, Nurit Melnik & Shuly Wintner. 2015. Development of maximally reusable grammars: Parallel development of Hebrew and Arabic grammars. In Stefan Müller (ed.), *Proceedings of the 22nd International Conference on Head-Driven Phrase Structure Grammar, Nanyang Technological University (NTU), Singapore*, 27–40. Stanford, CA: CSLI Publications. http://csli-publications.stanford.edu/HPSG/2015/ahmw.pdf.

Arends, Jacques. 2008. A demographic perspective on Creole formation. In Silvia Kouwenberg & John Victor Singler (eds.), *The handbook of pidgin and creole studies*, 309–331. Oxford/Cambridge: Blackwell Publishing Ltd.

Arka, I Wayan, Avery Andrews, Mary Dalrymple, Meladel Mistica & Jane Simpson. 2009. A linguistic and computational morphosyntactic analysis for the applicative *-i* in Indonesian. In Miriam Butt & Tracy Holloway King (eds.), *Proceedings of the LFG 2009 conference*, 85–105. Stanford, CA: CSLI Publications. http://csli-publications.stanford.edu/LFG/14/.

Arnold, Doug & Andrew Spencer. 2015. A constructional analysis for the skeptical. In Stefan Müller (ed.), *Proceedings of the 22nd International Conference on Head-Driven Phrase Structure Grammar, Nanyang Technological University (NTU), Singapore*, 41–60. Stanford, CA: CSLI Publications. http://csli-publications.stanford.edu/HPSG/2015/arnold-spencer.pdf.

Arnold, Jennifer E., Michael K. Tanenhaus, Rebecca J. Altmann & Maria Fagnano. 2004. The old and thee, uh, new. *Psychological Science* 15(9). 578–582.

Askedal, John Ole. 1986. Zur vergleichenden Stellungsfelderanalyse von Verbalsätzen und nichtverbalen Satzgliedern. *Deutsch als Fremdsprache* 23. 269–273 and 342–348.

Asudeh, Ash. 2004. *Resumption as resource management*: Stanford University dissertation.

Asudeh, Ash, Mary Dalrymple & Ida Toivonen. 2008. Constructions with lexical integrity: Templates as the lexicon-syntax interface. In Miriam Butt & Tracy Holloway King (eds.), *Proceedings of the LFG 2008 conference*, Stanford, CA: CSLI Publications. http://csli-publications.stanford.edu/LFG/13/.

Asudeh, Ash, Mary Dalrymple & Ida Toivonen. 2013. Constructions with lexical integrity. *Journal of Language Modelling* 1(1). 1–54.

Asudeh, Ash, Gianluca Giorgolo & Ida Toivonen. 2014. Meaning and valency. In Miriam Butt & Tracy Holloway King (eds.), *Proceedings of the LFG 2014 conference*, 68–88. Stanford, CA: CSLI Publications.

Asudeh, Ash & Ida Toivonen. 2014. *With* lexical integrity. *Theoretical Linguistics* 40(1–2). 175–186.

Attardi, Giuseppe. 2006. Experiments with a multilanguage non-projective dependency parser. In *Proceedings of the 10th Conference on Computational Natural Language Learning (CoNLL-X)*, 166–170. Association for Computational Linguistics.

Attia, Mohammed A. 2008. *Handling Arabic morphological and syntactic ambiguity within the LFG framework with a view to machine translation*: School of Languages, Linguistics and Cultures, University of Manchester dissertation.

Avgustinova, Tania & Yi Zhang. 2009. Exploiting the Russian national corpus in the development of a Russian Resource Grammar. In Núria Bel, Erhard Hinrichs, Kiril Simov & Petya Osenova (eds.), *Adaptation of language resources and technology to new domains at the RANLP 2009 Conference, Borovets, Bulgaria*, 1–11. Shoumen, Bulgaria: INCOMA Ltd.

Bach, Emmon. 1962. The order of elements in a Transformational Grammar of German. *Language* 8(3). 263–269.

Bach, Emmon. 1976. An extension of classical Transformation Grammar. In *Problems in linguistic metatheory, Proceedings of the 1976 Conference at the Michigan State University*, 183–224.

Bahrani, Mohammad, Hossein Sameti & Mehdi Hafezi Manshadi. 2011. A computational grammar for Persian based on GPSG. *Language Resources and Evaluation* 45(4). 387–408.

Baker, Carl Lee. 1978. *Introduction to Generative-Transformational Syntax.* Englewood Cliffs, NJ: Prentice-Hall.

Baker, Mark C. 2003. Linguistic differences and language design. *Trends in Cognitive Sciences* 7(8). 349–353.

Baker, Mark C. 2009. Language universals: Abstract but not mythological. *The Behavioral and Brain Sciences* 32(5). 448–449.

Baldridge, Jason. 2002. *Lexically specified derivational control in Combinatory Categorial Grammar*: University of Edinburgh dissertation.

Baldridge, Jason, Sudipta Chatterjee, Alexis Palmer & Ben Wing. 2007. DotCCG and VisCCG: Wiki and programming paradigms for improved grammar engineering with OpenCCG. In Tracy Holloway King & Emily M. Bender (eds.), *Grammar Engineering across Frameworks 2007* (Studies in Computational Linguistics ONLINE), 5–25. Stanford, CA: CSLI Publications. http://csli-publications.stanford.edu/GEAF/2007/.

Baldridge, Jason & Geert-Jan M. Kruijff. 2002. Coupling CCG and Hybrid Logic Dependency Semantics. In Pierre Isabelle (ed.), *40th Annual Meeting of the Association for Computational Linguistics: Proceedings of the conference*, 319–326. University of Pennsylvania, Philadelphia: Association for Computational Linguistics. http://aclanthology.info/events/acl-2002.

Ballweg, Joachim. 1997. Stellungsregularitäten in der Nominalphrase. In Hans-Werner Eroms, Gerhard Stickel & Gisela Zifonun (eds.), *Grammatik der deutschen Sprache*, vol. 7.3 (Schriften des Instituts für deutsche Sprache), 2062–2072. Berlin: Walter de Gruyter.

Baltin, Mark. 1981. Strict bounding. In Carl Lee Baker & John J. McCarthy (eds.), *The logical problem of language acquisition*, 257–295. Cambridge, MA/London, England: MIT Press.

Baltin, Mark. 2004. Remarks on the relation between language typology and Universal Grammar: Commentary on Newmeyer. *Studies in Language* 28(3). 549–553.

Baltin, Mark. 2006. Extraposition. In Martin Everaert, Henk van Riemsdijk, Rob Goedemans & Bart Hollebrandse (eds.), *The Blackwell companion to syntax* (Blackwell Handbooks in Linguistics), 237–271. Oxford: Blackwell Publishing Ltd.

Bangalore, Srinivas, Aravind K. Joshi & Owen Rambow. 2003. Dependency and valency in other theories: Tree Adjoining Grammar. In Vilmos Ágel, Ludwig M. Eichinger, Hans Werner Eroms, Peter Hellwig, Hans Jürgen Heringer & Henning Lobin (eds.), *Dependenz und Valenz / Dependency and valency: Ein internationales Handbuch der zeitgenössischen Forschung / An international handbook of contemporary research*, vol. 25.1 (Handbücher zur Sprach- und Kommunikationswissenschaft), 669–678. Berlin: Walter de Gruyter.

Bannard, Colin, Elena Lieven & Michael Tomasello. 2009. Modeling children's early grammatical knowledge. *Proceedings of the National Academy of Sciences* 106(41). 17284–17289.

Bar-Hillel, Yehoshua, Micha A. Perles & Eliahu Shamir. 1961. On formal properties of simple phrase-structure grammars. *Zeitschrift für Phonetik, Sprachwissenschaft und Kommunikationsforschung* 14(2). 143–172.

Bartsch, Renate & Theo Vennemann. 1972. *Semantic structures: A study in the relation between semantics and syntax* (Athenäum-Skripten Linguistik 9). Frankfurt/Main: Athenäum.

Barwise, Jon & John Perry. 1983. *Situations and attitudes*. Cambridge, MA/London, England: MIT Press.

Barwise, Jon & John Perry. 1987. *Situationen und Einstellungen – Grundlagen der Situationssemantik*. Berlin, New York: de Gruyter.

Baschung, K., G. G. Bes, A. Corluy & T. Guillotin. 1987. Auxiliaries and clitics in French UCG grammar. In Bente Maegaard (ed.), *Proceedings of the Third Conference of the European Chapter of the Association for Computational Linguistics*, 173–178. Copenhagen, Denmark: Association for Computational Linguistics.

Bates, Elizabeth A. 1984. Bioprograms and the innateness hypothesis. *The Behavioral and Brain Sciences* 7(2). 188–190.

Baumgärtner, Klaus. 1965. Spracherklärung mit den Mitteln der Abhängigkeitsstruktur. *Beiträge zur Sprachkunde und Informationsverarbeitung* 5. 31–53.

Baumgärtner, Klaus. 1970. Konstituenz und Dependenz: Zur Integration beider grammatischer Prinzipien. In Hugo Steger (ed.), *Vorschläge für eine strukturelle Grammatik des Deutschen* (Wege der Forschung 144), 52–77. Darmstadt: Wissenschaftliche Buchgesellschaft.

Bausewein, Karin. 1990. Haben kopflose Relativsätze tatsächlich keine Köpfe? In Gisbert Fanselow & Sascha W. Felix (eds.), *Strukturen und Merkmale syntaktischer Kategorien* (Studien zur deutschen Grammatik 39), 144–158. Tübingen: originally Gunter Narr Verlag now Stauffenburg Verlag.

Bayer, Josef & Jaklin Kornfilt. 1989. Restructuring effects in German. DYANA Report University of Edinburgh.

Beavers, John. 2003. A CCG implementation for the LKB. LinGO Working Paper 2002-08 CSLI Stanford Stanford, CA. http://lingo.stanford.edu/pubs/WP-2002-08.ps.gz.

Beavers, John. 2004. Type-inheritance Combinatory Categorial Grammar. In *Proceedings of COLING 2004*, 57–63. Geneva, Switzerland: Association for Computational Linguistics.

Beavers, John, Elias Ponvert & Stephen Mark Wechsler. 2008. Possession of a controlled substantive. In T. Friedman & S. Ito (eds.), *Proceedings of Semantics and Linguistic Theory (SALT) XVIII*, 108–125. Ithaca, NY: Cornell University.

Beavers, John & Ivan A. Sag. 2004. Coordinate ellipsis and apparent non-constituent coordination. In Stefan Müller (ed.), *Proceedings of the 11th International Conference on Head-Driven Phrase Structure Grammar, Center for Computational Linguistics, Katholieke Universiteit Leuven*, 48–69. Stanford, CA: CSLI Publications. http://csli-publications.stanford.edu/HPSG/2004/.

Bech, Gunnar. 1955. *Studien über das deutsche Verbum infinitum* (Linguistische Arbeiten 139). Tübingen: Max Niemeyer Verlag. 2nd unchanged edition 1983.

Becker, Tilman, Aravind K. Joshi & Owen Rambow. 1991. Long-distance scrambling and Tree Adjoining Grammars. In *Fifth Conference of the European Chapter of the Association for Computational Linguistics. Proceedings of the conference*, 21–26. Berlin: Association for Computational Linguistics. http://www.aclweb.org/anthology/E91-1005.pdf.

Beermann, Dorothee & Lars Hellan. 2004. A treatment of directionals in two implemented HPSG grammars. In Stefan Müller (ed.), *Proceedings of the 11th International Conference on Head-Driven Phrase Structure Grammar, Center for Computational Linguistics, Katholieke Universiteit Leuven*, 357–377. Stanford, CA: CSLI Publications. http://csli-publications.stanford.edu/HPSG/2004/.

Beghelli, Filippo & Timothy Stowell. 1997. Distributivity and negation: The syntax of *each* and *every*. In Anna Szabolcsi (ed.), *Ways of scope taking*, 71–107. Dordrecht: Kluwer Academic Publishers.

Behaghel, Otto. 1909. Beziehung zwischen Umfang und Reihenfolge von Satzgliedern. *Indogermanische Forschungen* 25. 110–142.

Behaghel, Otto. 1930. Von deutscher Wortstellung. *Zeitschrift für Deutschkunde* 44. 81–89.

Behrens, Heike. 2009. Konstruktionen im Spracherwerb. *Zeitschrift für Germanistische Linguistik* 37(3). 427–444.

Bellugi, Ursula, Liz Lichtenberger, Wendy Jones, Zona Lai & Marie St. George. 2000. The neurocognitive profile of Williams Syndrome: A complex pattern of strengths and weaknesses. *Journal of Cognitive Neuroscience* 12. 7–29.

Bender, Emily & Daniel P. Flickinger. 1999. Peripheral constructions and core phenomena: Agreement in tag questions. In Gert Webelhuth, Jean-Pierre Koenig & Andreas Kathol (eds.), *Lexical and Constructional aspects of linguistic explanation* (Studies in Constraint-Based Lexicalism 1), 199–214. Stanford, CA: CSLI Publications.

Bender, Emily M. 2000. *Syntactic variation and linguistic competence: The case of AAVE copula absence*: Stanford University dissertation. http://faculty.washington.edu/ebender/dissertation/.

Bender, Emily M. 2008a. Evaluating a crosslinguistic grammar resource: A case study of Wambaya. In Johanna D. Moore, Simone Teufel, James Allan & Sadaoki Furui (eds.), *Proceedings of the 46th Annual Meeting of the Association for Computational Linguistics: Human Language Technologies*, 977–985. Columbus, Ohio: Association for Computational Linguistics. http://aclweb.org/anthology-new/P/P08/P08-1111.pdf.

Bender, Emily M. 2008b. Grammar engineering for linguistic hypothesis testing. In Nicholas Gaylord, Alexis Palmer & Elias Ponvert (eds.), *Proceedings of the Texas Linguistics Society X Conference: Computational linguistics for less-studied languages*, 16–36. Stanford CA: CSLI Publications ONLINE.

Bender, Emily M. 2008c. Radical non-configurationality without shuffle operators: An analysis of Wambaya. In Stefan Müller (ed.), *Proceedings of the 15th International Conference on Head-Driven Phrase Structure Grammar*, 6–24. Stanford, CA: CSLI Publications. http://csli-publications.stanford.edu/HPSG/2008/.

Bender, Emily M. 2010. Reweaving a grammar for Wambaya: A case study in grammar engineering for linguistic hypothesis testing. *Linguistic Issues in Language Technology – LiLT* 3(3). 1–34. http://journals.linguisticsociety.org/elanguage/lilt/article/view/662/523.html.

Bender, Emily M., Daniel P. Flickinger & Stephan Oepen. 2002. The Grammar Matrix: An open-source starter-kit for the rapid development of cross-linguistically consistent broad-coverage precision grammars. In John Carroll, Nelleke Oostdijk & Richard Sutcliffe (eds.), *Proceedings of the Workshop on Grammar Engineering and Evaluation at the 19th International Conference on Computational Linguistics*, 8–14. Taipei, Taiwan.

Bender, Emily M. & Melanie Siegel. 2005. Implementing the syntax of Japanese numeral classifiers. In Keh-Yih Su, Oi Yee Kwong, Jn'ichi Tsujii & Jong-Hyeok Lee (eds.), *Natural language processing IJCNLP 2004* (Lecture Notes in Artificial Intelligence 3248), 626–635. Berlin: Springer Verlag.

Bergen, Benjamin K. & Nancy Chang. 2005. Embodied Construction Grammar in simulation-based language understanding. In Jan-Ola Östman & Mirjam Fried (eds.),

Construction Grammars: Cognitive grounding and theoretical extensions, 147–190. Amsterdam: John Benjamins Publishing Co.

Berman, Judith. 1996. Eine LFG-Grammatik des Deutschen. In *Deutsche und französische Syntax im Formalismus der LFG* (Linguistische Arbeiten 344), 11–96. Tübingen: Max Niemeyer Verlag.

Berman, Judith. 1999. Does German satisfy the Subject Condition? In Miriam Butt & Tracy Holloway King (eds.), *Proceedings of the LFG '99 conference, University of Manchester*, Stanford, CA: CSLI Publications. http://csli-publications.stanford.edu/LFG/4/.

Berman, Judith. 2003a. *Clausal syntax of German* (Studies in Constraint-Based Lexicalism). Stanford, CA: CSLI Publications.

Berman, Judith. 2003b. Zum Einfluss der strukturellen Position auf die syntaktische Funktion der Komplementsätze. *Deutsche Sprache* 3. 263–286.

Berman, Judith. 2007. Functional identification of complement clauses in German and the specification of COMP. In Annie Zaenen, Jane Simpson, Tracy Holloway King, Jane Grimshaw, Joan Maling & Chris Manning (eds.), *Architectures, rules, and preferences: Variations on themes by Joan W. Bresnan*, 69–83. Stanford, CA: CSLI Publications.

Berwick, Robert C. 1982. Computational complexity and Lexical-Functional Grammar. *American Journal of Computational Linguistics* 8(3–4). 97–109.

Berwick, Robert C. & Samuel David Epstein. 1995. On the convergence of the 'Minimalist' Syntax and Categorial Grammar. In Anton Nijholt, Giuseppe Scollo & Rene Steetskamp (eds.), *Algebraic methods in language processing*, 143–148. Enschede: University of Twente. http://eprints.eemcs.utwente.nl/9555/01/twlt10.pdf.

Berwick, Robert C. & Partha Niyogi. 1996. Learning from triggers. *Linguistic Inquiry* 27. 605–622.

Berwick, Robert C., Paul Pietroski, Beracah Yankama & Noam Chomsky. 2011. Poverty of the Stimulus revisited. *Cognitive Science* 35(7). 1207–1242.

Bick, Eckhard. 2001. En Constraint Grammar parser for dansk. In Peter Widell & Mette Kunøe (eds.), *8. Møde om Udforskningen af Dansk Sprog, 12.–13. October 2000*, vol. 8, 40–50. Århus: Århus University.

Bick, Eckhard. 2003. A Constraint Grammar-based question answering system for Portuguese. In Fernando Moura Pires & Salvador Abreu (eds.), *Progress in artificial intelligence: 11th Protuguese Conference on Artificial Intelligence, EPIA 2003, Beja, Portugal, December 4–7, 2003, proceedings* (Lecture Notes in Computer Science 2902), 414–418. Berlin: Springer Verlag.

Bick, Eckhard. 2006. A Constraint Grammar parser for Spanish. In *Proceedings of TIL 2006 – 4th Workshop on Information and Human Language Technology (Ribeirão Preto, October 27–28, 2006)*, 3–10. http://www.nilc.icmc.usp.br/til/til2006/.

Bick, Eckhard. 2009. A Dependency Constraint Grammar for Esperanto. In Eckhard Bick, Kristin Hagen, Kaili Müürisep & Trond Trosterud (eds.), *Constraint Grammar and robust parsing: Proceedings of the NODALIDA 2009 workshop* (NEALT Proceedings Series 8), 8–12. Northern European Association for Language Technologie Tartu: Tartu University Library.

Bick, Eckhard. 2010. FrAG: A hybrid Constraint Grammar parser for French. In Nicoletta Calzolari, Khalid Choukri, Bente Maegaard, Joseph Mariani, Jan Odijk, Stelios Piperidis, Mike Rosner & Daniel Tapias (eds.), *Proceedings of the Seventh International Conference on Language Resources and Evaluation (LREC'10)*, 794–798. Valletta, Malta: European Language Resources Association (ELRA).

Bick, Eckhard & Lars Nygaard. 2007. Using Danish as a CG interlingua: A wide-coverage Norwegian-English machine translation system. In Joakim Nivre, Heiki-Jaan Kaalep, Kadri Muischnek & Mare Koit (eds.), *Proceedings of the 16th Nordic Conference of Computational Linguistics*, 21–28. Forlag uden navn.

Bickerton, Derek. 1984a. Creol is still king. *The Behavioral and Brain Sciences* 7(2). 212–218.

Bickerton, Derek. 1984b. The Language Bioprogram Hypothesis. *The Behavioral and Brain Sciences* 7(2). 173–188.

Bickerton, Derek. 1997. How to acquire language without positive evidence: What acquisitionists can learn from Creoles. In Michel DeGraff (ed.), *Language creation and language change: Creolization, diachrony, and development* (Learning, Development, and Conceptual Change), 49–74. Cambridge, MA: MIT Press.

Bierwisch, Manfred. 1963. *Grammatik des deutschen Verbs* (studia grammatica 2). Berlin: Akademie Verlag.

Bierwisch, Manfred. 1966. Strukturalismus: Geschichte, Probleme und Methoden. *Kursbuch* 5. 77–152.

Bierwisch, Manfred. 1992. Grammatikforschung in der DDR: Auch ein Rückblick. *Linguistische Berichte* 139. 169–181.

Bildhauer, Felix. 2008. *Representing information structure in an HPSG grammar of Spanish*: Universität Bremen Dissertation.

Bildhauer, Felix. 2011. Mehrfache Vorfeldbesetzung und Informationsstruktur: Eine Bestandsaufnahme. *Deutsche Sprache* 39(4). 362–379.

Bildhauer, Felix. 2014. Head-Driven Phrase Structure Grammar. In Andrew Carnie, Yosuke Sato & Dan Siddiqi (eds.), *The Routledge handbook of syntax*, 526–555. Oxford: Routledge.

Bildhauer, Felix & Philippa Helen Cook. 2010. German multiple fronting and expected topic-hood. In Stefan Müller (ed.), *Proceedings of the 17th International Conference on Head-Driven Phrase Structure Grammar, Université Paris Diderot*, 68–79. Stanford, CA: CSLI Publications.

Bird, Steven & Ewan Klein. 1994. Phonological analysis in typed feature systems. *Computational Linguistics* 20(3). 455–491.

Bishop, Dorothy V. M. 2002. Putting language genes in perspective. *TRENDS in Genetics* 18(2). 57–59.

Bjerre, Tavs. 2006. Object positions in a topological sentence model for Danish: A linearization-based HPSG approach. Presentation at Ph.D.-Course at Sandbjerg, Denmark. http://www.hum.au.dk/engelsk/engsv/objectpositions/workshop/Bjerre.pdf.

Blackburn, Patrick & Johan Bos. 2005. *Representation and inference for natural language: A first course in computational semantics.* Stanford, CA: CSLI Publications.

Blackburn, Patrick, Claire Gardent & Wilfried Meyer-Viol. 1993. Talking about trees. In Steven Krauwer, Michael Moortgat & Louis des Tombe (eds.), *Sixth Conference of the European Chapter of the Association for Computational Linguistics. Proceedings of the conference*, 21–29. Uetrecht: Association for Computational Linguistics.

Błaszczak, Joanna & Hans-Martin Gärtner. 2005. Intonational phrasing, discontinuity, and the scope of negation. *Syntax* 8(1). 1–22.

Blevins, James P. 2003. Passives and impersonals. *Journal of Linguistics* 39(3). 473–520.

Block, Hans-Ulrich & Rudolf Hunze. 1986. Incremental construction of c- and f-structure in a LFG-parser. In Makoto Nagao (ed.), *Proceedings of COLING 86*, 490–493. University of Bonn: Association for Computational Linguistics.

Blom, Corrien. 2005. *Complex predicates in Dutch: Synchrony and diachrony* (LOT Dissertation Series 111). Utrecht: Utrecht University.

Bloom, Paul. 1993. Grammatical continuity in language development: The case of subjectless sentences. *Linguistic Inquiry* 24(4). 721–734.

Boas, Hans C. 2003. *A Constructional approach to resultatives* (Stanford Monographs in Linguistics). Stanford, CA: CSLI Publications.

Boas, Hans C. 2014. Lexical approaches to argument structure: Two sides of the same coin. *Theoretical Linguistics* 40(1–2). 89–112.

Bobaljik, Jonathan. 1999. Adverbs: The hierarchy paradox. *Glot International* 4(9/10). 27–28.

Bod, Rens. 2009a. Constructions at work or at rest? *Cognitive Linguistics* 20(1). 129–134.

Bod, Rens. 2009b. From exemplar to grammar: Integrating analogy and probability in language learning. *Cognitive Science* 33(4). 752–793.

Bögel, Tina, Miriam Butt & Sebastian Sulger. 2008. Urdu ezafe and the morphology-syntax interface. In Miriam Butt & Tracy Holloway King (eds.), *Proceedings of the LFG 2008 conference*, 129–149. Stanford, CA: CSLI Publications. http://csli-publications.stanford.edu/LFG/13/.

Bohnet, Bernd. 2010. Very high accuracy and fast Dependency Parsing is not a contradiction. In Chu-Ren Huang & Dan Jurafsky (eds.), *Proceedings of the 23rd International Conference on Computational Linguistics*, 89–97. Stroudsburg, PA, USA: Association for Computational Linguistics.

Bolc, Leonard, Krzysztof Czuba, Anna Kupść, Małgorzata Marciniak, Agnieszka Mykowiecka & Adam Przepiórkowski. 1996. A survey of systems for implementing HPSG grammars. Tech. Rep. 814 Institute of Computer Science, Polish Academy of Sciences Warsaw, Poland. http://www.cs.cmu.edu/~kczuba/systems-wide.ps.gz.

Booij, Geert E. 2002. Separable complex verbs in Dutch: A case of periphrastic word formation. In Nicole Dehé, Ray S. Jackendoff, Andrew McIntyre & Silke Urban (eds.), *Verb-particle explorations* (Interface Explorations 1), 21–41. Berlin: Mouton de Gruyter.

Booij, Geert E. 2005. Construction-Dependent Morphology. *Lingue e linguaggio* 4. 31–46.

Booij, Geert E. 2009. Lexical integrity as a formal universal: A Constructionist view. In Sergio Scalise, Elisabetta Magni & Antonietta Bisetto (eds.), *Universals of language today* (Studies in Natural Language and Linguistic Theory 76), 83–100. Berlin: Springer Verlag.

Booij, Geert E. 2010. Construction morphology. *Language and Linguistics Compass* 4(7). 543–555. DOI:10.1111/j.1749-818X.2010.00213.x.

Booij, Geert E. 2012. Construction morphology. Ms. Leiden University.

Borer, Hagit. 1994. The projection of arguments. In E. Benedicto & J. Runner (eds.), *Functional projections* (UMass Occasional Papers in Linguistics (UMOP) 17), 19–47. Massachusetts: University of Massachusetts Graduate Linguistic Student Association.

Borer, Hagit. 2003. Exo-skeletal vs. endo-skeletal explanations: Syntactic projections and the lexicon. In John Moore & Maria Polinsky (eds.), *The nature of explanation in linguistic theory*, 31–67. Stanford, CA: CSLI Publications.

Borer, Hagit. 2005. *Structuring sense: In name only*, vol. 1. Oxford: Oxford University Press.

Borsley, Robert D. 1987. Subjects and complements in HPSG. Report No. CSLI-87-107 Center for the Study of Language and Information Stanford, CA.

Borsley, Robert D. 1989. Phrase-Structure Grammar and the Barriers conception of clause structure. *Linguistics* 27(5). 843–863.

Borsley, Robert D. 1991. *Syntactic theory: A unified approach.* London: Edward Arnold.

Borsley, Robert D. 1999. *Syntactic theory: A unified approach.* London: Edward Arnold 2nd edn.

Borsley, Robert D. 2005. Against ConjP. *Lingua* 115(4). 461–482.

Borsley, Robert D. 2006. Syntactic and lexical approaches to unbounded dependencies. Essex Research Reports in Linguistics 49 University of Essex. http://core.ac.uk/download/pdf/4187949.pdf#page=35.

Borsley, Robert D. 2007. Hang on again! Are we 'on the right track'? In Andrew Radford (ed.), *Martin Atkinson – the Minimalist muse* (Essex Research Reports in Linguistics 53), 43–69. Essex: Department of Language and Linguistics, University of Essex.

Borsley, Robert D. 2012. Don't move! *Iberia: An International Journal of Theoretical Linguistics* 4(1). 110–139.

Bos, Johan. 1996. Predicate logic unplugged. In Paul J. E. Dekker & M. Stokhof (eds.), *Proceedings of the Tenth Amsterdam Colloquium*, 133–143. Amsterdam: ILLC/Department of Philosophy, University of Amsterdam.

Boukedi, Sirine & Kais Haddar. 2014. HPSG grammar treating of different forms of Arabic coordination. *Research in Computing Science* 86: Advances in Computational Linguistics and Intelligent Decision Making. 25–41.

Boullier, Pierre & Benoît Sagot. 2005a. Analyse syntaxique profonde à grande échelle: SxLfg. *Traitement Automatique des Langues (T.A.L.)* 46(2). 65–89.

Boullier, Pierre & Benoît Sagot. 2005b. Efficient and robust LFG parsing: SxLfg. In *Proceedings of IWPT 2005*, 1–10. Vancouver, Canada: Association for Computational Linguistics.

Boullier, Pierre, Benoît Sagot & Lionel Clément. 2005. Un analyseur LFG efficace pour le français: SxLfg. In *Actes de TALN 05*, 403–408. Dourdan, France.

Bouma, Gosse. 1996. Extraposition as a nonlocal dependency. In Geert-Jan Kruijff, Glynn V. Morrill & Dick Oehrle (eds.), *Proceedings of Formal Grammar 96*, 1–14. Prag. http://www.let.rug.nl/gosse/papers.html.

Bouma, Gosse, Robert Malouf & Ivan A. Sag. 2001a. Satisfying constraints on extraction and adjunction. *Natural Language and Linguistic Theory* 19(1). 1–65.

Bouma, Gosse & Gertjan van Noord. 1994. Constraint-based Categorial Grammar. In James Pustejovsky (ed.), *32th Annual Meeting of the Association for Computational Linguistics. Proceedings of the conference*, 147–154. Las Cruses: Association for Computational Linguistics.

Bouma, Gosse & Gertjan van Noord. 1998. Word order constraints on verb clusters in German and Dutch. In Erhard W. Hinrichs, Andreas Kathol & Tsuneko Nakazawa (eds.), *Complex predicates in nonderivational syntax* (Syntax and Semantics 30), 43–72. San Diego: Academic Press. http://www.let.rug.nl/~vannoord/papers/.

Bouma, Gosse, Gertjan van Noord & Robert Malouf. 2001b. Alpino: Wide-coverage computational analysis of Dutch. In Walter Daelemans, Khalil Sima'an, Jorn Veenstra & Jakub Zavrel (eds.), *Computational linguistics in the Netherlands 2000: Selected papers from the Eleventh CLIN Meeting* (Language and Computers 37), Amsterdam/New York, NY: Rodopi.

Bragmann, Sascha. 2015. Syntactically flexible VP-idioms and the N-after-N Construction. Poster presentation at the 5th General Meeting of PARSEME, Iasi, 23–24 September 2015.

Braine, Martin D. S. 1987. What is learned in acquiring word classes—A step toward an acquisition theory. In Brian MacWhinny (ed.), *Mechanisms of language acquisition*, 65–87. Hillsdale, NJ: Lawrence Erlbaum Associates, Publishers.

Branco, António & Francisco Costa. 2008a. A computational grammar for deep linguistic processing of Portuguese: LXGram, version A.4.1. Tech. Rep. TR-2008-17 Universidade de Lisboa, Faculdade de Ciências, Departamento de Informática.

Branco, António & Francisco Costa. 2008b. LXGram in the shared task 'comparing semantic representations' of STEP 2008. In Johan Bos & Rodolfo Delmonte (eds.), *Semantics in text processing: STEP 2008 conference proceedings*, vol. 1 (Research in Computational Semantics), 299–314. London: College Publications. http://www.aclweb.org/anthology/W08-2224.

Brants, Sabine, Stefanie Dipper, Peter Eisenberg, Silvia Hansen-Schirra, Esther König, Wolfgang Lezius, Christian Rohrer, George Smith & Hans Uszkoreit. 2004. TIGER: Linguistic interpretation of a German corpus. *Research on Language and Computation* 2(4). 597–620.

Bresnan, Joan. 1974. The position of certain clause-particles in phrase structure. *Linguistic Inquiry* 5(4). 614–619.

Bresnan, Joan. 1978. A realistic Transformational Grammar. In M. Halle, J. Bresnan & G. A. Miller (eds.), *Linguistic theory and psychological reality*, 1–59. Cambridge, MA: MIT Press.

Bresnan, Joan. 1982a. Control and complementation. *Linguistic Inquiry* 13(3). 343–434.

Bresnan, Joan. 1982b. The passive in lexical theory. In Joan Bresnan (ed.), *The mental representation of grammatical relations* (MIT Press Series on Cognitive Theory and Mental Representation), 3–86. Cambridge, MA/London: MIT Press.

Bresnan, Joan. 2001. *Lexical-Functional Syntax*. Oxford, UK/Cambridge, USA: Blackwell.

Bresnan, Joan & Jane Grimshaw. 1978. The syntax of free relatives in English. *Linguistic Inquiry* 9. 331–392.

Bresnan, Joan & Jonni M. Kanerva. 1989. Locative inversion in Chichewa: A case study of factorization in grammar. *Linguistic Inquiry* 20(1). 1–50.

Bresnan, Joan & Ronald M. Kaplan. 1982. Introduction: Grammars as mental representations of language. In Joan Bresnan (ed.), *The mental representation of grammatical relations* (MIT Press Series on Cognitive Theory and Mental Representation), xvii–lii. Cambridge, MA/London: MIT Press.

Bresnan, Joan & Sam A. Mchombo. 1995. The Lexical Integrity Principle: Evidence from Bantu. *Natural Language and Linguistic Theory* 13. 181–254.

Bresnan, Joan & Annie Zaenen. 1990. Deep unaccusativity in LFG. In Katarzyna Dziwirek, Patrick Farrell & Errapel Mejías-Bikandi (eds.), *Grammatical relations: A cross-theoretical perspective*, 45–57. Stanford, CA: CSLI Publications.

Brew, Chris. 1995. Stochastic HPSG. In Steven P. Abney & Erhard W. Hinrichs (eds.), *Proceedings of the Seventh Conference of the European Chapter of the Association for Computational Linguistics*, 83–89. Dublin: Association for Computational Linguistics.

Briscoe, Ted J. 1997. Review of Edward P. Stabler, Jr., The logical approach to syntax: Foundations, specifications, and implementations of theories of Government and Binding. *Journal of Linguistics* 33(1). 223–225.

Briscoe, Ted J. 2000. Grammatical acquisition: Inductive bias and coevolution of language and the language acquisition device. *Language* 76(2). 245–296.

Briscoe, Ted J. & Ann Copestake. 1999. Lexical rules in constraint-based grammar. *Computational Linguistics* 25(4). 487–526.

Bröker, Norbert. 2003. Formal foundations of Dependency Grammar. In Vilmos Ágel, Ludwig M. Eichinger, Hans Werner Eroms, Peter Hellwig, Hans Jürgen Heringer & Henning Lobin (eds.), *Dependenz und Valenz / Dependency and valency: Ein internationales Handbuch der zeitgenössischen Forschung / An international handbook of contemporary research*, vol. 25.1 (Handbücher zur Sprach- und Kommunikationswissenschaft), 294–310. Berlin: Walter de Gruyter.

Brosziewski, Ulf. 2003. *Syntactic derivations: A nontransformational view* (Linguistische Arbeiten 470). Tübingen: Max Niemeyer Verlag.

Brown, Roger & Camille Hanlon. 1970. Derivational complexity and order of acquisition in child speech. In John R. Hayes (ed.), *Cognition and the development of language*, 11–53. New York: John Wiley & Sons, Inc.

Bruening, Benjamin. 2009. Selectional asymmetries between CP and DP suggest that the DP hypothesis is wrong. In Laurel MacKenzie (ed.), *Proceedings of the 32th Annual Penn Linguistics Colloquium* (Penn Working Papers in Linguistics 15.1), 26–35. Philadelphia.

Bryant, John. 2003. *Constructional analysis*. University of Califorma at Berkeley MA thesis. http://www.icsi.berkeley.edu/~jbryant/old-analyzer.html.

Budde, Monika. 2010. Konstruktionen integrativ: Topik-Konstruktionen als rein-syntaktisches Pendant zu den lexikalisch verankerten Komplement-Konstruktionen. Vortrag auf der Tagung Konstruktionsgrammatik: Neue Perspektiven zur Untersuchung des Deutschen und Englischen. Internationale Fachtagung an der Christian-Albrechts-Universität zu Kiel vom 18. bis 20. Februar 2010.

Bungeroth, Jan. 2002. *A formal description of Sign Language using HPSG.* Karlsruhe Department of Computer Science, University of Stellenbosch, Lehrstuhl Informatik für Ingenieure und Naturwissenschaftler, Universität Karlsruhe (TH) Diploma thesis. http://www-i6.informatik.rwth-aachen.de/~bungeroth/diplarb.pdf.

Burzio, Luigi. 1981. *Intransitive verbs and Italian auxiliaries*: MIT dissertation.

Burzio, Luigi. 1986. *Italian syntax: A Government-Binding approach* (Studies in Natural Language and Linguistic Theory 1). Dordrecht: D. Reidel Publishing Company.

Busemann, Stephan. 1992. *Generierung natürlicher Sprache mit generalisierten Phrasenstrukturgrammatiken*, vol. 313 (Informatik-Fachberichte). Berlin: Springer Verlag.

Bußmann, Hadumod (ed.). 1983. *Lexikon der Sprachwissenschaft* (Kröners Taschenausgabe 452). Stuttgart: Alfred Kröner Verlag.

Bußmann, Hadumod (ed.). 1990. *Lexikon der Sprachwissenschaft* (Kröners Taschenausgabe 452). Stuttgart: Alfred Kröner Verlag 2nd edn.

Butt, Miriam. 2003. The light verb jungle. In C. Quinn, C. Bowern & G. Aygen (eds.), *Papers from the Harvard/Dudley House light verb workshop* (Harvard Working Papers in Linguistics 9), 1–49. Harvard University, Department of Linguistics.

Butt, Miriam, Stefanie Dipper, Anette Frank & Tracy Holloway King. 1999a. Writing large-scale parallel grammars for English, French and German. In Miriam Butt & Tracy Holloway King (eds.), *Proceedings of the LFG '99 conference, University of Manchester*, Stanford, CA: CSLI Publications. http://csli-publications.stanford.edu/LFG/4/.

Butt, Miriam, Helge Dyvik, Tracy Holloway King, Hiroshi Masuichi & Christian Rohrer. 2002. The Parallel Grammar Project. In *Proceedings of COLING-2002 Workshop on Grammar Engineering and Evaluation*, 1–7.

Butt, Miriam, Tracy Holloway King, María-Eugenia Niño & Frédérique Segond. 1999b. *A grammar writer's cookbook* (CSLI Lecture Notes 95). Stanford, CA: CSLI Publications.

Butt, Miriam, Tracy Holloway King & Sebastian Roth. 2007. Urdu correlatives: Theoretical and implementational issues. In Miriam Butt & Tracy Holloway King (eds.), *Proceedings of the LFG 2007 conference*, 107–127. Stanford, CA: CSLI Publications. http://csli-publications.stanford.edu/LFG/12/.

Cahill, Aoife, Michael Burke, Martin Forst, Ruth O'Donovan, Christian Rohrer, Josef van Genabith & Andy Way. 2005. Treebank-based acquisition of multilingual unification grammar resources. *Research on Language and Computation* 3(2). 247–279.

Cahill, Aoife, Michael Burke, Ruth O'Donovan, Stefan Riezler, Josef van Genabith & Andy Way. 2008. Wide-coverage deep statistical parsing using automatic dependency structure annotation. *Computational Linguistics* 34(1). 81–124.

Calder, Jonathan, Ewan Klein & Henk Zeevat. 1988. Unification Categorial Grammar: A concise, extendable grammar for natural language processing. In Dénes Vargha (ed.), *Proceedings of COLING 88*, 83–86. University of Budapest: Association for Computational Linguistics.

Callmeier, Ulrich. 2000. PET—A platform for experimentation with efficient HPSG processing techniques. *Journal of Natural Language Engineering* 1(6). 99–108. (Special Issue on Efficient Processing with HPSG: Methods, Systems, Evaluation).

Candito, Marie-Hélène. 1996. A principle-based hierarchical representation of LTAGs. In Jun-ichi Tsuji (ed.), *Proceedings of COLING-96. 16th International Conference on Computational Linguistics COLING96). Copenhagen, Denmark, August 5–9, 1996*, 194–199. Copenhagen, Denmark: Association for Computational Linguistics.

Candito, Marie-Hélène. 1998. Building parallel LTAG for French and Italian. In *Proceedings of the 36th Annual Meeting of the Association for Computational Linguistics and 17th International Conference on Computational Linguistics*, 211–217. Montreal, Quebec, Canada: Association for Computational Linguistics.

Candito, Marie-Hélène. 1999. *Organisation modulaire et paramétrable de grammaires électroniques lexicalisées. Application au français et à l'italien*: Université Paris 7 dissertation.

Candito, Marie-Hélène & Sylvain Kahane. 1998. Can the TAG derivation tree represent a semantic graph? An answer in the light of Meaning-Text Theory. In *TAG+4*, 25–28.

Cappelle, Bert. 2006. Particle placement and the case for "allostructions". *Constructions online* 1(7). 1–28.

Cappelle, Bert, Yury Shtyrov & Friedemann Pulvermüller. 2010. *Heating up* or *cooling up* the brain? MEG evidence that phrasal verbs are lexical units. *Brain and Language* 115. 189–201.

Carlson, Gregory N. & Michael K. Tanenhaus. 1988. Thematic roles and language comprehension. In Wendy Wilkins (ed.), *Thematic relations* (Syntax and Semantics 21), 263–289. San Diego: Academic Press.

Carpenter, Bob. 1992. *The logic of typed feature structures* (Tracts in Theoretical Computer Science). Cambridge: Cambridge University Press.

Carpenter, Bob. 1994. A natural deduction theorem prover for type-theoretic Categorial Grammars. Tech. rep. Carnegie Mellon Laboratory for Computational Linguistics. http://www.essex.ac.uk/linguistics/external/clmt/papers/cg/carp_cgparser_doc.ps.

Carpenter, Bob. 1998. *Type-logical semantics*. Cambridge, MA/London, England: MIT Press.

Carpenter, Bob & Gerald Penn. 1996. Efficient parsing of compiled typed attribute value logic grammars. In Harry Bunt & Masaru Tomita (eds.), *Recent advances in parsing technology* (Text, Speech and Language Technology 1), 145–168. Dordrecht: Kluwer Academic Publishers.

Çetinoğlu, Özlem & Kemal Oflazer. 2006. Morphology-syntax interface for Turkish LFG. In Nicoletta Calzolari, Claire Cardie & Pierre Isabelle (eds.), *Proceedings of the 21st International Conference on Computational Linguistics and 44th Annual Meeting of the Association for Computational Linguistics*, 153–160. Sydney, Australia: Association for Computational Linguistics.

Chang, Nancy Chih-Lin. 2008. Constructing grammar: A computational model of the emergence of early constructions. Technical Report UCB/EECS-2009-24 Electrical Engineering and Computer Sciences, University of California at Berkeley.

Chaves, Rui P. 2009. Construction-based cumulation and adjunct extraction. In Stefan Müller (ed.), *Proceedings of the 16th International Conference on Head-Driven Phrase Structure Grammar, University of Göttingen, Germany*, 47–67. Stanford, CA: CSLI Publications.

Choi, Hye-Won. 1999. *Optimizing structure in scrambling: Scrambling and information structure* (Dissertations in Linguistics). Stanford, CA: CSLI Publications.

Chomsky, Noam. 1956. Three models for the description of language. *IRE Transactions on Information Theory* 2. 113–124.

Chomsky, Noam. 1957. *Syntactic structures* (Janua Linguarum / Series Minor 4). The Hague/Paris: Mouton.

Chomsky, Noam. 1959. On certain formal properties of grammars. *Information and Control* 2(2). 137–167.

Chomsky, Noam. 1964a. *Current issues in linguistic theory* (Janua Linguarum / Series Minor 38). The Hague/Paris: Mouton.

Chomsky, Noam. 1964b. Degrees of grammaticalness. In Jerry A. Fodor & Jerrold J. Katz (eds.), *The structure of language*, 384–389. Englewood Cliffs, NJ: Prentice-Hall.

Chomsky, Noam. 1965. *Aspects of the theory of syntax*. Cambridge, MA: MIT Press.

Chomsky, Noam. 1968. Language and the mind. *Psychology Today* 1(9). 48–68. Reprint as: Chomsky (1976a).

Chomsky, Noam. 1970. Remarks on nominalization. In Roderick A. Jacobs & Peter S. Rosenbaum (eds.), *Readings in English Transformational Grammar*, chap. 12, 184–221. Waltham, MA/Toronto/London: Ginn and Company.

Chomsky, Noam. 1971. *Problems of knowledge and freedom*. London: Fontana.

Chomsky, Noam. 1973. Conditions on transformations. In Stephen R. Anderson & Paul Kiparski (eds.), *A festschrift for Morris Halle*, 232–286. New York: Holt, Rinehart & Winston.

Chomsky, Noam. 1975. *The logical structure of linguistic theory*. New York: Plenum Press.

Chomsky, Noam. 1976a. Language and the mind. In Diane D. Borstein (ed.), *Readings in the theory of grammar: From the 17th to the 20th century*, 241–251. Cambridge, MA: Winthrop. Reprint from: Chomsky (1968).

Chomsky, Noam. 1976b. *Reflections on language*. New York: Pantheon Books.

Chomsky, Noam. 1977. *Essays on form and interpretation*. New York: North Holland.

Chomsky, Noam. 1980. *Rules and representations*. Oxford: Basil Blackwell.

Chomsky, Noam. 1981a. *Lectures on government and binding*. Dordrecht: Foris Publications.

Chomsky, Noam. 1981b. Reply to comments of Thompson. *Philosophical Transactions of the Royal Society of London. Series B, Biological Sciences* 295(1077). 277–281.

Chomsky, Noam. 1982. *Some concepts and consequences of the theory of Government and Binding* (Linguistic Inquiry Monographs 5). Cambridge, MA/London, England: MIT Press.

Chomsky, Noam. 1986a. *Barriers* (Linguistic Inquiry Monographs 13). Cambridge, MA/London, England: MIT Press.

Chomsky, Noam. 1986b. *Knowledge of language: Its nature, origin, and use* (Convergence). New York/Westport, Connecticut/London: Praeger.

Chomsky, Noam. 1988. *Language and problems of knowledge: The Managua lectures* (Current Studies in Linguistics 16). Cambridge, MA: MIT Press.

Chomsky, Noam. 1989. Some notes on economy of derivation and representation. In I. Laka & Anoop Mahajan (eds.), *Functional heads and clause structure* (MIT Working Papers in Linguistics 10), 43–74. Cambridge, MA: Department of Linguistics and Philosophy.

Chomsky, Noam. 1990. On formalization and formal linguistics. *Natural Language and Linguistic Theory* 8(1). 143–147.

Chomsky, Noam. 1991. Some notes on economy of derivation and representation. In Robert Freidin (ed.), *Principles and parameters in Generative Grammar*, 417–454. Cambridge, MA: MIT Press. Reprint as: Chomsky (1995b: 129–166).

Chomsky, Noam. 1993. A Minimalist Program for linguistic theory. In Kenneth Hale & Samuel Jay Keyser (eds.), *The view from building 20: Essays in linguistics in honor of Sylvain Bromberger* (Current Studies in Linguistics 24), 1–52. Cambridge, MA/London: MIT Press.

Chomsky, Noam. 1995a. Bare phrase structure. In Hector Campos & Paula Kempchinsky (eds.), *Evolution and revolution in linguistic theory: Essays in honor of Carlos Otero*, 51–109. Washington, DC: Georgetown U Press.

Chomsky, Noam. 1995b. *The Minimalist Program* (Current Studies in Linguistics 28). Cambridge, MA/London, England: MIT Press.

Chomsky, Noam. 1998. Noam Chomsky's Minimalist Program and the philosophy of mind: An interview [with] Camilo J. Cela-Conde and Gisde Marty. *Syntax* 1(1). 19–36.

Chomsky, Noam. 1999. Derivation by phase. MIT Occasional Papers in Linguistics 18 MIT. Reprint in: Michael Kenstowicz, ed. 2001. Ken Hale. A Life in Language. Cambridge, MA: MIT Press, 1–52.

Chomsky, Noam. 2000. *New horizons in the study of language and mind.* Cambridge, UK: Cambridge University Press.

Chomsky, Noam. 2001. Derivation by phase. In Michael Kenstowicz (ed.), *Ken Hale: A life in language*, 1–52. Cambridge, MA: MIT Press.

Chomsky, Noam. 2002. *On nature and language.* Cambridge, UK: Cambridge University Press.

Chomsky, Noam. 2005. Three factors in language design. *Linguistic Inquiry* 36(1). 1–22.

Chomsky, Noam. 2007. Approaching UG from below. In Uli Sauerland & Hans-Martin Gärtner (eds.), *Interfaces + recursion = language? Chomsky's Minimalism and the view from syntax-semantics* (Studies in Generative Grammar 89), 1–29. Berlin: Mouton de Gruyter.

Chomsky, Noam. 2008. On phases. In Robert Freidin, Carlos P. Otero & Maria Luisa Zubizarreta (eds.), *Foundational issues in linguistic theory: Essays in honor of Jean-Roger Vergnaud*, 133–166. Cambridge, MA: MIT Press.

Chomsky, Noam. 2010. Restricting stipulations: Consequences and challenges. Talk given in Stuttgart.

Chomsky, Noam. 2013. Problems of projection. *Lingua* 130. 33–49.

Chomsky, Noam & George A. Miller. 1963. Introduction to the formal analysis of natural languages. In R. Duncan Luce, Robert R. Bush & Eugene Galanter (eds.), *Handbook of mathematical psychology*, vol. 2, 269–321. New York: John Wiley & Sons, Inc.

Chouinard, Michelle M. & Eve V. Clark. 2003. Adult reformulations of child errors as negative evidence. *Journal of Child Language* 30. 637–669.

Chrupala, Grzegorz & Josef van Genabith. 2006. Using machine-learning to assign function labels to parser output for Spanish. In Nicoletta Calzolari, Claire Cardie & Pierre Isabelle (eds.), *Proceedings of the 21st International Conference on Computational Linguistics and 44th Annual Meeting of the Association for Computational Linguistics*, 136–143. Sydney, Australia: Association for Computational Linguistics.

Chung, Sandra & James McCloskey. 1983. On the interpretation of certain island facts in GPSG. *Linguistic Inquiry* 14. 704–713.

Church, Kenneth. 2011. A pendulum swung too far. *Linguistic Issues in Language Technology* 6(5). 1–27. http://journals.linguisticsociety.org/elanguage/lilt/article/view/2581.html. Special Issue on Interaction of Linguistics and Computational Linguistics.

Cinque, Guglielmo. 1994. On the evidence for partial N movement in the Romance DP. In Guglielmo Cinque, Jan Koster, Jean-Yves Pollock, Luigi Rizzi & Raffaella Zanuttini (eds.), *Paths towards Universal Grammar: Studies in honor of Richard S. Kayne*, 85–110. Washington, D.C.: Georgetown University Press.

Cinque, Guglielmo. 1999. *Adverbs and functional heads: A cross-linguistic perspective.* New York, Oxford: Oxford University Press.

Cinque, Guglielmo & Luigi Rizzi. 2010. The cartography of syntactic structures. In Bernd Heine & Heiko Narrog (eds.), *The Oxford handbook of linguistic analysis*, 51–65. Oxford: Oxford University Press.

Citko, Barbara. 2008. Missing labels. *Lingua* 118(7). 907–944.

Clark, Alexander. 2000. Inducing syntactic categories by context distribution clustering. In *Proceedings CoNLL 2000*, 91–94. Stroudsburg, PA: Association for Computational Linguistics.

Clark, Herbert H. & Jean E. Fox Tree. 2002. Using *uh* and *um* in spontaneous speaking. *Cognition* 84(1). 73–111.

Clark, Herbert H. & Thomas Wasow. 1998. Repeating words in spontaneous speech. *Cognitive Psychology* 37(3). 201–242.

Clark, Stephen & James Curran. 2007. Wide-coverage efficient statistical parsing with CCG and log-linear models. *Computational Linguistics* 33(4). 493–552.

Clark, Stephen, Julia Hockenmaier & Mark J. Steedman. 2002. Building deep dependency structures with a wide-coverage CCG parser. In Pierre Isabelle (ed.), *40th Annual Meeting of the Association for Computational Linguistics: Proceedings of the conference*, 327–334. University of Pennsylvania, Philadelphia: Association for Computational Linguistics. http://aclanthology.info/events/acl-2002.

Clément, Lionel. 2009. XLFG5 documentation. Translated from French by Olivier Bonami. http://www.xlfg.org/.

Clément, Lionel & Alexandra Kinyon. 2001. XLFG—An LFG parsing scheme for French. In Miriam Butt & Tracy Holloway King (eds.), *Proceedings of the LFG 2001 conference*, Stanford, CA: CSLI Publications. http://csli-publications.stanford.edu/LFG/6/.

Clément, Lionel & Alexandra Kinyon. 2003. Generating parallel multilingual LFG-TAG grammars from a MetaGrammar. In Erhard Hinrichs & Dan Roth (eds.), *Proceedings of the 41st Annual Meeting of the Association for Computational Linguistics*, 184–191. Sapporo, Japan: Association for Computational Linguistics.

Clifton, Charles Jr. & Penelope Odom. 1966. Similarity relations among certain English sentence constructions. *Psychological Monographs: General and Applied* 80(5). 1–35.

Coch, Jose. 1996. Overview of AlethGen. In *Demonstrations and posters of the Eighth International Natural Language Generation Workshop (INLG'96)*, 25–28.

Cook, Philippa Helen. 2001. *Coherence in German: An information structure approach*: Departments of Linguistics and German, University of Manchester dissertation.

Cook, Philippa Helen. 2006. The datives that aren't born equal: Beneficiaries and the dative passive. In Daniel Hole, André Meinunger & Werner Abraham (eds.), *Datives and similar cases: Between argument structure and event structure*, 141–184. Amsterdam: John Benjamins Publishing Co.

Cooper, Robin, Kuniaki Mukai & John Perry (eds.). 1990. *Situation Theory and its applications*, vol. 1 (CSLI Lecture Notes 22). Stanford, CA: CSLI Publications.

Coopmans, Peter. 1989. Where stylistic and syntactic processes meet: Locative inversion in English. *Language* 65(4). 728–751.

Copestake, Ann. 2002. *Implementing typed feature structure grammars* (CSLI Lecture Notes 110). Stanford, CA: CSLI Publications.

Copestake, Ann. 2007. Applying robust semantics. In *Proceedings of the 10th Conference of the Pacific Assocation for Computational Linguistics (PACLING)*, 1–12.

Copestake, Ann & Ted Briscoe. 1995. Semi-productive polysemy and sense extension. *Journal of Semantics* 12(1). 15–67.

Copestake, Ann & Ted J. Briscoe. 1992. Lexical operations in a unification based framework. In James Pustejovsky & Sabine Bergler (eds.), *Lexical semantics and knowledge representation* (Lecture Notes in Artificial Intelligence 627), 101–119. Berlin: Springer Verlag.

Copestake, Ann & Daniel P. Flickinger. 2000. An open-source grammar development environment and broad-coverage English grammar using HPSG. In *Proceedings of the second Linguistic Resources and Evaluation Conference*, 591–600. Athens, Greece.

Copestake, Ann, Daniel P. Flickinger, Carl J. Pollard & Ivan A. Sag. 2005. Minimal Recursion Semantics: An introduction. *Research on Language and Computation* 4(3). 281–332.

Correa, Nelson. 1987. An Attribute-Grammar implementation of Government-Binding Theory. In Candy Sidner (ed.), *25th Annual Meeting of the Association for Computational Linguistics*, 45–51. Stanford, CA: Association for Computational Linguistics.

Costa, Francisco & António Branco. 2010. LXGram: A deep linguistic processing grammar for Portuguese. In Thiago A.S. Pardo (ed.), *Computational processing of the Portuguese language: 9th International Conference, PROPOR 2010, Porto Alegre, RS, Brazil,*

April 27–30, 2010. Proceedings (Lecture Notes in Artificial Intelligence 6001), 86–89. Berlin: Springer Verlag.

Covington, Michael A. 1990. Parsing discontinuous constituents in Dependency Grammar. *Computational Linguistics* 16(4). 234–236.

Crabbé, Benoit. 2005. *Représentation informatique de grammaires d'arbres fortement lexicalisées: le cas de la grammaire d'arbres adjoints*: Université Nancy 2 dissertation.

Crain, Stephen, Drew Khlentzos & Rosalind Thornton. 2010. Universal Grammar versus language diversity. *Lingua* 120(12). 2668–2672.

Crain, Stephen & Mineharu Nakayama. 1987. Structure dependence in grammar formation. *Language* 63(3). 522–543.

Crain, Stephen & Mark J. Steedman. 1985. On not being led up the garden path: The use of context by the psychological syntax processor. In David R. Dowty, Lauri Karttunen & Arnold M. Zwicky (eds.), *Natural language processing*, 320–358. Cambridge, UK: Cambridge University Press.

Crain, Stephen, Rosalind Thornton & Drew Khlentzos. 2009. The case of the missing generalizations. *Cognitive Linguistics* 20(1). 145–155.

Cramer, Bart & Yi Zhang. 2009. Construction of a German HPSG grammar from a detailed treebank. In Tracy Holloway King & Marianne Santaholma (eds.), *Proceedings of the 2009 Workshop on Grammar Engineering Across Frameworks (GEAF 2009)*, 37–45. Suntec, Singapore: Association for Computational Linguistics. http://www.aclweb.org/anthology/W/W09/#2600.

Crocker, Matthew Walter & Ian Lewin. 1992. Parsing as deduction: Rules versus principles. In Bernd Neumann (ed.), *ECAI 92. 10th European Conference on Artificial Intelligence*, 508–512. John Wiley & Sons, Inc.

Croft, William. 2001. *Radical Construction Grammar: Syntactic theory in typological perspective.* Oxford: Oxford University Press.

Croft, William. 2003. Lexical rules vs. constructions: A false dichotomy. In Hubert Cuyckens, Thomas Berg, René Dirven & Klaus-Uwe Panther (eds.), *Motivation in language: Studies in honour of Günter Radden*, 49–68. Amsterdam: John Benjamins Publishing Co.

Croft, William. 2009. Syntax is more diverse, and evolutionary linguistics is already here. *The Behavioral and Brain Sciences* 32(5). 457–458.

Crysmann, Berthold. 2001. Clitics and coordination in linear structure. In Birgit Gerlach & Janet Grijzenhout (eds.), *Clitics in phonology, morphology and syntax* (Linguistik Aktuell/Linguistics Today 36), 121–159. Amsterdam: John Benjamins Publishing Co.

Crysmann, Berthold. 2002. *Constraint-based co-analysis: Portuguese cliticisation and morphology-syntax interaction in HPSG* (Saarbrücken Dissertations in Computational Linguistics and Language Technology 15). Saarbrücken: Deutsches Forschungszentrum für Künstliche Intelligenz und Universität des Saarlandes.

Crysmann, Berthold. 2003. On the efficient implementation of German verb placement in HPSG. In *Proceedings of RANLP 2003*, 112–116. Borovets, Bulgaria.

Crysmann, Berthold. 2004. Underspecification of intersective modifier attachment: Some arguments from German. In Stefan Müller (ed.), *Proceedings of the 11th Interna-*

tional Conference on Head-Driven Phrase Structure Grammar, Center for Computational Linguistics, Katholieke Universiteit Leuven, 378–392. Stanford, CA: CSLI Publications. http://csli-publications.stanford.edu/HPSG/2004/.

Crysmann, Berthold. 2005a. An inflectional approach to Hausa final vowel shortening. In Geert Booij & Jaap van Marle (eds.), *Yearbook of morphology 2004*, 73–112. Dordrecht: Kluwer Academic Publishers.

Crysmann, Berthold. 2005b. Relative clause extraposition in German: An efficient and portable implementation. *Research on Language and Computation* 1(3). 61–82.

Crysmann, Berthold. 2005c. Syncretism in German: A unified approach to underspecification, indeterminacy, and likeness of case. In Stefan Müller (ed.), *Proceedings of the 12th International Conference on Head-Driven Phrase Structure Grammar, Department of Informatics, University of Lisbon*, 91–107. Stanford, CA: CSLI Publications. http://csli-publications.stanford.edu/HPSG/2005/.

Crysmann, Berthold. 2008. An asymmetric theory of peripheral sharing in HPSG: Conjunction reduction and coordination of unlikes. In Gerhard Jäger, Paola Monachesi, Gerald Penn & Shuly Wintner (eds.), *Proceedings of Formal Grammar 2003, Vienna, Austria*, 47–62. Stanford, CA: CSLI Publications.

Crysmann, Berthold. 2009. Autosegmental representations in an HPSG of Hausa. In Tracy Holloway King & Marianne Santaholma (eds.), *Proceedings of the 2009 Workshop on Grammar Engineering Across Frameworks (GEAF 2009)*, 28–36. Suntec, Singapore: Association for Computational Linguistics. http://www.aclweb.org/anthology/W/W09/#2600.

Crysmann, Berthold. 2011. A unified account of Hausa genitive constructions. In Philippe de Groote, Markus Egg & Laura Kallmeyer (eds.), *Formal Grammar: 14th International Conference, FG 2009, Bordeaux, France, July 25–26, 2009, revised selected papers* (Lecture Notes in Artificial Intelligence 5591), 102–117. Berlin: Springer Verlag.

Crysmann, Berthold. 2012. HaG: A computational grammar of Hausa. In Michael R. Marlo, Nikki B. Adams, Christopher R. Green, Michelle Morrison & Tristan M. Purvis (eds.), *Selected proceedings of the 42nd Annual Conference on African Linguistics (ACAL 42)*, 321–337. Somerville, MA: Cascadilla Press. http://www.lingref.com/cpp/acal/42/paper2780.pdf.

Culicover, Peter W. 1999. *Syntactic nuts: Hard cases, syntactic theory, and language acquisition*, vol. 1 (Foundations of Syntax). Oxford: Oxford University Press.

Culicover, Peter W. & Ray S. Jackendoff. 2005. *Simpler Syntax*. Oxford: Oxford University Press.

Culy, Christopher. 1985. The complexity of the vocabulary of Bambara. *Linguistics and Philosophy* 8. 345–351.

Curtiss, Susan. 1977. *Genie: A psycholinguistic study of a modern-day "wild child"*. New York: Academic Press.

Dąbrowska, Ewa. 2001. From formula to schema: The acquisition of English questions. *Cognitive Linguistics* 11(1–2). 83–102.

Dąbrowska, Ewa. 2004. *Language, mind and brain: Some psychological and neurological constraints on theories of grammar*. Washington, D.C.: Georgetown University Press.

Dahl, Östen & Viveka Velupillai. 2013a. The past tense. In Matthew S. Dryer & Martin Haspelmath (eds.), *The world atlas of language structures online*, Leipzig: Max Planck Institute for Evolutionary Anthropology. http://wals.info/chapter/66.

Dahl, Östen & Viveka Velupillai. 2013b. Perfective/imperfective aspect. In Matthew S. Dryer & Martin Haspelmath (eds.), *The world atlas of language structures online*, Leipzig: Max Planck Institute for Evolutionary Anthropology. http://wals.info/chapter/65.

Dahllöf, Mats. 2002. Token dependency semantics and the paratactic analysis of intensional constructions. *Journal of Semantics* 19(4). 333–368.

Dahllöf, Mats. 2003. Two reports on computational syntax and semantics. Reports from Uppsala University (RUUL) 36 Department of Linguistics. http://stp.ling.uu.se/~matsd/pub/ruul36.pdf.

Dalrymple, Mary. 1993. *The syntax of anaphoric binding* (CSLI Lecture Notes 36). Stanford, CA: CSLI Publications.

Dalrymple, Mary (ed.). 1999. *Semantics and syntax in Lexical Functional Grammar: The Resource Logic approach*. Cambridge, MA: MIT Press.

Dalrymple, Mary. 2001. *Lexical Functional Grammar* (Syntax and Semantics 34). New York: Academic Press.

Dalrymple, Mary. 2006. Lexical Functional Grammar. In Keith Brown (ed.), *The encyclopedia of language and linguistics*, 82–94. Oxford: Elsevier Science Publisher B.V. (North-Holland) 2nd edn.

Dalrymple, Mary, Ronald M. Kaplan & Tracy Holloway King. 2004. Linguistic generalizations over descriptions. In Miriam Butt & Tracy Holloway King (eds.), *Proceedings of the LFG 2004 conference*, 199–208. Stanford, CA: CSLI Publications. http://csli-publications.stanford.edu/LFG/9/.

Dalrymple, Mary, Ronald M. Kaplan, John T. Maxwell III & Annie Zaenen (eds.). 1995. *Formal issues in Lexical-Functional Grammar* (CSLI Lecture Notes 47). Stanford, CA: CSLI Publications.

Dalrymple, Mary, John Lamping & Vijay Saraswat. 1993. LFG semantics via constraints. In Steven Krauwer, Michael Moortgat & Louis des Tombe (eds.), *Sixth Conference of the European Chapter of the Association for Computational Linguistics. Proceedings of the conference*, 97–105. Uetrecht: Association for Computational Linguistics. DOI:10.3115/976744.976757.

Dalrymple, Mary, Maria Liakata & Lisa Mackie. 2006. Tokenization and morphological analysis for Malagasy. *Computational Linguistics and Chinese Language Processing* 11(4). 315–332.

Dalrymple, Mary & Helge Lødrup. 2000. The grammatical functions of complement clauses. In Miriam Butt & Tracy Holloway King (eds.), *Proceedings of the LFG 2000 conference*, Stanford, CA: CSLI Publications. http://csli-publications.stanford.edu/LFG/5/lfg00dalrympl-lodrup.pdf.

Davidson, Donald. 1967. The logical form of action sentences. In Nicholas Rescher (ed.), *The logic of decision and action*, 81–95. Pittsburg: Pittsburg University Press.

Davis, Anthony R. 1996. *Lexical semantics and linking in the hierarchical lexicon*: Stanford University dissertation.

Davis, Anthony R. & Jean-Pierre Koenig. 2000. Linking as constraints on word classes in a hierarchical lexicon. *Language* 76(1). 56–91.

De Kuthy, Kordula. 2000. *Discontinuous NPs in German — A case study of the interaction of syntax, semantics and pragmatics*. Saarbrücken: Universität des Saarlandes dissertation.

De Kuthy, Kordula. 2001. Splitting PPs from NPs. In Walt Detmar Meurers & Tibor Kiss (eds.), *Constraint-based approaches to Germanic syntax* (Studies in Constraint-Based Lexicalism 7), 31–76. Stanford, CA: CSLI Publications.

De Kuthy, Kordula. 2002. *Discontinuous NPs in German* (Studies in Constraint-Based Lexicalism 14). Stanford, CA: CSLI Publications.

De Kuthy, Kordula, Vanessa Metcalf & Walt Detmar Meurers. 2004. Documentation of the implementation of the Milca English Resource Grammar in the Trale system. Ohio State University, ms.

De Kuthy, Kordula & Walt Detmar Meurers. 2001. On partial constituent fronting in German. *Journal of Comparative Germanic Linguistics* 3(3). 143–205.

De Kuthy, Kordula & Walt Detmar Meurers. 2003a. Dealing with optional complements in HPSG-based grammar implementations. In Stefan Müller (ed.), *Proceedings of the 10th International Conference on Head-Driven Phrase Structure Grammar, Michigan State University, East Lansing*, 88–96. Stanford, CA: CSLI Publications. http://csli-publications.stanford.edu/HPSG/2003/.

De Kuthy, Kordula & Walt Detmar Meurers. 2003b. The secret life of focus exponents, and what it tells us about fronted verbal projections. In Stefan Müller (ed.), *Proceedings of the 10th International Conference on Head-Driven Phrase Structure Grammar, Michigan State University, East Lansing*, 97–110. Stanford, CA: CSLI Publications. http://csli-publications.stanford.edu/HPSG/2003/.

de Saussure, Ferdinand. 1916a. *Cours de linguistique générale* (Bibliothèque Scientifique Payot). Paris: Payot. Edited by Charles Bally and Albert Sechehaye.

de Saussure, Ferdinand. 1916b. *Grundfragen der allgemeinen Sprachwissenschaft*. Berlin: Walter de Gruyter & Co. 2nd edition 1967.

Delmonte, Rodolfo. 1990. Semantic parsing with an LFG-based lexicon and conceptual representations. *Computers and the Humanities* 24(5–6). 461–488.

Demberg, Vera & Frank Keller. 2008. A psycholinguistically motivated version of TAG. In *Proceedings of the 9th International Workshop on Tree Adjoining Grammars and Related Formalisms TAG+9*, 25–32. Tübingen.

Demske, Ulrike. 2001. *Merkmale und Relationen: Diachrone Studien zur Nominalphrase des Deutschen* (Studia Linguistica Germanica 56). Berlin: Walter de Gruyter Verlag.

den Besten, Hans. 1983. On the interaction of root transformations and lexical deletive rules. In Werner Abraham (ed.), *On the formal syntax of the Westgermania: Papers from the 3rd Groningen Grammar Talks, Groningen, January 1981* (Linguistik Aktuell/Linguistics Today 3), 47–131. Amsterdam: John Benjamins Publishing Co.

den Besten, Hans. 1985. Some remarks on the Ergative Hypothesis. In Werner Abraham (ed.), *Erklärende Syntax des Deutschen* (Studien zur deutschen Grammatik 25), 53–74. Tübingen: originally Gunter Narr Verlag now Stauffenburg Verlag.

Deppermann, Arnulf. 2006. Construction Grammar – eine Grammatik für die Interaktion? In Arnulf Deppermann, Reinhard Fiehler & Thomas Spranz-Fogasy (eds.), *Grammatik und Interaktion*, 43–65. Radolfzell: Verlag für Gesprächsforschung.

Derbyshire, Desmond C. 1979. *Hixkaryana* (Lingua Descriptive Series 1). Amsterdam: North Holland.

Devlin, Keith. 1992. *Logic and information*. Cambridge: Cambridge University Press.

Dhonnchadha, E. Uí & Josef van Genabith. 2006. A part-of-speech tagger for Irish using finite-state morphology and Constraint Grammar disambiguation. In *Proceedings of lrec'06*, 2241–2244.

Diesing, Molly. 1992. *Indefinites*. Cambridge, MA/London, England: MIT Press.

Dione, Cheikh Mouhamadou Bamba. 2013. Handling Wolof Clitics in LFG. In Christine Meklenborg Salvesen & Hans Petter Helland (eds.), *Challenging clitics* (Linguistik Aktuell/Linguistics Today 206), 87–118. Amsterdam: John Benjamins Publishing Co.

Dione, Cheikh Mouhamadou Bamba. 2014. An LFG approach to Wolof cleft constructions. In Miriam Butt & Tracy Holloway King (eds.), *Proceedings of the LFG 2014 conference*, 157–176. Stanford, CA: CSLI Publications.

Dipper, Stefanie. 2003. *Implementing and documenting large-scale grammars – German LFG*: IMS, University of Stuttgart dissertation. Arbeitspapiere des Instituts für Maschinelle Sprachverarbeitung (AIMS), Volume 9, Number 1.

Donati, C. 2006. On *wh*-head-movement. In Lisa Lai-Shen Cheng & Norbert Corver (eds.), Wh*-movement: Moving on* (Current Studies in Linguistics 42), 21–46. Cambridge, MA: MIT Press.

Donohue, Cathryn & Ivan A. Sag. 1999. Domains in Warlpiri. In *Sixth International Conference on HPSG–Abstracts. 04–06 August 1999*, 101–106. Edinburgh.

Doran, Christine, Beth Ann Hockey, Anoop Sarkar, Bangalore Srinivas & Fei Xia. 2000. Evolution of the XTAG system. In Anne Abeillé & Owen Rambow (eds.), *Tree Adjoining Grammars: Formalisms, linguistic analysis and processing* (CSLI Lecture Notes 156), 371–403. Stanford, CA: CSLI Publications.

Dörre, Jochen & Michael Dorna. 1993. CUF: A formalism for linguistic knowledge representation. DYANA 2 deliverable R.1.2A IMS Stuttgart, Germany.

Dörre, Jochen & Roland Seiffert. 1991. A formalism for natural language — STUF. In Otthein Herzog & Claus-Rainer Rollinger (eds.), *Text understanding in LILOG* (Lecture Notes in Artificial Intelligence 546), 29–38. Berlin: Springer Verlag.

Dowty, David. 1997. Non-constituent coordination, wrapping, and Multimodal Categorial Grammars: Syntactic form as logical form. In Maria Luisa Dalla Chiara, Kees Doets, Daniele Mundici & Johan Van Benthem (eds.), *Structures and norms in science* (Synthese Library 260), 347–368. Springer.

Dowty, David R. 1978. Governed transformations as lexical rules in a Montague Grammar. *Linguistic Inquiry* 9(3). 393–426.

Dowty, David R. 1979. *Word meaning and Montague Grammar* (Synthese Language Library 7). Dordrecht: D. Reidel Publishing Company.

Dowty, David R. 1988. Type raising, functional composition, and nonconstituent coordination. In Richard Oehrle, Emmon Bach & Deirdre Wheeler (eds.), *Categorial Grammars and natural language structures*, 153–198. Dordrecht: D. Reidel Publishing Company.

Dowty, David R. 1989. On the semantic content of the notion 'thematic role'. In Gennaro Chierchia, Barbara H. Partee & Raymond Turner (eds.), *Properties, types and meaning*, vol. 2 (Studies in Linguistics and Philosophy), 69–130. Dordrecht: Kluwer Academic Publishers.

Dowty, David R. 1991. Thematic proto-roles and argument selection. *Language* 67(3). 547–619.

Dowty, David R. 2003. The dual analysis of adjuncts and complements in Categorial Grammar. In Ewald Lang, Claudia Maienborn & Cathrine Fabricius-Hansen (eds.), *Modifying adjuncts* (Interface Explorations 4), 33–66. Berlin: Mouton de Gruyter.

Dras, Mark, François Lareau, Benjamin Börschinger, Robert Dale, Yasaman Motazedi, Owen Rambow, Myfany Turpin & Morgan Ulinski. 2012. Complex predicates in Arrernte. In Miriam Butt & Tracy Holloway King (eds.), *Proceedings of the LFG 2012 conference*, 177–197. Stanford, CA: CSLI Publications.

Drellishak, Scott. 2009. *Widespread but not universal: Improving the typological coverage of the Grammar Matrix*: University of Washington Doctoral dissertation.

Drosdowski, Günther. 1984. *Duden: Grammatik der deutschen Gegenwartssprache*, vol. 4. Mannheim, Wien, Zürich: Dudenverlag 4th edn.

Drosdowski, Günther. 1995. *Duden: Die Grammatik*, vol. 4. Mannheim, Leipzig, Wien, Zürich: Dudenverlag 5th edn.

Dryer, Matthew S. 1992. The Greenbergian word order correlations. *Language* 68(1). 81–138.

Dryer, Matthew S. 1997. Are grammatical relations universal? In Joan Bybee, John Haiman & Sandra Thompson (eds.), *Essays on language function and language type: Dedicated to T. Givon*, 115–143. Amsterdam: John Benjamins Publishing Co.

Dryer, Matthew S. 2013a. Order of adposition and noun phrase. In Matthew S. Dryer & Martin Haspelmath (eds.), *The world atlas of language structures online*, Leipzig: Max Planck Institute for Evolutionary Anthropology. http://wals.info/chapter/85.

Dryer, Matthew S. 2013b. Order of object and verb. In Matthew S. Dryer & Martin Haspelmath (eds.), *The world atlas of language structures online*, Leipzig: Max Planck Institute for Evolutionary Anthropology. http://wals.info/chapter/83.

Dryer, Matthew S. 2013c. Order of subject, object and verb. In Matthew S. Dryer & Martin Haspelmath (eds.), *The world atlas of language structures online*, Leipzig: Max Planck Institute for Evolutionary Anthropology. http://wals.info/chapter/81.

Dürscheid, Christa. 1989. *Zur Vorfeldbesetzung in deutschen Verbzweit-Strukturen* (FOKUS 1). Trier: Wissenschaftlicher Verlag.

Dyvik, Helge, Paul Meurer & Victoria Rosén. 2005. LFG, Minimal Recursion Semantics and translation. Paper presented at the LFG conference 2005.

Egg, Markus. 1999. Derivation and resolution of ambiguities in *wieder*-sentences. In Paul J. E. Dekker (ed.), *Proceedings of the 12th Amsterdam Colloquium*, 109–114.

Eisele, Andreas & Jochen Dorre. 1986. A Lexical Functional Grammar system in Prolog. In Makoto Nagao (ed.), *Proceedings of COLING 86*, 551–553. University of Bonn: Association for Computational Linguistics.

Eisenberg, Peter. 1992. Platos Problem und die Lernbarkeit der Syntax. In Peter Suchsland (ed.), *Biologische und soziale Grundlagen der Sprache* (Linguistische Arbeiten 280), 371–378. Tübingen: Max Niemeyer Verlag.

Eisenberg, Peter. 1994a. German. In Ekkehard König & Johan van der Auwera (eds.), *The Germanic languages* (Routledge Language Family Descriptions), 349–387. London / New York: Routledge.

Eisenberg, Peter. 1994b. *Grundriß der deutschen Grammatik*. Stuttgart, Weimar: Verlag J. B. Metzler 3rd edn.

Eisenberg, Peter. 2004. *Grundriß der deutschen Grammatik*, vol. 2. Der Satz. Stuttgart, Weimar: Verlag J. B. Metzler 2nd edn.

Eisenberg, Peter, Jörg Peters, Peter Gallmann, Cathrine Fabricius-Hansen, Damaris Nübling, Irmhild Barz, Thomas A. Fritz & Reinhard Fiehler. 2005. *Duden: Die Grammatik*, vol. 4. Mannheim, Leipzig, Wien, Zürich: Dudenverlag 7th edn.

Ellefson, Michelle R. & Morten Christiansen. 2000. Subjacency constraints without Universal Grammar: Evidence from artificial language learning and connectionist modeling. In *Proceedings of the 22nd Annual Conference of the Cognitive Science Society*, 645–650. Mahwah, NJ: Lawrence Erlbaum Associates.

Elman, Jeffrey L. 1993. Learning and development in neural networks: The importance of starting small. *Cognition* 48(1). 71–99.

Elman, Jeffrey L., Elizabeth A. Bates, Mark H. Johnson, Annette Karmiloff-Smith, Domenico Parisi & Kim Plunkett. 1996. *Rethinking innateness: A connectionist perspective on development*. Cambridge, MA: Bradford Books/MIT Press.

Embick, David. 2004. On the structure of resultative participles in English. *Linguistic Inquiry* 35(3). 355–392.

Emirkanian, Louisette, Lyne Da Sylva & Lorne H. Bouchard. 1996. The implementation of a computational grammar of French using the Grammar Development Environment. In Jun-ichi Tsuji (ed.), *Proceedings of COLING-96. 16th International Conference on Computational Linguistics COLING96). Copenhagen, Denmark, August 5–9, 1996*, 1024–1027. Copenhagen, Denmark: Association for Computational Linguistics.

Engdahl, Elisabet & Enric Vallduví. 1996. Information packaging in HPSG. In Claire Grover & Enric Vallduví (eds.), *Edinburgh Working Papers in Cognitive Science, vol. 12: Studies in HPSG*, chap. 1, 1–32. Scotland: Centre for Cognitive Science, University of Edinburgh. ftp://ftp.cogsci.ed.ac.uk/pub/CCS-WPs/wp-12.ps.gz.

Engel, Ulrich. 1970. Regeln zur Wortstellung. Forschungsberichte des Instituts für deutsche Sprache 5 Institut für deutsche Sprache Mannheim.

Engel, Ulrich. 1977. *Syntax der deutschen Gegenwartssprache*, vol. 22 (Grundlagen der Germanistik). Berlin: Erich Schmidt Verlag.

Engel, Ulrich. 1996. Tesnière mißverstanden. In Gertrud Gréciano & Helmut Schumacher (eds.), *Lucien Tesnière – Syntaxe Structurale et Opèrations Mentales. Akten des deutsch-französischen Kolloquiums anläßlich der 100. Wiederkehr seines Geburtstages. Strasbourg 1993* (Linguistische Arbeiten 348), 53–61. Tübingen: Max Niemeyer Verlag.

Engel, Ulrich. 2014. Die dependenzielle Verbgrammatik (DVG). In Jörg Hagemann & Sven Staffeldt (eds.), *Syntaxtheorien: Analysen im Vergleich* (Stauffenburg Einführungen 28), 43–62. Tübingen: Stauffenburg Verlag.

Erbach, Gregor. 1995. ProFIT: Prolog with features, inheritance and templates. In Steven P. Abney & Erhard W. Hinrichs (eds.), *Proceedings of the Seventh Conference of the European Chapter of the Association for Computational Linguistics*, 180–187. Dublin: Association for Computational Linguistics.

Ernst, Thomas. 1992. The phrase structure of English negation. *The Linguistic Review* 9(2). 109–144.

Eroms, Hans-Werner. 1985. Eine reine Dependenzgrammatik für das Deutsche. *Deutsche Sprache* 13. 306–326.

Eroms, Hans-Werner. 1987. Passiv und Passivfunktionen im Rahmen einer Dependenzgrammatik. In Centre de Recherche en Linguistique Germanique (Nice) (ed.), *Das Passiv im Deutschen* (Linguistische Arbeiten 183), 73–95. Tübingen: Max Niemeyer Verlag.

Eroms, Hans-Werner. 2000. *Syntax der deutschen Sprache* (de Gruyter Studienbuch). Berlin: Walter de Gruyter Verlag.

Eroms, Hans-Werner & Hans Jürgen Heringer. 2003. Dependenz und lineare Ordnung. In Vilmos Ágel, Ludwig M. Eichinger, Hans Werner Eroms, Peter Hellwig, Hans Jürgen Heringer & Henning Lobin (eds.), *Dependenz und Valenz / Dependency and valency: Ein internationales Handbuch der zeitgenössischen Forschung / An international handbook of contemporary research*, vol. 25.1 (Handbücher zur Sprach- und Kommunikationswissenschaft), 247–263. Berlin: Walter de Gruyter.

Eroms, Hans-Werner, Gerhard Stickel & Gisela Zifonun (eds.). 1997. *Grammatik der deutschen Sprache*, vol. 7 (Schriften des Instituts für deutsche Sprache). Berlin: Walter de Gruyter.

Erteschik-Shir, Nomi. 1973. *On the nature of island constraints*. Cambridge, MA: MIT dissertation.

Erteschik-Shir, Nomi. 1981. More on extractability from quasi-NPs. *Linguistic Inquiry* 12(4). 665–670.

Erteschik-Shir, Nomi & Shalom Lappin. 1979. Dominance and the functional explanation of island phenomena. *Theoretical Linguistics* 6(1–3). 41–86.

Estigarribia, Bruno. 2009. Facilitation by variation: Right-to-left learning of English yes/no questions. *Cognitive Science* 34(1). 68–93.

Evans, Nicholas & Stephen C. Levinson. 2009a. The myth of language universals: Language diversity and its importance for cognitive science. *The Behavioral and Brain Sciences* 32(5). 429–448.

Evans, Nicholas & Stephen C. Levinson. 2009b. With diversity in mind: Freeing the language sciences from Universal Grammar. *The Behavioral and Brain Sciences* 32(5). 472–492.

Evans, Roger. 1985. ProGram: A development tool for GPSG grammars. *Linguistics* 23(2). 213–244.

Everett, Daniel L. 2005. Cultural constraints on grammar and cognition in Pirahã. *Current Anthropology* 46(4). 621–646.

Everett, Daniel L. 2009. Pirahã culture and grammar: A response to some criticisms. *Language* 85(2). 405–442.

Evers, Arnold. 1975. *The transformational cycle in Dutch and German*: University of Utrecht dissertation.

Faaß, Gertrud. 2010. *A morphosyntactic description of Northern Sotho as a basis for an automated translation from Northern Sotho into English.* Pretoria, South Africa: University of Pretoria dissertation. http://hdl.handle.net/2263/28569.

Fabregas, Antonio, Tom Stroik & Michael Putnam. 2016. Is simplest merge too simple? Ms. Penn State University.

Falk, Yehuda N. 1984. The English auxiliary system: A Lexical-Functional analysis. *Language* 60(3). 483–509.

Fan, Zhenzhen, Sanghoun Song & Francis Bond. 2015. An HPSG-based shared-grammar for the Chinese languages: ZHONG [|]. In Emily M. Bender, Lori Levin, Stefan Müller, Yannick Parmentier & Aarne Ranta (eds.), *Proceedings of the Grammar Engineering Across Frameworks (GEAF) Workshop*, 17–24. The Association for Computational Linguistics.

Fang, Ji & Tracy Holloway King. 2007. An LFG Chinese grammar for machine use. In Tracy Holloway King & Emily M. Bender (eds.), *Grammar Engineering across Frameworks 2007* (Studies in Computational Linguistics ONLINE), 144–160. Stanford, CA: CSLI Publications. http://csli-publications.stanford.edu/GEAF/2007/.

Fanselow, Gisbert. 1981. *Zur Syntax und Semantik der Nominalkomposition* (Linguistische Arbeiten 107). Tübingen: Max Niemeyer Verlag.

Fanselow, Gisbert. 1987. *Konfigurationalität* (Studien zur deutschen Grammatik 29). Tübingen: originally Gunter Narr Verlag now Stauffenburg Verlag.

Fanselow, Gisbert. 1988. Aufspaltung von NPn und das Problem der ‚freien' Wortstellung. *Linguistische Berichte* 114. 91–113.

Fanselow, Gisbert. 1990. Scrambling as NP-movement. In Günther Grewendorf & Wolfgang Sternefeld (eds.), *Scrambling and Barriers* (Linguistik Aktuell/Linguistics Today 5), 113–140. Amsterdam: John Benjamins Publishing Co.

Fanselow, Gisbert. 1992a. „Ergative" Verben und die Struktur des deutschen Mittelfelds. In Ludger Hoffmann (ed.), *Deutsche Syntax: Ansichten und Aussichten* (Institut für deutsche Sprache, Jahrbuch 1991), 276–303. Berlin: de Gruyter.

Fanselow, Gisbert. 1992b. Zur biologischen Autonomie der Grammatik. In Peter Suchsland (ed.), *Biologische und soziale Grundlagen der Sprache* (Linguistische Arbeiten 280), 335–356. Tübingen: Max Niemeyer Verlag.

Fanselow, Gisbert. 1993. Die Rückkehr der Basisgenerierer. *Groninger Arbeiten zur Germanistischen Linguistik* 36. 1–74.

Fanselow, Gisbert. 2000a. Does constituent length predict German word order in the Middle Field? In Josef Bayer & Christine Römer (eds.), *Von der Philologie zur Grammatiktheorie: Peter Suchsland zum 65. Geburtstag*, 63–77. Tübingen: Max Niemeyer Verlag.

Fanselow, Gisbert. 2000b. Optimal exceptions. In Barbara Stiebels & Dieter Wunderlich (eds.), *The lexicon in focus* (studia grammatica 45), 173–209. Berlin: Akademie Verlag.

Fanselow, Gisbert. 2001. Features, θ-roles, and free constituent order. *Linguistic Inquiry* 32(3). 405–437.

Fanselow, Gisbert. 2002. Against remnant VP-movement. In Artemis Alexiadou, Elena Anagnostopoulou, Sjef Barbiers & Hans-Martin Gärtner (eds.), *Dimensions of movement: From features to remnants* (Linguistik Aktuell/Linguistics Today 48), 91–127. Amsterdam: John Benjamins Publishing Co.

Fanselow, Gisbert. 2003a. Free constituent order: A Minimalist interface account. *Folia Linguistica* 37(1–2). 191–231.

Fanselow, Gisbert. 2003b. Münchhausen-style head movement and the analysis of verb second. In Anoop Mahajan (ed.), *Proceedings of the workshop on head movement* (UCLA Working Papers in Linguistics 10), Los Angeles: UCLA, Linguistics Department.

Fanselow, Gisbert. 2003c. Zur Generierung der Abfolge der Satzglieder im Deutschen. *Neue Beiträge zur Germanistik* 112. 3–47.

Fanselow, Gisbert. 2004a. Cyclic phonology-syntax-interaction: PPT Movement in German (and other languages). In Shinichiro Ishihara, Michaela Schmitz & Anne Schwarz (eds.), *Interdisciplinary studies on information structure* (Working Papers of the SFB 632 1), 1–42. Potsdam: Universitätsverlag.

Fanselow, Gisbert. 2004b. Fakten, Fakten, Fakten! *Linguistische Berichte* 200. 481–493.

Fanselow, Gisbert. 2004c. Münchhausen-style head movement and the analysis of verb second. In Ralf Vogel (ed.), *Three papers on German verb movement* (Linguistics in Potsdam 22), 9–49. Universität Potsdam.

Fanselow, Gisbert. 2006. On pure syntax (uncontaminated by information structure). In Patrick Brandt & Eric Fuss (eds.), *Form, structure and grammar: A festschrift presented to Günther Grewendorf on occasion of his 60th birthday* (Studia grammatica 63), 137–157. Berlin: Akademie Verlag.

Fanselow, Gisbert. 2009. Die (generative) Syntax in den Zeiten der Empiriediskussion. *Zeitschrift für Sprachwissenschaft* 28(1). 133–139.

Fanselow, Gisbert & Sascha W. Felix. 1987. *Sprachtheorie 2. Die Rektions- und Bindungstheorie* (UTB für Wissenschaft: Uni-Taschenbücher 1442). Tübingen: A. Francke Verlag GmbH.

Fanselow, Gisbert, Matthias Schlesewsky, Damir Cavar & Reinhold Kliegl. 1999. Optimal parsing, syntactic parsing preferences, and Optimality Theory. Rutgers Optimality Archive (ROA) 367 Universität Potsdam. http://roa.rutgers.edu/view.php3?roa=367.

Feldhaus, Anke. 1997. Eine HPSG-Analyse ausgewählter Phänomene des deutschen *w*-Fragesatzes. Working Papers of the Institute for Logic and Linguistics 27 Institute for Logic and Linguistics IBM Scientific Center Heidelberg.

Feldman, Jerome. 1972. Some decidability results on grammatical inference and complexity. *Information and Control* 20(3). 244–262.

Fillmore, Charles J. 1968. The case for case. In Emmon Bach & Robert T. Harms (eds.), *Universals of linguistic theory*, 1–88. New York: Holt, Rinehart, and Winston.

Fillmore, Charles J. 1971. Plädoyer für Kasus. In Werner Abraham (ed.), *Kasustheorie* (Schwerpunkte Linguistik und Kommunikationswissenschaft 2), 1–118. Frankfurt/Main: Athenäum.

Fillmore, Charles J. 1988. The mechanisms of "Construction Grammar". In Shelley Axmaker, Annie Jaisser & Helen Singmaster (eds.), *Proceedings of the 14th Annual Meeting of the Berkeley Linguistics Society*, 35–55. Berkeley, CA: Berkeley Linguistics Society.

Fillmore, Charles J. 1999. Inversion and Constructional inheritance. In Gert Webelhuth, Jean-Pierre Koenig & Andreas Kathol (eds.), *Lexical and Constructional aspects of linguistic explanation* (Studies in Constraint-Based Lexicalism 1), 113–128. Stanford, CA: CSLI Publications.

Fillmore, Charles J., Paul Kay & Mary Catherine O'Connor. 1988. Regularity and idiomaticity in grammatical constructions: The case of *let alone*. *Language* 64(3). 501–538.

Fillmore, Charles J., Russell R. Lee-Goldmann & Russell Rhomieux. 2012. The FrameNet constructicon. In Hans C. Boas & Ivan A. Sag (eds.), *Sign-based Construction Grammar* (CSLI Lecture Notes 193), 309–372. Stanford, CA: CSLI Publications.

Fischer, Ingrid & Martina Keil. 1996. Parsing decomposable idioms. In Jun-ichi Tsuji (ed.), *Proceedings of COLING-96. 16th International Conference on Computational Linguistics COLING96). Copenhagen, Denmark, August 5–9, 1996*, 388–393. Copenhagen, Denmark: Association for Computational Linguistics.

Fischer, Kerstin & Anatol Stefanowitsch (eds.). 2006. *Konstruktionsgrammatik: Von der Anwendung zur Theorie* (Stauffenburg Linguistik 40). Tübingen: Stauffenburg Verlag.

Fisher, Simon E. & Gary F. Marcus. 2005. The eloquent ape: Genes, brains and the evolution of language. *Nature Reviews Genetics* 7(1). 9–20.

Fisher, Simon E., Faraneh Vargha-Khadem, Kate E. Watkins, Anthony P. Monaco & Marcus E. Pembrey. 1998. Localisation of a gene implicated in a severe speech and language disorder. *Nature Genetics* 18(2). 168–170.

Fitch, W. Tecumseh. 2010. Three meanings of "recursion": Key distinctions for biolinguistics. In Richard K. Larson, Viviane Déprez & Hiroko Yamakido (eds.), *The evolution of human language: Biolinguistic perspectives* (Approaches to the Evolution of Language 2), 73–90. Cambridge, UK: Cambridge University Press.

Fitch, W. Tecumseh, Marc D. Hauser & Noam Chomsky. 2005. The evolution of the language faculty: Clarifications and implications. *Cognition* 97(2). 179–210.

Flickinger, Daniel P. 1983. Lexical heads and phrasal gaps. In *Proceedings of the West Coast Conference on Formal Linguistics*, vol. 2, Stanford University Linguistics Dept.

Flickinger, Daniel P. 1987. *Lexical rules in the hierarchical lexicon*: Stanford University dissertation.

Flickinger, Daniel P. 2000. On building a more efficient grammar by exploiting types. *Natural Language Engineering* 6(1). 15–28.

Flickinger, Daniel P. 2008. Transparent heads. In Stefan Müller (ed.), *Proceedings of the 15th International Conference on Head-Driven Phrase Structure Grammar*, 87–94. Stanford, CA: CSLI Publications. http://csli-publications.stanford.edu/HPSG/2008/abstr-flickinger.shtml.

Flickinger, Daniel P. & Emily M. Bender. 2003. Compositional semantics in a multilingual grammar resource. In Emily M. Bender, Daniel P. Flickinger, Frederik Fouvry & Melanie Siegel (eds.), *Proceedings of the ESSLLI 2003 Workshop "Ideas and Strategies for Multilingual Grammar Development"*, 33–42. Vienna, Austria.

Flickinger, Daniel P., Ann Copestake & Ivan A. Sag. 2000. HPSG analysis of English. In Wolfgang Wahlster (ed.), *Verbmobil: Foundations of speech-to-speech translation* (Artificial Intelligence), 254–263. Berlin: Springer Verlag.

Flickinger, Daniel P., Carl J. Pollard & Thomas Wasow. 1985. Structure-sharing in lexical representation. In William C. Mann (ed.), *Proceedings of the Twenty-Third Annual Meeting of the Association for Computational Linguistics*, 262–267. Chicago, IL: Association for Computational Linguistics.

Fodor, Janet Dean. 1998a. Parsing to learn. *Journal of Psycholinguistic Research* 27(3). 339–374.

Fodor, Janet Dean. 1998b. Unambiguous triggers. *Linguistic Inquiry* 29(1). 1–36.

Fodor, Janet Dean. 2001. Parameters and the periphery: Reflections on *syntactic nuts*. *Journal of Linguistics* 37. 367–392.

Fodor, Jerry A., Thomas G. Bever & Merrill F. Garrett. 1974. *The psychology of language: An introduction to psycholinguistics and Generative Grammar*. New York: McGraw-Hill Book Co.

Fokkens, Antske. 2011. Metagrammar engineering: Towards systematic exploration of implemented grammars. In *Proceedings of the 49th Annual Meeting of the Association for Computational Linguistics: Human Language Technologies*, 1066–1076. Portland, Oregon, USA: Association for Computational Linguistics. http://www.aclweb.org/anthology/P11-1107.

Fokkens, Antske, Laurie Poulson & Emily M. Bender. 2009. Inflectional morphology in Turkish VP coordination. In Stefan Müller (ed.), *Proceedings of the 16th International Conference on Head-Driven Phrase Structure Grammar, University of Göttingen, Germany*, 110–130. Stanford, CA: CSLI Publications.

Fong, Sandiway. 1991. *Computational properties of principle-based grammatical theories*: MIT Artificial Intelligence Lab dissertation.

Fong, Sandiway. 2014. Unification and efficient computation in the Minimalist Program. In L. Francis & L. Laurent (eds.), *Language and recursion*, 129–138. Berlin: Springer Verlag.

Fong, Sandiway & Jason Ginsburg. 2012. Computation with doubling constituents: Pronouns and antecedents in Phase Theory. In Anna Maria Di Sciullo (ed.), *To-*

wards a Biolinguistic understanding of grammar: Essays on interfaces (Linguistik Aktuell/Linguistics Today 194), 303–338. Amsterdam: John Benjamins Publishing Co.

Fordham, Andrew & Matthew Walter Crocker. 1994. Parsing with principles and probabilities. In Judith L. Klavans Philip Resnik (ed.), *The balancing act: Combining symbolic and statistical approaches to language*, Las Cruces, New Mexico, USA: Association for Computational Linguistics.

Forst, Martin. 2006. COMP in (parallel) grammar writing. In Miriam Butt & Tracy Holloway King (eds.), *Proceedings of the LFG 2006 conference*, Stanford, CA: CSLI Publications. http://csli-publications.stanford.edu/LFG/11/lfg06forst.pdf.

Forst, Martin & Christian Rohrer. 2009. Problems of German VP coordination. In Miriam Butt & Tracy Holloway King (eds.), *Proceedings of the LFG 2009 conference*, 297–316. Stanford, CA: CSLI Publications. http://csli-publications.stanford.edu/LFG/14/.

Fortmann, Christian. 1996. *Konstituentenbewegung in der DP-Struktur: Zur funktionalen Analyse der Nominalphrase im Deutschen* (Linguistische Arbeiten 347). Tübingen: Max Niemeyer Verlag.

Fourquet, Jean. 1957. Review of: Heinz Anstock: Deutsche Syntax – Lehr- und Übungsbuch. *Wirkendes Wort* 8. 120–122.

Fourquet, Jean. 1970. *Prolegomena zu einer deutschen Grammatik* (Sprache der Gegenwart – Schriften des Instituts für deutsche Sprache in Mannheim 7). Düsseldorf: Pädagogischer Verlag Schwann.

Fouvry, Frederik. 2003. Lexicon acquisition with a large-coverage unification-based grammar. In *Proceedings of EACL 03, 10th Conference of the European Chapter of the Association for Computational Linguistics, research notes and demos, April 12–17, 2003, Budapest, Hungary*, 87–90.

Fraj, Fériel Ben, Chiraz Zribi & Mohamed Ben Ahmed. 2008. ArabTAG: A Tree Adjoining Grammar for Arabic syntactic structures. In *Proceedings of the International Arab Conference on Information Technology*, Sfax, Tunisia.

Frank, Anette. 1994. Verb second by lexical rule or by underspecification. Arbeitspapiere des SFB 340 No. 43 IBM Deutschland GmbH Heidelberg. ftp://ftp.ims.uni-stuttgart.de/pub/papers/anette/v2-usp.ps.gz.

Frank, Anette. 1996. Eine LFG-Grammatik des Französischen. In *Deutsche und französische Syntax im Formalismus der LFG* (Linguistische Arbeiten 344), 97–244. Tübingen: Max Niemeyer Verlag.

Frank, Anette. 2006. (Discourse-) functional analysis of asymmetric coordination. In Miriam Butt, Mary Dalrymple & Tracy Holloway King (eds.), *Intelligent linguistic architectures: Variations on themes by Ronald M. Kaplan*, 259–285. Stanford, CA: CSLI Publications.

Frank, Anette & Uwe Reyle. 1995. Principle based semantics for HPSG. In Steven P. Abney & Erhard W. Hinrichs (eds.), *Proceedings of the Seventh Conference of the European Chapter of the Association for Computational Linguistics*, 9–16. Dublin: Association for Computational Linguistics.

Frank, Anette & Annie Zaenen. 2002. Tense in LFG: Syntax and morphology. In Hans Kamp & Uwe Reyle (eds.), *How we say when it happens: Contributions to the theory of temporal reference in natural language*, 17–52. Tübingen: Max Niemeyer Verlag. Reprint as: Frank & Zaenen (2004).

Frank, Anette & Annie Zaenen. 2004. Tense in LFG: Syntax and morphology. In Louisa Sadler & Andrew Spencer (eds.), *Projecting morphology*, 23–66. Stanford, CA: CSLI Publications.

Frank, Robert. 2002. *Phrase structure composition and syntactic dependencies* (Current Studies in Linguistics 38). Cambridge, MA/London: MIT Press.

Franks, Steven. 1995. *Parameters in Slavic morphosyntax.* New York, Oxford: Oxford University Press.

Frazier, Lyn. 1985. Syntactic complexity. In David R. Dowty, Lauri Karttunen & Arnold M. Zwicky (eds.), *Natural language processing*, 129–189. Cambridge, UK: Cambridge University Press.

Frazier, Lyn & Charles Clifton. 1996. *Construal.* Cambridge, MA: MIT Press.

Freidin, Robert. 1975. The analysis of passives. *Language* 51(2). 384–405.

Freidin, Robert. 1997. Review article: The Minimalist Program. *Language* 73(3). 571–582.

Freidin, Robert. 2009. A note on methodology in linguistics. *The Behavioral and Brain Sciences* 32(5). 454–455.

Freudenthal, Daniel, Julian M. Pine, Javier Aguado-Orea & Fernand Gobet. 2007. Modeling the developmental patterning of finiteness marking in English, Dutch, German, and Spanish using MOSAIC. *Cognitive Science* 31(2). 311–341.

Freudenthal, Daniel, Julian M. Pine & Fernand Gobet. 2006. Modeling the development of children's use of optional infinitives in Dutch and English using MOSAIC. *Cognitive Science* 30(2). 277–310.

Freudenthal, Daniel, Julian M. Pine & Fernand Gobet. 2009. Simulating the referential properties of Dutch, German, and English root infinitives in MOSAIC. *Language Learning and Development* 5(1). 1–29.

Frey, Werner. 1993. *Syntaktische Bedingungen für die semantische Interpretation: Über Bindung, implizite Argumente und Skopus* (studia grammatica 35). Berlin: Akademie Verlag.

Frey, Werner. 2000. Über die syntaktische Position der Satztopiks im Deutschen. In Ewald Lang, Marzena Rochon, Kerstin Schwabe & Oliver Teuber (eds.), *Issues on topics* (ZAS Papers in Linguistics 20), 137–172. Berlin: ZAS, Humboldt-Universität zu Berlin.

Frey, Werner. 2001. About the whereabouts of indefinites. *Theoretical Linguistics* 27(2/3). 137–161. DOI:10.1515/thli.2001.27.2-3.137. Special Issue: NP Interpretation and Information Structure, Edited by Klaus von Heusinger and Kerstin Schwabe.

Frey, Werner. 2004a. The grammar-pragmatics interface and the German prefield. Forschungsprogramm Sprache und Pragmatik 52 Germanistisches Institut der Universität Lund.

Frey, Werner. 2004b. A medial topic position for German. *Linguistische Berichte* 198. 153–190.

Frey, Werner. 2005. Pragmatic properties of certain German and English left peripheral constructions. *Linguistics* 43(1). 89–129.

Frey, Werner & Hans-Martin Gärtner. 2002. On the treatment of scrambling and adjunction in Minimalist Grammars. In Gerhard Jäger, Paola Monachesi, Gerald Penn & Shuly Wintner (eds.), *Proceedings of Formal Grammar 2002*, 41–52. Trento.

Frey, Werner & Uwe Reyle. 1983a. Lexical Functional Grammar und Diskursrepräsentationstheorie als Grundlagen eines sprachverarbeitenden Systems. *Linguistische Berichte* 88. 79–100.

Frey, Werner & Uwe Reyle. 1983b. A Prolog implementation of Lexical Functional Grammar as a base for a natural language processing system. In Antonio Zampolli (ed.), *First Conference of the European Chapter of the Association for Computational Linguistics: Proceedings of the conference*, 52–57. Pisa, Italy: Association for Computational Linguistics. http://aclweb.org/anthology/E/E83/.

Fried, Mirjam. 2013. Principles of constructional change. In Thomas Hoffmann & Graeme Trousdale (eds.), *The Oxford handbook of Construction Grammar* (Oxford Handbooks), 419–437. Oxford: Oxford University Press.

Fried, Mirjam. 2015. Construction Grammar. In Tibor Kiss & Artemis Alexiadou (eds.), *Syntax – theory and analysis: An international handbook*, vol. 42 (Handbooks of Linguistics and Communication Science), 974–1003. Berlin: Mouton de Gruyter 2nd edn.

Friederici, Angela D. 2009. Pathways to language: Fiber tracts in the human brain. *Trends in Cognitive Sciences* 13(4). 175–181.

Friedman, Joyce. 1969. Applications of a computer system for Transformational Grammar. In Research Group for Quantitative Linguistics (ed.), *Proceedings of COLING 69*, 1–27.

Friedman, Joyce, Thomas H. Bredt, Robert W. Doran, Bary W. Pollack & Theodore S. Martner. 1971. *A computer model of Transformational Grammar* (Mathematical Linguistics and Automatic Language Processing 9). New York: Elsevier.

Fries, Norbert. 1988. Über das Null-Topik im Deutschen. Forschungsprogramm Sprache und Pragmatik 3 Germanistisches Institut der Universität Lund.

Fukui, Naoki & Margaret Speas. 1986. Specifiers and projection. In N. Fukui, T. R. Rapoport & E. Sagey (eds.), *Papers in theoretical linguistics* (MIT Working Papers 8), 128–172. Cambridge, MA: MIT.

Gaifman, Haim. 1965. Dependency systems and phrase-structure systems. *Information and Control* 8. 304–397.

Gallmann, Peter. 2003. Grundlagen der deutschen Grammatik. Lecture notes Friedrich-Schiller-Universität Jena. http://www.syntax-theorie.de.

Gardner, R. Allen. 1957. Probability-learning with two and three choices. *The American Journal of Psychology* 70(2). 174–185.

Gärtner, Hans-Martin & Jens Michaelis. 2007. Some remarks on locality conditions and Minimalist Grammars. In Uli Sauerland & Hans-Martin Gärtner (eds.), *Interfaces + recursion = language? Chomsky's Minimalism and the view from syntax-semantics* (Studies in Generative Grammar 89), 161–195. Berlin: Mouton de Gruyter.

Gärtner, Hans-Martin & Markus Steinbach. 1997. Anmerkungen zur Vorfeldphobie pronominaler Elemente. In Franz-Josef d'Avis & Uli Lutz (eds.), *Zur Satzstruktur im*

Deutschen (Arbeitspapiere des SFB 340 No. 90), 1–30. Tübingen: Eberhard-Karls-Universität Tübingen.

Gazdar, Gerald. 1981a. On syntactic categories. *Philosophical Transactions of the Royal Society of London. Series B, Biological Sciences* 295(1077). 267–283.

Gazdar, Gerald. 1981b. Unbounded dependencies and coordinate structure. *Linguistic Inquiry* 12. 155–184.

Gazdar, Gerald, Ewan Klein, Geoffrey K. Pullum & Ivan A. Sag. 1985. *Generalized Phrase Structure Grammar*. Cambridge, MA: Harvard University Press.

Gazdar, Gerald, Geoffrey K. Pullum, Bob Carpenter, Ewan Klein, Thomas E. Hukari & Robert D. Levine. 1988. Category structures. *Computational Linguistics* 14(1). 1–19.

Geach, Peter Thomas. 1970. A program for syntax. *Synthese* 22. 3–17.

Geißler, Stefan & Tibor Kiss. 1994. Erläuterungen zur Umsetzung einer HPSG im Basisformalismus STUF III. Tech. Rep. 19 IBM Informationssysteme GmbH – Institut für Logik und Linguistik (Verbundvorhaben Verbmobil) Heidelberg.

Gerdes, Kim. 2002a. DTAG? In *Proceedings of the Sixth International Workshop on Tree Adjoining Grammar and Related Frameworks (TAG+6)*, 242–251. Universitá di Venezia.

Gerdes, Kim. 2002b. *Topologie et grammaires formelles de l'allemand*: Ecole doctorale Science du langage, UFR de linguistique, Université Paris 7 dissertation.

Gerdes, Kim & Sylvain Kahane. 2001. Word order in German: A formal Dependency Grammar using a topological hierarchy. In *Proceedings of the 39th Annual Meeting on Association for Computational Linguistics*, 220–227. Stroudsburg, PA, USA: Association for Computational Linguistics. DOI:10.3115/1073012.1073041.

Gerken, LouAnn. 1991. The metrical basis for children's subjectless sentences. *Journal of Memory and Language* 30. 431–451.

Gibson, Edward. 1998. Linguistic complexity: Locality of syntactic dependencies. *Cognition* 68(1). 1–76.

Gibson, Edward & James Thomas. 1999. Memory limitations and structural forgetting: The perception of complex ungrammatical sentences as grammatical. *Language and Cognitive Processes* 14(3). 225–248.

Gibson, Edward & Kenneth Wexler. 1994. Triggers. *Linguistic Inquiry* 25(3). 407–454.

Ginzburg, Jonathan & Ivan A. Sag. 2000. *Interrogative investigations: The form, meaning, and use of English interrogatives* (CSLI Lecture Notes 123). Stanford, CA: CSLI Publications.

Gold, Mark E. 1967. Language identification in the limit. *Information and Control* 10(5). 447–474.

Goldberg, Adele E. 1995. *Constructions: A Construction Grammar approach to argument structure* (Cognitive Theory of Language and Culture). Chicago/London: The University of Chicago Press.

Goldberg, Adele E. 2003a. Constructions: A new theoretical approach to language. *Trends in Cognitive Sciences* 7(5). 219–224.

Goldberg, Adele E. 2003b. Words by default: The Persian Complex Predicate Construction. In Elaine J. Francis & Laura A. Michaelis (eds.), *Mismatch: Form-function incon-*

gruity and the architecture of grammar (CSLI Lecture Notes 163), 117–146. Stanford, CA: CSLI Publications.

Goldberg, Adele E. 2006. *Constructions at work: The nature of generalization in language* (Oxford Linguistics). Oxford, New York: Oxford University Press.

Goldberg, Adele E. 2009. Constructions work. [response]. *Cognitive Linguistics* 20(1). 201–224.

Goldberg, Adele E. 2013a. Argument structure Constructions vs. lexical rules or derivational verb templates. *Mind and Language* 28(4). 435–465.

Goldberg, Adele E. 2013b. Explanation and Constructions: Response to Adger. *Mind and Language* 28(4). 479–491.

Goldberg, Adele E. 2014. Fitting a slim dime between the verb template and argument structure construction approaches. *Theoretical Linguistics* 40(1–2). 113–135.

Goldberg, Adele E., Devin Casenhiser & Nitya Sethuraman. 2004. Learning argument structure generalizations. *Cognitive Linguistics* 15(3). 289–316.

Goldberg, Adele E. & Ray S. Jackendoff. 2004. The English resultative as a family of Constructions. *Language* 80(3). 532–568.

Gopnik, Myrna & Martha B. Cargo. 1991. Familial aggregation of a developmental language disorder. *Cognition* 39(1). 1–50.

Gordon, Peter. 1986. Level ordering in lexical development. *Cognition* 21(2). 73–93.

Gosch, Angela, Gabriele Städing & Rainer Pankau. 1994. Linguistic abilities in children with Williams-Beuren Syndrome. *American Journal of Medical Genetics* 52(3). 291–296.

Götz, Thilo, Walt Detmar Meurers & Dale Gerdemann. 1997. The ConTroll manual: (ConTroll v.1.0 beta, XTroll v.5.0 beta). User's manual Seminar für Sprachwissenschaft Universität Tübingen. http://www.sfs.uni-tuebingen.de/controll/code.html.

Grebe, Paul & Helmut Gipper. 1966. *Duden: Grammatik der deutschen Gegenwartssprache*, vol. 4. Mannheim, Wien, Zürich: Dudenverlag 2nd edn.

Green, Georgia M. 2011. Modelling grammar growth: Universal Grammar without innate principles or parameters. In Robert D. Borsley & Kersti Börjars (eds.), *Non-transformational syntax: Formal and explicit models of grammar: A guide to current models*, 378–403. Oxford, UK/Cambridge, MA: Blackwell Publishing Ltd.

Grewendorf, Günther. 1983. Reflexivierungen in deutschen A.c.I.-Konstruktionen – kein transformationsgrammatisches Dilemma mehr. *Groninger Arbeiten zur Germanistischen Linguistik* 23. 120–196.

Grewendorf, Günther. 1985. Anaphern bei Objekt-Koreferenz im Deutschen: Ein Problem für die Rektions-Bindungs-Theorie. In Werner Abraham (ed.), *Erklärende Syntax des Deutschen* (Studien zur deutschen Grammatik 25), 137–171. Tübingen: originally Gunter Narr Verlag now Stauffenburg Verlag.

Grewendorf, Günther. 1987. Kohärenz und Restrukturierung: Zu verbalen Komplexen im Deutschen. In Brigitte Asbach-Schnitker & Johannes Roggenhofer (eds.), *Neuere Forschungen zur Wortbildung und Histographie: Festgabe für Herbert E. Brekle zum 50. Geburtstag* (Tübinger Beiträge zur Linguistik 284), 123–144. Tübingen: Gunter Narr Verlag.

Grewendorf, Günther. 1988. *Aspekte der deutschen Syntax: Eine Rektions-Bindungs-Analyse* (Studien zur deutschen Grammatik 33). Tübingen: originally Gunter Narr Verlag now Stauffenburg Verlag.

Grewendorf, Günther. 1989. *Ergativity in German* (Studies in Generative Grammar 35). Dordrecht: Foris Publications.

Grewendorf, Günther. 1993. German: A grammatical sketch. In Joachim Jacobs, Arnim von Stechow, Wolfgang Sternefeld & Theo Vennemann (eds.), *Syntax – Ein internationales Handbuch zeitgenössischer Forschung*, vol. 9.2 (Handbücher zur Sprach- und Kommunikationswissenschaft), 1288–1319. Berlin: Walter de Gruyter Verlag.

Grewendorf, Günther. 2002. *Minimalistische Syntax* (UTB für Wissenschaft: Uni-Taschenbücher 2313). Tübingen, Basel: A. Francke Verlag GmbH.

Grewendorf, Güther. 2009. The left clausal periphery: Clitic left dislocation in Italian and left dislocation in German. In Benjamin Shear, Philippa Helen Cook, Werner Frey & Claudia Maienborn (eds.), *Dislocated elements in discourse: Syntactic, semantic, and pragmatic perspectives* (Routledge Studies in Germanic Linguistics), 49–94. New York: Routledge.

Grimshaw, Jane. 1986. Subjacency and the S/S′ Parameter. *Linguistic Inquiry* 17(2). 364–369.

Grimshaw, Jane. 1997. Projections, heads, and optimality. *Linguistic Inquiry* 28. 373–422.

Grinberg, Dennis, John D. Lafferty & Daniel Dominic Sleator. 1995. A robust parsing algorithm for Link Grammars. In *Proceedings of the Fourth International Workshop on Parsing Technologies*, http://arxiv.org/abs/cmp-lg/9508003. Also as Carnegie Mellon University Computer Science Technical Report CMU-CS-95-125.

Groos, Anneke & Henk van Riemsdijk. 1981. Matching effects in free relatives: A parameter of core grammar. In A. Belletti, L. Brandi & L. Rizzi (eds.), *Theory of markedness in Generative Grammar*, 171–216. Pisa: Scuola Normale Superiore.

Groß, Thomas M. & Timothy Osborne. 2009. Toward a practical Dependency Grammar theory of discontinuities. *SKY Journal of Linguistics* 22. 43–90.

Groß, Thomas Michael. 2003. Dependency Grammar's limits – and ways of extending them. In Vilmos Ágel, Ludwig M. Eichinger, Hans Werner Eroms, Peter Hellwig, Hans Jürgen Heringer & Henning Lobin (eds.), *Dependenz und Valenz / Dependency and valency: Ein internationales Handbuch der zeitgenössischen Forschung / An international handbook of contemporary research*, vol. 25.1 (Handbücher zur Sprach- und Kommunikationswissenschaft), 331–351. Berlin: Walter de Gruyter.

Grosu, Alexander. 1973. On the status of the so-called Right Roof Constraint. *Language* 49(2). 294–311.

Grover, Claire, John Carroll & Ted J. Briscoe. 1993. The Alvey Natural Language Tools grammar (4th release). Technical Report 284 Computer Laboratory, Cambridge University, UK.

Grubačić, Emilija. 1965. *Untersuchungen zur Frage der Wortstellung in der deutschen Prosadichtung der letzten Jahrzehnte.* Zagreb: Philosophische Fakultät dissertation.

Gruber, Jeffrey. 1965. *Studies in lexical relations*: MIT dissertation.

Gunji, Takao. 1986. Subcategorization and word order. In William J. Poser (ed.), *Papers from the Second International Workshop on Japanese Syntax*, 1–21. Stanford, CA: CSLI Publications.

Günther, Carsten, Claudia Maienborn & Andrea Schopp. 1999. The processing of information structure. In Peter Bosch & Rob van der Sandt (eds.), *Focus: Linguistic, cognitive, and computational perspectives* (Studies in Natural Language Processing), 18–42. Cambridge, UK: Cambridge University Press. Rev. papers orig. presented at a conference held 1994, Schloss Wolfsbrunnen, Germany.

Guo, Yuqing, Haifeng Wang & Josef van Genabith. 2007. Recovering non-local dependencies for Chinese. In *Proceedings of the Joint Conference on Empirical Methods in Natural Language Processing and Natural Language Learning, (EMNLP-CoNLL 2007)*, 257–266. Prague, Czech Republic: Association for Computational Linguistics.

Guzmán Naranjo, Matías. 2015. Unifying everything: Integrating quantitative effects into formal models of grammar. In *Proceedings of the 6th Conference on Quantitative Investigations in Theoretical Linguistics*, DOI:10.15496/publikation-8636.

Haddar, Kais, Sirine Boukedi & Ines Zalila. 2010. Construction of an HPSG grammar for the Arabic language and its specification in TDL. *International Journal on Information and Communication Technologies* 3(3). 52–64.

Haegeman, Liliane. 1994. *Introduction to Government and Binding Theory* (Blackwell Textbooks in Linguistics 1). Oxford, UK/Cambridge, USA: Blackwell Publishing Ltd 2nd edn.

Haegeman, Liliane. 1995. *The syntax of negation*. Cambridge, UK: Cambridge University Press.

Haftka, Brigitta. 1995. Syntactic positions for topic and contrastive focus in the German middlefield. In Inga Kohlhof, Susanne Winkler & Hans-Bernhard Drubig (eds.), *Proceedings of the Göttingen Focus Workshop, 17 DGfS, March 1–3* (Arbeitspapiere des SFB 340 No. 69), 137–157. Eberhard-Karls-Universität Tübingen.

Haftka, Brigitta. 1996. Deutsch ist eine V/2-Sprache mit Verbendstellung und freier Wortfolge. In Ewald Lang & Gisela Zifonun (eds.), *Deutsch – typologisch* (Institut für deutsche Sprache, Jahrbuch 1995), 121–141. Berlin: Walter de Gruyter.

Hagen, Kristin, Janne Bondi Johannessen & Anders Nøklestad. 2000. A constraint-based tagger for Norwegian. In C.-E. Lindberg & S. N. Lund (eds.), *17th Scandinavian Conference of Linguistic, Odense*, vol. I (Odense Working Papers in Language and Communication 19), 1–15.

Hahn, Michael. 2011. Null conjuncts and bound pronouns in Arabic. In Stefan Müller (ed.), *Proceedings of the 18th International Conference on Head-Driven Phrase Structure Grammar, University of Washington*, 60–80. Stanford, CA: CSLI Publications. http://csli-publications.stanford.edu/HPSG/2011/.

Haider, Hubert. 1982. Dependenzen und Konfigurationen: Zur deutschen V-Projektion. *Groninger Arbeiten zur Germanistischen Linguistik* 21. 1–60.

Haider, Hubert. 1984. Was zu haben ist und was zu sein hat – Bemerkungen zum Infinitiv. *Papiere zur Linguistik* 30(1). 23–36.

Haider, Hubert. 1985a. The case of German. In Jindřich Toman (ed.), *Studies in German grammar* (Studies in Generative Grammar 21), 23–64. Dordrecht: Foris Publications.

Haider, Hubert. 1985b. Über *sein* oder nicht *sein*: Zur Grammatik des Pronomens *sich*. In Werner Abraham (ed.), *Erklärende Syntax des Deutschen* (Studien zur deutschen Grammatik 25), 223–254. Tübingen: originally Gunter Narr Verlag now Stauffenburg Verlag.

Haider, Hubert. 1986a. Fehlende Argumente: Vom Passiv zu kohärenten Infinitiven. *Linguistische Berichte* 101. 3–33.

Haider, Hubert. 1986b. Nicht-sententiale Infinitive. *Groninger Arbeiten zur Germanistischen Linguistik* 28. 73–114.

Haider, Hubert. 1990a. Pro-bleme? In Gisbert Fanselow & Sascha W. Felix (eds.), *Strukturen und Merkmale syntaktischer Kategorien* (Studien zur deutschen Grammatik 39), 121–143. Tübingen: originally Gunter Narr Verlag now Stauffenburg Verlag.

Haider, Hubert. 1990b. Topicalization and other puzzles of German syntax. In Günther Grewendorf & Wolfgang Sternefeld (eds.), *Scrambling and Barriers* (Linguistik Aktuell/ Linguistics Today 5), 93–112. Amsterdam: John Benjamins Publishing Co.

Haider, Hubert. 1991. Fakultativ kohärente Infinitivkonstruktionen im Deutschen. Arbeitspapiere des SFB 340 No. 17 IBM Deutschland GmbH Heidelberg.

Haider, Hubert. 1993. *Deutsche Syntax – generativ: Vorstudien zur Theorie einer projektiven Grammatik* (Tübinger Beiträge zur Linguistik 325). Tübingen: Gunter Narr Verlag.

Haider, Hubert. 1994. (Un-)heimliche Subjekte: Anmerkungen zur Pro-drop Causa, im Anschluß an die Lektüre von Osvaldo Jaeggli & Kenneth J. Safir, eds., The Null Subject Parameter. *Linguistische Berichte* 153. 372–385.

Haider, Hubert. 1995. Studies on phrase structure and economy. Arbeitspapiere des SFB 340 No. 70 Universität Stuttgart Stuttgart.

Haider, Hubert. 1997a. Projective economy: On the minimal functional structure of the German clause. In Werner Abraham & Elly van Gelderen (eds.), *German: Syntactic problems—Problematic syntax* (Linguistische Arbeiten 374), 83–103. Tübingen: Max Niemeyer Verlag.

Haider, Hubert. 1997b. Typological implications of a directionality constraint on projections. In Artemis Alexiadou & T. Alan Hall (eds.), *Studies on Universal Grammar and typological variation* (Linguistik Aktuell/Linguistics Today 13), 17–33. Amsterdam: John Benjamins Publishing Co.

Haider, Hubert. 1999. The license to license: Structural case plus economy yields Burzio's Generalization. In Eric Reuland (ed.), *Arguments and case: Explaining Burzio's Generalization* (Linguistik Aktuell/Linguistics Today 34), 31–55. Amsterdam: John Benjamins Publishing Co.

Haider, Hubert. 2000. OV is more basic than VO. In Peter Svenonius (ed.), *The derivation of VO and OV*, 45–67. Amsterdam: John Benjamins Publishing Co.

Haider, Hubert. 2001. Parametrisierung in der Generativen Grammatik. In Martin Haspelmath, Ekkehard König, Wulf Oesterreicher & Wolfgang Raible (eds.), *Sprachtypologie und sprachliche Universalien – Language typology and language universals: Ein internationales Handbuch – An international handbook*, 283–294. Berlin: Mouton de Gruyter.

Haider, Hubert. 2014. Scientific ideology in grammar theory. Ms. Universität Salzburg, Dept. of Linguistics and Centre for Cognitive Neuroscience.

Hajičová, Eva & Petr Sgall. 2003. Dependency Syntax in Functional Generative Description. In Vilmos Ágel, Ludwig M. Eichinger, Hans Werner Eroms, Peter Hellwig, Hans Jürgen Heringer & Henning Lobin (eds.), *Dependenz und Valenz / Dependency and valency: Ein internationales Handbuch der zeitgenössischen Forschung / An international handbook of contemporary research*, vol. 25.1 (Handbücher zur Sprach- und Kommunikationswissenschaft), 570–592. Berlin: Walter de Gruyter.

Hakuta, Kenji, Ellen Bialystok & Edward Wiley. 2003. Critical evidence: A test of the Critical-Period Hypothesis for second-language acquisition. *Psychological Science* 14(1). 31–38.

Hale, Kenneth. 1976. The adjoined relative clause in Australia. In R.M.W. Dixon (ed.), *Grammatical catgeories of Australian languages* (Linguistic Series 22), 78–105. New Jersey: Humanities Press.

Hale, Kenneth & Samuel Jay Keyser. 1993. On argument structure and the lexical expression of syntactic relations. In Kenneth Hale & Samuel Jay Keyser (eds.), *The view from building 20: Essays in linguistics in honor of Sylvain Bromberger* (Current Studies in Linguistics 24), 53–109. Cambridge, MA/London: MIT Press.

Hale, Kenneth & Samuel Jay Keyser. 1997. On the complex nature of simple predicators. In Alex Alsina, Joan Bresnan & Peter Sells (eds.), *Complex predicates* (CSLI Lecture Notes 64), 29–65. Stanford, CA: CSLI Publications.

Han, Chung-hye, Juntae Yoon, Nari Kim & Martha Palmer. 2000. A feature-based Lexicalized Tree Adjoining Grammar for Korean. Technical Report IRCS-00-04 University of Pennsylvania Institute for Research in Cognitive Science. http://repository.upenn.edu/ircs_reports/35/.

Harbour, Daniel. 2011. Mythomania? Methods and morals from 'The myth of language universals'. *Lingua* 121(12). 1820–1830.

Harley, Heidi & Rolf Noyer. 2000. Formal versus encyclopedic properties of vocabulary: Evidence from nominalizations. In Bert Peeters (ed.), *The lexicon–encyclopedia interface*, 349–374. Amsterdam: Elsevier.

Harman, Gilbert. 1963. Generative grammars without transformation rules: A defence of phrase structure. *Language* 39. 597–616.

Harris, Zellig S. 1957. Co-occurrence and transformation in linguistic structure. *Language* 33(3). 283–340.

Haspelmath, Martin. 2008. Parametric versus functional explanations of syntactic universals. In T. Biberauer (ed.), *The limits of syntactic variation*, 75–107. Amsterdam: John Benjamins Publishing Co.

Haspelmath, Martin. 2009. The best-supported language universals refer to scalar patterns deriving from processing costs. *The Behavioral and Brain Sciences* 32(5). 457–458.

Haspelmath, Martin. 2010a. Comparative concepts and descriptive categories in crosslinguistic studies. *Language* 86(3). 663–687.

Haspelmath, Martin. 2010b. Framework-free grammatical theory. In Bernd Heine & Heiko Narrog (eds.), *The Oxford handbook of grammatical analysis*, 341–365. Oxford: Oxford University Press.

Haspelmath, Martin. 2010c. The interplay between comparative concepts and descriptive categories (reply to Newmeyer). *Language* 86(3). 696–699.

Haugereid, Petter. 2007. Decomposed phrasal constructions. In Stefan Müller (ed.), *Proceedings of the 14th International Conference on Head-Driven Phrase Structure Grammar*, 120–129. Stanford, CA: CSLI Publications. http://csli-publications.stanford.edu/HPSG/2007/.

Haugereid, Petter. 2009. *Phrasal subconstructions: A Constructionalist grammar design, exemplified with Norwegian and English*: Norwegian University of Science and Technology dissertation.

Haugereid, Petter, Nurit Melnik & Shuly Wintner. 2013. Nonverbal predicates in Modern Hebrew. In Stefan Müller (ed.), *Proceedings of the 20th International Conference on Head-Driven Phrase Structure Grammar, Freie Universität Berlin*, 69–89. Stanford, CA: CSLI Publications. http://csli-publications.stanford.edu/HPSG/2013/hmw.pdf.

Hauser, Marc D., Noam Chomsky & W. Tecumseh Fitch. 2002. The faculty of language: What is it, who has it, and how did it evolve? *Science* 298. 1569–1579. DOI:10.1126/science.298.5598.1569.

Hausser, Roland. 1992. Complexity in left-associative grammar. *Theoretical Computer Science* 106(2). 283–308.

Hawkins, John A. 1999. Processing complexity and filler-gap dependencies across grammars. *Language* 75(2). 244–285.

Hawkins, John A. 2004. *Efficiency and complexity in grammars*. Oxford: Oxford University Press.

Hays, David G. 1964. Dependency Theory: A formalism and some observations. *Language* 40(4). 511–525.

Hays, David G. & T. W. Ziehe. 1960. Studies in machine translation: 10–Russian sentence-structure determination. Tech. rep. Rand Corporation.

Heinecke, Johannes, Jürgen Kunze, Wolfgang Menzel & Ingo Schröder. 1998. Eliminative parsing with graded constraints. In Pierre Isabelle (ed.), *Proceedings of the 36th Annual Meeting of the Association for Computational Linguistics and 17th International Conference on Computational Linguistics*, 526–530. Montreal, Quebec, Canada: Association for Computational Linguistics. DOI:10.3115/980845.980953.

Heinz, Wolfgang & Johannes Matiasek. 1994. Argument structure and case assignment in German. In John Nerbonne, Klaus Netter & Carl J. Pollard (eds.), *German in Head-Driven Phrase Structure Grammar* (CSLI Lecture Notes 46), 199–236. Stanford, CA: CSLI Publications.

Helbig, Gerhard & Joachim Buscha. 1969. *Deutsche Grammatik: Ein Handbuch für den Ausländerunterricht*. Leipzig: VEB Verlag Enzyklopädie.

Helbig, Gerhard & Joachim Buscha. 1998. *Deutsche Grammatik: Ein Handbuch für den Ausländerunterricht*. Leipzig Berlin München: Langenscheidt Verlag Enzyklopädie 18th edn.

Helbig, Gerhard & Wolfgang Schenkel. 1969. *Wörterbuch zur Valenz und Distribution deutscher Verben*. Leipzig: VEB Bibliographisches Institut Leipzig.

Hellan, Lars. 1986. The headedness of NPs in Norwegian. In Peter Muysken & Henk van Riemsdijk (eds.), *Features and projections*, 89–122. Dordrecht/Cinnaminson, U.S.A.: Foris Publications.

Hellan, Lars. 2007. On 'deep evaluation' for individual computational grammars and for cross-framework comparison. In Tracy Holloway King & Emily M. Bender (eds.), *Grammar Engineering across Frameworks 2007* (Studies in Computational Linguistics ONLINE), 161–181. Stanford, CA: CSLI Publications. http://csli-publications.stanford.edu/GEAF/2007/.

Hellan, Lars & Dorothee Beermann. 2006. The 'specifier' in an HPSG grammar implementation of Norwegian. In S. Werner (ed.), *Proceedings of the 15th NODALIDA Conference, Joensuu 2005* (Ling@JoY: University of Joensuu electronic publications in linguistics and language technology 1), 57–64. Joensuu: University of Joensuu.

Hellan, Lars & Petter Haugereid. 2003. Norsource – An excercise in the Matrix Grammar building design. In Emily M. Bender, Daniel P. Flickinger, Frederik Fouvry & Melanie Siegel (eds.), *Proceedings of the ESSLLI 2003 Workshop "Ideas and Strategies for Multilingual Grammar Development"*, Vienna, Austria.

Hellwig, Peter. 1978. PLAIN – Ein Programmsystem zur Sprachbeschreibung und maschinellen Sprachbearbeitung. *Sprache und Datenverarbeitung* 1(2). 16–31.

Hellwig, Peter. 1986. Dependency Unification Grammar. In Makoto Nagao (ed.), *Proceedings of COLING 86*, 195–198. University of Bonn: Association for Computational Linguistics.

Hellwig, Peter. 2003. Dependency Unification Grammar. In Vilmos Ágel, Ludwig M. Eichinger, Hans Werner Eroms, Peter Hellwig, Hans Jürgen Heringer & Henning Lobin (eds.), *Dependenz und Valenz / Dependency and valency: Ein internationales Handbuch der zeitgenössischen Forschung / An international handbook of contemporary research*, vol. 25.1 (Handbücher zur Sprach- und Kommunikationswissenschaft), 593–635. Berlin: Walter de Gruyter.

Hellwig, Peter. 2006. Parsing with Dependency Grammars. In Vilmos Ágel, Ludwig M. Eichinger, Hans Werner Eroms, Peter Hellwig, Hans Jürgen Heringer & Henning Lobin (eds.), *Dependenz und Valenz / Dependency and valency: Ein internationales Handbuch der zeitgenössischen Forschung / An international handbook of contemporary research*, vol. 25.2 (Handbücher zur Sprach- und Kommunikationswissenschaft), 1081–1109. Berlin: Walter de Gruyter.

Her, One-Soon, Dan Higinbotham & Joseph Pentheroudakis. 1991. An LFG-based machine translation system. *Computer Processing of Chinese and Oriental Languages* 5(3–4). 285–297.

Heringer, Hans-Jürgen. 1996. *Deutsche Syntax dependentiell* (Stauffenburg Linguistik). Tübingen: Stauffenburg Verlag.

Higginbotham, James. 1985. On semantics. *Linguistic Inquiry* 16(4). 547–593.

Hinrichs, Erhard W., Walt Detmar Meurers, Frank Richter, Manfred Sailer & Heike Winhart (eds.). 1997. *Ein HPSG-Fragment des Deutschen. Teil 1: Theorie*, vol. No. 95 (Arbeitspapiere des SFB 340). Tübingen: Eberhard-Karls-Universität Tübingen.

Hinrichs, Erhard W. & Tsuneko Nakazawa. 1989a. Flipped out: AUX in German. In *Aspects of German VP structure* (SfS-Report-01-93), Tübingen: Eberhard-Karls-Universität Tübingen.

Hinrichs, Erhard W. & Tsuneko Nakazawa. 1989b. Subcategorization and VP structure in German. In *Aspects of German VP structure* (SfS-Report-01-93), Tübingen: Eberhard-Karls-Universität Tübingen.

Hinrichs, Erhard W. & Tsuneko Nakazawa. 1994. Linearizing AUXs in German verbal complexes. In John Nerbonne, Klaus Netter & Carl J. Pollard (eds.), *German in Head-Driven Phrase Structure Grammar* (CSLI Lecture Notes 46), 11–38. Stanford, CA: CSLI Publications.

Hinterhölzel, Roland. 2004. Language change versus grammar change: What diachronic data reveal about the interaction between core grammar and periphery. In Carola Trips & Eric Fuß (eds.), *Diachronic clues to synchronic grammar*, 131–160. Amsterdam: John Benjamins Publishing Co.

Hoberg, Ursula. 1981. *Die Wortstellung in der geschriebenen deutschen Gegenwartssprache* (Heutiges Deutsch. Linguistische Grundlagen. Forschungen des Instituts für deutsche Sprache 10). München: Max Hueber Verlag.

Hockett, Charles F. 1960. The origin of speech. *Scientific American* 203. 88–96.

Hoeksema, Jack. 1991. Theoretische Aspekten van Partikelvooropplaatsing. *TABU Bulletin voor Taalwetenschap* 21(1). 18–26.

Hoffman, Beryl Ann. 1995. *The computational analysis of the syntax and interpretation of "free" word order in Turkish*: University of Pennsylvania dissertation.

Höhle, Tilman N. 1978. *Lexikalische Syntax: Die Aktiv-Passiv-Relation und andere Infinitkonstruktionen im Deutschen* (Linguistische Arbeiten 67). Tübingen: Max Niemeyer Verlag.

Höhle, Tilman N. 1982. Explikationen für „normale Betonung" und „normale Wortstellung". In Werner Abraham (ed.), *Satzglieder im Deutschen – Vorschläge zur syntaktischen, semantischen und pragmatischen Fundierung* (Studien zur deutschen Grammatik 15), 75–153. Tübingen: originally Gunter Narr Verlag now Stauffenburg Verlag. Republished as Höhle (2016c).

Höhle, Tilman N. 1983. Topologische Felder. Köln, ms, Published as Höhle (2016g).

Höhle, Tilman N. 1986. Der Begriff „Mittelfeld", Anmerkungen über die Theorie der topologischen Felder. In Walter Weiss, Herbert Ernst Wiegand & Marga Reis (eds.), *Akten des VII. Kongresses der Internationalen Vereinigung für germanische Sprach-und Literaturwissenschaft. Göttingen 1985. Band 3. Textlinguistik contra Stilistik? – Wortschatz und Wörterbuch – Grammatische oder pragmatische Organisation von Rede?* (Kontroversen, alte und neue 4), 329–340. Tübingen: Max Niemeyer Verlag. Republished as Höhle (2016b).

Höhle, Tilman N. 1988. Verum-Fokus. Netzwerk Sprache und Pragmatik 5 Universität Lund, Germananistisches Institut Lund. Republished as Höhle (2016h).

Höhle, Tilman N. 1991a. On reconstruction and coordination. In Hubert Haider & Klaus Netter (eds.), *Representation and derivation in the theory of grammar* (Studies in Natural Language and Linguistic Theory 22), 139–197. Dordrecht: Kluwer Academic Publishers. Republished as Höhle (2016d).

Höhle, Tilman N. 1991b. Projektionsstufen bei V-Projektionen: Bemerkungen zu F/T. Ms. Published as Höhle (2016e).

Höhle, Tilman N. 1994. Spuren in HPSG. Vortrag auf der GGS-Tagung in Tübingen am 14. Mai 1994, published as Höhle (2016f).

Höhle, Tilman N. 1997. Vorangestellte Verben und Komplementierer sind eine natürliche Klasse. In Christa Dürscheid, Karl Heinz Ramers & Monika Schwarz (eds.), *Sprache im Fokus: Festschrift für Heinz Vater zum 65. Geburtstag*, 107–120. Tübingen: Max Niemeyer Verlag. Republished as Höhle (2016i).

Höhle, Tilman N. 1999. An architecture for phonology. In Robert D. Borsley & Adam Przepiórkowski (eds.), *Slavic in Head-Driven Phrase Structure Grammar*, 61–90. Stanford, CA: CSLI Publications. Republished as Höhle (2016a).

Höhle, Tilman N. 2016a. An architecture for phonology. In Stefan Müller, Marga Reis & Frank Richter (eds.), *Beiträge zur Grammatik des Deutschen* (Classics in Linguistics), Berlin: Language Science Press. Originally published as Höhle (1999).

Höhle, Tilman N. 2016b. Der Begriff „Mittelfeld", Anmerkungen über die Theorie der topologischen Felder. In Stefan Müller, Marga Reis & Frank Richter (eds.), *Beiträge zur Grammatik des Deutschen* (Classics in Linguistics), Berlin: Language Science Press. First published as Höhle (1986).

Höhle, Tilman N. 2016c. Explikationen für „normale Betonung" und „normale Wortstellung". In Stefan Müller, Marga Reis & Frank Richter (eds.), *Beiträge zur Grammatik des Deutschen* (Classics in Linguistics), Berlin: Language Science Press. In Preparation.

Höhle, Tilman N. 2016d. On reconstruction and coordination. In Stefan Müller, Marga Reis & Frank Richter (eds.), *Beiträge zur Grammatik des Deutschen* (Classics in Linguistics), Berlin: Language Science Press. In Preparation.

Höhle, Tilman N. 2016e. Projektionsstufen bei V-Projektionen: Bemerkungen zu F/T. In Stefan Müller, Marga Reis & Frank Richter (eds.), *Beiträge zur Grammatik des Deutschen* (Classics in Linguistics), Berlin: Language Science Press. First circulated in 1991.

Höhle, Tilman N. 2016f. Spuren in HPSG. In Stefan Müller, Marga Reis & Frank Richter (eds.), *Beiträge zur Grammatik des Deutschen* (Classics in Linguistics), Berlin: Language Science Press. Vortrag auf der GGS-Tagung in Tübingen am 14. Mai 1994.

Höhle, Tilman N. 2016g. Topologische Felder. In Stefan Müller, Marga Reis & Frank Richter (eds.), *Beiträge zur Grammatik des Deutschen* (Classics in Linguistics), Berlin: Language Science Press. First circulated as draft in 1983.

Höhle, Tilman N. 2016h. Verum-Fokus. In Stefan Müller, Marga Reis & Frank Richter (eds.), *Beiträge zur Grammatik des Deutschen* (Classics in Linguistics), Berlin: Language Science Press. Originally published as Höhle (1988).

Höhle, Tilman N. 2016i. Vorangestellte Verben und Komplementierer sind eine natürliche Klasse. In Stefan Müller, Marga Reis & Frank Richter (eds.), *Beiträge zur*

Grammatik des Deutschen (Classics in Linguistics), Berlin: Language Science Press. First published as Höhle (1997).

Holler, Anke. 2005. *Weiterführende Relativsätze: Empirische und theoretische Aspekte* (studia grammatica 60). Berlin: Akademie Verlag.

Hornstein, Norbert. 2013. Three grades of grammatical involvement: Syntax from a Minimalist perspective. *Mind and Language* 28(4). 392–420.

Hornstein, Norbert, Jairo Nunes & Kleantes K. Grohmann. 2005. *Understanding Minimalism* (Cambridge Textbooks in Linguistics). Cambridge, UK: Cambridge University Press.

Hudson, Carla L. & Elissa L. Newport. 1999. Creolization: Could adults really have done it all? In Annabel Greenhill, Heather Littlefield & Cheryl Tano (eds.), *Proceedings of the Boston University Conference on Language Development*, vol. 23, 265–276. Somerville, MA: Cascadilla Press.

Hudson, Richard. 1980. Constituency and dependency. *Linguistics* 18. 179–198.

Hudson, Richard. 1984. *Word grammar.* Oxford: Basil Blackwell.

Hudson, Richard. 1989. Towards a computer-testable Word Grammar of English. *UCL Working Papers in Linguistics* 1. 321–339.

Hudson, Richard. 1990. *English Word Grammar.* Oxford: Basil Blackwell.

Hudson, Richard. 1991. *English Word Grammar.* Oxford: Basil Blackwell.

Hudson, Richard. 2003. Mismatches in default inheritance. In Elaine J. Francis & Laura A. Michaelis (eds.), *Mismatch: Form-function incongruity and the architecture of grammar* (CSLI Lecture Notes 163), 355–402. Stanford, CA: CSLI Publications.

Hudson, Richard. 2004. Are determiners heads? *Functions of Language* 11(1). 7–42.

Hudson, Richard. 2010a. Reaction to: "The myth of language universals and cognitive science": On the choice between phrase structure and dependency structure. *Lingua* 120(12). 2676–2679.

Hudson, Richard. 2015. Pied piping in cognition. Ms. London. http://dickhudson.com/papers/.

Hudson, Richard A. 1988. Coordination and grammatical relations. *Journal of Linguistics* 24(2). 303–342.

Hudson, Richard A. 1997. German partial VP fronting. Ms. University College London. http://dickhudson.com/papers/.

Hudson, Richard A. 2000. Discontinuity. *Dependency Grammars, TAL* 41(1). 15–56.

Hudson, Richard A. 2007. *Language networks: The new Word Grammar.* Oxford: Oxford University Press.

Hudson, Richard A. 2010b. *An introduction to Word Grammar* (Cambridge Textbooks in Linguistics). Cambridge, UK: Cambridge University Press.

Hudson Kam, Carla L. & Elissa L. Newport. 2005. Regularizing unpredictable variation: The roles of adult and child learners in language formation and change. *Language Learning and Development* 1. 151–195.

Humboldt, Wilhelm von. 1988. *Gesammelte Werke.* Berlin, New York: Walter de Gruyter.

Hurford, James R. 2002. Expression/induction models of language evolution: Dimensions and issues. In Ted J. Briscoe (ed.), *Linguistic evolution through language acquisition*, 301–344. Cambridge, UK: Cambridge University Press.

Hurskainen, Arvi. 2006. Constraint Grammar in unconventional use: Handling complex Swahili idioms and proverbs. *Suominen, Mickael et.al.: A Man of Measure: Festschrift in Honour of Fred Karlsson on his 60th Birthday. Special Supplement to SKY Jounal of Linguistics* 19. 397–406.

Ingram, David & William Thompson. 1996. Early syntactic acquisition in German: Evidence for the modal hypothesis. *Language* 72(1). 97–120.

Iordanskaja, L., M. Kim, R. Kittredge, B. Lavoie & A. Polguère. 1992. Generation of extended bilingual statistical reports. In Antonio Zampolli (ed.), *14th International Conference on Computational Linguistics (COLING '92), August 23–28*, vol. 3, 1019–1023. Nantes, France: Association for Computational Linguistics.

Islam, Md. Asfaqul, K. M. Azharul Hasan & Md. Mizanur Rahman. 2012. Basic HPSG structure for Bangla grammar. In *15th International Conference on Computer and Information Technology (ICCIT)*, 185–189. Curran Associates. DOI:10.1109/ICCITechn.2012.6509749.

Jackendoff, Ray S. 1972. *Semantic interpretation in Generative Grammar.* Cambridge, MA/London, England: MIT Press.

Jackendoff, Ray S. 1975. Morphological and semantic regularities in the lexikon. *Language* 51(3). 639–671.

Jackendoff, Ray S. 1977. *$\overline{X}$ syntax: A study of phrase structure.* Cambridge, MA/London, England: MIT Press.

Jackendoff, Ray S. 1997. *The architecture of the language faculty* (Linguistic Inquiry Monographs 28). Cambridge, MA/London: MIT Press.

Jackendoff, Ray S. 2000. Fodorian modularity and representational modularity. In Yosef Grodzinsky, Lewis P. Shapiro & David Swinney (eds.), *Language and the brain: Representation and processing* (Foundations of Neuropsychology), 3–30. San Diego: Academic Press.

Jackendoff, Ray S. 2002. *Foundations of language.* Oxford: Oxford University Press.

Jackendoff, Ray S. 2007. A parallel architecture perspective on language processing. *Brain Research* 1146. 2–22.

Jackendoff, Ray S. 2008. Construction after Construction and its theoretical challenges. *Language* 84(1). 8–28.

Jackendoff, Ray S. 2011. What is the human language faculty? Two views. *Language* 87(3). 586–624.

Jackendoff, Ray S. & Steven Pinker. 2005. The nature of the language faculty and its implications for evolution of language (reply to Fitch, Hauser, and Chomsky). *Cognition* 97(2). 211–225.

Jackendoff, Ray S. & Steven Pinker. 2009. The reality of a universal language faculty. *The Behavioral and Brain Sciences* 32(5). 465–466.

Jacobs, Joachim. 1986. The syntax of focus and adverbials in German. In Werner Abraham & S. de Meij (eds.), *Topic, focus, and configurationality: Papers from the 6th Gronin-*

gen Grammar Talks, Groningen, 1984 (Linguistik Aktuell/Linguistics Today 4), 103–127. Amsterdam: John Benjamins Publishing Co.

Jacobs, Joachim. 1991. Bewegung als Valenztransfer. SFB 282: Theorie des Lexikons 1 Heinrich Heine Uni/BUGH Düsseldorf/Wuppertal.

Jacobs, Joachim. 2008. Wozu Konstruktionen? *Linguistische Berichte* 213. 3–44.

Jacobson, Pauline. 1987a. Phrase structure, grammatical relations, and discontinuous constituents. In Geoffrey J. Huck & Almerindo E. Ojeda (eds.), *Discontinuous constituency* (Syntax and Semantics 20), 27–69. New York: Academic Press.

Jacobson, Pauline. 1987b. Review of generalized phrase structure grammar. *Linguistics and Philosophy* 10(3). 389–426.

Jaeggli, Osvaldo A. 1986. Passive. *Linguistic Inquiry* 17(4). 587–622.

Jäger, Gerhard & Reinhard Blutner. 2003. Competition and interpretation: The German adverb *wieder* 'again'. In Ewald Lang, Claudia Maienborn & Cathrine Fabricius-Hansen (eds.), *Modifying adjuncts* (Interface Explorations 4), 393–416. Berlin: Mouton de Gruyter.

Jäppinen, H., A. Lehtola & K. Valkonen. 1986. Functional structures for parsing dependency constraints. In Makoto Nagao (ed.), *Proceedings of COLING 86*, 461–463. University of Bonn: Association for Computational Linguistics. DOI:10.3115/991365.991501.

Johnson, David E. & Shalom Lappin. 1997. A critique of the Minimalist Programm. *Linguistics and Philosophy* 20(3). 273–333.

Johnson, David E. & Shalom Lappin. 1999. *Local constraints vs. economy* (Stanford Monographs in Linguistics). Stanford, CA: CSLI Publications.

Johnson, David E. & Paul M. Postal. 1980. *Arc Pair Grammar*. Princeton, NJ: Princeton University Press.

Johnson, Jacqueline S. & Elissa L. Newport. 1989. Critical period effects in second language learning: The influence of maturational state on the acquisition of English as a second language. *Cognitive Psychology* 21(1). 60–99.

Johnson, Kent. 2004. Gold's theorem and cognitive science. *Philosophy of Science* 71(4). 571–592.

Johnson, Mark. 1986. A GPSG account of VP structure in German. *Linguistics* 24(5). 871–882.

Johnson, Mark. 1988. *Attribute-value logic and the theory of grammar* (CSLI Lecture Notes 14). Stanford, CA: CSLI Publications.

Johnson, Mark. 1989. Parsing as deduction: The use of knowledge of language. *Journal of Psycholinguistic Research* 18(1). 105–128.

Johnson, Mark, Stuart Geman, Stephen Canon, Zhiyi Chi & Stefan Riezler. 1999. Estimators for stochastic "unification-based" grammars. In Robert Dale & Ken Church (eds.), *Proceedings of the Thirty-Seventh Annual Meeting of the ACL*, 535–541. Association for Computational Linguistics.

Joshi, Aravind K. 1985. Tree Adjoining Grammars: How much context-sensitivity is required to provide reasonable structural descriptions? In David Dowty, Lauri Karttunen & Arnold Zwicky (eds.), *Natural language parsing*, 206–250. Cambridge University Press.

Joshi, Aravind K. 1987a. Introduction to Tree Adjoining Grammar. In Alexis Manaster-Ramer (ed.), *The mathematics of language*, 87–114. Amsterdam: John Benjamins Publishing Co.

Joshi, Aravind K. 1987b. Word-order variation in natural language generation. In *AAAI 87, Sixth National Conference on Artificial Intelligence*, 550–555. Seattle.

Joshi, Aravind K., Tilman Becker & Owen Rambow. 2000. Complexity of scrambling: A new twist to the competence-performance distinction. In Anne Abeillé & Owen Rambow (eds.), *Tree Adjoining Grammars: Formalisms, linguistic analysis and processing* (CSLI Lecture Notes 156), 167–181. Stanford, CA: CSLI Publications.

Joshi, Aravind K., Leon S. Levy & Masako Takahashi. 1975. Tree Adjunct Grammar. *Journal of Computer and System Science* 10(2). 136–163.

Joshi, Aravind K. & Yves Schabes. 1997. Tree-Adjoning Grammars. In G. Rozenberg & A. Salomaa (eds.), *Handbook of formal languages*, 69–123. Berlin: Springer Verlag.

Joshi, Aravind K., K. Vijay Shanker & David Weir. 1990. The convergence of mildly context-sensitive grammar formalisms. Tech. Rep. MS-CIS-90-01 Department of Computer and Information Science, University of Pennsylvania. http://repository.upenn.edu/cis_reports/539/.

Jungen, Oliver & Horst Lohnstein. 2006. *Einführung in die Grammatiktheorie* (UTB 2676). München: Wilhelm Fink Verlag.

Jurafsky, Daniel. 1996. A probabilistic model of lexical and syntactic access and disambiguation. *Cognitive Science* 20(2). 137–194.

Kahane, Sylvain. 1997. Bubble trees and syntactic representations. In Tilman Becker & Hans-Ulrich Krieger (eds.), *Proceedings of Mathematics of Language (MOL5) Meeting*, 70–76. Saarbrücken: DFKI.

Kahane, Sylvain. 2003. The Meaning-Text Theory. In Vilmos Ágel, Ludwig M. Eichinger, Hans Werner Eroms, Peter Hellwig, Hans Jürgen Heringer & Henning Lobin (eds.), *Dependenz und Valenz / Dependency and valency: Ein internationales Handbuch der zeitgenössischen Forschung / An international handbook of contemporary research*, vol. 25.1 (Handbücher zur Sprach- und Kommunikationswissenschaft), 546–570. Berlin: Walter de Gruyter.

Kahane, Sylvain. 2009. On the status of phrases in Head-Driven Phrase Structure Grammar: Illustration by a fully lexical treatment of extraction. In Alain Polguère & Igor A. Mel'čuk (eds.), *Dependency in linguistic description* (Studies in Language Companion Series 111), 111–150. Amsterdam: John Benjamins Publishing Co.

Kahane, Sylvain, Alexis Nasr & Owen Rambow. 1998. Pseudo-projectivity: A polynomially parsable non-projective Dependency Grammar. In Pierre Isabelle (ed.), *Proceedings of the 36th Annual Meeting of the Association for Computational Linguistics and 17th International Conference on Computational Linguistics*, 646–652. Montreal, Quebec, Canada: Association for Computational Linguistics. DOI:10.3115/980845.980953. http://www.aclweb.org/anthology/P98-1106.

Kallmeyer, Laura. 2005. Tree-local Multicomponent Tree Adjoining Grammars with shared nodes. *Computational Linguistics* 31(2). 187–225.

Kallmeyer, Laura & Aravind K. Joshi. 2003. Factoring predicate argument and scope semantics: Underspecified semantics with LTAG. *Research on Language and Computation* 1(1–2). 3–58. DOI:10.1023/A:1024564228892.

Kallmeyer, Laura, Timm Lichte, Wolfgang Maier, Yannick Parmentier, Johannes Dellert & Kilian Evang. 2008. TuLiPA: Towards a multi-formalism parsing environment for grammar engineering. In Stephen Clark & Tracy Holloway King (eds.), *Coling 2008: Proceedings of the Workshop on Grammar Engineering Across Frameworks*, 1–8. Manchester, England: Association for Computational Linguistics.

Kallmeyer, Laura & Rainer Osswald. 2012. A frame-based semantics of the dative alternation in Lexicalized Tree Adjoining Grammars. In Christopher Piñón (ed.), *Empirical issues in syntax and semantics*, vol. 9, 167–184. Paris: CNRS.

Kallmeyer, Laura & Maribel Romero. 2008. Scope and situation binding in LTAG using semantic unification. *Research on Language and Computation* 6(1). 3–52.

Kallmeyer, Laura & Sinwon Yoon. 2004. Tree-local MCTAG with shared nodes: An analysis of word order variation in German and Korean. *Traitement automatique des langues TAL* 45(3). 49–69.

Kamp, Hans & Uwe Reyle. 1993. *From discourse to logic: Introduction to modeltheoretic semantics of natural language, formal logic and Discourse Representation Theory* (Studies in Linguistics and Philosophy 42). Dordrecht: Kluwer Academic Publishers.

Kaplan, Ronald M. 1995. The formal architecture of Lexical-Functional Grammar. In Dalrymple et al. (1995) 7–27.

Kaplan, Ronald M. & Joan Bresnan. 1982. Lexical-Functional Grammar: A formal system for grammatical representation. In Joan Bresnan (ed.), *The mental representation of grammatical relations* (MIT Press Series on Cognitive Theory and Mental Representation), 173–281. Cambridge, MA/London: MIT Press. Reprint in: Dalrymple et al. (1995: 29–130).

Kaplan, Ronald M. & John T. Maxwell III. 1996. LFG grammar writer's workbench. Tech. rep. Xerox PARC.

Kaplan, Ronald M., Stefan Riezler, Tracy Holloway King, John T. Maxwell III, Alexander Vasserman & Richard Crouch. 2004. Speed and accuracy in shallow and deep stochastic parsing. In *Proceedings of the Human Language Technology Conference and the 4th Annual Meeting of the North American Chapter of the Association for Computational Linguistics (HLT-NAACL'04)*, Boston, MA: Association for Computational Linguistics.

Kaplan, Ronald M. & Annie Zaenen. 1989. Long-distance dependencies, constituent structure and functional uncertainty. In Mark R. Baltin & Anthony S. Kroch (eds.), *Alternative conceptions of phrase structure*, 17–42. Chicago/London: The University of Chicago Press.

Karimi, Simin. 2005. *A Minimalist approach to scrambling: Evidence from Persian* (Studies in Generative Grammar 76). Berlin, New York: Mouton de Gruyter.

Karimi-Doostan, Gholamhossein. 2005. Light verbs and structural case. *Lingua* 115(12). 1737–1756.

Karlsson, Fred. 1990. Constraint Grammar as a framework for parsing running text. In Hans Karlgren (ed.), *COLING-90: Papers presented to the 13th International Conference on Computational Linguistics*, 168–173. Helsinki: Association for Computational Linguistics.

Karmiloff-Smith, Annette. 1998. Development itself is the key to understanding developmental disorders. *Trends in Cognitive Sciences* 2(10). 389–398.

Karmiloff-Smith, Annette, Julia Grant, Ioanna Berthoud, Mark Davies, Patricia Howlin & Orlee Udwin. 1997. Language in Williams Syndrome: How intact is 'intact'? *Child Development* 68(2). 246–262.

Karttunen, Lauri. 1986. Radical lexicalism. Report No. CSLI-86-68 Center for the Study of Language and Information.

Karttunen, Lauri. 1989. Radical lexicalism. In Mark R. Baltin & Anthony S. Kroch (eds.), *Alternative conceptions of phrase structure*, 43–65. Chicago/London: The University of Chicago Press.

Kasper, Robert T. 1994. Adjuncts in the Mittelfeld. In John Nerbonne, Klaus Netter & Carl J. Pollard (eds.), *German in Head-Driven Phrase Structure Grammar* (CSLI Lecture Notes 46), 39–70. Stanford, CA: CSLI Publications.

Kasper, Robert T., Bernd Kiefer, Klaus Netter & Vijay K. Shanker. 1995. Compilation of HPSG to TAG. In Hans Uszkoreit (ed.), *33rd Annual Meeting of the Association for Computational Linguistics. Proceedings of the conference*, 92–99. Cambridge, MA: Association for Computational Linguistics.

Kathol, Andreas. 1995. *Linearization-based German syntax*: Ohio State University dissertation.

Kathol, Andreas. 2000. *Linear syntax*. New York, Oxford: Oxford University Press.

Kathol, Andreas. 2001. Positional effects in a monostratal grammar of German. *Journal of Linguistics* 37(1). 35–66.

Kathol, Andreas & Carl J. Pollard. 1995. Extraposition via complex domain formation. In Hans Uszkoreit (ed.), *33rd Annual Meeting of the Association for Computational Linguistics. Proceedings of the conference*, 174–180. Cambridge, MA: Association for Computational Linguistics.

Kaufmann, Ingrid & Dieter Wunderlich. 1998. Cross-linguistic patterns of resultatives. SFB 282: Theorie des Lexikons 109 Heinrich Heine Uni/BUGH Düsseldorf.

Kaufmann, Tobias. 2009. *A rule-based language model for speech recognition*: Computer Engineering and Networks Laboratory, ETH Zürich dissertation.

Kaufmann, Tobias & Beat Pfister. 2007. Applying licenser rules to a grammar with continuous constituents. In Stefan Müller (ed.), *Proceedings of the 14th International Conference on Head-Driven Phrase Structure Grammar*, 150–162. Stanford, CA: CSLI Publications. http://csli-publications.stanford.edu/HPSG/2007/.

Kaufmann, Tobias & Beat Pfister. 2008. Applying a grammar-based language model to a broadcast-news transcription task. In Johanna D. Moore, Simone Teufel, James Allan & Sadaoki Furui (eds.), *Proceedings of the 46th Annual Meeting of the Association for Computational Linguistics: Human Language Technologies*, 106–113. Columbus, Ohio: Association for Computational Linguistics. http://www.aclweb.org/anthology/P/P08/P08-1013.pdf.

Kay, Martin. 1967. Experiments with a powerful parser. In *Proceedings of Conference Internationale Sur Le Traitement Automatique Des Langues (COLING 1967)*, Grenoble. http://aclweb.org/anthology/C/C67/C67-1009.pdf.

Kay, Martin. 2000. David G. Hays. In William J. Hutchins (ed.), *Early years in machine translation* (Amsterdam Studies in the Theory and History of Linguistics Science Series 3), 165–170. Amsterdam: John Benjamins Publishing Co.

Kay, Martin. 2011. Zipf's law and *L'Arbitraire du Signe. Linguistic Issues in Language Technology* 6(8). 1–25. http://journals.linguisticsociety.org/elanguage/lilt/article/view/2584.html. Special Issue on Interaction of Linguistics and Computational Linguistics.

Kay, Paul. 2002. An informal sketch of a formal architecture for Construction Grammar. *Grammars* 5(1). 1–19.

Kay, Paul. 2005. Argument structure constructions and the argument-adjunct distinction. In Mirjam Fried & Hans C. Boas (eds.), *Grammatical constructions: Back to the roots* (Constructional Approaches to Language 4), 71–98. Amsterdam: John Benjamins Publishing Co.

Kay, Paul & Charles J. Fillmore. 1999. Grammatical Constructions and linguistic generalizations: The What's X Doing Y? Construction. *Language* 75(1). 1–33.

Kay, Paul, Ivan A. Sag & Daniel P. Flickinger. 2015. A lexical theory of phrasal idioms. Ms. CSLI Stanford.

Kayne, Richard S. 1994. *The antisymmetry of syntax* (Linguistic Inquiry Monographs 25). Cambridge, MA: MIT Press.

Kayne, Richard S. 2011. Why are there no directionality parameters? In Mary Byram Washburn, Katherine McKinney-Bock, Erika Varis, Ann Sawyer & Barbara Tomaszewicz (eds.), *Proceedings of the 28th West Coast Conference on Formal Linguistics*, 1–23. Somerville, MA: Cascadilla Press.

Keenan, Edward L. & Bernard Comrie. 1977. Noun phrase accessibility and Universal Grammar. *Linguistic Inquiry* 8(1). 63–99.

Keller, Frank. 1994. German functional HPSG – An experimental CUF encoding. Tech. rep. Institut für Maschinelle Sprachverarbeitung Stuttgart.

Keller, Frank. 1995. Towards an account of extraposition in HPSG. In Steven P. Abney & Erhard W. Hinrichs (eds.), *Proceedings of the Seventh Conference of the European Chapter of the Association for Computational Linguistics*, Dublin: Association for Computational Linguistics.

Kettunen, Kimmo. 1986. On modelling dependency-oriented parsing. In Fred Karlsson (ed.), *Papers from the Fifth Scandinavian Conference of Computational Linguistics*, 113–120. Helsinki.

Kiefer, Bernd, Hans-Ulrich Krieger & Mark-Jan Nederhof. 2000. Efficient and robust parsing of word hypotheses graphs. In Wolfgang Wahlster (ed.), *Verbmobil: Foundations of speech-to-speech translation* (Artificial Intelligence), 280–295. Berlin: Springer Verlag.

Kifle, Nazareth Amlesom. 2012. *Tigrinya applicatives in Lexical-Functional Grammar*: University of Bergen dissertation. http://hdl.handle.net/1956/5730.

Kim, Jong-Bok & Peter Sells. 2008. *English syntax: An introduction* (CSLI Lecture Notes 185). Stanford, CA: CSLI Publications.

Kim, Jong-Bok, Peter Sells & Jaehyung Yang. 2007. Parsing two types of multiple nominative constructions: A Constructional approach. *Language and Information* 11(1). 25–37.

Kim, Jong-Bok & Jaehyung Yang. 2003. Korean phrase structure grammar and its implementations into the LKB system. In Dong Hong Ji & Kim Teng Lua (eds.), *Proceedings of the 17th Pacific Asia Conference on Language, Information and Computation*, 88–97. National University of Singapore: COLIPS Publications.

Kim, Jong-Bok & Jaehyung Yang. 2004. Projections from morphology to syntax in the Korean Resource Grammar: Implementing typed feature structures. In Alexander Gelbukh (ed.), *Computational linguistics and intelligent text processing: 5th International Conference, CICLing 2004, Seoul, Korea, February 15-21, 2004, Proceedings* (Lecture Notes in Computer Science 2945), 13–24. Berlin: Springer Verlag.

Kim, Jong-Bok & Jaehyung Yang. 2006. Coordination structures in a typed feature structure grammar: Formalization and implementation. In Tapio Salakoski, Filip Ginter, Sampo Pyysalo & Tapio Pahikkala (eds.), *Advances in natural language processing: 5th International Conference, FinTAL 2006 Turku, Finland, August 23-25, 2006 proceedings* (Lecture Notes in Artificial Intelligence 4139), 194–205. Berlin: Springer Verlag.

Kim, Jong-Bok & Jaehyung Yang. 2009. Processing three types of Korean cleft constructions in a typed feature structure grammar. *Korean Journal of Cognitive Science* 20(1). 1–28.

Kim, Jong-Bok, Jaehyung Yang, Sanghoun Song & Francis Bond. 2011. Deep processing of Korean and the development of the Korean Resource Grammar. *Linguistic Research* 28(3). 635–672.

Kimball, John P. 1973. *The formal theory of grammar* (Foundations of Modern Linguistics). Englewood Cliffs, NJ: Prentice-Hall.

King, Paul. 1994. An expanded logical formalism for Head-Driven Phrase Structure Grammar. Arbeitspapiere des SFB 340 No. 59 Eberhard-Karls-Universität Tübingen. http://www.sfs.uni-tuebingen.de/sfb/reports/berichte/59/59abs.html.

King, Paul. 1999. Towards truth in Head-Driven Phrase Structure Grammar. In Valia Kordoni (ed.), *Tübingen studies in Head-Driven Phrase Structure Grammar* (Arbeitsberichte des SFB 340 No. 132), 301–352. Tübingen: Universität Tübingen. http://www.sfs.uni-tuebingen.de/sfb/reports/berichte/132/132abs.html.

King, Tracy Holloway & John T. Maxwell III. 2007. Overlay mechanisms for multi-level deep processing applications. In Tracy Holloway King & Emily M. Bender (eds.), *Grammar Engineering across Frameworks 2007* (Studies in Computational Linguistics ONLINE), 182–202. Stanford, CA: CSLI Publications. http://csli-publications.stanford.edu/GEAF/2007/.

Kinyon, Alexandra, Owen Rambow, Tatjana Scheffler, SinWon Yoon & Aravind K. Joshi. 2006. The Metagrammar goes multilingual: A cross-linguistic look at the V2-phenomenon. In Laura Kallmeyer & Tilman Becker (eds.), *TAG+8: The Eighth Inter-*

national Workshop on Tree Adjoining Grammar and Related Formalisms: Proceedings of the workshop, 17–24. Sydney, Australia: Association for Computational Linguistics.

Kiparsky, Paul. 1987. Morphology and grammatical relations. Unpublished paper, Stanford University, Stanford.

Kiparsky, Paul. 1988. Agreement and linking theory. Unpublished paper, Stanford University, Stanford.

Kiparsky, Paul & Carol Kiparsky. 1970. Fact. In Manfred Bierwisch & Karl Erich Heidolph (eds.), *Progress in linguistics*, 143–173. The Hague/Paris: Mouton.

Kiss, Katalin E. 2003. Argument scrambling, focus movement and topic movement in Hungarian. In Simin Karimi (ed.), *Word order and scrambling*, 22–43. London: Blackwell.

Kiss, Tibor. 1991. The grammars of LILOG. In Otthein Herzog & Claus-Rainer Rollinger (eds.), *Text understanding in LILOG* (Lecture Notes in Artificial Intelligence 546), 183–199. Berlin: Springer Verlag.

Kiss, Tibor. 1992. Variable Subkategorisierung: Eine Theorie unpersönlicher Einbettungen im Deutschen. *Linguistische Berichte* 140. 256–293.

Kiss, Tibor. 1993. Infinite Komplementation – Neue Studien zum deutschen Verbum infinitum. Arbeiten des SFB 282 No. 42 Bergische Universität Gesamthochschule Wuppertal.

Kiss, Tibor. 1995. *Infinite Komplementation: Neue Studien zum deutschen Verbum infinitum* (Linguistische Arbeiten 333). Tübingen: Max Niemeyer Verlag.

Kiss, Tibor. 2001. Configurational and relational scope determination in German. In Walt Detmar Meurers & Tibor Kiss (eds.), *Constraint-based approaches to Germanic syntax* (Studies in Constraint-Based Lexicalism 7), 141–175. Stanford, CA: CSLI Publications.

Kiss, Tibor. 2005. Semantic constraints on relative clause extraposition. *Natural Language and Linguistic Theory* 23(2). 281–334.

Kiss, Tibor & Birgit Wesche. 1991. Verb order and head movement. In Otthein Herzog & Claus-Rainer Rollinger (eds.), *Text understanding in LILOG* (Lecture Notes in Artificial Intelligence 546), 216–242. Berlin: Springer Verlag.

Klann-Delius, Gisela. 2008. *Spracherwerb*. Stuttgart: J.B. Metzler–Verlag 2nd edn.

Klein, Wolfgang. 1971. *Parsing: Studien zur maschinellen Satzanalyse mit Abhängigkeitsgrammatiken und Transformationsgrammatiken*, vol. 2. Frankfurt a. M.: Athenäum Verlag.

Klein, Wolfgang. 1985. Ellipse, Fokusgliederung und thematischer Stand. In Reinhard Meyer-Hermann & Hannes Rieser (eds.), *Ellipsen und fragmentarische Ausdrücke*, 1–24. Tübingen: Max Niemeyer Verlag.

Klein, Wolfgang. 1986. *Second language acquisition* (Cambridge Textbooks in Linguistics). Cambridge, UK: Cambridge University Press.

Klein, Wolfgang. 2009. Finiteness, Universal Grammar and the language faculty. In Jiansheng Guo, Elena Lieven, Nancy Budwig, Susan Ervin-Tripp, Keiko Nakamura & Seyda Ozcaliskan (eds.), *Cross-linguistic approaches to the study of language: Research in the tradition of Dan Isaac Slobin* (Psychology Press Festschrift Series), 333–344. New York: Psychology Press.

Klenk, Ursula. 2003. *Generative Syntax* (Narr Studienbücher). Tübingen: Gunter Narr Verlag.

Kluender, Robert. 1992. Deriving island constraints from principles of predication. In Helen Goodluck & Michael Rochemont (eds.), *Island constraints: Theory, acquisition, and processing*, 223–258. Dordrecht: Kluwer Academic Publishers.

Kluender, Robert & Marta Kutas. 1993. Subjacency as a processing phenomenon. *Language and Cognitive Processes* 8(4). 573–633.

Knecht, Laura. 1985. *Subject and object in Turkish*: M.I.T. dissertation.

Kobele, Gregory M. 2008. Across-the-board extraction in Minimalist Grammars. In *Proceedings of the Ninth International Workshop on Tree Adjoining Grammar and Related Formalisms (TAG+9)*, 113–128.

Koenig, Jean-Pierre. 1999. *Lexical relations* (Stanford Monographs in Linguistics). Stanford, CA: CSLI Publications.

Koenig, Jean-Pierre & Karin Michelson. 2010. Argument structure of Oneida kinship terms. *International Journal of American Linguistics* 76(2). 169–205.

Koenig, Jean-Pierre & Karin Michelson. 2012. The (non)universality of syntactic selection and functional application. In Christopher Piñón (ed.), *Empirical issues in syntax and semantics*, vol. 9, 185–205. Paris: CNRS.

Kohl, Dieter. 1992. Generation from under- and overspecified structures. In Antonio Zampolli (ed.), *14th International Conference on Computational Linguistics (COLING '92), August 23–28*, 686–692. Nantes, France: Association for Computational Linguistics.

Kohl, Dieter, Claire Gardent, Agnes Plainfossé, Mike Reape & Stefan Momma. 1992. Text generation from semantic representation. In Gabriel G. Bes & Thierry Guillotin (eds.), *The construction of a natural language and graphic interface: Results and perspectives from the ACORD project*, 94–161. Berlin: Springer Verlag.

Kohl, Karen T. 1999. *An analysis of finite parameter learning in linguistic spaces*. Massachusetts Institute of Technology MA thesis. http://karentkohl.org/papers/SM.pdf.

Kohl, Karen T. 2000. Language learning in large parameter spaces. In *Proceedings of the Seventeenth National Conference on Artificial Intelligence and Twelfth Conference on Innovative Applications of Artificial Intelligence*, 1080. AAAI Press / The MIT Press.

Kolb, Hans-Peter. 1997. GB blues: Two essays on procedures and structures in Generative Syntax. Arbeitspapiere des SFB 340 No. 110 Eberhard-Karls-Universität Tübingen.

Kolb, Hans-Peter & Craig L. Thiersch. 1991. Levels and empty categories in a Principles and Parameters based approach to parsing. In Hubert Haider & Klaus Netter (eds.), *Representation and derivation in the theory of grammar* (Studies in Natural Language and Linguistic Theory 22), 251–301. Dordrecht: Kluwer Academic Publishers.

Konieczny, Lars. 1996. *Human sentence processing: A semantics-oriented parsing approach*: Universität Freiburg Dissertation. IIG-Berichte 3/96.

König, Esther. 1999. LexGram: A practical Categorial Grammar formalism. *Journal of Language and Computation* 1(1). 33–52.

Koopman, Hilda & Dominique Sportiche. 1991. The position of subjects. *Lingua* 85(2–3). 211–258.

Kordoni, Valia (ed.). 1999. *Tübingen studies in Head-Driven Phrase Structure Grammar* (Arbeitspapiere des SFB 340, No. 132, Volume 1). Tübingen: Eberhard-Karls-Universität Tübingen.

Kordoni, Valia. 2001. Linking experiencer-subject psych verb constructions in Modern Greek. In Daniel P. Flickinger & Andreas Kathol (eds.), *Proceedings of the HPSG-2000 Conference, University of California, Berkeley*, 198–213. CSLI Publications. http://csli-publications.stanford.edu/HPSG/1/.

Kordoni, Valia & Julia Neu. 2005. Deep analysis of Modern Greek. In Keh-Yih Su, Oi Yee Kwong, Jn'ichi Tsujii & Jong-Hyeok Lee (eds.), *Natural language processing IJCNLP 2004* (Lecture Notes in Artificial Intelligence 3248), 674–683. Berlin: Springer Verlag.

Kornai, András & Geoffrey K. Pullum. 1990. The X-bar Theory of phrase structure. *Language* 66(1). 24–50.

Koster, Jan. 1975. Dutch as an SOV language. *Linguistic Analysis* 1(2). 111–136.

Koster, Jan. 1978. *Locality principles in syntax*. Dordrecht: Foris Publications.

Koster, Jan. 1986. The relation between pro-drop, scrambling, and verb movements. *Groningen Papers in Theoretical and Applied Linguistics* 1. 1–43.

Koster, Jan. 1987. *Domains and dynasties: The radical autonomy of syntax*. Dordrecht: Foris Publications.

Kratzer, Angelika. 1984. On deriving syntactic differences between German and English. TU Berlin, ms.

Kratzer, Angelika. 1996. Severing the external argument from its verb. In Johan Rooryck & Laurie Zaring (eds.), *Phrase structure and the lexicon*, 109–137. Dordrecht: Kluwer Academic Publishers.

Krieger, Hans-Ulrich & John Nerbonne. 1993. Feature-based inheritance networks for computational lexicons. In Ted Briscoe, Ann Copestake & Valeria de Paiva (eds.), *Inheritance, defaults, and the lexicon*, 90–136. Cambridge, UK: Cambridge University Press. A version of this paper is available as DFKI Research Report RR-91-31. Also published in: Proceedings of the ACQUILEX Workshop on Default Inheritance in the Lexicon, Technical Report No. 238, University of Cambridge, Computer Laboratory, October 1991.

Kroch, Anthony S. 1987. Unbounded dependencies and subjacency in a Tree Adjoining Grammar. In Alexis Manaster-Ramer (ed.), *Mathematics of language*, 143–172. Amsterdam: John Benjamins Publishing Co.

Kroch, Anthony S. & Aravind K. Joshi. 1985. The linguistic relevance of Tree Adjoining Grammar. Tech. Rep. MS-CIS-85-16 University of Pennsylvania. http://repository.upenn.edu/cgi/viewcontent.cgi?article=1706&context=cis_reports.

Kroch, Anthony S. & Aravind K. Joshi. 1987. Analyzing extraposition in a Tree Adjoining Grammar. In Geoffrey J. Huck & Almerindo E. Ojeda (eds.), *Discontinuous constituency* (Syntax and Semantics 20), 107–149. New York: Academic Press.

Kropp Dakubu, Mary Esther, Lars Hellan & Dorothee Beermann. 2007. Verb sequencing constraints in Ga: Serial verb constructions and the extended verb complex. In Stefan

Müller (ed.), *Proceedings of the 14th International Conference on Head-Driven Phrase Structure Grammar*, 99–119. Stanford, CA: CSLI Publications. http://csli-publications.stanford.edu/HPSG/2007/.

Kruijff-Korbayová, Ivana & Mark J. Steedman. 2003. Discourse and information structure. *Journal of Logic, Language and Information: Special Issue on Discourse and Information Structure* 12(3). 249–259.

Kübler, Sandra, Ryan McDonald & Joakim Nivre. 2009. *Dependency Parsing* (Synthesis Lectures on Human Language Technologies 2). San Rafael, U.S.A: Morgan & Claypool Publishers.

Kuhn, Jonas. 1995. Information packaging in German: Some motivation from HPSG-based translation. Universität Stuttgart, ms. ftp://ftp.ims.uni-stuttgart.de/pub/papers/kuhn/Info-Pack.pdf.

Kuhn, Jonas. 1996. An underspecified HPSG representation for information structure. In Jun-ichi Tsuji (ed.), *Proceedings of COLING-96. 16th International Conference on Computational Linguistics COLING96). Copenhagen, Denmark, August 5–9, 1996*, 670–675. Copenhagen, Denmark: Association for Computational Linguistics.

Kuhn, Jonas. 2007. Interfaces in constraint-based theories of grammar. In Gillian Ramchand & Charles Reiss (eds.), *The Oxford handbook of linguistic interfaces*, 613–650. Oxford: Oxford University Press.

Kuhn, Jonas & Christian Rohrer. 1997. Approaching ambiguity in real-life sentences: The application of an Optimality Theory-inspired constraint ranking in a large-scale LFG grammar. In *Proceedings of DGfS/CL 97*, Heidelberg.

Kuhns, Robert J. 1986. A PROLOG implementation of Government-Binding Theory. In Alan W. Biermann (ed.), *Proceedings of the Twenty-Fourth Annual Meeting of the Association for Computational Linguistics*, 546–550. Columbia University, New York: Association for Computational Linguistics.

Kunze, Jürgen. 1968. The treatment of non-projective structures in the syntactic analysis and synthesis of English and German. *Computational Linguistics* 7. 67–77.

Kunze, Jürgen. 1975. *Abhängigkeitsgrammatik* (studia grammatica 12). Berlin: Akademie Verlag.

Kunze, Jürgen. 1991. *Kasusrelationen und semantische Emphase* (studia grammatica XXXII). Berlin: Akademie Verlag.

Kunze, Jürgen. 1993. *Sememstrukturen und Feldstrukturen* (studia grammatica 36). Berlin: Akademie Verlag. Unter Mitarbeit von Beate Firzlaff.

Labelle, Marie. 2007. Biolinguistics, the Minimalist Program, and psycholinguistic reality. *Snippets* 14. 6–7. http://www.ledonline.it/snippets/.

Laczkó, Tibor, György Rákosi & Ágoston Tóth. 2010. HunGram vs. EngGram in ParGram: On the comparison of Hungarian and English in an international computational linguistics project. In Irén Hegedűs & Sándor Martsa (eds.), *Selected papers in linguistics from the 9th HUSSE Conference*, vol. 1, 81–95. Pécs: Institute of English Studies, Faculty of Humanities, University of Pécs.

Laenzlinger, Christoph. 2004. A feature-based theory of adverb syntax. In Jennifer R. Austin, Stefan Engelberg & Gisa Rauh (eds.), *Adverbials: The interplay between mean-*

ing, context, and syntactic structure (Linguistik Aktuell/Linguistics Today 70), 205–252. Amsterdam: John Benjamins Publishing Co.

Lai, Cecilia S. L., Simon E. Fisher, Jane A. Hurst, Faraneh Vargha-Khadem & Anthony P. Monaco. 2001. A forkhead-domain gene is mutated in a severe speech and language disorder. *Nature* 413(6855). 519–523. DOI:10.1038/35097076.

Lakoff, George. 1987. *Women, fire, and dangerous things: What categories reveal about the mind.* Chicago: The University of Chicago Press.

Langacker, Ronald W. 1987. *Foundations of Cognitive Grammar*, vol. 1. Stanford, CA: Stanford University Press.

Langacker, Ronald W. 2000. A dynamic usage-based model. In Michael Barlow & Suzanne Kemmer (eds.), *Usage-based models of language*, 1–63. Stanford, CA: CSLI Publications.

Langacker, Ronald W. 2008. *Cognitive Grammar: A basic introduction.* Oxford: Oxford University Press.

Langacker, Ronald W. 2009. Cognitive (Construction) Grammar. *Cognitive Linguistics* 20(1). 167–176.

Lappin, Shalom, Robert D. Levine & David E. Johnson. 2000a. The revolution confused: A response to our critics. *Natural Language and Linguistic Theory* 18(4). 873–890.

Lappin, Shalom, Robert D. Levine & David E. Johnson. 2000b. The structure of unscientific revolutions. *Natural Language and Linguistic Theory* 18(3). 665–671.

Lappin, Shalom, Robert D. Levine & David E. Johnson. 2001. The revolution maximally confused. *Natural Language and Linguistic Theory* 19(4). 901–919.

Larson, Richard K. 1988. On the double object construction. *Linguistic Inquiry* 19(3). 335–391.

Lascarides, Alex & Ann Copestake. 1999. Default representation in constraint-based frameworks. *Computational Linguistics* 25(1). 55–105.

Lasnik, Howard & Mamoru Saito. 1992. *Move α: Conditions on its application and output* (Current Studies in Linguistics 22). Cambridge, MA: MIT Press.

Lasnik, Howard & Juan Uriagereka. 2002. On the poverty of the challenge. *The Linguistic Review* 19(1–2). 147–150.

Lavoie, Benoit & Owen Rambow. 1997. RealPro–A fast, portable sentence realizer. In *Proceedings of the Conference on Applied Natural Language Processing (ANLP'97)*, .

Le, Hong Phuong, Thi Minh Huyen Nguyen & Azim Roussanaly. 2008. Metagrammar for Vietnamese LTAG. In *Proceedings of the Ninth International Workshop on Tree Adjoining Grammars and Related Formalisms (TAG+9)*, 129–132. Tübingen.

Legate, Julie & Charles D. Yang. 2002. Empirical re-assessment of stimulus poverty arguments. *The Linguistic Review* 19(1–2). 151–162.

Lehtola, Aarno. 1986. DPL: A computational method for describing grammars and modelling parsers. In Fred Karlsson (ed.), *Papers from the Fifth Scandinavian Conference of Computational Linguistics*, 151–159. Helsinki.

Leiss, Elisabeth. 2003. Empirische Argumente für Dependenz. In Vilmos Ágel, Ludwig M. Eichinger, Hans Werner Eroms, Peter Hellwig, Hans Jürgen Heringer & Henning Lobin (eds.), *Dependenz und Valenz / Dependency and valency: Ein internationales*

Handbuch der zeitgenössischen Forschung / An international handbook of contemporary research, vol. 25.1 (Handbücher zur Sprach- und Kommunikationswissenschaft), 311–324. Berlin: Walter de Gruyter.

Leiss, Elisabeth. 2009. *Sprachphilosophie* (de Gruyter Studienbuch). Berlin: Walter de Gruyter.

Lenerz, Jürgen. 1977. *Zur Abfolge nominaler Satzglieder im Deutschen* (Studien zur deutschen Grammatik 5). Tübingen: originally Gunter Narr Verlag now Stauffenburg Verlag.

Lenerz, Jürgen. 1994. Pronomenprobleme. In Brigitta Haftka (ed.), *Was determiniert Wortstellungsvariation? Studien zu einem Interaktionsfeld von Grammatik, Pragmatik und Sprachtypologie*, 161–174. Opladen: Westdeutscher Verlag.

Lenneberg, Eric H. 1964. The capacity for language acquisition. In Jerry A. Fodor & Jerrold J. Katz (eds.), *The structure of language*, 579–603. Englewood Cliffs, NJ: Prentice-Hall.

Lenneberg, Eric H. 1967. *Biological foundations of language.* New York: John Wiley & Sons, Inc.

Levelt, Willem J. M. 1989. *Speaking: From intonation to articulation* (ACL-MIT Press Series in Natural Language Processing). Cambridge, MA: MIT Press.

Levin, Beth. 1993. *English verb classes and alternations: A preliminary investigation.* Chicago, Illinois: University of Chicago Press.

Levin, Beth & Malka Rappaport Hovav. 2005. *Argument realization.* Cambridge University Press.

Levine, Robert D. 2003. Adjunct valents, cumulative scopings and impossible descriptions. In Jongbok Kim & Stephen Mark Wechsler (eds.), *The proceedings of the 9th International Conference on Head-Driven Phrase Structure Grammar*, 209–232. Stanford, CA: CSLI Publications. http://csli-publications.stanford.edu/HPSG/3/.

Levine, Robert D. & Thomas E. Hukari. 2006. *The unity of unbounded dependency constructions* (CSLI Lecture Notes 166). Stanford, CA: CSLI Publications.

Levine, Robert D. & Walt Detmar Meurers. 2006. Head-Driven Phrase Structure Grammar: Linguistic approach, formal foundations, and computational realization. In Keith Brown (ed.), *The encyclopedia of language and linguistics*, 237–252. Oxford: Elsevier Science Publisher B.V. (North-Holland) 2nd edn.

Lewis, Geoffrey L. 1967. *Turkish grammar.* Oxford: Clarendon Press.

Lewis, John D. & Jeffrey L. Elman. 2001. Learnability and the statistical structure of language: Poverty of Stimulus arguments revisited. In Barbora Skarabela, Sarah Fish & Anna H.-J. Do (eds.), *Proceedings of the 26th Annual Boston University Conference on Language Development*, 359–370. http://crl.ucsd.edu/~elman/Papers/BU2001.pdf.

Li, Charles N. & Sandra A. Thompson. 1981. *Mandarin Chinese: A functional reference grammar.* Berkeley and Los Angeles: University of California Press.

Li, Wei. 1996. Esperanto inflection and its interface in HPSG. Working papers of the linguistics circle University of Victoria.

Lichte, Timm. 2007. An MCTAG with tuples for coherent constructions in German. In Laura Kallmeyer, Paola Monachesi, Gerald Penn & Giorgio Satta (eds.), *Proceedings of the 12th Conference on Formal Grammar 2007*, Dublin, Ireland.

Lieb, Hans-Heinrich. 1983. *Integrational linguistics: Vol. I.: General outline* (Current Issues in Linguistic Theory 17). Amsterdam: John Benjamins Publishing Co.

Lightfoot, David W. 1997. Catastrophic change and learning theory. *Lingua* 100(1). 171–192.

Link, Godehard. 1984. Hydras: On the logic of relative constructions with multiple heads. In Fred Landmann & Frank Veltman (eds.), *Varieties of formal semantics*, 245–257. Dordrecht: Foris Publications.

Lipenkova, Janna. 2009. *Serienverbkonstruktionen im Chinesischen und ihre Analyse im Rahmen von HPSG*. Institut für Sinologie, Freie Universität Berlin MA thesis.

Liu, Gang. 1997. *Eine unifikations-basierte Grammatik für das moderne Chinesisch – dargestellt in der HPSG*: FG Sprachwissenschaft, Universität Konstanz dissertation. http://www.ub.uni-konstanz.de/kops/volltexte/1999/191/.

Liu, Haitao. 2009. *Dependency Grammar: From theory to practice*. Beijing: Science Press.

Liu, Haitao & Wei Huang. 2006. Chinese Dependency Syntax for treebanking. In *Proceedings of the Twentieth Pacific Asia Conference on Language, Information and Computation*, 126–133. Beijing: Tsinghua University Press.

Lloré, F. Xavier. 1995. *Un Método de 'Parsing' para Gramáticas Categoriales Multimodales*: I.C.E. de la Universidad Politécnica de Catalunya dissertation.

Lobin, Henning. 1993. *Koordinationssyntax als strukturales Phänomen* (Studien zur Grammatik 46). Tübingen: Gunter Narr Verlag.

Lobin, Henning. 2003. Dependenzgrammatik und Kategorialgrammatik. In Vilmos Ágel, Ludwig M. Eichinger, Hans Werner Eroms, Peter Hellwig, Hans Jürgen Heringer & Henning Lobin (eds.), *Dependenz und Valenz / Dependency and valency: Ein internationales Handbuch der zeitgenössischen Forschung / An international handbook of contemporary research*, vol. 25.1 (Handbücher zur Sprach- und Kommunikationswissenschaft), 325–330. Berlin: Walter de Gruyter.

Löbner, Sebastian. 1986. In Sachen Nullartikel. *Linguistische Berichte* 101. 64–65. http://user.phil-fak.uni-duesseldorf.de/~loebner/publ/Nullartikel.html.

Lohndal, Terje. 2012. Toward the end of argument structure. In María Cristina Cuervo & Yves Roberge (eds.), *The end of argument structure?*, vol. 38 (Syntax and Semantics), 155–184. Bingley, UK: Emerald Group Publishing.

Lohnstein, Horst. 1993. *Projektion und Linking: Ein prinzipienbasierter Parser fürs Deutsche* (Linguistische Arbeiten 287). Tübingen: Max Niemeyer Verlag.

Lohnstein, Horst. 2014. Artenvielfalt in freier Wildbahn: Generative Grammatik. In Jörg Hagemann & Sven Staffeldt (eds.), *Syntaxtheorien: Analysen im Vergleich* (Stauffenburg Einführungen 28), 165–185. Tübingen: Stauffenburg Verlag.

Longobardi, Giuseppe & Ian Roberts. 2010. Universals, diversity and change in the science of language: Reaction to "The myth of language universals and cognitive science". *Lingua* 120(12). 2699–2703.

Lorenz, Konrad. 1970. *Studies in human and animal behavior*, vol. I. Cambridge, MA: Harvard University Press.

Lötscher, Andreas. 1985. Syntaktische Bedingungen der Topikalisierung. *Deutsche Sprache* 13(3). 207–229.

Loukam, Mourad, Amar Balla & Mohamed Tayeb Laskri. 2015. Towards an open platform based on HPSG formalism for the Standard Arabic language. *International Journal of Speech Technology* DOI:10.1007/s10772-015-9314-4.

Lüdeling, Anke. 2001. *On particle verbs and similar constructions in German* (Dissertations in Linguistics). Stanford, CA: CSLI Publications.

Luuk, Erkki & Hendrik Luuk. 2011. The redundancy of recursion and infinity for natural language. *Cognitive Processing* 12(1). 1–11.

Maas, Heinz Dieter. 1977. The Saarbrücken Automatic Translation System (SUSY). In Eric James Coates (ed.), *Proceedings of the Third European Congress on Information Systems and Networks: Overcoming the Language Barrier*, vol. 1, 585–592. München: Verlag Dokumentation.

Maché, Jakob. 2010. Towards a compositional analysis of verbless directives in German. Paper presented at the HPSG 2010 Conference.

Machicao y Priemer, Antonio. 2015. SpaGram: An implemented grammar fragment of Spanish. Ms. Humboldt Universität zu Berlin. In Preparation.

MacWhinney, Brian. 1995. *The CHILDES project: Tools for analyzing talk*. Hillsdale, NJ: Erlbaum 2nd edn.

Maess, Burkhard, Stefan Koelsch, Thomas C. Gunter & Angela D. Friederici. 2001. Musical syntax is processed in Broca's area: An MEG study. *Nature Neuroscience* 4(5). 540–545.

Marantz, Alec. 1984. *On the nature of grammatical relations* (Linguistic Inquiry Monographs 10). Cambridge, MA: MIT Press.

Marantz, Alec. 1997. No escape from syntax: Don't try morphological analysis in the privacy of your own lexicon. *U. Penn Working Papers in Linguistics* 4(2). 201–225. http://www.ling.upenn.edu/papers/v4.2-contents.html.

Marantz, Alec. 2005. Generative linguistics within the cognitive neuroscience of language. *The Linguistic Review* 22(2–4). 429–445.

Marcus, Gary F. 1993. Negative evidence in language acquisition. *Cognition* 46(1). 53–85.

Marcus, Gary F. & Simon E. Fisher. 2003. FOXP2 in focus: What can genes tell us about speech and language? *TRENDS in Cognitive Sciences* 7(6). 257–262.

Marcus, Mitchell P. 1980. *A theory of syntactic recognition for natural language*. London, England/Cambridge, MA: MIT Press.

Marimon, Montserrat. 2013. The Spanish DELPH-IN grammar. *Language Resources and Evaluation* 47(2). 371–397. DOI:10.1007/s10579-012-9199-7.

Marshall, Ian & Éva Sáfár. 2004. Sign Language generation in an ALE HPSG. In Stefan Müller (ed.), *Proceedings of the 11th International Conference on Head-Driven Phrase Structure Grammar, Center for Computational Linguistics, Katholieke Universiteit Leuven*, 189–201. Stanford, CA: CSLI Publications. http://csli-publications.stanford.edu/HPSG/2004/.

Marslen-Wilson, William. 1975. Sentence perception as an interactive parallel process. *Science* 189(4198). 226–228.

Masuichi, Hiroshi & Tomoko Ohkuma. 2003. Constructing a practical Japanese parser based on Lexical-Functional Grammar. *Journal of Natural Language Processing* 10. 79–109. In Japanese.

Masum, Mahmudul Hasan, Muhammad Sadiqul Islam, M. Sohel Rahman & Reaz Ahmed. 2012. HPSG analysis of type-based Arabic nominal declension. In *The 13th International Arab Conference*, 272–279.

Mayo, Bruce. 1997. Die Konstanzer LFG-Umgebung. Arbeitspapier 82 des Fachbereichs Sprachwissenschaft der Universität Konstanz Universität Konstanz.

Mayo, Bruce. 1999. *A computational model of derivational morphology*: Universität Hamburg dissertation. http://www.sub.uni-hamburg.de/opus/volltexte/1999/386/.

Meinunger, André. 2000. *Syntactic aspects of topic and comment* (Linguistik Aktuell/ Linguistics Today 38). Amsterdam: John Benjamins Publishing Co.

Meisel, Jürgen. 1995. Parameters in acquisition. In Paul Fletcher & Brian MacWhinny (eds.), *The handbook of child language*, 10–35. Oxford: Blackwell Publishing Ltd.

Mel'čuk, Igor A. 1964. *Avtomatičeskij sintaksičeskij analiz*, vol. 1. Novosibirsk: Izdatel´stvo SO AN SSSR.

Mel'čuk, Igor A. 1981. Meaning-Text Models: A recent trend in Soviet linguistics. *Annual Review of Anthropology* 10. 27–62.

Mel'čuk, Igor A. 1988. *Dependency Syntax: Theory and practice* (SUNY Series in Linguistics). Albany, NY: SUNY Press.

Mel'čuk, Igor A. 2003. Levels of dependency description: Concepts and problems. In Vilmos Ágel, Ludwig M. Eichinger, Hans Werner Eroms, Peter Hellwig, Hans Jürgen Heringer & Henning Lobin (eds.), *Dependenz und Valenz / Dependency and valency: Ein internationales Handbuch der zeitgenössischen Forschung / An international handbook of contemporary research*, vol. 25.1 (Handbücher zur Sprach- und Kommunikationswissenschaft), 188–230. Berlin: Walter de Gruyter.

Melnik, Nurit. 2007. From "hand-written" to computationally implemented HPSG theories. *Research on Language and Computation* 5(2). 199–236.

Mensching, Guido & Eva-Maria Remberger. 2011. Syntactic variation and change in Romance: A Minimalist approach. In Peter Siemund (ed.), *Linguistic universals and language variation* (Trends in Linguistics. Studies and Monographs 231), 361–403. Berlin: Mouton de Gruyter.

Menzel, Wolfgang. 1998. Constraint satisfaction for robust parsing of spoken language. *Journal of Experimental & Theoretical Artificial Intelligence* 10(1). 77–89.

Menzel, Wolfgang & Ingo Schröder. 1998a. Constraint-based diagnosis for intelligent language tutoring systems. In *Proceedings of the ITF & KNOWS Conference at the IFIP '98 Congress*, Wien/Budapest.

Menzel, Wolfgang & Ingo Schröder. 1998b. Decision procedures for Dependency Parsing using graded constraints. In Alain Polguère & Sylvain Kahane (eds.), *Processing of dependency-based grammars: Proceedings of the workshop at COLING-ACL'98*, 78–

87. Association for Computational Linguistics. http://www.aclweb.org/anthology/W/W98/#0500.

Meurer, Paul. 2009. A computational grammar for Georgian. In Peter Bosch, David Gabelaia & Jérôme Lang (eds.), *Logic, language, and computation: 7th International Tbilisi Symposium on Logic, Language, and Computation, TbiLLC 2007, Tbilisi, Georgia, October 2007, revised selected papers* (Lecture Notes in Artificial Intelligence 5422), 1–15. Berlin: Springer Verlag.

Meurers, Walt Detmar. 1994. On implementing an HPSG theory. In Erhard W. Hinrichs, Walt Detmar Meurers & Tsuneko Nakazawa (eds.), *Partial-VP and split-NP topicalization in German – An HPSG analysis and its implementation* (Arbeitspapiere des SFB 340 No. 58), 47–155. Tübingen: Eberhard-Karls-Universität. http://www.sfs.uni-tuebingen.de/~dm/papers/on-implementing.html.

Meurers, Walt Detmar. 1999a. German partial-VP fronting revisited. In Gert Webelhuth, Jean-Pierre Koenig & Andreas Kathol (eds.), *Lexical and Constructional aspects of linguistic explanation* (Studies in Constraint-Based Lexicalism 1), 129–144. Stanford, CA: CSLI Publications.

Meurers, Walt Detmar. 1999b. *Lexical generalizations in the syntax of German non-finite constructions*. Tübingen: Eberhard-Karls-Universität dissertation.

Meurers, Walt Detmar. 1999c. Raising spirits (and assigning them case). *Groninger Arbeiten zur Germanistischen Linguistik (GAGL)* 43. 173–226. http://www.sfs.uni-tuebingen.de/~dm/papers/gagl99.html.

Meurers, Walt Detmar. 2000. Lexical generalizations in the syntax of German non-finite constructions. Arbeitspapiere des SFB 340 No. 145 Eberhard-Karls-Universität Tübingen. http://www.sfs.uni-tuebingen.de/~dm/papers/diss.html.

Meurers, Walt Detmar. 2001. On expressing lexical generalizations in HPSG. *Nordic Journal of Linguistics* 24(2). 161–217.

Meurers, Walt Detmar, Kordula De Kuthy & Vanessa Metcalf. 2003. Modularity of grammatical constraints in HPSG-based grammar implementations. In Emily M. Bender, Daniel P. Flickinger, Frederik Fouvry & Melanie Siegel (eds.), *Proceedings of the ESSLLI 2003 Workshop "Ideas and Strategies for Multilingual Grammar Development"*, 83–90. Vienna, Austria. http://www.sfs.uni-tuebingen.de/~dm/papers/meurers-dekuthy-metcalf-03.html.

Meurers, Walt Detmar & Stefan Müller. 2009. Corpora and syntax. In Anke Lüdeling & Merja Kytö (eds.), *Corpus linguistics: An international handbook*, vol. 29 (Handbücher zur Sprach- und Kommunikationswissenschaft), chap. 42, 920–933. Berlin: Mouton de Gruyter.

Meurers, Walt Detmar, Gerald Penn & Frank Richter. 2002. A web-based instructional platform for constraint-based grammar formalisms and parsing. In Dragomir Radev & Chris Brew (eds.), *Effective tools and methodologies for teaching NLP and CL*, 18–25. Association for Computational Linguistics. Proceedings of the Workshop held at 40th Annual Meeting of the Association for Computational Linguistics. Philadelphia, PA.

Micelli, Vanessa. 2012. Field topology and information structure: A case study for German constituent order. In Luc Steels (ed.), *Computational issues in Fluid Construction Grammar* (Lecture Notes in Computer Science 7249), 178–211. Berlin: Springer Verlag.

Michaelis, Jens. 2001. *On formal properties of Minimalist Grammars*: Universität Potsdam dissertation.

Michaelis, Laura A. 2006. Construction Grammar. In Keith Brown (ed.), *The encyclopedia of language and linguistics*, 73–84. Oxford: Elsevier Science Publisher B.V. (North-Holland) 2nd edn.

Michaelis, Laura A. & Josef Ruppenhofer. 2001. *Beyond alternations: A Constructional model of the German applicative pattern* (Stanford Monographs in Linguistics). Stanford, CA: CSLI Publications.

Miller, George A. & Kathryn Ojemann McKean. 1964. A chronometric study of some relations between sentences. *Quarterly Journal of Experimental Psychology* 16(4). 297–308.

Mittendorf, Ingo & Louisa Sadler. 2005. Numerals, nouns and number in Welsh NPs. In Miriam Butt & Tracy Holloway King (eds.), *Proceedings of the LFG 2005 conference*, 294–312. Stanford, CA: CSLI Publications. http://csli-publications.stanford.edu/LFG/10/.

Miyao, Yusuke, Takashi Ninomiya & Jun'ichi Tsujii. 2005. Corpus-oriented grammar development for acquiring a Head-Driven Phrase Structure Grammar from the Penn Treebank. In Keh-Yih Su, Oi Yee Kwong, Jn'ichi Tsujii & Jong-Hyeok Lee (eds.), *Natural language processing IJCNLP 2004* (Lecture Notes in Artificial Intelligence 3248), 684–693. Berlin: Springer Verlag.

Miyao, Yusuke & Jun'ichi Tsujii. 2008. Feature forest models for probabilistic HPSG parsing. *Computational Linguistics* 34(1). 35–80.

Moens, Marc, Jo Calder, Ewan Klein, Mike Reape & Henk Zeevat. 1989. Expressing generalizations in unification-based grammar formalisms. In Harold Somers & Mary McGee Wood (eds.), *Proceedings of the Fourth Conference of the European Chapter of the Association for Computational Linguistics*, 174–181. Manchester, England: Association for Computational Linguistics.

Montague, Richard. 1974. *Formal philosophy*. New Haven: Yale University Press.

Moortgat, Michael. 1989. *Categorical investigations: Logical and linguistic aspects of the Lambek Calculus* (Groningen Amsterdam Studies in Semantics 9). Dordrecht/Cinnaminson, U.S.A.: Foris Publications.

Moortgat, Michael. 2011. Categorial type logics. In Johan F. A. K. van Benthem & G. B. Alice ter Meulen (eds.), *Handbook of logic and language*, 95–179. Amsterdam: Elsevier 2nd edn.

Moot, Richard. 2002. *Proof nets for linguistic analysis*: University of Utrecht dissertation.

Morgan, James L. 1989. Learnability considerations and the nature of trigger experiences in language acquisition. *Behavioral and Brain Sciences* 12(2). 352–353.

Morin, Yves Ch. 1973. A computer tested Transformational Grammar of French. *Linguistics* 116(11). 49–114.

Morrill, Glyn V. 1994. *Type Logical Grammars: Categorial logic of signs*. Dordrecht: Kluwer Academic Publishers.

Morrill, Glyn V. 1995. Discontinuity in Categorial Grammar. *Linguistics and Philosophy* 18(2). 175–219.

Morrill, Glyn V. 2012. CatLog: A Categorial parser/theorem-prover. In *Logical aspects of computational linguistics: System demonstrations*, 13–16. Nantes, France: University of Nantes.

Müller, Gereon. 1996a. A constraint on remnant movement. *Natural Language and Linguistic Theory* 14(2). 355–407.

Müller, Gereon. 1996b. On extraposition and successive cyclycity. In Uli Lutz & Jürgen Pafel (eds.), *On extraction and extraposition in German* (Linguistik Aktuell/Linguistics Today 11), 213–243. Amsterdam: John Benjamins Publishing Co.

Müller, Gereon. 1998. *Incomplete category fronting: A derivational approach to remnant movement in German* (Studies in Natural Language and Linguistic Theory 42). Dordrecht: Kluwer Academic Publishers.

Müller, Gereon. 2000. *Elemente der optimalitätstheoretischen Syntax* (Stauffenburg Linguistik 20). Tübingen: Stauffenburg Verlag.

Müller, Gereon. 2009a. There are no Constructions. Handout Ringvorlesung: *Algorithmen und Muster: Strukturen in der Sprache*. Freie Universität Berlin, 20. Mai.

Müller, Gereon. 2011. Regeln oder Konstruktionen? Von verblosen Direktiven zur sequentiellen Nominalreduplikation. In Stefan Engelberg, Anke Holler & Kristel Proost (eds.), *Sprachliches Wissen zwischen Lexikon und Grammatik* (Institut für Deutsche Sprache, Jahrbuch 2010), 211–249. Berlin: de Gruyter.

Müller, Gereon. 2014a. Syntactic buffers. Linguistische Arbeitsberichte 91 Institut für Linguistic Universität Leipzig. http://www.uni-leipzig.de/~muellerg/mu765.pdf.

Müller, Natascha & Beate Riemer. 1998. *Generative Syntax der romanischen Sprachen: Französisch, Italienisch, Portugiesisch, Spanisch* (Stauffenburg Einführungen 17). Tübingen: Stauffenburg Verlag.

Müller, Stefan. 1995. Scrambling in German – Extraction into the *Mittelfeld*. In Benjamin K. T'sou & Tom Bong Yeung Lai (eds.), *Proceedings of the Tenth Pacific Asia Conference on Language, Information and Computation*, 79–83. City University of Hong Kong.

Müller, Stefan. 1996c. The Babel-System—An HPSG fragment for German, a parser, and a dialogue component. In *Proceedings of the Fourth International Conference on the Practical Application of Prolog*, 263–277. London.

Müller, Stefan. 1996d. Yet another paper about partial verb phrase fronting in German. In Jun-ichi Tsuji (ed.), *Proceedings of COLING-96: 16th International Conference on Computational Linguistics (COLING96). Copenhagen, Denmark, August 5–9, 1996*, 800–805. Copenhagen, Denmark: Association for Computational Linguistics.

Müller, Stefan. 1999a. *Deutsche Syntax deklarativ: Head-Driven Phrase Structure Grammar für das Deutsche* (Linguistische Arbeiten 394). Tübingen: Max Niemeyer Verlag.

Müller, Stefan. 1999b. An HPSG-analysis for free relative clauses in German. *Grammars* 2(1). 53–105.

Müller, Stefan. 1999c. Restricting discontinuity. In *Proceedings of the 5th Natural Language Processing Pacific Rim Symposium 1999 (NLPRS'99)*, 85–90. Peking.

Müller, Stefan. 1999d. Restricting discontinuity. Verbmobil Report 237 Deutsches Forschungszentrum für Künstliche Intelligenz Saarbrücken. This report is also published in the Proceedings Proceedings of GLDV 99 (Frankfurt/Main). The initial part is contained in the proceedings of the 5th Natural Language Processing Pacific Rim Symposium 1999 (NLPRS'99).

Müller, Stefan. 2001. Case in German – towards an HPSG analysis. In Walt Detmar Meurers & Tibor Kiss (eds.), *Constraint-based approaches to Germanic syntax* (Studies in Constraint-Based Lexicalism 7), 217–255. Stanford, CA: CSLI Publications.

Müller, Stefan. 2002a. *Complex predicates: Verbal complexes, resultative constructions, and particle verbs in German* (Studies in Constraint-Based Lexicalism 13). Stanford, CA: CSLI Publications.

Müller, Stefan. 2002b. Multiple frontings in German. In Gerhard Jäger, Paola Monachesi, Gerald Penn & Shuly Wintner (eds.), *Proceedings of Formal Grammar 2002*, 113–124. Trento.

Müller, Stefan. 2002c. Syntax or morphology: German particle verbs revisited. In Nicole Dehé, Ray S. Jackendoff, Andrew McIntyre & Silke Urban (eds.), *Verb-particle explorations* (Interface Explorations 1), 119–139. Berlin: Mouton de Gruyter.

Müller, Stefan. 2003a. Mehrfache Vorfeldbesetzung. *Deutsche Sprache* 31(1). 29–62.

Müller, Stefan. 2003b. Object-to-subject-raising and lexical rule: An analysis of the German passive. In Stefan Müller (ed.), *Proceedings of the 10th International Conference on Head-Driven Phrase Structure Grammar, Michigan State University, East Lansing*, 278–297. Stanford, CA: CSLI Publications.

Müller, Stefan. 2003c. Solving the bracketing paradox: An analysis of the morphology of German particle verbs. *Journal of Linguistics* 39(2). 275–325.

Müller, Stefan. 2004a. An analysis of depictive secondary predicates in German without discontinuous constituents. In Stefan Müller (ed.), *Proceedings of the 11th International Conference on Head-Driven Phrase Structure Grammar, Center for Computational Linguistics, Katholieke Universiteit Leuven*, 202–222. Stanford, CA: CSLI Publications.

Müller, Stefan. 2004b. Complex NPs, subjacency, and extraposition. *Snippets* 8. 10–11.

Müller, Stefan. 2004c. Continuous or discontinuous constituents? A comparison between syntactic analyses for constituent order and their processing systems. *Research on Language and Computation, Special Issue on Linguistic Theory and Grammar Implementation* 2(2). 209–257.

Müller, Stefan. 2004d. An HPSG analysis of German depictive secondary predicates. In Lawrence S. Moss & Richard T. Oehrle (eds.), *Proceedings of the joint meeting of the 6th Conference on Formal Grammar and the 7th Conference on Mathematics of Language* (Electronic Notes in Theoretical Computer Science 53), 233–245. Helsinki: Elsevier Science Publisher B.V. (North-Holland). DOI:10.1016/S1571-0661(05)82585-X.

Müller, Stefan. 2005a. Resultative Constructions: Syntax, world knowledge, and collocational restrictions: Review of Hans C. Boas: A Constructional approach to resultatives. *Studies in Language* 29(3). 651–681.

Müller, Stefan. 2005b. Zur Analyse der deutschen Satzstruktur. *Linguistische Berichte* 201. 3–39.

Müller, Stefan. 2005c. Zur Analyse der scheinbar mehrfachen Vorfeldbesetzung. *Linguistische Berichte* 203. 297–330.

Müller, Stefan. 2006. Phrasal or lexical Constructions? *Language* 82(4). 850–883.

Müller, Stefan. 2007a. The Grammix CD Rom: A software collection for developing typed feature structure grammars. In Tracy Holloway King & Emily M. Bender (eds.), *Grammar Engineering across Frameworks 2007* (Studies in Computational Linguistics ONLINE), 259–266. Stanford, CA: CSLI Publications. http://csli-publications.stanford.edu/GEAF/2007/.

Müller, Stefan. 2007b. *Head-Driven Phrase Structure Grammar: Eine Einführung* (Stauffenburg Einführungen 17). Tübingen: Stauffenburg Verlag 1st edn.

Müller, Stefan. 2007c. Phrasal or lexical Constructions: Some comments on underspecification of constituent order, compositionality, and control. In Stefan Müller (ed.), *Proceedings of the 14th International Conference on Head-Driven Phrase Structure Grammar*, 373–393. Stanford, CA: CSLI Publications.

Müller, Stefan. 2007d. Qualitative Korpusanalyse für die Grammatiktheorie: Introspektion vs. Korpus. In Gisela Zifonun & Werner Kallmeyer (eds.), *Sprachkorpora – Datenmengen und Erkenntnisfortschritt* (Institut für Deutsche Sprache Jahrbuch 2006), 70–90. Berlin: Walter de Gruyter.

Müller, Stefan. 2008. Depictive secondary predicates in German and English. In Christoph Schroeder, Gerd Hentschel & Winfried Boeder (eds.), *Secondary predicates in Eastern European languages and beyond* (Studia Slavica Oldenburgensia 16), 255–273. Oldenburg: BIS-Verlag.

Müller, Stefan. 2009b. A Head-Driven Phrase Structure Grammar for Maltese. In Bernard Comrie, Ray Fabri, Beth Hume, Manwel Mifsud, Thomas Stolz & Martine Vanhove (eds.), *Introducing Maltese linguistics: Papers from the 1st International Conference on Maltese Linguistics (Bremen/Germany, 18–20 October, 2007)* (Studies in Language Companion Series 113), 83–112. Amsterdam: John Benjamins Publishing Co.

Müller, Stefan. 2009c. On predication. In Stefan Müller (ed.), *Proceedings of the 16th International Conference on Head-Driven Phrase Structure Grammar, University of Göttingen, Germany*, 213–233. Stanford, CA: CSLI Publications.

Müller, Stefan. 2010a. *Grammatiktheorie* (Stauffenburg Einführungen 20). Tübingen: Stauffenburg Verlag.

Müller, Stefan. 2010b. Persian complex predicates and the limits of inheritance-based analyses. *Journal of Linguistics* 46(3). 601–655.

Müller, Stefan. 2012a. On the copula, specificational constructions and type shifting. Ms. Freie Universität Berlin.

Müller, Stefan. 2012b. A personal note on open access in linguistics. *Journal of Language Modelling* 0(1). 9–39.

Müller, Stefan. 2013a. The CoreGram project: A brief overview and motivation. In Denys Duchier & Yannick Parmentier (eds.), *Proceedings of the workshop on high-level methodologies for grammar engineering (HMGE 2013), Düsseldorf*, 93–104.

Müller, Stefan. 2013b. *Grammatiktheorie* (Stauffenburg Einführungen 20). Tübingen: Stauffenburg Verlag 2nd edn.

Müller, Stefan. 2013c. Unifying everything: Some remarks on Simpler Syntax, Construction Grammar, Minimalism and HPSG. *Language* 89(4). 920–950.

Müller, Stefan. 2014b. Artenvielfalt und Head-Driven Phrase Structure Grammar. In Jörg Hagemann & Sven Staffeldt (eds.), *Syntaxtheorien: Analysen im Vergleich* (Stauffenburg Einführungen 28), 187–233. Tübingen: Stauffenburg Verlag.

Müller, Stefan. 2014c. Elliptical constructions, multiple frontings, and surface-based syntax. In Paola Monachesi, Gerhard Jäger, Gerald Penn & Shuly Wintner (eds.), *Proceedings of Formal Grammar 2004, Nancy*, 91–109. Stanford, CA: CSLI Publications.

Müller, Stefan. 2014d. Kernigkeit: Anmerkungen zur Kern-Peripherie-Unterscheidung. In Antonio Machicao y Priemer, Andreas Nolda & Athina Sioupi (eds.), *Zwischen Kern und Peripherie* (studia grammatica 76), 25–39. Berlin: de Gruyter.

Müller, Stefan. 2015a. The CoreGram project: Theoretical linguistics, theory development and verification. *Journal of Language Modelling* 3(1). 21–86. DOI:10.15398/jlm.v3i1.91.

Müller, Stefan. 2015b. *German sentence structure: An analysis with special consideration of so-called multiple fronting* (Empirically Oriented Theoretical Morphology and Syntax). Berlin: Language Science Press. Submitted.

Müller, Stefan. 2015c. HPSG – A synopsis. In Tibor Kiss & Artemis Alexiadou (eds.), *Syntax – Theory and analysis: An international handbook* (Handbooks of Linguistics and Communication Science 42.2), 937–973. Berlin: Walter de Gruyter 2nd edn.

Müller, Stefan. 2016a. *Germanic syntax* (Textbooks in Language Sciences). Berlin: Language Science Press. In Preparation.

Müller, Stefan. 2016b. Satztypen: Lexikalisch oder/und phrasal. In Rita Finkbeiner & Jörg Meibauer (eds.), *Satztypen und Konstruktionen im Deutschen* (Linguistik – Impulse und Tendenzen 65), 72–105. Berlin, Boston: de Gruyter.

Müller, Stefan & Masood Ghayoomi. 2010. PerGram: A TRALE implementation of an HPSG fragment of Persian. In *Proceedings of 2010 IEEE International Multiconference on Computer Science and Information Technology – Computational Linguistics Applications (CLA'10). Wisła, Poland, 18–20 October 2010*, vol. 5, 461–467. Polnish Information Processing Society.

Müller, Stefan & Martin Haspelmath. 2013. Language Science Press: A publication model for open-access books in linguistics. Grant Proposal to the DFG.

Müller, Stefan & Walter Kasper. 2000. HPSG analysis of German. In Wolfgang Wahlster (ed.), *Verbmobil: Foundations of speech-to-speech translation* (Artificial Intelligence), 238–253. Berlin: Springer Verlag.

Müller, Stefan & Janna Lipenkova. 2009. Serial verb constructions in Chinese: An HPSG account. In Stefan Müller (ed.), *Proceedings of the 16th International Conference on Head-Driven Phrase Structure Grammar, University of Göttingen, Germany*, 234–254. Stanford, CA: CSLI Publications.

Müller, Stefan & Janna Lipenkova. 2013. ChinGram: A TRALE implementation of an HPSG fragment of Mandarin Chinese. In Huei ling Lai & Kawai Chui (eds.), *Proceedings of the 27th Pacific Asia Conference on Language, Information, and Computation*

(PACLIC 27), 240–249. Taipei, Taiwan: Department of English, National Chengchi University.

Müller, Stefan & Janna Lipenkova. 2016. *Mandarin Chinese in Head-Driven Phrase Structure Grammar* (Empirically Oriented Theoretical Morphology and Syntax). Berlin: Language Science Press. In Preparation.

Müller, Stefan & Bjarne Ørsnes. 2011. Positional expletives in Danish, German, and Yiddish. In Stefan Müller (ed.), *Proceedings of the 18th International Conference on Head-Driven Phrase Structure Grammar, University of Washington, U.S.A.*, 167–187. Stanford, CA: CSLI Publications.

Müller, Stefan & Bjarne Ørsnes. 2013a. Passive in Danish, English, and German. In Stefan Müller (ed.), *Proceedings of the 20th International Conference on Head-Driven Phrase Structure Grammar, Freie Universität Berlin*, 140–160. Stanford, CA: CSLI Publications.

Müller, Stefan & Bjarne Ørsnes. 2013b. Towards an HPSG analysis of object shift in Danish. In Glyn Morrill & Mark-Jan Nederhof (eds.), *Formal Grammar: 17th and 18th International Conferences, FG 2012, Opole, Poland, August 2012, revised selected papers, FG 2013, Düsseldorf, Germany, August 2013: Proceedings* (Lecture Notes in Computer Science 8036), 69–89. Berlin: Springer Verlag.

Müller, Stefan & Bjarne Ørsnes. 2015. *Danish in Head-Driven Phrase Structure Grammar* (Empirically Oriented Theoretical Morphology and Syntax). Berlin: Language Science Press. In Preparation.

Müller, Stefan & Stephen Mark Wechsler. 2014a. Lexical approaches to argument structure. *Theoretical Linguistics* 40(1–2). 1–76.

Müller, Stefan & Stephen Mark Wechsler. 2014b. Two sides of the same slim Boojum: Further arguments for a lexical approach to argument structure. *Theoretical Linguistics* 40(1–2). 187–224.

Muraki, Kazunori, Shunji Ichiyama & Yasutomo Fukumochi. 1985. Augmented Dependency Grammar: A simple interface between the grammar rule and the knowledge. In Maghi King (ed.), *Proceedings of the 2nd European Meeting of the Association for Computational Linguistics*, 198–204. Geneva: Association for Computational Linguistics. http://aclweb.org/anthology/E/E85/.

Musso, Mariacristina, Andrea Moro, Volkmar Glauche, Michel Rijntjes, Jürgen Reichenbach, Christian Büchel & Cornelius Weiller. 2003. Broca's area and the language instinct. *Nature Neuroscience* 6(7). 774–781.

Müürisep, Kaili. 1999. Determination of syntactic functions in Estonian Constraint Grammar. In Henry S. Thompson & Alex Lascarides (eds.), *Ninth conference of the European Chapter of the Association for Computational Linguistics*, 291–292. Bergen, Norway.

Müürisep, Kaili, Tiina Puolakainen, Kadri Muischnek, Mare Koit, Tiit Roosmaa & Heli Uibo. 2003. A new language for Constraint Grammar: Estonian. In *International Conference Recent Advances in Natural Language Processing*, 304–310.

Muysken, Peter. 1982. Parameterizing the notion of "head". *Journal of Linguistic Research* 2. 57–75.

Mykowiecka, Agnieszka, Małgorzata Marciniak, Adam Przepiórkowski & Anna Kupść. 2003. An implementation of a Generative Grammar of Polish. In Peter Kosta, Joanna

Błaszczak, Jens Frasek, Ljudmila Geist & Marzena Żygis (eds.), *Investigations into formal Slavic linguistics: Contributions of the Fourth European Conference on Formal Description of Slavic Languages – FDSL IV held at Potsdam University, November 28–30, 2001*, 271–285. Frankfurt am Main: Peter Lang.

Naumann, Sven. 1987. Ein einfacher Parser für generalisierte Phrasenstrukturgrammatiken. *Zeitschrift für Sprachwissenschaft* 6(2). 206–226.

Naumann, Sven. 1988. *Generalisierte Phrasenstrukturgrammatik: Parsingstrategien, Regelorganisation und Unifikation* (Linguistische Arbeiten 212). Tübingen: Max Niemeyer Verlag.

Neeleman, Ad. 1994. *Complex predicates*. Utrecht: Onderzoeksinstituut voor Taal en Spraak (OTS) dissertation.

Nelimarkka, Esa, Harri Jäppinen & Aarno Lehtola. 1984. Two-way finite automata and Dependency Grammar: A parsing method for inflectional free word order languages. In Yorick Wilks (ed.), *Proceedings of the 10th International Conference on Computational Linguistics and 22nd Annual Meeting of the Association for Computational Linguistics*, 389–392. Stanford University, California: Association for Computational Linguistics.

Nerbonne, John. 1986a. 'Phantoms' and German fronting: Poltergeist constituents? *Linguistics* 24(5). 857–870.

Nerbonne, John. 1986b. A phrase-structure grammar for German passives. *Linguistics* 24(5). 907–938.

Nerbonne, John. 1993. A feature-based syntax/semantics interface. *Annals of Mathematics and Artificial Intelligence* 8(1–2). 107–132. Special issue on Mathematics of Language edited by Alexis Manaster-Ramer and Wlodek Zadrozsny, selected from the 2nd Conference on Mathematics of Language. Also published as DFKI Research Report RR-92-42.

Nerbonne, John, Klaus Netter & Carl J. Pollard (eds.). 1994. *German in Head-Driven Phrase Structure Grammar* (CSLI Lecture Notes 46). Stanford, CA: CSLI Publications.

Netter, Klaus. 1991. Clause union phenomena and complex predicates in German. DYANA Report, Deliverable R1.1.B University of Edinburgh.

Netter, Klaus. 1992. On non-head non-movement: An HPSG treatment of finite verb position in German. In Günther Görz (ed.), *Konvens 92. 1. Konferenz „Verarbeitung natürlicher Sprache". Nürnberg 7.–9. Oktober 1992* (Informatik aktuell), 218–227. Berlin: Springer Verlag.

Netter, Klaus. 1993. Architecture and coverage of the DISCO Grammar. In Stephan Busemann & Karin Harbusch (eds.), *DFKI Workshop on Natural Language Systems: Re-Usability and Modularity, October 23* (DFKI Document D-93-03), 1–10. Saarbrücken, Germany: DFKI.

Netter, Klaus. 1994. Towards a theory of functional heads: German nominal phrases. In John Nerbonne, Klaus Netter & Carl J. Pollard (eds.), *German in Head-Driven Phrase Structure Grammar* (CSLI Lecture Notes 46), 297–340. Stanford, CA: CSLI Publications.

Netter, Klaus. 1996. *Functional categories in an HPSG for German*. Saarbrücken: Universität des Saarlandes Dissertation.

Netter, Klaus. 1998. *Functional categories in an HPSG for German* (Saarbrücken Dissertations in Computational Linguistics and Language Technology 3). Saarbrücken: Deutsches Forschungszentrum für Künstliche Intelligenz Universität des Saarlandes.

Neville, Anne & Patrizia Paggio. 2004. Developing a Danish grammar in the GRASP project: A construction-based approach to topology and extraction in Danish. In Lawrence S. Moss & Richard T. Oehrle (eds.), *Proceedings of the joint meeting of the 6th Conference on Formal Grammar and the 7th Conference on Mathematics of Language* (Electronic Notes in Theoretical Computer Science 53), 246–259. Helsinki: Elsevier Science Publisher B.V. (North-Holland).

Nevins, Andrew Ira, David Pesetsky & Cilene Rodrigues. 2009. Pirahã exceptionality: A reassessment. *Language* 85(2). 355–404.

Newmeyer, Frederick J. 2004a. Against a parameter-setting approach to language variation. *Linguistic Variation Yearbook* 4. 181–234.

Newmeyer, Frederick J. 2004b. Typological evidence and Universal Grammar. *Studies in Language* 28(3). 527–548.

Newmeyer, Frederick J. 2005. *Possible and probable languages: A Generative perspective on linguistic typology*. Oxford: Oxford University Press.

Newmeyer, Frederick J. 2010. On comparative concepts and descriptive categories: A reply to Haspelmath. *Language* 86(3). 688–695.

Newport, Elissa L. 1990. Maturational constraints on language learning. *Cognitive Science* 14(1). 11–28.

Ng, Say Kiat. 1997. *A double-specifier account of Chinese NPs using Head-Driven Phrase Structure Grammar*. University of Edinburgh, Department of Linguistics MSc speech and language processing.

Nivre, Joakim. 2003. An efficient algorithm for projective dependency parsing. In Gertjan van Noord (ed.), *Proceedings of the 8th International Workshop on Parsing Technologies (IWPT 03)*, Nancy.

Nolda, Andreas. 2007. *Die Thema-Integration: Syntax und Semantik der gespaltenen Topikalisierung im Deutschen* (Studien zur deutschen Grammatik 72). Tübingen: Stauffenburg Verlag.

Noonan, Michael. 1994. A tale of two passives in Irish. In Barbara Fox & Paul J. Hopper (eds.), *Voice: Form and function* (Typological Studies in Language 27), 279–311. Amsterdam: John Benjamins Publishing Co.

van Noord, Gertjan & Gosse Bouma. 1994. The scope of adjuncts and the processing of lexical rules. In Makoto Nagao (ed.), *Proceedings of COLING 94*, 250–256. Kyoto, Japan: Association for Computational Linguistics.

Nordgård, Torbjørn. 1994. E-Parser: An implementation of a deterministic GB-related parsing system. *Computers and the Humanities* 28(4–5). 259–272.

Nordlinger, Rachel. 1998. *Constructive case: Evidence from Australia* (Dissertations in Linguistics). Stanford, CA: CSLI Publications.

Nowak, Martin A., Natalia L. Komarova & Partha Niyogi. 2001. Evolution of Universal Grammar. *Science* 291(5501). 114–118.

Nozohoor-Farshi, R. 1986. On formalizations of Marcus' parser. In Makoto Nagao (ed.), *Proceedings of COLING 86*, 533–535. University of Bonn: Association for Computational Linguistics.

Nozohoor-Farshi, R. 1987. Context-freeness of the language accepted by Marcus' parser. In Candy Sidner (ed.), *25th Annual Meeting of the Association for Computational Linguistics*, 117–122. Stanford, CA: Association for Computational Linguistics.

Nunberg, Geoffrey. 1995. Transfers of meaning. *Journal of Semantics* 12(2). 109–132.

Nunberg, Geoffrey, Ivan A. Sag & Thomas Wasow. 1994. Idioms. *Language* 70(3). 491–538.

Nunes, Jairo. 2004. *Linearization of chains and Sideward Movement* (Linguistic Inquiry Monographs 43). Cambridge, MA/London, England: MIT Press.

Ochs, Elinor. 1982. Talking to children in Western Samoa. *Language and Society* 11(1). 77–104.

Ochs, Elinor & Bambi B. Schieffelin. 1985. Language acquisition and socialization: Three developmental stories. In Richard A. Shweder & Robert A. LeVine (eds.), *Culture theory: Essays in mind, self and emotion*, 276–320. Cambridge, UK: Cambridge University Press.

O'Donovan, Ruth, Michael Burke, Aoife Cahill, Josef van Genabith & Andy Way. 2005. Large-scale induction and evaluation of lexical resources from the Penn-II and Penn-III Treebanks. *Computational Linguistics* 31(3). 328–365.

Oepen, Stephan & Daniel P. Flickinger. 1998. Towards systematic grammar profiling: Test suite technology ten years after. *Journal of Computer Speech and Language* 12(4). 411–436. http://www.delph-in.net/itsdb/publications/profiling.ps.gz. (Special Issue on Evaluation).

Özkaragöz, İnci. 1986. Monoclausal double passives in Turkish. In Dan I. Slobin & Karl Zimmer (eds.), *Studies in Turkish linguistics* (Typological Studies in Language 8), 77–91. Amsterdam: John Benjamins Publishing Co.

Oliva, Karel. 1992. Word order constraints in binary branching syntactic structures. CLAUS-Report 20 Universität des Saarlandes Saarbrücken.

Oliva, Karel. 2003. Dependency, valency and Head-Driven Phrase-Structure Grammar. In Vilmos Ágel, Ludwig M. Eichinger, Hans Werner Eroms, Peter Hellwig, Hans Jürgen Heringer & Henning Lobin (eds.), *Dependenz und Valenz / Dependency and valency: Ein internationales Handbuch der zeitgenössischen Forschung / An international handbook of contemporary research*, vol. 25.1 (Handbücher zur Sprach- und Kommunikationswissenschaft), 660–668. Berlin: Walter de Gruyter.

O'Neill, Michael & Randall Wood. 2012. The grammar of happiness. Essential Media & Entertainment / Smithsonian Networks. https://www.youtube.com/watch?v=er2VAk4uXUs#t=1519.

Oppenrieder, Wilhelm. 1991. *Von Subjekten, Sätzen und Subjektsätzen* (Linguisitische Arbeiten 241). Tübingen: Max Niemeyer Verlag.

Orgun, Cemil Orhan. 1996. *Sign-based morphology and phonology*: University of California, Berkeley dissertation.

Osborne, Miles & Ted J. Briscoe. 1997. Learning Stochastic Categorial Grammars. In T. Mark Ellison (ed.), *CoNLL97: Computational Natural Language Learning: Proceedings of the 1997 meeting of the ACL Special Interest Group in Natural Language Learning*, 80–87. Madrid: Association for Computational Linguistics. http://www.aclweb.org/anthology-new/signll.html#1997-0.

Osborne, Timothy. 2014. Dependency Grammar. In Andrew Carnie, Yosuke Sato & Dan Siddiqi (eds.), *The Routledge handbook of syntax*, 604–626. Oxford: Routledge.

Osborne, Timothy. 2016. Ellipsis in Dependency Grammar. In Jeroen van Craenenbrok (ed.), *Oxford handbook of ellipsis*, Oxford: Oxford University Press. To appear.

Osborne, Timothy & Thomas M. Groß. 2012. Constructions are catenae: Construction Grammar meets Dependency Grammar. *Cognitive Linguistics* 23(1). 165–216.

Osborne, Timothy & Sylvain Kahane. 2015. Translators' introduction. In *Elements of structural syntax*, xxix–lxxiii. Amsterdam: John Benjamins Publishing Co. Translated by Timothy Osborne and Sylvain Kahane.

Osborne, Timothy, Michael Putnam & Thomas M. Groß. 2011. Bare Phrase Structure, label-less trees, and specifier-less syntax: Is Minimalism becoming a Dependency Grammar? *The Linguistic Review* 28(3). 315–364.

Osenova, Petya. 2010a. Bulgarian Resource Grammar – efficient and realistic (BURGER). Tech. rep. LingoLab, CSLI Stanford. http://www.bultreebank.org/BURGER/BURGER3.pdf.

Osenova, Petya. 2010b. *Bulgarian Resource Grammar: Modeling Bulgarian in HPSG*. Saarbrücken: VDM Verlag Dr. Müller.

Osenova, Petya. 2011. Localizing a core HPSG-based grammar for Bulgarian. In Hanna Hedeland, Thomas Schmidt & Kai Wörner (eds.), *Multilingual resources and multilingual applications: Proceedings of the Conference of the German Society for Computational Linguistics and Language Technology (GSCL) 2011* (Arbeiten zur Mehrsprachigkeit/Working Papers in Multilingualism, Folge B/Series B 96), 175–182. Hamburg: Universitat Hamburg.

Ott, Dennis. 2011. A note on free relative clauses in the theory of Phases. *Linguistic Inquiry* 42(1). 183–192.

Ørsnes, Bjarne. 1995. *The derivation and compounding of complex event nominals in Modern Danish: An HPSG approach with an implementation in Prolog*: University of Copenhagen dissertation.

Ørsnes, Bjarne. 2002. Case marking and subject extraction in Danish. In Miriam Butt & Tracy Holloway King (eds.), *Proceedings of the LFG 2002 conference*, 333–353. Stanford, CA: CSLI Publications. http://csli-publications.stanford.edu/LFG/7/.

Ørsnes, Bjarne. 2009a. Das Verbalfeldmodell: Ein Stellungsfeldermodell für den kontrastiven DaF-Unterricht. *Deutsch als Fremdsprache* 46(3). 143–149.

Ørsnes, Bjarne. 2009b. Preposed negation in Danish. In Stefan Müller (ed.), *Proceedings of the 16th International Conference on Head-Driven Phrase Structure Grammar, University of Göttingen, Germany*, 255–275. Stanford, CA: CSLI Publications.

Ørsnes, Bjarne & Jürgen Wedekind. 2003. Paralelle datamatiske grammatikker for Norsk og Dansk [parallel computational grammars for Norwegian and Danish]. In Henrik Holmboe (ed.), *Årbog for nordisk sprogteknologisk forskningsprogram 2000–2004*, 113–130. Kopenhagen: Museum Tusculanums Forlag.

Ørsnes, Bjarne & Jürgen Wedekind. 2004. Paralelle datamatiske grammatikker for Norsk og Dansk: Analyse og disambiguering af modalverber [parallel computational grammars for Norwegian and Danish: Analysis and disambiguation of modal verbs]. In Henrik Holmboe (ed.), *Årbog for Nordisk Sprogteknologisk forskningsprogram 2000–2004*, 165–182. Kopenhagen: Museum Tusculanums Forlag.

Pafel, Jürgen. 1993. Ein Überblick über die Extraktion aus Nominalphrasen im Deutschen. In Franz-Josef d'Avis, Sigrid Beck, Uli Lutz, Jürgen Pafel & Susanne Trissler (eds.), *Extraktion im Deutschen I* (Arbeitspapiere des SFB 340 No. 34), 191–245. Tübingen: Eberhard-Karls-Universität Tübingen.

Paggio, Patrizia. 2005. Representing information structure in a formal grammar of Danish. In *Proceedings of the 2nd International Workshop on Logic and Engineering of Natural Language Semantics (LENLS2005). Kitakyushu, Japan. June 13–14*, .

Parmentier, Yannick, Laura Kallmeyer, Wolfgang Maier, Timm Lichte & Johannes Dellert. 2008. TuLiPA: A syntax-semantics parsing environment for mildly context-sensitive formalisms. In *Proceedings of the Ninth International Workshop on Tree Adjoining Grammars and Related Formalisms (TAG+9)*, 121–128. Tübingen. http://www.sfs.uni-tuebingen.de/~lk/papers/tag+9-parmentier-et-al.pdf.

Partee, Barbara H. 1987. Noun phrase interpretation and type-shifting principles. In Jeroen A. G. Groenendijk, Dick de Jongh & Martin J. B. Stokhof (eds.), *Studies in Discourse Representation Theory and the theory of generalized quantifiers*, 115–143. Dordrecht: Foris Publications.

Patejuk, Agnieszka & Adam Przepiórkowski. 2012. Towards an LFG parser for Polish: An exercise in parasitic grammar development. In *Proceedings of the Eighth International Conference on Language Resources and Evaluation, LREC 2012*, 3849–3852. Istanbul, Turkey: ELRA.

Paul, Hermann. 1919. *Deutsche Grammatik. Teil IV: Syntax*, vol. 3. Halle an der Saale: Max Niemeyer Verlag. 2nd unchanged edition 1968, Tübingen: Max Niemeyer Verlag.

Paul, Soma. 2004. *An HPSG account of Bangla compound verbs with LKB implementation.* Hyderabad, India: CALTS, University of Hyderabad, India dissertation.

Penn, Gerald. 2004. Balancing clarity and efficiency in typed feature logic through delaying. In Donia Scott (ed.), *Proceedings of the 42nd Meeting of the Association for Computational Linguistics (ACL'04), main volume*, 239–246. Barcelona, Spain.

Penn, Gerald & Bob Carpenter. 1999. ALE for speech: A translation prototype. In Géza Gordos (ed.), *Proceedings of the 6th Conference on Speech Communication and Technology (EUROSPEECH)*, Budapest, Hungary.

Perlmutter, David M. 1978. Impersonal passives and the Unaccusative Hypothesis. In *Proceedings of the 4th Annual Meeting of the Berkeley Linguistics Society*, 157–189. Berkeley Linguistic Society.

Perlmutter, David M. (ed.). 1983. *Studies in relational grammar*, vol. 1. Chicago: The University of Chicago Press.

Perlmutter, David M. (ed.). 1984. *Studies in relational grammar*, vol. 2. Chicago: The University of Chicago Press.

Perlmutter, David M. & John Robert Ross. 1970. Relative clauses with split antecedents. *Linguistic Inquiry* 1(3). 350.

Pesetsky, David. 1996. *Zero syntax: Experiencers and cascades*. Cambridge, MA: MIT Press.

Peters, Stanley & R. W. Ritchie. 1973. On the generative power of Transformational Grammar. *Information Sciences* 6(C). 49–83.

Petrick, Stanley Roy. 1965. *A recognition procedure for Transformational Grammars*: Massachusetts Institute of Technology. Dept. of Modern Languages dissertation. http://hdl.handle.net/1721.1/13013.

Phillips, Colin. 2003. Linear order and constituency. *Linguistic Inquiry* 34(1). 37–90.

Phillips, John D. 1992. A computational representation for Generalised Phrase Structure Grammars. *Linguistics and Philosophy* 15(3). 255–287.

Phillips, John D. & Henry S. Thompson. 1985. GPSGP – A parser for Generalized Phrase Structure Grammar. *Linguistics* 23(2). 245–261.

Piattelli-Palmarini, Massimo (ed.). 1980. *Language and learning: The debate between Jean Piaget and Noam Chomsky*. Cambridge: Harvard University Press.

Pickering, Martin & Guy Barry. 1993. Dependency Categorial Grammar and coordination. *Linguistics* 31(5). 855–902.

Pienemann, Manfred. 2005. An introduction to Processability Theory. In Manfred Pienemann (ed.), *Cross-linguistic aspects of processablity theory*, 1–60. Amsterdam: John Benjamins Publishing Co.

Piñango, Maria Mercedes, Jennifer Mack & Ray S. Jackendoff. 2006. Semantic combinatorial processes in argument structure: Evidence from light-verbs. In *Proceedings of the 32nd Annual Meeting of the Berkeley Linguistics Society: Theoretical approaches to argument structure*, vol. 32, Berkeley, CA: BLS.

Pineda, Luis Alberto & Iván V. Meza. 2005a. A computational model of the Spanish clitic system. In Alexander Gelbkuh (ed.), *Computational linguistics and intelligent language processing*, 73–82. Berlin: Springer Verlag.

Pineda, Luis Alberto & Iván V. Meza. 2005b. The Spanish pronominal clitic system. *Procesamiento del Lenguaje Natural* 34. 67–103.

Pinker, Steven. 1984. *Learnability and cognition: The acquisition of argument structure*. London/Cambridge, MA: MIT Press.

Pinker, Steven. 1994. *The language instinct: How the mind creates language*. New York: William Morrow.

Pinker, Steven & Ray S. Jackendoff. 2005. The faculty of language: What's special about it? *Cognition* 95(2). 201–236.

Pittner, Karin. 1995. Regeln für die Bildung von freien Relativsätzen: Eine Antwort an Oddleif Leirbukt. *Deutsch als Fremdsprache* 32(4). 195–200.

Plank, Frans & Elena Filimonova. 2000. The universals archive: A brief introduction for prospective users. *Sprachtypologie und Universalienforschung* 53(1). 109–123.

Poletto, Cecilia. 2000. *The higher functional field: Evidence from Northern Italian Dialects*. Oxford: Oxford University Press.

Pollard, Carl J. 1984. *Generalized Phrase Structure Grammars, Head Grammars, and natural language*: Stanford University dissertation.
Pollard, Carl J. 1988. Categorial Grammar and Phrase Structure Grammar: An excursion on the syntax-semantics frontier. In Richard Oehrle, Emmon Bach & Deirdre Wheeler (eds.), *Categorial Grammars and natural language structures*, 391–415. Dordrecht: D. Reidel Publishing Company.
Pollard, Carl J. 1994. Toward a unified account of passive in German. In John Nerbonne, Klaus Netter & Carl J. Pollard (eds.), *German in Head-Driven Phrase Structure Grammar* (CSLI Lecture Notes 46), 273–296. Stanford, CA: CSLI Publications.
Pollard, Carl J. 1996a. The nature of constraint-based grammar. Paper presented at the Pacific Asia Conference on Language, Information, and Computation, Kyung Hee University, Seoul, Korea. http://lingo.stanford.edu/sag/L221a/pollard-96.txt.
Pollard, Carl J. 1996b. On head non-movement. In Harry Bunt & Arthur van Horck (eds.), *Discontinuous constituency* (Natural Language Processing 6), 279–305. Berlin: Mouton de Gruyter. Published version of a Ms. dated January 1990.
Pollard, Carl J. 1999. Strong generative capacity in HPSG. In Gert Webelhuth, Jean-Pierre Koenig & Andreas Kathol (eds.), *Lexical and Constructional aspects of linguistic explanation* (Studies in Constraint-Based Lexicalism 1), 281–298. Stanford, CA: CSLI Publications.
Pollard, Carl J. & Andrew M. Moshier. 1990. Unifying partial descriptions of sets. In Philip P. Hanson (ed.), *Information, language and cognition* (Vancouver Studies in Cognitive Science 1), 285–322. Vancouver: University of British Columbia Press.
Pollard, Carl J. & Ivan A. Sag. 1987. *Information-based syntax and semantics* (CSLI Lecture Notes 13). Stanford, CA: CSLI Publications.
Pollard, Carl J. & Ivan A. Sag. 1992. Anaphors in English and the scope of Binding Theory. *Linguistic Inquiry* 23(2). 261–303.
Pollard, Carl J. & Ivan A. Sag. 1994. *Head-Driven Phrase Structure Grammar* (Studies in Contemporary Linguistics). Chicago: The University of Chicago Press.
Pollock, Jean-Yves. 1989. Verb movement, Universal Grammar and the structure of IP. *Linguistic Inquiry* 20(3). 365–424.
Popowich, Fred & Carl Vogel. 1991. A logic based implementation of Head-Driven Phrase Structure Grammar. In Charles Grant Brown & Gregers Koch (eds.), *Natural Language Understanding and Logic Programming, III. The 3rd International Workshop, Stockholm, Sweden, 23–25 Jan., 1991*, 227–246. Amsterdam: Elsevier, North-Holland.
Porzel, Robert, Vanessa Micelli, Hidir Aras & Hans-Peter Zorn. 2006. Tying the knot: Ground entities, descriptions and information objects for Construction-based information extraction. In *Proceedings of the OntoLex Workshop at LREC, May 2006. Genoa, Italy*, 35–40.
Postal, Paul M. 2004. *Skeptical linguistic essays.* Oxford: Oxford University Press.
Postal, Paul M. 2009. The incoherence of Chomsky's 'Biolinguistic' ontology. *Biolinguistics* 3(1). 104–123.
Postal, Paul M. & Geoffrey K. Pullum. 1986. Misgovernment. *Linguistic Inquiry* 17(1). 104–110.

Prince, Alan & Paul Smolensky. 1993. Optimality Theory: Constraint interaction in Generative Grammar. RuCCS Technical Report 2 Center for Cognitive Science, Rutgers University, Piscataway, N.J., and Computer Science Department, University of Colorado, Boulder. http://roa.rutgers.edu/files/537-0802/537-0802-PRINCE-0-0.PDF.

Przepiórkowski, Adam. 1999a. *Case assignment and the complement-adjunct dichotomy: A non-configurational constraint-based approach*: Eberhard-Karls-Universität Tübingen dissertation. https://publikationen.uni-tuebingen.de/xmlui/handle/10900/46147.

Przepiórkowski, Adam. 1999b. On case assignment and "adjuncts as complements". In Gert Webelhuth, Jean-Pierre Koenig & Andreas Kathol (eds.), *Lexical and Constructional aspects of linguistic explanation* (Studies in Constraint-Based Lexicalism 1), 231–245. Stanford, CA: CSLI Publications.

Przepiórkowski, Adam & Anna Kupść. 2006. HPSG for Slavicists. *Glossos* 8. 1–68.

Przepiórkowski, Adam, Anna Kupść, Małgorzata Marciniak & Agnieszka Mykowiecka. 2002. *Formalny opis języka polskiego: Teoria i implementacja*. Warsaw: Akademicka Oficyna Wydawnicza EXIT.

Pullum, Geoffrey K. 1977. Word order universals and grammatical relations. In Peter Cole & Jerrold M. Sadock (eds.), *Grammatical relations* (Syntax and Semantics 8), 249–277. New York, San Francisco, London: Academic Press.

Pullum, Geoffrey K. 1982. Free word order and phrase structure rules. In James Pustejovsky & Peter Sells (eds.), *Proceedings of the 12th Anual Meeting of the Northeast Linguistic Society*, 209–220. Amherst: Graduate Linguistics Student Association.

Pullum, Geoffrey K. 1983. How many possible human languages are there? *Linguistic Inquiry* 14(3). 447–467.

Pullum, Geoffrey K. 1984. Stalking the perfect journal. *Natural Language and Linguistic Theory* 2(2). 261–267.

Pullum, Geoffrey K. 1985. Assuming some version of X-bar Theory. In *Papers from the 21st Annual Meeting of the Chicago Linguistic Society*, 323–353.

Pullum, Geoffrey K. 1986. Footloose and context-free. *Natural Language and Linguistic Theory* 4(3). 409–414.

Pullum, Geoffrey K. 1988. Citation etiquette beyond thunderdome. *Natural Language and Linguistic Theory* 6(4). 579–588.

Pullum, Geoffrey K. 1989a. Formal linguistics meets the Boojum. *Natural Language and Linguistic Theory* 7(1). 137–143. DOI:10.1007/BF00141350.

Pullum, Geoffrey K. 1989b. The incident of the node vortex problem. *Natural Language and Linguistic Theory* 7(3). 473–479.

Pullum, Geoffrey K. 1991. *The great Eskimo vocabulary hoax and other irreverent essays on the study of language*. Chicago: The University of Chicago Press.

Pullum, Geoffrey K. 1996. Learnability, hyperlearning, and the Poverty of the Stimulus. In J. Johnson, M. L. Juge & J. L. Moxley (eds.), *Proceedings of the 22nd Annual Meeting of the Berkeley Linguistics Society: General session and parasession on the role of learnability in grammatical theory*, 498–513. Berkeley, CA: Berkeley Linguistic Society. http://users.ecs.soton.ac.uk/harnad/Papers/Py104/pullum.learn.html.

Pullum, Geoffrey K. 2003. Learnability: Mathematical aspects. In William J. Frawley (ed.), *Oxford international encyclopedia of linguistics*, 431–434. Oxford: Oxford University Press 2nd edn.

Pullum, Geoffrey K. 2007. The evolution of model-theoretic frameworks in linguistics. In James Rogers & Stephan Kepser (eds.), *Model-theoretic syntax at 10 – Proceedings of the ESSLLI 2007 MTS@10 Workshop, August 13–17*, 1–10. Dublin: Trinity College Dublin.

Pullum, Geoffrey K. 2009. Response to Anderson. *Language* 85(2). 245–247.

Pullum, Geoffrey K. 2013. The central question in comparative syntactic metatheory. *Mind and Language* 28(4). 492–521.

Pullum, Geoffrey K. & Barbara C. Scholz. 2001. On the distinction between Generative-Enumerative and Model-Theoretic syntactic frameworks. In Philippe de Groote, Glyn Morrill & Christian Retor (eds.), *Logical Aspects of Computational Linguistics: 4th International Conference* (Lecture Notes in Computer Science 2099), 17–43. Berlin: Springer Verlag.

Pullum, Geoffrey K. & Barbara C. Scholz. 2002. Empirical assessment of stimulus poverty arguments. *The Linguistic Review* 19(1–2). 9–50.

Pullum, Geoffrey K. & Barbara C. Scholz. 2010. Recursion and the infinitude claim. In Harry van der Hulst (ed.), *Recursion in human language* (Studies in Generative Grammar 104), 113–138. Berlin: Mouton de Gruyter.

Pulman, Stephen G. 1985. A parser that doesn't. In Maghi King (ed.), *Proceedings of the 2nd European Meeting of the Association for Computational Linguistics*, 128–135. Geneva: Association for Computational Linguistics. http://aclweb.org/anthology/E/E85/.

Pulvermüller, Friedemann. 2003. *The neuroscience of language: On brain circuits of words and serial order.* Cambridge, UK: Cambridge University Press.

Pulvermüller, Friedemann. 2010. Brain embodiment of syntax and grammar: Discrete combinatorial mechanisms spelt out in neuronal circuits. *Brain & Language* 112(3). 167–179.

Pulvermüller, Friedemann, Bert Cappelle & Yury Shtyrov. 2013. Brain basis of meaning, words, constructions, and grammar. In Thomas Hoffmann & Graeme Trousdale (eds.), *The Oxford handbook of Construction Grammar* (Oxford Handbooks), 397–416. Oxford: Oxford University Press.

Quaglia, Stefano. 2014. On the syntax of some apparent spatial particles in Italian. In Miriam Butt & Tracy Holloway King (eds.), *Proceedings of the LFG 2014 conference*, 503–523. Stanford, CA: CSLI Publications.

Radford, Andrew. 1990. *Syntactic theory and the acquisition of English syntax.* Cambridge, MA: Blackwell Publishing Ltd.

Radford, Andrew. 1997. *Syntactic theory and the structure of English: A Minimalist approach* (Cambridge Textbooks in Linguistics). Cambridge, UK: Cambridge University Press.

Rákosi, György, Tibor Laczkó & Gábor Csernyi. 2011. On English phrasal verbs and their Hungarian counterparts: From the perspective of a computational linguistic project. *Argumentum* 7. 80–89.

Rambow, Owen. 1994. *Formal and computational aspects of natural language syntax*: University of Pennsylvania dissertation.

Ramchand, Gillian. 2005. Post-Davidsonianism. *Theoretical Linguistics* 31(3). 359–373.

Randriamasimanana, Charles. 2006. Simple sentences in Malagasy. In Henry Y. Chang, Lillian M. Huang & Dah ah Ho (eds.), *Streams converging into an ocean: Festschrift in honor of Professor Paul Jen-kuei Li on his 70th birthday*, 71–96. Taipei, Taiwan: Institute of Linguistics, Academia Sinica.

Raposo, Eduardo & Juan Uriagereka. 1990. Long-distance case assignment. *Linguistic Inquiry* 21(4). 505–537.

Rappaport, Malka. 1983. On the nature of derived nominals. In Lori S. Levin, Malka Rappaport & Annie Zaenen (eds.), *Papers in Lexical Functional Grammar*, 113–42. Indiana: Indiana University Linguistics Club.

Rauh, Gisa. 2013. Linguistic categories and the syntax-semantics interface: Evaluating competing approaches. Ms. Universität Wuppertal.

Reape, Mike. 1991. Word order variation in Germanic and parsing. DYANA Report Deliverable R1.1.C University of Edinburgh.

Reape, Mike. 1992. *A formal theory of word order: A case study in West Germanic*: University of Edinburgh dissertation.

Reape, Mike. 1994. Domain union and word order variation in German. In John Nerbonne, Klaus Netter & Carl J. Pollard (eds.), *German in Head-Driven Phrase Structure Grammar* (CSLI Lecture Notes 46), 151–198. Stanford, CA: CSLI Publications.

Reape, Mike. 2000. Formalisation and abstraction in linguistic theory II: Toward a radical Linearisation Theory of German. unpublished paper.

Redington, Martin, Nick Chater & Steven Finch. 1998. Distributional information: A powerful cue for acquiring syntactic categories. *Cognitive Science* 22(4). 425–469.

Reis, Marga. 1974. Syntaktische Hauptsatzprivilegien und das Problem der deutschen Wortstellung. *Zeitschrift für Germanistische Linguistik* 2(3). 299–327.

Reis, Marga. 1980. On justifying topological frames: 'Positional field' and the order of nonverbal constituents in German. *Documentation et Recherche en Linguistique Allemande Contemporaine* 22/23. 59–85.

Reis, Marga. 1982. Zum Subjektbegriff im Deutschen. In Werner Abraham (ed.), *Satzglieder im Deutschen – Vorschläge zur syntaktischen, semantischen und pragmatischen Fundierung* (Studien zur deutschen Grammatik 15), 171–211. Tübingen: originally Gunter Narr Verlag now Stauffenburg Verlag.

Remberger, Eva-Maria. 2009. Null subjects, expletives and locatives in Sardinian. In Georg A. Kaiser & Eva-Maria Remberger (eds.), *Proceedings of the workshop* Null-Subjects, Expletives, and Locatives in Romance (Arbeitspapier 123), 231–261. Konstanz: Fachbereich Sprachwissenschaft, Universität Konstanz.

Resnik, Philip. 1992. Probabilistic Tree-Adjoining Grammar as a framework for statistical natural language processing. In Antonio Zampolli (ed.), *14th International Conference on Computational Linguistics (COLING '92), August 23–28*, 418–424. Nantes, France: Association for Computational Linguistics.

Reyle, Uwe. 1993. Dealing with ambiguities by underspecification: Construction, representation and deduction. *Journal of Semantics* 10(2). 123–179.

Richards, Marc. 2015. Minimalism. In Tibor Kiss & Artemis Alexiadou (eds.), *Syntax – theory and analysis: An international handbook*, vol. 42 (Handbooks of Linguistics and Communication Science), 803–839. Berlin: Mouton de Gruyter 2nd edn.

Richter, Frank. 2004. *A mathematical formalism for linguistic theories with an application in Head-Driven Phrase Structure Grammar*: Eberhard-Karls-Universität Tübingen Phil. Dissertation (2000). https://publikationen.uni-tuebingen.de/xmlui/handle/10900/46230.

Richter, Frank. 2007. Closer to the truth: A new model theory for HPSG. In James Rogers & Stephan Kepser (eds.), *Model-theoretic syntax at 10 – Proceedings of the ESSLLI 2007 MTS@10 Workshop, August 13–17*, 101–110. Dublin: Trinity College Dublin.

Richter, Frank & Manfred Sailer. 1999a. A lexicalist collocation analysis of sentential negation in French. In Valia Kordoni (ed.), *Tübingen studies in Head-Driven Phrase Structure Grammar* (Arbeitspapiere des SFB 340, No. 132, Volume 1), 231–300. Tübingen: Eberhard-Karls-Universität Tübingen.

Richter, Frank & Manfred Sailer. 1999b. Lexicalizing the left periphery of German finite sentences. In Valia Kordoni (ed.), *Tübingen studies in Head-Driven Phrase Structure Grammar* (Arbeitspapiere des SFB 340, No. 132, Volume 1), 116–154. Tübingen: Eberhard-Karls-Universität Tübingen.

Richter, Frank & Manfred Sailer. 2004. Basic concepts of lexical resource semantics. In Arnold Beckmann & Norbert Preining (eds.), *ESSLLI 2003 – Course material I* (Collegium Logicum 5), 87–143. Wien: Kurt Gödel Society.

Richter, Frank & Manfred Sailer. 2009. Phraseological clauses as Constructions in HPSG. In Stefan Müller (ed.), *Proceedings of the 16th International Conference on Head-Driven Phrase Structure Grammar, University of Göttingen, Germany*, 297–317. Stanford, CA: CSLI Publications.

Riehemann, Susanne. 1993. *Word formation in lexical type hierarchies: A case study of* bar*-adjectives in German*. Eberhard-Karls-Universität Tübingen MA thesis. Also published as SfS-Report-02-93, Seminar für Sprachwissenschaft, University of Tübingen.

Riehemann, Susanne Z. 1998. Type-based derivational morphology. *Journal of Comparative Germanic Linguistics* 2(1). 49–77.

Riemsdijk, Henk van. 1978. *A case study in syntactic markedness: The binding nature of prepositional phrases*. Lisse: The Peter de Ridder Press.

Riezler, Stefan, Tracy Holloway King, Ronald M. Kaplan, Richard Crouch, John T. Maxwell III & Mark Johnson. 2002. Parsing the Wall Street Journal using a Lexical-Functional Grammar and discriminative estimation techniques. In Pierre Isabelle (ed.), *40th Annual Meeting of the Association for Computational Linguistics: Proceedings of the conference*, 271–278. University of Pennsylvania, Philadelphia: Association for Computational Linguistics. http://aclanthology.info/events/acl-2002.

Rizzi, Luigi. 1982. Violations of the *wh* island constraint and the Subjacency Condition. In Luigi Rizzi (ed.), *Issues in Italian syntax* (Studies in Generative Grammar 11), 49–76. Dordrecht: Foris Publications.

Rizzi, Luigi. 1986. Null objects in Italian and the theory of *pro*. *Linguistic Inquiry* 17(3). 501–577.

Rizzi, Luigi. 1997. The fine structure of the left periphery. In Liliane Haegeman (ed.), *Elements of grammar*, 281–337. Dordrecht: Kluwer Academic Publishers.

Rizzi, Luigi. 2009a. The discovery of language invariance and variation, and its relevance for the cognitive sciences. *The Behavioral and Brain Sciences* 32(5). 467–468.

Rizzi, Luigi. 2009b. Language variation and universals: Some notes on N. Evans and S. C. Levinson (2009) "The myth of language universals: Language diversity and its importance for cognitive science". In Paola Cotticelli-Kurras & Alessandra Tomaselli (eds.), *La Grammatica tra storia e teoria. Studi in onore di Giorgio Graffi*, 153–162. Alessandra: Edizioni dell'Orso.

Roberts, Ian F. & Anders Holmberg. 2005. On the role of parameters in Universal Grammar: A reply to Newmeyer. In Hans Broekhuis, N. Corver, Riny Huybregts, Ursula Kleinhenz & Jan Koster (eds.), *Organizing grammar: Linguistic studies in honor of Henk van Riemsdijk* (Studies in Generative Grammar 86), 538–553. Berlin: Mouton de Gruyter.

Robins, Robert Henry. 1997. *A short history of linguistics* (Longman Linguistics Library). London: Routledge 4th edn.

Rogers, James. 1994. Obtaining trees from their descriptions: An application to Tree-Adjoining Grammars. *Computational Intelligence* 10(4). 401–421.

Rogers, James. 1997. "Grammarless" Phrase Structure Grammar. *Linguistics and Philosophy* 20. 721–746.

Rogers, James. 1998. *A descriptive approach to language-theoretic complexity* (Studies in Logic, Language and Information). Stanford, CA: CSLI Publications.

Rohrer, Christian. 1996. Fakultativ kohärente Infinitkonstruktionen im Deutschen und deren Behandlung in der Lexikalisch Funktionalen Grammatik. In Gisela Harras & Manfred Bierwisch (eds.), *Wenn die Semantik arbeitet: Klaus Baumgärtner zum 65. Geburtstag*, 89–108. Tübingen: Max Niemeyer Verlag.

Rohrer, Christian & Martin Forst. 2006. Improving coverage and parsing quality of a large-scale LFG for German. In *Proceedings of the Language Resources and Evaluation Conference (LREC-2006)*, Genoa, Italy.

Ross, John Robert. 1967. *Constraints on variables in syntax*: MIT dissertation. http://files.eric.ed.gov/fulltext/ED016965.pdf. Reproduced by the Indiana University Linguistics Club and later published as Ross (1986).

Ross, John Robert. 1986. *Infinite syntax!* Norwood, New Jersey: Ablex Publishing Corporation.

Rothkegel, Annely. 1976. *Valenzgrammatik* (Linguistische Arbeiten 19). Saarbrücken, Germany: Sonderforschungsbereich Elektronische Sprachforschung, Universität des Saarlandes.

Sabel, Joachim. 1999. Das Passiv im Deutschen: Derivationale Ökonomie vs. optionale Bewegung. *Linguistische Berichte* 177. 87–112.

Sáfár, Éva & John Glauert. 2010. Sign Language HPSG. In *Proceedings of the 4th Workshop on the Representation and Processing of Sign Languages: Corpora and Sign Language Technologies, LREC 2010, 22–23 May 2010, Malta*, 204–207.

Sáfár, Éva & Ian Marshall. 2002. Sign language translation via DRT and HPSG. In Alexander Gelbukh (ed.), *Computational linguistics and intelligent text processing: Third International Conference, CICLing 2002 Mexico City, Mexico, February 17–23, 2002 Proceedings* (Lecture Notes in Computer Science 2276), 58–68. Berlin: Springer Verlag.

Sag, Ivan A. 1997. English relative clause constructions. *Journal of Linguistics* 33(2). 431–484.

Sag, Ivan A. 2000. Another argument against *Wh*-trace. Jorge Hankamer Webfest. http://ling.ucsc.edu/Jorge/sag.html.

Sag, Ivan A. 2007. Remarks on locality. In Stefan Müller (ed.), *Proceedings of the 14th International Conference on Head-Driven Phrase Structure Grammar*, 394–414. Stanford, CA: CSLI Publications. http://csli-publications.stanford.edu/HPSG/2007/.

Sag, Ivan A. 2010. English filler-gap constructions. *Language* 86(3). 486–545.

Sag, Ivan A. 2012. Sign-Based Construction Grammar: An informal synopsis. In Hans C. Boas & Ivan A. Sag (eds.), *Sign-based Construction Grammar* (CSLI Lecture Notes 193), 69–202. Stanford, CA: CSLI Publications.

Sag, Ivan A., Hans C. Boas & Paul Kay. 2012. Introducing Sign-Based Construction Grammar. In Hans C. Boas & Ivan A. Sag (eds.), *Sign-based Construction Grammar* (CSLI Lecture Notes 193), 1–29. Stanford, CA: CSLI Publications.

Sag, Ivan A., Philip Hofmeister & Neal Snider. 2007. Processing complexity in subjacency violations: The Complex Noun Phrase Constraint. In Malcolm Elliott, James Kirby, Osamu Sawada, Eleni Staraki & Suwon Yoon (eds.), *Proceedings of the 43rd Annual Meeting of the Chicago Linguistic Society*, 215–229. Chicago: Chicago Linguistic Society.

Sag, Ivan A. & Carl J. Pollard. 1991. An integrated theory of complement control. *Language* 67(1). 63–113.

Sag, Ivan A. & Thomas Wasow. 2011. Performance-compatible competence grammar. In Robert D. Borsley & Kersti Börjars (eds.), *Non-transformational syntax: Formal and explicit models of grammar: A guide to current models*, 359–377. Oxford, UK/Cambridge, MA: Blackwell Publishing Ltd.

Sag, Ivan A., Thomas Wasow & Emily M. Bender. 2003. *Syntactic theory: A formal introduction* (CSLI Lecture Notes 152). Stanford, CA: CSLI Publications 2nd edn.

Sag, Ivan A. & Tom Wasow. 2015. Flexible processing and the design of grammar. *Journal of Psycholinguistic Research* 44(1). 47–63.

Sailer, Manfred. 2000. *Combinatorial semantics and idiomatic expressions in Head-Driven Phrase Structure Grammar*: Eberhard-Karls-Universität Tübingen Dissertation. https://publikationen.uni-tuebingen.de/xmlui/handle/10900/46191.

Samarin, William J. 1984. Socioprogrammed linguistics. *The Behavioral and Brain Sciences* 7(2). 206–207.

Sampson, Geoffrey. 1989. Language acquisition: Growth or learning? *Philosophical Papers* 18(3). 203–240.

Samvelian, Pollet. 2007. A (phrasal) affix analysis of the Persian Ezafe. *Journal of Linguistics* 43. 605–645.

Sarkar, Anoop & Aravind K. Joshi. 1996. Coordination in Tree Adjoining Grammars: Formalization and implementation. In Jun-ichi Tsuji (ed.), *Proceedings of COLING-96. 16th International Conference on Computational Linguistics COLING96). Copenhagen, Denmark, August 5–9, 1996*, 610–615. Copenhagen, Denmark: Association for Computational Linguistics.

Sato, Yo. 2006. Constrained free word order parsing with Lexicalised Linearisation Grammar. In *Proceedings of 9th Annual CLUK Research Colloquium*, Open University, UK.

Sato, Yo. 2008. *Implementing Head-Driven Linearisation Grammar*: King's College London dissertation.

Sauerland, Uli & Paul Elbourne. 2002. Total reconstruction, PF movement, and derivational order. *Linguistic Inquiry* 33(2). 283–319.

Savin, Harris B. & Ellen Perchonock. 1965. Grammatical structure and the immediate recall of English sentences. *Journal of Verbal Learning and Verbal Behavior* 4(5). 348–353.

Schein, Barry. 1993. *Plurals and events* (Current Studies in Linguistics 23). Cambridge, MA: MIT Press.

Scherpenisse, Wim. 1986. *The connection between base structure and linearization restrictions in German and Dutch* (Europäische Hochschulschriften, Reihe XXI, Linguistik 47). Frankfurt/M.: Peter Lang.

Schluter, Natalie & Josef van Genabith. 2009. Dependency parsing resources for French: Converting acquired Lexical Functional Grammar f-structure annotations and parsing f-structures directly. In Kristiina Jokinen & Eckhard Bick (eds.), *Nodalida 2009 conference proceedings*, 166–173.

Schmidt, Paul, Sibylle Rieder & Axel Theofilidis. 1996a. Final documentation of the German LS-GRAM lingware. Deliverable DC-WP6e (German) IAI Saarbrücken.

Schmidt, Paul, Axel Theofilidis, Sibylle Rieder & Thierry Declerck. 1996b. Lean formalisms, linguistic theory, and applications: Grammar development in ALEP. In Jun-ichi Tsuji (ed.), *Proceedings of COLING-96. 16th International Conference on Computational Linguistics COLING96). Copenhagen, Denmark, August 5–9, 1996*, 286–291. Copenhagen, Denmark: Association for Computational Linguistics. DOI:10.3115/992628.992679.

Scholz, Barbara C. & Geoffrey K. Pullum. 2002. Searching for arguments to support linguistic nativism. *The Linguistic Review* 19(1–2). 185–223.

Schubert, K. 1987. *Metataxis: Contrastive Dependency Syntax for machine translation.* Dordrecht: Foris Publications.

Schumacher, Helmut, Jacqueline Kubczak, Renate Schmidt & Vera de Ruiter. 2004. *VALBU – Valenzwörterbuch deutscher Verben.* Tübingen: Gunter Narr Verlag.

Schütz, Jörg. 1996. The ALEP formalism in a nutshell. Tech. rep. IAI Saarbrücken. http://www.iai-sb.de/docs/alep-nutshell.pdf.

Schwarze, Christoph & Leonel de Alencar. 2016. *Lexikalisch-funktionale Grammatik: Eine Einführung am Beispiel des Französischen, mit computerlinguistischer Implementierung* (Stauffenburg Einführungen 30). Tübingen: Stauffenburg Verlag.

Seiss, Melanie & Rachel Nordlinger. 2012. An electronic dictionary and translation system for Murrinh-Patha. *The EUROCALL Review: Proceedings of the EUROCALL 2011 Conference* 20(1). 135–138.

Sengupta, Probal & B. B. Chaudhuri. 1997. A delayed syntactic-encoding-based LFG parsing strategy for an Indian language—Bangla. *Computational Linguistics* 23(2). 345–351.

Seuren, Pieter A. M. 1984. The Bioprogram Hypothesis: Facts and fancy. *The Behavioral and Brain Sciences* 7(2). 208–209.

Seuren, Pieter A. M. 2004. *Chomsky's Minimalism*. Oxford: Oxford University Press.

Shieber, Stuart M. 1985. Evidence against the context-freeness of natural language. *Linguistics and Philosophy* 8(3). 333–343.

Shieber, Stuart M. 1986. *An introduction to unification-based approaches to grammar* (CSLI Lecture Notes 4). Stanford, CA: CSLI Publications.

Shieber, Stuart M. & Mark Johnson. 1993. Variations on incremental interpretation. *Journal of Psycholinguistic Research* 22(2). 287–318.

Shieber, Stuart M., Hans Uszkoreit, Fernando Pereira, Jane Robinson & Mabry Tyson. 1983. The formalism and implementation of PATR-II. In *Research on interactive acquisition and use of knowledge*, 39–79. Menlo Park, CA: Artificial Intelligence Center, SRI International.

Shtyrov, Y., E. Pihko & F. Pulvermüller. 2005. Determinants of dominance: Is language laterality explained by physical or linguistic features of speech? *Neuroimage* 27(1). 37–47.

Siegel, Melanie. 2000. HPSG analysis of Japanese. In Wolfgang Wahlster (ed.), *Verbmobil: Foundations of speech-to-speech translation* (Artificial Intelligence), 264–279. Berlin: Springer Verlag.

Siegel, Melanie & Emily M. Bender. 2002. Efficient deep processing of Japanese. In *Proceedings of the 3rd Workshop on Asian Language Resources and International Standardization at the 19th International Conference on Computational Linguistics. Taipei, Taiwan*, http://www.aclweb.org/anthology-new/W/W02/W02-1210.pdf.

Simov, Kiril, Petya Osenova, Alexander Simov & Milen Kouylekov. 2004. Design and implementation of the Bulgarian HPSG-based treebank. *Research on Language and Computation* 2(4). 495–522.

Simpson, Jane. 1983. Resultatives. In Lori S. Levin, Malka Rappaport & Annie Zaenen (eds.), *Papers in Lexical Functional Grammar*, 143–157. Indiana: Indiana University Linguistics Club. Reprint: Simpson (2005b).

Simpson, Jane. 2005a. Depictives in English and Warlpiri. In Nikolaus P. Himmelmann & Eva Schultze-Berndt (eds.), *Secondary predication and adverbial modification: The typology of depictives*, 69–106. Oxford: Oxford University Press.

Simpson, Jane. 2005b. Resultatives. In Miriam Butt & Tracy Holloway King (eds.), *Lexical semantics in LFG*, 149–161. Stanford, CA: CSLI Publications.

Singleton, Jenny L. & Elissa L. Newport. 2004. When learners surpass their models: The acquisition of American Sign Language from inconsistent input. *Cognitive Psychology* 49(4). 370–407.

Sleator, Daniel D. K. & Davy Temperley. 1991. Parsing English with a Link Grammar. CMU-CS-TR-91-126 School of Computer Science, Carnegie Mellon University.

Smith, Carlota S. 1970. Jespersen's "move and change" class and causative verbs in English. In Bert Peeters (ed.), *The lexicon–encyclopedia interface*, 101–109. Amsterdam: Elsevier.

Smith, Carlota S. 1972. On causative verbs and derived nominals in English. *Linguistic Inquiry* 3(1). 136–138.

Snyder, William. 2001. On the nature of syntactic variation: Evidence from complex predicates and complex word-formation. *Language* 77(2). 324–342.

Soehn, Jan-Philipp & Manfred Sailer. 2008. At first blush on tenterhooks: About selectional restrictions imposed by nonheads. In Gerhard Jäger, Paola Monachesi, Gerald Penn & Shuly Wintner (eds.), *Proceedings of Formal Grammar 2003, Vienna, Austria*, 149–161. Stanford, CA: CSLI Publications. http://csli-publications.stanford.edu/FG/2003/soehn.pdf.

Son, Minjeong. 2007. Directionality and resultativity: The cross-linguistic correlation revisited. *Tromsø University Working Papers on Language & Linguistics* 34. 126–164. http://hdl.handle.net/10037/3191.

Son, Minjeong & Peter Svenonius. 2008. Microparameters of cross-linguistic variation: Directed motion and resultatives. In Natasha Abner & Jason Bishop (eds.), *Proceedings of the 27th West Coast Conference on Formal Linguistics*, 388–396. Somerville, MA: Cascadilla Proceedings Project.

Song, Sanghoun, Jong-Bok Kim, Francis Bond & Jaehyung Yang. 2010. Development of the Korean Resource Grammar: Towards grammar customization. In *Proceedings of the 8th Workshop on Asian Language Resources, Beijing, China, 21–22 August 2010*, 144–152. Asian Federation for Natural Language Processing.

Sorace, Antonella. 2003. Near-nativeness. In Catherine J. Doughty & Michael H. Long (eds.), *The handbook of second language acquisition* (Blackwell Handbooks in Linguistics), 130–151. Oxford, UK/Cambridge, USA: Blackwell Publishing Ltd.

Stabler, Edward P. 1987. Restricting logic grammars with Government-Binding Theory. *Computational Linguistics* 13(1–2). 1–10.

Stabler, Edward P. 1991. Avoid the pedestrian's paradox. In Robert C. Berwick, Steven P. Abney & Carol Tenny (eds.), *Principle-based parsing: Computation and psycholinguistics*, 199–237. Dordrecht: Kluwer Academic Publishers.

Stabler, Edward P. 1992. *The logical approach to syntax: Foundations, specifications, and implementations of theories of Government and Binding* (ACL-MIT Press Series in Natural Language Processing). Cambridge, MA: MIT Press.

Stabler, Edward P. 2001. Minimalist Grammars and recognition. In Christian Rohrer, Antje Rossdeutscher & Hans Kamp (eds.), *Linguistic form and its computation* (Studies in Computational Linguistics 1), 327–352. Stanford, CA: CSLI Publications.

Stabler, Edward P. 2011a. After Governement and Binding Theory. In Johan F. A. K. van Benthem & G. B. Alice ter Meulen (eds.), *Handbook of logic and language*, 395–414. Amsterdam: Elsevier 2nd edn.

Stabler, Edward P. 2011b. Computational perspectives on Minimalism. In Cedric Boeckx (ed.), *The Oxford handbook of linguistic Minimalism* (Oxford Handbooks in Linguistics), chap. 27, 616–641. Oxford: Oxford University Press.

Starosta, Stanley. 1988. *The case for Lexicase* (Open Linguistics Series). London: Pinter Publishers.

Starosta, Stanley & Hirosato Nomura. 1986. Lexicase parsing: A lexicon-driven approach to syntactic analysis. In Makoto Nagao (ed.), *Proceedings of COLING 86*, 127–132. University of Bonn: Association for Computational Linguistics. DOI:10.3115/991365.991400.

von Stechow, Arnim. 1979. Deutsche Wortstellung und Montague-Grammatik. In Jürgen M. Meisel & Martin D. Pam (eds.), *Linear order and Generative theory*, 317–490. Amsterdam: John Benjamins Publishing Co.

von Stechow, Arnim. 1989. Distinguo: Eine Antwort auf Dieter Wunderlich. *Linguistische Berichte* 122. 330–339.

von Stechow, Arnim. 1996. The different readings of *wieder* 'again': A structural account. *Journal of Semantics* 13(2). 87–138.

von Stechow, Arnim & Wolfgang Sternefeld. 1988. *Bausteine syntaktischen Wissens: Ein Lehrbuch der Generativen Grammatik.* Opladen/Wiesbaden: Westdeutscher Verlag.

Steedman, Mark J. 1985. Dependency and coordination in the grammar of Dutch and English. *Language* 61(3). 523–568.

Steedman, Mark J. 1989. Constituency and coordination in a Combinatory Grammar. In Mark R. Baltin & Anthony S. Kroch (eds.), *Alternative conceptions of phrase structure*, 201–231. Chicago/London: The University of Chicago Press.

Steedman, Mark J. 1991. Structure and intonation. *Language* 67(2). 260–296.

Steedman, Mark J. 1997. *Surface structure and interpretation* (Linguistic Inquiry Monographs 30). Cambridge, MA/London, England: MIT Press.

Steedman, Mark J. 2000. *The syntactic process* (Language, Speech, and Communication). Cambridge, MA/London, England: MIT Press.

Steedman, Mark J. 2011. Romantics and revolutionaries. *Linguistic Issues in Language Technology* 6(11). 1–20. http://journals.linguisticsociety.org/elanguage/lilt/article/view/2587.html. Special Issue on Interaction of Linguistics and Computational Linguistics.

Steedman, Mark J. & Jason Baldridge. 2006. Combinatory Categorial Grammar. In Keith Brown (ed.), *Encyclopedia of language and linguistics*, 610–621. Oxford: Elsevier 2nd edn.

Steels, Luc. 2003. Evolving grounded communication for robots. *Trends in Cognitive Science* 7(7). 308–312.

Steels, Luc (ed.). 2011. *Design patterns in Fluid Construction Grammar* (Constructional Approaches to Language 11). Amsterdam: John Benjamins Publishing Co.

Steels, Luc (ed.). 2012. *Computational issues in Fluid Construction Grammar* (Lecture Notes in Computer Science 7249). Berlin: Springer Verlag.

Steels, Luc. 2013. Fluid Construction Grammar. In Thomas Hoffmann & Graeme Trousdale (eds.), *The Oxford handbook of Construction Grammar* (Oxford Handbooks), 153–167. Oxford: Oxford University Press.

Steels, Luc. 2015. *The Talking Heads experiment: Origins of words and meanings* (Computational Models of Language Evolution 1). Berlin: Language Science Press.

Steels, Luc & Joachim De Beule. 2006. A (very) brief introduction to Fluid Construction Grammar. Paper presented at the Third International Workshop on Scalable Natural Language Understanding (ScaNaLU 2006) June 8, 2006, following HLT/NAACL, New York City.

Steels, Luc & Remi van Trijp. 2011. How to make Construction Grammars fluid and robust. In Luc Steels (ed.), *Design patterns in Fluid Construction Grammar* (Constructional Approaches to Language 11), 301–330. Amsterdam: John Benjamins Publishing Co.

Stefanowitsch, Anatol. 2008. Negative entrenchment: A usage-based approach to negative evidence. *Cognitive Linguistics* 19(3). 513–531.

Stefanowitsch, Anatol & Kerstin Fischer (eds.). 2008. *Konstruktionsgrammatik II: Von der Konstruktion zur Grammatik* (Stauffenburg Linguistik 47). Tübingen: Stauffenburg Verlag.

Stefanowitsch, Anatol & Stephan Th. Gries. 2009. Corpora and grammar. In Anke Lüdeling & Merja Kytö (eds.), *Corpus linguistics: An international handbook*, vol. 29 (Handbücher zur Sprach- und Kommunikationswissenschaft), chap. 43, 933–952. Berlin: Mouton de Gruyter.

Sternefeld, Wolfgang. 1985a. Deutsch ohne grammatische Funktionen: Ein Beitrag zur Rektions- und Bindungstheorie. *Linguistische Berichte* 99. 394–439.

Sternefeld, Wolfgang. 1985b. On case and binding theory. In Jindřich Toman (ed.), *Studies in German grammar* (Studies in Generative Grammar 21), 231–285. Dordrecht: Foris Publications.

Sternefeld, Wolfgang. 1995. Voice phrases and their specifiers. *FAS Papers in Linguistics* 3. 48–85.

Sternefeld, Wolfgang. 2006. *Syntax: Eine morphologisch motivierte generative Beschreibung des Deutschen* (Stauffenburg Linguistik 31). Tübingen: Stauffenburg Verlag.

Sternefeld, Wolfgang & Frank Richter. 2012. Wo stehen wir in der Grammatiktheorie? – Bemerkungen anläßlich eines Buchs von Stefan Müller. *Zeitschrift für Sprachwissenschaft* 31(2). 263–291.

Stiebels, Barbara. 1996. *Lexikalische Argumente und Adjunkte: Zum semantischen Beitrag verbaler Präfixe und Partikeln* (studia grammatica 39). Berlin: Akademie Verlag.

Stowell, Timothy. 1981. *Origins of phrase structure*: MIT dissertation. http://hdl.handle.net/1721.1/15626.

Strunk, Jan & Nil Snider. 2013. Subclausal locality constraints on relative clause extraposition. In Gert Webelhuth, Manfred Sailer & Heike Walker (eds.), *Rightward movement in a comparative perspective* (Linguistik Aktuell/Linguistics Today 200), 99–143. Amsterdam: John Benjamins Publishing Co.

Suchsland, Peter. 1997. *Syntax-Theorie: Ein zusammengefaßter Zugang* (Konzepte der Sprach- und Literaturwissenschaft 55). Tübingen: Max Niemeyer Verlag. Deutsche Bearbeitung von Borsley (1991) durch Peter Suchsland.

Sulger, Sebastian. 2009. Irish clefting and information-structure. In Miriam Butt & Tracy Holloway King (eds.), *Proceedings of the LFG 2009 conference*, 562–582. Stanford, CA: CSLI Publications. http://csli-publications.stanford.edu/LFG/14/.

Sulger, Sebastian. 2010. Analytic and synthetic verb forms in Irish – An agreement-based implementation in LFG. In Manfred Pinkal, Ines Rehbein, Sabine Schulte im Walde & Angelika Storrer (eds.), *Semantic approaches in natural language processing: Proceedings of the Conference on Natural Language Processing 2010*, 169–173. Saarbrücken: Saarland University Press (universaar).

Svenononius, Peter. 2004. Slavic prefixes inside and outside VP. *Nordlyd. Special Issue on Slavic Prefixes* 32(2). 205–253.

Takami, Ken-ichi. 1988. Preposition stranding: Arguments against syntactic analyses and an alternative functional explanation. *Lingua* 76(4). 299–335.

Tanenhaus, Michael K., Michael J. Spivey-Knowlton, Kathleen M. Eberhard & Julie C. Sedivy. 1995. Integration of visual and linguistic information in spoken language comprehension. *Science* 268(5217). 1632–1634.

Tanenhaus, Michael K., Michael J. Spivey-Knowlton, Kathleen M. Eberhard & Julie C. Sedivy. 1996. Using eye movements to study spoken language comprehension: Evidence for visually mediated incremental interpretation. In Toshio Inui & James L. McClelland (eds.), *Information integration in perception and communication* (Attention and Performance XVI), 457–478. Cambridge, MA: MIT Press.

ten Hacken, Pius. 2007. *Chomskyan linguistics and its competitors*. London: Equinox Publishing Ltd.

Tesnière, Lucien. 1959. *Eléments de syntaxe structurale*. Paris: Librairie C. Klincksieck.

Tesnière, Lucien. 1980. *Grundzüge der strukturalen Syntax*. Stuttgart: Klett-Cotta. Translated by Ulrich Engel.

Tesnière, Lucien. 2015. *Elements of structural syntax*. Amsterdam: John Benjamins Publishing Co. Translated by Timothy Osborne and Sylvain Kahane.

Thiersch, Craig L. 1978. *Topics in German syntax*: M.I.T. Dissertation.

Thompson, Henry S. 1982. Handling metarules in a parser for GPSG. D.A.I. Research 175 University of Edinburgh.

Timberlake, Alan. 1982. The impersonal passive in Lithuanian. In Monica Macaulay, Orin D. Gensler, Claudia Brugmann, Inese Čivkulis, Amy Dahlstrom, Katherine Krile & Rob Sturm (eds.), *Proceedings of the Eighth Annual Meeting of the Berkeley Linguistics Society*, 508–524. Berkeley: University of California.

Tomasello, Michael. 1995. Language is not an instinct. *Cognitive Development* 10(1). 131–156.

Tomasello, Michael. 2000. Do young children have adult syntactic competence? *Cognition* 74(3). 209–253.

Tomasello, Michael. 2003. *Constructing a language: A usage-based theory of language acquisition*. Cambridge, MA: Harvard University Press.

Tomasello, Michael. 2005. Beyond formalities: The case of language acquisition. *The Linguistic Review* 22(2–4). 183–197.

Tomasello, Michael. 2006a. Acquiring linguistic constructions. In Deanna Kuhn & Robert Siegler (eds.), *Handbook of child psychology*, vol. 2, New York: John Wiley & Sons, Inc. 6th edn.

Tomasello, Michael. 2006b. Construction Grammar for kids. *Constructions* Special Volume 1. http://www.constructions-journal.com/.

Tomasello, Michael. 2006c. Konstruktionsgrammatik und früher Erstspracherwerb. In Kerstin Fischer & Anatol Stefanowitsch (eds.), *Konstruktionsgrammatik: Von der Anwendung zur Theorie* (Stauffenburg Linguistik 40), 19–37. Tübingen: Stauffenburg Verlag.

Tomasello, Michael. 2009. Universal Grammar is dead. *The Behavioral and Brain Sciences* 32(5). 470–471.

Tomasello, Michael, Nameera Akhtar, Kelly Dodsen & Laura Rekau. 1997. Differential productivity in young children's use of nouns and verbs. *Journal of Child Language* 24(2). 373–387.

Tomasello, Michael, Malinda Carpenter, Josep Call, Tanya Behne & Henrike Moll. 2005. Understanding and sharing intentions: The origins of cultural cognition. *The Behavioral and Brain Sciences* 28(5). 675–735.

Travis, Lisa. 1984. *Parameters and effects of word order variation*. Cambridge, MA: M.I.T. Dissertation.

Trosterud, Trond. 2009. A Constraint Grammar for Faroese. In Eckhard Bick, Kristin Hagen, Kaili Müürisep & Trond Trosterud (eds.), *Constraint Grammar and robust parsing: Proceedings of the NODALIDA 2009 workshop*, vol. 8 (NEALT Proceedings Series 8), 1–7. Northern European Association for Language Technologie Tartu: Tartu University Library.

Tseng, Jesse (ed.). 2000. *Aspekte eines HPSG-Fragments des Deutschen* (Arbeitspapiere des SFB 340 No. 156). Tübingen: Eberhard-Karls-Universität Tübingen. http://www.sfs.uni-tuebingen.de/sfb/reports/berichte/156/156abs.html.

Tseng, Jesse L. 2003. LKB grammar implementation: French and beyond. In Emily M. Bender, Daniel P. Flickinger, Frederik Fouvry & Melanie Siegel (eds.), *Proceedings of the ESSLLI 2003 Workshop "Ideas and Strategies for Multilingual Grammar Development"*, 91–97. Vienna, Austria. http://w3.erss.univ-tlse2.fr/textes/pagespersos/tseng/Pubs/mgd03.pdf.

Tseng, Jesse L. 2007. English prepositional passive constructions. In Stefan Müller (ed.), *Proceedings of the 14th International Conference on Head-Driven Phrase Structure Grammar*, 271–286. Stanford, CA: CSLI Publications. http://csli-publications.stanford.edu/HPSG/2007/.

Umemoto, Hiroshi. 2006. Implementing a Japanese semantic parser based on glue approach. In *Proceedings of The 20th Pacific Asia Conference on Language, Information and Computation*, 418–425. http://dspace.wul.waseda.ac.jp/dspace/handle/2065/29076.

Uszkoreit, Hans. 1986a. Categorial Unification Grammars. In Makoto Nagao (ed.), *Proceedings of COLING 86*, 187–194. University of Bonn: Association for Computational Linguistics. http://aclweb.org/anthology-new/C/C86/C86-1045.pdf.

Uszkoreit, Hans. 1986b. Linear precedence in discontinuous constituents: Complex fronting in German. Report No. CSLI-86-47 Center for the Study of Language and Information Stanford, CA.

Uszkoreit, Hans. 1987. *Word order and constituent structure in German* (CSLI Lecture Notes 8). Stanford, CA: CSLI Publications.

Uszkoreit, Hans. 1990. Extraposition and adjunct attachment in Categorial Unification Grammar. In Werner Bahner, Joachim Schildt & Dieter Viehweger (eds.), *Proceedings of the Fourteenth International Congress of Linguists, Berlin/GDR, August 10–15, 1987*, vol. 3, 2331–2336. Berlin: Akademie Verlag.

Uszkoreit, Hans, Rolf Backofen, Stephan Busemann, Abdel Kader Diagne, Elizabeth A. Hinkelman, Walter Kasper, Bernd Kiefer, Hans-Ulrich Krieger, Klaus Netter, Günter Neumann, Stephan Oepen & Stephen P. Spackman. 1994. DISCO—An HPSG-based NLP system and its application for appointment scheduling. In Makoto Nagao (ed.), *Proceedings of COLING 94*, 436–440. Kyoto, Japan: Association for Computational Linguistics.

Uszkoreit, Hans, Rolf Backofen, Jo Calder, Joanne Capstick, Luca Dini, Jochen Dörre, Gregor Erbach, Dominique Estival, Suresh Manandhar, Anne-Marie Mineur & Stephan Oepen. 1996. The EAGLES formalisms working group: Final report Expert Advisory Group on Language Engineering Standards. Technical Report LRE 61–100. http://www.coli.uni-sb.de/publikationen/softcopies/Uszkoreit:1996:EFW.pdf.

Valian, Virginia. 1991. Syntactic subjects in the early speech of American and Italian children. *Cognition* 40(1–2). 21–81.

Van Eynde, Frank. 2015. Sign-Based Construction Grammar: A guided tour. *Journal of Linguistics* DOI:10.1017/S0022226715000341.

Van Langendonck, Willy. 1994. Determiners as heads? *Cognitive Linguistics* 5. 243–259.

van Trijp, Remi. 2011. A design pattern for argument structure constructions. In Luc Steels (ed.), *Design patterns in Fluid Construction Grammar* (Constructional Approaches to Language 11), 115–145. Amsterdam: John Benjamins Publishing Co.

van Trijp, Remi. 2013. A comparison between Fluid Construction Grammar and Sign-Based Construction Grammar. *Constructions and Frames* 5(1). 88–116.

van Trijp, Remi. 2014. Long-distance dependencies without filler–gaps: A cognitive-functional alternative in Fluid Construction Grammar. *Language and Cognition* 6(2). 242–270.

Van Valin, Robert D. Jr. (ed.). 1993. *Advances in Role and Reference Grammar*. Amsterdam: John Benjamins Publishing Co.

Van Valin, Robert D. Jr. 1998. The acquisition of *wh*-questions and the mechanisms of language acquisition. In Michael Tomasello (ed.), *The new psychology of language: Cognitive and functional approaches to language structure*, 221–249. Hillsdale, NJ: Lawrence Erlbaum.

Vancoppenolle, Jean, Eric Tabbert, Gerlof Bouma & Manfred Stede. 2011. A German grammar for generation in Open CCG. In Hanna Hedeland, Thomas Schmidt & Kai Wörner (eds.), *Multilingual resources and multilingual applications: Proceedings of the Conference of the German Society for Computational Linguistics and Language Technology (GSCL) 2011* (Arbeiten zur Mehrsprachigkeit/Working Papers in Multilingualism, Folge B/Series B 96), 145–150. Hamburg: Universität Hamburg.

Vargha-Khadem, Faraneh, Kate E. Watkins, Katie Alcock, Paul Fletcher & Richard Passingham. 1995. Praxic and nonverbal cognitive deficits in a large family with a genetically transmitted speech and language disorder. In *Proceedings of the National Academy of Sciences of the United States of America*, vol. 92, 930–933.

Vasishth, Shravan & Richard L. Lewis. 2006. Human language processing: Symbolic models. In Keith Brown (ed.), *The encyclopedia of language and linguistics*, vol. 5, 410–419. Oxford: Elsevier Science Publisher B.V. (North-Holland) 2nd edn.

Vasishth, Shravan, Katja Suckow, Richard L. Lewis & Sabine Kern. 2010. Short-term forgetting in sentence comprehension: Crosslinguistic evidence from verb-final structures. *Language and Cognitive Processes* 25(4). 533–567.

Vater, Heinz. 2010. Strukturalismus und generative Grammatik in Deutschland. In Hans-Harald Müller, Marcel Lepper & Andreas Gardt (eds.), *Strukturalismus in Deutschland: Literatur- und Sprachwissenschaft 1910–1975* (Marbacher Schriften. Neue Folge 5), 125–160. Göttingen: Wallstein Verlag.

Veenstra, Mettina Jolanda Arnoldina. 1998. *Formalizing the Minimalist Program*: Rijksuniversiteit Groningen Ph.d. thesis.

Vennemann, Theo & Ray Harlow. 1977. Categorial Grammar and consistent basic VX serialization. *Theoretical Linguistics* 4(1–3). 227–254.

Verhagen, Arie. 2010. What do you think is the proper place of recursion? Conceptual and empirical issues. In Harry van der Hulst (ed.), *Recursion in human language* (Studies in Generative Grammar 104), 93–110. Berlin: Mouton de Gruyter.

Verspoor, Cornelia Maria. 1997. *Contextually-dependent lexical semantics*: University of Edinburgh dissertation. ftp://ftp.cogsci.ed.ac.uk/pub/kversp/thesis.ps.gz.

Vierhuff, Tilman, Bernd Hildebrandt & Hans-Jürgen Eikmeyer. 2003. Effiziente Verarbeitung deutscher Konstituentenstellung mit der Combinatorial Categorial Grammar. *Linguistische Berichte* 194. 213–237.

Vijay-Shanker, K. & Aravind K. Joshi. 1988. Feature structures based Tree Adjoining Grammars. In Dénes Vargha (ed.), *Proceedings of COLING 88*, vol. 1, 714–719. University of Budapest: Association for Computational Linguistics. http://www.aclweb.org/anthology-new/C/C88/C88-2147.pdf.

Villavicencio, Aline. 2002. The acquisition of a unification-based Generalised Categorial Grammar. UCAM-CL-TR-533 University of Cambridge Computer Laboratory.

Vogel, Ralf. 2001. Case conflict in German free relative constructions: An Optimality Theoretic treatment. In Gereon Müller & Wolfgang Sternefeld (eds.), *Competition in syntax*, 341–375. Berlin: Mouton de Gruyter.

Vogel, Ralf & Markus Steinbach. 1998. The dative – An oblique case. *Linguistische Berichte* 173. 65–91.

Volk, Martin. 1988. *Parsing German with GPSG: The problem of separable-prefix verbs.* University of Georgia MA thesis.
Voutilainen, Atro, Juha Heikkilä & Arto Anttila. 1992. *Constraint Grammar of English: A performance-oriented introduction* (Publications of the Department of General Linguistics 21). Helsinki: University of Helsinki.
Wada, Hajime & Nicholas Asher. 1986. BUILDRS: An implementation of DR Theory and LFG. In Makoto Nagao (ed.), *Proceedings of COLING 86*, 540–545. University of Bonn: Association for Computational Linguistics.
Wahlster, Wolfgang (ed.). 2000. *Verbmobil: Foundations of speech-to-speech translation* (Artificial Intelligence). Berlin: Springer Verlag.
Walther, Markus. 1999. *Deklarative prosodische Morphologie: Constraint-basierte Analysen und Computermodelle zum Finnischen und Tigrinya* (Linguistische Arbeiten 399). Tübingen: Max Niemeyer Verlag.
Webelhuth, Gert. 1985. German is configurational. *The Linguistic Review* 4(3). 203–246.
Webelhuth, Gert. 1990. Diagnostics for structure. In Günther Grewendorf & Wolfgang Sternefeld (eds.), *Scrambling and Barriers* (Linguistik Aktuell/Linguistics Today 5), 41–75. Amsterdam: John Benjamins Publishing Co.
Webelhuth, Gert. 1995. X-bar Theory and Case Theory. In Gert Webelhuth (ed.), *Government and Binding Theory and the Minimalist Program: Principles and Parameters in syntactic theory* (Generative Syntax), 15–95. Oxford, UK & Cambrigde, USA: Blackwell Publishing Ltd.
Webelhuth, Gert. 2011. Paradigmenwechsel rückwärts: Die Renaissance der grammatischen Konstruktion. In Stefan Engelberg, Anke Holler & Kristel Proost (eds.), *Sprachliches Wissen zwischen Lexikon und Grammatik* (Institut für Deutsche Sprache, Jahrbuch 2010), 149–180. Berlin: de Gruyter.
Weber, Heinz J. 1997. *Dependenzgrammatik: Ein interaktives Arbeitsbuch* (Narr Studienbücher). Tübingen: Gunter Narr Verlag 2nd edn.
Wechsler, Stephen Mark. 1991. *Argument structure and linking*: Stanford University dissertation.
Wechsler, Stephen Mark. 1995. *The semantic basis of argument structure* (Dissertations in Linguistics). Stanford, CA: CSLI Publications.
Wechsler, Stephen Mark. 1997. Resultative predicates and control. In Ralph C. Blight & Michelle J. Moosally (eds.), *Texas Linguistic Forum 38: The syntax and semantics of predication: Proceedings of the 1997 Texas Linguistics Society Conference*, 307–321. Austin, Texas: University of Texas, Department of Linguistics.
Wechsler, Stephen Mark. 2005. What is right and wrong about little v. In *Grammar and beyond—Essays in honour of Lars Hellan*, 179–195. Oslo, Norway: Novus Press.
Wechsler, Stephen Mark. 2008a. A diachronic account of English deverbal nominals. In Charles B. Chang & Hannah J. Haynie (eds.), *Proceedings of the 26th West Coast Conference on Formal Linguistics*, 498–506. Somerville, MA: Cascadilla Proceedings Project.

Wechsler, Stephen Mark. 2008b. Dualist syntax. In Stefan Müller (ed.), *Proceedings of the 15th International Conference on Head-Driven Phrase Structure Grammar*, 294–304. Stanford, CA: CSLI Publications. http://csli-publications.stanford.edu/HPSG/2008/.

Wechsler, Stephen Mark & Bokyung Noh. 2001. On resultative predicates and clauses: Parallels between Korean and English. *Language Sciences* 23(4). 391–423.

Wegener, Heide. 1985. *Der Dativ im heutigen Deutsch* (Studien zur deutschen Grammatik 28). Tübingen: originally Gunter Narr Verlag now Stauffenburg Verlag.

Weir, Morton W. 1964. Developmental changes in problem-solving strategies. *Psychological Review* 71(6). 473–490.

Weissgerber, Monika. 1983. *Valenz und Kongruenzbeziehungen: Ein Modell zur Vereindeutigung von Verben in der maschinellen Analyse und Übersetzung*. Frankfurt a. M.: Peter Lang.

Weisweber, Wilhelm. 1987. Ein Dominanz-Chart-Parser für generalisierte Phrasenstrukturgrammatiken. KIT-Report 45 Technische Universität Berlin Berlin.

Weisweber, Wilhelm & Susanne Preuss. 1992. Direct parsing with metarules. In Antonio Zampolli (ed.), *14th International Conference on Computational Linguistics (COLING '92), August 23–28*, 1111–1115. Nantes, France: Association for Computational Linguistics.

Welke, Klaus. 1988. *Einführung in die Valenz- und Kasustheorie*. Leipzig: Bibliographisches Institut.

Welke, Klaus. 2009. Konstruktionsvererbung, Valenzvererbung und die Reichweite von Konstruktionen. *Zeitschrift für Germanistische Linguistik* 37(3). 514–543.

Welke, Klaus. 2011. *Valenzgrammatik des Deutschen: Eine Einführung* (De Gruyter Studium). Berlin: de Gruyter.

Wells, Rulon S. 1947. Immediate constituents. *Language* 23(2). 81–117.

Werner, Edeltraud. 1993. *Translationstheorie und Dependenzmodell: Kritik und Reinterpretation des Ansatzes von Lucien Tesnière* (Kultur und Erkenntnis: Schriften der Philosophischen Fakultät der Heinrich-Heine-Universität Düsseldorf 10). Tübingen: Francke Verlag.

Wetta, Andrew C. 2011. A Construction-based cross-linguistic analysis of V2 word order. In Stefan Müller (ed.), *Proceedings of the 18th International Conference on Head-Driven Phrase Structure Grammar, University of Washington*, 248–268. Stanford, CA: CSLI Publications. http://csli-publications.stanford.edu/HPSG/2011/.

Wexler, Kenneth. 1998. Very early parameter setting and the unique checking constraint: A new explanation of the optional infinitive stage. *Lingua* 106(1–4). 23–79.

Wexler, Kenneth & Peter W. Culicover. 1980. *Formal principles of language acquisition*. Cambridge, MA/London: MIT Press.

Weydt, Harald. 1972. „Unendlicher Gebrauch von endlichen Mitteln": Mißverständnisse um ein linguistisches Theorem. *Poetica* 5(3/4). 249–267.

Wharton, R. M. 1974. Approximate language identification. *Information and Control* 26(3). 236–255.

White, Mike & Jason Baldridge. 2003. Adapting chart realization to CCG. In Ehud Reiter, Helmut Horacek & Kees van Deemter (eds.), *Proceedings of the 9th European Workshop on Natural Language Generation (ENLG-2003) at EACL 2003*, 119–126.

Wijnen, Frank, Masja Kempen & Steven Gillis. 2001. Root infinitives in Dutch early child language: An effect of input? *Journal of Child Language* 28(3). 629–660.

Wiklund, Anna-Lena, Gunnar Hrafn Hrafnbjargarson, Kristine Bentzen & Þorbjörg Hróarsdóttir. 2007. Rethinking Scandinavian verb movement. *Journal of Comparative Germanic Linguistics* 10(3). 203–233.

Wilcock, Graham. 2001. Towards a discourse-oriented representation of information structure in HPSG. In *13th Nordic Conference on Computational Linguistics, Uppsala, Sweden*, http://www.ling.helsinki.fi/~gwilcock/Pubs/2001/Nodalida-01.pdf.

Wilder, Chris. 1991. Small clauses and related objects. *Groninger Arbeiten zur Germanistischen Linguistik* 34. 215–236.

Williams, Edwin. 1984. Grammatical relations. *Linguistic Inquiry* 15(4). 639–673.

Winkler, Susanne. 1997. *Focus and secondary predication* (Studies in Generative Grammar 43). Berlin, New York: Mouton de Gruyter.

Wittenberg, Eva, Ray S. Jackendoff, Gina Kuperberg, Martin Paczynski, Jesse Snedeker & Heike Wiese. 2014. The processing and representation of light verb constructions. In Asaf Bachrach, Isabelle Roy & Linnaea Stockall (eds.), *Structuring the argument* (Language Faculty and Beyond 10), 61–80. Amsterdam: John Benjamins Publishing Co.

Wittenberg, Eva & Maria Mercedes Piñango. 2011. Processing light verb constructions. *The Mental Lexicon* 6(3). 393–413.

Wöllstein, Angelika. 2010. *Topologisches Satzmodell* (Kurze Einführungen in die Germanistische Linguistik 8). Heidelberg: Universitätsverlag Winter.

Wunderlich, Dieter. 1987. Vermeide Pronomen – Vermeide leere Kategorien. *Studium Linguistik* 21. 36–44.

Wunderlich, Dieter. 1989. Arnim von Stechow, das Nichts und die Lexikalisten. *Linguistische Berichte* 122. 321–333.

Wunderlich, Dieter. 1992. CAUSE and the structure of verbs. Arbeiten des SFB 282 No. 36 Heinrich Heine Uni/BUGH Düsseldorf/Wuppertal.

Wunderlich, Dieter. 1997. Argument extension by lexical adjunction. *Journal of Semantics* 14(2). 95–142.

Wunderlich, Dieter. 2004. Why assume UG? *Studies in Language* 28(3). 615–641.

Wunderlich, Dieter. 2008. Spekulationen zum Anfang von Sprache. *Zeitschrift für Sprachwissenschaft* 27(2). 229–265.

Wurmbrand, Susanne. 2003a. *Infinitives: Restructuring and clause structure* (Studies in Generative Grammar 55). Berlin: Mouton de Gruyter.

Wurmbrand, Susanne. 2003b. Long passive (corpus search results).

XTAG Research Group. 2001. A lexicalized Tree Adjoining Grammar for English. Tech. rep. Institute for Research in Cognitive Science Philadelphia. ftp://ftp.cis.upenn.edu/pub/xtag/release-2.24.2001/tech-report.pdf.

Yamada, Hiroyasu & Yuji Matsumoto. 2003. Statistical dependency analysis with support vector machines. In Gertjan van Noord (ed.), *Proceedings of the 8th International Workshop on Parsing Technologies (IWPT 03)*, Nancy.

Yamada, Jeni. 1981. Evidence for the independence of language and cognition: Case study of a "hyperlinguistic" adolescent. UCLA Working Papers in Cognitive Linguistics 3 University of California, Los Angeles.

Yampol, Todd & Lauri Karttunen. 1990. An efficient implementation of PATR for Categorial Unification Grammar. In Hans Karlgren (ed.), *COLING-90: Papers presented to the 13th International Conference on Computational Linguistics*, 419–424. Helsinki: Association for Computational Linguistics.

Yang, Charles D. 2004. Universal Grammar, statistics or both? *Trends in Cognitive Sciences* 8(10). 451–456. DOI:10.1016/j.tics.2004.08.006.

Yasukawa, Hidekl. 1984. LFG System in Prolog. In Yorick Wilks (ed.), *Proceedings of the 10th International Conference on Computational Linguistics and 22nd Annual Meeting of the Association for Computational Linguistics*, 358–361. Stanford University, California: Association for Computational Linguistics.

Yip, Moira, Joan Maling & Ray S. Jackendoff. 1987. Case in tiers. *Language* 63(2). 217–250.

Yoshinaga, Naoki, Yusuke Miyao, Kentaro Torisawa & Jun'ichi Tsujii. 2001. Resource sharing amongst HPSG and LTAG communities by a method of grammar conversion between FB-LTAG and HPSG. In *Proceedings of ACL/EACL workshop on Sharing Tools and Resources for Research and Education*, 39–46. Toulouse, France.

Zaenen, Annie & Ronald M. Kaplan. 1995. Formal devices for linguistic generalizations: West Germanic word order in LFG. In Dalrymple et al. (1995) 215–239.

Zaenen, Annie, Joan Maling & Höskuldur Thráinsson. 1985. Case and grammatical functions: The Icelandic passive. *Natural Language and Linguistic Theory* 3(4). 441–483.

Zappa, Frank. 1986. Does humor belong in music? EMI Music Germany GmbH & Co.KG.

Zucchi, Alessandro. 1993. *The language of propositions and events: Issues in the syntax and the semantics of nominalization* (Studies in Linguistics and Philosophy 51). Berlin: Springer Verlag.

Zwart, C. Jan-Wouter. 1994. Dutch is head-initial. *The Linguistic Review* 11(3–4). 377–406.

Zweigenbaum, Pierre. 1991. Un analyseur pour grammaires lexicales-fonctionnelles. *TA Informations* 32(2). 19–34.

Zwicky, Arnold M., Joyce Friedman, Barbara C. Hall & Donald E. Walker. 1965. The MITRE syntactic analysis procedure for Transformational Grammars. In *Proceedings – FALL Joint Computer Conference*, 317–326. DOI:10.1109/AFIPS.1965.108.

Name index

Abbott, Barbara, 588
Abeillé, Anne, 118, 157, 158, 403, 543, 544, 625
Abney, Steven P., 29, 114, 115, 117, 468, 484, 501, 521, 669
Abraham, Werner, 12, 148
Abzianidze, Lasha, 256
Ackerman, Farrell, 114, 518, 654, 669
Adams, Marianne, 449
Ades, Anthony E., 506
Adger, David, xvi, 123, 128, 129, 132–138, 145, 161, 168, 172, 540, 569, 571, 573
Ágel, Vilmos, 355
Aguado-Orea, Javier, 477, 522
Ahmed, Mohamed Ben, 403
Ahmed, Reaz, 255
Ajdukiewicz, Kasimir, 155, 158, 237, 355
Akhtar, Nameera, 523
Alcock, Katie, 463
Alsina, Alex, 38, 304, 438, 579, 584, 591
Altmann, Hans, 48
Altmann, Rebecca J., 505
Ambridge, Ben, 447–449, 471, 476, 483, 528
Anderson, John M., 355
Anderson, Stephen R., 223
Andrews, Avery, 214
Anttila, Arto, 357
Aoun, Joseph, 116
Arad Greshler, Tali, 255, 256
Aras, Hidir, 330
Arends, Jacques, 460
Arka, I Wayan, 214
Arnold, Doug, 549
Arnold, Jennifer E., 505
Asher, Nicholas, 213
Askedal, John Ole, 43
Asudeh, Ash, 222, 234, 299, 304, 579, 591–593, 595, 596
Attardi, Giuseppe, 356
Attia, Mohammed A., 213
Avgustinova, Tania, 256
Bach, Emmon, 62, 99
Backofen, Rolf, 255
Bahrani, Mohammad, 175
Baker, Carl Lee, 464, 469
Baker, Mark C., 434, 438, 442, 512
Baldridge, Jason, xvi, 158, 237, 238, 242, 245, 250, 253, 287, 558
Balla, Amar, 255
Ballweg, Joachim, 530
Baltin, Mark, 442, 443, 450
Bangalore, Srinivas, 402
Bannard, Colin, 305, 548
Bar-Hillel, Yehoshua, 549, 551
Barry, Guy, 253
Bartsch, Renate, 101, 156
Barwise, Jon, 270
Barz, Irmhild, 13, 23–25, 42, 48, 71
Baschung, K., 237
Bates, Elizabeth A., 457, 458, 461, 487
Baumgärtner, Klaus, 355, 359, 388
Bausewein, Karin, 152, 153, 276
Bayer, Josef, 97, 114
Beavers, John, 157, 158, 237, 296, 331, 627, 630
Bech, Gunnar, 47, 409, 421
Becker, Tilman, 94, 409, 410, 419–422
Beermann, Dorothee, 256
Beghelli, Filippo, 142
Behaghel, Otto, 539
Behne, Tanya, 459, 460, 468
Behrens, Heike, 354, 457, 526, 628
Bellugi, Ursula, 462
Bender, Emily, 322, 542
Bender, Emily M., xvi, 6, 27, 116, 256, 257, 294, 300, 318, 319, 507, 542, 545, 550
Bentzen, Kristine, 142
Bergen, Benjamin K., 94, 303, 313, 314, 330, 332, 333, 524, 613
Berman, Judith, 38, 75, 97, 99, 213, 225–230, 233, 235, 419, 438, 440

Berthoud, Ioanna, 462
Berwick, Robert C., 155, 167, 171, 471, 513, 514, 529
Bes, G. G., 237
Bever, Thomas G., 502
Bialystok, Ellen, 458
Bick, Eckhard, 357
Bickerton, Derek, 460
Bierwisch, Manfred, 6, 81, 99, 113–115, 453
Bildhauer, Felix, xvi, 17, 145, 149, 257, 258, 301, 314, 339, 384
Bird, Steven, 258, 328
Bishop, Dorothy V. M., 461, 463
Bjerre, Tavs, 633
Blackburn, Patrick, 80, 491, 558
Błaszczak, Joanna, 142, 172
Blevins, James P., 311
Block, Hans-Ulrich, 213
Blom, Corrien, 620, 632
Bloom, Paul, 114, 513, 515
Blutner, Reinhard, 557
Boas, Hans C., 318, 344, 353, 580
Bobaljik, Jonathan, 143
Bod, Rens, 471, 477, 478, 635
Bögel, Tina, 214
Bohnet, Bernd, 356
Bolc, Leonard, 255
Bond, Francis, 255, 256
Booij, Geert E., 571, 594, 620, 632, 634
Borer, Hagit, 150, 579, 586, 597, 603, 607, 611, 612
Börschinger, Benjamin, 213
Borsley, Robert D., 119, 121, 156, 157, 166, 172, 283, 329, 353, 392, 647, 775
Bos, Johan, 80, 558
Bouchard, Lorne H., 175
Boukedi, Sirine, 255
Boullier, Pierre, 213
Bouma, Gerlof, 237
Bouma, Gosse, 163, 165, 167, 237, 256, 274, 293, 313, 325, 341, 370, 376, 491, 549, 550, 564, 574, 617
Bragmann, Sascha, 401, 650
Braine, Martin D. S., 450, 484
Branco, António, 256
Brants, Sabine, 445
Bredt, Thomas H., 117
Bresnan, Joan, 97, 121, 152, 157, 166, 213, 216, 218, 223, 224, 226, 228, 235, 311, 339, 435, 438, 529, 541, 546, 550, 563, 588, 589, 591, 592, 600
Brew, Chris, 257, 350
Briscoe, Ted, 583
Briscoe, Ted J., 119, 175, 238, 245, 253, 350, 450, 565, 583, 597, 668
Bröker, Norbert, 363
Brosziewski, Ulf, 127
Brown, Roger, 485
Bruening, Benjamin, 29, 169
Bryant, John, 304
Büchel, Christian, 462, 663
Budde, Monika, xvi, 642
Bühler, Karl, 452
Bungeroth, Jan, 257
Burke, Michael, 214
Burzio, Luigi, 91, 110
Buscha, Joachim, 355
Busemann, Stephan, 196, 255
Butt, Miriam, 213, 214, 630

Cahill, Aoife, 214
Calder, Jo, 255, 668
Calder, Jonathan, 237
Call, Josep, 459, 460, 468
Callmeier, Ulrich, 255
Candito, Marie-Hélène, 308, 403, 404, 406, 413, 613
Canon, Stephen, 214
Cappelle, Bert, 313, 337, 631–634
Capstick, Joanne, 255
Cargo, Martha B., 463
Carlson, Gregory N., 628
Carpenter, Bob, 197, 211, 237, 255, 491
Carpenter, Malinda, 459, 460, 468
Carroll, John, 175
Casenhiser, Devin, 582
Cavar, Damir, 501
Çetinoğlu, Özlem, 214
Chang, Nancy, 94, 303, 304, 313, 314, 330, 332, 333, 524, 613
Chang, Nancy Chih-Lin, 333
Chater, Nick, 484
Chatterjee, Sudipta, 237, 238
Chaudhuri, B. B., 213

Chaves, Rui P., 326, 377, 550
Chi, Zhiyi, 214
Choi, Hye-Won, 226, 227
Chomsky, Noam, 4, 6, 74, 75, 81–84, 87, 90–92, 94, 95, 107, 108, 114, 116, 119, 123, 124, 129, 139–142, 149–157, 160, 165–167, 169, 171–173, 175, 303, 311, 419, 431, 433, 434, 436–438, 440, 442, 450–457, 459, 461, 463, 464, 468, 471, 484, 485, 492, 499, 502, 504, 507, 508, 511, 512, 517, 519–521, 529, 536, 550, 590, 595, 601–603, 667, 704, 705
Chouinard, Michelle M., 485
Christiansen, Morten, 449
Chrupala, Grzegorz, 214
Chung, Sandra, 449
Church, Kenneth, 669
Cinque, Guglielmo, 140–142, 145, 147, 169, 450, 664
Citko, Barbara, 152, 154
Clark, Alexander, 484
Clark, Eve V., 485
Clark, Herbert H., 504
Clark, Stephen, 237, 238
Clément, Lionel, 213, 308, 613
Clifton, Charles, 508
Clifton, Charles Jr., 501
Coch, Jose, 357
Cole, Jennifer, 117, 501
Comrie, Bernard, 153, 158, 276
Cook, Philippa Helen, xvi, 17, 39, 149, 213, 339, 384, 448
Coopmans, Peter, 549
Copestake, Ann, 255, 256, 262, 272, 307, 318, 347, 350, 352, 407, 558, 565, 583, 597
Corluy, A., 237
Correa, Nelson, 117
Costa, Francisco, 256
Covington, Michael A., 357, 387
Crabbé, Benoit, 403
Crain, Stephen, 440, 441, 449, 476, 483, 506
Cramer, Bart, 257
Crocker, Matthew Walter, 117, 119
Croft, William, 303, 304, 438, 451, 524, 536, 579, 580, 585, 612, 615, 617, 629, 661
Crouch, Richard, 213, 214
Crysmann, Berthold, 17, 101, 157, 158, 256, 258, 296, 331, 627, 632
Csernyi, Gábor, 214
Culicover, Peter W., 42, 81, 156, 161, 440, 456, 503, 520, 551, 579, 617, 618, 630
Culy, Christopher, 195, 403, 529
Curran, James, 237
Curtiss, Susan, 459
Czuba, Krzysztof, 255

Da Sylva, Lyne, 175
Dąbrowska, Ewa, 303, 354, 461–463, 475, 523, 579
Dahl, Östen, 450
Dahllöf, Mats, 255, 256
Dale, Robert, 213
Dalrymple, Mary, 38, 97, 214, 215, 219–221, 226, 234, 235, 299, 304, 363, 438, 441, 536, 556, 579, 591, 593, 596
Davidson, Donald, 597
Davies, Mark, 462
Davis, Anthony R., 272, 308, 613
de Alencar, Leonel, 213, 214, 235
De Beule, Joachim, 304
De Kuthy, Kordula, 15, 17, 115, 166, 256, 314, 339, 448, 530, 531
de Saussure, Ferdinand, 3, 258, 452
Declerck, Thierry, 255
Dellert, Johannes, 403
Delmonte, Rodolfo, 213, 214
Demberg, Vera, 346
Demske, Ulrike, 29
den Besten, Hans, 113, 114, 156
Deppermann, Arnulf, 353, 464, 594
Derbyshire, Desmond C., 455
Devlin, Keith, 270
Dhonnchadha, E. Uí, 357
Diagne, Abdel Kader, 255
Diesing, Molly, 97
Dini, Luca, 255
Dione, Cheikh Mouhamadou Bamba, 214
Dipper, Stefanie, 213, 445
Dodsen, Kelly, 523
Donati, C., 151
Donohue, Cathryn, 296

Doran, Christine, 403
Doran, Robert W., 117
Dorna, Michael, 255
Dörre, Jochen, 255
Dowty, David, 238
Dowty, David R., 6, 90, 156, 237, 242, 311, 337, 557, 563, 586, 592, 597, 598, 602, 605, 624
Dras, Mark, 213
Drellishak, Scott, 257
Drosdowski, Günther, 25, 41
Dryer, Matthew S., 99, 434, 435, 661
Dürscheid, Christa, 113, 530
Dyvik, Helge, xvii, 214

Eberhard, Kathleen M., 504, 505
Egg, Markus, 557, 559
Eikmeyer, Hans-Jürgen, 237
Eisele, Andreas, 213
Eisenberg, Peter, xvi, 13, 23–26, 28, 33, 35, 37, 42, 47, 48, 64, 71, 156, 445, 468
Elbourne, Paul, 112, 113, 171, 509, 667
Ellefson, Michelle R., 449
Elman, Jeffrey L., 458, 461, 471, 475, 487
Embick, David, 597
Emirkanian, Louisette, 175
Engdahl, Elisabet, 339
Engel, Ulrich, 355, 358, 360, 361, 363, 368, 386, 393, 402, 531, 550
Epstein, Samuel David, 155, 167
Erbach, Gregor, 255
Ernst, Thomas, 147, 148
Eroms, Hans-Werner, 94, 355, 360, 363–366, 368, 369, 375, 381, 400, 550
Erteschik-Shir, Nomi, 449
Estigarribia, Bruno, 476
Estival, Dominique, 255
Evang, Kilian, 403
Evans, Nicholas, 435, 438, 441, 450, 451, 455, 664
Evans, Roger, 175
Everett, Daniel L., 454
Evers, Arnold, 114, 115, 611
Evert, Stefan, xvi

Faaß, Gertrud, 214
Fabregas, Antonio, 154
Fabricius-Hansen, Cathrine, 13, 23–25, 42, 48, 71
Fagnano, Maria, 505
Falk, Yehuda N., 118
Fan, Zhenzhen, 255, 256
Fang, Ji, 214
Fanselow, Gisbert, xvi, 81, 107, 112–115, 117, 121, 148, 149, 165, 166, 173, 237, 246, 287, 289, 386, 424, 439, 441, 448, 459, 501, 530, 575, 664
Feldhaus, Anke, 99
Feldman, Jerome, 466
Felix, Sascha W., 81, 107, 121
Fiehler, Reinhard, 13, 23–25, 42, 48, 71
Filimonova, Elena, 433
Fillmore, Charles J., 68, 79, 118, 167, 303–305, 307, 314–317, 330, 475, 544, 551, 583, 585, 613
Finch, Steven, 484
Fischer, Ingrid, 543
Fischer, Klaus, 355
Fisher, Simon E., 461–463
Fitch, W. Tecumseh, 84, 140, 442, 450, 451, 453–456, 461, 463, 484
Fletcher, Paul, 463
Flickinger, Daniel P., 116, 202, 256, 257, 262, 272, 300, 307, 318, 322, 336, 407, 542, 558, 566
Fodor, Janet Dean, 500, 512, 513, 517, 518, 520
Fodor, Jerry A., 502
Fokkens, Antske, 256, 257
Fong, Sandiway, xvi, 117, 170, 171
Fordham, Andrew, 117, 119
Forst, Martin, 38, 213, 214, 438
Fortmann, Christian, 530
Fourquet, Jean, 99
Fouvry, Frederik, 257
Fox Tree, Jean E., 504
Fraj, Fériel Ben, 403
Frank, Anette, 99, 213, 558, 721
Frank, Robert, 403
Franks, Steven, 474, 511
Frazier, Lyn, 500, 508
Freidin, Robert, 117, 175, 442, 664
Freudenthal, Daniel, 477, 521–523
Frey, Werner, 111, 113, 119, 148, 155, 162, 213, 219, 299, 530

Fried, Mirjam, 303, 305
Friederici, Angela D., 459, 461, 462
Friedman, Joyce, 117, 118
Fries, Norbert, 276
Fritz, Thomas A., 13, 23–25, 42, 48, 71
Fukui, Naoki, 97
Fukumochi, Yasutomo, 356, 357

Gaifman, Haim, 359, 387, 388
Gallmann, Peter, xviii, 13, 23–25, 42, 48, 71, 120
Gardent, Claire, 213, 491
Gardner, R. Allen, 461
Garrett, Merrill F., 502
Gärtner, Hans-Martin, 12, 142, 155, 162, 172, 530
Gazdar, Gerald, 117–119, 121, 158, 166, 175, 176, 178, 182, 183, 187–189, 193, 196, 300, 311, 343, 489, 491, 550
Geach, Peter Thomas, 166, 195
Geißler, Stefan, 256
Geman, Stuart, 214
George, Marie St., 462
Gerdemann, Dale, 255
Gerdes, Kim, xvi, 357, 362, 403
Gerken, LouAnn, 515
Ghayoomi, Masood, 256, 658
Gibson, Edward, 287, 420, 434, 449, 500, 501, 512–514, 611
Gillis, Steven, 521, 522
Ginsburg, Jason, 117, 171
Ginzburg, Jonathan, 118, 158, 164, 167, 262, 270, 298, 389, 399, 475, 477, 520, 647
Giorgolo, Gianluca, 595
Gipper, Helmut, 41
Glauche, Volkmar, 462, 663
Glauert, John, 257
Gobet, Fernand, 477, 521–523
Gold, Mark E., 465
Goldberg, Adele, xvi
Goldberg, Adele E., 303–305, 313, 335, 337, 346, 353, 447–449, 485, 487, 521, 524, 528, 548, 551, 579–582, 584–586, 591, 593, 620, 628–631, 665
Gopnik, Myrna, 463
Gordon, Peter, 464, 468
Gosch, Angela, 462
Götz, Thilo, 255
Grant, Julia, 462
Grebe, Paul, 41
Green, Georgia M., 526
Grewendorf, Günther, 81, 91, 92, 105, 109, 113–115, 121, 123, 140, 141, 148, 172, 276, 439, 444, 530, 549, 618
Grewendorf, Güther, 140, 148
Gries, Stephan Th., 635, 638
Grimshaw, Jane, xvi, 152, 449, 630
Grinberg, Dennis, 356
Grohmann, Kleantes K., 145, 172, 453, 454
Groos, Anneke, 153
Groß, Thomas M., 153, 191, 364, 366, 368–370, 380, 384, 385, 397, 402, 550, 575, 576, 633
Groß, Thomas Michael, 35
Grosu, Alexander, 449
Grover, Claire, 175
Grubačić, Emilija, 633
Guillotin, T., 237
Gunji, Takao, 575
Gunter, Thomas C., 462
Günther, Carsten, 339
Guo, Yuqing, 214
Guzmán Naranjo, Matías, 350

Haddar, Kais, 255
Haegeman, Liliane, 121, 143, 535, 536, 539, 570
Haftka, Brigitta, 92, 148
Hagen, Kristin, 357
Hahn, Michael, 255
Haider, Hubert, 75, 81, 97, 100, 107, 110, 113, 114, 119, 143, 146, 147, 166, 226, 234, 275, 278, 280, 287, 299, 413, 438, 439, 444, 511, 530, 545, 549, 575, 605, 664, 667
Hajičová, Eva, 355
Hakuta, Kenji, 458
Hale, Kenneth, 128, 454, 591, 597
Hall, Barbara C., 117, 118
Han, Chung-hye, 404
Hanlon, Camille, 485
Hansen-Schirra, Silvia, 445
Harley, Heidi, 601–603

Harlow, Ray, 29
Harman, Gilbert, 80, 175
Harris, Zellig S., 4
Hasan, K. M. Azharul, 255
Haspelmath, Martin, xvi, xix, 93, 431, 451, 512, 661, 662
Haugereid, Petter, 256, 275, 298, 597, 605, 607, 608, 610, 669
Hauser, Marc D., 84, 140, 442, 450, 451, 453, 455, 456, 461, 463, 484
Hausser, Roland, 506
Hawkins, John A., 287, 435, 446, 449
Hays, David G., 356, 357, 359, 388
Heikkilä, Juha, 357
Heinecke, Johannes, 357
Heinz, Wolfgang, 106, 234, 605
Helbig, Gerhard, 355
Hellan, Lars, 29, 256, 669
Hellwig, Peter, 355–357, 362, 364, 387, 396, 397, 402, 529, 667
Her, One-Soon, 213, 214
Heringer, Hans Jürgen, 365, 368, 369
Herzig Sheinfux, Livnat, 255, 256
Higginbotham, James, 300, 546
Higinbotham, Dan, 213, 214
Hildebrandt, Bernd, 237
Hinkelman, Elizabeth A., 255
Hinrichs, Erhard W., 115, 166, 279, 300, 327, 364, 421, 566, 574, 577, 611
Hinterhölzel, Roland, 148
Hoberg, Ursula, 422, 573
Hockenmaier, Julia, 237, 238
Hockett, Charles F., 455
Hockey, Beth Ann, 403
Hoeksema, Jack, 621
Hoffman, Beryl Ann, 237, 246, 287
Hofman, Ute, 48
Hofmeister, Philip, 449
Höhle, Tilman N., 43, 51, 97, 100, 111, 245, 258, 281, 326, 495, 574, 731–733
Holler, Anke, 262
Holmberg, Anders, 512
Hornstein, Norbert, 145, 169, 172, 450, 453, 454, 457
Howlin, Patricia, 462
Hrafnbjargarson, Gunnar Hrafn, 142
Hróarsdóttir, Þorbjörg, 142
Huang, Wei, 357
Hudson, Carla L., 461
Hudson Kam, Carla L., 461
Hudson, Richard, xvi, 29, 355–358, 363–365, 393, 395–399, 456
Hudson, Richard A., 356, 358, 363–365, 368, 370–372, 375, 380, 550
Hukari, Thomas E., 326, 491, 549, 550
Humboldt, Wilhelm von, 451
Hunze, Rudolf, 213
Hurford, James R., 457, 476
Hurskainen, Arvi, 357
Hurst, Jane A., 463

Ibbotson, Paul, 663
Ichiyama, Shunji, 356, 357
Ingram, David, 523
Iordanskaja, L., 357
Islam, Md. Asfaqul, 255
Islam, Muhammad Sadiqul, 255

Jackendoff, Ray S., 42, 74, 81, 92, 94, 115, 139, 156, 158, 161, 278, 304, 346, 353, 400, 435, 440, 450, 456, 476, 503, 507, 509, 510, 520, 551, 565, 579, 591, 617, 618, 620, 630, 640, 649, 650, 654
Jacobs, Joachim, 99, 188, 244, 353, 639, 654
Jacobson, Pauline, 188, 196, 283
Jaeggli, Osvaldo A., 570
Jäger, Gerhard, 557
Jäppinen, H., 356, 357
Jäppinen, Harri, 357
Johannessen, Janne Bondi, 357
Johnson, David E., 117, 139, 454, 490
Johnson, Jacqueline S., 458, 459
Johnson, Kent, 466, 467
Johnson, Mark, 119, 192, 194, 197, 211, 213, 214, 346, 426, 506–508, 529
Johnson, Mark H., 458, 461, 487
Jones, Wendy, 462
Joshi, Aravind K., 94, 331, 402–404, 406–411, 413, 415, 419–422, 425, 426, 605, 625
Jungen, Oliver, xv
Jurafsky, Daniel, 305, 548

Kahane, Sylvain, xvi, 355, 357, 360, 362, 368, 375, 378–380, 389, 400, 406
Kallmeyer, Laura, xvi, 308, 403, 404, 406–408, 425, 426, 550, 613, 615
Kamp, Hans, 219
Kanerva, Jonni M., 224
Kaplan, Ronald M., 119, 121, 213, 214, 218, 223, 227, 230, 232, 234, 299, 315, 438, 454, 491, 529, 563
Karimi, Simin, 143
Karimi-Doostan, Gholamhossein, 143
Karlsson, Fred, 356
Karmiloff-Smith, Annette, 458, 461–463, 487
Karttunen, Lauri, 228, 237
Kasper, Robert T., 101, 185, 285, 313, 389, 425, 538
Kasper, Walter, 255, 256, 350
Kathol, Andreas, 47, 191, 279, 285, 296, 331, 338, 345, 386, 392, 621, 632, 633
Kaufmann, Ingrid, 592
Kaufmann, Tobias, 255, 256, 669
Kay, Martin, 117, 118, 356, 669
Kay, Paul, xvi, 303–305, 307, 314–318, 322, 330, 353, 475, 544, 583, 585, 592, 613, 616
Kayne, Richard S., 142, 143, 156, 157, 170, 287, 653, 663
Keenan, Edward L., 153, 158, 276
Keil, Martina, 543
Keller, Frank, 167, 256, 344, 346
Kempen, Masja, 521, 522
Kern, Sabine, 501
Kettunen, Kimmo, 357
Keyser, Samuel Jay, 128, 591, 597
Khlentzos, Drew, 440, 441, 449
Kiefer, Bernd, 255, 352, 425
Kifle, Nazareth Amlesom, 214
Kim, Jong-Bok, 4, 121, 256, 452, 453
Kim, M., 357
Kim, Nari, 404
Kimball, John P., 464, 468
King, Paul, 197, 211, 454, 491, 629
King, Tracy Holloway, 213, 214, 234, 299
Kinyon, Alexandra, 213, 308, 404, 413, 613
Kiparsky, Carol, 448
Kiparsky, Paul, 448, 581
Kiss, Katalin E., 143
Kiss, Tibor, xvi, 80, 99, 112, 113, 115, 245, 256, 276, 437, 444, 575, 673
Kittredge, R., 357
Klann-Delius, Gisela, 528
Klein, Ewan, 117, 118, 158, 175, 176, 178, 182, 183, 187, 188, 196, 237, 258, 300, 311, 328, 489, 491, 493, 550, 668
Klein, Wolfgang, 156, 276, 356, 372, 456, 458, 468
Klenk, Ursula, 84
Kliegl, Reinhold, 501
Kluender, Robert, 449, 457
Knecht, Laura, 311
Kobele, Gregory M., 166
Koelsch, Stefan, 462
Koenig, Jean-Pierre, 272, 295, 304, 308, 310, 351, 613, 617, 644, 660
Kohl, Dieter, 213
Kohl, Karen T., 514
Koit, Mare, 357
Kolb, Hans-Peter, 117–119, 139
Komarova, Natalia L., 4, 452, 512
Konieczny, Lars, 342, 346
König, Esther, 237, 445, 550
Koopman, Hilda, 97
Kordoni, Valia, 256, 308, 613
Kornai, András, 76, 117, 436, 454
Kornfilt, Jaklin, 97, 114
Koster, Jan, 99, 101, 109, 110, 113, 119, 299, 443, 444
Kouylekov, Milen, 255
Kratzer, Angelika, 113, 530, 540, 597–600
Krieger, Hans-Ulrich, 255, 312, 352, 594, 614
Krifka, Manfred, 456
Kroch, Anthony S., 403, 411, 413, 426, 550, 605
Kropp Dakubu, Mary Esther, 256
Kruijff, Geert-Jan M., 558
Kruijff-Korbayová, Ivana, 216
Kubczak, Jacqueline, 355
Kübler, Sandra, 356
Kuhn, Jonas, xvi, 121, 172, 213, 223, 224, 234, 339, 509, 510, 520
Kuhns, Robert J., 117
Kunze, Jürgen, 355–357, 368, 380, 605
Kuperberg, Gina, 630
Kutas, Marta, 449

Labelle, Marie, 502
Laczkó, Tibor, 214
Laenzlinger, Christoph, 138, 142, 144, 148, 287, 653
Lafferty, John D., 356
Lai, Cecilia S. L., 463
Lai, Zona, 462
Lakoff, George, 303, 490
Lamping, John, 219, 363
Langacker, Ronald W., 303, 333, 579, 580
Lappin, Shalom, 117, 139, 446–448
Lareau, François, 213
Larson, Richard K., 107, 128, 129, 155, 161, 549, 569
Lascarides, Alex, 565
Laskri, Mohamed Tayeb, 255
Lasnik, Howard, 472, 508
Lavoie, B., 357
Lavoie, Benoit, 357
Le, Hong Phuong, 404
Lee-Goldmann, Russell R., 68, 79
Legate, Julie, 472–474
Lehtola, A., 356, 357
Lehtola, Aarno, 357
Leiss, Elisabeth, 4, 393, 499, 547
Lenerz, Jürgen, 12, 108, 113, 115, 137, 573
Lenneberg, Eric H., 458, 459
Levelt, Willem J. M., 235
Levin, Beth, 605
Levine, Robert D., xvi, 117, 139, 301, 326, 347, 350, 375, 376, 491, 549, 550
Levinson, Stephen C., 435, 438, 441, 450, 451, 455, 664
Levy, Leon S., 403, 426
Lewin, Ian, 117, 119
Lewis, Geoffrey L., 311, 614
Lewis, John D., 471, 475
Lewis, Richard L., 501
Lezius, Wolfgang, 445
Li, Charles N., 646
Li, Wei, 256
Liakata, Maria, 214
Lichte, Timm, xvi, 403, 411, 424
Lichtenberger, Liz, 462
Lieb, Hans-Heinrich, xvi
Lieven, Elena, 305, 548
Lieven, Elena V. M., 528
Lightfoot, David W., 116, 521
Link, Godehard, 437
Lipenkova, Janna, 256, 353, 646, 647, 658
Liu, Gang, 256
Liu, Haitao, xvi, 357
Lloré, F. Xavier, 237
Lobin, Henning, 253, 355, 402
Löbner, Sebastian, 549
Lødrup, Helge, 38, 438
Lohndal, Terje, 597, 598, 606
Lohnstein, Horst, xv, 109, 117, 119, 120, 502, 549, 570
Longobardi, Giuseppe, 456
Lorenz, Konrad, 458
Lötscher, Andreas, 545
Loukam, Mourad, 255
Lüdeling, Anke, 635
Luuk, Erkki, 453, 456
Luuk, Hendrik, 453, 456

Maas, Heinz Dieter, 357
Maché, Jakob, xvi, 642, 646
Machicao y Priemer, Antonio, 658
Mack, Jennifer, 630
Mackie, Lisa, 214
MacWhinney, Brian, 470
Maess, Burkhard, 462
Maienborn, Claudia, 339
Maier, Wolfgang, 403
Maling, Joan, 37, 115, 185, 225, 278, 604
Malouf, Robert, 165, 256, 274, 293, 313, 325, 341, 370, 376, 549, 550, 564, 617
Manandhar, Suresh, 255
Manshadi, Mehdi Hafezi, 175
Marantz, Alec, 150, 502, 505, 590, 597, 599, 601, 602, 641
Marciniak, Małgorzata, 255, 256
Marcus, Gary F., 461–463, 485
Marcus, Mitchell P., 117
Marimon, Montserrat, 257
Marshall, Ian, 257
Marslen-Wilson, William, 504
Martinet, André, 452
Martner, Theodore S., 117
Masuichi, Hiroshi, 214
Masum, Mahmudul Hasan, 255
Matiasek, Johannes, 106, 234, 605

Matsumoto, Yuji, 356
Maxwell III, John T., 213, 214
Mayo, Bruce, 213, 214
McCloskey, James, 449
McDonald, Ryan, 356
Mchombo, Sam A., 223, 591
McIntyre, Andrew, xvi
McKean, Kathryn Ojemann, 501
Meinunger, André, 113, 138, 142, 563
Meisel, Jürgen, 435, 460, 511, 527
Mel'čuk, Igor A., 355–357, 363, 396, 550
Melnik, Nurit, 255, 256
Mensching, Guido, xvi, xvii, 519
Menzel, Wolfgang, 357
Metcalf, Vanessa, 256
Meurer, Paul, 213, 214
Meurers, Walt Detmar, 17, 99, 115, 166, 255, 256, 277–279, 285, 300, 301, 326, 336, 347, 350, 392, 421, 445, 542, 545, 565, 621, 669
Meyer-Viol, Wilfried, 491
Meza, Iván V., 257
Micelli, Vanessa, 305, 312, 330
Michaelis, Jens, xvi, 159, 162, 529, 530
Michaelis, Laura, xvi
Michaelis, Laura A., 234, 304, 308, 317, 318, 353, 551, 613, 667
Michelson, Karin, 295, 351, 660
Miller, George A., 419, 499, 501
Mineur, Anne-Marie, 255
Mistica, Meladel, 214
Mittendorf, Ingo, 214
Miyao, Yusuke, 257, 425
Moens, Marc, 668
Mohanan, KP, 38, 438
Mohanan, Tara, 38, 438
Mok, Eva, 304
Moll, Henrike, 459, 460, 468
Momma, Stefan, 213
Monaco, Anthony P., 463
Montague, Richard, 182, 237
Moortgat, Michael, 237, 238
Moot, Richard, 237
Morgan, James L., 467
Morin, Yves Ch., 117
Moro, Andrea, 462, 663
Morrill, Glyn V., 237, 238, 252
Moshier, Andrew M., 310
Motazedi, Yasaman, 213
Muischnek, Kadri, 357
Müller, Gereon, xvi, 92, 114, 115, 138, 166, 169, 403, 530, 641–643, 651
Müller, Max, 456
Müller, Natascha, 457
Müller, Stefan, xv, xix, 6, 15, 29, 35, 42, 99, 107, 115, 116, 151–153, 155, 158, 159, 162, 163, 165–167, 172, 173, 210, 234, 244, 255–257, 261, 264, 271, 275, 276, 278–280, 283, 285, 286, 294, 296–301, 303–305, 309–312, 315, 320, 325, 326, 329, 331, 335, 336, 338, 344, 345, 347, 350–353, 384–386, 392, 400, 413, 421, 424, 431, 438, 439, 441, 443, 445, 453, 496, 497, 524, 530, 542, 545, 549, 552, 563, 565, 566, 574, 580, 582, 585, 587, 591, 592, 594, 596, 597, 601, 605, 609–611, 616–622, 628–630, 632–635, 645–648, 656, 658, 662, 669, 673, 684
Muraki, Kazunori, 356, 357
Musso, Mariacristina, 462, 663
Muysken, Peter, 76, 157
Mykowiecka, Agnieszka, 255, 256

Nakayama, Mineharu, 476, 483
Nakazawa, Tsuneko, 115, 166, 279, 300, 327, 364, 421, 566, 574, 577, 611
Nasr, Alexis, 368, 380
Naumann, Sven, 175
Nederhof, Mark-Jan, 352
Neeleman, Ad, 304
Nelimarkka, Esa, 357
Nerbonne, John, 192, 194, 270, 312, 439, 558, 594, 614
Netter, Klaus, 29, 80, 99, 244, 255, 256, 421, 425, 662, 672
Neu, Julia, 256
Neumann, Günter, 255
Neville, Anne, 255
Nevins, Andrew Ira, 454
Newmeyer, Frederick J., 114, 143, 435, 436, 442, 450, 457, 512, 520, 521, 549, 661

Newport, Elissa L., 458, 459, 461
Ng, Say Kiat, 256
Nguyen, Thi Minh Huyen, 404
Niño, María-Eugenia, 214
Ninomiya, Takashi, 257
Nivre, Joakim, 356
Niyogi, Partha, 4, 452, 512–514
Noh, Bokyung, 565, 592, 610
Nøklestad, Anders, 357
Nolda, Andreas, xvi
Nomura, Hirosato, 356, 357
Noonan, Michael, 311, 614
Nordgård, Torbjørn, 117
Nordhoff, Sebastian, xvi
Nordlinger, Rachel, 214, 300, 544
Nowak, Martin A., 4, 452, 512
Noyer, Rolf, 601–603
Nozohoor-Farshi, R., 117
Nübling, Damaris, 13, 23–25, 42, 48, 71
Nunberg, Geoffrey, 520, 583, 600, 601, 616, 632
Nunes, Jairo, 145, 166, 172, 453, 454
Nygaard, Lars, 357

Ochs, Elinor, 475, 485
O'Connor, Mary Catherine, 303, 585
Odom, Penelope, 501
O'Donovan, Ruth, 214
Oepen, Stephan, 116, 255, 257
Özkaragöz, İnci, 311, 614
Oflazer, Kemal, 214
Ohkuma, Tomoko, 214
Oliva, Karel, 99, 283, 387, 396, 402
O'Neill, Michael, 4, 452
Oppenrieder, Wilhelm, 113, 574
Orgun, Cemil Orhan, 258
Ørsnes, Bjarne, xvi
Osborne, Miles, 238
Osborne, Timothy, xvi, 153, 191, 364, 366, 368–370, 378–380, 384, 385, 397, 400, 402, 550, 575, 576, 633
Osenova, Petya, 255
Osswald, Rainer, 308, 613, 615
Ott, Dennis, 153

Paczynski, Martin, 630
Pafel, Jürgen, 530
Paggio, Patrizia, 255, 339
Palmer, Alexis, 237, 238
Palmer, Martha, 404
Pankau, Andreas, xvi, xviii
Pankau, Rainer, 462
Parisi, Domenico, 458, 461, 487
Parmentier, Yannick, 403
Partee, Barbara H., 566
Passingham, Richard, 463
Patejuk, Agnieszka, 214
Paul, Hermann, 46
Paul, Soma, 255
Pembrey, Marcus E., 463
Penn, Gerald, 255, 347
Pentheroudakis, Joseph, 213, 214
Perchonock, Ellen, 501
Pereira, Fernando, 330
Perles, Micha A., 549, 551
Perlmutter, David M., 91, 115, 135, 275, 437
Perry, John, 270
Pesetsky, David, 454, 601, 603, 663
Peters, Jörg, 13, 23–25, 42, 48, 71
Peters, Stanley, 84
Petrick, Stanley Roy, 117
Pfister, Beat, 256, 669
Phillips, Colin, 501, 507
Phillips, John D., 175
Pickering, Martin, 253
Pienemann, Manfred, 235
Pietroski, Paul, 171, 471
Pietsch, Christian, xvi
Pihko, E., 634
Piñango, Maria Mercedes, 630, 631
Pine, Julian M., 471, 476, 477, 483, 521–523
Pineda, Luis Alberto, 257
Pinker, Steven, 84, 139, 235, 433–435, 438, 449, 450, 453, 456, 461, 487, 640
Pittner, Karin, 276
Plainfossé, Agnes, 213
Plank, Frans, 433
Plunkett, Kim, 458, 461, 487
Poletto, Cecilia, 142, 148
Polguère, A., 357
Pollack, Bary W., 117
Pollard, Carl J., 29, 35, 151, 158, 164–166, 196, 197, 202, 248, 249, 251, 255, 257, 262, 264, 270–272, 274, 276, 279, 287, 290, 293–295, 297, 298, 300,

307, 310, 311, 318, 319, 325, 329, 345, 386, 399, 400, 407, 454, 509, 518, 529, 536, 542, 544, 545, 550, 556, 558, 564, 605, 629
Pollock, Jean-Yves, 142, 143, 223
Ponvert, Elias, 630
Popowich, Fred, 255
Porzel, Robert, 330
Postal, Paul M., 116, 453, 454, 490, 549
Poulson, Laurie, 257
Preuss, Susanne, 175, 185, 187
Prince, Alan, xvi
Przepiórkowski, Adam, 115, 214, 255, 256, 278, 300, 301, 542, 545
Pullum, Geoffrey K., xvi, xix, 4, 76, 91, 116–118, 153, 158, 175, 176, 178, 179, 182, 183, 187, 188, 195, 196, 276, 300, 311, 403, 436, 453–455, 463, 466, 468–471, 474, 477, 478, 485, 487, 489–493, 511, 550
Pulman, Stephen G., 506
Pulvermüller, F., 634
Pulvermüller, Friedemann, 4, 476, 487, 631–634
Puolakainen, Tiina, 357
Putnam, Michael, 153, 154, 402

Quaglia, Stefano, 214

Radford, Andrew, 145, 172, 434, 521
Rahman, M. Sohel, 255
Rahman, Md. Mizanur, 255
Rákosi, György, 214
Rambow, Owen, 94, 213, 357, 368, 380, 402–404, 409–411, 413, 415, 417, 419–422, 424–426, 550
Ramchand, Gillian, 566
Randriamasimanana, Charles, 214
Raposo, Eduardo, 474, 511
Rappaport Hovav, Malka, 605
Rappaport, Malka, 602
Rauh, Gisa, 150
Reape, Mike, 94, 213, 286, 296, 314, 331, 338, 345, 352, 389, 530, 632, 633, 668
Redington, Martin, 484
Reichenbach, Jürgen, 462, 663
Reis, Marga, 35, 36, 43, 49, 51, 99, 101, 113, 439
Rekau, Laura, 523
Remberger, Eva-Maria, 474, 519
Resnik, Philip, 404
Reyle, Uwe, 213, 219, 558
Rhomieux, Russell, 68, 79
Richards, Marc, 139, 140, 502, 505
Richter, Frank, xvi, xvii, 172, 197, 211, 255, 270, 296, 320, 322, 324, 329, 347, 350, 379, 454, 542, 546, 664
Rieder, Sibylle, 255
Riehemann, Susanne, 194, 571
Riehemann, Susanne Z., 194, 571
Riemer, Beate, 457
Riemsdijk, Henk van, 93
Riezler, Stefan, 213, 214
Rijntjes, Michel, 462, 663
Ritchie, R. W., 84
Rizzi, Luigi, 140, 141, 145, 148, 169, 440, 442, 450, 511, 664
Roberts, Ian, 456
Roberts, Ian F., 512
Robins, Robert Henry, xv
Robinson, Jane, 330
Rodrigues, Cilene, 454
Rogers, James, 119, 454, 491
Rohrer, Christian, 213, 214, 445
Romero, Maribel, 426
Roosmaa, Tiit, 357
Rosén, Victoria, 214
Ross, John Robert, 115, 193, 251, 343, 437, 442, 446, 768
Roth, Sebastian, 214
Rothkegel, Annely, 356
Roussanaly, Azim, 404
Rowland, Caroline F., 471, 476, 483
Ruiter, Vera de, 355
Ruppenhofer, Josef, 234, 304, 308, 317, 551, 613, 667

Sabel, Joachim, 530
Sadler, Louisa, 214
Sáfár, Éva, 257
Sag, Ivan A., xvi, 27, 29, 117, 118, 148, 151, 157, 158, 164–167, 175, 176, 178, 182, 183, 187, 188, 196, 197, 202, 251, 255, 256, 262, 264, 270–272, 274, 276, 287, 290, 293–298, 300, 304,

307, 310, 311, 313, 318, 319, 322, 325–331, 339, 341, 346, 349, 353, 370, 376, 389, 399, 400, 407, 449, 475, 477, 489, 501, 504, 506, 507, 509, 510, 518, 520, 536, 542, 544, 545, 549, 550, 558, 564, 591, 600, 601, 605, 616, 617, 621, 627, 629, 632, 635, 647, 648
Sagot, Benoît, 213
Sailer, Manfred, 270, 296, 320, 322, 329, 542, 543, 546
Saito, Mamoru, 508
Samarin, William J., 460
Sameti, Hossein, 175
Sampson, Geoffrey, 457, 471, 472
Samvelian, Pollet, 437
Saraswat, Vijay, 219, 363
Sarkar, Anoop, 331, 403, 625
Sato, Yo, 255, 296
Sauerland, Uli, xvi, 112, 113, 171, 509, 667
Savin, Harris B., 501
Schabes, Yves, 426, 543, 544
Schäfer, Roland, xviii, 242
Scheffler, Tatjana, 404, 413
Schein, Barry, 597, 598
Schenkel, Wolfgang, 355
Scherpenisse, Wim, 105, 113, 191, 367
Schieffelin, Bambi B., 475, 485
Schlesewsky, Matthias, 501
Schluter, Natalie, 214
Schmidt, Paul, 255
Schmidt, Renate, 355
Scholz, Barbara C., 4, 453–455, 463, 466, 468–471, 474, 477, 478, 485, 487, 490–493, 511
Schopp, Andrea, 339
Schröder, Ingo, 357
Schubert, K., 355
Schumacher, Helmut, 355
Schütz, Jörg, 255
Schwarze, Christoph, xvi, 213, 235
Sedivy, Julie C., 504, 505
Segond, Frédérique, 214
Seiffert, Roland, 255
Seiss, Melanie, 214
Sells, Peter, 4, 121, 256, 452, 453
Sengupta, Probal, 213
Sethuraman, Nitya, 582
Seuren, Pieter A. M., 139, 460
Sgall, Petr, 355
Shamir, Eliahu, 549, 551
Shanker, K. Vijay, 409
Shanker, Vijay K., 425
Shieber, Stuart M., 195, 197, 211, 330, 346, 403, 426, 506, 507, 529
Shtyrov, Y., 634
Shtyrov, Yury, 631–634
Siegel, Melanie, 256
Simov, Alexander, 255
Simov, Kiril, 255
Simpson, Jane, 214, 304, 545, 592, 771
Singleton, Jenny L., 461
Sleator, Daniel D. K., 356, 357
Sleator, Daniel Dominic, 356
Smith, Carlota S., 602, 603
Smith, George, 445
Smolensky, Paul, xvi
Snedeker, Jesse, 630
Snider, Neal, 449
Snider, Nil, 446
Snyder, William, 511
Soehn, Jan-Philipp, 329
Son, Minjeong, 512, 519
Song, Sanghoun, 255, 256
Spackman, Stephen P., 255
Speas, Margaret, 97
Spencer, Andrew, 549
Spivey-Knowlton, Michael J., 504, 505
Sportiche, Dominique, 97, 116
Srinivas, Bangalore, 403
Stabler, Edward P., 117, 119, 140, 155, 159, 160, 162, 170–172, 300, 440, 506, 508, 509, 529, 546, 667
Städing, Gabriele, 462
Stark, Elisabeth, xvii
Starosta, Stanley, 356, 357, 550
Stede, Manfred, 237
Steedman, Mark J., 155, 156, 158, 163, 216, 237, 238, 240, 243, 245, 246, 248–251, 253, 287, 312, 493, 506, 509, 623–625, 637, 669
Steels, Luc, 304, 305, 334, 337, 338, 352
Stefanowitsch, Anatol, 486, 635, 638
Steinbach, Markus, 12, 114, 530

Sternefeld, Wolfgang, xvii, 81, 97, 113, 114, 121, 140, 142, 145, 172, 226, 379, 438, 505, 549, 664
Stiebels, Barbara, 632
Stowell, Timothy, 142, 447
Stroik, Tom, 154
Strunk, Jan, xvi, 446
Suchsland, Peter, 530
Suckow, Katja, 501
Sulger, Sebastian, 214
Svenonius, Peter, 512, 519
Svenononius, Peter, 143

Tabbert, Eric, 237
Takahashi, Masako, 403, 426
Takami, Ken-ichi, 448
Tanenhaus, Michael K., 504, 505, 628
Temperley, Davy, 356, 357
ten Hacken, Pius, 119, 494
Tesnière, Lucien, 31, 355, 362, 372, 373, 379, 400, 402
Theofilidis, Axel, 255
Thiersch, Craig L., 99, 113, 117–119
Thomas, James, 500
Thompson, Henry S., 121, 175, 184
Thompson, Sandra A., 646
Thompson, William, 523
Thornton, Rosalind, 440, 441, 449
Thráinsson, Höskuldur, 37, 185, 225, 604
Timberlake, Alan, 311, 614
Toivonen, Ida, 234, 299, 304, 579, 591–593, 595, 596
Tomasello, Michael, 84, 114, 305, 353, 433, 451, 455, 459, 460, 463, 468, 485, 487, 521, 523, 524, 528, 548, 579–582, 584, 585, 663
Torisawa, Kentaro, 425
Tóth, Ágoston, 214
Travis, Lisa, 435
Trosterud, Trond, 357
Tseng, Jesse L., 256, 275
Tsujii, Jun'ichi, 257, 425
Turpin, Myfany, 213
Tyson, Mabry, 330

Udwin, Orlee, 462
Uibo, Heli, 357
Ulinski, Morgan, 213
Umemoto, Hiroshi, 214
Uriagereka, Juan, 472, 474, 511
Uszkoreit, Hans, 94, 175, 176, 184, 188, 189, 195, 196, 237, 245, 255, 330, 408, 420, 445, 500, 550

Valian, Virginia, 515–517
Valkonen, K., 356, 357
Vallduví, Enric, 339
Van Eynde, Frank, 329
van Genabith, Josef, 214, 357
Van Langendonck, Willy, 29, 358
van Noord, Gertjan, 163, 237, 256, 313, 325, 491, 574
van Riemsdijk, Henk, 153
van Trijp, Remi, 333–339, 341, 344–347, 353
Van Valin, Robert D. Jr., 448
Vancoppenolle, Jean, 237
Vargha-Khadem, Faraneh, 463
Vasishth, Shravan, xvi, 501
Vasserman, Alexander, 214
Vater, Heinz, 81
Veenstra, Mettina Jolanda Arnoldina, 117, 119, 161, 170, 197, 440, 491, 550, 667
Velupillai, Viveka, 450
Vennemann, Theo, 29, 101, 156
Verhagen, Arie, 547
Verspoor, Cornelia Maria, 565, 592
Vierhuff, Tilman, 237
Vijay-Shanker, K., 415
Villavicencio, Aline, 237, 238, 245, 253, 451, 475, 668
Vogel, Carl, 255
Vogel, Ralf, 114, 153, 530
Volk, Martin, 175
von Stechow, Arnim, 81, 114, 121, 142, 237, 549, 557, 563
Voutilainen, Atro, 357

Wada, Hajime, 213
Walker, Donald E., 117, 118
Walther, Markus, 258, 328
Wang, Haifeng, 214
Wasow, Thomas, 27, 202, 255, 257, 294, 300, 318, 319, 346, 501, 504, 506, 507, 520, 550, 600, 601, 616, 632
Wasow, Tom, xvi, 255, 507, 510
Watkins, Kate E., 463

Way, Andy, 214
Webelhuth, Gert, 110, 113, 114, 142, 518, 647, 654, 669
Weber, Heinz J., 355, 372, 377
Wechsler, Stephen Mark, xvi, 151, 155, 162, 272, 304, 312, 335, 345, 353, 413, 524, 565, 580, 581, 590–592, 596, 600–603, 610, 630
Wedekind, Jürgen, 213
Wegener, Heide, 423
Weiller, Cornelius, 462, 663
Weir, David, 409
Weir, Morton W., 461
Weissgerber, Monika, 356
Weisweber, Wilhelm, 175, 185, 187
Welke, Klaus, 355, 358, 655
Wells, Rulon S., 331, 632
Werner, Edeltraud, 355
Wesche, Birgit, 99, 245
Wetta, Andrew C., 191, 296, 621, 633
Wexler, Kenneth, 156, 434, 512–514, 521
Weydt, Harald, 452
Wharton, R. M., 466
White, Mike, 237
Wiese, Heike, 630
Wijnen, Frank, 521, 522
Wiklund, Anna-Lena, 142
Wilcock, Graham, 339
Wilder, Chris, 113
Wiley, Edward, 458
Williams, Edwin, 234, 438
Wing, Ben, 237, 238
Winkler, Susanne, 114, 300, 338, 546
Wintner, Shuly, 255, 256
Wittenberg, Eva, xvi, 630, 631
Wöllstein, Angelika, 43, 48
Wood, Randall, 4, 452
Wunderlich, Dieter, 84, 304, 450, 549, 551, 592
Wurmbrand, Susanne, 169, 574

Xia, Fei, 403
XTAG Research Group, 403

Yamada, Hiroyasu, 356
Yamada, Jeni, 462
Yampol, Todd, 237
Yang, Charles D., 472–474, 514, 519
Yang, Jaehyung, 256
Yankama, Beracah, 171, 471
Yasukawa, Hidekl, 213
Yatsushiro, Kazuko, 112
Yip, Moira, 115, 278
Yoon, Juntae, 404
Yoon, SinWon, 404, 413
Yoshinaga, Naoki, 425

Zaenen, Annie, 37, 185, 213, 223, 225, 226, 230, 232, 315, 604, 721
Zalila, Ines, 255
Zappa, Frank, 432
Zeevat, Henk, 237, 668
Zhang, Yi, 256, 257
Ziehe, T. W., 356, 357
Zorn, Hans-Peter, 330
Zribi, Chiraz, 403
Zucchi, Alessandro, 590
Zwart, C. Jan-Wouter, 143
Zweigenbaum, Pierre, 213
Zwicky, Arnold M., 117, 118

Language index

Abaza, 441
Akan, 446
Akkadian, 455
Arabic, 99, 213, 238, 255, 403
Arrernte, 213

Basque, 357, 512, 557, 563
Bengali, 213, 255
Bulgarian, 255

Cantonese, 255
Catalan, 357
Chamorro, 293
Czech, 512

Danish, 99, 100, 213, 255, 257, 356, 357, 446, 449, 474
Dutch, 109n19, 110, 143, 169, 237, 243, 256, 356, 443n13, 521–523, 574, 611, 620, 621
Dyirbal, 435, 455

English, 3, 27, 68n10, 73, 83–85, 96, 99, 108, 110, 114, 147, 171, 183, 187, 213, 219, 223, 237, 246, 256, 283n16, 287, 300n26, 305, 322, 356, 357, 392n31, 395, 403, 414–415, 434, 441, 443, 449, 458, 468–477, 484–486, 513, 515, 518, 521–523, 542, 545, 548, 549, 564, 572, 623, 640, 644, 647–649, 655, 658
Esperanto, 256, 356, 357, 372
Estonian, 357
Ewe, 293

Faroese, 357
Finnish, 228n10, 237, 356, 357
French, 27, 99, 213, 235, 237, 256, 257, 293, 356, 357, 377, 403, 485, 658

Ga, 256
Galician, 474, 511n1
Georgian, 213, 256
German, 171, 257, 356, 357, 484, 523, 657, 658
Greek, 256
Guugu Yimidhirr, 441

Hausa, 256
Hawaiian Creole English, 460
Hebrew, 256, 512
Hindi, 214
Hixkaryána, 454
Hungarian, 146, 214, 435

Icelandic, 37, 293, 574
Indonesian, 214
Irish, 214, 293, 357, 614
Iroquoian, 295n23
Italian, 142, 148, 214, 356, 357, 403, 462, 474, 511n1, 515, 515

Jakaltek, 435
Japanese, 85, 112, 113n23, 114, 169, 171, 214, 246, 256, 287, 356, 357, 434, 446, 462, 512
Javanese, 512
Jiwarli, 435

Kikuyu, 293
Korean, 214, 256, 404, 446, 512

Latin, 3, 246, 357
Lithuanian, 614

Malagasy, 214
Malayalam, 435, 512
Maltese, 256, 257, 658
Mandarin Chinese, 214, 256, 257, 357, 450, 458, 484, 515, 646–647, 658
Moore, 293
Murrinh-Patha, 214

Northern Sotho, 214
Norwegian, 214, 256, 356, 357, 446, 474

Old Icelandic, 357
Oneida, 295n23, 660

Palauan, 293
Persian, 256, 257, 434, 658
Pirahã, 454
Polish, 214, 256
Portuguese, 214, 256, 356, 357
Proto-Uralic, 455

Russian, 228n10, 256, 356, 357

Sahaptin, 257
Sami, 357
sign language, 460–461
    American (ASL), 459, 512
    British, 257
    French, 257
    German, 257
    Greek, 257
    South African, 257
Slavic, 355
Sorbian
    Lower, 474, 511n1
    Upper, 474, 511n1
Spanish, 149, 214, 257, 293, 314, 356, 357, 458, 522–523, 658
Straits Salish, 450
Swahili, 357
Swedish, 356, 357, 446, 591n19

Tagalog, 237, 246, 435
Tamil, 446
Thompson Salish, 293
Tigrinya, 214
Turkish, 214, 237, 246, 257, 312, 614

Urdu, 214

Vietnamese, 404

Wambaya, 257, 300, 435, 544
Warlpiri, 435, 454
Welsh, 99, 214, 392n31
Wolof, 214

Yiddish, 256, 257, 293, 404, 658

Subject index

+, 401, 651
\, 239, 245
○, 389
↓, 219, 252, 404
∃, 89
∀, 89
λ-calculus, 60
⊕, 264
→, 53
↑, 219, 248, 252
↑↑, 249
∨, 203
|, 229, 245
*, 9n2, 64, 75, 130, 184, 232, 404
/, 189, 238–239, 245
#, 9n2
§, 9n2
⇒, 263, 268
⊸, 220

a-structure, 225
accent, 258
accomplishment, 584
acquisition, 4, 458–459, 463–487, 509, 511–527, 655
    second language, 458
    speed, 457–458
Across the Board Extraction, 166, 193, 343, 633n49
actant, 31, 360
activity, 584
adjacency, 55
adjective, 18–19, 21, 23, 92, 273, 450
    depictive, 41
    predicative, 41
adjunct, 30–35, 63–65, 75, 90, 98, 149, 183–185, 223, 241, 264, 272–275, 307, 404–405, 447, 537
    head, 75
adjunction, 404–405
    ban, 544
    obligatory, 415–417
adjuncts, 222
adposition, 22, 450
adverb, 18, 22, 92
    pronominal-, 24
    relative, 25
adverbial, 34n15, 40–41
adverbs, 22
agent, 31, 90, 224
Agree, 126, 148, 170, 540, 573n1
agreement, 5, 35, 56–58, 146, 171, 203, 364, 375
    object, 142, 557, 563
ambiguity, 421, 422
    spurious, 71, 76, 497, 596
analogy, 484
animacy, 90
antipassive, 641–645
apparent multiple fronting, 191n14
Arc Pair Grammar, 454
argument, 30–35, 89, 238, 264, 271, 447
    designated, 234, 275, 308n5, 667
    external, 90, 97, 234
    internal, 90, 234
    position, 90
argument structure, 89
article, 18, 53
aspect, 584
attribute-value matrix (AVM), 197
attribute-value structure, 197
automaton
    finite, 484
auxiliary inversion, 95, 117, 167, 283n16, 470–485, 521

back-formation, 100
backward application, 163, 239
base generation, 113
benefactive, 595–597

beneficiary, 90, 225, 226
β-reduction, 61, 240
bias, 521
binary, 55
Binding Theory, 88, 139, 271, 276n14, 440–442, 536, 537, 549
Biolinguistics, 346
bit vector, 352
blocking, 485
bounding node, 442
branching, 55
binary, 55, 155, 455n27, 478, 484, 535–538, 608, 660
unary, 55
Broca's area, 461
Burzio's Generalization, 110, 641

c-command, 133, 287n20, 440
c-structure, 185n2, 215, 219
capacity
generative, 159, 184, 195, 425, 529–533
cartography, 140n6, 450
case, 20, 23, 33, 58, 234, 270, 300, 421
absolutive, 656
accusative, 20, 38, 40, 43, 106, 656
agreement, 42, 106n16
dative, 20, 107
ergative, 656
filter, 107
genitive, 20, 106, 107, 278
lexical, 106–225
nominative, 20, 35, 106, 656
semantic, 40
structural, 106–438
Case Theory, 139, 234
Categorial Grammar (CG), 159–167, 171, 188, 195, 196, 237–252, 258, 280, 283n16, 297, 298, 300, 304, 307, 355, 364, 421, 426, 437, 438, 455, 474, 489, 491, 493, 501, 505, 507, 509n13, 536, 550, 558, 563, 566n5, 669
category
functional, 91, 140, 149, 169, 450
−Pol, 142
μ, 142
+Pol, 142
%Pol, 142
Adverb, 142, 147
Agr, 224
AgrA, 142
AgrIO, 142, 438
AgrN, 142
AgrO, 142, 438, 557, 563
AgrS, 142, 438, 557
AgrV, 142
Asp, 142, 143
Aux, 142
C, 93, 450
Clitic Voices, 142
Color, 142n9
D, 93
Dist, 142, 143
Fin, 141
Foc, 141, 148
Force, 141
Gender, 142
Hearer, 142, 148
Honorific, 142
I, 93, 95–97, 107, 450
Intra, 143
Kontr, 148
Mod, 142
Mood, 142
Nationality, 142n9
Neg, 142, 143, 224, 381
Number, 142
Obj, 143
OuterTop, 142
Pass, 571
Passive, 136
PassP, 569
PathP, 143
Perf, 571
Perfect(?), 142
Person, 142
PlaceP, 143
Predicate, 142
Quality, 142n9
Shape, 142n9
Share, 142
Size, 142n9
Speaker, 142, 148
Subj, 143

T, 93, 142, 224, 557
Tense, 129, 142
Top, 141, 143, 148
Tra, 143
v, 127–129, 569, 598–601
Voice, 142, 540, 557
Z, 142
lexical, 28, 91, 450
syntactic, 28
causative construction, 312
CAUSE, 557
change of state, 584
CHILDES, 470, 471n35, 471, 473, 474, 484
chimpanzee, 459
classifier, 450
clitic, 522
CoGETI, 257
Cognitive Grammar, 303, 432, 475, 523, 551
coherence, 227, 231, 233
coindexation, 270
comparative, 21, 23
competence, 346, 419–424, 452, 499–510, 515, 526
complement, 35, 75, 90, 155–160
complementizer, 102, 245, 281
completeness, 227, 231, 233
Complex NP Constraint, 442, 446
complexity class, 83, 403, 485, 529–533
composition, 247, 468
backward, 246, 247, 624
forward, 246, 247
compositionality, 272, 457
computer science, 116
configurationality, 113
conjunction, 22, 53, 150n14
constituent, 7, 13
discontinuous, 44, 94, 313–314, 331, 627
constituent order, 113, 180, 227, 230, 245–287, 314, 408–411
fixed, 245, 287
free, 245, 287
constituent position, 285
Constraint Language for Lambda-Structures (CLLS), 557
constraint-based grammar, 454
construction
Active Ditransitive, 332
Caused-Motion, 337, 338, 586, 591, 596, 631, 632
Determiner Noun, 330
linking, 307
N-P-N, 400–401, 403n2, 649–651
passive, 308
resultative, 304, 548, 565–566, 592–610
subject, 308
transitive, 308
verb phrase, 306
Construction Grammar (CxG), 94, 113, 150, 167, 170n38, 188, 194, 195, 228n10, 234, 269, 272, 275n11, 298, 303–354, 403, 432, 475, 501n3, 507, 509n13, 523–526, 536, 544, 547, 551, 571, 580, 594n22, 620, 651, 667, 669
Fluid, 312, 395
Sign-Based, 330, 345–352
Construction Grammar(CxG), 615
context, 476
context-free grammar, 195, 403, 464, 465, 529
probabilistic (PCFG), 305, 548
context-sensitive grammar, 403, 465, 466, 529
context-free grammar, 83
contraction, 88
contrast, 505
control, 35, 216
Control Theory, 89, 139
conversion, 27
cooperativeness, 421
coordination, 16–17, 48n23, 65, 78, 118, 162–163, 191n14, 249, 263, 331n26, 455, 507n11, 525
-test, 10–11, 16
copula, 44, 550
Copy Theory of Movement, 150n13, 151, 166, 171n41
core grammar, 91, 303, 511, 519
CoreGram, 257
corpus, 6
corpus annotation, 356
corpus linguistics, 486, 669
coverb, 435, 450
creole language, 460–461
critical period, 458–459

cycle
in feature description, 205, 285, 333, 390
transformational, 447, 503, 539

D-structure, 85, 139, 299
declarative clause, 102
Deep Structure, *see* D-Structure, 296, 299
Definite Clause Grammar (DCG), 80, 211
deletion, 502
DELPH-IN, 255
dependency, 456
Dependency Categorial Grammar, 253
Dependency Grammar (DG), 94, 113, 167, 188, 191n14, 426, 499n1, 626n45, 633n49
Dependency Unification Grammar (DUG), 397, 529, 667
depictive predicate, 276n14, 300n26, 545–547
derivation, 27, 119, 312, 656
derivation tree, 406
Derivational Theory of Complexity (DTC), 501n3, 501–504
descriptive adequacy, 431
determiner, 23, 53
as head, 29
directive, 639
disjunction, 202–203, 229
Distributed Morphology, 641
do-Support, 523
dominance, 54
immediate, 55, 179, 258, 313

economy
transderivational, 139
elementary tree, 404
ellipsis, 276n14, 502, 507n11, 536, 549, 641
empty element, 15n8, 68, 109, 149, 155, 161, 165, 285, 298, 304, 314, 325, 410, 419, 425, 436, 439, 440, 536, 549–566, 636, 647
PRO, *see* PRO
empty head, 640, 649
endocentricity, 94
entity, 182
epsilon, 551
epsilon production, 68

escape hatch, 444
event, 271
evidence
negative
indirect, 485
evokes operator, 333
Exceptional Case Marking (ECM), 540
experiencer, 31, 90, 225
explanatory adequacy, 431
Extended Projection Principle (EPP), 438, 517
external argument, 91
extraction, 376, 442, 446–449, 550
from adjuncts, 530
from specifier, 530
island, 446
subject, 511
extraction path marking, 293, 341, 370
extraposition, 101n11, 143n10, 166, 386, 421, 442, 446
Extraposition, 442

f-structure, 185n2, 215, 219, 536, 539, 544
Faculty of Language
in the Broad Sense (FLB), 456
in the Narrow Sense (FLN), 456
feature
checking, 125
deletion, 125
strong, 123
weak, 123
feature checking, 140
feature description, 197–209
feature structure, 207–209
feature-value structure, 197
feral child, 459
field
middle-, 44, 98
post-, 44
pre-, 44, 98
filler, 190, 306
focus, 103, 140, 148–149, 215–216, 231, 448
Foot Feature Principle, 192
foot node, 415
formal language, 478
formalization, 6, 304, 524
forward application, 163, 238

FoxP2, 463
fronting, 10–16
  apparent multiple, 17n9, 149, 166, 384, 386, 621n39, 633n49
function composition, 258, 300
functional application, 182
functional uncertainty, 232, 315, 544, 611
functor, 238, 526
future, 20, 522

gap, 87
gender, 20, 23, 58, 270, 300, 494–496, 539
gene, 463, 664
Generalized Phrase Structure Grammar (GPSG), 74, 99n9, 119, 121, 211, 227n8, 228, 238, 252, 259, 264, 266, 280, 285, 297–299, 314, 318, 332, 370, 389n29, 403, 405, 409, 426, 454, 489, 491, 501, 507, 509n13, 550, 667
Generative Grammar, 54, 453, 489
genitive, 38, 547
Gesetz der wachsenden Glieder, 539
glue language, 220
glue semantics, 219–222, 363
goal, 225
government, 33, 116
Government and Binding (GB), xviii, 74, 82, 84, 85, 87, 88, 99, 105, 119, 186, 188n5, 215, 217, 218, 220, 226, 227, 238, 241, 244, 246, 252, 259, 280, 296, 299, 304, 384, 405, 410, 421, 438, 440, 470, 501n3, 501, 503, 536, 539, 542, 546, 549, 557, 623n44, 641, 648, 669
gradability, 491–492
Grammar Matrix, 257
grammatical function, 143, 223, 275, 306, 438–440, 668
  governable, 215
Greediness Constraint, 513, 514n2, 514

head, 28–30, 219, 264
head domain
  extended, 227, 300
head feature, 30
Head Feature Convention (HFC), 176, 266
Head-Driven Phrase Structure Grammar (HPSG), 74, 94, 97n8, 113n23, 119, 121, 140n6, 149, 150, 157, 163, 167, 185n2, 188, 191n14, 195, 234, 244n6, 246, 255–300, 304, 307, 308, 319, 331, 332, 345–353, 364, 370, 372, 376, 384, 386, 399, 403, 413, 426, 438, 441, 454, 475, 491, 494, 501, 503, 507, 509n13, 510, 518, 529, 536–538, 541, 542, 545, 550, 552, 558, 564, 566n5, 625, 627, 633n49, 654, 658, 667, 669
  Constructional, 325
Heavy-NP-Shift, 314
Hole Semantics, 558
hydra clause, 437
hypotenuse, 333

iambus, 515
Icelandic, 278n15
ID/LP grammar, 179, 227n8, 258, 408
identification in the limit, 465–468
ideophone, 450
idiom, 330, 519, 542–547, 615
imperative, 20, 35
implication, 263, 268
index, 149
indicative, 20
inflection, 19–22, 27, 86, 656
  -paradigm, 20
inflectional class, 21, 58
information structure, 103, 148–149, 215, 339, 448, 594n21
inheritance, 234, 271, 306, 307, 312, 594, 615–617, 649, 668
  default, 398, 616
  multiple, 202, 413
instrument, 225
Integrational Linguistics, xvi
interface, 346
interjection, 22, 23
interrogative clause, 48–649
intervention, 133
introspection, 669
inversion, 549
IQ, 462

Kleene star, 184

label, 149–155, 164
λ-abstraction, 61
λ-conversion, 61
language
  formal, 116, 464
language acquisition, 114, 129, 238, 304, 431, 442n11, 535
language evolution, 304
learnability, 467
learning theory, 478
left associativity, 239
lexeme, 27
Lexical Decomposition Grammar, 304
Lexical Functional Grammar (LFG), 38, 39, 74, 97n8, 121, 149, 167, 171, 172, 185n2, 188, 194, 211, 280, 297–300, 304, 314, 362, 372, 419, 438, 440, 454, 489, 491, 501n3, 501, 507, 509n13, 510, 529, 536, 537, 541, 542, 544, 550, 554, 556, 584, 594n22, 620, 625, 654, 667, 669
lexical integrity, 223, 304
Lexical Mapping Theory (LMT), 224–226, 280
Lexical Resource Semantics (LRS), 270n9
lexical rule, 187, 243, 275–566
  verb-initial position, 283–285
lexicon, 86–269
linear logic, 220
linear precedence, 179, 258, 313
Linear Precedence Rule, 180
linearization rule, 165, 223, 332
Linguistic Knowledge Builder (LKB), 255
Link Grammar, 356
linking, 91, 224–226, 271–272, 307–312, 362
list, 199, 679
  difference, 680
local maximum, 514
locality, 148, 262, 318–325, 330, 405, 425, 538–547
  of matching, 133
locative alternation, 629
Logical Form (LF), 86, 88–89, 299, 426
long-distance dependency, 102–105, 189–192, 230–233, 249, 283n16, 288–293, 297, 314–315, 318, 414–415
long-Distance dependency, 246–372
LP-rule, 180

macaque, 459
machine translation, 356
macro, 234, 298
Mainstream Generative Grammar, 81
Mandarin Chinese, 435, 468
Markov model, 484
matryoshka, 4, 7
maturation, 514
Meaning–Text Theory (MTT), 355, 356n2, 363, 396n35
meaning constructor, 220
memory, 502n4
Merge, 140, 149, 437, 451n23, 455n27, 459
  External, 140, 660
  Internal, 140
metarule, 180–182, 187–188, 538
metrical grid, 258
metrics, 515
Middle Construction, 310, 312
middle field, *see* field
mildly context-sensitive grammar, 403, 425
Minimal Recursion Semantics (MRS), 262, 270, 274n10, 307, 318, 407, 558, 610
Minimalist Grammar (MG), 140n6, 159–167, 171, 300, 529, 530
Minimalist Program (MP), 123–169, 186, 346, 381, 436, 437, 455, 491, 493, 504, 505, 566n5, 623n44, 648, 667, 669
Missing VP effect, 500
model, 207–209
model-theoretic grammar, 81, 454, 489–497
modifier, 34, 90
modularity, 505
module, 509
modus ponens, 221
mood, 20
morphology, 86, 171, 223–654
Move, 140
movement
  altruistic, 148
  covert, 146
  feature-driven, 148
  permutation, 13
movement test, 9

Move α, 87
Multi-Component TAG, 408–410
music, 456, 462

nativism, 432
negative evidence, 465, 466, 470, 472, 485–486
Neo-Davidsonian semantics, 609
neural network, 475–476
neutral order, 111
New Prague School, 355
Nirvana, 516
No Tampering Condition (NTC), 507n11
node, 54
  daughter, 55
  mother, 55
  sister, 55
nominalization, 106, 485
Non-Tangling Condition, 94
noun, 18, 20, 23, 53, 68, 91, 450
  common, 330
  mass, 69
  relational, 66
NP-split, 14
nucleus, 358
number, 20, 56, 58, 270, 300
numeration, 170

o-command, 287n20
object, 299, 438–440
  direct, 38, 39
  indirect, 38, 39
obliqueness, 276n14, 438
Obliqueness, 287n20
observational adequacy, 431
Off-Line Parsability, 529
Optimality Theory (OT), xvi, 501n3
optional infinitive, 521
optionality, 32, 34
order
  unmarked, 111
organ, 461

paradigm, 27
parameter, 84, 511–519, 655
  default value, 513, 514, 517
  head direction, 434–435
  head position, 84
  pro-drop, 473, 474, 511, 515–517
  subjacency, 449, 511
  subject article drop, 515
  SV, 512
  topic drop, 515
  V2, 512, 514
parameters, 460
parser, 530
Parsing as Deduction, 119
partial verb phrase fronting, 194–195, 326, 662
participle
  adjectival, 135
particle, 22, 23
passive, 106, 110, 135–137, 185–188, 223–226, 242, 275–312, 317, 363–364, 411–413, 502, 543, 563, 594n21, 595–596, 654
  impersonal, 107, 109, 187, 188, 279, 549
  long, 299n25, 301
  remote, 574
path, 198
path equation, 330
patient, 31, 90, 225
PATR-II, 211, 330
performance, 305, 346, 419–424, 446, 449, 452, 499–510, 515, 526, 611, 663
periphery, 91n4, 303, 519
permutation test, 9
person, 20, 56
Person, 270
phase, 124, 346, 504
phenomenon, 207
Phenomenon, 209
Phonetic Form (PF), 86–88
phonology, 258
phrase, 7
phrase structure grammar, 53–59, 238, 259, 260, 489, 549
pidgin language, 460
pied-piping, 250, 400n37
pivot schema, 523
plural, 20, 68
Polish, 542
polygraph, 379
positional, 450
postfield, *see* field

postposition, 22
Poverty of the Stimulus, 441, 442n11, 460, 463–487
predicate, 89
predicate logic, 30
predicate-argument structure, 456
predicative, 41–42
prefield, *see* field
  ellipsis, 276n14
preposition, 18, 22, 73, 92
present, 20
presupposition, 448
preterite, 20
principle
  case, 656
  Case, 278–280
  Generalized Head Feature, 399
  Head Feature, 266
  NONLOC-, 291
  Semantics, 272, 656
  Sign, 319n15
  Subject-Mapping, 225
Principles & Parameters, 84–85, 511–519
PRO, 410
Probability Matching, 461
progressive, 523
projection, 29, 94
  maximal, 29, 76, 94
  of features, 30
projectivity, 362, 367, 382, 389–396, 409, 575
pronominalization test, 8
pronoun, 24–656
  expletive, 11–12, 26, 31, 103, 109, 439, 473, 516, 549
  reflexive, 270, 537
  relative, 550
prosody, 249, 493, 505

quantification, 222
quantifier
  existential, 89
  universal, 89, 183
question tag, 542

raising, 278n15, 413, 541, 610
Random Step, 514
Rangprobe, 47
recursion, xvii, 4n1, 50, 65, 425, 484, 499n1, 499, 547–548
recursively enumerable language, 466
reference, 11, 12
regular language, 465, 529
relation, 538
  ○, 389
  append, 210, 264, 287
Relational Grammar, xvi, 490
relative clause, 48–649
  free, 152–153, 276n14
remote passive, 364n11
repetitive, 557
representational model, 119
restitutive, 557
resultative construction, 512, 565
rewrite grammar, 464
Right Roof Constraint, 442
right to left elaboration, 477
Right-Node-Raising, 157
rising, 370, 575
Role and Reference Grammar, xvi, 150
root, 655
root Infinitive, 521
rule-to-rule hypothesis, 62, 183

S-structure, 85, 139, 299
S-Structure, 426
satellite, 358
Satzglied, 13n4
schema
  Filler-Head, 292
  head-adjunct, 274
  head-argument, 263
Schema
  Specifier-Head-, 294
scope, 101–113, 191n14, 223, 314, 408, 549, 633n49
segmentation, 521
selection, 31
  restriction, 421
self-embedding, 452n25, 499, 547, 548
semantic role, 31, 90, 224–226, 271, 307, 362, 607
semantics, 171, 272
sentence bracket, 44, 98
sentence symbol, 269

set, 199, 315–317
sexus, 495
Shortest Move Constraint (SMC), 160n30, 530
sideward movement, 166
sign language, 461
  American (ASL), 461
signature, 207
Single Value Constraint, 513, 514
singular, 20
Situation Semantics, 270n9
specifier, 75, 95, 155–160, 530
statistics, 214, 238, 305, 404, 476, 478–486, 635
stem, 656
strength, 123
Structure Preservation, 507n11
structure sharing, 203–205, 260, 280, 327, 330, 370, 503
subcategorization, 89, 176, 260
subcategorization frame, 89
subjacency, 442–449, 511
Subjacency, 139
subject, 35–38, 95, 107, 299, 306, 438–440, 542
Subject Condition, 438
subjunctive, 20
substitution, 404
substitution test, 7, 8
subsumption, 316
superlative, 21
Surface Structure, *see* S-structure
SVO, 513
symbol
  non-terminal, 464
  terminal, 464
syntax-semantics interface, 60

T model, 85–87
TAG
  Free Order (FO-TAG), 409
Tamagotchi, 457
tense, 20, 23
text, 454n26
that-t, 511
the-clause, 648
thematic grid, 89
theme, 90, 225
theory, 207–209
Theta-Criterion, 90, 139, 218, 234
θ-grid, 89, 215
θ-role, 90
θ-Theory, 119, 234, 508
third construction, 662
Tiger corpus, 445
topic, 140, 148–149, 215–216, 231
Topic Drop, 276n14
topicalization, 103, 248, 249, 648
topology, 43–50, 97
trace, 87
  extraction trace, 290–291, 293
  verb, 15n8, 283, 285
TRALE, 255, 347
transderivational constraint, 153, 169, 170
transformation, 82–84, 296, 304, 425, 426, 474, 501–504, 507, 563–566
  fact-Deletion, 448
Transformational Grammar, 499n1, 81–499
Tree Adjoining Grammar (TAG), 94, 159, 162, 167, 188n5, 298, 308, 331n26, 403–426, 489, 491, 507, 509n13, 518, 529, 547, 550, 563, 625, 627, 654, 667, 669
  Feature Structure-Based (FTAG), 415
  Synchronous (STAG), 426
  Feature Structure-Based (FTAG), 415–417
  Multi-Component (MC-TAG), 409–410
  Tree Tuple MC-TAG (TT-MC-TAG), 411, 424
  Vector (V-TAG), 411, 417–419, 424, 426, 550
trigger, 519
trochee, 515
truth value, 182
type, 200–203
  atomic, 201
type hierarchy, 201–202, 271
type raising, 246, 247, 550, 566n5
  backward, 624

unary, 55
underspecification, 557

Underspecified Discourse Representation Theory (UDRT), 558
unification, 205–207, 240, 316
uniformity, 440, 549
universal, 433–457
  implicational, 433n4
  implicative, 664
Universal Base Hypothesis, 667
Universal Grammar (UG), 140, 142, 238, 432, 573, 643
  as a toolkit, 450
  falsifiability, 449n19, 451, 455
unrestricted grammars, 529
Unsupervised Data-Oriented Parsing (U-DOP), 478–485, 635–637

valence, 31–35, 57, 176, 215, 238–239, 259–260, 271, 404
  change, 648
  classes, 86
valence frame, 89
verb, 18, 19, 23, 53, 91, 450, 655
  -final, 43
  -first, 43
  -second, 43
  AcI, 106
  auxiliary, 468
  bivalent, 43
  ditransitive, 42, 107n18, 512
  ergative, 91n3
  inherent reflexives, 16, 31
  intransitive, 42
  modal, 468, 523
  monovalent, 161–162
  particle, 502, 512
  perception, 106n17
  serial, 646–647
  subjectless, 316
  transitive, 42, 275n12
  unaccusative, 91, 113, 135, 226, 275n12, 602, 655
  unergative, 275n12, 655
verb position, 102, 189, 226, 243–245, 280–314, 411, 642, 644
  -second-, 102
Verb position, 188
verb-final language, 102, 227
verb-second language, 103
verb-particle, 5
verbal complex, 115, 611
Verb*mobil*, 171, 257, 350n36
visual perception, 456
Vorfeld, 17n9

Wernicke's area, 461
wh-exclamative, 648
Williams Syndrome, 462
word, 656
Word Grammar (WG), 356, 358, 359, 364n11, 365n12, 370, 396n35
word sequence, 7

$\overline{\text{X}}$ theory, 73–76, 79, 82, 91–94, 114, 119, 123, 127, 139, 150, 155–159, 165, 241n3, 272, 435–438, 508, 535, 536, 539, 650
XP, 75